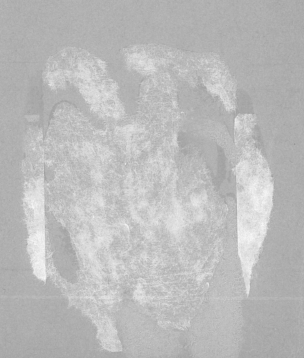

Industrial
Psychology

THE IRWIN SERIES IN MANAGEMENT

CONSULTING EDITOR   JOHN F. MEE   *Indiana University*

12-25

Industrial
Psychology

LAURENCE SIEGEL, Ph.D.

Chairman, Department of Psychology
Professor of Psychology
Louisiana State University

Revised Edition
1969

RICHARD D. IRWIN, INC., Homewood, Illinois
IRWIN-DORSEY LIMITED, Georgetown, Ontario

Revised Edition

First Printing, March, 1969

Library of Congress Catalog Card No. 69–17163

Printed in the United States of America

To Lila

Preface

This revision, like the original edition, is intended primarily for students enrolled in courses variously designated *Business Psychology* or *Industrial Psychology*. I am hopeful also that it will prove useful to persons functioning in the field as personnel managers, training directors, and so on. My intention has been to provide an overview of industrial psychology broadly conceived. Instead of restricting the scope to personnel problems or management problems, I have organized the content about the three major parties to industrial activity: workers, managers, and consumers.

A background in introductory psychology will probably prove helpful to the reader but is not indispensable. While preparing the manuscript I have attempted to keep in mind the kind of student likely to enroll in the course. For a few students, this course will be a first contact with an offering in psychology; most will have had a prior course in introductory psychology. It has been my experience that both groups benefit when certain "bridges" between the content regarded as *general* psychology and that as *industrial* psychology are provided.

Such bridges appear at various points in the text: the viewpoint and methods of present-day psychology are presented in the first chapters; certain principles of measurement are discussed in the chapter on testing; pertinent concepts of learning are presented in the training chapter; motivation is discussed preliminary to consideration of job satisfaction; and some rudimentary principles of social psychology, with elaboration of those particularly pertinent to leadership and organizations, precede the consideration of their applications in industry. These bridges are relatively brief and are not intended to duplicate the content of an introductory psychology course. Rather, they were designed to facilitate the transition from discussions of behavior in general to a discussion of industrial behavior.

I have had the frustrating feeling as teacher and author that the arbitrary compartmentalization of knowledge into topics or chapters is too often reflected in a genuine compartmentalization by the student. He sometimes considers a topic as if it were a discrete element unrelated to what has preceded it, what will follow it, or to any macrocosmic view of the subject. Therefore, I have introduced him in the first chapter to an overview of the book and to the S–I–R concept as an organizing notion. I return to the latter often and deliberately throughout the succeeding chapters.

This revision differs from the original edition of the book in a number of significant ways. Some of these differences reflect changes in the field during the intervening years; others, primarily in the organization and depth of coverage of traditional topics, were suggested by questionnaire replies from approximately 75 colleagues familiar with the original edition. Of the changes made in the revision, aside from integrating recent research literature, I call your attention particularly to the following:

The revised edition is a considerably longer book than the original, in spite of the fact that four chapters of the latter are now compressed into two. The additional length results from expanded treatment, here as chapters, of "Performance Criteria and Predictive Validity," "Engineering Psychology," "Organizational Theories and Structures," and "Management Development." By breaking these topics out for chapter-length treatment, it became possible to extend the discussions at many other points to include more in the way of theoretical content and illustrative applications. A fifth additional chapter, "Statistical Computation," is presented as an Appendix supplement for use by instructors desiring it.

Aside from added chapters and expanded topical coverage, some of the major differences in organization are these: The importance of criterion development and associated problems is emphasized by the placement of this discussion in a separate chapter introducing Part II. Performance rating is treated as a particular form of performance appraisal generally, and is placed in the context of personnel selection, placement, training, and appraisal in Part II. The importance of employee motivation and of organizational psychology is recognized by according each of these topical areas status as separate Parts of the book. Many other more subtle changes in topical placement and coverage will be apparent to users of the first edition.

I am under no delusion that this book will satisfy all psychologists with respect to breadth of coverage, depth of treatment, or topical emphasis. The instructor will sometimes undoubtedly wish I had expanded the treatment of this issue and reduced the treatment of that issue, included this topic and excluded that one. However, I hopefully anticipate that the book will contribute effectively to the instructional partnership formed by teacher and author. A textbook, after all, is not a course. It may serve as the skeleton for a course and even provide some of the muscle for it; but the lifeblood of a subject is infused into it by the teacher.

I am indebted to many persons for assistance in preparing and refining the manuscript. The details of manuscript preparation were greatly simplified for me through the efforts of Mrs. Vera M. Foil and Mrs. Mary Kay Grimes.

Many colleagues have, of course, influenced my thinking about the field in subtle ways reflected in anything I write. Of these, I must particularly acknowledge the professional and personal contributions of Dr. Lila Corkland Siegel.

Finally, the entire manuscript for this revision was read and evaluated by Dr. Richard H. Henneman, University of Virginia; and Dr. Donald D. Glad, Louisiana State University. In addition, several colleagues critically read the manuscript for the original edition, portions of which are retained herein, and others made helpful comments about the original edition during the past several years. All of these persons will recognize, in the finished work, some evidence that certain of their suggestions were implemented.

Baton Rouge, Louisiana   LAURENCE SIEGEL
February, 1969

Foreword to the Student

You are undoubtedly approaching this subject matter with certain expectations. Perhaps you plan a career in sales and would like to learn about the "psychologist's-eye view" of the potential purchaser of soap or diesel equipment or breadboxes. You may be planning a career in industrial management and seeking "rules" for increasing production without increasing costs. Or you may anticipate some kind of work in the broad area of personnel and would like, therefore, to learn something about "getting along with people." Maybe you haven't yet decided upon a vocation and anticipate that this book will familiarize you with career opportunities and offer guidance that may be of assistance in making your occupational choice. In view of the disparity in expectations of individual readers, it will be useful at the outset to clarify the objectives of this book and to provide an overview of its contents.

Let us begin with two basic premises. In the first place, psychology is concerned with the behavior of organisms. Secondly, these organisms are systematically studied by psychologists using techniques that are *scientific* in the same sense that techniques of investigation in physics or chemistry are scientific. Organisms are, to be sure, extremely complicated. Unlike atoms of hydrogen, people are not identical to each other. There is considerable variation in behavior from person to person, and the behavior of a single individual may vary from one occasion to another. The unique individuality and personal dignity of every human being is prized above all else in a democratic society. People are not like interchangeable units on a piece of mechanical equipment. The fact that organisms, and most particularly human beings, are complex and variable does not, however, imply that psychology must perforce be unscientific. The essence of science is not *what* it studies but the *methods* by which it studies.

If psychology is the scientific study of behavior, industrial psychology is simply the scientific study of behavior as it occurs in business and industry. We may conveniently class the behaving organisms in this setting into three groups: workers, management, and consumers. This classification does not imply that each of these groups is homogeneous. Workers differ, for example, with respect to occupational level, age, sex, personal aspirations, physical health, home environment, and many other factors. Management and consumers may be similarly classified into subgroups that are psychologically important. This broad classification, *workers, management, consumers,* forms the backbone of the organization of the book.

You will undoubtedly be somewhat disappointed by the exclusion of certain topics and perhaps you will be surprised by the inclusion of certain others. You may be dismayed by the fact that nowhere in the book is there a list of "rules" for getting along with people or for impressing a recruitment interviewer. It is important to recognize at the outset that the book focuses upon human relationships in business and industry and not upon oversimplified prescriptions for particular sets of circumstances.

You will encounter discussions of technique from time to time in your reading. You will, for example, learn something about the procedures involved in the construction of psychological tests, development of attitude surveys, and the conduct of market research. These techniques are not described for the purpose of training you to do the work of an industrial psychologist. Rather they are presented because of the conviction that the proper interpretation of research findings is dependent upon an understanding of the ways in which research is conducted. A degree of familiarity with the techniques employed by the industrial psychologist will better enable you to evaluate the worth of his contribution to industry and will highlight both the specific areas in which extensive knowledge is now available and the areas in which present knowledge is, at best, incomplete.

L. S.

Table of Contents

Weighted Checklist. Forced-Choice Ratings. Sources of Error in Performance Rating: *Format of the Rating Scale. Halo Effect. Systematic Bias. Ratings Based upon Inadequate Information. Ratings Reflecting Uncontrolled Factors.* Feedback to the Ratee: *The Need for Feedback. Kinds of Feedback.*

I.

Introduction

In the course of a single day, the psychologist working in an industrial setting may find himself called upon to administer tests, confer with supervisors, attend a training conference, design an experiment to test the effectiveness of a new advertising campaign, perform the statistical analysis of questionnaire data from a morale survey, and counsel an employee who is experiencing some kind of personal difficulty. This list of functions is by no means exhaustive; it represents just a sample of the industrial psychologist's sphere of activity.

The chapters in this section are designed to provide a base for subsequent discussions. These chapters will introduce you to the field of industrial psychology by indicating something of the scope of psychological services available to business and industry, the training and employment of industrial psychologists, and the research methods employed by them. In short, the three chapters which ensue focus upon what the industrial psychologist does and how he goes about doing it.

1. Scope of Industrial Psychology

[Psychology is usually defined as the scientific study of behavior.] As such it has matured considerably during the past 50 years or so. Its maturity is evidenced by its increased reliance upon the appropriate application of scientific methods and [its increased devotion to studying "behavior."] Thus it is relatively uncommon now for even moderately sophisticated persons to confuse the methods and concerns of scientific psychology with those of such *pseudo*psychologies as physiognomy, phrenology, and palmistry. Whereas the latter attempted to relate personality to facial characteristics (physiognomy), bumps on the head (phrenology), or lines in the palm (palmistry), psychology attempts systematically to understand how and why people act as they do.

One of the consequences of the maturation of scientific psychology is a growing demand for the application of psychological knowledge and the consequent development of psychological *practice*. To the extent that behavior can be scientifically understood, it may be predicted in advance of its occurrence and sometimes may be modified. Such applications of psychological knowledge are clearly relevant to people at work and constitute the subject matter of industrial psychology.

[Whereas not all company executives are "sold" on the desirability of consulting with an industrial psychologist, their receptivity seems gradually to be increasing.] One survey, taken a little over 20 years ago, reported 53 percent of a sample of corporate executives as favoring the employment of industrial psychologists.[1] In a more

---

[1] R. Stagner, "Attitudes of Corporate Executives Regarding Psychological Methods in Personnel Work," *American Psychologist,* Vol. 1 (1946) , pp. 540–41.

recent survey of another sample of executives, this percentage had increased to 66 percent.[2] Furthermore, among those executives holding favorable attitudes toward employing industrial psychologists, the latter study revealed[greater acceptance of the psychologist's potential contribution to solving problems in the areas of personnel selection, personnel training, and morale than to problems in such areas as production efficiency and accident control.] Apparently in these latter areas management has not been apprised of some of the significant developments in industrial psychology.

Rather than view this failure of total acceptance pessimistically, it is significant that acceptance is so high in view of the short history of scientific psychology. The first laboratory for studying psychological phenomena was initiated about 90 years ago; and the first major book dealing with *industrial* psychology was written only about 55 years ago.

In spite of this very short history of scientific psychology, people have undoubtedly always evidenced a concern for how and why human beings behave as they do. Until recently this concern was largely speculative. It was based upon opinion and casual observation which gave rise to a considerable body of folklore and "common sense" about behavior.

One needs only to point to the endless series of "psychological" articles appearing in newspapers, magazines, and Sunday supplements offering prescriptions for child care, advice to the lovelorn, and helpful hints for happy homes, to verify that there is yet today considerable confusion between common sense and psychology. One writer maintains that children must never be spanked because in so doing the parent descends to the child's level; another maintains that spanking itself may be beneficial because it establishes the parent as an authority figure. Whereas one writer advises her female readers to take an active interest in their husbands' activities and hobbies in order better to experience "togetherness," another advises wives not to pry into their husbands' activities lest the husband resent the invasion of his sense of privacy. The more he reads such articles, the more confused the reader becomes until he is forced to conclude that it's all just so much hogwash. The problem arises, of course, because most of these articles are based upon idle speculation rather than upon scientific evidence. They are in most cases written by professional writers capitalizing upon man's desire to understand himself.

One of our purposes in this chapter is to distinguish between common sense and scientific psychology. We will describe the activities of psychologists in general, regardless of whether they function in clinics, schools, research organizations, government agencies, or industries. Furthermore, within the general field of psychology, we will bring into clear focus the role of the psychologist in business and industry. To do this we must begin with the broad problem of defining the subject matter of psychology.

THE SUBJECT MATTER OF PSYCHOLOGY

Conceptions about psychology held by most of the public fall somewhere in the vast middle ground between two extreme viewpoints. At one of these extremes still a few people confuse psychologists with mystics. These people fail to distinguish between scientific psychology and the pseudopsychologies; they may even naïvely attribute special "mental powers" to psychologists! At the other extreme, still a few people regard "psychology" as merely a fancy way of spelling "common sense."

Although most persons today take a moderate position between these extremes, they have a rather hazy notion about what it is that psychologists study. This notion usually equates psychology with the study of "mental functions" like intelligence, thinking, and attitudes.

Although fundamentally correct, this notion is a gross oversimplification of the psychologist's activities. We must recognize at the outset that such an important psychological concept as "attitude" is not directly observable. A person's attitudes cannot be seen or bottled for laboratory analysis. They are not immediately apparent to anyone else, even though this someone else may be a psychologist.

We become aware of the existence and operation of such factors by inference. We judge from something a person does or says that he feels and thinks in certain ways. Thus, when dealing with psychological phenomena, we must begin with something observable. However, even when our observations are carefully made we may arrive at a number of alternative inferences or explanations, each of which seems reasonable or tenable. These in turn must be further studied in order to reject all but the most promising of them. The psychologist's orientation throughout the process of observation, inference, and subsequent test of the inference is one of rigorous scientific verification.

To illustrate, an industrial psychologist might hypothesize from an employee's record of abnormal absence from work that he may be dissatisfied with the job for some reason, or that he may be experiencing personal difficulties in his home environment, or that the work itself may be either too demanding or too unstimulating for his intellectual abilities. This by no means exhausts the list of possible explanations, but it will serve for the present illustration. Once made, these hypotheses would have to be examined and sifted until the most likely ones are isolated for the particular case in question, and remedial steps would follow.

The observable factor studied by the psychologist in the instance noted above is the employee's *behavior*. First, attention is focused upon this particular employee because of undesirable industrial behavior, that is, high rate of absence and sickness reports. The psychologist formulates possible explanations and verifies or discards each by noting other behavioral indices. The suspicion of a discrepancy between level of ability and level of required job performance may be checked by administering intelligence and aptitude tests. Such tests provide a sample of the employee's behavior in a controlled setting designed to determine the level of his abilities. The employee may be interviewed and his responses evaluated with respect to job attitudes and personal adjustment. Supervisors or fellow workers may be called upon to record their observations of the employee's behavior on the job.

Emergence of Scientific Psychology

Man has, to be sure, speculated about phenomena of a psychological nature for a long, long time. One can almost imagine Eve selecting from her wardrobe of fig leaves the ones she calculated to make the most favorable impression upon Adam. A *scientific* approach as opposed to a speculative approach, however, awaited a definition of psychological phenomena in terms that were amenable to observation and experimentation. The key to the development of a scientific body of information in the area was the realization that the only phenomenon that could be directly studied was behavior. And this delineation of the subject matter of psychology as "the study of behavior" is generally identified with the establishment of the first laboratory for the study of psychological phenomena by Wilhelm Wundt in 1879.

Psychologists in the early 20th century adopted a systematic approach to understanding behavior. Instead of correlating external signs with character traits as the pseudopsychologists did, the early scientific psychologists studied the responses made by organisms to particular environmental conditions. The basic approach of these early psychologists was systematically to vary some aspect of the environment, thereby providing a *stimulus,* and noting corresponding changes in the organism's *response.* This approach is sometimes referred to as *S-R* psychology.

Perhaps the two most outstanding characteristics of the early scientific approach to psychology were first its emphasis upon rigorous scientific methodology rather than speculation and second its preoccupation with the study of stimulus conditions and the physiology of the receptors. Neither of these characteristics is surprising in view of the fact that early psychologists received most of their formal training in physiology and physics. The effect of this training was to cause them to apply the research methods of these disciplines to the investigation of behavior and to seek the explanation of response in terms of physical stimuli and physiological functions.

This approach to understanding behavior contrasted markedly with the unscientific approach of the pseudopsychologies. It removed behavior from the realm of mere speculation and made it accessible for study by investigators grounded in the rigors of verification. Thus, the early psychologists made enormous strides by establishing the legitimacy and feasibility of a science of behavior and developing a methodology appropriate to this science.

Although the *S-R* approach to behavior marked a vigorous beginning for psychology, its long-range utility was somewhat limited. Some of the difficulties inherent in this early approach to psychology stemmed from the fact that it attempted to become scientific by emulating the procedures and approaches of the older sciences. Rigorous laboratory investigation can be both a strength and a weakness. It is unrealistic to assume that data uncovered in a laboratory can always be generalized to an environment outside the laboratory. Our attitude toward work, for example, differs when we are required to produce in an industrial setting and when we are required to produce in a laboratory. In the latter instance, we are participating in an experiment; in the former, we are doing our job and earning our income. The incentives for performance in these two situations may be quite different even though the physical setting in the laboratory may attempt to duplicate the work setting.

In addition, stimulus-response relationships are exceedingly complex. A given stimulus may evoke different responses from different persons, or even from the same person on different occasions. To understand behavior it is necessary to discover and understand the roles of the variables intervening between stimuli and responses.

Modern Psychology

A clue to the subject matter of psychology as viewed by present-day psychologists is the observation that a given stimulus typically

FIGURE 1-1

Associations to Stimulus Word *"Round"*

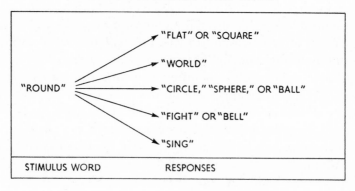

evokes quite a range and variety of responses. This can be simply illustrated by word association in which respondents are asked to reply with the first word that they think of in response to a stimulus word like "round." Some of the responses to this stimulus are cited in Figure 1–1. You can probably think of others.

If individual respondents were asked to explain their association between stimulus and response, we might get such varied explanations as "Columbus thought the world was round, not flat"; "I heard the word 'round' and thought of its opposite, 'square' "; "It made me think of a prizefight"; and so on. Without further laboring the point, it is apparent that the respondents were not replying to a single stimulus word which was uniformly interpreted. Rather, they responded in terms of their personal interpretations of the stimulus word.

An S-I-R Formulation. It is therefore convenient to think of modern psychology as fitting more nearly into an *S-I-R* formulation as opposed to the earlier *S-R* formulation. The response (R) is a function of both the stimulus (S) and the respondent's interpretation (I) of that stimulus. Almost any stimulus, whether it be a word or a more involved stimulus pattern like a memorandum from the supervisor exhorting employees to use safety equipment provided on their machines, may produce a variety of responses depending upon the significance of that stimulus for, and the interpretation of the stimulus by, each individual respondent.

Let us apply the *S-I-R* framework to exploring the range of potential responses employees might make to the aforementioned memorandum regarding safety practices. The stimulus condition (S) is identical for all employees; they all receive the same memorandum. This stimulus is evaluated by each employee against the background of his own past experience and attitudes. This evaluation leads each employee to a personal interpretation of the significance of the memorandum for him (I) and to a consequent response (R). Several alternative interpretative frameworks and consequent responses are schematically indicated in Figure 1–2.

The relationship between the interpretation of the stimulus condition and the consequent response is considerably oversimplified in the illustration outlined in Figure 1–2. First, many gradations of response other than those indicated in the illustration would be anticipated. And secondly, the memorandum would be interpreted by each employee in the light of other factors in addition to the ones of attitude and past experience. The employee's general satisfaction or dissatisfaction with the job, his physical and mental health, his mood as a result of specific experiences during the day, as well as other variables, may influence his reaction to this apparently simple stimulus condition.

An Elaborated S-I-R Formulation. Thus far we have said that each person's unique interpretation (I) of stimulus conditions (S) determines how he will respond (R) to those conditions. As indicated above, the interpretations made by different people vary with a tremendous number and variety of personal characteristics (like

FIGURE 1–2

Multiple Responses to a Uniform Stimulus Condition

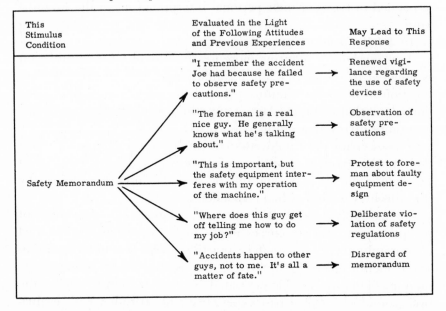

This Stimulus Condition	Evaluated in the Light of the Following Attitudes and Previous Experiences	May Lead to This Response
Safety Memorandum	"I remember the accident Joe had because he failed to observe safety precautions."	Renewed vigilance regarding the use of safety devices
	"The foreman is a real nice guy. He generally knows what he's talking about."	Observation of safety precautions
	"This is important, but the safety equipment interferes with my operation of the machine."	Protest to foreman about faulty equipment design
	"Where does this guy get off telling me how to do my job?"	Deliberate violation of safety regulations
	"Accidents happen to other guys, not to me. It's all a matter of fate."	Disregard of memorandum

intellectual ability, motivation, emotional state) and previous experiences. Clearly, a person's behavior is flexible. More appropriate responses are substituted for less appropriate ones, implying that the interpretations of stimulus conditions can be modified by experience. In short, people learn.

To indicate something of the influence of past experience upon present behavior requires an elaboration of the *S-I-R* formulation. What occurs after a person behaves in some way? Typically, his behavior is followed by some type of *reinforcement;* that is, an indication of whether his response is appropriate or inappropriate, desirable or undesirable, deserving of praise or reproof, and so on. Such reinforcement may be provided by the responses evoked from other people by his behavior or may be provided by the person himself as he assesses the outcomes of his behavior.

Thus, referring back to Figure 1–2, the employee who disregards the safety memorandum may receive a rebuff from his supervisor for not following instructions. Alternatively, he may suffer an injury which he quite properly attributes to having disregarded the safety

memorandum. In either case the employee's behavior has had consequences. Since these consequences are unfavorable, we refer to them
as *negative* reinforcements. Obviously, praise from a supervisor, a
financial bonus, approval from other workers, or a personal sense of
achievement are all instances of *positive* reinforcements.

An elaborated *S-I-R* formulation showing the influence of reinforcement *(Re)* is given below:

As shown in this scheme, the stimulus condition as interpreted by
the person evokes a response. This response, in turn, is followed by
some kind of reinforcement *(Re)*, the effects of which are "fed
back" into his interpretative framework. If the reinforcement is
positive, the feedback strengthens the existing interpretive framework. However if the reinforcement is negative, the feedback tends
to weaken, and perhaps to modify, the original interpretive framework. Once the *I* is modified, subsequent confrontation by this *S* will
likely generate a modified *R*. This sequence is shown in Figure 1–3
for an employee who learns that accidents can indeed happen to
him.

Of course, the same sequence as outlined in Figure 1–3 can occur
without actual injury as the reinforcement. Hearing about someone
else's injury or experiencing a near-accident can serve the same
ends.

There is an interesting and useful parallel between the *S-I-R-Re*
scheme with a feedback loop as described above and the concept of a
system which is further elaborated in the chapter on engineering
psychology. A system, like an electric circuit to a lamp, has certain
inputs (electric current), controls (a switch), and outputs (glowing
bulb). Viewing the human organism as a system, the stimuli are
inputs, the interpretative conditions are controls, and the responses
are outputs.

Furthermore, certain kinds of mechanical systems (that is, closed
loop systems) are self-regulating. Suppose the electric circuit includes a photoelectric cell sensing the daylight outside and activating the control switch only when outside illumination falls below a

FIGURE 1-3

An Illustration of Changed Response Following Reinforcement

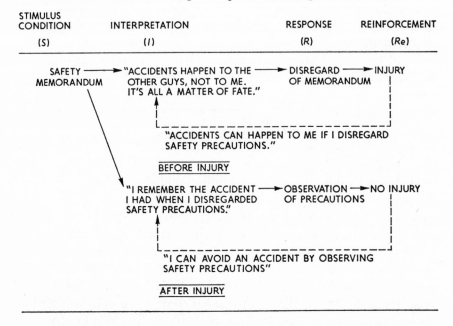

twilight level. This cell would then be performing a function similar to that of reinforcement in the human system by activating or deactivating the switch through a feedback circuit.

PSYCHOLOGY APPLIED TO INDUSTRIAL PROBLEMS

The foregoing discussion has merely hinted at the complexity of human behavior and the challenge of working within the vital and dynamic area of human behavior. Let us now bring the activities of the industrial psychologist, as opposed to specialists in other areas of psychology, into somewhat sharper focus.

We have already defined psychology as "the study of behavior" and have indicated that the industrial psychologist specializes in studying human behavior as it occurs in business and industrial settings. Perhaps the greatest barrier to understanding the functions of the industrial psychologist is the fairly prevalent confusion between industrial psychologists and "efficiency experts." The latter term calls to mind an image of a man more stopwatch than human.

The stereotype of an "efficiency expert" is that he equates efficiency with production and regards acceleration or speedup of the activities of each employee as the least expensive road to increased productivity.

Such a stereotype is invalid, bearing no relationship to the activities of the industrial psychologist. He is committed to promoting individual initiative and strengthening personal dignity. The successful realization of these objectives may, of course, be reflected in higher productivity, decreased absenteeism, and other objective criteria of improved performance. The essential point, however, is that the psychologist is interested in maximizing the realization of potential for accomplishment and personal satisfaction. Thus, he has a responsibility to all men, employees as well as employers.

History of Industrial Psychology

It is difficult to date the beginnings of activity that might properly be designated as industrial psychology. The most reasonable date to assign to the formulation of this as an area of specialization within the broader framework of general psychology is 1913 when Hugo Munsterberg's *Psychology and Industrial Efficiency* was published.[3] Efficiency as defined in it involved the dual notions of output or productivity as a function of input or effort.

Although the professional interests of early applied psychologists were rather diverse, American psychologists tended to concentrate most heavily on problems of personnel selection and placement. This emphasis was characteristic of most applied psychological work in the Army during World War I. The successful use of psychological tests for military classification and placement did much to familiarize large segments of the public with the efficacy of psychological testing.

A few years after the end of World War I, the Psychological Corporation was founded to develop and distribute psychological tests and to provide consultative services to industrial and other organizations. In the years since its formation in 1921, the Psychological Corporation has been joined in providing such services by many other such firms both in the United States and abroad.

A noteworthy departure from the early American emphasis upon

---

[3] H. Munsterberg, *Psychology and Industrial Efficiency* (Boston: Houghton Mifflin Co., 1913) .

personnel selection and placement can be dated to 1924 when the Hawthorne studies were undertaken. As elaborated in Chapter 10, these studies were designed to determine the relationship between working conditions (like illumination, temperature) and worker efficiency defined by the incidence of fatigue and monotony.[4] While unique in this country, this focus upon the conditions of work had been anticipated somewhat in Great Britain during World War I by the organization of the Industrial Fatigue Research Board.

The significant thing about the Hawthorne studies is that they opened a new era of psychological research in industry. What appeared at first to be a simple problem requiring a brief research program became progressively more involved as the studies continued for the next 15 years. These studies were singularly responsible for bringing the *I* aspects of the *S-I-R* formulation into industrial psychology. They raised questions and provided considerable methodology as well as some solutions to issues concerning attitudes, communication, leadership, and organizational structure. These issues, along with personnel matters, are central to contemporary industrial psychology.

The extensive requirements of the military during World War II for improved personnel assessment and training procedures added further impetus to the development of industrial psychology as we know it today. Enormous methodological advances were made in these areas, including refinements of procedures for personnel classification and performance appraisal. In addition, the rapid rate of technological change during and subsequent to World War II led to the formulation of a new area of specialization within industrial psychology—that of engineering psychology. This area is concerned with designing equipment in accord with the capabilities and limitations of the prospective human operators.

The postwar period has seen a continued development of industrial psychology in all of the areas already mentioned—personnel selection and classification, performance appraisal, working conditions, training, leadership, organizational psychology, and engineering psychology. Of these, the last three have probably captured the attention of recent researchers in the field to a somewhat greater extent than the others.

---

[4] F. J. Roethlisberger and W. J. Dickson, *Management and the Worker—An Account of a Research Program Conducted by the Western Electric Company, Chicago* (Cambridge: Harvard University Press, 1939).

As industry increasingly accepted psychologists' contributions, the industrial psychologist has come more and more to be consulted on matters affecting all aspects of the industrial enterprise. Whereas the field was initially restricted in scope to studying employee behavior, it has now been extended also to include studies of management and consumer behavior. Whereas early industrial psychologists were limited to studies of behavior within the context of a limited work setting, the field now includes consultations leading to changes in the organizational structures subsuming such settings.

There is every reason to believe that the growth and expansion of activity by industrial psychologists will continue in the future. Most of society's significant problems are at least in part psychological. Likewise many of society's significant goals require for their attainment the kinds of knowledge that psychologists have generated in the past and will generate to an even greater extent in the future. With astronauts, automation, the war on poverty, shorter workweeks, increased requirements for technical and managerial personnel, increasing populations, the consequent possibility of serious food shortages, and the ever-present issues of ethnic, racial, and international relations, there is no shortage of meaningful problems for the field of industrial psychology.

An Overview of the Field

The specific kinds of problems industrial psychologists are called upon to solve are extensive in scope. It will be convenient to indicate something of the range of industrial problems amenable to psychological analysis by presenting what is in essence an overview of the chapters that follow.

Although a book is of necessity divided into chapters and topics, we all realize that people and problems are not neatly segmented in similar fashion. The industrial complex involves interactions cutting across the specific chapter headings and topical organization of any book. Realizing this, let us preview the major topics with which we will subsequently be concerned.

Part I: Scope and Methods. Before we can plunge into a discussion of the applications of psychological principles and methods to industrial problems, we need to know something about psychologists and the ways in which they work. A statement like: "The importance of salary as a determinant of job satisfaction has been vastly overrated by management" is meaningless if the conclusion is predicated upon incomplete or faulty evidence. Thus, the present chapter and the two following are designed to familiarize you with the psychologist's orientation and discipline. These chapters discuss the subject matter and methodology of psychology in general and industrial psychology in particular.

[Industrial psychology is an applied discipline] Its practitioner makes direct applications of sound principles underlying knowledge about human behavior gained both from other areas within the broad field of psychology (for example, clinical, experimental, and social psychology) and such other disciplines as sociology, economics, and physiology. These applications are ultimately directed either toward predicting behavior in advance of its occurrence or toward invoking some kind of change in behavior as presently constituted. These two objectives, prediction and change, are a kind of payoff. They represent a practical test of theory.

The point of view taken in this book is that the science and profession of psychology can contribute positively to all elements of the industrial complex. It is for this reason that separate sections are devoted to discussions of psychological problems related to employee recruitment and efficiency, management efficiency, and consumer behavior.

Part II: Selecting, Placing, Training, and Appraising Employees. This part focuses upon the job applicant and the new employee. The company is often confronted first by the problem of selecting from a group of job applicants those who will best fulfill certain requirements. Which applicants if hired will most likely prove to be efficient and reasonably well-satisfied employees and which ones will find the job too easy, too difficult, or otherwise unsuited to their particular needs and desires?

This is a prediction problem requiring that the psychologist be familiar with the tools and techniques of personnel selection and placement. It may lead him into studies of the predictive efficiency of tests, inventories, interviews, application blanks, and letters of recommendation. He may have to devise new predictive instruments or to modify already existing devices. He must also develop adequate criteria of the outcomes he is attempting to predict, including industrial efficiency and job satisfaction.

Most companies place considerable emphasis upon training programs of various kinds for both new and experienced employees.

The primary purpose of industrial training is to develop certain knowledges, skills, and attitudes and to alter working behaviors demonstrated to be relatively inefficient.

A systematic training program is mandatory when a company is compelled to hire inexperienced employees. New employees with prior job experience also benefit from training with respect to company policies and practices. Psychologists can make important contributions to the conduct of such programs. Problems concerning training methods, simulation of working conditions, and teaching approaches have been of significant concern to psychologists for many years.

Industrial training is by no means restricted to new employees. Management may have a number of problems for which a continual program of training for employees already on the job is the only feasible solution. Among these we may simply list as representative the problems of job enlargement, development of potential supervisory personnel, maintenance and improvement of quality as well as output, management development, and preparing employees to take on new jobs created by an ever-expanding technocracy.

Finally, the performance of employees once selected, placed, and trained must be appraised. Such performance appraisals (a) guide subsequent personnel decisions including promotion, transfer, and merit increases; (b) permit diagnostic feedback to the employee concerning the quality of his performance and areas of possible improvement; and (c) provide criteria for determining the efficiency of selection, classification, and training programs.

Part III. Worker Efficiency. This series of chapters is concerned with a constellation of factors affecting the efficiency of employees on the job.

The physical working environment presents a number of problems concerning such things as optimal ventilation, illumination, machine location, and so on. More recently, psychologists have contributed significantly to problems of machine design and the structure of man-machine systems. This activity is particularly critical whenever the complexity of the equipment is such that careless design would strain or exceed human capability. Consider, for example, some of the design problems in developing high-speed aircraft in which a five-second delay during which the pilot fumbles to find a particular lever, knob, button, or dial may well represent a traveled distance of one mile. Less dramatic perhaps but equally

important are engineering psychology studies of the optimal location of controls and dials on automobile dashboards and industrial
equipment.

In spite of technological advances, and often because of them,
fatigue and boredom are often characteristic of work. The deleterious effect of these conditions upon morale, output, and safety are
self-evident as problems for psychological analysis.

Part IV: Motivation for Work. In order for them to perform
satisfactorily, employees must have the prerequisite knowledge and
ability. In addition, the working environment must be comfortable
and the equipment must be appropriately designed.

However these factors alone are insufficient to insure either high
productivity or the worker's sense of job satisfaction. Employees
must be motivated; they must want to invest the effort required for
maximum performance if they are to work most efficiently. And they
must regard their work as personally fulfilling if they are to derive a
sense of satisfaction from it. These matters are considered in Part
IV.

Motivation is a complex matter. At any moment in time, the goals
toward which a person strives reflect the interaction between the
present situation and his entire past history. Thus there are widespread individual differences between employees in their attitudes
toward work and the satisfactions they derive from it. Employees
who feel secure, enjoy their work, and feel amply rewarded in terms
of personal recognition and in terms of salary are predisposed to
react favorably to management policies and practices. Thus one of
the tasks for the industrial psychologist is to discover principles of
motivation transcending individual differences in specific work-
related drives.

Highly motivated employees do not, of course, always agree with
or endorse decisions by management. As a matter of fact they may
feel sufficiently comfortable in their working environment to be
quite vociferous in voicing objections or criticisms to particular
practices. They do not, however, regard every new decision with the
suspicion and mistrust characteristic of employees who are dissatisfied with their jobs. Consequently, industrial psychologists are frequently called upon to investigate the sources of dissatisfaction in a
particular working environment.

The context for work is a social one for most employees. With the
exception of a few solitary jobs, most workers are required to interact with one another. Furthermore, an employee brings a social

history to the job with him. Outside of work he has many group affiliations including his family, neighborhood, and church, to name just three. Industrial behavior is often clarified by studying the group affiliations and allegiances of the employees. Union and non-union employees, for example, may react quite differently to salary and promotion policies. Similarly, subgroups of employees by sex, seniority, and level of skill may be responding from different frames of reference.

V. Organizational Psychology. Our emphasis shifts in this part from individual workers to the organizational context in which work is performed, and to management. Management has a responsibility for facilitating both employee satisfaction and organizational efficiency.

The fact that a man occupies a leadership position by no means guarantees that he will have a willing group of followers. The selection and training of management personnel are generally regarded as critical problems in most companies. This statement is not limited to line supervision. Industrial psychologists are increasingly being called upon to develop programs for appraising and developing mid- and top-management personnel.

Although effective leadership at all levels of the company hierarchy is a requirement for industrial harmony, it does not guarantee such harmony. Every company is segmented to some degree into management and worker subgroups. Each of these subgroups is in turn further segmented into smaller subgroups by such things as type of work, amount and kind of influence, age, experience, pay, and so on. Yet together, and in spite of subgroup and sub-subgroup identification, all of these people are members of a single organization: the company. Organizational psychology seeks to effect a synthesis of these diverse influences in understanding behavior within the company.

One aspect of organizational psychology is the study of conflicts arising between the needs and vested interests of organizational subgroups, including disputes between labor and management. Industrial disharmony is always costly both to labor and management. The field of social psychology in particular has made noteworthy contributions to understanding the dynamics of such conflict.

Part VI: Consumer Behavior. A company survives because consumers buy its products or services. Thus, all parties to the manufacture, distribution, and sale of products or services have a vital interest in predicting and controlling consumer behavior.

One of the psychologist's unique contributions in this general area is his application of rigorous scientific methods of inquiry to such diverse problems as the size and constituency of markets, the effectiveness of advertising campaigns, consumer reactions to the product and the company manufacturing it, and the needs and motives underlying consumer behavior, to list a few.

To the extent that there is a psychology of consumer behavior, it has been significantly bolstered by activities of psychologists in the clinical and experimental areas. Clinical tools have been used by motivation researchers to discover the "hidden" or unconscious reasons underlying consumer behavior. Advertising has capitalized for years upon well-established findings from traditional laboratory-type research in experimental psychology.

Although psychologists have to the present devoted relatively little attention to studying the process of salesmanship, considerable research has been directed toward the problems of selecting and training salesmen.

INDUSTRIAL PSYCHOLOGY AS A PROFESSION

We have thus far described something of the scope of activities of the industrial psychologist. It is apparent from the foregoing discussion that he must possess general knowledge about human behavior and the factors influencing it. In addition, he must have at his command certain rather specific skills. He is a researcher and consequently must be conversant with techniques of assessment including psychological tests, attitude scales, and performance appraisal. He must know how to design experiments and evaluate the results in the broad area of industrial behavior. He must know how to draw representative samples from a population in order to perform certain kinds of market research and opinion studies. And we could list other skills as well. It is appropriate now to inquire into the development of these skills. How is the industrial psychologist trained, and how may we differentiate between the well-qualified practitioner and the glib but untrained charlatan?

Certification and Licensing

The classified section of the telephone directory for almost any large city contains listings under "psychologist." Unfortunately, it is legal in many states for anyone to represent himself to the public through the classified directory or any other outlet as a psychologist. This unhappy state of affairs is gradually being rectified by legislation. Thus, some states *license* psychologists in the same way as physicians, dentists, and lawyers are licensed. It is a criminal offense in such states for an individual without a license to practice psychology or to offer psychological service to the public. Other states *certify* psychologists. Certification involves less legislative control than licensing since it prohibits unqualified persons merely from representing themselves as "psychologists" or as "certified psychologists." It is perfectly legal in some of the states with certification laws for an untrained and unqualified person to represent himself as a "psychologist" as long as he makes no claim to certification.

Although the number is growing each year, many states still do not either license or certify psychologists. This means that if you were seeking the services of a bona fide industrial psychologist solely from the listing in a telephone directory in most communities, you might come up with a totally unqualified person. It is important, then, to know something about the training and professional affiliations of qualified industrial psychologists.

Professional Training

Since the public is not adequately protected against fraudulent psychological practice, the primary responsibility for specifying and maintaining standards rests with the psychological profession itself. Most qualified psychologists in this country are members of the American Psychological Association, which is the professional counterpart of such organizations as the American Medical Association and the American Dental Association. The purpose of the American Psychological Association is ". . . to advance psychology as a science, as a profession and as a means of promoting human welfare."[5] Although the Association does not endorse the professional qualifications of any of its members, it has developed a code of ethical practice to which all of its members are required to adhere. The minimum standard for acceptability as a *member* is roughly the doctorate in psychology from an accredited institution and engagement in work primarily psychological in nature. *Fellows* of the

---

[5] Bylaws for the American Psychological Association, Article I.1.

Association usually have the Ph.D. degree and a minimum of five years of postdoctoral professional experience. The total of both classes of members is approximately 25,000.

The Association is composed of 28 divisions representing specialized fields of interest and activities of the members. One of these is designated the Division of Industrial Psychology, which in 1968 was composed of approximately 900 members. The Division has as its stated purposes:

1. Establishing and maintaining high standards of practice in business, industry, public service, and related fields.
2. Encouraging research and publication in these fields.
3. Facilitating the exchange of information and experience among its members and with the general public.
4. Expediting the development of professional opportunities.
5. Fostering cooperative relations with allied professions.
6. Protecting the public from untrained and/or unethical practitioners.
7. Contributing to the advancement of psychology in general.[6]

An additional kind of professional recognition is the diploma awarded by the American Board of Examiners for Professional Psychology. This diploma is awarded to psychologists who are judged to be well-trained, highly competent, and very responsible practitioners. The requirements for status as a diplomate in the fields of clinical psychology, counseling, and guidance, or industrial psychology are the Ph.D. and five years of professional experience.

Employment of Industrial Psychologists

Industrial psychologists typically are employed in one of three kinds of settings. They may be employed as full-time staff members of a particular industry; they may be a full-time member of an organization of consulting psychologists; or they may hold an academic position in a university or college. Many industrial psychologists employed in the academic setting also consult on a part-time basis.

Industrial psychologists are employed as full-time staff members of quite a variety of industries, including oil companies, automotive companies, insurance companies, and so on. These psychologists are

---

[6] Bylaws of Division 14 of the American Psychological Association, Article I.2.

TABLE 1–1

Job Duties Performed by a Sample of Industrial Psychologists

Job Duty	*Percent*
Consulting with management	67
Personnel (management) development	47
Training	40
Test interpretation	38
Test validation	35
Personnel counseling	34
Organization planning	33
Criterion development	31
Research on personnel policies and practices	31
Attitude research and measurement	30
Personnel administration	30
Recruiting and employment	26
Test development and construction	24
Job studies and job analysis	24
Test administration	21
Wage and salary administration	14
Human engineering	14
Marketing and consumer research	13
Collective bargaining	5
Other specified duties	27

most often designated by some title other than "industrial psychologist." Several are Personnel Directors, Vice Presidents, and Directors of Research.

A number of organizations of psychologists offer consultive service to industry. These organizations typically perform studies under contract to a particular industry, business, or government agency. An industrial corporation may, for example, let a contract to a consulting organization to conduct a morale survey, or to develop a personnel selection battery, or to establish a training program. A member or team from the consulting group is then assigned to work on the problem for the contracting agency on a temporary basis. They are reassigned when the project is completed.

An analysis of the job duties reported by a sample of 246 industrial psychologists, including some who were employed full time in industry and some whose primary employment was academic, is summarized in Table 1–1. The primary work roles of these respondents were subsumed under four major headings:

1. Personnel administration (including recruiting, and wage and salary administration) ;

(2) Test research;

(3) Working with people (including personnel counseling, test administration, test interpretation, and management development) ;

(4). Organizational analysis (including attitude measurement, and advising management concerning personnel policy) . Other important areas of activity were human engineering and training.[7]

Although the primary emphasis in the employment of industrial psychologists is an *applied* emphasis involving a service commitment, this does not imply the absence of theoretical or pure research in this area. Industrial psychologists, whether employed by industry, a consulting organization, or a university have a commitment to further the development of psychology as a science. Thus, they continuously maintain a research orientation toward such basic problems in the field as improving the techniques of test construction and evaluation procedures, furthering scientific knowledge about human motivation, gaining a more comprehensive understanding of the learning process and, in fact, toward the entire vista of human behavior.

SUMMARY

Industrial psychology is the study of behavior as it occurs in business and industrial settings. Thus, it is concerned with the behavior of three broad classifications of individuals: workers, management, and consumers. It is a technology and an applied science, both using the findings of the behavioral sciences in general to improve organizational effectiveness and contributing in its own right to furthering the understanding of human behavior.

The application of sound psychological principles differs from both the pseudopsychologies and the stereotype of the "efficiency expert." Pseudopsychologies are founded upon a presumed relationship between character traits and external signs like lines in the palm or size of the ears. This presumption is entirely unfounded.

Modern industrial psychology studies behavior with a view to maximizing the realization of potential for accomplishment and personal satisfaction. Thus, it has a responsibility to employees as well as to employers. The psychologist views behavior as a function of precipitating factors (the stimulus conditions) and of intervening

---

[7] A. C. Mackinney and M. D. Dunnette, "The Industrial Psychologist's Job," *Personnel Psychology*, Vol. 17 (1964) , pp. 271–80.

variables which determine the way in which particular individuals will perceive and interpret the stimulus.

Many states have no legislation designed to protect the public from fraudulent psychological practice. Consequently, the primary responsibility for specifying and maintaining standards rests with the profession of psychology itself. Most qualified psychologists in this country are members of the American Psychological Association. Membership in this organization is predicated upon satisfactory completion of certain minimum requirements of graduate training and experience.

An industrial psychologist may be employed as a full-time staff member of a particular industrial organization, as a full-time consultant, or as a faculty member in a university or college.

2. How the Industrial Psychologist Works

Frequent reference was made in the previous chapter to the fact that psychology is the *scientific* study of behavior. Some persons find it difficult to conceive of a "science" without the trappings of a laboratory, including sparkling glassware, bunsen burners, microscopes, and perhaps a cyclotron or two. Reference to a scientific study of behavior is regarded by them as a basic contradiction in terms. They argue that the complexity and variability of human behavior precludes its study in scientific fashion.

Reasoning like this is erroneous because it rests upon an incorrect definition of "science." A science is characterized by the methods it employs rather than by the phenomena it studies or the physical setting in which it operates. The complexity of human behavior creates special problems for the psychologist to be sure, but it does not itself dictate the application of methods that are unscientific. In essence, the methods employed by psychologists are identical with those employed by researchers in such disciplines as chemistry and physics.

It will be helpful to know something about the characteristics of scientific method in general before considering the specific ways in which the industrial psychologist employs these methods.

ESSENTIALS OF SCIENTIFIC METHOD

You will recall that the pseudopsychologies were primarily based upon speculation rather than upon observation. There is nothing inherently wrong with speculation in itself. Many brilliant ideas originate as figments of someone's vivid imagination. So, too, do many ideas that are not so brilliant! Consider, for example, some of the delusions experienced by certain mental patients who believe they have discovered the secret of perpetual life or have "proven" that the world is flat after all.

Scientific method requires that we go one step beyond speculation. The investigator's educated guess about relationships between phenomena must be cast into the form of an hypothesis. The hypothesis is a statement of possible relationship that is amenable to investigation by observation.

Objectivity

Scientific observations for the purpose of substantiating or refuting hypotheses must be made in objective rather than subjective fashion. The investigator does not have an axe to grind. He attempts to discover whether or not a hypothesized relationship exists. He is not committed to proving the existence of the relationship.

During the course of everyday living, most of us make observations that are quite subjective in nature and hence are unscientific. We hold certain biases and preconceived notions which color our observations. If, for example, you fear airplane travel, you may find support for your fear in newspaper accounts of airplane accidents. In so doing, however, you are failing to consider all of the data. What about the vast majority of flights which are successful and hence are not newsworthy?

Subjectivity may influence our observations in yet another way. The observer's biases and misconceptions may actually cause him to misinterpret what he sees and hears. Suppose that an employee is convinced that his supervisor is unfair and guilty of favoritism. The fact that this supervisor recommends pay raises for certain of his subordinates and not for others may be incorrectly interpreted by this employee as another sign of favoritism rather than as a reflection of the fact that some employees are truly more deserving of salary increases than others.

Controlled Observation

In addition to objectivity, scientific methods require the exertion of careful controls. It is insufficient, for example, merely to speculate that older employees are more safety-conscious than younger ones.

And casual observations of a few older employees at work would not contribute to the scientific validity of this speculative conclusion.

Instead, what is required is a systematic investigation of the injury records of employees of different ages. The influence of factors other than the critical one of age would have to be *controlled* (eliminated or held constant) if the investigation were to have meaning. Such "control variables" might include length of job experience, nature of the work with respect to exposure to potential hazards, and so on.

The Independent Variable. The elements of scientific method—observation, objectivity, and control—are translated by the researcher into an investigation of the relationship between two basic kinds of variables. One of these, the independent variable, is the factor whose effects are being investigated.

The range of independent variables of interest to the industrial psychologist is quite extensive. He may, for example, be interested in studying the effects of changes in the physical working environment, or of a new safety program, or of a training program for supervisors. Any factor that is systematically controlled so that it operates under certain circumstances and not under others (or is operative for certain groups and not for others) may be investigated as an independent variable.

The Dependent Variable. The behaviors studied as possible functions of the independent variable are referred to as dependent variables. The investigator is interested in determining whether certain aspects of behavior can be shown to depend upon manipulation of the independent variable.

The dependent variables of greatest concern to industrial psychologists have been classified as (*a*) performance and (*b*) satisfaction.[1] The importance of performance measures as dependent variables is almost self-evident. In investigating the effect of some change in the working environment or some new job practice it is logical to inquire whether performance is improved, diminished, or unaffected as a consequence of the change. The kinds of performance measures used for this purpose are exceedingly diverse, including such things as productivity, absenteeism, turnover, spoilage, suspensions, and accidents.

---

[1] R. A. Katzell, "Industrial Psychology," in P. R. Farnsworth and Quinn McNemar (eds.), *Annual Review of Psychology*, Vol. 8 (Palo Alto, Calif.: Annual Reviews, Inc., 1957), p. 237.

The importance of "satisfaction" as a dependent variable may not be quite as obvious unless we recognize that management and workers do not always share similar objectives. Although increased output may be regarded by management as a desirable consequence of altered working conditions, such alterations sometimes lead to considerable worker dissatisfaction. Dissatisfaction can be fertile soil for low morale, increased turnover, and absenteeism. Hence, it often is imperative to ascertain the impact of independent variable manipulations upon criteria of both satisfaction and output.

Causality?

The scientist is acutely aware of the fact that he may demonstrate a relationship between two variables but can never actually prove that one *causes* the other. Cause-effect relationships are, to be sure, frequently inferred from a set of observations. Quite often, however, we can demonstrate a relationship between variables without having any indication of which one is cause and which is effect.

Suppose, for example, that the psychologist makes the observation that in general, insurance salesmen who have been with a company for more than one year sell more insurance (that is, are more productive) than salesmen who have been with the company for less than a year. The factors of length of time with the company and productivity are thus related, but which is cause and which is effect? Does experience with the company improve selling technique? Perhaps. It is just as plausible, however, to hypothesize that highly productive salesmen are rewarded both in terms of salary and job satisfaction, causing them to remain with the company for a relatively long period of time. Unproductive salesmen, on the other hand, may receive lower commissions and become sufficiently discouraged with the job to seek employment elsewhere within a year or less. Finally, we cannot discount the possibility that *neither* experience nor productivity is a causal factor since both may themselves be caused by some third factor held in common.

The foregoing discussion has been offered in the nature of a hasty overview of some of the essentials of scientific methodology. Let us now see how the industrial psychologist applies scientific methods to the study of human behavior in three basic ways: naturalistic observation, experimental observation, and clinical observation.

NATURALISTIC OBSERVATION

We have already stated that the scientist attempts to discover relationships between independent and dependent variables. This requires that the independent variable be so manipulated as to reveal corresponding variations in the dependent variable.

Some kinds of independent variables, however, are not amenable to manipulation by the investigator. This situation is perhaps most apparent in astronomy where the observer cannot alter the course of the stars and planets to fulfill the needs of his experimentation. The independent variables of interest to the astronomer are manipulated, so to speak, by nature. The scientist makes his observations whenever conditions existing in their natural state are favorable to the study of the particular phenomenon that he wishes to investigate. Naturalistic observation, then, is characterized by the fact that the researcher does not control the independent variable. Rather, he is compelled to study it as and when it occurs in its natural state.

An Illustration of Naturalistic Observation

Naturalistic observations are frequently made by psychologists. One investigation of this type was concerned with studying the relative effectiveness of a stop sign and a red blinker light at an intersection.[2] State law required that a driver bring his car to a full stop at or before such a sign or blinker light.

The independent variable in this study was the signal to stop (sign or light) ; the dependent variable was the action of the driver in adhering to or disobeying these signals. It would have been extremely difficult for the investigators to study the relationship between these variables in any setting other than the natural environment. Consequently, observations were made at two intersections in the same neighborhood: one intersection had a stop sign while the other had a red blinker light. The observations were made from a sheltered doorway, and the responses of the drivers were classified and tabulated as illustrated in Table 2–1.

The investigators drew the following conclusions: (1) Only

---

[2] C. F. Hummel and G. R. Schmeidler, "Driver Behavior at Dangerous Intersections Marked by Stop Signs or by Red Blinker Lights," *Journal of Applied Psychology,* Vol. 39, No. 1 (1955) , pp. 17–19.

TABLE 2-1

Stops and Slowdowns of Cars at Intersections with a Stop Sign and with a
Blinker Light

Category of Response	Stop Sign 3–4 Weeks after Erection	Stop Sign 3–4 Months after Erection	Red Blinker Light
Full stop with no more than half the car past the intersection line	22%	29%	44%
Full stop with more than half the car past the intersection line	30	19	9
Slowing down but not a full stop	31	35	25
No perceptible slowing down	17	17	22
Total	100%	100%	100%

about one half of the drivers in the neighborhood studied stopped their cars completely when required to do so by the stop sign or blinker light. (2) A significantly greater percentage of drivers stopped too late (past the intersection) at the stop sign than at the blinker light. (This is interpreted as meaning that the blinker is more readily visible from a distance.) (3) The percentage of drivers who stopped or slowed down for a newly erected sign was about the same as the percentage stopping or slowing down for a sign that had been standing for several months.

The fact that investigators employing naturalistic observation do not themselves manipulate the independent variable does not make the method or the findings unscientific. As long as observations are made systematically and objectively and as long as extraneous factors are controlled, the results of naturalistic investigations can be both meaningful and useful.

Extraneous factors are those potentially affecting the dependent variable but not currently the subject of investigation. Hence, the control of these factors is extremely important and sometimes difficult to achieve in natural situations. The investigators comparing the relative effectiveness of the stop sign and blinker light had to control at least four such factors which might have influenced driver behavior. First, they had to take reasonable precautions to prevent drivers from knowing that their behavior was being studied. It is likely that a higher percentage of drivers would have complied with the law had they known that they were being observed. Secondly, the neighborhood was controlled by making observations at two intersections in the same vicinity. There are undoubtedly differences between neighborhoods in the extent to which drivers adhere to the letter of the law. A third controlled variable was the factor of restraints apart from the stop sign and blinker light. Obviously the experimenters would have contaminated their findings if they had selected one intersection that was regularly patrolled by a policeman (in addition to having a stop sign) and another intersection not similarly patrolled. Finally, the investigators observed that some drivers were compelled to slow down or to stop at the intersection in order to avoid a collision with the car in front. Since it was impossible to determine whether these drivers would have stopped or slowed down for the sign or blinker light, these cases were eliminated from the data analysis.

Evaluation of the Naturalistic Method

The psychologist has certain reservations about using the naturalistic method. Since he has not directly manipulated the independent variable, it is difficult to repeat a set of naturalistic observations under exactly the same conditions as prevailed the first time. What would happen, for example, if we wished to verify the findings cited in Table 2–1? Even if we followed a procedure identical with that originally used and made our observations at the same two intersections, we might obtain different results because of changes in the natural situation. A series of accidents, for example, at the stop sign intersection might have led to the posting of a policeman at this intersection for several weeks. Even though he were no longer present when we recorded driver behavior, his former presence there may have encouraged better driving habits. Furthermore, the sign itself will have been up for a longer time when we repeat our observations. The time of the year at which observations are made may influence our findings. Many high school students take part-time jobs requiring that they drive a car or truck during the summer. Their behavior may be quite different from that of older, more experienced drivers. You can undoubtedly think of other subtle variations that may creep into the natural situation, making it difficult or even impossible to repeat and verify a set of naturalistic observations.

There are nevertheless situations in which the naturalistic method is the best method available to the industrial psychologist. Persons who know that they are being observed in an experimental situation will sometimes deliberately behave in a way calculated to impress the investigator. Such alterations of behavior might be noted, for example, if we were to conduct a study of the kinds of programs TV viewers prefer to watch. We could administer a questionnaire dealing with viewing habits, but the obtained responses might not be trustworthy. An alternative procedure would be to develop an experimental situation in which viewers have access to several TV channels under controlled circumstances and to tabulate the percentage of viewers watching each kind of program. Here again, though, the investigator could not be certain that the viewers had not altered their behavior because they knew they were being observed. Consequently, naturalistic observation would be the method of choice for the study of this problem. Persons might be interviewed in their homes to determine whether or not they were watching TV at the moment and if so, the particular program being viewed.

THE EXPERIMENTAL METHOD

The primary difference between the experimental and naturalistic methods is that the former places the investigator in charge of the situation. He manipulates the independent variable and controls extraneous factors. This kind of regulation by the experimenter makes it possible to repeat observations under identical conditions in order to verify the findings. It also means that the investigator is in a somewhat stronger position to infer cause-effect relationships because he may systematically vary one factor at a time and note corresponding changes, if any, in other factors that he suspects might be affected.

Experimental Design

The experimental method may be employed in either a laboratory setting or in a real-life setting like an office or industrial plant. The advantage of doing research in a laboratory is that the investigator can arrange his materials and experimental conditions with precision. Since the laboratory is, however, an artificial environment, generalizations from laboratory findings to the industrial setting may be erroneous. Therefore, the industrial psychologist most often accepts laboratory findings as suggestive and attempts to verify them in the plant, office, or other work setting before attempting to apply the results of his experimentation.

The simplest kind of experimental design requires a study of two groups of *subjects* (persons being investigated) . One of these groups, the *control group,* serves as a standard for comparative purposes. The *experimental group,* on the other hand, is the one in which the independent variable is manipulated. A simple illustration will serve to clarify the difference between these groups.

Let us assume that we wish to investigate the effect of increased illumination upon the typewriting proficiency of secretaries. The independent variable is level of illumination. Hence, secretaries working under the changed level of illumination would constitute the experimental group. The effectiveness of this variable would be investigated by comparing the typing proficiency of subjects in the experimental group with the performance of secretaries working under normal illumination. Consequently a second group of subjects working under normal illumination conditions would constitute the control group.

The dependent variable in this investigation would be some criterion of typing proficiency like the number of words typed per unit of time and corrected for errors or erasures. It is apparent, however, that many factors aside from the specific independent variable under investigation (illumination) may affect typing speed. Such factors as finger dexterity, length of experience as a typist, and kind of copy being typed may be reflected in speed and accuracy of secretarial performance but are really extraneous to the specific problem under investigation. It would therefore be necessary to insure the similarity of the experimental and control groups with respect to all such extraneous factors before we could attribute any observed differences in typing speed solely to the independent variable.

Matched Group Design. One procedure for eliminating the effects of extraneous factors is to match or equate the groups of subjects on the basis of such factors. For example, if we wish to investigate only the effects of illumination, it would be necessary somehow to eliminate the potential effect of differences in finger dexterity. This would be accomplished in a matched-groups design by administering a finger dexterity test to a pool of available subjects before assigning anyone to the experimental or control group. Pairs of persons with identical scores would be identified, and one member of the pair would be assigned to the experimental group while her counterpart would be assigned to the control group.

It is exceedingly difficult to implement a matched-groups design for a number of reasons. First, it is necessary to have a large pool of potential subjects available in order to identify pairs that match. Second, the process of constructing equated groups becomes increasingly difficult as the number of extraneous variables to be controlled increases. You will recall that our hypothetical investigation requires that we eliminate from consideration both the factors of finger dexterity and length of experience. Thus, we would have to identify pairs of subjects who not only have the same scores on a finger dexterity test but also are identical in length of secretarial experience. As we attempt to match for still more variables, the process becomes unmanageable. Third, we have been considering a design involving only two groups of subjects. If, however, our design required more than two groups (and many *do*), the task of matching is still further complicated. Finally, even when a matched-groups design is feasible, it would be erroneous to assume that matching has really accomplished what we set out to do; that is, to eliminate the effects of potentially contaminating factors. There is always the possibility that factors other than the ones on which we equated our groups will exert some consistent and uncontrolled effect upon the dependent variable.

It is for these reasons that most experimental investigations utilize a random group design rather than a matched group design.

Random Group Design. In this procedure, subjects are randomly assigned to the experimental and control groups. Randomization requires that every subject have an equal chance for assignment to each of the groups required for an experiment. Since no biases of any kind are permitted into the assignment of subjects to groups, we may assume that each randomly constructed group is essentially like every other randomly constructed group drawn from the same orginal pool of subjects.

Once the subjects are randomly assigned to groups, there remains only the decision about which should be treated experimentally and which should serve as a control. This again should be decided without bias, perhaps by flipping a coin.

An Illustrative Laboratory Experiment

A considerable amount of research in the general area of improving machine design has, as you might suspect, been directed toward facilitating aircraft pilot efficiency. As aircraft become increasingly complex and as their speed increases, the pilot must make correct decisions with increased rapidity. This in turn means that new techniques must be discovered for relaying information about the functioning of aircraft components to the pilot in a way that is readily comprehensible.

The location of various kinds of dials and the "normal" position of the pointers has been shown to be a critical factor affecting the speed and accuracy with which the dials are read. The best configuration of 16 dials in multiengined aircraft has been demonstrated to be four banks of four dials each, with the normal position of each pointer at the "nine o'clock" position as indicated in Figure 2–1.

Starting with this arrangement of dials, an experiment was performed to determine whether or not speed and accuracy of dial reading could be further improved by combining a deviating pointer (indicating some kind of malfunction or condition that must be corrected) with a change in illumination of the specific dial in question.[3]

The independent variable, then, was change in illumination accompanying a deviating dial pointer. Cockpit dials are normally illuminated in red. The illuminant of deviating dials changed from red to green.

One of the dependent variables was the speed with which the subjects could identify the number of deviating dials (which was varied by the investigator between 1 and 8) in each cluster of 16.

The control condition consisted of presenting the clusters of 16 dials with varying numbers and configurations of discrepancies but without changing the illuminant. The experimental condition consisted of the presentation of the same configuration of discrepancies with a red-to-green illuminant for discrepant dials. The same sub-

---

[3] A. E. Bartz, "Attention Value as a Function of Illuminant Color Change," *Journal of Applied Psychology,* Vol. 41 (1957), pp. 82–84.

FIGURE 2–1

Optimal Arrangement of 16 Aircraft Dials, Each Pointing
to the Normal Condition

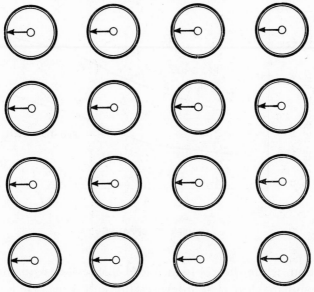

Source: M. J. Warrick and W. F. Grether, "The Effect of Pointer
Alignment on Check Reading of Instrument Panels," Aero Medical
Laboratory, *AMCMCREXD 694–17* (June, 1948).

jects were used under the two conditions, making it unnecessary to
equate the experimental and control groups on extraneous factors.

The average times required to count the number of deviating
dials under the experimental and control conditions are graphed in
Figure 2–2.

Two conclusions follow from these data. First, the time required
to count deviant dials increases as a function of the number of such
dials. Secondly, this time is considerably reduced when deviation of
the pointer is accompanied by changing the illuminant from red to
green. The implication of these findings for the design of aircraft
instrument panels is obvious.

Speed of discrepancy identification was not the only dependent
variable investigated. The experimenter was interested also in comparing the *accuracy* of identification under the experimental and
control conditions. He noted that the subjects averaged 1.05 errors
(in identifying a total of 36 discrepant dials) with constant red

FIGURE 2–2

Average Response Times to Configurations Containing
One through Eight Error Dials

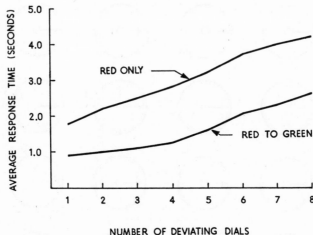

NUMBER OF DEVIATING DIALS

illumination, while they only averaged 0.38 errors with the red-to-green illuminant shift. The interpretation of the average number of errors under these two conditions required a statistical analysis in order to determine that the difference between them was attributable to the experimental conditions rather than to chance. The types and applications of statistics are discussed later in this chapter.

CLINICAL OBSERVATION

Several procedures for gathering and interpreting data are derived from techniques more usually associated with clinical than with industrial psychology. This is most evident in certain studies seeking to relate personality to employee, management, and consumer behavior using depth interviews, projective tests, and the clinical case history. Such procedures have been used for such diverse projects as morale assessments, investigations of personality patterns associated with "accident-proneness," and analysis of the impact of advertising appeals and product design upon consumers' unconscious needs.

A distinguishing characteristic of clinical observation as a method is its emphasis upon gathering information "in depth" about one person at a time. This focus upon the dynamics of an individual's behavior does not preclude generalizations about groups of persons.

In order to make such generalizations, clinical observations must be collated across people.

Although clinical observation can be a useful supplement to the naturalistic and experimental methods, it suffers certain limitations when applied to problems in industrial psychology.

First, there is the matter of the appropriateness in industry of procedures developed for application in treatment settings. This may impinge upon the employee's right to privacy. A person seeking psychological treatment voluntarily places himself in the role of patient and accepts the fact that it is in his own best interest to aid the clinical diagnostician by revealing his needs, fears, and wishes—both conscious and unconscious. However, there is a legitimate question about the propriety of requiring employees to be similarly revealing.

Second, some of the tools of clinical observation lack refinement by the standards imposed upon scientific methods in general. This is a somewhat less serious problem when these techniques are used for their intended diagnostic purpose by experienced clinical psychologists than when they are used by relatively untrained or inexperienced researchers. This is a less serious problem also when these clinical tools are used to generate leads for further investigation than when they alone provide the data for generalizing about industrial behavior.

The foregoing paragraphs do not deny the usefulness of some kinds of clinical observation in industrial settings. Indeed, two essentially clinical procedures—the personal interview and the life history—are extensively and profitably used in industrial psychology. However, other clinical procedures which seek to probe personality "in depth" must be used cautiously both in industrial research and practice.

STATISTICS

Statistics of various kinds are used in conjunction with almost any experiment performed by the industrial psychologist. The investigator typically measures change in the dependent variable associated with manipulation of the independent variable. Hence, the outcome of an experiment is usually expressed in numerical form; that is, test scores, production records, accident rates, numbers of persons answering "yes" to a questionnaire item, and so on. The summary and interpretation of numerical results is facilitated by statistical analysis.

Statistical techniques fall generally into three classes: descriptive statistics, statistical inference, and correlation.

Descriptive statistics provide a kind of shorthand description of a mass of data. This is a kind of statistic with which you are most familiar. When we speak of an average score or a range of scores, we are really summarizing a mass of data in a simple and convenient way.

A second kind of statistic is required to facilitate the interpretation of obtained averages or ranges of scores. You will recall that the results of the dial reading experiment indicated that subjects made fewer errors when the illuminant was changed then when it remained constant. Before interpreting these findings as indicative of the superiority of illuminant change, however, we must be certain that the difference between the number of errors under the two conditions did not arise solely as a function of chance. *Statistical inference* provides us with an indication of the likelihood that our experimental findings are merely chance findings. As the likelihood of attributing obtained findings to chance is reduced, we may have increased confidence in the conclusion that these findings resulted from the manipulation of the independent variable.

A third statistical procedure is that of *correlation*. Correlational analysis reveals the magnitude and direction of the relationship between variables. If measures of these variables parallel each other closely, they are strongly correlated. However, when there is little or no parallelism between these measures, correlation is weak or absent. Thus, correlational analysis could be used, for example, to determine whether there is a relationship between seniority and supervisory ratings of employee proficiency, between preemployment test scores and a subsequently obtained performance measure, between age and accident frequency, and so on.

The ensuing discussion concerns some of the simpler statistics. The computation of these statistics is not considered in this chapter. Rather, we will illustrate some of the ways in which descriptive and inferential statistics and correlation are applied. The reader interested in computational procedures is referred to Appendix A.

Descriptive Statistics

Many kinds of data may be conveniently summarized by counting the number of persons (or computing the percentage of persons) obtaining each score. This summary may be visually presented by plotting a *frequency polygon* or a *histogram* as illustrated in Figure 2–3.

Both of the plots in Figure 2–3 were derived from the same set of IQ data. They show the percentage of youngsters earning IQs within each 10-point interval starting with the interval 40 to 49.

The Normal Distribution Curve. As the number of observations plotted on a graph is increased, the resultant distribution tends

FIGURE 2–3

Frequency Distribution of Intelligence Quotients of 2,904 Children

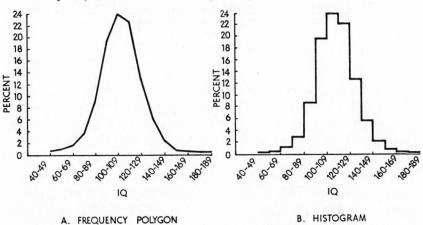

A. FREQUENCY POLYGON   B. HISTOGRAM

Source: L. M. Terman and Maud A. Merrill, *Measuring Intelligence* (Cambridge: Riverside Press, 1937), p. 37.

more and more to approximate a curve rather than a polygon. When we have made a substantial number of observations free of biasing factors, the obtained curve often has the characteristics of the normal distribution. Such a normal distribution curve is illustrated in Figure 2–4. You will note that very few persons have IQs as low as 40 or as high as 160. The highest percentage of persons have IQs which cluster closely about 100.

Graphed data do not always take the form of a normal distribution. Some characteristics are not normally distributed even when data are plotted for the entire population. In addition, when the sample of persons is not randomly selected (that is, is somehow biased), the resultant distribution of data is usually asymmetrical.

FIGURE 2-4

A Normal Distribution Curve Obtained from Measurement of IQ

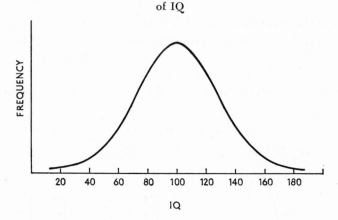

Suppose, for example, we administered a 180-point test of blueprint reading knowledge to a group of job applicants and separated these applicants into two subgroups: one with previous work experience entailing some sort of blueprint reading, and the other without such experience. The resultant test score distributions would look like those in Figure 2-5. These distributions are *skewed* (unsymmetrical) because we have plotted measurements for selected groups of persons. We expect the distribution to be normal only when selective factors are absent.

The curve for inexperienced applicants shows that whereas most earned relatively low scores, a few earned atypically high scores

FIGURE 2-5

Skewed Distributions

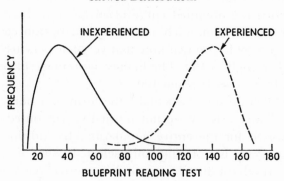

perhaps because of formal training in blueprint reading or hobbies requiring such knowledge. This curve is *positively* skewed. In contrast, the curve for experienced applicants is *negatively* skewed. In spite of previous work experience which ought to be helpful to performance on this test, some of these applicants apparently know relatively little about reading a blueprint. This is probably the reason they are seeking another job!

Although it is possible to summarize a set of data by graphing the distribution, this kind of summary can be rather inconvenient. Alternatively, we can pretty well summarize the data presented in Figure 2–4, for example, in terms of two critical features: the "average" IQ, and the spread of IQs away from this "average." The typical or "average" score is statistically expressed by a measure of *central tendency*. The spread of scores is expressed by a measure of *variability*.

Central Tendency. The three primary measures of central tendency are the mean, median, and mode.

The *mean* ($\bar{X}$) is the measure with which you are probably most familiar. It is simply the arithmetic average computed by adding the scores and dividing by the number of cases or observations. The computational formula for the mean is written

$$\bar{X} = \frac{\Sigma X}{N}$$

where X is used to denote a score, Σ is the process of summing, and N is the number of cases.

The *median* (*Med*) is the score falling precisely at the middle of the distribution. If a distribution of IQs earned by 501 employees were arranged in order from lowest to highest, the median IQ would be the one earned by the 251st worker. Two hundred fifty employees will have earned IQs below the median and 250 would have earned IQs above the median.

The *mode* (*Mo*) is simply the score that occurs most frequently within a distribution. It is little used as a measure of central tendency except under special circumstances. A shoe buyer, for example, would find it useful to know the modal shoe size worn by men in order to place his orders wisely.

The mean, median, and mode are identical when the distribution of data is normal. These three measures of central tendency diverge,

however, when the distribution is skewed. The relationships between mean, median, and mode in normal and skewed distributions
are illustrated in Figure 2–6.

You will note that the mean is more sensitive to the "tail" of the
distribution than is the median. The fact that the mean is highly
influenced by extreme or unusual cases in a distribution implies that
its use should be limited to situations in which the distribution of
data is not seriously skewed. You can readily see that the median,
which is less influenced by extreme cases in a distribution, is a more
representative measure of central tendency than the mean when
distributions are skewed.

FIGURE 2–6

Measures of Central Tendency in Normal and in Skewed Distributions

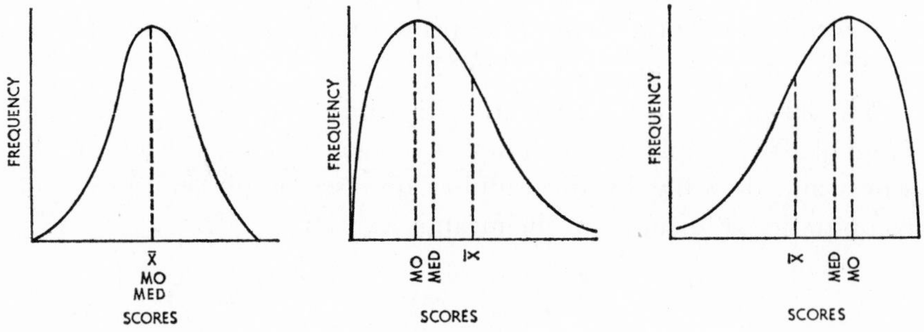

| Normal Distribution | Positively Skewed Distribution | Negatively Skewed Distribution |

Consider, for example, the interpretation of the statement that
the average annual income of 10 secretaries in a company is $5,550.
The first question we might raise concerns the type of "average"
computed. Was it a mean, median, or mode? Secondly, the interpretation of this "average" would depend upon the shape of the distribution. Is it normal or skewed? Suppose $5,550 represents the mean
income derived from the following set of figures: $4,000, $4,200,
$4,300, $4,500, $5,000, $5,000, $5,500, $6,500, $6,500 and $10,000.
The fact that one of these 10 women (the president's personal secretary) is receiving an atypically high salary has acted to increase the
mean for the group to a figure that does not truly reflect typical earnings. A more realistic kind of average under such circumstances
would be the median, here computed as $5,000.

A Measure of Variability. An indication of central tendency does not by itself provide an adequate description of a distribution of scores. It is perfectly possible, for example, for the means of two normal distributions to be identical even though these distributions may be quite different with respect to variability (or spread of scores away from the mean). This kind of situation is illustrated in Figure 2–7, in which the data in the dotted-line distribution cluster more closely about the mean than do the data in the solid line distribution.

FIGURE 2–7

Two Normal Distributions with Identical Means but Different Variabilities

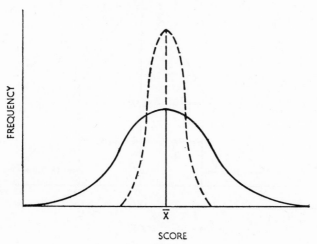

There are a number of different statistical measures of variability, all of which describe the spread of data away from the measure of central tendency. The statistic most often used for this purpose and the only one with which we will be here concerned is the *standard deviation* (σ). Its computation is described in Appendix A.

Approximately 68 percent (actually 68.26 percent) of the scores in a normal distribution fall within the scores delimited by one standard deviation on either side of the mean. This percentage is constant regardless of the type of score that is plotted and of the computed mean, *provided that the distribution of data is normal.*

Suppose we have calculated the mean of a set of mechanical

aptitude test scores as 50 and the standard deviation of the distribution of scores as 10. The limits defined by $\pm 1\sigma$ (one standard deviation on either side of the mean) are thus 40 and 60, and approximately 68 percent of the obtained scores fall between these limits. The remaining 32 percent of the scores are equally divided, with 16 percent falling below the score corresponding to -1σ (40) and 16 percent falling above the scores corresponding to $+1\sigma$ (60). The distribution of scores obtained on this test of mechanical aptitude is schematically represented in Figure 2–8.

FIGURE 2–8

A Distribution of Test Scores in Which the Mean Is 50 and the Standard Deviation Is 10

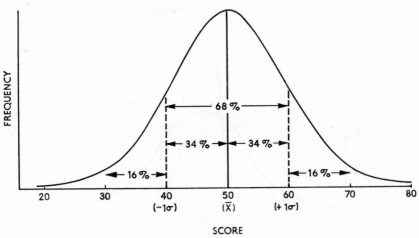

If we administered the same test to another group of persons and found here that the mean was still 50 but that the standard deviation was only 5, the middle 68 percent of the scores would fall between the limits of 45 to 55. Similarly, if we had a third distribution of data also with a mean of 50 but with a standard deviation of 15, the middle 68 percent of the cases would fall between scores of 35 and 65. Thus, the larger the standard deviation the greater is the spread of scores away from the mean. Conversely, as the size of the standard deviation decreases, the scores cluster more tightly about the mean.

Just as the percentage of cases between the limits of $\pm 1\sigma$ is constant for normal distributions, so too is the percentage of cases between the limits defined by two and three standard deviations on either side of the mean. The scores between -2σ and $+2\sigma$ include 95.44 percent of the cases, while virtually all of the cases in normal distributions (99.74 percent) are included between the score limits defined by three standard deviations on either side of the mean.

Knowledge about the standard deviation of a distribution of data is useful in a number of ways. One application of this statistic relates to the interpretation of test scores. Let us assume that we have administered two tests to an individual, a test of mechanical aptitude and a test of manual dexterity. We will further assume that this person earned a score of 80 on the mechanical aptitude test and a score of 115 on the dexterity test. Did he score better on the mechanical or manual test? It is obvious that the information thus far presented is insufficient to make a judgment.

A partial answer to this question is provided by comparing his performance with the mean performance of large groups of persons who have previously taken both tests. Suppose the mean mechanical aptitude score earned by such groups was 60 and the mean manual dexterity score was 105. It is apparent now that this person scored somewhat better than average on both the mechanical aptitude and on the dexterity test. In order to find out *how much* better than average he scored on these tests we might want to examine the standard deviations of the two distributions of test scores. We will assume that the standard deviation as computed for the mechanical aptitude test is 20 while the standard deviation for the manual dexterity test is 30. The distributions of scores for these two tests are shown in Figure 2–9.

When the test scores are converted to standard deviation units as shown in Figure 2–9, this person's mechanical aptitude score converts to $+1\sigma$ (1 standard deviation above the mean) while his manual dexterity score converts to $+0.33\sigma$ (one third of a standard deviation above the mean). Since a standard deviation is uniformly interpreted regardless of the test or the unit of measurement, provided that the distributions are normal, it is apparent that this person scored better on the mechanical test than on the manual test. In addition, we can see how much better he scored on mechanical aptitude by comparing the percentage of persons scoring below $+1\sigma$ (84 percent) with the percentage scoring below $+0.33\sigma$ (62 percent).

By way of summary to the present point, then, we can completely

FIGURE 2–9

Distributions of Scores on a Test of Mechanical Aptitude and a Test of
Manual Dexterity Showing the Relative Position of Individual X in
Each Distribution

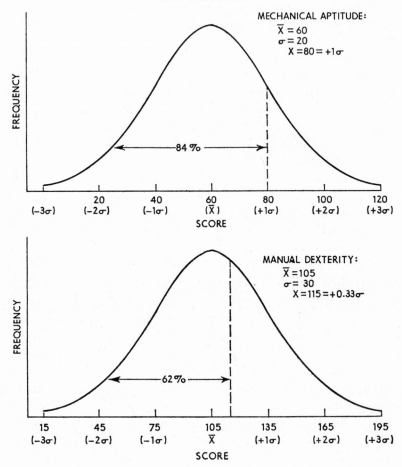

describe any set of normally distributed data by indicating the mean
and standard deviation of the distribution and the number of subjects upon whom observations were made. The typical experiment
yields at least two distributions of data: one for the experimental
group and one for the control group. These distributions must be
evaluated by the investigator in order to determine whether they are
similar or dissimilar. It is to this matter of interpreting the outcomes
of experimentation that we next turn our attention.

Statistical Inference

The usual control-group experiment illustrates the need for statistical inference. Here, the investigator has made two sets of observations: one in the experimental group and one in the control group. He wishes to determine whether differences between the distributions of data in these two groups can be attributed to the influence of the independent variable.

The Difference between Means. One way in which to evaluate the effectiveness of an industrial training program is periodically to test the employees' knowledge as the training progresses. This is quite comparable to the usual practice in colleges and universities of testing students' knowledge during the course of the academic year.

Suppose we were interested in comparing the effectiveness of two kinds of industrial training programs. The first kind, which we will refer to as "distributed training," requires that employees attend training sessions two hours a day for five days. The second kind of program, "massed training," also offers a total of 10 hours of instruction. Employees under this program, however, attend class five hours a day for two consecutive days. The trainees are randomly assigned to the two groups to control extraneous factors, and a test of their knowledge at the end of 10 hours of training yields a mean score in the distributed group of 52.5 while the mean for the massed group is only 50.0. Although it appears upon superficial examination that distributed training is superior to massed training, it is impossible to interpret these data properly until we apply a test of statistical significance to the obtained difference between means.

The fundamental problem underlying statistical inference stems from the fact that experimental data are accumulated over a finite period of time and from limited numbers of experimental subjects. In the illustrative training program experiment we are dealing with *samples* of employees receiving massed and distributed training rather than with the *population* (all employees to whom such training might be given). Furthermore, the criterion measure of knowledge after 10 hours of training must, of necessity, sample this knowledge rather than measure all of its components. Thus, the criterion instrument itself samples from the population of information and skills constituting "job knowledge."

However, our interest in experimental findings is not limited to the performance of samples of persons upon samples of possible test questions. We wish instead to make inferences of a more general nature from our data. We want to be able, for example, to formulate generalizations about the performance on the *population* of test questions measuring job knowledge by the *population* of employees.

The extent to which we can confidently make such generalizations is largely dependent upon the magnitude of our sampling errors. The smaller such errors, the more confidence we may place in generalizations about the population. When we statistically test the significance of the difference between means, we are in effect asking: "What is the probability of obtaining a difference between means as great or greater than the one we have noted for our samples *when there is actually no difference between the population means?*" In other words, what is the likelihood that we have obtained a chance rather than a statistically significant difference?

In addition to the magnitude of sampling errors influencing the means, the answer to this question is dependent upon the errors of measurement itself (which are usually small) and the size of the obtained difference between sample means. Sampling and measurement errors affect the accuracy of the mean, and their influence can be estimated by formula from the standard deviation of the scores in the distribution and the number of subjects in the group.

Let us assume that there were 100 trainees in each group, that the standard deviation as computed for the distributed group was 17.0, and that the standard deviation as computed for the massed group was 18.0. The distributions of data for the two groups are shown in Figure 2–10.

The two distributions shown in Figure 2–10 overlap to a considerable extent. A statistic for estimating *percentage overlap* between two such distributions is described in Appendix A. Applying this statistic, the actual amount of overlap is estimated as 94 percent. This means that virtually every test score was earned by some persons from both training groups. Only 6 percent of the cases were clearly distinguishable on the basis of the training they had received. Since the distributions overlap to such a great extent, it is evident in this instance that performance was not affected by the nature of the training program.

What can we say about the obtained difference between the means of the massed and distributed training groups? Since the distributions are so much alike (94 percent overlap), we cannot be

FIGURE 2–10

Distributions of Test Scores after Massed and Distributed Training Sessions:
The Effect of Large Standard Deviations

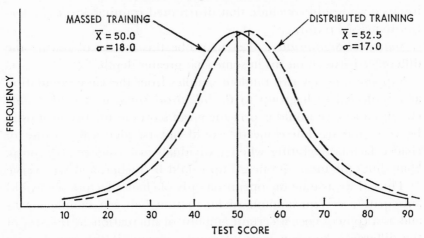

at all confident that the 2.5-point difference between means would be obtained again if the experiment were repeated.

By way of contrast, however, if the standard deviations were smaller, say 0.5 for the distributed group and 0.4 for the massed group, the plotted distributions of scores would look like those illustrated in Figure 2–11. You notice in this instance that the distributions of scores are quite independent of one another. Little overlap (less than 1 percent) exists, indicating that most of the

FIGURE 2–11

Distributions of Test Scores after Massed and Distributed Training Sessions:
The Effect of Relatively Small Standard Deviations

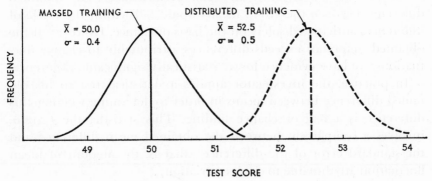

scores were obtained either by trainees in the distributed group or the massed group, but not by trainees in both groups. Such data indicate that the two distributions of scores are independent. In this instance we would conclude that distributed training is really superior to massed training.

Statistical Significance. Let us probe this matter of testing the difference between means in somewhat greater depth.

Suppose we drew two random samples from the same population and subjected each group to the *identical* condition. Under such circumstances we would expect the mean scores in the two groups to be very similar. These means would not be identical because of chance factors operating when individuals are assigned to groups. Sometimes the mean of one group would be higher, and vice versa.

Thus, if we assume the operation only of chance factors, we would anticipate a certain amount of fluctuation between sample means and as a consequence a certain amount of fluctuation in the size of the difference between pairs of sample means. If the samples are randomly drawn from the same population, the differences between pairs of means should be distributed closely about a value of zero.

Expectations about the fluctuation of mean differences attributable *solely to chance* can be determined statistically. The "standard error of the difference" tells us how much chance variation to anticipate in a distribution of differences between pairs of means for groups randomly drawn from the same population. The standard error of the difference is in effect a standard deviation of a distribution of mean differences attributable to chance when groups are randomly drawn from the same population.

In actual experimentation, we begin with random groups and subject them to *different* conditions. What would happen if these conditions had no effect at all upon performance? The obtained difference between the group means would fall within the range of differences anticipated solely on the basis of chance. However, if the obtained difference exceeds differences attributable to chance fluctuations, we have evidence for a "statistically significant" difference.

In practice, the investigator applies a statistical test to his obtained difference between means in order to determine whether this difference is a real or chance finding. This statistic, the *t ratio*, involves a comparison between the obtained mean difference and the standard error of the difference (that is, the amount of mean fluctuation attributable to chance variation) .

The *t* ratio indicates the likelihood that the mean difference for samples drawn from a single population is *smaller* than the one actually obtained from the experimental samples. Convention dictates that when this probability exceeds 5 percent, we regard the obtained difference as not significant. We must, in other words, have evidence that a difference as great or greater than the one we obtained would occur by chance only five times in a hundred before attributing this difference to manipulation of the independent variable rather than to chance. Although a probability of 0.05 is generally accepted as indicating a statistically significant difference, lower probabilities on the order of 0.01 or 0.001 often are obtained and give cause for still greater confidence in the experimental conclusion.

Statistical versus Practical Significance. The distinction between statistical and practical significance is of great importance in applied research. To illustrate, consider again the hypothetical investigation of the effects of increased illumination upon typing speed. Even if the mean performance in the experimental group (with increased illumination) was statistically superior to that in the control group, we still must inquire whether the amount of improvement justifies the expense of rewiring and installing new fixtures in the office.

A relatively small difference between means may be statistically significant when the groups are large but may lack statistical significance when the groups are small. If very large groups are required to demonstrate statistical significance, the practical utility of the finding may be questionable.

Correlation

As we have previously said, correlation is a statistical procedure for determining the strength and direction of relationship between variables. This relationship is statistically expressed by the coefficient of correlation (r).

Although the ensuing discussion of correlation is limited to its application when two variables are involved, correlational studies need not be limited in this way. The usual predictive study, for example, involves an attempt to maximize the efficiency with which the criterion (say, job performance) is predicted from combined scores on several preemployment measures (tests, interviews, personal history data, and so on), each weighted optimally. The statistical technique appropriate to this kind of problem is *multiple corre-lation.*

It must be emphasized that although correlation implies a rela-tionship between scores or events, it does not provide evidence re-garding causation. Assuming the existence of a correlation between two variables, either one may be cause and the other effect. Further-more, it is quite possible to obtain a correlation when *neither* of them is cause or effect. This occurs whenever the correlated variables are themselves dependent upon some third or fourth variable un-derlying the two particular ones correlated by the investigator.

A Perfect Positive Correlation. Two sets of observations made under comparable circumstances may be conveniently presented in the form of a crossplot or *scattergram.* Such a scattergram showing the relationship between inches and centimeters is illustrated in Figure 2–12. Measurement of distance in inches is shown on the Y-axis; corresponding distances in centimeters show on X-axis.

This scattergram shows eight pairs of observations, each indicated by a dot. Each of these points shows the distance on a centimeter scale corresponding to a particular distance on an inch scale.

You will note that all of the plotted points in this scattergram can be joined by a straight line. The fact that all pairs of observations

FIGURE 2–12

A Scattergram for Inches Plotted against
Centimeters

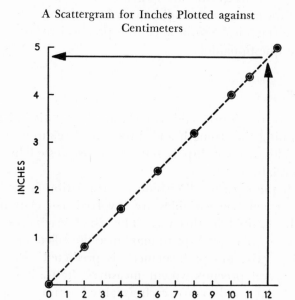

fall on this line indicates the existence of a perfect correlation between the two variables under consideration. When computed, the numerical value of the coefficient of correlation would be 1.00, which is the maximum value that this statistic may attain.

What does a correlation coefficient of 1.00 tell us? It indicates in the first place that there is a complete and inflexible relationship between the two variables. One centimeter, for example, always corresponds to 0.3937 inch, two centimeters to 0.7874 inch, and so on. Secondly, differences between pairs of measurements of one variable are reflected in proportional differences between pairs of measurements of the second variable. In our illustration, every increase or decrease of 1 centimeter corresponds to an increase or decrease of 0.3937 inch. The effect of proportional change in the two variables is to produce the straight line relationship illustrated in Figure 2–12.

A perfect relationship, like the one illustrated, enables us to predict one variable from the other without error. Suppose, for example, that we lost the ruler that measures in inches and had only the one that measures in centimeters. We could transform a measured distance of 12 centimeters to 4.72 inches simply by inspection of the scattergram. We could, in other words, predict what the measurement would have been if we had used a scale calibrated in inches. As long as the correlation between the variables is perfect (1.00), such predictions will be entirely free of error.

In addition to being perfect, the correlation for data like those presented in Figure 2–12 is positive; the computed value of the coefficient will be +1.00. The fact that the obtained correlation carries a + sign indicates that there is a *direct* relationship between the two variables. Increases in score on either of the variables are paralleled by increases in score on the other variable. Similarly, a decrease in score on one variable is paralleled by a corresponding decrease on the other variable.

A Perfect Negative Correlation. Correlation coefficients are not always positive. An illustration of a scattergram yielding a perfect negative correlation (−1.00) is presented in Figure 2–13.

Again, all pairs of observations fall on a straight line indicating a perfect relationship between variables X and Y and hence errorless predictability of one variable from the other. Knowing, for example, that an individual scored 7.0 on variable X we would predict that his score on variable Y would be 4.5.

The variables in this illustration are, however, inversely rather

FIGURE 2–13

Scattergram Indicating a Perfect Negative Correlation

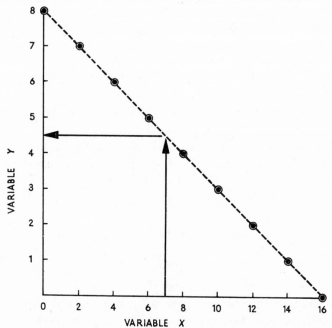

than directly related. An increase in scores on variable X is paralleled by a corresponding decrease in Y-scores; and a decrease in X-scores is paralleled by a corresponding increase in Y-scores. This inverse relationship would be reflected in the computation of r by the assignment of a negative sign to the correlation coefficient.

A High Correlation.   Perfect correlations do not occur when we deal with psychological phenomena. Let us assume that we have constructed a test for selecting personnel and wish to validate it against the criterion of supervisor's rating of efficiency at the end of six months of employment. We would administer the test to all new employees and correlate the scores with the supervisor's ratings which would be available six months later. Figure 2–14 shows a hypothetical scattergram of such data.

This scattergram indicates that 4 of the 36 employees tested earned test scores of 60; their ratings six months later ranged between 5.50 and 7.00. Similarly, five employees earned test scores of 50 and received ratings ranging between 4.30 and 6.50 and so on.

FIGURE 2–14

A Crossplot of Scores on a Personnel Selection Test against Supervisory Ratings of Efficiency

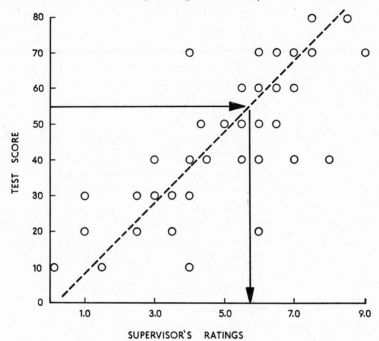

It is obvious that the 36 points do not fall on a straight line; hence the correlation between the two variables is not perfect. The points do, however, tend to cluster about a line as indicated in Figure 2–14. The computed correlation would be somewhat less than perfect, and it would be positive, indicating that as test scores increase, supervisor's ratings tend to be more favorable. The actual coefficient in this illustration is +0.74.

Can we use an imperfect correlation like this one as a basis for making predictions? Yes, but our predictions will contain a certain amount of error. If a job applicant scored 55 on the test, our best point prediction about his efficiency rating is that it will be 5.70. The more closely the observations cluster about a line (the higher the correlation), the more confidence we can have in the accuracy of this prediction. Conversely, the more dispersed are the observations from a line (the lower the correlation), the less confident we will be of the accuracy of this prediction.

What would happen to the obtained correlation coefficient if we had plotted the test scores in terms of the number of items answered incorrectly instead of in terms of the number of correct answers. The strength of the relationship between the test and criterion would be unaffected. The direction of this relationship would, however, be reversed. In other words, as error scores increased, efficiency ratings would decrease. The resultant value of r would be negative, although the numerical value of the coefficient would be unchanged. Thus, the coefficient computed under these circumstances would be -0.74.

A Zero Correlation. Suppose we wish to determine the extent of relationship between the heights of college students and their grade-point averages. We could plot these variables against each other and would obtain results approximating those displayed in Figure 2–15. This scattergram indicates that there is no relationship between the two variables in question. The grade-point averages of tall students are no different from those of short students, and in consequence, the computed r is 0.00. This minimum value of the correlation

FIGURE 2–15

Heights of College Students Plotted against Grade-Point Averages Indicating a Correlation Coefficient of 0.00

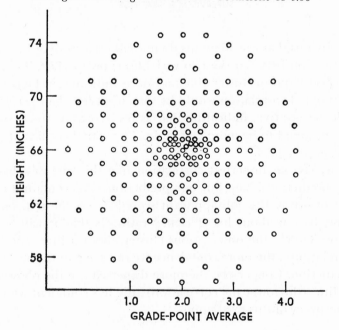

coefficient indicates that it is impossible to fit any line to the data. As a result, predictions of one variable from the other will have only chance accuracy.

Interpretation of Correlation Coefficients. A correlation coefficient is most properly interpreted in the light of the purpose for which it was computed. When estimating the validity of a test, coefficients in the vicinity of 0.40 are generally acceptable. Reliability studies, however, must demonstrate the existence of a more substantial correlation. The manuals for most published tests generally report reliability coefficients within the range 0.80–0.95.

As indicated earlier, correlational analysis has numerous applications aside from those related to the reliability and validity of tests. One such application utilizes the coefficient to provide an index of the amount of overlapping variance. The higher the correlation, the greater is the amount of overlap between variables. When the obtained correlation is 1.00, the variances overlap completely; when the correlation is 0.00, the variables do not overlap at all.

It is unfortunate that correlation coefficients look like percentages. The resemblance is entirely superficial. The percentage of overlapping variance is given by the *coefficient of determination* (r^2) rather than by the r itself. A correlation of 0.60, for example, indicates 36 percent overlapping variance. Conversely, the *coefficient of nondetermination* $(1 - r^2)$ in this instance indicates that 64 percent of the variance is independent (that is, does not overlap).

We have already said that correlations do not imply causality. Thus, the coefficient of determination must be interpreted cautiously. Although, a correlation of 0.60 means we have 36 percent overlapping variance, this amount of overlap might have resulted from any one of four conditions:

1. Changes in one variable caused changes to occur in the second variable.

2. Changes in the second variable caused changes to occur in the first variable.

3. The two correlated variables covary as a function of changes in some third, more basic underlying variable, but are themselves unrelated in causative fashion.

4. The relationship between the correlated variables is interactive in nature. An obtained correlation between productivity of piece-rate workers and their job satisfaction might reflect such an interaction. High productivity results in higher pay and may there-

fore lead to increased job satisfaction. Dissatisfaction with the job, however, may be responsible for diminished interest in the work and hence for lowered output.

Regardless of the conditions responsible for correlation, covariation enables us to predict scores on one variable from knowledge about scores on the other variable. The accuracy of these predictions is a function of the magnitude of r. As the numerical value of r decreases, our predictions become less and less accurate until with a correlation of 0.00 all predictions have chance accuracy.

Assume, for example, we find a 0.00 correlation between students' heights and their grade-point averages. This means that 50 percent of the students who are taller than average earn above-average grade points, and 50 percent of the shorter than average students also earn above-average grade points. Clearly, then, knowledge about height will not aid us in predicting grade point.

If, however, we used a test of academic ability as a predictor of scholastic performance we could make predictions with better than chance accuracy. Suppose we obtain a correlation between the test and grade point of 0.40. It has been shown that with such a correlation 63 percent of the students earning above-average predictor scores also earn above-average criterion scores. If the correlation were 0.60, 70 percent of the students earning above-average test scores also earn above-average grade points.

We will mention just one other application of the correlation coefficient. Sometimes the investigator merely wishes to determine whether the relationship between variables exceeds expectations on the basis of chance. Any r in excess of what would be expected as a chance deviation from a correlation of 0.00 would be statistically significant under such circumstances. As is the case with the t ratio discussed earlier, convention requires a probability level of 5 percent or better. In other words, for an obtained correlation to be regarded as statistically significant from 0.00, the probability of its occurrence as a chance variation from a true value of 0.00 must be 5 percent or less. Table 2–1 shows the value of r required for statistical significance at both the 5 and 1 percent levels for selected N's (number of pairs of observations).

Note that the size of r required for *statistical significance* decreases as the number of pairs of observations from which r is computed increases. Thus when the correlation is calculated from 1,000 pairs of observations, a value of only 0.06 is statistically significant at the 5 percent level.

TABLE 2–1

Values of *r* Required for Significance at the
5 and 1 Percent Levels*

N	5 Percent Level	1 Percent Level
10......................0.63		0.77
25......................0.40		0.51
50......................0.28		0.36
75......................0.23		0.30
100......................0.20		0.26
500......................0.09		0.12
1,000......................0.06		0.08

* After Lyle D. Edmison in J. E. Wert, C. O. Neidt, and J. S. Ahmann, *Statistical Methods in Educational and Psychological Research* (New York: Appleton-Century-Crofts, Inc., 1954).

In this regard it is important to recall the distinction made earlier between statistical and practical significance. A relatively low correlation may be statistically different from a correlation of 0.00 but lack practical significance for predictive applications.

SUMMARY

The basic approaches to the study of behavior utilized by the industrial psychologist are identical to the methodological approaches utilized in any of the other sciences. These methods are characterized by observation rather than by speculation, by objectivity rather than subjectivity, and by controls making it possible to repeat a set of observations and to draw meaningful conclusions. These elements of scientific method are translated by the researcher into an investigation of the relationship between two basic kinds of variables. One of these, the independent variable, is the factor whose effects are being investigated. The behaviors studied as possible functions of the independent variable are referred to as dependent variables. Thus, in an experiment concerning the effects of illumination upon industrial productivity, illumination is the independent variable and productivity is the dependent variable.

The relationship between independent and dependent variables may be studied by means of the naturalistic method, the experimental method, and by clinical observation. Naturalistic observations are made whenever the independent variable is not amenable to manipulation by the investigator. Under these circumstances the effects of the independent variable must be studied in natural surroundings without interference by the researcher. The experimental method, on the other hand, requires that the investigator manipulate the independent variable and control extraneous factors. The simplest kind of experimental design utilizes two groups of subjects: a control group, which serves as a standard for comparative purposes; and an experimental group, in which the independent variable is manipulated. Clinical observation emphasizes studies "in depth" of the subject's personality and motivation.

The summary and interpretation of research data requires that they be submitted to a statistical analysis. Data may be statistically summarized by measures of central tendency and variability. Measures of central tendency indicate the typical or "average" score; measures of variability indicate the spread of scores away from this "average." The primary measures of central tendency are the mean (the arithmetic average), the median (the middle score in the distribution), and the mode (the score that occurs most frequently). The only measure of variability discussed in the chapter is the standard deviation.

The t ratio is a statistical technique aiding data interpretation. It is a test of the likelihood that an obtained difference between means is attributable to chance rather than to the independent variable.

Correlational analysis reveals the magnitude and direction of the relationship between two or more variables.

3. Job Analysis

As we saw in Chapter 1, industrial psychology is concerned with the human side of work. It seeks to improve the conditions and outcomes of work, and to increase the satisfactions afforded by the job. The pursuit of these goals may involve the psychologist in studies of employee selection and training, the physical and social conditions of work, performance appraisal, and organizational management.

Job analysis is an indispensible starting place for many such studies. Its purpose is to provide information about the duties entailed in performing the job and the surroundings in which these duties are performed. Such an analysis involves a comprehensive description of the job and in turn leads to an understanding of the characteristics required of an employee if he is to perform satisfactorily.

WAYS IN WHICH JOB ANALYSIS IS USED

It will be useful to know something about the range of applications for the kind of thorough description of job duties provided by job analyses. The following discussion of some of these applications previews much of the topical content of the remainder of the book.

Personnel Selection and Placement

It would be utterly impossible to fit men to jobs unless we knew a good deal about the jobs we were attempting to fill. The specific duties to be performed by an employee and the circumstances under which these duties are to be performed lead to the specification of necessary employee characteristics. Such specifications dictate the utilization of certain kinds of selection devices and criteria rather than others. Thus, a job involving the use of an electronic computer can be satisfactorily filled only by an employee who either knows how to operate such a computer or has demonstrated the abilities prerequisite to learning the job. A job, like paint mixing, that requires employees to make very fine color discriminations cannot be satisfactorily filled by a color-blind job applicant.

Job analysis sometimes reveals that existent criteria for personnel selection and placement are quite inappropriate. A personnel director may, for example, automatically reject applicants who have not graduated from high school while analysis of the job may reveal that it only requires an eighth-grade education. Conversely, in the absence of a thoroughgoing job analysis, the personnel director may place his requirements for selection and placement at an unrealistically low level.

Training Programs

New employees frequently receive some kind of training during the initial period of their employment. The nature of training programs varies extensively from one industry to another and even between jobs within the same industry. Such training may be a highly formalized program consisting of several hours a week of classroom-type instruction. It may, on the other hand, be a relatively informal program in which new employees work "under the wing" of more experienced employees for a period.

The object of any training program may be to teach certain skills required to do a job, to develop certain attitudes (perhaps with respect to safety practices), or to provide other kinds of information of value to new employees. In any event, it is apparent that the structure and objectives of a training program must depend to a large extent upon a thoroughgoing job analysis. It is necessary to know what a job entails before employees can be properly trained for satisfactory job performance.

Job Evaluation

The purpose of job evaluation is to determine the relative worth of each job in an industrial organization. One of the primary applications of such an evaluation is the establishment of equitable salary ranges for various jobs within a company. By way of simple illustration, some jobs may expose employees to hazardous working conditions but may not require much in the way of formal education.

Other jobs may require graduate training of some sort but do not expose employees to undue hazards. A job evaluation under such circumstances would lead to a weighting of the factors of working conditions and educational requirements in order to establish an equitable basis for paying employees on both kinds of jobs.

The determination of the worth of each job within an industrial organization is dependent upon a comparative study of the job duties and the working conditions. Thus, job evaluation must be preceded by an analysis of every job to be evaluated.

Efficient Work Methods

A job analysis may be performed as a preliminary to motion studies designed to develop more efficient methods of work. An analysis for such purposes may reveal, for example, that a particular job requires employees to do considerable walking or an excessive amount of heavy lifting. Rearrangement of the working environment or of materials may reduce the extent of such nonproductive physical activity, leading to a consequent reduction in fatigue and an increase in productivity.

Health, Safety, and Equipment Design

Certain jobs, by their very nature, expose employees to personal danger. Unnecessary exposure to noxious fumes or radiation, for example, may be discovered by the job analyst and the working conditions revised in order to reduce or eliminate such conditions. Similarly, job analysis may reveal that certain features of machine operation are unduly hazardous, leading thereby to redesign of the equipment.

Performance Appraisal

Performance appraisals entail assessments of the employee's job proficiency. Such appraisals are used both as partial determinants of personnel actions (salary increase, promotion, and so on) and in the development of criteria for psychological investigations of such things as working conditions and predictor effectiveness. Data for performance appraisals come from several sources including production and personnel records, proficiency tests, job simulator performance, and supervisory ratings, to name a few.

The development and utilization of any criterion of job proficiency must, of course, be preceded by a job analysis in order to identify those aspects of job performance that are critical to employee success. Consider, for example, the unfortunate practice sometimes followed of administering generalized rating scales wherein the supervisor evaluates each employee in "shotgun" fashion on various characteristics ranging from *initiative* to *personal appearance*. Such rating scales may have little or no bearing upon the specific job being performed by a particular employee. It is doubtful, for example, that a rating of a lathe operator's "personal appearance" will indicate anything about his proficiency as a lathe operator.

Delimitation of Functions

Even small businesses and offices employing relatively few workers may utilize job analyses. A major source of bickering and discontent in such organizations results from the lack of clarification of duties of individual employees and delimitation of authority. An analysis leading to the definition of duties of each position may serve to eliminate this source of discontent.

The delimitation of personnel functions may likewise be helpful to larger industrial organizations by suggesting changes in current administrative patterns. Over the years, the areas of responsibility assumed by a manager are likely to reflect his personal interests and strengths. This is particularly true of companies at the forefront of technological change. Such companies are continually creating new jobs not even conceptualized several months or years earlier. Once created, the job is usually subsumed under some existing administrative unit of the company. Hence a periodic reassessment of all jobs in a company with a view toward their most appropriate administrative allocations may suggest needed changes in present management patterns.

The foregoing descriptions of applications of job analysis is not exhaustive. It is sufficient, however, to indicate the diversity of uses for information of the type provided by such analyses. The specific emphasis in any given job analysis will, of course, reflect the purpose for which the analysis has been performed. Job analyses written to provide clues to more efficient industrial operation will highlight different aspects of the job than will analyses prepared for the purpose of evaluating the relative worth of jobs within an industrial organization. However, aside from minor differences in emphasis as a function of intended application, all job analyses are basically alike in that they are designed to provide a detailed description of the analyzed jobs.

SOURCES OF INFORMATION FOR JOB ANALYSIS

The analyst is frequently required to study jobs with which he is initially unfamiliar, in industries about which he may have relatively little prior knowledge. Thus he must utilize many different sources of information in order to insure the accuracy and meaningfulness of his findings, including questionnaires, checklists, individual and group interviews, observations, technical conferences, daily diaries, work participation, and critical incidents.[1] Although we will discuss many of these methods separately, it should be recognized that they are typically combined to provide information for the job analysis.

Preliminaries to Job Analysis

The Dictionary of Occupational Titles. A useful preliminary to almost any job analysis is to consult analyses of similar jobs prepared in other industries and to review pertinent job descriptions prepared on a national basis. A comprehensive reference for the latter type of job description is the *Dictionary of Occupational Titles* (*D.O.T.*)[2] which is published in two volumes. Volume I alphabetically lists almost 22,000 job titles and defines each in a brief paragraph. An additional 14,000 alternate titles are listed and cross-indexed.

All titles are assigned a six-digit code number wherein the first digit designates the major occupational category, the second and third digits designate subgroups within that category, and the last three digits designate specific occupations within the subgroups. For example, the code number 633.281 refers to *office-machine service-*

[1] J. E. Morsh, "Job Analysis in the United States Air Force," *Personnel Psychology*, Vol. 37 (1962), pp. 7–17.

[2] United States Employment Service, *Dictionary of Occupational Titles*, Vol. I, *Definition of Titles*; Vol. II, *Occupational Classification and Industry Index*. (3d ed.; Washington, D.C.: U.S. Government Printing Office, 1965).

man apprentice. The "6" designates the general category "machine trades occupations;" the second and third digits, "33," indicate the subgroup "business and commercial machine repairman;" and the last three digits are specific to the title "office-machine serviceman apprentice."

Volume II of the D.O.T. lists all titles according to their code numbers whereas Volume I lists the titles alphabetically.

The descriptions in the D.O.T. are rather terse and somewhat general in nature. They represent a synthesis of the duties encompassed by a particular job title as performed by employees in a number of different industries. However, these descriptions may serve to familiarize the analyst with some of the vocabulary he is likely to encounter from employees and supervisors. Here, for example, is the description of an educational placement officer as presented in the D.O.T.

PLACEMENT OFFICER (education) 166.268. manager, student employment; placement counselor; placement interviewer; student-employment officer. Provides job placement service for students and graduates: Interviews applicants for full- or part-time employment to determine their qualifications on basis of education, ability, interest, and other employment factors, and eligibility for employment in accordance with school and municipal policies. Matches qualifications to job requirements as indicated by employer and refers applicant to job opening. Gives information to students regarding job opportunities, vocational choice, and desirable qualifications. Maintains file of applicants and record of placement and counseling activities. Develops job openings through employer contact. May arrange for administration and scoring of selected psychological tests. Assembles and maintains current labor market information and assists in developing library of occupational information. May specialize in placing specific groups, such as law students or undergraduates seeking part-time employment.[3]

Previous Job Analyses. The job analyst occasionally finds that the job he is asked to study has previously been submitted to analysis in the same industry, plant, or business in which he is working. Plant modernization and equipment changes may make it necessary to revise and update job analyses performed several years earlier. Furthermore, an analysis originally written for one purpose (for example, improving safety practices) is not always useful for other

---

[3] *Ibid.,* p. 537.

purposes. Nevertheless the job analyst may profitably study these written analyses as a preliminary to preparing his own analysis.

As was indicated earlier, the job analyst may follow these preliminaries by applying many different methods for assembling the data he needs. We will discuss three of these methods in particular: observation and/or work participation, questionnaire and/or interview, and critical incidents. These approaches are best regarded as supplemental to one another rather than as mutually exclusive. Specific elements of the job not detected by one method may be revealed by another.

Observation and Work Participation

It is clearly useful for the analyst to watch employees as they work. While so doing he must be careful to be as unobtrusive as possible. Generally he restricts notetaking to a minimum while making the observation, expanding his notes immediately after the observation is completed.

The observer must be constantly aware of the fact that he is to note characteristics of the job and not characteristics of individual employees. Personal idiosyncrasies will cause subtle discrepancies in the ways in which individual workers perform the same job.

An adequate sample of workers on the same job must be observed at various times during the work period. In order to generalize about the job requirements, the analyst must guard against observing only the best or worst workers, or limiting his observations to periods when workers are performing at their maximum or minimum levels.

The observations will suggest many questions to the analyst about what is being done, why it is done in a particular way, and about the skills, past training, and other prerequisites to satisfactory job performance. The purpose of interviews and questionnaires is both to elicit new information about the job as suggested by such questions and to verify the observations.

Questionnaires and Interviews

In gathering information for a job analysis, various persons may be interviewed and asked to complete questionnaires. These may include the workers, their subordinates (if any), their immediate supervisors, higher level management, service personnel, and so on. The employees themselves are often aware of small details of job performance that may pass unnoticed by their supervisors or by the job analyst. The supervisor, on the other hand, is in a somewhat better position by virtue of his responsibility for several employees to separate out job characteristics from worker characteristics.

The use of a job analysis questionnaire can be illustrated by a study of the work done by production foremen. The questionnaire consisted of four parts: one concerned the frequency with which the respondent influenced what went *into* the production (for example, "An employee asks me for a work assignment") ; a second concerned the frequency with which the respondent influenced job *output* (for example, "I check quality standards with the quality control people") ; a third concerned job activities involving *communication;* and the fourth required the respondent to rank such areas of *job responsibility* as production planning, cost control, and so on, with respect both to the time devoted to each and the importance of each.[4]

The primary advantage of utilization of a questionnaire rather than an interview for eliciting job information is that the former is more economical of time. Persons completing a questionnaire may do so at their leisure, and if the accompanying directions are self-explanatory, without the guidance of the job analyst. This advantage is more than offset, however, by two potential deficiencies in the questionnaire approach. First, it may be difficult to motivate respondents to fill out the questionnaire with the necessary accuracy and care. Secondly, responses to questionnaire items may be lacking in the essential detail needed by the job analyst. Consequently, wherever possible, the personal interview either by itself or in combination with administration of a questionnaire is a more desirable method for eliciting information of value to the job analyst.

The conduct of an interview is not a simple matter. The completeness of the information elicited during an interview depends in large measure upon the care with which the interviewer phrases his questions and upon the rapport (mutual respect and understanding) developed between interviewer and interviewee. Certain fun-

---

[4] E. Kay and H. H. Meyer, "The Development of a Job Activity Questionnaire for Production Foremen," *Personnel Psychology*, Vol. 15 (1962) , pp. 411–18.

damental "rules" for the conduct of the job analysis interview have been suggested as follows:[5]

1. Make sure the interviewee knows whom you represent, what your name is, and what you are there for, so he will have a broad idea of what is required of him.
2. Show that his cooperation in giving information is helping to find facts.
3. Carefully think out and word questions before asking them.
4. Be interested in the information which you are receiving.
5. Secure specific and full information as directly as possible.
6. Respect the judgment of the interviewee since he, not the analyst, is the expert.
7. Close the interview promptly.
8. Express appreciation to the one who has granted the interview.

Critical Incidents

This technique emphasizes the specific factors critical to job success or failure.[6] The technique has numerous applications in psychological evaluation and is particularly well suited to job analysis.

Almost any job analysis will reveal something about the factors differentiating between efficient and inefficient workers, and hence will suggest specifications for satisfactory job performance. However the critical incidents technique was developed in order to overcome the relatively slipshod way in which some of this information is obtained. It focuses the observer's attention specifically upon the critical behaviors differentiating between satisfactory and unsatisfactory job performance.

In essence the critical incidents technique requires that the supervisor and others familiar with a job carefully observe and record employees' behaviors which are critical to satisfactory job performance. The respondent also records specific incidents in which workers have performed unsatisfactorily.

The critical incidents report usually includes a description of the

---

[5] United States Employment Service, Department of Labor, *Training and Reference Manual for Job Analysis* (Washington, D.C.: U.S. Government Printing Office, 1944), p. 57.

[6] J. C. Flanagan, "Critical Requirements: A New Approach to Employee Evaluation," *Personnel Psychology,* Vol. 2 (1949), pp. 419–25.

conditions leading up to the incident, the exact nature of the incident, and its consequences. The unique advantage of this approach to characterizing the duties involved in successful job performance is that it is based upon reports of *actual behavior* rather than upon opinions or other subjective impressions about how the job "ought" to be done. Typically, after a large number of critical incidents are collected, these serve as the basis for developing a checklist which can be completed by each incumbent and his supervisor.

One illustrative application of the critical incidents procedure identified the behavior associated with successful salesmanship. The investigators collected over 100 critical incidents in selling as reported by sales managers. These incidents were summarized by classifying them into 13 behavioral categories like being truthful with customers and managers, persisting with "tough customers," keeping up with new sales techniques and methods, calling on all accounts, and so on.[7]

ASSEMBLING JOB ANALYSIS INFORMATION

The job information obtained from all sources is assembled to provide a verbal summary of the job duties and requirements. The organization of this summary varies somewhat with the nature of the job being analyzed and the purpose for which the analysis is made. Essentially, though, all job analyses include certain basic elements. The format for assembling job analysis information used by the United States Employment Service emphasizes the following items:

1. *Work Performed—Physical and Mental*
    a) *What* the worker does, including physical and mental responses made in the work situation.
    b) *How* he does it. What tools, machinery, equipment, and so on does the worker use? What kinds of calculations, formulas, judgments, and so on must the worker make?
    c) *Why* is the job done? What is its overall purpose and how does each task performed relate to this purpose?
2. *Skill Involved*
    a) *Responsibility.* What is the extent of the worker's super-

---

[7] W. K. Kirchner and M. D. Dunnette, "Identifying the Critical Factors in Salesmanship," *Personnel*, Vol. 34 (1957), pp. 54–59.

FIGURE 3-1

Job Analysis Schedule Used by the United States Employment Office

---

Form USES-546
(2-44)

U. S. DEPARTMENT OF LABOR
BUREAU OF EMPLOYMENT SECURITY
UNITED STATES EMPLOYMENT SERVICE

Budget Bureau No. 44-R577.3

JOB ANALYSIS SCHEDULE

1. Job title __Bank Clerk's Wife__   2. Number __102__

3. Number employed M __0__   F __1__   4. Establishment No. _____

6. Alternate titles _____   5. Date __1944__

___Spouse___   Number of sheets _____

___Darling___   8. Industry __Family__

___Battleaxe___   9. Branch __Local__

7. Dictionary title and code _____   10. Department __Uxorial__

11. WORK PERFORMED:

Under supervision of Husband (101) and/or Children (104, 105, 106) maintains household. Allocates funds. Purchases supplies. Contrives, invents means and methods of making Bank Clerk's (101) salary support family. (This is considered impossible, or at least improbable, by careful statisticians.) Entertains intelligentsia (friends and own family) and Morons (husband's friends and family). Supervises Dog (103) and other livestock including Husband (101) and Children (104, 105, 106).

Daily Duties:
1. Awakes Clerk (101). Selects suit (selection limited to one). Selects shirt (selection limited to one clean, one soiled and two frayed). Searches for shoes, keys, handkerchiefs, studs. Gives detailed instructions for day's program.
2. Prepares meal. Disburses carfare and/or lunch funds.
3. Dresses children (104, 105, 106).
4. Washes dishes. Scrubs floors, windows, paintwork. Polishes silver, brass, furniture.
5. Plans day's marketing. Calculates expenditures. Compares calculations with available funds. Recalculates. Goes to market with Children (104, 105, 106). Destroys market list as impractical. Improvises new menu according to availability of materials.
6. Arbitrates differences of opinion expressed vociferously and belligerently by Children (104, 105, 106).
7. Washes and irons sheets, shirts, blankets, rugs, underwear.
8. Mends and repairs sheets, shirts, blankets, rugs, underwear, tables, chairs, beds, radio.
9. Compromises differences of opinion. Accepts her own opinion. Rejects Husband's.
10. Exercises Dog (103). Wards off seasonal acquaintances. Takes Dog out when Dog prefers to stay in. Takes Dog in when Dog insists upon staying out. Separates Dog from fights and other turmoils. Relegates Husband (101) to dog-house.

(CONTINUE ON SUPPLEMENTARY SHEETS)

Analyst __A. Clurk__   Reviewer _____

FIGURE 3–1—*Continued*

SOURCES OF WORKERS

12. Experience: None .... Acceptable .Charm,.poise,.amatory.efficiency.--.past. ..experience.not.divulged..Complete.knowledge.of.French,.piano,.ballet,.opera,. ...literature..Ability.to.handle.butlers,.personal.servants.etc.

13. Training data: Minimum training time—(a) Inexperienced workers.   Varies
     (b) Experienced workers.   Varies

TRAINING	SPECIFIC JOB SKILLS ACQUIRED THROUGH TRAINING
In-plant (on job) training Continual during the period of employment.	Ability to render first aid, medical advice and treatment and minor surgical assistance. Veterinarian ability. Ability to haggle, wash diapers, iron shirts etc.
Vocational training Continual prior to employment.	twelve hours a day and still look lovely in the evening. Ability to do the work of carpenter, painter, electrician, plumber, cleaning woman, dishwasher, chef, CPA,
Technical training Varies	arbitrator, fashion designer, advisor.
SRW Eng. General education Ability to please, charm and fascinate.	
Activities and hobbies	

14. Apprenticeship: Formal ..No.. Informal .No... Length required ....
15. Relation to other jobs:
    (a) Promotions from and to, transfers, etc.: ..Promotion.from.'Teen..Eventual.promotion.to. ......mother-in-law.

    (b) Supervision received: General .... Close ...X...... By ..Husband.(101)................
                                                                                    (Title)

    (c) Supervision given: None .... Number supervised ....5..... Titles ..Husband.(101),.Children. ......(104,.105,.106).and.Dog.(103)..
The following items must be covered on supplementary sheets.

PERFORMANCE REQUIREMENTS

16. Responsibility (consider material or product, safety of others, equipment or process, cooperation with others, instruction of others, public contacts, and the like).
17. Job knowledge (consider pre-employment and on-the-job knowledge of equipment, materials, working procedures, techniques, and processes).
18. Mental application (consider initiative, adaptability, independent judgment, and mental alertness).
19. Dexterity and accuracy (consider speed and degree of precision, dexterity, accuracy, coordination, expertness, care, and deftness of manipulation, operation, or processing of materials, tools, instruments, or gages used).

COMMENTS

20. Equipment, materials, and supplies. : Electrical equipment, vacuum cleaner, duster, mop, broom,
21. Definition of terms.   sewing machine, rolling pin, pressure cooker, snow shovel,
22. General comments.   ash cans, washing machine, black lace and other deceptive
                                            devices, eyelashes, girdles, sweaters, lipstick and
                                            perfumes.

GPO 883463

visory responsibility for the activities of other employees? What is the extent of his nonsupervisory responsibility for preventing damage to equipment and materials, for making personal contacts (of the type made by salesmen) , and for cooperating with other employees?

b) *Job knowledge.* This factor includes knowledge of equipment, materials, techniques, and processes. The amount of job knowledge required is inversely related to the degree of supervision and guidance received by the employee.

c) *Mental application.* This general designation includes such factors as versatility, judgment, and intellectual alertness.

d) *Dexterity and accuracy.* What kind of manual or manipulative ability is required to perform the work to the degree of accuracy and precision required by the job?

3. *Selection Factors*

a) *Experience and training,* including prior job experience, or experience on related jobs, or educational requirements.

b) *Physical demands.* The physical activities required by the job, the environmental conditions in which the job is performed, and exposure to hazards and dangers.

c) *Worker characteristics* of any kind (both physical and mental) that are related to satisfactory job performance.

This format has been used to provide the analysis of the job of Bank Clerk's Wife shown in Figure 3–1 (pp. 73–74) using a description anonymously prepared after World War II.[8]

JOB SPECIFICATION

The information obtained from a job analysis is rarely used in its original form. The data as recorded on the job analysis schedule is generally too cumbersome for practical purposes. It must be organized and edited in order to make pertinent information readily accessible to the reader. The resultant statement of duties, qualifications, and other information developed from a job analysis is referred to as a *job description.* When the job description is primarily prepared for specifying worker characteristics to be considered when hiring and placing employees, it is called a *job specification.* A sample job specification presenting a brief job description followed by detailed information about worker characteristics required for satisfactory job performance is shown in Figure 3–2.

The purpose of specifications, like those shown in this figure, is to delineate personnel characteristics differentiating between satisfac-

---

[8] Anonymous, "Job Description of a Bank Clerk's Wife," *The Dime,* Union Dime Savings Bank. Reprinted in *Personnel Journal,* Vol. 27 (1948), pp. 79–80.

FIGURE 3–2

Job Specification for Hand Burner; John Doe Shipbuilding Company

PAYROLL TITLE ___Hand Burner___

CLASSIFICATION TITLE _____

Acetylene Burner Operator

DEPARTMENT _____

OCCUPATIONAL CODE _____

Plate Shop

6-85.219

FOREMAN ___John Jones___

TELEPHONE ___158___

JOB SUMMARY: Cuts mild steel plates into various shapes with an oxyacetylene cutting torch guided by layout markings on the material. With an oxyacetylene cutting torch, cuts steel plates and shapes to various dimensions and sizes as marked and laid out by LAYOUT MAN, manually moving the cutting torch along prescribed lines so that flame will cut plates squarely or with a specified bevel, as indicated by layout symbols; occasionally heats metal to dry surface, or preheats metal for cutting, bending or shaping, or to burn off paint, rust or scale, preparatory to Arc Welding,

Works under supervision of LEADERMAN (BURNING).

EDUCATIONAL STATUS ___Speak, read, write English___

EXPERIENCE REQUIRED ___3 months as hand burner helper___

KNOWLEDGE AND SKILLS: Must know oxyacetylene cutting and heating procedure and how to adjust fuel pressure; must be able to select proper burning tips, to clean and adjust torch and torch tips.

PHYSICAL REQUIREMENTS ___Standard physical examination___

PERSONAL REQUIREMENTS ___None___   MARITAL STATUS ___Open___

SEX ___Male___   AGE RANGE ___18 and over___   CITIZENSHIP ___Open___

REFERENCES REQUIRED: WORK ___Yes___   CHARACTER ___None___

WORKER MUST FURNISH ___8" pliers; 10" crescent wrench; gloves; helmet.___

WAGE CODE ___3a___

HOURS ___8___   DAYS ___6___   SHIFT ___Day; swing; graveyard___

TESTS: APTITUDE ___None___   TRADE ___Performance burning test___

Source: Carroll L. Shartle, *Occupational Information* (New York: Prentice-Hall, Inc., 1952), p. 66.

tory and unsatisfactory employees. Such information contributes to selection and placement by clarifying the nature of the demands imposed by the work. For example, if the job requires a high level of motor coordination, assessment of this ability ought to be included in the personnel selection program.

There are two basic procedures for extrapolating information about worker requirements from the job analysis: (1) estimation and (2) measurement.

Estimation

The earliest approaches were based simply upon the analyst's estimate of the job's requirements derived from his observations and interviews. The characteristics thus delimited tended to be rather vague and ambiguous. Furthermore, it was virtually impossible to arrange the worker characteristics identified in this fashion into a hierarchy of relative importance.

More recent attempts subjectively to delineate worker specifications use more systematic procedures. In general, these begin with a list of job skills, abilities, and traits that might be important for *any* job. Each item in the list is carefully defined and accompanied by a rating scale on which the analyst estimates the degree of importance of each characteristic for the job in question. The pattern of ratings for a given job constitutes its "profile," and a comparison of profiles for various jobs indicates the relative importance of the various worker characteristics across jobs.[9]

One such analysis of generalized job variables cutting across specific jobs identified activities engaged in to a greater or lesser degree by workers at about 400 jobs relatively representative of the range of jobs in general. Some of the variables identified were: (*a*) varied intellectual activities versus structured, repetitive activities; (*b*) decisions directly affecting people; (*c*) gross muscular activities; (*d*) public contact activities; (*e*) persuasive communication activities; and so on.[10] This type of analysis is useful in directing the job

[9] M. S. Viteles, "Job Specifications and Diagnostic Tests of Job Competency Designed for the Auditing Division of a Street Railway Company," *Psychological Clinic,* Vol. 14 (1923), pp. 83–105.

[10] G. G. Gordon and E. J. McCormick, *The Identification, Measurement and Factor Analysis of "Worker-Oriented" Job Variables* (Lafayette, Ind.: Occupational Research Center, Purdue University, July, 1963); and J. W. Cunningham and E. J. McCormick, *Worker-Oriented Job Variables: Their Factor Structure* (Lafayette, Ind.: Occupational Research Center, Purdue University, July, 1964).

FIGURE 3–3

Form ES-267 (Reverse)
(Rev. 2-44)

PHYSICAL DEMANDS FORM

Job Title_____Occupational Code_____
Dictionary Title_____
Firm Name & Address_____
Industry_____Industrial Code_____
Branch_____Department _____
Company Officer_____Analyst_____ Date_____

PHYSICAL ACTIVITIES		WORKING CONDITIONS	
1 Walking	16 Throwing	51 Inside	66 Mechanical Hazards
2 Jumping	17 Pushing	52 Outside	67 Moving Objects
3 Running	18 Pulling	53 Hot	68 Cramped Quarters
4 Balancing	19 Handling	54 Cold	69 High Places
5 Climbing	20 Fingering	55 Sudden Temp. Changes	70 Exposure to Burns
6 Crawling	21 Feeling	56 Humid	71 Electrical Hazards
7 Standing	22 Talking	57 Dry	72 Explosives
8 Turning	23 Hearing	58 Wet	73 Radiant Energy
9 Stooping	24 Seeing	59 Dusty	74 Toxic Conditions
10 Crouching	25 Color Vision	60 Dirty	75 Working With Others
11 Kneeling	26 Depth Perception	61 Odors	76 Working Around Others
12 Sitting	27 Working Speed	62 Noisy	77 Working Alone
13 Reaching	28	63 Adequate Lighting	78
14 Lifting	29	64 Adequate Ventilation	79
15 Carrying	30	65 Vibration	80

DETAILS OF PHYSICAL ACTIVITIES:

7-5507 bu-final

analyst's attention to a common core of possible worker activities. By considering these activities as they relate to each job under consideration, his judgments concerning worker specification are given direction.

Another approach to guiding the analyst in extrapolating worker specifications from job analyses is that taken by the United States Employment Service. Here the analyst uses a uniform checklist in describing all jobs under consideration. The breadth of this checklist, and hence its appropriateness to a wide range of jobs, is illustrated by the form for noting "physical demands" reproduced in Figure 3–3.

Such generalized lists of work activities and forms for rating job requirements are distinct improvements upon more subjective approaches to estimating requisite worker characteristics. The former eliminate some of the ambiguity from these estimates and facilitate the placement of the requirements in a hierarchy of relative importance.

Measurement

All estimates of worker requirements suffer one major shortcoming. Whenever a procedure rests upon estimates made by human beings it is susceptible to subjective errors in judgment. The suggestion was made about 50 years ago that job profiles could be objectively developed by relying upon the results of measurement instead of judgment. Instead of requiring analysts to estimate worker requirements, a battery of psychological tests could be administered to workers on different jobs and the resultant scores used to develop profiles of the abilities and traits associated with job performance.[11] This procedure, or some variant of it, is designated the "measurement" approach to worker specification.

A number of difficulties are inherent in the measurement approach to job specification. Foremost among these is the matter of deciding which tests ought to be included in the battery. In attempting to strike a reasonable balance between cost of the program, time available for test administration, and comprehensive coverage of the psychological characteristics measured, there is always the danger that tests measuring important characteristics will not be included in the battery. Thus, although the measurement approach is more objective than the estimating approach to job specification, the latter may provide increased breadth of trait coverage.

The utilization of test scores for constructing job profiles presents another problem. One technique develops the profile from the

---

[11] H. C. Link, *Employment Psychology* (New York: The Macmillan Co., 1920).

average scores earned by groups of workers on a given job. This average is presumed to indicate the relative importance of each trait or characteristic: when it is high, the trait is important; when it is low, the trait is unimportant. However, it has been shown that groups of workers may average relatively high scores on tests that are quite unrelated to job performance.[12]

An alternative to using average scores as indications of relative importance is to weight the abilities or characteristics measured by the tests in terms of their validities. Validity is indicated by the correlation between predictor scores and a performance criterion. Tests correlating substantially with a criterion of job performance may be presumed to be measuring more important characteristics than those measured by tests yielding low validity coefficients.

Although the validity approach holds promise, it is limited on the one hand by the scope of the test battery and on the other by the adequacy of the criterion of job success. The former limitation was discussed earlier as it applied to job specification by measurement in general. The matter of establishing suitable criteria of job performance requires considerably more attention and is discussed in detail in Chapter 4.

SUMMARY

Studies of employee selection and training, the conditions of work, and organizational management typically begin with pertinent job analyses. The purpose of job analysis is to provide information about the duties entailed in job performance and the surroundings in which these duties are performed. Job analysis ultimately leads to specification of worker skills, abilities, and characteristics prerequisite to satisfactory job performance.

The job analyst obtains his information from several sources. Those discussed in this chapter include the *Dictionary of Occupational Titles,* observation, work participation, questionnaire administration, interview, and application of the critical incidents procedure.

The information obtained from a job analysis usually suggests worker characteristics associated with effective personnel selection.

---

[12] W. H. Stead and C. L. Shartle, *Occupational Counseling Techniques* (New York: American Book Co., 1940).

The analyst sometimes *estimates* the personnel requirements on the basis of his familiarity with the activities entailed in efficient job performance. Alternatively, he may administer psychological tests to *measure* personnel characteristics differentiating between effective and ineffective employees.

II.

Selecting, Placing, Training, and Appraising Employees

The fundamental objective of selection, placement, and training programs in industry is to best utilize the specific capabilities and interests of the employees. Every individual is unique with respect to the pattern of his abilities and his history of past experiences. Such individual differences result from the interaction of inherited predispositions and environmental influences. The former may, for example, impose maximum limits upon intellectual and physical capabilities. The latter may determine the extent to which these capabilities are realized. Both hereditarian and environmental factors determine our interests, which in turn influence the kinds of satisfactions we seek from work and from life in general.

Employers generally consider several factors when hiring a new worker. First, there must be some evidence that the applicant has the capabilities and knowledges required for satisfactory job performance and completion of the company's training program. Second, employers seek workers who will be interested in and stimulated by their work to the maximum extent possible. A third consideration in many instances is the applicant's potential for advancement to positions of greater responsibility within the company.

The reasons for regarding both ability and satisfaction as important elements in personnel selection and placement are fairly obvious. Employees who lack the required abilities, regardless of whether these requisites are intellectual or personal, simply cannot work efficiently. The salesman who cannot converse easily, the supervisor who cannot direct the activities of subordinates, the laborer who lacks the necessary physical stamina, and the teacher who does not know her subject matter are all relatively ineffectual as employees. Similarly, employees who are capable of doing their work but do not regard it as enjoyable or stimulating may reflect their dissatisfaction in lowered productivity and in high absenteeism and turnover.

The primary problem, then, in the selection and placement of personnel is predictive in nature. The employer needs to know in advance which of several job applicants will if hired be most efficient as an employee. Furthermore, he must be guided in placing employees in order to best utilize their abilities, skills, knowledge, and personal characteristics.

The relationship between selection-placement programs and training programs is almost self-evident. A fundamental purpose of training is to develop job-related knowledges, skills, and attitudes. In addition, in-service training programs often provide educational experiences of a more-or-less formal nature and are designed to provide employees with opportunities for job enlargement and intracompany promotion.

Sound selection, placement, and training programs yield substantial financial dividends. Every new employee represents a monetary investment by management. In addition to the costs of recruitment and training programs, a number of other expenses are incidental to hiring procedures. Every time an employee voluntarily terminates employment or must be fired, this investment is lost.

One of the purposes of this section is to discuss the major techniques of personnel selection and placement, including the use of interviews, application forms, letters of recommendation, and psychological tests. We will be specifically concerned with the ways in which these techniques are developed, utilized, and improved. In addition, the section includes a discussion of industrial training which when properly conceived should permeate all levels and activities of the organization.

Another purpose of this section is to clarify the nature of performance criteria as they relate to selection, placement, training, personnel decisions, and industrial psychological research in general. The more objective forms of performance appraisal, like output, spoilage, turnover, and so on, are discussed in Chapter 4. Subjective performance appraisal by rating is discussed in Chapter 9.

4. Performance Criteria and Prediction

Virtually everything the industrial psychologist does necessitates his concern with some sort of criterion of job performance. Whether he is engaged in developing techniques for selecting or training personnel, improving the work environment, developing promotional procedures, doing research on conditions contributing to job satisfaction, or anything else, he must come to grips with criterion definition and development. It is insufficient from a research standpoint to speak of improving efficiency or job performance. These can be variously defined; the ways in which they are measured are functions of their definitions; and conditions leading to improvement judged by one criterion may prove ineffective when judged by some other criterion.

The discussion of criteria in this chapter is specifically oriented toward developing measures of job performance suitable for personnel selection and training programs. However, the issues raised in this discussion are sufficiently general to apply to the broader problem of assessing industrial efficiency for any purpose. Specific criterion problems encountered in evaluating training programs, appraising workers on the job, and measuring job satisfaction are described in context throughout subsequent chapters; special considerations unique to subjectively made performance appraisals (ratings) are discussed in Chapter 9.

INDIVIDUAL DIFFERENCES

The discussion of descriptive statistics in Chapter 2 concerned procedures for summarizing sets of data like test scores, performance measures, and so on. You will recall that when such data are graphed or arranged in a frequency distribution, some of the persons in the sample are seen to perform at higher levels than others. Thus, some employees are more "efficient" than others; some job applicants earn higher preemployment test scores than others; some students are "brighter" than others; some persons are taller than others; and so on.

These differences between individuals reflect the interaction between hereditary predispositions and environmental influences. We need not be concerned here with the relative contributions of these two sets of factors in generating individual differences. It is sufficient here to note that whereas the influence of heredity is particularly strong in generating certain kinds of individual differences (like those of height and weight), environmental factors are primary determinants of others (for example, interests). Furthermore, the interaction between these two general determinants of individual differences is inescapable. Thus, whereas genetic factors may be the primary determinants of height, environmental conditions like climate and nutrition also cause variations in this characteristic. Likewise, whereas environmental factors may be the primary determinants of interests, it is unlikely that an interest will develop in the absence of a genetic predisposition to perform satisfactorily in the interest area. Students with low aptitude for learning mathematics, for example, are unlikely to become interested in graduate training in this area.

The purpose of any criterion is to make evident the differences between individuals. In industry, criteria of job performance are designed to clarify and display the differences between employees who do well and those who do poorly—for example, those who are highly productive and those who are relatively unproductive. Criteria effectively making this distinction are obviously useful as guides to promotion, salary determination, identification of training needs, and related personnel actions. Such criteria also are the dependent variables in research programs designed to determine the effects of altered work environments and training programs.

Since the primary focus in Part II is on personnel selection and placement, this chapter is concerned with yet another application of performance criteria. These measures are what we wish to predict whenever personnel selection devices are administered. The purpose of personnel selection procedures is to identify individual differences between job applicants on measures associated with individual differences between employees on performance criteria. If, for example, the performance criterion that interests us is some measure of productivity, we will wish to use preemployment devices that allow us to identify those persons who if hired will be most likely to rank high in the distribution of productivity.

ADEQUACY OF CRITERIA

A criterion is a standard against which we evaluate something. The effectiveness of a test battery for selecting workers, for example, is judged by the accuracy of hiring decisions following its use. If the battery is effective, the personnel manager basing his decisions upon it will hire mostly persons who subsequently prove to be "efficient" workers; most of those he rejects would subsequently have proven to be "inefficient" workers. In this instance the criterion would have to be some measure of "efficiency."

Particular criteria are often chosen merely because they are readily available, or have been used by other investigators confronted by a similar problem, or are thought by management to be relevant to the problem at hand.[1] Without minimizing the importance of these considerations, they are insufficient by themselves to insure adequacy of the criterion.

Whenever anything is measured, the investigator needs assurance that his yardstick is both reliable and valid. We have already given one definition of reliability, that is, the consistency of measurement. Validity has been defined as the relevance of measurement to whatever it is we intend to measure.

The significance of these concepts for test development will be discussed at some length in Chapter 6. The important point here is that the criteria we expect our tests to predict must themselves be reliable and valid. It is not possible accurately to predict an unstable criterion. Furthermore, there is not much wisdom in predicting a criterion of something other than the thing we really wish to predict.

KINDS OF CRITERIA

The "ultimate" criterion of job success would have to reflect an individual's productive efficiency throughout his working life.[2] It

---

[1] J. Weitz, "Criteria for Criteria," *American Psychologist*, Vol. 16 (1961), pp. 228–31.

[2] L. E. Albright, J. R. Glennon, W. J. Smith, *The Use of Psychological Tests in Industry* (Cleveland: Howard Allen, Inc., 1963), p. 21.

clearly is infeasible to attempt to develop such an "ultimate" criterion. People change jobs during their lifetimes, and "productive efficiency" means different things for different jobs. Even for a single job, the definition of "productive efficiency" may change over a period of time. The components of productive efficiency for any job are typically beyond comprehensive identification in terms amenable to evaluation. And if the foregoing were not enough to discourage a search for "ultimate" criteria, the simple fact that by definition they are unavailable until the end of an employee's productive lifetime would itself prove discouraging.

Characteristically, then, industrial psychologists develop some sort of intermediate criteria of performance which have components in common with (and therefore are presumed to correlate with) the "ultimate" criterion. These intermediate criteria are more immediately available and are restricted to performance on the employee's present or prospective job.

The diversity of available criteria of job performance is tremendous. One listing of such criteria includes items bearing upon (a) output per unit of time; (b) quality of production; (c) time lost by personnel because of sickness, accidents, and so on; (d) personnel turnover; (e) training time; (f) promotability; and (g) employee satisfaction.[3] Data germane to these criteria are often available in one form or another in already existing company records. The problem from a research standpoint is that often the form in which they have been collected precludes reliability and/or validity.

Production

Undoubtedly some sort of production index is one of the most widely used criteria for industrial research. This is so in part because of expediency; most companies maintain production records, and thus they are immediately available to the researcher. Also, management generally considers high productivity to be synonymous with efficiency.

Criteria of productivity ordinarily combine two elements: quantity and quality of output. The quantitative components of production records can often be readily tabulated and statistically analyzed; for example, the number of armatures wound by assembly

---

[3] R. J. Wherry, "Criteria and Validity," in D. H. Fryer and E. R. Henry (eds.), *Handbook of Applied Psychology* (New York: Holt, Rinehart & Winston, Inc., 1950), Vol. I, chap. xxvii.

line workers during a shift, the number of words per minute typed by a secretary, or the monthly sales record of an insurance salesman.

However output records are often invalid in their raw form. Productivity may be a meaningless criterion unless it is corrected for spoilage. Some adjustment is necessary when comparing a secretary averaging 70 words per minute but with three errors with one averaging 60 errorless words per minute. Similarly, in evaluating monthly insurance sales records, it is necessary to include some indication of policy cancellations.

Contamination. Even a measure of output corrected for spoilage and obtained for employees doing what superficially appears to be the same kind of work may not be a satisfactory criterion of job performance because of contamination. *Contamination* refers to the effect upon the criterion of factors which are really extraneous to the measure being sought.

One source of criterion contamination may be the working environment itself. Typing speed and accuracy, for example, are affected by the amount of noise and other distractions in the office. Likewise, for assembly tasks, output may be limited by such things as the output rate of fellow workers, maximum machine speed, and availability of raw materials. Output for salesmen undoubtedly reflects the size of the sales territory and the socioeconomic status of the residents as contaminating factors.

A second source of criterion contamination is subtle differences in the nature of the job itself. A secretary typing a technical manuscript is not doing the same kind of work as one typing letters; an insurance salesman is not doing the same type of work as an automobile salesman. In both instances it would be erroneous to attempt direct comparisons of productivity.

Finally, criteria may be contaminated by variations in job experience. Since there often is a correlation between length of experience and productivity, output measures obtained for relatively new employees cannot be directly compared with those for more experienced employees.

Sampling Errors. Another possible source of error in developing production criteria results from the fact that production records are not used in their entirety. Instead, these criteria ordinarily are derived from samples of job performance. Samples of output will not accurately reflect fluctuations in performance unless they are drawn from periods representative of the entire shift or in the case of sales positions, from periods representative of the entire year. If each output sample spans only a brief time period, or if too few samples are drawn to insure representativeness, the criterion may lack reliability.

Interpreting Productivity. Another kind of problem is encountered when the attempt is made to convert performance records to a criterion of "goodness" or "efficiency." This is somewhat analagous to the evaluative problem faced by a teacher when he attempts to judge student performance on an examination. He may be able to convert the student's answers to a numerical score (that is, an output record), but he still must decide whether the score is good enough to merit a grade of A or whether it really deserves only a B or C. The standards for such a judgment, whether it be made for a class or a group of workers, may be relativistic (median output is defined as "average") or absolutistic (anyone performing better than some specified level, like 90 percent of capacity, is "superior"). The latter kind of industrial output evaluation often uses time study results for defining "capacity."

Performance Rating

Although highly valued, an index of production suitably corrected for contamination and based upon an adequate sample of work still may be inappropriate for criterion purposes. There are many jobs for which it is either impossible to count units of production or the units when counted reveal relatively little about job performance.

What production measure should be counted, for example, to appraise supervisory or managerial proficiency? One possibility might be to use an aggregate of the output by workers in the supervisor's department or the manager's section. But such a criterion would be contaminated by factors other than the critical one of "quality of supervision." It might also neglect certain important aspects of managerial proficiency not readily revealed in subordinates' productivity.

When objective indices of proficiency are unobtainable or insufficient because of the nature of the job, it may be necessary to build criteria upon subjective appraisals of performance. These appraisals usually involve some sort of rating procedure. The ratings may be solicited from co-workers; most often they are made by the worker's immediate superior. These ratings may require a judgment about overall job performance or some more specific aspect of job perform-ance like "attitude toward supervision," "perseverance," "creativ-ity," and so on. Reliance upon subjective performance appraisals as criteria is particularly characteristic of technical, professional, super-visory, and managerial assessments.

The problem encountered in rating and possible refinements of rating procedures are discussed at length in Chapter 9. It should be apparent that such subjectively derived criteria can be extremely unreliable because raters may disagree among themselves. Also, since the bases upon which such ratings are made may be unrelated to the actual quality of work performed by the ratee, these criteria may be relatively invalid.

Miscellaneous Criteria

Still another type of criterion measure may be derived from the *job sample*. This is a test of job performance under very carefully controlled conditions. It is designed to get at very much the same type of behavior as a production criterion, but without the danger of contamination sometimes present for the latter.

Criterion measures are intended to reflect performance differ-ences between employees attributable to differences in their abili-ties, motivation, level of experience, and other personal characteris-tics. As was indicated earlier, measures of performance may be contaminated by factors other than the ones specifically under con-sideration. Such potentially contaminating factors can often be more easily controlled in a job sample than in the actual work situation.

Productivity, objectively or subjectively appraised, is neither the only nor always the most desirable indication of job performance. Consider, for example, a job requiring a very lengthy initial train-ing period at considerable expense to the company. No company likes to contemplate the prospect of an employee accepting a job offered by a competitor shortly after completing such a training program. Job tenure may actually be a more meaningful criterion than productivity in this instance.

There are a number of jobs in which the range of productivity is so narrow that the difference in output between the best and worst producer is relatively insignificant. This is particularly true of highly repetitive work paid on a piece rate for departments in which the workers have established a "gentleman's agreement" among themselves about how much they will produce. Under these circumstances management may be more interested in predicting such criteria as absenteeism, tardiness, and turnover than output.

CRITERION COMBINATION

Which of the criteria described above is the "best" or "most useful" index of job performance. Obviously, this question is not answered easily. Whereas productivity or output somehow corrected for spoilage is extremely relevant for some positions, it is irrelevant for others. Furthermore, even when relevant, a measure of productivity may not tell the whole story. A highly productive employee who has a record of excessive absenteeism or who lacks the necessary skills for eventual promotion to a supervisory position may be less valuable to the company than one who, although less productive, is hardly ever absent and is trainable for a supervisory position.

Thus most jobs are not unidimensional. Instead, they have various dimensions each reflecting one of the several goals of "satisfactory" job performance.[4] One analysis of supervisory behavior, for example, identified the following six dimensions of effective supervision: (a) establishment of an effective climate for work, (b) ethics in managing subordinates, (c) self-development, (d) personal maturity and sensitivity, (e) knowledge and execution of corporate policies and procedures, and (f) technical job knowledge.[5] All of these dimensions of effective supervisory behavior must somehow be included in a criterion for supervisors. Evidence of this sort raises two alternative possibilities for criterion development: one is to develop multiple criteria for each job; the other is somehow to combine such multiple criteria into a single index of overall employee effectiveness.

Multiple Criteria

The development of multiple criteria of job success implicitly assumes that a search for *the* criterion is futile. Instead, what is required is the development and utilization of several criteria each

---

[4] E. E. Ghiselli, "Dimensional Problems of Criteria," *Journal of Applied Psychology,* Vol. 40 (1956), pp. 1–4.

[5] H. Peres, "Performance Dimensions of Supervisory Positions," *Personnel Psychology,* Vol. 15 (1962), pp. 405–10.

reflecting a particular dimension of job performance.[6] According to this line of reasoning, the combination of several criteria into a single measure of "overall effectiveness" obscures important information. Thus, referring to the dimensions of supervisory behavior, two supervisors judged to be about equal by a composite criterion of overall effectiveness might really function quite differently. One, for example, might have a high level of technical job knowledge but be relatively immature and insensitive; the other may be relatively mature and sensitive but know little about the technical aspects of job performance.

The Single Overall Criterion

The other alternative for criterion development is, of course, somehow to evolve a single overall index of job performance. The practical importance of deriving a single overall criterion is undeniable in certain circumstances; for example, as an aid to making personnel decisions including those related to promotion and salary increase.

A single criterion can be developed in two ways: by combining the several dimensional criterion measures into a single index or by developing some new criterion index underlying a number of separate performance subcriteria.

Combining Subcriteria. When several subcriteria are to be combined into a single overall performance index, each of the subcriteria must somehow be weighted in terms of its contribution to the composite. Such weights are often subjectively assigned by having judges assess the importance of each subcriterion as a partial determinant of overall job performance.

Alternatively, such weights may be statistically determined either by weighting more heavily the more reliable subcriteria or by weighting more heavily those subcriteria which correlate most highly with some overall assessment of job performance.

In either case, the combination of subcriteria into a single criterion index cannot be effected routinely without regard for the intercorrelations between the subcriteria themselves.[7] Such combination

---

[6] M. A. Dunnette, "A Note on *the* Criterion," *Journal of Applied Psychology,* Vol. 47 (1963), pp. 251–54.

[7] R. M. Guion, "Criterion Measurement and Personnel Judgments," *Personnel Psychology,* Vol. 14 (1961), pp. 141–49.

makes the most sense when the subcriteria are somewhat intercorrelated, indicating that they share a common underlying behavioral core. Subcriterion combination makes less sense when the components are relatively uncorrelated with each other. In this case, without evidence for a common behavioral core underlying the various subcriteria, their combination into a single index would be illogical.

Deriving a New Overall Criterion. The issue of subcriterion intercorrelation is circumvented in a proposed single overall criterion evolved from cost accounting procedures.[8] Instead of seeking a common *behavioral* core underlying the subcriteria, this procedure assumes that there is another type of common element reflected in all subcriteria; that is, that of dollar worth to the company.

In these terms, the purpose of a criterion is to reflect the employee's dollar value to the company. Since this value can be viewed as the employee's contribution to helping the company make money, the proponents of the "dollar criterion" suggest that the effect of each subcriterion can be traced out by cost accounting procedures to determine its monetary impact. Those subcriteria related to production of goods or services would thus be positively weighted because they yield a monetary gain. Conversely, errors, spoilage, and so on that result in a dollar loss for the company would be negatively weighted.

PREDICTIVE VALIDITY

When making hiring decisions, the responsible company officer will wish to select from the pool of job applicants those who are most likely to perform satisfactorily. The problem is that of predicting job behavior in advance of its occurrence. Criterion scores related to personnel selection are those performance measures which are to be predicted by the tests, interviews, and so on that are administered to job applicants.

The strength of the relationship between predictor and criterion is termed *predictive validity*. (Other kinds of validity are discussed in Chapter 6.) In its simplest form, predictive validity is determined by correlating the scores on some preemployment measure adminis-

---

[8] H. E. Brogden and E. K. Taylor, "The Dollar Criterion-Applying the Cost Accounting Concept to Criterion Construction," *Personnel Psychology*, Vol. 3 (1950), pp. 133–54.

tered to job applicants with the criterion scores earned by these same people some time later. If this correlation is high, the predictor instrument may be used for personnel selection with some degree of confidence; persons who are high scorers on the predictor are the ones most likely to maintain satisfactory job performance. Conversely, if the predictor-criterion correlation is low, the predictor cannot be included in the preemployment selection program.

How high a predictor-criterion correlation is needed in order for the preemployment measure to be useful in a practical sense? Such correlations rarely exceed 0.55 or 0.60. In order to determine whether a validity coefficient of, say, 0.30 or 0.35 signifies that the predictor ought to be included in or excluded from the preemployment selection program, we must take into account two other considerations: (a) the proportion of workers selected without the predictor in question who are regarded as "superior" employees and (b) the selection ratio.

Present Proportion of Superior Employees

Suppose of the present group of employees selected without the predictor in question, only 30 percent is regarded as superior, that is, in the high criterion group. The remaining employees (70 percent) are in the low criterion group. There clearly is room for improvement of the selection process. And some improvement can be anticipated even by adding a selection device with only moderately high predictive validity.

However, the situation is quite different when a high proportion (say, 80 percent) of the present employees are in the high criterion group. With the existing selection program the chances are only 2 in 10 of making an incorrect hiring decision. To reduce this chance of an erroneous hiring decision even further requires insertion into the selection program of a test with very high predictive validity.

Selection Ratio

The selection ratio is simply:

$$\frac{\text{the number of applicants hired}}{\text{the number of applicants available for hiring}}.$$

A company that must hire 80 of each 100 applicants in order to fill its vacant positions cannot afford to be as discriminating as one that hires only 20 of each 100 applicants. The latter company is in the advantageous position of having a low selection ratio. Therefore, it can afford to be stringent in setting the "passing score" for any new test considered for inclusion in the preemployment program. When the selection ratio is high, the company is compelled by its need to fill vacant positions, to hire most applicants—even those with relatively low preemployment test scores.

Relationship between Selection Ratio and Proportion of Successful Employees

The relationship between the selection ratio, proportion of successful employees, and passing score on a preemployment test is clarified in Figure 4–1.

This figure shows a scatterplot of test scores against criterion performance for 100 employees in a company wherein 30 percent of the employees are regarded as successful (in the high criterion group). If we disregarded the new test and selected on the old basis,

FIGURE 4–1

The Relationship between Selection Ratio and the Proportion of Successful Employees

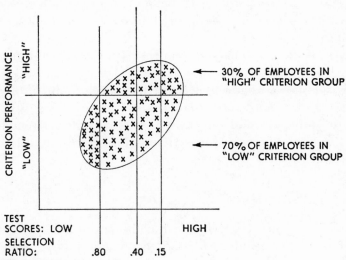

it is likely that we would continue to find that 30 percent of our newly hired employees would prove to be in the high criterion group.

Note what happens to the proportions of high and low criterion employees as a function of establishing various passing scores on this test. A high selection ratio (say, 0.80) signifies proportionately few applicants relative to the number of vacant positions. As shown in Figure 4–1, of each 80 applicants thus selected, we will obtain 30 who will eventually be in the high criterion group and 50 who will eventually be in the low criterion group. Given this selection ratio, the new test will improve the proportion of high criterion employees selected from the present level of 30 percent to 37.5 percent (30/80).

Predictive efficiency is improved further as the passing score can be set for a lower selection ratio. Suppose we had a sufficient number of applicants relative to position vacancies to select only 40 of each 100 applicants. As shown in Figure 4–1, this will have two effects. First, a number of applicants will be rejected who would have proven to be high criterion employees. However, the number of such potentially high criterion rejects will be much lower than the number of potentially low criterion employees simultaneous rejected. Thus the second effect of this more stringent passing score will be to improve the selection program still further. In this case we would obtain 20 employees who will eventually be in the high criterion group and 20 who will eventually be in the low criterion group. The selective efficiency is here improved from its present level of 30 percent to 50 percent.

Finally, if the labor market permits, a still greater gain in predictive efficiency will come from setting the passing score still higher. Figure 4–1 shows what will happen if the selection ratio can be reduced to 0.15. For every 15 applicants selected, 10 will be high criterion employees and only 5 will be low criterion employees. Predictive efficiency under these circumstances has risen to 10/15, or 67 percent.

GROUP PREDICTIONS

Returning to the question raised at the beginning of the discussion of predictive validity, what is the practical importance of a validity coefficient of, say, 0.30 compared with one of, say, 0.50? One helpful way in which to rephrase this question is to ask: "Given present conditions in terms of selection ratio and proportion of successful employees, what improvement in selection accuracy can be anticipated from expanding the battery to include a test with a given predictive validity coefficient?" To make the question specific, let us assume that by whatever means employees are now selected, we have a 70 percent "batting average"; that is, 70 percent of the applicants we select prove after a period of employment to be high criterion employees. Suppose further that our selection ratio is 0.60. Finally, suppose we are considering inclusion in the selection program of a new test with a predictive validity of 0.55. To what extent will inclusion of this test improve the selection program?

The answer to this kind of question is provided by referring to the *Taylor-Russell Tables*.[9] These tables are reproduced in Appendix B. The Taylor-Russell Tables indicate the proportion of applicants likely to be in the high criterion group under various conditions. Thus these tables facilitate so-called "institutional," or group, prediction.

Note that there is one such table for each decile (unit of 10 percentage points) of high criterion employees selected by present methods. Thus, the answer to the illustrative question above is provided in the table headed by 0.70 as the proportion of employees considered satisfactory. Portions of this table are reproduced as Table 4-1.

Entering this table for the appropriate column (a selection ratio of 0.60) and row (predictive validity of 0.55), we see that by adding this new test to the existing selection program, our predictive efficiency will be 85 percent. According to the information provided for this illustration, 70 percent of the employees selected *without* this new test now prove to be in the high criterion group. Therefore, since inclusion of this new test in the selection program would increase this proportion to 85 percent, we would have a 21 percent improvement in predictive efficiency (0.15/0.70).

Examine the entries in Table 4-1 for other combinations of selection ratio and predictive validity.

A validity coefficient of 0.00 means that there is no correlation between the test and criterion scores. A test yielding this validity

---

[9] H. C. Taylor and J. T. Russell, "The Relationship of Validity Coefficients to the Practical Effectiveness of Tests in Selection: Discussion and Tables," *Journal of Applied Psychology*, Vol. 23 (1939), pp. 567–78.

TABLE 4–1

Portions of the Taylor-Russell Table Where Proportion
of Employees Considered Satisfactory Is 0.70

					Selection Ratio						
r	0.05	0.10	0.20	0.30	0.40	0.50	0.60	0.70	0.80	0.90	0.95
0.00	0.70	0.70	0.70	0.70	0.70	0.70	0.70	0.70	0.70	0.70	0.70
0.05	0.73	0.73	0.72	0.72	0.72	0.71	0.71	0.71	0.71	0.70	0.70
0.10	0.77	0.76	0.75	0.74	0.73	0.73	0.72	0.72	0.71	0.71	0.70
0.15	0.80	0.79	0.77	0.76	0.75	0.74	0.73	0.73	0.72	0.71	0.71
0.45	0.94	0.93	0.90	0.87	0.85	0.83	0.81	0.78	0.76	0.73	0.72
0.50	0.96	0.94	0.91	0.89	0.88	0.86	0.83	0.81	0.78	0.74	0.72
0.55	0.97	0.96	0.93	0.91	0.90	0.87	0.85	0.82	0.79	0.75	0.73
0.60	0.98	0.97	0.95	0.92	0.92	0.89	0.86	0.83	0.80	0.75	0.73
0.90	1.00	1.00	1.00	1.00	0.99	0.98	0.95	0.91	0.85	0.78	0.74
0.95	1.00	1.00	1.00	1.00	1.00	0.99	0.98	0.94	0.86	0.78	0.74
1.00	1.00	1.00	1.00	1.00	1.00	1.00	1.00	1.00	0.88	0.78	0.74

coefficient cannot increase the proportion of employees considered satisfactory irrespective of the selection ratio.

Holding the selection ratio constant, the proportion of successful employees increases as a function of the magnitude of the validity coefficient. Note, for example, that with a selection ratio of 0.60, the proportion of satisfactory employees increases from 70 percent to 73 percent by adding a test with a validity of 0.15. However, with the same selection ratio but with a validity coefficient of 0.60 instead of 0.15, this proportion increases from 70 percent to 86 percent. Thus the magnitude of the validity coefficient is one of the determinants of selective efficiency.

The selection ratio is another determinant of predictive efficiency. For a particular validity coefficient, the proportion of successful identification of high criterion employees increases and management can exercise greater selectivity in choosing employees. For example, when the test-criterion correlation is 0.55, the proportion of high criterion employees selected is 97 percent with a selection ratio of 0.05, but only 73 percent with a selection ratio of 0.95.

One final point about predicting employee success needs elaboration. By examining the full set of Taylor-Russell Tables in Appendix B, you will note that it is easier to obtain gains in predictive efficiency when the present selection program is relatively ineffective than when it is relatively effective for selecting high criterion employees.

INDIVIDUAL PREDICTION

The Taylor-Russell Tables permit predictions about the proportion of successful employees from a *group* of applicants. It is possible also to predict the likelihood of success of an *individual* job applicant from theoretical charts developed for this purpose by Lawshe *et al.*[10] These charts are exhibited in Appendix C.

The use of the tables for individual prediction requires much the same information as required for the Taylor-Russell Tables. Both sets of tables are entered with (*a*) the proportion of present employees considered satisfactory and (*b*) the validity of the test. The third piece of required information is slightly different for the two sets of tables. Whereas the tables for group prediction require information about the selection ratio, the tables for individual prediction require information about the applicant's test score.

To illustrate the use of the tables for individual prediction, let us assume we are dealing with a situation wherein 30 percent of the employees are considered satisfactory, and further assume we are using a test with a predictive validity of 0.65. Referring to the appropriate table in Appendix C (30 percent of employees considered satisfactory) and checking the entries for the appropriate row ($r = 0.65$), we find the following: An applicant scoring in the upper fifth on the selection test has 68 chances in 100 of being a successful employee, whereas an applicant scoring in the bottom fifth on this test has only 4 chances in 100 of being a successful employee. Intermediate degrees of probable success are associated with intermediate test score categories.

Individual and group predictions are not interchangeable; they serve different purposes for the company. When a decision must be made about whether or not to include a new test in the preemployment program, the answer is given in part by group predictions. These provide information about the probable improvement in efficiency of the selection program to be anticipated with the test in

[10] C. H. Lawshe, R. A. Bolda, R. L. Brune. G. Auclair, "Expectancy Charts III: Their Theoretical Development," *Personnel Psychology,* Vol. 11 (1958), pp. 545–99

question. In contrast, when the company needs information about the probable success of a particular job applicant, tables for individual prediction will prove useful.

SUMMARY

Criteria make explicit the differences between individuals. Thus they define what is meant by employee "success." It is insufficient to select criteria solely on the basis of expediency or perceived relevance by management. Criterion measures must meet acceptable standards of reliability and validity.

An ever-present danger in criterion development is the possibility of criterion contamination. Such contamination results whenever the criterion measure reflects the influence of factors which are really extraneous to the particular measure being sought. Such contamination may be a function of the working environment, subtle differences in the nature of work, and variations in job experience of the employees.

Another possible source of error in criterion development is that associated with an inadequate or inappropriate sampling of production records.

Although output is most frequently used as a performance criterion, it must often be supplemented by or replaced with such criteria as quality, turnover, lost time, and worker satisfaction. Such behavior cannot always be objectively assessed. There are many occasions when the criteria of job performance rest upon supervisory judgments of employee effectiveness.

It is unrealistic to think of a single best or most appropriate criterion of employee effectiveness for any job. This is so because virtually all jobs are multidimensional. Hence employee effectiveness must be assessed by developing criteria for each of the job's most important dimensions. Such multiple criteria may either be used without combination or may be combined to provide a single index of the employee's overall job performance.

Since Chapter 4 was particularly oriented toward the use of criteria for personnel selection and placement, considerable attention was given to predicting criterion performance from preemployment selection programs. Three factors determine the magnitude of improvements in the efficiency of a selection program: (*a*) the selection ratio, (*b*) the proportion of superior employees selected by the

existing program, and (c) the predictive validity of new tests considered for inclusion in the program. The interaction of these three
factors as summarized in the Taylor-Russell Tables permit predictions about the probable increase in selective efficiency to be obtained under specific conditions. Using essentially the same three
factors, Lawshe *et al.* developed charts permitting predictions about
the probable success of individual job applicants.

5. Application Blank and Employment Interview

The specific procedures employed for selecting and placing personnel vary from one industrial or business organization to another as a function of the requirements of the specific job to be filled and of the selection ratio. In spite of variability in selection procedures, virtually all industrial organizations use at least the two devices discussed in this chapter—an application form and some kind of interview—as a partial basis for selection decisions. Indeed, many organizations rely upon these devices as the sole basis for selecting personnel, neglecting such other sources of information available to prospective employers as letters of reference and psychological tests of various kinds.

The widespread use of application blanks and employment interviews is predicated upon the notion that job success depends upon certain critical background factors (like past experience and education) and interpersonal factors (like the ability to create and maintain a favorable impression and to converse easily).

The interpretation of the significance of replies on the application form and of certain kinds of behavior during the interview is highly subjective. The efforts of industrial psychologists to improve these devices have been directed toward reducing this subjectivity. This is accomplished by (1) relating interview questions and items on the application blank to the results of a thoroughgoing job analysis suggesting critical items of information to be elicited by these devices; and (2) research demonstrating that such information does, in fact, correlate with a meaningful criterion of job success, that is, that it has predictive validity.

APPLICATION FORMS

Letters of application and responses to formalized application blanks are generally used as preliminary hurdles in the selection process. If, for example, the job specification indicates that a tenth-grade education is prerequisite to satisfactory job performance and the letter of application is written by someone who is virtually illiterate or the "schooling" section of the application form indicates that the applicant possesses a lesser degree of education, further investigation of the applicant's qualifications is unwarranted.

The typical application blank contains items pertaining to the applicant's age, marital status, dependents, schooling, past experience, and references. Portions of an application form for sales applicants are shown in Figure 5–1.

The Weighted Application Blank

There is considerable evidence that careful evaluation of the kind of information elicited by the application blank can result in the selection of better qualified employees and the reduction of employee turnover. The application blank is most useful when it is developed and analyzed in accordance with standard research procedures.

This implies that the investigator must determine the extent, if any, of the relationship between responses to the items on the application blank and some criterion of the employee's success. Items which are shown to be related to a criterion, for example, industrial productivity, are weighted to reflect the extent of this relationship, and the total blank is "scored" by summing the weights of responses to the items.

You will note, from the above description of the various procedures for constructing a standardized application blank, the essential similarity of the steps involved in developing these forms and many other kinds of psychological tests and inventories in this area. (These

FIGURE 5-1. Portions of Application for Employment, Radio Corporation of America

NAME

| LAST | FIRST | MIDDLE |

INSTRUCTIONS

1. TYPE OR PRINT IN INK
2. EACH QUESTION MUST BE FULLY AND ACCURATELY ANSWERED. (USE ADDITIONAL SHEET IF NECESSARY)
3. SIGN AND DATE (LAST PAGE)

(RCA logo) ®

QUALIFICATION RECORD

RADIO CORPORATION OF AMERICA

| ADDRESS NEXT THREE MONTHS | NUMBER | STREET | CITY | ZONE | STATE | PHONE |

| PERMANENT ADDRESS | NUMBER | STREET | CITY | ZONE | STATE | PHONE |

| SOCIAL SECURITY NUMBER | U. S. CITIZEN? ☐ YES ☐ NO | ARE YOU PREPARED TO SUBMIT PROOF OF U. S. CITIZENSHIP IF EMPLOYED WITHIN NEXT 3 MONTHS? ☐ YES ☐ NO | | MARITAL STATUS |

| AGE | BIRTH DATE | NUMBER OF DEPENDENTS (INCLUDE YOURSELF) | AGES OF CHILDREN | HEALTH ☐ EXCELLENT ☐ GOOD ☐ FAIR ☐ POOR | HEIGHT | WEIGHT |

| LIST HANDICAPS | | % DISABILITY | LIST CHRONIC AILMENTS | | % DISABILITY |

| NAMES OF RELATIVES EMPLOYED BY RCA | | PREVIOUS RCA EMPLOYMENT APPLICATION MADE? ☐ YES ☐ NO |
| | | WHERE? WHEN? |

IN CASE OF EMERGENCY, NOTIFY

| NAME (LAST, FIRST, MIDDLE) | | | | |
| ADDRESS | NUMBER | STREET | CITY | ZONE | STATE | PHONE |

| HAVE YOU EVER BEEN ARRESTED? ☐ YES ☐ NO | IF YES, EXPLAIN: |

| LOCATION PREFERENCE | ARE YOU WILLING TO RELOCATE? ☐ YES ☐ NO |

| EARLIEST DATE AVAILABLE FOR EMPLOYMENT | LATEST DATE AVAILABLE FOR EMPLOYMENT | MINIMUM SALARY REQUIREMENT FOR 40 HOUR WEEK (PER MONTH) $ |

NAME OR DESCRIBE THE TYPE POSITION YOU DESIRE NOW

NAME OR DESCRIBE THE TYPE POSITION YOU DESIRE EVENTUALLY

FIGURE 5-1—*Continued*

APPLICANTS FOR SCIENTIFIC OR ENGINEERING POSITIONS PLEASE COMPLETE THIS SECTION

CHECK FIELD(S) OF PROFESSIONAL INTEREST

☐ Electrical Engineering ☐ Physics ☐ Ceramics
☐ Mechanical Engineering ☐ Chemistry ☐ Industrial Engineering
☐ Mathematics

Other _____

CHECK FIELDS OF PRODUCT INTEREST BELOW

☐ Radar   ☐ Gas Tubes   ☐ Receiving Tubes   ☐ Component Design   ☐ Aviation Electronics
☐ Computer   ☐ Television   ☐ Phototubes   ☐ Radio and TV Receivers ☐ Industrial Electronics
☐ Acoustics   ☐ Power Tubes.   ☐ Semi-Conductors   ☐ Solid State Physics   ☐ Electronics of Solids
☐ Chemistry   ☐ Camera Tubes   ☐ Machine Design   ☐ Communications   ☐ General Circuit Design
☐ Standards   ☐ Storage Tubes   ☐ Mechanical Design   ☐ Other _____

INDICATE SPECIFICALLY YOUR INTEREST IN THE ABOVE PRODUCT FIELDS: EXAMPLE—STORAGE TECHNIQUES, DIGITAL COMPUTER, OR, FIRE CONTROL DESIGN AIRBORNE RADAR

LISTED BELOW ARE RCA SCIENTIFIC OR ENGINEERING CATEGORIES. PLEASE INDICATE THE INFORMATION REQUESTED IN THE THREE COLUMNS TO THE RIGHT.

	INDICATE PREFERENCE (1, 2, 3)	NUMBER OF MONTHS EXPERIENCE	MONTHS OF SUPERVISORY EXPERIENCE
FUNDAMENTAL PURE RESEARCH—Scientific study to discover new principles			
APPLIED RESEARCH—Application of the results of fundamental research to possible useful ends			
SYSTEMS—Integration of theory, equipments and environment to create and optimize major electronic concepts			
ADVANCED DEVELOPMENT—Integration of major innovations into systems or components (model)			
DEVELOPMENT—Reduction of new ideas to practice (model)			
DESIGN—Engineering to produce a product to specifications			
FACTORY FOLLOW-UP—Liaison to reconcile design and manufacturing problems			
MANUFACTURING OR INDUSTRIAL—Factory Layout, Production Planning, Process, Time and Motion Study, Quality, Control, etc.			
SALES—Technical product representation to the customer			
APPLICATION—Determination and solution of customers' technical requirements			
FIELD SERVICE OR INSTALLATION—Erection, instruction, modification, maintenance, operation			
THESIS, PAPERS, PUBLICATIONS, PATENTS			
SUPERVISORY EXPERIENCE IN DETAIL			

Have you a currently effective agreement with employers or others concerning inventions you make?   Yes_____   No_____

If yes, how long is agreement effective after termination of services? _____ (Furnish copy of agreements)

procedures are further elaborated in Chapter 6.) Once the criterion-related application blank items are identified and weighted for scoring purposes, the entire form must be validated against an external criterion.

The usefulness of this general technique has been demonstrated for predicting various criteria of success for a wide range of positions, including sales personnel,[1] seasonably employed production workers,[2] and office-clerical personnel.[3]

In one of these investigations a weighted application blank was devised to predict turnover of clerical and secretarial employees in a university setting. The replies to each item on an application form completed by employees hired several years earlier were studied. Although all of these employees had been hired on a "permanent" basis, it was possible to identify "long-tenure" and "short-tenure" subgroups. Persons in the former subgroup had been working from two to four years and were still on the job. Those in the "short-tenure" group had terminated employment within two years. Each of the items on the application blank was analyzed to determine the extent to which it differentiated between the long- and short-tenure subgroups.

The responses for each group were classified, tallied, and converted to percentages. For some items the percentage of response within each classification was virtually identical for both groups. Since such items did not discriminate, they were weighted zero and hence did not contribute to the score. When it was evident that an item *did* discriminate between the long- and short-tenure groups, it was weighted to reflect both the magnitude and direction of its discrimination. Illustrative data for some discriminatory and non-discriminatory items are shown in Table 5–1. As the table shows,

---

[1] O. A. Ohmann, "A Report of Research in the Selection of Salesmen at the Tremco Manufacturing Company," *Journal of Applied Psychology*, Vol. 25 (1941), pp. 18–19; and R. W. Scollay, "Personal History Data as a Predictor of Success," *Personnel Psychology*, Vol. 10 (1957), pp. 23–26.

[2] M. D. Dunnette and J. Maetzold, "Use of a Weighted Application Blank in Hiring Seasonal Employees," *Journal of Applied Psychology*, Vol. 39 (1955), pp. 308–10.

[3] P. H. Kreidt and M. S. Gadel, "Prediction of Turnover among Clerical Workers," *Journal of Applied Psychology*, Vol. 37 (1953), pp. 338–40; W. K. Kirschner and M. D. Dunnette, "Applying the Weighted Application Blank Technique to a Variety of Office Jobs," *Journal of Applied Psychology*, Vol. 41 (1957), pp. 206–08; and E. A. Fleishman and J. Berniger, "One Way to Reduce Office Turnover," *Personnel*, Vol. 37 (1960), pp. 63–69.

TABLE 5-1

Comparison of Item Responses of Long- and Short-Tenure Office Employees

Application Blank Items	Short-Tenure Group	Long-Tenure Group	Weight Assigned to Response
Local address:			
Within city	39%	62%	+2
Outlying suburbs	50	36	−2
Age:			
Under 20	35	8	−3
21–25	38	32	−1
26–30	8	2	−1
31–35	7	10	0
35 and over	11	48	+3
Previous salary:			
Under $2,000	31	30	0
$2,000–$3,000	41	38	0
$3,000–$4,000	13	12	0
Over $4,000	4	4	0
Age of children:			
Preschool	12	4	−3
Public school	53	33	−3
High school or older	35	63	+3

local address differentiated effectively between the groups but previous salary was an ineffective differentiator.[4]

The application blanks of a second sample of long- and short-tenure employees were then scored, utilizing the weights derived from this analysis. The total score was obtained simply by adding or subtracting the weights assigned to categories of response for the items. The correlation between application blank scores and subsequent tenure for this sample was 0.57. If a critical (passing) score of 4 had been used as the basis for hiring or rejecting these women when they were job applicants, it would have been possible to reduce office turnover considerably (see Figure 5–2).

It is not possible to structure a weighted application blank that will be usable for all jobs in all organizations or even for very similar jobs in different organizations. Every selection program presents a unique problem both with respect to the phrasing of items

---

[4] For a more detailed discussion of procedures for developing a weighted application blank, see G. W. England, *Development and Use of Application Blanks* (Dubuque, Iowa: Wm. C. Brown Co., 1961).

FIGURE 5–2

Percentages of Correct and Incorrect Hiring Decisions that
Would Have Been Obtained for Office Employees

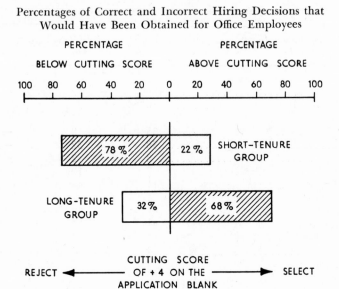

for inclusion in the blank and the weighting of responses to these
items. Consequently, to be most effective, application forms should
be tailored to the needs of the specific business or industry desiring
to use such a device.

Biographical Information Blank

The usual weighted application blank yields a single overall score
which has some predictive usefulness. However, the meaning of this
score is uncertain; it does not contribute to understanding the relationship between personal history and job performance.[5]

The Biographical Information Blank (BIB) is a refinement of
the weighted application blank. It is uniquely suited both to prediction and to research on the relationship between factors in the
employee's past history and his level of job performance.

In appearance, the BIB looks like a psychological inventory. It
typically consists of a series of items pertaining to the respondent's

---

[5] R. M. Guion, "Personnel Selection," *Annual Review of Psychology*, Vol. 18 (1967),
p. 200.

personal background and present status. For the most part these items concern matters of fact (for example, age, schooling, number of dependents), although some may require expressions of interest or attitude. The BIB usually uses a multiple choice answer format.

By correlating each alternative for every BIB item with the criterion, it is possible to eliminate the invalid items and to develop a scoring key using only the valid items. This process is similar to the one discussed earlier for identifying those application blank items which are to be weighted. Although it is possible similarly to weight BIB items, this is not ordinarily done. Instead, most biographical information blanks are scored by assigning unit weights to the valid items: +1 if the item correlates positively with the criterion and −1 if the item correlates negatively with the criterion. The evidence of the desirability of differentially weighting BIB items is conflictual. Some studies have demonstrated that differential weighting permits the inclusion of fewer items in the scoring key.[6] Others support the use of unit weights.

In addition to correlating BIB items with a criterion in an effort to develop a scorable predictive instrument, the interrelationships between the BIB items themselves may be analyzed. By means of statistical procedures beyond the scope of the present discussion, it is possible to group these items into subsets, or clusters, based upon certain traits, or factors, common to all of the items in a subset. Each of these factors, consisting of *homogeneous* (that is, with a common element) items, may then be scored as a biographical subtest and correlated with the criterion.

The common element defining a cluster of biographical items may be the type of activity common to all items in that cluster. This was the case, for example, with items administered to high school seniors and clustered into subsets concerned with social activities, religious activities, economic independence, and so on.[7] Alternatively, it has been suggested that our understanding of the personal backgrounds contributing to employee effectiveness can be enhanced by developing clusters of biographical items about such

---

[6] R. A. Ehrle, "Quantification of Biographical Data for Predicting Vocational Rehabilitation Success," *Journal of Applied Psychology*, Vol. 48 (1964), pp. 171–74.

[7] L. Siegel, "A Biographical Inventory for Students," *Journal of Applied Psychology*, Vol. 40 (1956), pp. 5–10.

traits as level of maturity, rate of maturation, social adaptability, job interest, and energy level.[8]

A special value of this kind of analysis is that it permits additional understanding of the relationship between personal history and job success. Instead of merely contributing to improved prediction, this analysis facilitates the discovery of answers to *why*, in terms of personal history, some persons are more satisfactory employees than others. Further, by comparing biographical factor scores earned by employees in different positions, it becomes possible to hypothesize about the relationship between differences in personal histories and success or failure in various kinds of positions.

THE EMPLOYMENT INTERVIEW

The primary function of the employment interview is to allow the interviewer to meet the applicant in a face-to-face relationship, thereby better permitting the interviewer to evaluate certain of the applicant's qualifications. The interview may be justified as a selection device when personal characteristics, physical appearance, and social factors are critical job requirements. Even under such circumstances, however, the subjectivity of employment interviewing seriously limits its usefulness. The interview should never be considered a substitute for psychological tests specifically designed to measure such factors as intelligence or job knowledge.

When placed in proper perspective, the employment interview serves two functions in addition to the primary one of accepting or rejecting the applicant. Besides securing information bearing upon the applicant's status, the interviewer gives certain information to the applicant about the job and the company and he establishes a friendly relationship with the interviewee. The latter function of employment interviewing is particularly important in situations in which rejected job applicants are potential customers.

Many personnel directors pride themselves on what they consider to be their unique and uncanny ability to select employees by means of an interview. Most generally, however, the validity of their interviewing procedures has never been ascertained.[9] A validity study

---

[8] E. R. Henry, Chmn., *Research Conference on the Use of Autobiographical Data as Psychological Predictors* (Greensboro, N.C.: The Richardson Foundation, 1965).

[9] M. D. Dunnette and B. M. Bass, "Behavioral Scientists and Personnel Management," *Industrial Relations*, Vol. 2 (1963), pp. 115–30.

would require data on the number of rejected applicants who would have been successful if they had been hired and the number of accepted applicants who later prove to be unsuccessful employees. When attempted, the results of such studies sometimes indicate that the well-meaning but untrained interviewer might better make his selections on the basis of revelations from a ouija board or crystal ball.[10]

Another disturbing feature of the employment interview as usually conducted is its unreliability. Several interviewers may differ markedly in their appraisal of the same job applicant. One of the early studies of the reliability of employment interviews compared the ratings assigned to 57 applicants by 12 different interviewers.

TABLE 5–2

Ranks Assigned to Job Applicants by 12 Sales Managers Who Interviewed Them*

	Interviewer												
Applicant	I	II	III	IV	V	VI	VII	VIII	IX	X	XI	XII	Range
A	33	46	6	56	26	32	12	38	23	22	22	9	6–56
B	36	50	43	17	51	47	38	20	38	55	39	9	9–55
C	53	10	6	21	16	9	20	2	57	28	1	26	1–57

* A rank of 1 signifies that the interviewer believed the applicant to be the most suitable for the position; a rank of 57 means that the applicant was rated as the least suitable for the position.

The interviewers were sales managers, each of whom was allowed to conduct the interview in whatever manner he wished. Each interviewer's ratings were transformed to numerical ranks ranging from 1 to 57 in terms of the suitability of the applicant for the job of salesman. The ranks assigned by the 12 interviewers to several of the applicants are shown in Table 5–2.[11] Note particularly the spread or range of ranks assigned to each interviewee. In spite of the fact that the interviewers were sales managers, each with considerable interviewing experience, they disagreed extensively in their appraisal of each applicant.

Although evidence like this is disquieting, it must be remembered

---

[10] J. R. Hinrichs, "Technical Selection: How to Improve Your Batting Average," *Personnel*, Vol. 37 (1960), pp. 56–60.

[11] H. L. Hollingworth, *Vocational Psychology and Character Analysis* (New York: D. Appleton & Co., 1923), pp. 115–19.

that the interviewers were not restricted either with respect to procedure or to the bases upon which their evaluations were to be made. This was an *unstructured* interview situation. As we will discuss later, standardization of interviewing techniques, structuring the interview, and training of interviewers with respect to the proper criteria for evaluating job applicants does much to improve both the reliability and validity of employment interviews.

There are two general kinds of conditions acting to lower the reliability and validity of interviews, hence limiting their usefulness. These conditions are those associated with the interviewing procedure itself, and with the kind of perceptual distortion that may occur in any interpersonal situation. It will be convenient to separate these two limiting conditions for the purpose of our discussion and to indicate for each the appropriate remedial steps.

Procedure as a Limiting Factor

The unstructured interview is one in which the pattern of questions, the circumstances under which these questions are asked, and the bases for evaluation of replies to these questions are not standardized. These factors vary from one interviewer to another and from one applicant to another. In short, the unstructured interview is subjective in the extreme. This subjectivity may lead different interviewers to disagree quite markedly about the suitability of a particular applicant. Such disagreement adversely affects both the reliability and validity of unstructured interviews.

Reliability and Validity of the Unstructured Interview. Reliability has been defined as consistency of measurement. When applied to the interview, high reliability requires a high degree of interrater agreement. In other words, different interviewers independently interviewing the same candidate would have substantially to agree about that candidate's suitability for employment. As has been previously indicated, interrater *dis*agreement is more common than agreement in interpreting interview performance.

Of the several conditions responsible for the low reliability of the unstructured interview, an important one is the fact that different interviewers are free to cover different material.[12] When 109 submariners were interviewed, it was found that the items most consistently

---

[12] For an excellent review of research on the selection interview, see E. C. Mayfield, "The Selection Interview—A Re-evaluation of Published Research," *Personnel Psychology*, Vol. 17 (1964), pp. 239-60.

covered by different interviewers were of the factual, biographical type. Interviewee attitudes on the other hand were assessed very inconsistently.[13] The simple fact is that different interviewers are interested in different features of the applicant's background and attitudes. And the unstructured interview does not guide the procedure in any way to insure that common questions are asked and that the interviewers are thereby provided with a common basis for assessment.[14]

A related condition contributing to the low interrater reliability of the unstructured interview is the fact that such procedures fail to standardize the way in which the information obtained is to be weighted by the interviewers. Even when interviewers obtain the same information, they are likely to interpret and weigh it differently.[15]

Even in the unusual circumstance where high reliability can be demonstrated, this cannot be construed as evidence for satisfactory *validity*. The fact that raters agree among themselves in assessing a candidate does not insure that their assessment will permit satisfactory predictions of performance. Furthermore, we have already indicated that the reliability of the unstructured interview tends to be low. Given low reliability, it is impossible to demonstrate high validity. An assessment instrument simply cannot accurately predict a subsequently obtained criterion (that is, cannot be valid) when it measures inconsistently.

In view of the statement above, it is not surprising to note little evidence supporting the validity of the unstructured interview. One source of invalidity is that the interviewers tend to form their judgments about interviewees early, and on the basis of such often irrelevant characteristics as personal dress.[16] Furthermore, their judgments are more easily influenced by unfavorable than by favorable information.[17]

---

[13] S. Pashalian and W. J. E. Crissy, "The Interview, IV. The Reliability and Validity of the Assessment Interview as a Screening and Selection Technique in the Submarine Service," *MLR Report No. 216*, Vol. 12, No. 1 (January, 1953).

[14] E. C. Webster, *Factors Pertaining to Decision Making in the Personnel Interview*, Final Report, Canadian Defense Research Board Grant 9435–53, (April, 1962).

[15] P. Wentworth, "How to Improve Employment Interviews," *Personnel Journal*, Vol. 32 (1953), pp. 46–49.

[16] B. M. Springbett, "Factors Affecting the Final Decision in the Employment Interview," *Canadian Journal of Psychology*, Vol. 12 (1958), pp. 13–22.

[17] B. I. Bolster and B. M. Springbett, "The Reaction of Interviewers to Favorable and Unfavorable Information," *Journal of Applied Psychology*, Vol. 45 (1961), pp. 97–103.

The Structured Interview: An Improvement.   As discussed above, the basic objection to the unstructured interview is its low reliability and validity. In the absence of standardization of the questions asked, the sequence in which they are asked, and the way in which replies are interpreted, the relative qualifications of the various applicants cannot be compared. The interview must be *structured* (that is, controlled or standardized) with respect to these factors in order to obtain meaningful comparisons across interviewers and between interviewees.[18] Thus it is clear that structured interviews tend to be more reliable than unstructured interviews and therefore to have greater *potential* (although not always *actual*) validity.

Structured interviews most typically are developed for specific jobs in particular companies. In addition, two types of structured interview forms have been devised for use across companies and jobs: the "patterned interview" and the "diagnostic interviewer's guide." Both techniques were designed to overcome some of the deficiencies of uncontrolled interviewing.

The *patterned interview* consists of special interview schedules (lists of questions) which were developed as guides to the interviewer in his search for relevant information about the applicant and his previous work history. This procedure focuses upon such character traits as "stability," "industry," "perseverance," and "leadership." It does not attempt to provide information about the applicant's level of job skill; this can be better appraised by methods other than the interview.

A portion of a patterned interview schedule is reproduced in Figure 5–3. Notice that there is a provision on this form for the interviewer to make notations about the applicant's responses. The questions under each response position are designed as guides for the interviewer in helping him appraise what the applicant is saying.

The patterned interview program as outlined by McMurry also includes a telephone check designed to verify statements made by the applicant on his application form, to obtain previous employer's estimates of the applicant's strengths and weaknesses, and to indicate to the interviewer the areas in which additional information must be elicited during the interview. A telephone check form for sales applicants is reproduced in Figure 5–4.

The specific advantage of the patterned interview procedure is

---

[18] Mayfield, *op. cit.*

FIGURE 5–3

Patterned Interview Form

PATTERNED INTERVIEW
(Short Form)

Name_____ Sex: ☐ M, ☐ F; Date of Birth_____ Soc. Sec. No._____

Address _____

| SUMMARY | Rating: | 1 | 2 | 3 | 4 | Comments:_____ |

Rating: | 1 | 2 | 3 | 4 | Comments:_____
In making final rating, be sure to consider applicant's stability, industry, perseverance, loyalty, ability
to get along with others, self-reliance, leadership, maturity, motivation: also, domestic situation and health.

Interviewer:_____ Job Considered for:_____ Date_____

Why are you applying for work in this Company?_____
Is his underlying reason a desire for prestige, security, or earnings?

If you were hired, how long
would it take you to get to work?_____ How would you do it?_____
Is there anything undesirable here?

WORK EXPERIENCE. Cover all positions. This information is very important. Interviewer should record last position first. Every month since leaving school
should be accounted for. Note military service in work record in continuity with jobs held since that time.

	LAST OR PRESENT POSITION	NEXT TO LAST POSITION	SECOND FROM LAST POSITION
Name of Company			
Address			
Dates of employment	From To	From To	From To
		Do these dates check with his application?	
Nature of work			
		Will his previous experience be helpful on this job?	
Starting salary			
Salary at leaving			
Was anything especially liked about the job?	Has he made good work progress?		General or merit increases?
		Has he been happy and contented in his work?	
Was there anything especially disliked?			
	Were his dislikes justified?		Is he chronically dissatisfied?
Reasons for leaving			
		Are his reasons for leaving reasonable and consistent?	

OTHER POSITIONS

Name of Company	Type of Work	Salary	Date Started	Date Left	Reasons for Leaving
	Has he stayed in one line of work for the most part?				
	Has he gotten along well on his jobs?				
	Are his attitudes toward his employers loyal?				
	Was he interested in creative work? In work requiring activity?				
	Has he improved himself and his position?				

FIGURE 5-3—*Continued*

How much unemployment compensation have you drawn?________ When?________ Why?________
Does he depend on himself?

How many weeks have you been unemployed in the past five years?________ How did you spend this time?________
Did conditions in his occupation justify this time? Did he use his time profitably?

What accidents have you had in recent years?________
Is he "accident-prone"? Any disabilities which will interfere with his work?

SCHOOLING

How far did you go in school? Grade: 1 2 3 4 5 6 7 8 High School: 1 2 3 4 College: 1 2 3 4 Date of leaving school________
Is his schooling adequate for the job?

If you did not graduate from high school or college, why not?________ Who paid for your schooling?________
Are his reasons for not finishing sound? Self-reliant?

What special training have you taken?________
Will this be helpful? Indications of perseverance? Industry?

Extracurricular activities________ What offices did you hold in these groups?________
Did he get along well with others? Indications of leadership?

FAMILY BACKGROUND	FINANCIAL SITUATION	DOMESTIC AND SOCIAL SITUATION
Father living?___ Mother living?___ Normal background?	Own home: $___ Mortgage: $___ Stability?	Single?___ Engaged?___
Father's occupation___	Rent House: $___ Apt.: $___	Married?___ When?___
Average earnings___	Live with friends: $___ Relatives: $___	Widowed?___ Divorced?___
Number brothers or sisters older___ Younger___ Has he been babied?	Own furniture___ Number of Rooms___	Ages of children___ Motivation?
Financial aid to family___	Cost of living per month $___ Realistic?	How do you and your wife get along?___ Maturity?
Leisure time activities___ Habits of industry?	Any current debts?___ Mature financially?	Recreation___ Maturity?
Summer vacations___ Did he keep busy?	Wages ever garnisheed?___	Hobbies___ Will these help?
Church activities___ (Do not ask what church)	Borrow from small loan agency?___ Judgment?	Entertain at home?___ Get along well with others?
Group activities___ (Exclude racial, religious, and nationality groups)	Savings on last job $___ Net Worth $___	Group activities___ (Exclude racial, religious, nationality groups)
	Wife employed?___ Her earnings: $___ Effect on motivation?	When did you have last drink?___ Sensible?
Positions of leadership___ Leader?	Other income $___	What types of people rub you the wrong way?___ Bias?
How old when fully self-supporting?___ Self-reliant?	Life insurance $___ Accident insurance $___ Is he provident?	Ever arrested?___ Charges___ Immaturity?

HEALTH

What serious illnesses, operations, or accidents did you have as a child?________
Has he retained any infantile personality traits due to childhood illnesses?

What illnesses, operations, or accidents have you had in recent years?________
Are his illnesses legitimate rather than indicating a desire to "enjoy ill health"?

How much time have you lost from work because of illness during past year?________
Will he be able to do the job?

Does anyone in your home suffer ill health?________
Are his wife, children, or family relatively healthy?

Do you suffer from:
- ☐ Poor Eyesight
- ☐ Rupture
- ☐ Rheumatism
- ☐ Asthma
- ☐ Heart Trouble
- ☐ Diabetes
- ☐ Ulcers
- ☐ Hay Fever
- ☐ Flat Feet
- ☐ Nervousness

ADDITIONAL INFORMATION:________

Form No. OP-202

Source: The Dartnell Corporation, Chicago, 1949. Developed by Robert N. McMurry & Co.

FIGURE 5–4

Telephone Check on Sales Applicant

TELEPHONE CHECK ON SALES APPLICANT _____

Name of Applicant

Person Contacted	Position

Company	City and State	Telephone Number

1. I wish to *verify* some of the information given to us by Mr. (name) who has applied for a position with our firm. Do you remember him? What were the dates of his employment with your Company?
From_____ 19____ To_____ *Do dates check?* 19_____

2. What was he doing when he started? _____ *Did he exaggerate?*

   When he left? _____ *Did he progress?*

3. He says he was earning $_____ per_____when he left. Is that right?   ☐ Yes,   ☐ No; $_____ *Did he falsify?*

4. How much of this was salary? $_____

   How much commission? $_____

5. How was his attendance? _____ *Conscientious?   Health problems?*

6. What type of selling did he do? _____ *To whom?   How did he get his contacts?*

7. How did his sales results compare with others? _____ *Industrious?   Competitive?*

8. Did he supervise anyone else?   ☐ No,   ☐ Yes; How many?_____ *Does this check?*

   (If yes) How well did he handle it? _____ *Is he a leader or a driver?*

9. How closely was he supervised? _____ *Was he hard to manage?*

10. How hard did he work? _____ *Is he habitually industrious?*

11. How well did he get along with other people? _____ *Is he a troublemaker?*

12. What arguments did he have with customers? _____ *Does he like selling?   Can he control his temper?*

13. What did you think of him? _____ *Did he get along with his superiors?*

14. Why did he leave? _____ *Good reasons?   Do they check?*

15. Would you rehire him?   ☐ Yes,   ☐ No; Why Not?_____ *Does this affect his suitability with us?*

16. Did he have any domestic or financial difficulties that interfered with work?   ☐ No,   ☐ Yes; What?_____ *Immaturity?*

17. How about drinking or gambling?   ☐ No,   ☐ Yes; What?_____ *Immaturity?*

18. What are his outstanding strong points? _____

19. What type of saleswork do you feel he would do best? _____

20. What are his weak points? _____

Checked by_____   Date_____

Form No. ST-108

Copyright 1949, The Dartnell Corporation, Chicago, Printed in U. S. A. Developed by Robert N. McMurry & Company

Source: The Dartnell Corporation, Chicago, 1949. Developed by Robert N. McMurry & Co.

that it provides the interviewer with a set of carefully worded questions and a sequence in which these questions are to be asked. This eliminates some of the variability of procedure between interviewers. In addition, the interview schedule contains questions designed to guide the interviewer in making his appraisal of the applicant's qualifications. The effect of this is to direct the interviewer's attention to the critical factors to be considered in making his judgment, thereby reducing the effects of personal bias and halo effect.

One indication of the validity of the patterned interview was obtained from a study of the usefulness of the technique for predict-

TABLE 5–3

Comparison of Ratings from the Patterned Interview and Success on the Job

| | Patterned Interview Rating | | | |
Success on the Job	*1* *Outstanding*	*2* *Good*	*3* *Average*	*4* *Poor*
Successful: Still in service......75%		38.5%	26.1%	13.3%
Failure: Left service for any reason...................25		61.5	73.9	86.7

ing the probable success of truck drivers.[19] One hundred and eight applicants were interviewed, and all were hired regardless of the rating assigned by the interviewers. The data comparing the initial rating by the interviewer and a criterion of employee success determined after 11 weeks are shown in Table 5–3. It is apparent that the patterned interview was quite effective in predicting the ultimate success or failure of the applicants.

The Diagnostic Interviewer's Guide (D.I.G.). The D.I.G.[20] is a device which, like the patterned interview, provides a set of standardized questions to be asked of job applicants. In addition, the *Guide* contains a "scoring" system which enables the interviewer to quantify his impressions of each applicant.

The D.I.G. questions are arranged into four areas covering the applicant's work, family, social, and personal history. The questions in the *Work History* section seek information about the applicant's

---

[19] R. N. McMurry, "Validating the Patterned Interview," *Personnel*, Vol. 23, No. 4 (1947), pp. 270–71.

[20] C. I. Hovland and E. F. Wonderlic, "Prediction of Success from a Standardized Interview," *Journal of Applied Psychology*, Vol. 33 (1939), pp. 537–46.

ability to analyze tasks assigned to him and his ability to profit from his work experience. *Family History* items relate to his social, economic, and educational background for the job. The section on *Social History* seeks to determine level of sociability and interest in people. Motivational factors like ambition and persistence are covered in the section on *Personal History*.

At the end of each section, there is a series of questions to be answered by the *interviewer*. One such question in the *Work History* section, for example, is: "Has the applicant indicated a serious and sincere attitude toward the work he has been doing?" The

TABLE 5–4

Percentage of Employees Still on the Job, Resigned, or Dismissed by Category of Score on the D.I.G.

	D.I.G. *Score Category*				
Criterion	*0–10*	*12–16*	*18–22*	*24–28*	*30–34*
Still on job.........	38.9%	42.9%	47.2%	48.6%	59.2%
Resigned...........	22.2	25.7	29.2	29.4	34.7
Dismissed..........	38.9	31.4	23.6	22.0	6.1

interviewer answers either "yes" or "no"; and this answer is transformed to a + or − weight. The algebraic sum of the weights of all of the interviewer's answers to the summary questions constitutes the applicant's "score."

An indication of the validity of the D.I.G. is given by a study conducted at the Household Finance Corporation. The *Guide* was completed and scored for 300 applicants, all of whom were hired. The percentages of employees who were still on the job, who had resigned, and who had been dismissed during the course of their employment are summarized in Table 5–4. These data clearly indicate that the percentage of persons still on the job is greater, the higher the D.I.G. score. Note also the marked decrease in the percentage of persons dismissed as the D.I.G. score increases.

More recently the question has been raised whether the relative success of techniques like the patterned interview and the D.I.G. is attributable primarily to control over the sequence and phraseology of questions or simply to the fact that they focus attention upon specific well-defined traits. It has been suggested that undue control over sequence and phraseology may obscure important characteristics that might become evident in a somewhat freer and more dynamic interaction between interviewer and interviewee. In a pilot study utilizing a standardized but less static format than the typical patterned interview, interviewer ratings of small groups of pharmaceutical employees were correlated with composite supervisors' ratings of job performance. The obtained validity coefficients were statistically significant for three of the five groups and positive though not significant for two of the groups. The investigator concludes that a properly used interview can play a reliable part in overall assessment of an individual's qualities.[21]

Distorted Interpersonal Perception

The implications of subjectivity were outlined earlier in conjunction with the discussion of the *S-I-R* concept. You will recall from that discussion that responses are functions not only of the precipitating stimuli but also of the interpretation of those stimuli by the respondent. This interpretative factor is the subjective element. The employment interview involves two sets of psychologically significant responses: those made by the interviewer and those made by the job applicant. The stimuli for the interviewer's responses are provided by the applicant's replies to questions, his physical appearance, and personal mannerisms. The ways in which the applicant replies to the questions (the applicant's responses) are in turn a function of stimuli provided by the interviewer—the questions he asks, *his* physical appearance, and *his* personal mannerisms.

The interview, then, involves a very dynamic interpersonal relationship. The two parties react in terms of their perceptions of one another. The factors influencing these perceptions may be quite subtle and not always deliberate, but their effects are manifest in the relatively low reliability and validity of the interview. The human factors operative on both sides of the interviewer's desk which will concern us here are (*a*) lack of rapport, (*b*) bias, and (*c*) halo effect.

Lack of Rapport. Virtually every job applicant experiences some degree of anxiety and tension during the employment interview. His "nervousness" is well founded! The decision about whether or not

---

[21] K. A. Yonge, "The Value of the Interview: An Orientation and a Pilot Study," *Journal of Applied Psychology,* Vol. 40 (1956), pp. 25–31.

he is employed rests at least in part upon the impression he makes upon the interviewer. Thus, a normally fluent individual may be quite lost for words during an interview; and a normally calm person may temporarily become a finger drummer, toe tapper, or ear scratcher. The extent to which these behaviors are excused by the interviewer as being atypical and a result of an unusually tense situation varies considerably from one interviewer to another. Similarly, there is considerable variation in the extent to which different interviewers attempt to establish *rapport*—a feeling of warmth, understanding, and relaxation—at the beginning of the interview.

The behavior of any job applicant may be quite different under circumstances in which he is interviewed by a personnel director who is himself calm, relaxed, unhurried, and gives the impression that he truly understands the kind of tension engendered by the situation, from what it is under circumstances in which the interviewer is obviously rushed, tense, and either too busy, disinclined, or personally unable to establish rapport.

Bias. We all have certain biases or preconceptions about people. There are certain characteristics that immediately "rub us the wrong way." These may be physical characteristics such as overweight, red hair, dimunitive height, or a physical infirmity of some kind, or some mannerism like gum chewing or smoking. These biases vary from one interviewer to another, influencing their appraisal of the applicant in an uncontrolled fashion. The 10 personal traits listed by untrained interviewers as being most objectionable are cited in Table 5–5.

Like the rest of us, interviewers may respond in biased fashion because they identify the applicant with some group about which they have certain preconceptions or *stereotypes.* The interviewer who rejects the blonde applicant for a secretarial position because ". . . blondes are dumb" and the student who knows that ". . . professors are absent-minded" are both victims of stereotyped thinking. They subscribe to rather sweeping generalizations about groups of people which have no basis in fact. Stereotyped judgments about persons are, of course, most dangerous when any individual's qualifications are "evaluated" on the basis of ill-conceived generalizations about his particular ethnic or religious group.

The effect of personal bias is to introduce into the employment interview a highly subjective basis for the selection or rejection of particular applicants. The criteria employed by a particular interviewer may be totally unrelated to the abilities required for satisfactory job performance.

Another source of bias is the form in which the questions are asked. One of the early studies of the influence of the form of the questions upon replies involved repeated showings of movies to subjects until they grasped the essential details of the films. Then each person was asked a series of questions about the contents of the film. The form of the inquiry was varied in order to discover the

TABLE 5-5

Personal Traits Listed as Most Objectionable by Three Interviewers*

Interviewer I	Interviewer II	Interviewer III
Biting fingernails	Chewing and snapping gum	Short arms
Talking with cigarette in mouth	Being jittery or fidgety	Bad breath
Interrupting you	Nonstop talking	Shifty-eyed
Playing with articles on person	Too aggressive	Too well-groomed
Smoking chain fashion	Loud clothing	Sloppy
Being pretentious or bragging	Not meticulous about personal hygiene	Ugly
Using "I" continuously	Fresh and "smart alecky"	Jiggling legs continuously
Inconsideration	Making gestures with hands	Tapping
Avoids looking you in the eye	Foreign looking	Doodling
"Alibi"	Mousy and bashful	Acne

* American Management Association, *Manual of Employment Interviewing*, Research Report No. 9 (1946), p. 15.

influence of the wording of the questions upon responses. The investigator found that the poorest kind of question was one in which the phraseology implied something about the nature of the desired response. A question like, "Was the man carrying the umbrella?" led to fewer correct answers and fewer responses of "I don't remember" than did the question "Did you see an umbrella?" The former wording cued a response by implying that there was a man and there was an umbrella.[22]

In similar fashion, responses are distorted when the interviewer leads a job applicant to make a particular response. Quite different

[22] B. Muscio, "The Influence of the Form of the Question," *British Journal of Psychology*, Vol. 8 (1916), pp. 351–89.

replies may be anticipated to the following questions, each of which is phrased to determine the reasons for which the applicant left his previous employment:

Why did you leave your previous job?

Did you leave your previous job voluntarily or were you fired?

You weren't fired from your last job, were you?

Halo Effect. The tendency to generalize from some specific characteristic or trait to an overall evaluation of the suitability of a job applicant is referred to as the "halo effect." Halo may be positive or negative. The interviewee who is neatly dressed, knocks on the door before entering the office, does not sit down until invited to do so, and is relatively free from nervous mannerisms creates a favorable initial impression. This impression may color the interviewer's perception of the entire interview, leading him to a positive evaluation of the applicant in spite of the fact that he may really be rather poorly qualified for the job in question.

Conversely, the applicant who gives the impression of being overly cocky may create negative halo. The interviewer may fail to perceive such an applicant's strengths of training and past experience because the entire proceedings are unfavorably colored by his perception of the interviewee as a "brash young man."

Certain traits are, to be sure, sufficiently important by themselves to be used as a basis for rejecting a candidate for the job. Some jobs, for example, require that the employee be tactful. An applicant who demonstrates a noticeable lack of tact could legitimately be rejected for this reason alone. An undesirable negative halo effect would be operating, however, when a tactless applicant is rejected for this reason alone in spite of the fact that he is being interviewed for a job in which personal diplomacy is not a critical requirement.

SUMMARY

The application blank and interview are the two most frequently used devices for selecting and placing personnel. The efforts of the industrial psychologist to improve these devices have for the most part been directed toward overcoming their inherent subjectivity.

One approach to improving the validity of application blanks is to weight the responses to individual items (for example, age, years of schooling, and so on) and to "score" the blank by summing these weights. Such weights are derived from an investigation of the relationship between specific responses and some criterion of employee success. The stronger this relationship, the higher is the weight assigned to a particular response.

The Biographical Information Blank is a refinement of the weighted application blank. It is a type of psychological inventory uniquely suited both to prediction and to research on the relationship between factors in the employee's past history and his level of job performance.

The employment interview serves two purposes in addition to the primary one of providing a basis for accepting or rejecting the applicant. The interviewer gives certain information to the applicant about the job and the company, and he strives to establish a friendly relationship with the applicant. The latter function is important because even rejected applicants are potential consumers of the product or service offered.

Interviews may be conducted in either unstructured or structured fashion.

In the unstructured interview, the pattern of questions, the circumstances under which these questions are asked, and the bases for evaluating the replies are not standardized. These factors vary from one interviewer to another and from one interviewee to another. Thus, the unstructured interview is subjective in the extreme. Such procedures tend to be markedly unreliable and invalid.

The structured interview is one in which the procedure is so controlled as to reduce the extent to which interviewer biases operate. The pattern of questions to be asked of all applicants by all interviewers is specified. In addition, the factors upon which the interviewer is to base his evaluation of the applicant are clarified.

Several suggestions for improving interviewing technique are discussed in this chapter. These suggestions relate to the influence of rapport, personal bias, halo effect, and contagious bias.

6. Principles of Psychological Testing

We have thus far described the two methods most often used for making predictions about a job applicant's likelihood of succeeding as an employee: the personal interview and the application form. Although widely used for personnel selection, both of these methods are inherently subjective. This means that the decision about whether or not to hire an applicant on the basis of information of this sort may unduly reflect the personal biases and prejudgments of the hiring official.

The purpose of testing is to provide an *objective* assessment of various kinds of psychological characteristics. When such tests are used for personnel selection, the measured characteristics are those known to be related to success on the job. Thus, a personnel testing program involves first a preliminary study designed to identify measurable characteristics thought to be associated with job success; second, the identification (or sometimes, construction) of a test or *battery* (group) of tests designed to measure these characteristics; and finally, a follow-up study to determine the extent to which the measured characteristics are, in fact, related to employee efficiency. The present chapter is specifically concerned with the kinds of research implied in these three phases of testing for personnel selection.

Psychological tests are used in two general ways: as devices for *predicting* subsequent job performance, and as bases for *evaluating* the employee's present level of job performance and the abilities, knowledge, and personality characteristics related to such performance.

The predictive application is most apparent in the case of preemployment testing for personnel selection. Here, the test and other data contribute to the decision about whether or not to employ a job applicant. Another application also involving predictions from test scores is personnel placement. The placement function requires that test and other data contribute to the decision about *where* within a company the applicant is most likely to demonstrate satisfactory job performance.

On occasion the potential contribution of testing to placement decisions may be even more important than its contribution to selection decisions. This would clearly be the case when a company has an urgent need to fill a variety of job openings and has only relatively few applicants. In such instances the urgency of the need for personnel may reduce the value of tests for *selection;* virtually all applicants must be hired. But correspondingly, the need for proper *placement* is thereby enhanced.

Aside from their contributions to the efficiency of selection and placement programs, psychological tests provide evaluative information needed for other personnel decisions. When administered to present employees rather than job applicants, tests may be used diagnostically to facilitate decisions about employee reassignment, training, or counseling.

Given the broad applicability and usefulness of psychological tests, two points need emphasis at the outset of this discussion.

First, psychological tests are fallible. In regarding them as valuable aids to making personnel decisions, we mean merely that the appropriate use of well-designed tests makes possible more accurate decisions than those made without such test data. We do not mean to imply that these decisions will be faultless, or that the test results upon which they are based are entirely free from error.

Second, psychological tests provide only one source of information pertinent to decisions about personnel. Additional useful information can be assembled from the preemployment interview, application blank, references, and previous job history, in addition to other sources. Furthermore, personnel decisions once made are not irrevocable. Employee performance ought continuously to be monitored by means of periodic performance reviews in order to insure that the most effective use is being made of each person's capabilities, needs, and interests.

THE NATURE OF PSYCHOLOGICAL TESTS

A psychological test is much more than an assemblage of questions, the answers to which are interpreted on the basis of "common sense" or informal observation.

In essence, a test is a yardstick uniformly and systematically applied in the same way to all persons being assessed. This assessment is made in terms of a common scale on which these persons are ordered along a continuum of the trait or characteristic measured by the test.

However, it is not enough merely to order persons from "high" to "low" with reference to some trait or characteristic. When we refer to personnel tests, we imply yardsticks with certain other well-defined qualities. These qualities include: (*a*) assessment of those specific characteristics shown clearly to be related to criteria of job success and (*b*) systems for interpreting test scores in ways calculated to improve the ratio of "successful" to "unsuccessful" employees.

Pseudotests

The notion of psychological testing has caught the public fancy to a rather considerable extent. Although this kind of popularity has made it somewhat easier for management to introduce testing programs in industry, it has also had certain rather unfortunate consequences. It has, for example, led to the dissemination of so-called "tests" purporting to measure virtually everything ranging from *Your Suitability as a Marriage Partner* to *Your Susceptibility to Advertising Appeals* in Sunday supplements and pulp magazines. The questions contained in them and the suggested interpretations of responses make interesting reading. They are, however, relatively valueless as a basis for personal evaluation.

The surprising thing about such popularized pseudotests is that they appeal to and hoodwink so many otherwise hardheaded and sophisticated persons. The typical businessman, for example, tends to consider expenditures associated with engineering and raw materials supply very carefully. He may, however, be amazingly naive in the purchase of an expensive "employee selection program" that is not properly justified by an accumulation of scientific evidence

TABLE 6–1

Evaluations of 13 Glittering Generalities by Personnel Managers Who Thought They Were Receiving a Personality Analysis

Item	Judgment on Accuracy of Item*				
	a	b	c	d	e
1. You have a great need for other people to like and admire you	39%	46%	13%	1%	1%
4. You have a tendency to be critical of yourself	46	36	15	3	0
5. You have a great deal of unused capacity which you have not turned to your advantage	37	36	18	4	1
7. While you have some personality weaknesses, you are generally able to compensate for them	34	55	9	0	0
9. Your sexual adjustment has presented problems for you	15	16	16	33	19
10. Disciplined and self-controlled outside, you tend to be worrisome and insecure inside	40	21	22	10	4
12. At times you have serious doubts as to whether you have made the right decision or done the right thing	27	31	19	18	4
15. You prefer a certain amount of change and variety and become dissatisfied when hemmed in by restrictions and limitations	63	28	7	1	1
16. You pride yourself as an independent thinker and do not accept others' statements without satisfactory proof	49	31	12	4	4
18. You have found it unwise to be too frank in revealing yourself to others	31	37	22	6	4
20. At times you are extroverted, affable, sociable, while at other times you are introverted, wary, reserved	43	25	18	9	5
21. Some of your aspirations tend to be pretty unrealistic	12	16	22	43	7
23. Security is one of your major goals in life	40	31	15	9	5

* Definitions of scale steps as follows: (a) amazingly accurate, (b) rather good, (c) about half and half, (d) more wrong than right, and (e) almost entirely wrong.

supportive of its worth. The following study of the gullibility of personnel managers will serve to illustrate the point.[1]

A legitimately published personality inventory was administered to a group of personnel managers attending a conference. They each then received a fake "personality analysis" ostensibly based upon their responses to the inventory but actually consisting of 13 glittering generalities. These generalities had been collected from dream

[1] Ross Stagner, "The Gullibility of Personnel Managers," *Personnel Psychology*, Vol. 11, No. 3 (1958), pp. 347–52.

books and astrology charts.[2] The 13 general statements were inter-spersed with other more specific statements about personality. Both kinds of statement, the general ones and the specific ones, were duplicated; the personnel manager's name was written at the top of the sheet; the 13 general statements were encircled on every sheet; and the sheets were passed out to the respondents. Thus, every personnel manager labored under the delusion that he was receiving a personality analysis based upon the results of the inventory. Fur-thermore, without knowing it, every personnel manager received the identical "analysis" of his personality.

The 13 encircled statements received by each manager are shown in Table 6–1. The data in this table following each statement summarize the judgments with respect to the accuracy of each state-ment. Each man was asked to read the items marked for him and to rate it with respect to accuracy on the following five-step scale: (a) amazingly accurate, (b) rather good, (c) about half and half, (d) more wrong than right, and (e) almost entirely wrong.

In addition, the personnel managers were asked to make an overall evaluation of the fake analysis. Fifty percent said that the overall description was amazingly accurate, 40 percent thought it was rather good, and only 10 percent rated it as about half and half.

Since the purpose of this demonstration was to educate rather than dupe the personnel men involved, the participants were then asked to compare the personality reports they had received. The author reports, "Upon discovering that all were identical they set up at a terrific noise apparently compounded of resentment at being duped and amazement at themselves for being tricked."

The demonstration proved to be extremely valuable for convinc-ing the participants to investigate a test or testing program thor-oughly before buying it. In this instance the "test" yielded glittering generalities which apply to virtually everyone and are distinctive for no one. Such generalities do not, of course, have differential value for selection, placement, or any other personnel function.

Characteristics of Useful Tests

Useful tests can be distinguished from pseudotests by the qualities of the former as devices for measurement. These qualities include,

---

[2] B. R. Forer, "The Fallacy of Personal Validations: A Classroom Demonstration of Gullibility," *Journal of Abnormal and Social Psychology,* Vol. 44 (1949), pp. 118–23.

as we have already said, the requirements that tests (*a*) be uniformly and systematically applied, (*b*) assess characteristics specifically related to job success, (*c*) permit a meaningful ordering of test performances along some kind of yardstick or scale, and (*d*) provide a system for translating the person's placement on the test score continuum into a prediction about job performance.

These qualities influence the procedures for test construction. In order to insure their presence, all psychological tests have certain well-defined characteristics. It will be helpful to outline these characteristics briefly before discussing the specifics of test construction.

Objectivity.   You will recall that the primary objection to the use of both the uncontrolled interview and the application blank for selecting personnel is that these techniques are highly subjective in nature. The usefulness of these techniques is improved when they are made more objective.

The distinction between subjective and objective appraisal is apparent also in the area of testing. A test requiring that the scorer exercise his judgment in appraising the quality of response (for example, an essay test) is subjective in nature. A test that may be scored independently of such judgment (for example, a multiple-choice test) is objective in nature.

Regardless of the merits of subjective tests for enabling the respondent to express himself and to display a sequence of thinking, such tests do suffer from one marked deficiency. The score assigned to the person being tested may reflect an assortment of factors totally unrelated to his qualifications. Bias, halo effect, mood of the reader, as well as other subjective factors may enter into the appraisal of essay responses.

In consequence, industrial tests tend for the most part to be objective. The score earned on such tests by the job applicant is unrelated to mood fluctuations and the personal opinions of the person scoring the test. An additional advantage of objective testing is that these tests may be scored easily and rapidly by clerks with minimal training. This factor materially reduces the cost of administering the testing program compared to what the cost would be if subjective tests were used.

Reliability and Validity.   The notions of reliability and validity were introduced earlier, and they are elaborated in detail later in this chapter. At this point it is necessary to make just two general observations about these characteristics of tests:

First, it is perfectly possible for a test to be reliable without being valid. A yardstick, for example, is an extremely reliable measuring device. When applied several times to the same object it will yield about the same "score" or reading in inches. However, it is totally invalid as a measure of employee efficiency except in very special circumstances (for example, professional basketball) where there is a relationship between height and employee success.

Second, a test may be valid for certain circumstances but not for others. The yardstick which is extremely valid as a measure of height is not at all valid as a measure of muscular coordination.

Uniformity of Interpretation.   Suppose we have developed a test and demonstrated that it is both reliable and valid for selecting personnel. We now administer this test to a job applicant and determine that his score on this test is 57. Such a score derived either from the number of correctly answered items or the number right less a correction for guessing is referred to as a *raw score*. It cannot be interpreted properly without reference to test *norms* which summarize the raw scores earned on the test by a large number of persons. Knowledge about the raw score does not in itself enable us to make a decision about whether or not the job applicant ought to be hired.

What kinds of additional information do we need before properly interpreting this score of 57? It might help, for example, to know the maximum possible score on the test. A score of 57 out of a possible 58 points probably means something quite different than does a score of 57 out of a possible 200 points.

A detailed statistical analysis of the distribution of scores earned on this test by persons previously tested would be even more helpful. This might involve the calculation of the mean and standard deviation of the distribution in order to provide an indication of whether the score of 57 is better or worse than average. In addition, the interpretation of this score is greatly facilitated when the data are prepared in such a way as to make possible a statement about the probability that an applicant with a score of 57 will if hired be a successful rather than an unsuccessful employee.

Standardization of Testing Conditions.   It is apparent that whenever a number of persons are to be compared with respect to test score, they must either take the same test or different forms of the same test. One cannot hope, for example, to compare the arithmetic test scores of two applicants, one of whom has taken a test requiring that he be familiar with concepts no more complex than long division, while the other has taken a test requiring mastery of fractions and decimals.

It is perhaps less obvious, however, that the mere fact that identical questions are presented to two applicants does not in itself guarantee that they are taking the same test! A test really consists of a set of questions administered under certain conditions of illumination, ventilation, working space, assistance from the proctors, and preliminary directions to the person tested, to name just a few. Test scores may be markedly affected by the conditions under which the test is given. Thus, one of the characteristics of good psychological tests is that the testing conditions are *standardized*. This means that the directions for administering and scoring the test are prescribed and specified so that they may be held relatively constant from one testing session to another. A departure from the standardized testing conditions may well invalidate the test norms. The manual of directions for administering a test will most often specify the specific wording of instructions and will indicate something about the amount of assistance (if any) to be given by the proctors, the kind of physical facilities to be used for testing, the time limit if there is one, and the way in which the test should be scored and interpreted.

TEST CONSTRUCTION

The foregoing description of the required characteristics of psychological tests implies that there is considerably more to constructing a test than merely putting pen to paper and writing questions. We will be concerned in the remainder of this chapter with the implementation of these characteristics.

Job Analysis and Item Development

Nothing concrete can be done in the way of writing test questions until a clear notion of the behavior or personal characteristics to be measured is formulated. This is only possible after a thoroughgoing job analysis designed to clarify the differences between efficient and inefficient employees has been performed. The job analysis will provide the clues about the critical psychological functions, including specific kinds of knowledges, abilities, and personal characteristics that ought to be measured in the selection test.

The Test Plan. Once the behavior or personal characteristic to be measured has been identified and defined, the test's architect formulates a test plan. By analogy with building construction, the test plan serves as the blueprint for the entire structure. The plan specifies the ultimate nature of the test being formulated with particular reference to the weight to be assigned to various kinds of tested behavior.

Suppose, for example, that we wish to assess arithmetic proficiency as an aid to selecting department store sales clerks. Obviously, the number of arithmetic questions that could be asked is limitless. Equally apparent is the fact that there are practical limits to the length of a test in order to optimize the efficiency of measurement.

Although we could easily write a large number of test items presenting combinations of two three-digit numbers for addition, there is little point to using all of the possible items in this universe. Instead, it makes sense to sample from the total universe of such combinations. If this sample of items is sufficiently large and is representative of the kinds of functions required to handle this type of addition problem, we will be able to generalize from test behavior to behavior with all other problems of this type. The rationale underlying test items as samples of behavior is clearly similar to that underlying sampling procedures in, for example, public opinion polling.

Thus, the plan for our arithmetic proficiency test requires that we consider three kinds of issues before beginning test construction. First, how do we wish to define arithmetic proficiency? What kinds of arithmetic *operations* are included in our definition? Second, upon what kinds of *content* must these operations be performed? Third, how do we wish to *weight* the various kinds of operations and contents?

Such a plan is shown in Table 6–2. This plan reflects the decision that the test will assess four different operations with five different contents (numerical combinations). The plan further indicates that certain operations-contents combinations were judged inappropriate to the purpose of the test and therefore need not be assessed. Finally, it shows the relative weights to be assigned to the several operation and content combinations, and translates these into specifications for the test items. Thus, 3 percent of the test items will require addition of pairs of decimals; 10 percent will require addition of pairs of fractions; and so on.

Item Construction. Once the plan is established, it guides the test constructor in his subsequent endeavors. He knows what kinds of items to write and has an overview of the final composition of the test.

Item construction requires a high level of skill. Even with considerable experience, the test constructor may set performance tasks that are unsuitable for personnel testing or write questions that are defective by virtue of ambiguity or of some internal cue as to the correct answer. Thus, he prepares a preliminary set of items or tasks which he will subsequently evaluate by means of an item analysis.

TABLE 6–2

A Test Plan for Measuring Arithmetic Proficiency
(entries indicate percent of items of each type required)

Content Combinations	Operations				Content Weight
	Addition	Subtraction	Multiplication	Division	
Decimals with decimals....	3%	8%	5%	9%	25%
Fractions with fractions....	10	..	..	..	10
Digits with digits..........	3	8	6	8	25
Decimals with digits.......	2	9	6	8	25
Fractions with digits.......	7	..	8	..	15
Operations weight....	25%	25%	25%	25%	100%

These items may be cast in a variety of formats including, but not limited to, the widely used multiple-choice format.

There are certain kinds of pitfalls in the construction of multiple-choice items that may be rather readily avoided. These are separately described for the *premise* (the question or phrase preceding the alternative choice) and the *alternatives* (the group of correct answer and incorrect choices).

Perhaps the criticism most often leveled against objective tests is that the items contained in them tend so often to be ambiguous. Ambiguities can be avoided in multiple-choice items only when the *premise* contains a clear statement of all of the conditions necessary to interpret the item properly. It would be impossible, for example, to respond to an item beginning, "The most appropriate measure of central tendency is:" because no measure is "most appropriate" under all circumstances. The respondent needs to know whether the distribution is normal or skewed, and something about the purpose for which the measure of central tendency is to be computed.

Another source of confusion in phrasing the premise results from failure to call attention in some way to negatives. Unless such words as *not* and *never* are italicized or capitalized, the respondent may fail to notice them because of the tension and anxiety surrounding the administration of a selection test.

The test constructor must also exercise care in phrasing the premise to prevent the appearance of a grammatical cue pinpointing the correct alternative. A premise ending in the word *an,* for example, cues an alternative beginning with a vowel rather than a consonent. Similarly, a premise ending with the word *these* cues a plural rather than a singular response. Such cues, of course, make it possible for respondents to answer correctly even in the absence of knowledge called for by the item.

Defects in the structure of the *alternatives* generally have the effect of cueing the correct answer. If the *distractors* (incorrect alternatives), for example, are not all plausible, they may be eliminated by the respondent on the basis of common sense rather than actual knowledge.

It is desirable to avoid structuring the alternatives so that one is atypical in length. The atypical alternative, which may be either unusually long or unusually short, is more often the correct answer than would be expected on the basis of chance. This is probably true because the test constructor finds it possible either to phrase the correct answer very succinctly or finds that he must add several qualifiers in order to eliminate the ambiguities.

Finally, partial parallelism should be avoided in the structure of the alternatives. "Parallel" alternatives are ones that are phrased alike with the exception of one or two key words. Often, but not always, the parallel alternatives are the converse of one another. The following alternatives are parallel:

a) The mean is higher than the median.
b) The mean is lower than the median.

A multiple-choice item with partial parallelism will often contain two parallel alternatives and two that are not parallel. In such cases, the correct answer is generally contained in the pair of parallel alternatives, thereby substantially increasing the likelihood of obtaining a correct response solely on the basis of a lucky guess.

The foregoing list of "rules" for the construction of multiple-choice items is by no means comprehensive. It serves, however, to indicate some of the kinds of errors that may creep into such items with the effect either of making the item ambiguous or of cueing the correct answer.

Item Analysis

An item analysis provides data enabling the test constructor to evaluate the worth of each of the preliminary items he has developed. The item analysis serves as the basis for selecting those items from the preliminary item pool which are to be included in the final version of the test. The typical item analysis provides two kinds of information about each item: (1) information about the discriminatory power of the item and (2) information about the relative ease or difficulty of the item.

Item Discrimination. Every item in a test should make its contribution to the test's power to differentiate between persons on the function the test is measuring. Item discrimination (or item validity) is an indication of the extent to which the test item differentiates between persons who rank at opposite ends of the continuum with respect to the particular characteristic being measured.

This phase of the item analysis requires that the preliminary set of items be administered to a sample of persons like those who will eventually be taking the test in its final form. The persons in this item analysis group are then subdivided into high and low criterion subgroups. In practice this assignment is most often based upon the criterion of total score on the test. Thus, the objective of this phase of the analysis is to determine the extent to which each test item is measuring the function measured by the total test.

It has been determined that the optimal split for constituting the criterion subgroups is obtained by assigning the 27 percent of the persons with the highest scores to the "high" criterion group and the 27 percent of the persons with the lowest scores to the "low" criterion group.[3] Thus, if a test to be item analyzed is administered to a total group of 185 persons, each of the criterion subgroups would contain 50 persons.

It is apparent from the foregoing discussion that an item which

[3] T. L. Kelley, "The Selection of Upper and Lower Groups for the Validation of Test Items," *Journal of Educational Psychology* (1939), pp. 17–24.

has good discriminating power is one that differentiates between the high and low criterion subgroups. So a perfectly valid item is one that is answered correctly by everyone in the high criterion group and answered incorrectly by everyone in the low criterion group. The correlation between item response ("correct" or "incorrect") and criterion subgroup ("high" or low") for such an item would, of course, be +1.00.

TABLE 6–3

Percentages within Each Criterion Subgroup Correctly and
Incorrectly Answering Items at Various Levels
of Item Discrimination

		Criterion Subgroup		
Item Number	Item Response	Low	High	Correlation*
1.	Right	—	100%	+1.00
	Wrong	100%	—	
2.	Right	15	90	+0.73
	Wrong	85	10	
3.	Right	20	70	+0.50
	Wrong	80	30	
4.	Right	30	60	+0.31
	Wrong	70	40	
5.	Right	40	40	0.00
	Wrong	60	60	

* Correlational values from J. C. Flanagan, "A Table of the Value of the Product Moment Coefficient of Correlation in a Normal Bivariate Population Corresponding to Given Proportions of Successes" (Pittsburgh: American Institute for Research, 1950).

Item analysis data indicative of various degrees of discrimination power are shown in Table 6–3. The entries for the five items in the Table show the percentage of respondents within each criterion subgroup answering the item correctly and incorrectly. The correlational values represent the strength of relationship between item-response and criterion subgroup assignment.

Note particularly that the correlation between item response and total test score (as reflected in criterion subgroup assignment) decreases as the percentage of respondents from each of the subgroups answering correctly becomes increasingly similar. Finally, in item 5, in which the percentage of correct responses is identical for the two criterion subgroups, the correlational value is 0.00. This item does not differentiate at all between the high and low criterion groups.

This discussion of item discrimination has been limited to item analyses against the internal criterion of total test score. It is quite possible, however, to establish the criterion groups on some basis that is external to the test itself. A measure of productivity, a rating of employee efficiency, or any other external index may serve as a basis for separating high and low criterion groups and hence for item analysis. The use of external criteria for item analysis is much less frequent than is the use of total test score as the criterion.

Item Difficulty.   Questions from the preliminary pool of items are considered for inclusion in the final version of the test only if they have demonstrated discriminative power. The items that have survived this phase of the analysis are further screened on the basis of their relative ease or difficulty before the ultimate selection of items for the final form of the test is made.

What would be the effect, for example, if a test of numerical ability contained items, all of which were extremely easy? Since most persons would be able to answer every item, the test scores would tend to run rather high. The effect of this would be to make it difficult to separate out from the total group of persons tested those who possess a moderately high degree of numerical ability from those who possess a very high degree of such ability. The test would not have enough "top."

Conversely, a test consisting entirely of very difficult items would have too much "top." Most persons would receive low scores, making it impossible to separate out the persons of moderately low ability from those of very low ability.

To avoid either of these extreme conditions, tests are generally structured so that they contain items distributed throughout the range of difficulty. The test as finally constituted will contain some rather easy items, some rather difficult items, and a considerable number of items that are in the midrange of difficulty.

Data regarding item difficulty are obtained by computing the percentage of persons in the total item analysis group answering each item correctly. Thus, the test in its final form will contain only those items that have been demonstrated to possess satisfactory discriminative power and a range of relative ease and difficulty. Several things remain to be done with this test, however, before it can be used for personnel selection.

RELIABILITY

From previous discussions it should now be apparent that demonstrated reliability is an essential requirement for psychological tests.

Broadly speaking, a reliable test is one providing a *consistent* yardstick. Thus, a fundamental objective of reliability studies is to demonstrate that the test scores do not fluctuate unduly over time as a result of something inherent in the test itself (including scorer subjectivity), the transitory nature of the function being assessed, or by factors extraneous to the particular behavior the test is designed to evaluate.

On occasion, the concept of reliability as "consistency of measurement" is given a somewhat different but related meaning. Here the reliability study focuses particularly upon the homogeneity of the test—its *internal* consistency—rather than upon consistency in the sense of stability of scores over time. If a test is not homogeneous, then it really is comprised of subsets of items each measuring a different human function.

These different definitions of reliability are reflected in the procedures whereby a test's reliability is estimated. Three such procedures are described below.

Test-Retest Method

A reliable test is one in which an individual will rank in about the same position on successive testings regardless of who administers the test. This definition of reliability suggests a simple method for determining the relative degree of consistency of measurement; that is, give the test twice to the same group of persons and correlate the scores earned on the two administrations. Ideally, the person who earned the highest score (ranked highest) when originally tested should also earn the highest score when retested. Similarly, the person who earned the lowest score the first time (ranked lowest) should earn the lowest score on the retest, and persons with intermediate scores the first time should maintain their same relative score positions the second time they take the test.

Such a perfect relationship between rankings on the original test and the retest would, of course, yield a correlation coefficient of +1.00. Although this perfect relationship is never achieved in practice, the requirement for test-retest estimates of reliability is generally set in the vicinity of +0.90.

Numerous objections have been raised to the test-retest method of estimating reliability. It is, in the first place, an uneconomical procedure since it requires that employees be excused from their work for experimental purposes on two separate occasions. Secondly, the period between original test and retest is not vacuous. New learning may occur during this time interval, causing relative rankings on the retest to be somewhat different from the rank position on the original test. Thirdly, employees may remember items from the original session when they are retested. This memory factor will enable them to respond rapidly to the remembered items and to devote proportionately more time to the items which caused them difficulty during the original testing.

The Equivalent Forms Method

This method overcomes some of the objections to the test-retest procedure, particularly those related to the possible operation of learning and memory factors. As the name implies, this method involves the administration of an equivalent form of the original test after a time interval rather than readministration of the original test itself.

Equivalent forms of a test are alike with respect to statistical characteristics (the distribution of item difficulty and item validity indices) and general content, although the specific items in the forms are different. The fact that the specific content of the items in equivalent forms of a test are different means that neither the memory factor nor the learning factor can operate when reliability is estimated by correlating the scores earned on the two forms.

Perhaps the primary objection to this procedure is that the expense of developing equivalent forms of a test is not justified when they are developed solely for a reliability study. There are, however, other reasons for which two or more forms of a test may be developed. It is advantageous, for example, to have multiple test forms for administration when one wishes to measure growth as a result of a formal training program or as a result of job experience. One of the forms can be given as a pretest to new employees while the other form can be given as a posttest after completion of the training program or after a certain period of time on the job. Furthermore, multiple forms of a test are extremely useful whenever a large group of persons is to be tested in a room that does not permit for adequate spacing between seats in order to prevent copying.

Split-Halves Method

A fundamental objection to both the test-retest and the equivalent forms method of estimating reliability is that these procedures require two testing sessions. The split-halves method makes it possible to estimate reliability from a single administration of a test and hence is widely used in the industrial setting.

This method requires that the total test be divided into halves in such a way that the items in each half constitute a miniature representation of the entire test. In practice, this is often accomplished by assigning the odd-numbered items to one half and the even numbered items to the other half, although any other procedure for splitting the test is acceptable provided that it yields halves that are comparable. The halves are scored separately, and the estimate of reliability is derived by correlating the scores earned by a group of persons on the halves of the test.

There are certain parallels between the split-halves method and the equivalent forms method for estimating reliability. Both procedures require the correlation of scores earned on two forms of a test. The equivalent forms method involves the correlation between two full-length forms while the split-halves method involves the correlation between two half-length forms. A fundamental difference between these procedures is the fact that while the forms are deliberately equated for the equivalent forms method the split-halves method correlates two forms that are, at best, crudely comparable.

In appraising the split-halves method, it must be remembered that there is no time interval between administration of halves of a test and that the correlation coefficient resulting from this procedure is based upon only half the number of items in the total test. Each of these unique aspects of the split-halves method has certain implications. The absence of a time interval has the desirable effect of eliminating the possible influences of memory and learning. It also, however, eliminates the possible effects of day-to-day fluctuations in mood, attentiveness, and attitude of the respondents. This latter factor is one that should be included in estimates of test reliability. The effect of eliminating the potential influence of these daily fluctuations is to spuriously increase the reliability coefficient.

A special problem arises when the split-halves method is used to estimate the reliability of speeded tests in which the imposed time limit prevents subjects from completing all questions. Computation of an odd-even reliability under such circumstances tends to overestimate the test's reliability. This is so because the unanswered questions are distributed evenly between the two halves of the test, thereby exerting a uniform effect upon the individual's relative rank position for each half. This problem is generally resolved either by application of correction formulas estimating the lower limit of reliability for speeded tests or by a rather simple experimental expedient. The latter requires that each half of the total test be separately administered with its own time limit.

The fact that this method yields an estimate of reliability based upon the correlation of scores on two halves of the test means that the resultant coefficient is an estimate of the reliability of a test only half as long as the one actually under consideration. Since reliability is in part a function of test length, estimates of reliability based upon the split-halves method must be adjusted upwards by means of a formula designed to indicate what the reliability would have been for the full-length test. The Spearman-Brown prophecy formula for a test doubled in length is:

$$R = \frac{2r_{11}}{1 + r_{11}}$$

where R is the reliability of the test doubled in length and r_{11} is the reliability of the half-length test. Thus, if the correlation between scores on the halves of a test is 0.80, the estimate of reliability for the total test would be 1.60/1.80, or 0.89.

Comparison between Methods

In the preceding sections we have described three methods for estimating the reliability of a test loosely defined as the "consistency of measurement." It is evident that each method is based upon a somewhat different concept of "consistency." Hence the methods do not yield comparable estimates of reliability.

For the test-retest procedure, consistency means *stability of scores* over a period of time. A low test-retest coefficient is evidence either for the fact that the function measured by the test is unstable over time, or that test performance is influenced by extraneous factors of an unstable nature.

The split-halves method utilizes quite a different concept of consistency. This method does not consider fluctuations over time; instead it estimates *internal consistency* or homogeneity of the test. As we have described this procedure, it indicates the extent to which one half of the test measures whatever it is that the other half measures. Variations of the general method may split the test into smaller fragments than halves. Thus it is possible when a test is fragmented into single items to inquire whether each item is measuring whatever is measured by each of the other items.

The equivalent forms method involves elements of both the stability and internal consistency concepts. The longer the time interval between the administration of the forms, the heavier is the emphasis upon stability over time. Conversely, with progressively shorter time intervals between test administrations, the coefficient tends increasingly to reflect internal consistency.

It is impossible, in the light of these differences, to single out a particular procedure as "best" under all circumstances. If we wish the reliability coefficient to reflect score stability over time, the split-halves method is clearly inappropriate. Since this method estimates consistency without a time interval, it overestimates stability. However, the practical consideration of available testing time may overshadow other factors and dictate the use of the split-halves method. Furthermore, there are occasions when the test constructor is more interested in estimating the internal consistency of his test than the stability of the resultant scores. When this is the case, the test-retest method and the equivalent forms method with a relatively long time interval may underestimate the kind of reliability he seeks.

Relationship of Reliability and Validity

When is reliability sufficiently high for practical purposes?

Clearly, the higher the test's reliability, the greater the confidence we can place in the stability of the scores it yields. On this basis, then, we must conclude that the higher the reliability, the better. And from this standpoint, tests yielding reliability coefficients in the range between 0.85–0.99 are usually regarded as being satisfactorily reliable.

Having stated this as a rule of thumb, we must note an exceptional circumstance where lower reliability coefficients are tolerated.

When the testing program requires an assessment of many different functions in a brief time period, the tests comprising the battery will obviously have to be short ones. Since, as we have already discussed, there is a relationship between test length and reliability, it is to be expected that these short tests will each be relatively unreliable. Their use is justified only when the components of the battery are measuring sufficiently independent and important functions that it is worth finding out *something* about each rather than assessing just a few of them more comprehensively and accurately. This is a compromise. When possible, it is far preferable to use tests with higher reliabilities.

Aside from confidence in the relative stability of the scores, there is another reason for ordinarily preferring to use tests with high (above 0.85) reliability. This follows from the relationship between reliability and validity. If test scores are unstable, the value of that test for predicting a criterion is thereby diminished. If the test produces predictor scores which fluctuate unduly for each person, then the correlation between these scores and a performance criterion is adversely affected. The predictor scores for some persons will be higher than they should be, and those for others will be lower than they should be. In the extreme case, where a test's reliability coefficient is estimated as 0.00, the relationship between test and criterion measures must be random; here the validity coefficient will have to be 0.00 also.

Theoretically, a test's maximum potential validity is given by the square root of its reliability. This means, for example, that a test for which reliability is estimated as 0.49 cannot generate a validity coefficient above 0.70. Likewise, if the test's reliability is 0.81, its validity cannot exceed 0.90.

This is *not* to say that a test with a reliability of 0.81 will have a validity of 0.90. In this instance, 0.90 is only the theoretical maximum limit upon the validity coefficient. How closely this theoretically maximum validity is approximated depends upon two characteristics of the *criterion:* relevance and criterion reliability.

No matter how reliable the predictor, it clearly cannot correlate highly with an irrelevant criterion. Thus, although we can measure people's heights with great reliability, these height "scores" are not valid for predicting, say, job tenure as a criterion. This criterion is irrelevant for this predictor.

Likewise, even a very reliable test cannot efficiently predict an unreliable criterion. Unless the behavior to be predicted is itself relatively stable, there is little point to attempting further to increase the validity coefficient by revising the predictor test to improve *its* reliability.

Since these two criterion conditions, perfect relevance and perfect reliability, can never be satisfied, obtained validity coefficients are always somewhat below the maximum theoretically possible. However, a point to remember is that the *possibility* of a high validity coefficient increases as the reliability of the test increases.

VALIDITY

Our discussions of validity thus far in this chapter and the related discussion in Chapter 4 have all been concerned with one particular definition of validity; that is, the correlation between a predictor test and a criterion of job performance. This definition is really only one of five different ones applicable to validity.[4] Of these five definitions, the first two require the availability of some kind of useful, relevant, and reliable criterion of job performance against which the test can be validated; the three remaining definitions of validity do not depend upon the availability of such criteria.

Involving Criteria of Job Performance

The two types of validity most pertinent to personnel selection tests are "predictive" and "concurrent" validity. These two types of validity are similar in that they are based upon the demonstration of a satisfactory correlation between test scores and job performance criterion measures.

Of the two, *predictive validity* is the more convincing. In order to demonstrate predictive validity, the test must be administered to job applicants, all of whom are hired regardless of test score. The scores are filed until some subsequent time when a criterion job performance measure becomes available. The scores earned on the test by the employees when they were applicants are then correlated with this criterion, thereby indicating the power of the test to predict subsequent performance.

The meaning of predictive validity is graphically shown in Figure 6–1. The data in this graph show the relationship between pilot

---

[4] American Psychological Association, "Technical Recommendations for Psychological Tests and Diagnostic Techniques," *Supplement to the Psychological Bulletin*, Vol. 51, No. 2, Part 2 (1954).

aptitude score and elimination rate during pilot training in the United States Army Air Force. It is apparent that the psychological aptitude test predicted fitness for flight training.

In spite of the desirability of obtaining evidence of predictive validity, resistance to the necessary procedure is often encountered in industry. Management may raise certain obvious objections to hiring all applicants regardless of their performance on the test be-

FIGURE 6–1

Relation between Elimination Rate and Pilot Aptitude Score

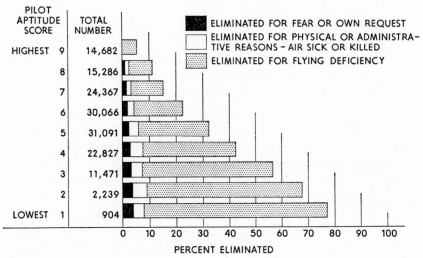

Source: "Psychological Activities in Training Command AAF," *Psychological Bulletin*, Vol. 42 (1945), p. 46.

ing validated and in spite of the results of all other selection techniques including the interview and application form. Consequently, industrial tests are often validated by administering them to employees on the job and correlating the scores with an immediately available criterion of efficiency. This procedure establishes *concurrent* rather than predictive validity because the test and criterion measures are available simultaneously.

Not Involving Criteria of Job Performance

Three other kinds of validity do not require test-criterion correlations: "face" validity, content validity, and construct validity.

When a test has the *appearance* of measuring factors germane to the job, it is said to have *face validity*. A pilot selection test, for example, possesses face validity when the item phraseology makes reference to aircraft and flight.

Such an appearance of validity is entirely independent of the statistical characteristics of a test. It is a matter solely of item content. Although conceptually independent of statistical validity, face validity is generally regarded as a desirable characteristic for industrial tests. Such tests look meaningful and therefore facilitate companywide acceptance of the testing program, and they heighten the motivation of persons tested.

Since they are somewhat irrelevant in the context of this discussion of personnel selection and placement, content and construct validity are described only briefly.

Content validity requires an assessment of the test's content to assure that the sample of questions comprising the test is representative of the universe of questions that might have been asked. It is, in short, an assessment of the adequacy of the plan underlying the construction of the test. This nonstatistical assessment is usually dependent upon the judgment of presumed "experts" and is most appropriate when developing achievement tests.

Construct validity procedures enable us to label the psychological functions measured by a new test. Suppose, for example, that we have developed a test we think measures "intelligence." One way to determine whether this new test does in fact measure the psychological construct "intelligence" is to correlate scores from it with scores obtained by the same people on other, generally accepted, intelligence tests.

Multiple Predictors

We now return to considering validity defined in predictive and concurrent terms. Although the preceding discussion of these kinds of validity was limited to the relationship between a single test and a single criterion of job performance, this is an oversimplification. In practice, the usual selection program uses applicant's scores on a battery, or group, of tests. Furthermore, as described in Chapter 4, this multiple predictor is often correlated with a multiple criterion; that is, one composed of several measures of employee performance.

There are two primary ways in which multiple predictors can be jointly used. By combining several separate tests each of which has moderate predictive validity, both methods attempt to make more accurate predictions than would be possible using any one of the predictors alone.

Successive Hurdles. This procedure, sometimes designated "multiple cutoff," combines economy with multiple prediction. Given several tests, each of which has predictive validity, applicants are required successively to "pass" the tests sequentially administered. Those applicants "failing" the first test in the battery are terminated at that point; the surviving applicants are given the second test, and again those "failing" it are terminated; the survivors are given the third test; and so on. After administration of the last test in the battery, the only remaining applicants are those who have "passed" every subtest.

Although useful, this procedure suffers two shortcomings. First, it does not allow for the circumstance where weakness in some tested function may be offset by strength in some other tested function. In presenting subtests as a series of successive hurdles, the assumption is made that job performance depends upon a summation of tested functions. This assumption is untenable where job performance really reflects the *interaction* of tested functions. Thus, "successful" secretarial performance may be possible both when moderate skill as a typist is combined with superior skill as a stenographer and when moderate stenographic skills are combined with superior typing skills.

Second, whereas the successive hurdles procedure identifies a group of "survivors" for employment, it provides no single index of the relative predictor standing of each one.

Multiple Correlation. This is a statistical technique indicating the maximum predictive validity obtainable from the optimal combination of scores on subtests comprising the battery. (The procedures for calculating multiple correlation are beyond the scope of this discussion.)

To arrive at the optimal combination of subtest scores, multiple correlation procedures weight the subtests in terms of the (*a*) validity of each separately considered and (*b*) the magnitude of the intercorrelations between these predictors.[5]

---

[5] M. R. Marks, R. E. Christal, and R. A. Bottenberg, "Simple Formula Aids for Understanding the Joint Action of Two Predictors," *Journal of Applied Psychology,* Vol. 45 (1961), pp. 285–88.

Moderator Variables

The general model for predictive or concurrent validity which has thus far been described and which most often serves as the basis for validation studies rests upon the supposition of a simple relationship between predictors and criteria. Starting with this supposition, personnel selection research requires the demonstration that predictor (or battery) X correlates with criterion (or criteria) Y. Selection practices proceed from such evidence to use scores on test (or battery) X to identify potentially successful employees.

This traditional model has recently been questioned and elaborated.

On the predictor side, it is clear that test performance varies between people only partly as a function of differences in whatever the test measures. In other words, only part of the variation in scores on, say, a mathematics test can be attributed to individual differences in mathematical ability. At least some of the variation is attributable to factors extraneous to mathematical ability, like motivation, anxiety over taking a test, and so on.

Variations in criterion performance can be similarly interpreted. In addition to reflecting job proficiency, criteria often reflect such extraneous factors as the employee's sex, age, education, job experience, and assorted personality characteristics.

Thus, validity studies never involve correlations between "pure" predictor and criterion measures. These measures are always contaminated by experience, attitudes, and so on, which intervene between performance on the predictor and the criterion. These intervening effects "moderate" the correlation between predictor and criterion; that is, they reduce it. In fact, validity coefficients above 0.50 are rarely obtained; typically, they range between 0.35–0.45.[6]

A "moderator variable" validity design differs from the classical model in that the former requires separate test-criterion correlations for each moderator variable subgroup. By thus controlling for (that is, eliminating the effects of) unwanted variation, such designs seek to increase the power of the predictor. In this way, for example, sex has been found to be a useful moderator variable when predicting scholastic grades. Irrespective of the predictor, grades can pretty much be more accurately predicted for women than for men.[7]

---

[6] E. E. Ghiselli, *The Measurement of Occupational Attitude* (Berkeley: University of California Press, 1955).

[7] H. G. Seashore, "Women Are More Predictable than Men," (presidential address, Division 17, American Psychological Association, September, 1961).

The use of moderator variables is not alone going to be a panacea for increasing predictive validity coefficients. There is some ambiguity in the professional literature in the meaning of the term itself. Furthermore, regardless of how it is used, many studies employing moderator variables have failed to demonstrate that validity is thereby increased.[8]

However, the introduction of the moderator variable concept and the consequent embellishment of the classical model for validating tests will have far-reaching effects, indeed. It now seems less important to inquire whether or not a particular test or procedure is any good and more important to inquire in the *circumstances* optimizing the usefulness of predictive tests and other procedures.[9]

INTERPRETING TEST SCORES

Raw test scores are not very useful in the practical situation because they cannot be interpreted meaningfully. The industrial psychologist who has developed a test for selection purposes must perform statistical analyses designed to answer two general types of questions about every applicant's score. First, how did his score compare to the scores of other applicants who have taken the test? Secondly, did he pass the test; that is, should he be hired? The first of these questions requires that the raw score be transformed to another kind of score reflecting the performance of the specific applicant under consideration in relation to the performance of other applicants who have taken the same test. It involves the development of test *norms*. The second question requires that a "passing" score be determined for the test.

Test Norms

Norms make possible the expression of an individual's raw test score relative to the distribution of scores earned by a group of persons known as the *standardization* or *norms* group. The development of test norms thus requires that the test first be administered to

---

[8] R. M. Guion, "Personnel Selection," *Annual Review of Psychology,* Vol. 18 (1967), pp. 105–216.

[9] M. D. Dunnette, "A Modified Model for Test Validation and Selection Research," *Journal of Applied Psychology,* Vol. 47 (1963), pp. 317–23; and L. Siegel, "The Instructional Gestalt: A Conceptual Framework," *Teachers College Record,* Vol. 62 (1960), pp. 202–13.

a sizable group of persons as nearly as possible like the applicants for whom the test is intended. Certain of the statistical operations required to effect the raw score transformations described below are discussed in Appendix A.

The distribution of scores earned by persons in the norms group may serve as the basis for converting raw scores to *percentiles*. A

FIGURE 6–2

Relationship between Raw Scores, Percentiles, and Standard Scores

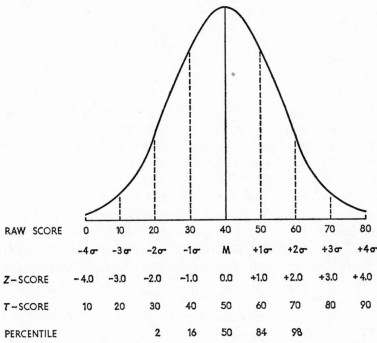

RAW SCORE	0	10	20	30	40	50	60	70	80
	-4σ	-3σ	-2σ	-1σ	M	$+1\sigma$	$+2\sigma$	$+3\sigma$	$+4\sigma$
Z–SCORE	−4.0	−3.0	−2.0	−1.0	0.0	+1.0	+2.0	+3.0	+4.0
T–SCORE	10	20	30	40	50	60	70	80	90
PERCENTILE			2	16	50	84	98		

percentile value indicates the percentage of persons who earned a raw score at or below the specific raw score in question. Thus, if it has been determined that a raw score of 35 corresponds to the sixty-second percentile, this would mean that 62 percent of the standardization group scored 35 or less on the test.

The interpretation of raw scores may also be facilitated by converting them to some kind of standard scores. Standard scores express test performance as a function of the central tendency and variability of the distribution of scores obtained in the norm group. The most obvious kind of standard score involves the transformation of raw scores to standard deviation units. Suppose, for example, that the mean score in the norms group is 40 and the standard deviation is 10. It follows then that a raw score of 50 would correspond to a transformed score of +1 standard deviation, a score of 30 to −1 standard deviation, and so on.

The relationships between raw scores, percentiles, and two kinds of standard scores (Z scores and T scores) are illustrated in Figure 6–2. You will note one of the major advantages of standard scores in comparison with percentiles: the former are spaced equidistantly along the measurement continuum. Hence, they are amenable to the usual kinds of arithmetic manipulations.

"Passing" Score

Although it is extremely useful in many situations to know how a person's test score compares with the scores earned by others who have previously taken the test, the process of personnel selection requires that the test score be interpreted along with other information to produce a decision about whether or not to hire the applicant.

This requirement can be most simply visualized in terms of the "critical" score. This score is set at the point where the probabilities of job success favor the applicant exceeding it over the applicant falling below it. This condition is summarized graphically in Figure 6–3 comparing test score distributions for successful and unsuccess-

FIGURE 6–3

Graphic Determination of the Critical Score on a Test

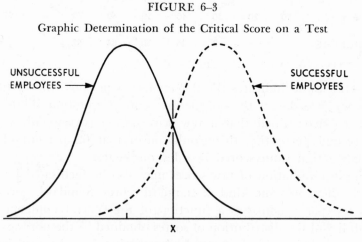

UNSUCCESSFUL EMPLOYEES ⟶

SUCCESSFUL EMPLOYEES ⟵

X

THE CRITICAL SCORE

ful employees. The point of intersection between these distributions gives the score optimizing selection when *no additional data are available*.

However, as discussed in Chapter 4, additional data *must* be provided in order properly to determine whether an applicant has "passed" the test. This determination rests upon a prediction expressed in terms of the probability that this applicant will be a successful employee. As you will recall, such predictions can be made for groups of applicants from the Taylor-Russell Tables and for individual applicants from the Lawshe Tables. These tables take into account the selection ratio, proportion of present employees considered satisfactory, and the validity of the test.

SUMMARY

A psychological test is a yardstick uniformly and systematically applied in the same way to all persons being assessed. This assessment is made in terms of a common scale on which all persons are ordered along a continuum of the trait or characteristic measured by the test. This chapter was concerned specifically with the development and application of preemployment tests for selecting and placing personnel.

The point of departure for constructing a preemployment test is the job analysis. This analysis provides clues about the critical psychological functions distinguishing between satisfactory and unsatisfactory employees. Once such a function is identified for assessment, the test constructor develops his test plan to guide item writing. The purpose of the test plan is to insure that the questions comprising the test are a truly representative sample of all such questions that *could* have been written.

The preliminary set of items written for the test is refined by "item analysis." This analysis identifies items for inclusion in the final version of the test on the basis of their utility for discriminating effectively between high and low criterion groups and their levels of item difficulty.

Before this collection of items can be considered suitable for preemployment testing, the test must be shown to be both reliable and valid.

Reliability studies supporting use of the test demonstrate that the scores on it do not fluctuate unduly over time as a result of something inherent in the test itself, the transitory nature of the function it assesses, or factors extraneous to the particular behavior the test is designed to evaluate.

Validity studies for preemployment tests are designed to demonstrate that the test scores do in fact correlate with a subsequently obtained performance criterion (predictive validity) or a criterion measure available simultaneously with the test score (concurrent validity).

Finally, before the test can be effectively used, norms must be developed for it. Normative studies provide a basis for interpreting raw test scores and permit determination of a "satisfactory" or "passing" score.

7. Using Psychological Tests

Let us assume that the decision has been made to incorporate a psychological testing program into a company's personnel selection and appraisal procedures. Job analyses have been performed, and some of the critical functions to be measured have been identified. There are now two courses of action to be considered. Either tests specifically designed to measure these functions can be custom-built for the company, or already existent tests available from commercial test publishers may be purchased. There is, as a matter of fact, quite a sizable pool of commercially available tests. A primary reference summarizing and reviewing virtually all developments in the field of testing is the series of *Mental Measurements Yearbooks* edited by Buros. The most recent volume in this series appeared in 1965.[1]

Several factors enter into the decision about whether to custom-build tests or to use commercially available standardized tests. Outstanding among the advantages of published instruments is the matter of economy. It is undoubtedly less expensive, particularly when the group is not too large, to purchase testing materials from a publisher than it is to engage in a program of test construction. Furthermore, the process of test development requires considerable time, thereby necessitating a delay in the actual introduction of the testing program. Commercially published tests, on the other hand, are available for virtually immediate use. Finally, many standardized tests have been administered to norms groups of various kinds,

---

[1] Oscar K. Buros (ed.) , *The Sixth Mental Measurements Yearbook* (Highland Park, N.J.: Gryphon Press, 1965) .

thereby facilitating the comparison between the employees now being tested with others who have previously taken the test.

In spite of these virtues, there are certain limitations to the use of commercially available tests. The fact that a test has proven valid in one industrial setting does not guarantee that it will be equally valid even for similar jobs in other settings. It is necessary, therefore, for any test to be validated under the particular circumstances in which it is to be used. Thus, a certain amount of research must be done within the company even when the decision is made to purchase standardized tests.

Secondly, an expanding technocracy implies the creation of new jobs with novel requirements. Testing programs for such jobs may necessitate the development of unique instruments simply because the commercially available tests are not appropriate.

Finally, standardized tests may lack face validity for a particular job within a particular company.

The choice between utilization of published tests and the development of special tests is one that must be made in each individual case. It is the purpose of the present chapter to indicate something of the range of standardized tests currently available.

TEST FORMATS

Psychological tests differ from one another in the way in which they are structured, administered, and scored. Every kind of format tends to have its own peculiar strengths and weaknesses, although some are more appropriate than others for industrial testing.

Subjective versus Objective Scoring

The primary advantages and disadvantages of subjective as opposed to objective testing were discussed in some detail earlier. Industrial tests are almost exclusively objective in nature because of considerations of reliability and ease of scoring. The skills needed to score an objective test are minimal. The scores obtained from such tests are free from scorer bias and halo effect and are rapidly obtainable after the testing session is terminated.

Speed versus Power Tests

A *speed* test is one with a fixed time limit beyond which the respondents are not permitted to work even though they may not

have attempted all of the questions, while a *power* test is administered without a time limit.

The conduct of a large-scale testing program is facilitated somewhat by the administration of time-limit tests. All of the papers are
due back within a fixed period of time, thereby permitting the
simultaneous scoring and processing of all of the answer sheets.

There are, in addition, certain circumstances in which speed is an
essential aspect of the function being measured. Various tests of
manual dexterity, for example, are designed to measure both the
accuracy and speed of motor activities. These tests are administered
with a time limit. Clerical speed is another function measured by
means of time-limit tests. The items contained in tests of clerical
speed are relatively simple, typically requiring that the respondent
examine pairs of names or numbers like those illustrated below and
indicate whether they are the same or different.

149278_____149228

192278_____192278

Mary L. Jones_____Mary L. Jones

John R. Smith_____John R. Smyth

The critical function such items measure is not solely the number of
pairs that the respondent can answer correctly. Given enough time,
most persons would answer almost all such items correctly. The key
factor here is the number that can be answered correctly within a
limited period of time.

It has been shown that older persons are placed in a somewhat
disadvantageous position on speed tests when compared with
younger persons, although the performance of these age groups on
power tests is quite comparable.[2] Aside from this finding, however,
the available evidence supports the use of time-limit tests in the
industrial setting.

Group versus Individual Tests

Group tests may be administered simultaneously to a large number of persons while individual tests require that an administrator
be present for each person being tested. Group tests are by far the
more economical to administer, provided that adequate facilities for
seating and proctoring the groups being tested are available.

---

[2] I. Lorge, "The Influence of the Test upon the Nature of Mental Decline as a
Function of Age," *Journal of Educational Psychology*, Vol. 27 (1936), pp. 100–110.

The unique advantages of individual testing are of greater import in clinical and vocational guidance testing than they are in industrial testing. It is easier to establish a relaxed atmosphere and to note the examinee's behavior during an individual test. It is possible to ask the kind of probing question that may be necessary during certain kinds of personality appraisals only in the individual testing situation. Most industrial testing, however, is the type that lends itself as readily to group as to individual testing.

Performance versus Paper-and-Pencil Tests

Paper-and-pencil tests require the respondent to reply by marking or writing an answer to written questions, while *performance* tests require him to manipulate apparatus or equipment. The apparatus involved in a performance test may duplicate a real-life situation. This is the case, for example, with flight simulators used for training and evaluating aircrews. A performance test may, on the other hand, require the manipulation of apparatus designed solely to measure some psychological function involving motor activity or manual dexterity.

The fact that performance tests require some kind of equipment means that such tests are generally more expensive to administer than are paper-and-pencil tests. Performance tests, furthermore, do not lend themselves readily to large-group testing. Thus, if a psychological function can be measured with equal effectiveness by means of a paper-and-pencil test and a performance test, the former will be the preferred method of measurement.

It should be apparent, however, that certain aspects of behavior can only be measured effectively by performance tests. How, for example, could a skill like typing proficiency be appraised otherwise? The only way in which to determine a typist's skill is to ask her to type a standardized passage under controlled conditions.

CHARACTERISTICS MEASURED BY TESTS

In addition to differences in format, psychological tests are differentiated from one another on the basis of the personal characteristics they measure. These functions are identified as intelligence, aptitude, achievement, interest, and personality. We will first distinguish between these areas of measurement and then in a later section describe a few specific tests of each type.

These several functions cannot be assessed with equal reliability. Physical characteristics, like height and weight, can be most accurately (reliably) measured; interests and personality traits are least reliably measured; and the reliability of intelligence, aptitude, and knowledge tests tends to fall between these extremes.

Intelligence

The definition of intelligence is complicated by the diversity of concepts included in this broad classification. Intelligence is regarded as a general kind of mental alertness. This may involve the ability to learn quickly, to solve problems not encountered previously, and to remember information learned sometime in the past. It certainly involves the ability to think in abstract as well as in concrete terms and to manipulate symbols such as mathematical and verbal concepts. The most outstanding feature of any definition of intelligence is that it involves the *general capacity* for learning and problem solving. Such potential is inferred by comparing a person's present level of cognitive attainment with the level achieved by other persons presumed to have experienced similar opportunities for such attainment.

The fact that intelligence tests purport to measure capacity rather than knowledge means that a high score on such tests is no guarantee of the possession of the specific skills necessary for satisfactory job performance. An applicant who scores high enough on an intelligence test to be considered for the position of bookkeeper or accountant, for example, may actually know very little about bookkeeping or accounting procedures. He has merely demonstrated that he has the capability for learning these skills provided that the appropriate opportunities for training are presented to him.

The notion of minimal intellectual requirements for various kinds of work is fairly obvious. It is not so obvious, however, that certain kinds of work may be performed best by employees below some specified maximum level of intelligence. The concept of optimal intellectual levels for certain kinds of work does not imply that the ability to do the work declines as a function of increased intelligence. Rather, the job may be insufficiently demanding of the employee's intellectual capabilities. This lack of total utilization of capability may be reflected in boredom, job dissatisfaction, absenteeism, and even in increased accident rate.

The factor of optimal intellectual level for certain jobs is illustrated by a study of the average length of service of cashiers and inspector wrappers as a function of their score on an intelligence test.[3] The resultant data are shown in Table 7–1. It is apparent that the greatest stability was found for employees in the middle range of intelligence. Similarly, evidence was accumulated in one company that salesmen with high scores on a mental ability test tended to be short-tenure employees.[4]

TABLE 7–1

Intelligence and Length of Service

Test Score	Average Length of Service in Days
10–19	3
20–29	91
30–39	156
40–49	142
50–59	107
60–69	100
70–79	96
80–89	87
90 and over	35

Aptitude

Aptitudes are specific capacities for acquiring particular knowledges or skills. One way of viewing the relationship between intelligence and aptitude is that the former is a kind of general aptitude. A number of studies have attempted to fragment general intelligence into component aptitudes. An early study of this type by Thurstone identified seven primary mental abilities (aptitudes): Memory, Number, Perceptual, Reasoning, Spatial, Verbal, and Word Fluency.[5] The identification of these aptitudes was accomplished by the statistical procedure known as *factor analysis* whereby the intercorrelations between test scores are examined in order to identify measured functions which cluster or "hang" together. These seven primary mental abilities cannot be regarded as the ultimate in

[3] M. J. Viteles, "Selecting Cashiers and Predicting Length of Service," *Journal of Personnel Research*, Vol. 2 (1924), pp. 467–73.

[4] L. E. Albright, W. J. Smith, and J. R. Glennon, "A Follow-Up on Some 'Invalid' Tests for Selecting Salesmen," *Personnel Psychology*, Vol. 12 (1959), pp. 105–12.

[5] L. L. Thurstone, *Primary Mental Abilities* (Chicago: University of Chicago Press, 1938).

aptitude identification. As greater variety is introduced into the battery of tests submitted to factor analysis, more and more specific aptitudes are identified. Thus, it has been suggested more recently that as many as 40 dimensions of intellect have now been discovered.[6]

Again, as is the case with intelligence, aptitude tests measure capacity but not necessarily knowledge. Tests of general mechanical aptitude attempt to measure capacity for learning to deal with mechanical devices and to perceive mechanical relationships. The person who earns a high mechanical aptitude score may not have had any experience that will qualify him for an industrial position. Similarly, a person who earns a high musical aptitude score may not know how to play a musical instrument or how to compose music. His test score reveals only a capability for learning in this area, provided that the opportunities are presented to him.

Achievement or Proficiency

Intelligence and aptitude tests are useful measures of potential. They are most helpful for selecting personnel whenever the job to be filled requires unique skills or knowledges which the company expects to teach to new employees. In addition these tests may be used for selecting personnel when the labor market is such that the company is compelled to hire employees who have certain capabilities even though these have not yet been augmented by training and experience, or when the company is specifically seeking persons who have the potential for growth and promotion within the organization.

Most often, however, the employment office will seek employees who now know how to do certain kinds of work. In such cases, the selection tests will measure achievement, knowledge, or proficiency. The specific skills or proficiencies necessary for success in particular occupations are measured by *trade tests*.

Interest

Measures of capacity (intelligence and aptitude tests) and of achievement are fundamental to a personnel testing program. How-

---

[6] J. P. Guilford, "The Structure of Intellect," *Psychological Bulletin*, Vol. 53 (1956), pp. 267–93.

ever, cognitive measures alone rarely yield validity coefficients in excess of 0.40. Thus, a number of job applicants selected for employment on the basis of scores on such tests will fail as employees and a number of rejected applicants would if hired have been successful employees.

The lack of perfect validity of cognitive measures is due in part to errors of measurement. Every kind of measuring instrument is subject to a certain amount of error. The lack of perfect validity is due in part also to the fact that factors other than capacity and achievement are partially responsible for employee success. Two such factors are measured by interest and personality inventories.

Interests are a product of the interaction of hereditary and environmental factors. It seems probable that human beings have capabilities which are never fully realized or exploited. The failure to reach the limits of our capacity in certain directions results primarily from lack of interest. The converse is also true to some extent. Heredity circumscribes the range of individual interests by limiting the range of possible achievement. Thus, we would hardly expect a color-blind person to display a strong interest in painting or other activity involving color perception or color matching. But the main limiting factor in the evolution of our interests is environmental rather than hereditary in nature.

Given two job applicants of about equal potential and prior experience, the one with the more significant vocational interests will probably be the better employee. Unfortunately, however, the measurement of interests is a much more satisfactory aid to vocational counseling with students than it is to selecting personnel. A fundamental objection to the use of interest inventories in the selection process is that the items in such inventories tend to be transparent. The applicant can often determine by reading the item which response will portray his interests most favorably for the job in question. He is thus able to make the "best" or "most appropriate" response even though it may not be indicative of his true interests.

Transparency is not regarded as a serious problem when students take an interest inventory for counseling purposes because it is likely that they are motivated to respond as carefully and accurately as possible. Job applicants, however, want to be accepted for employment. Thus, the validity of their replies to interest inventories may be open to question.

It follows, then, that interest inventories are probably of greater usefulness in a personnel testing program when the results are used for placement, classification, or counseling rather than selection. Once accepted for employment, the job applicant can probably be induced to respond as honestly as possible to an interest inventory on the grounds that it will facilitate his assignment to the kind of job in which he will most likely be successful.

The one noteworthy exception to this generalization is that the validity of interest inventories administered for the purpose of personnel selection has been demonstrated for certain groups of salesmen. The "salesmanship" scoring keys provided for standardized interest inventories contribute positively to selection in certain instances; in others, it has proven necessary to custom-tailor scoring keys for specific jobs.[7]

Personality

Many personnel officers regard personality as the crux of job success or failure. The feeling is rather widespread that for certain types of positions, particularly those requiring the exercise of supervision, personal characteristics may be even more important than skill or job knowledge. It is likely that an employment interviewer fancies as one of his primary functions, the determination of "what the applicant is really like." There is indeed little doubt that *personality traits* (characteristic modes of reaction) are vocationally significant. It is apparent also that adjustment, goal-directedness, and general mental health will all influence an employee's efficiency.

Of the several procedures for assessing personality, the two most often used are: paper-and-pencil inventories and projective techniques. *Paper-and-pencil inventories* contain a series of questions or statements like:

I worry a good deal about my health.
I frequently have headaches.
I concentrate easily.

The respondent is directed to reply to each statement by answering "yes" or "no" or "always," "sometimes," or "never." Standardized

---

[7] J. L. Hughes and W. J. McNamara, "Limitations on the Use of Strong Sales Keys for Selection and Counseling," *Journal of Applied Psychology*, Vol. 42 (1958), pp. 93–96.

paper-and-pencil personality inventories are as simple to administer and score as any other kind of objective group test. The results obtained from administration of such inventories for personnel selection have been, however, largely negative. The reason for this is that like interest inventories, paper-and-pencil personality inventories are highly transparent.

Projective techniques confront the examinee with a relatively unstructured or ambiguous set of stimuli which in the case of the Rorschach Test look like ink blots and in the Murray Thematic Apperception Test are pictures. He is encouraged to respond freely, telling what he sees in the blot or making up a story about the picture. Responses to such stimuli are presumed to be projections of the subject's thoughts, wishes, desires, and needs.

Projective devices are not transparent. The subject does not know what responses are desired and hence cannot fake his replies in meaningful fashion. Administering projective techniques and interpreting responses to them does, however, require a high level of training and skill. Such instruments are typically administered individually and are both time consuming and expensive. In addition, projective tests have consistently been shown to be less reliable than objective tests.

The transparency of paper-and-pencil inventories and the expense as well as relative unreliability of projective techniques has kept personality appraisal in industry to a minimum. More research is needed to develop such measures particularly for predicting success in different types of high-level jobs within a given professional area.[8] For such jobs, more of the variance of job success is attributable to personal noncognitive qualities; the cognitive attributes (ability, aptitude, knowledge) are pretty much assured by the education and training requirements imposed as qualification standards.

Note that we are speaking above only about high-level executive and managerial positions. For most industrial positions, personality assessment is of dubious validity and therefore may constitute an unwarranted invasion of privacy. This issue is discussed at length later in the chapter. Furthermore, even when personality assessments

---

[8] W. B. Michael, "Differential Testing of High Level Personnel," *Educational and Psychological Measurement*, Vol. 17 (1957), pp. 475–90.

may be regarded as appropriate, their present state of development does not usually justify their inclusion in selection batteries.[9]

SOME SPECIFIC TESTS

Literally thousands of psychological tests have been reported in the professional literature, reviewed in comprehensive test bibliographies, and are available for distribution to qualified persons by test publishers. It is possible here to present only a cursory overview of some of the standardized tests most often used in industry.

Intelligence Tests

The *Otis Quick-Scoring Mental Ability Tests*[10] is a rapidly administered, paper-and-pencil group measure which although relatively old is still widely used. It may be administered with a 20- or a 30-minute time limit, and an even briefer version has been developed by Wonderlic.[11] This test has demonstrated validity for selecting employees for quite a variety of occupations not requiring a really high level of intelligence. The *Otis* does not have sufficient "top," for example, for administration to college students.

The *Wechsler Adult Intelligence Scales*[12] is an individually administered intelligence test sometimes used for industrial purposes. The advantages of this test are related more to clinical than to industrial applications. The fact that the examiner can probably elicit a higher level of motivation from the respondent and can better observe his behavior while he responds in the individual than in the group testing situation probably leads to a more accurate appraisal of intelligence. Most industrial requirements can, however, be satisfied by the more economical procedure of group testing.

The fact that intelligence tests are designed to measure general rather than specific capacity implies that measures of intelligence have been found to correlate with success in quite a range of occupa-

---

[9] S. Biesheuval, "Personnel Selection," *Annual Review of Psychology*, Vol. 16 (1965), p. 300.

[10] A. S. Otis, *Manuals:* Gamma (1937), Alpha, Beta (1939) (Tarrytown-on-Hudson, N.Y.: Harcourt, Brace & World, Inc.).

[11] *Personnel Test* (Northfield, Ill., 1945).

[12] D. Wechsler (New York: Psychological Corp., 1955).

FIGURE 7–1

AGCT Scores for a Selected Group of Occupations

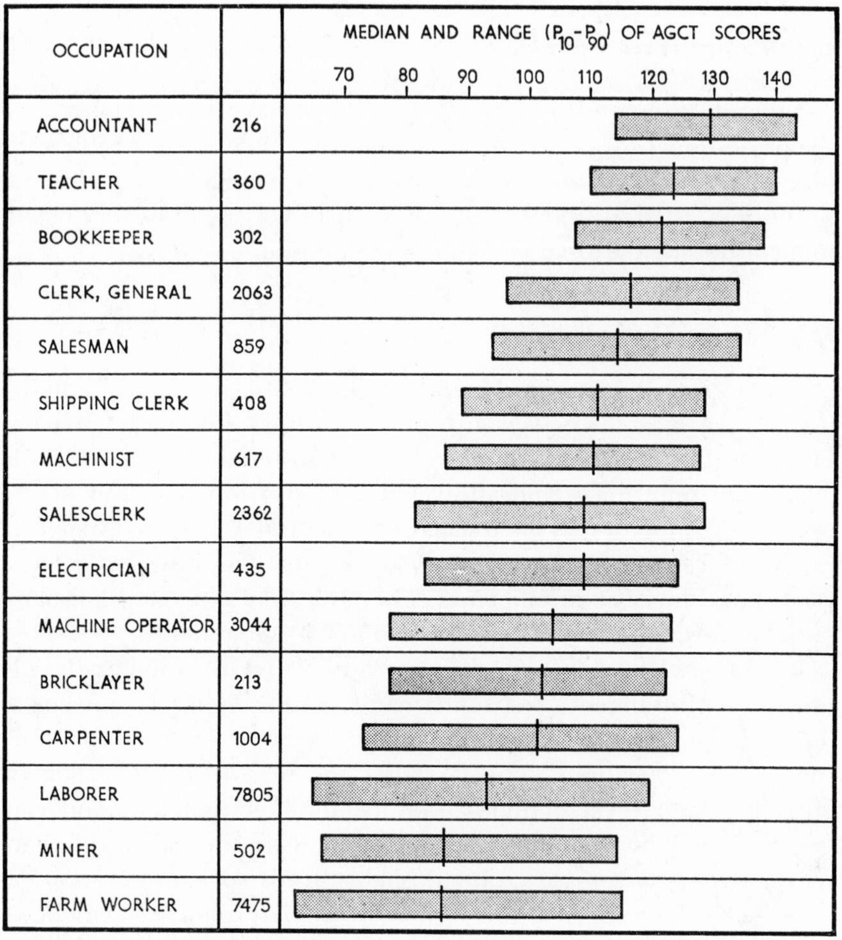

OCCUPATION		MEDIAN AND RANGE $(P_{10}-P_{90})$ OF AGCT SCORES
		70 80 90 100 110 120 130 140
ACCOUNTANT	216	
TEACHER	360	
BOOKKEEPER	302	
CLERK, GENERAL	2063	
SALESMAN	859	
SHIPPING CLERK	408	
MACHINIST	617	
SALESCLERK	2362	
ELECTRICIAN	435	
MACHINE OPERATOR	3044	
BRICKLAYER	213	
CARPENTER	1004	
LABORER	7805	
MINER	502	
FARM WORKER	7475	

Each bar shows the range of scores between the 10th and 90th percentiles for enlisted selectees in that occupation. The vertical bars represent median scores.

Source: N. Stewart, *Occupations*, Vol. 26 (1947), pp. 5–13. "AGCT scores of Army personnel grouped by occupations."

tions. The relationship between intelligence and occupational level is illustrated by the data in Figure 7–1. These data show the range of scores from the 10th to the 90th percentiles and the median scores earned by inducted enlisted men from various civilian occupations on the *Army General Classification Test* during World War II. The scores on this test are not to be confused with intelligence quotients (IQs).

If we assume that these data reflect intellectual requirements for various occupations, it can be seen that there is considerable overlap between occupations with respect to these requirements. Nevertheless, there is a marked tendency for measured intelligence to increase as occupational level increases.

Other more difficult tests have been designed particularly to assess the higher levels of mental ability required of executives and managers. One such device is Educational Testing Service's *In-Basket Test* discussed in greater detail in Chapter 17. This test presents the applicant with a standardized set of problems like those he might encounter in his in-basket. He responds by taking what he regards as appropriate action: dictating letters, organizing and calling a meeting, and so on.

Aptitude Tests

Various standardized aptitude batteries are available from test publishers. One such battery, representative of those published, is the *Flanagan Aptitude Classification (FACT)*.[13] The subtests comprising this battery are cited and defined in Figure 7–2.

It was not intended that substantial importance be given to any single test score in the *FACT* battery. Rather, various combinations of the subtests in the battery have been shown to measure the significant job elements associated with specific occupations. The combination of measures related to the job of accountant, for example, are Coding, Memory, Judgment and Comprehension, Arithmetic, and Tables. Similar patterns of aptitude based upon the significant job elements have been determined for quite a variety of occupations.

The Bennett, Seashore, and Wesman *Mechanical Reasoning Test*[14] is a paper-and-pencil measure of mechanical aptitude. The items in this test are similar to the illustration in Figure 7–3. It is rapidly administered and scored, and likely to be of value for jobs like engineering where understanding machines is of prime importance.

The *Clerical Aptitudes Test*[15] developed by Science Research Associates is representative of the kind of measure designed to iden-

---

[13] Science Research Associates, Inc. (Chicago, 1959).

[14] G. K. Bennett, H. G. Seashore, and A. G. Wesman (New York: The Psychological Corp., 1947).

[15] Science Research Associates, Inc., Chicago.

FIGURE 7-2

Description of the Flanagan Aptitude Classification Tests

DESCRIPTION OF THE FLANAGAN APTITUDE CLASSIFICATION TESTS

FACT NO.	NAME OF TEST	DESCRIPTION
1	INSPECTION	This test measures ability to spot flaws or imperfections in a series of articles quickly and accurately. The test was designed to measure the type of ability required in inspecting finished or semi-finished manufactured items.
2	CODING	This test measures speed and accuracy of coding typical office information. A high score can be obtained either by learning the codes quickly or by speed in performing a simple clerical task.
3	MEMORY	This test measures ability to remember the codes learned in test 2.
4	PRECISION	This test measures speed and accuracy in making very small circular finger movements with one hand and with both hands working together. The test samples ability to do precision work with small objects.
5	ASSEMBLY	This test measures ability to "see" how an object would look when put together according to instructions, without having an actual model to work with. The test samples ability to visualize the appearance of an object from a number of separate parts.
6	SCALES	This test measures speed and accuracy in reading scales, graphs, and charts. The test samples scale-reading of the type required in engineering and similar technical occupations.
7	COORDINATION	This test measures ability to coordinate hand and arm movements. It involves the ability to control movements in a smooth and accurate manner when these movements must be continually guided and readjusted in accordance with observations of their results.
8	JUDGMENT AND COMPREHENSION	This test measures ability to read with understanding, to reason logically, and to use good judgment in practical situations.
9	ARITHMETIC	This test measures skill in working with numbers—adding, subtracting, multiplying, and dividing.
10	PATTERNS	This test measures ability to reproduce simple pattern outlines in a precise and accurate way. Part of the test requires the ability to sketch a pattern as it would look if it were turned over.
11	COMPONENTS	This test measures ability to identify important component parts. The samples used are line drawings and blueprint sketches. It is believed this performance should be representative of ability to identify components in other types of complex situations.
12	TABLES	This test measures performance in reading two types of tables. The first consists entirely of numbers; the second contains only words and letters of the alphabet.
13	MECHANICS	This test measures understanding of mechanical principles and ability to analyze mechanical movements.
14	EXPRESSION	This test measures feeling for and knowledge of correct English. The test samples certain communication tasks involved in getting ideas across in writing and talking.

Flanagan Aptitude Classification Tests, *Examiner Manual* (Chicago: Science Research Associates, Inc., 1959), p. 5.

tify potentially successful office workers. It consists of three subtests: office vocabulary, office arithmetic, and office checking. The latter subtest is a measure of the speed and accuracy with which the respondent compares pairs of numbers.

Certain occupations, like drafting, require that the employee be able to visualize objects in space. Spatial visualization is measured by tests like the *Minnesota Paper Formboard (Revised)* [16] in which the individual responds to items similar to the ones illustrated in Figure 7–4. He must select the drawing that represents what the object will look like when the components are assembled.

A study performed by Surgent[17] will serve to indicate the kind of findings that may be obtained when aptitude test scores are correlated with a criterion of employee efficiency. Four aptitude tests

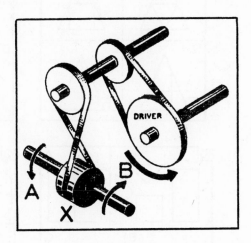

FIGURE 7–3

Sample Item from Form B of the Bennett, Seashore, and Wesman Mechanical Reasoning Test

The subject marks *A* or *B* in response to the question: "If the driver turns in the direction shown, which way will the pulley at 'X' turn?"

(yielding five scores) were administered to 233 female radio tube mounters. The predictor instruments, all of which measure manual and manipulative ability, were:

Minnesota Rate of Manipulation Test: A board with 60 round holes and 60 pegs. The "placing test" requires the subject to put each block in a hole. The "turning test" requires the subject to turn over each block.

O'Connor Finger Dexterity Test: A metal plate containing 100 holes. The subject is required to place three metal pins in each hole with his fingers.

O'Connor Tweezer Dexterity Test: Same apparatus as above. The subject uses tweezers to place one peg in each hole.

Purdue Pegboard: This test has two parts. The first measures

[16] New York: Psychological Corp., 1941.

[17] L. V. Surgent, "The Use of Aptitude Tests in the Selection of Radio Tube Mounters," *Psychological Monographs,* Vol. 41, No. 283 (1947), p. 40.

FIGURE 7–4

Items from the Revised Minnesota Paper Formboard Test

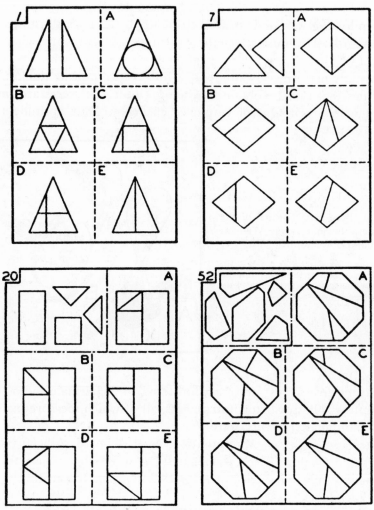

The subject must pick the figure (from *A* to *E*) which shows how the parts will look when assembled.

finger dexterity by requiring the subject to assemble pins, washers, and collars. The second measures manual dexterity by having subjects insert the pins in holes. (The latter part was used in this investigation.)

FIGURE 7-5

Minnesota Rate of Manipulation Test (Above); O'Connor Finger and Tweezer Dexterity Test (Right); Purdue Pegboard (Left)

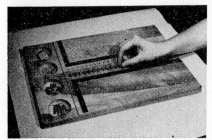 

Courtesy: Educational Test Bureau, Minneapolis; C. H. Stoelting Co., Chicago; Science Research Associates, Inc., Chicago.

The equipment required for these three tests is shown in Figure 7-5.

Test scores on these instruments were correlated with supervisory ratings of efficiency during the training period with the results shown in Table 7-2.

Although the Purdue Pegboard was the most efficient predictor of supervisory ratings, it was apparent that the other measures were also fairly effective predictors. Consequently, the tests were combined into a battery, and multiple correlations were computed to determine the predictive efficiency of the combined tests. The most

TABLE 7-2

Correlations between Test Scores and Supervisory Ratings
of Tube Mounters during the Training Periods

Test	Correlation
Minnesota Rate of Manipulation:	
Placing test	0.56
Turning test	0.50
O'Connor:	
Finger dexterity	0.48
Tweezer dexterity	0.59
Purdue Pegboard	0.64

efficient combination involving the Purdue Pegboard, the O'Conner Tweezer Dexterity Test, and the Minnesota Rate of Manipulation Placing Test yielded a multiple correlation of 0.76, which was considerably better than that obtained from any of the predictors used singly.

Achievement Tests

Many of the trade tests currently being used are not available for commercial distribution because they have been developed for and are the property of a specific company. Nevertheless, trade tests have been published in such areas as stenographic proficiency, machine-shop tools, equipment and procedures, blueprint reading, and industrial electricity.

A special form of achievement testing worthy of note even though not available from test publishers is the "job sample." Here, the applicant is given an opportunity either actually to do the work in question or to simulate the actual tasks.

Although job sample testing has the obvious advantages of face validity and assessment based upon doing rather than merely writing about the work, it also has the disadvantages typically associated with performance testing. Furthermore, a job can never be completely replicated in a test setting. Much of the ultimate job performance may depend heavily upon situational factors associated with the work: for example, differing styles of supervision, unwritten work rules and practices, and so on.[18]

---

[18] L. E. Albright, J. R. Glennon, W. J. Smith, *The Use of Psychological Tests in Industry* (Cleveland: Howard Allen, Inc., 1963), p. 128.

Interest Inventories

Interest inventories can, as was pointed out earlier, be extremely helpful for the purpose of vocational guidance even though they are of rather limited utility in the industrial setting. The two most widely used inventories are the Strong *Vocational Interest Blank* and the Kuder *Preference Record.*

The items in the Strong Vocational Interest Blank[19] list occupations, school subjects, amusements, activities, and so on, which the respondent must rank in order of preference or respond to in terms

TABLE 7–3

The Relationship between Vocational Interest Blank Score, Rate of
Retention, and Annual Sales by Life Insurance Salesmen

Score on Strong	Number of Salesmen Contracted	After One Year		After Two Years	
		Percent Remaining	*Median Sales*	*Percent Remaining*	*Median Sales*
A................228		66.5%	$155,414	42.5%	$206,680
B+................	72	59.1	112,839	32.4	144,446
B, B−, C..........	76	34.2	73,814	15.8	133,039

of "like," "dislike," or "indifferent." Every item in the inventory carries a positive or a negative weight based upon comprehensive statistical analyses. These weights are combined to produce occupational scoring keys. When the overall positive or negative weight is determined for each occupation, it is transformed to an indication of level of interest expressed as a letter grade (A, B+, B, B−, C+, or C). An A rating means that the individual's interests are similar to the pattern characteristic of persons successfully engaged in that type of work. A B rating means that his interests bear some resemblance to those of successful workers, while a C rating means that his interests bear little if any resemblance to those of successful workers.

This inventory has an exceedingly thorough and comprehensive research program behind it. One of the most impressive indications of the relationship between scores on the Strong Vocational Interest

---

[19] E. K. Strong, *Manual* (Stanford, Calif.: Stanford University Press, 1927, 1938, 1951).

Blank and an occupational criterion has been reported for life insurance salesmen.[20] The obtained relationship between score on the Life Insurance Salesman Key of the *Strong,* percent of salesmen retained after one and two years, and median amount of insurance sales during the first and second year is shown in Table 7–3. Salesmen who scored at the A level on the *Strong* were roughly twice as productive and much more likely to be retained than were the salesmen who scored at the B level or lower.

The Kuder *Preference Record*[21] consists of items arranged in triads (groups of three) requiring the examinee to select the one he likes most and the one he likes least. An illustrative item is cited below:

Visit an art gallery
Browse in a library
Visit a museum

The *Preference Record* yields scores indicative of strength of interest in nine vocational areas identified as Mechanical, Computational, Scientific, Persuasive, Artistic, Literary, Musical, Social Service, and Clerical. A fundamental difference between the interest inventories developed by Kuder and by Strong is that the former indicates the relative strength of each of nine interest areas within the individual while the latter yields comparisons between an individual's interests and those of successful employees within various occupational groups.

A newer form of the Kuder *Preference Record* scored by occupation rather than by vocational area has also been published.[22] Scoring keys for 22 specific occupations are thus far available. Additional research on this form is presently under way.

Personality Inventories

The *Guilford-Zimmerman Temperament Survey*[23] is a widely used paper-and-pencil device for assessing personality. The questions in this test are scored for 10 traits: general activity, restraint, ascend-

---

[20] Marion A. Bills, "A Tool for Selection That Has Stood the Test of Time," L. L. Thurstone (ed.), *Applications of Psychology* (New York: Harper & Bros., 1952), Table II, p. 133.

[21] G. F. Kuder, *Manual,* Short Industrial Form, 1948, (Chicago: Science Research Associates, 1939, 1943, 1953).

[22] Chicago: Science Research Associates, 1956.

[23] Beverly Hills, Calif.: Sheridan Supply Co.

ance, sociability, emotional stability, objectivity, friendliness, thoughtfulness, personal relations, and masculinity.

Also sometimes used is the *Bernreuter Personality Inventory*,[24] another paper-and-pencil inventory. This self-administering inventory yields scores for sociability, self-confidence, dominance, neurotic tendency, introversion, and self-sufficiency.

Transparency is a particular problem with all paper-and-pencil tests administered for preemployment purposes. It is sometimes possible for an applicant to "misrepresent" his personal characteristics by falsifying his test responses; understandably, he wishes to present himself in the most favorable light. Occasionally such tests are valid against job criteria in spite of their transparency. But such validity cannot be assumed; it must be demonstrated.

The *Edwards Personal Preference Schedule*[25] was developed as a "forced choice" inventory to help reduce the deleterious influence of transparency. The rationale underlying the forced-choice procedure is discussed in Chapter 9. It is sufficient here to indicate that the intent of this procedure is to reduce transparency by compelling respondents to choose between alternatives which appear to them to be equally attractive but actually differ in item validity. Thus, it is theoretically possible for a respondent to mark only alternatives that make him "look good" and still to earn an unfavorable score. The Edwards Personal Preference Schedule yields 15 scores on such personality variables as the need for achievement, deference, order, autonomy, and so on.

SOME TESTING ISSUES

Granted that psychological tests are valuable aids in selecting and placing personnel, several questions about their "fairness" and the morality of their use have been raised by job applicants, management, federal agencies, and the public press. It is appropriate to consider the issues most often raised by way of closing this discussion of personnel testing.

Issues Related to "Fairness"

Three questions most frequently raised in considering the fairness or legitimacy of testing are:[26]

---

[24] Stanford, Calif.: Stanford University Press.

[25] New York: The Psychological Corp.

[26] R. S. Barrett. "Guide to Using Psychological Tests," *Harvard Business Review*, September–October, 1963, pp. 138–46.

1. Because of their involvement with testing, are psychologists not thereby identifying themselves with the solution of management's rather than the applicant's or employee's problems?

2. Are not some applicants "unfairly" rejected on the basis of tests which have less than perfect validity?

3. Do not tests lead to the selection of "conformists" and the rejection of nonconformists?

Testing a "Management Tool"?   Virtually all employment and preemployment testing is paid for by management. Companies engage in these activities because good testing programs are economically sound. The company benefits by rejecting those applicants who stand little chance of satisfying performance standards and placing its employees in those particular positions where they are most likely to succeed.

However, the fact that testing is a sound economic procedure for management does not imply that job applicants or employees are thereby somehow penalized. The aim of testing is to help effect a match between an applicant's capabilities and knowledges on the one hand and the job's requirements on the other. To the extent that this match is effectively made, it clearly contributes to the employee's sense of satisfaction, dignity, and personal worth. Inappropriately placed employees are likely to experience frustration and a sense of personal inadequacy.

Thus, although testing is sponsored and paid for primarily by management in its own self-interest, this in no way implies a necessary conflict of interest with employees. An effective testing program benefits all parties to the industrial enterprise.

"Unfair Rejection?"   *All* personnel selection procedures are less than perfectly valid; hence, *all* lead to rejecting some applicants who if hired would have satisfied performance criteria. There is no known device for making perfectly accurate predictions of human performance. This fact provides the logic for using multiple predictors and assembling as much pertinent information about the applicants as is available when making hiring decisions.

Considering all available predictors of job performance, objective measures are clearly more fair than subjective ones. Test scores are generally immune to the influence of such factors as religion, skin color, and physical attractiveness. These factors are extraneous to the functions measured by tests. As discussed earlier, interviews differ from tests in that the former are susceptible to the very kinds of biases to which tests are relatively immune.

Thus, whereas measurement errors in testing are undeniable and cause some qualified applicants to be rejected, such errors and "unfair" rejections are much more prevalent without preemployment testing. The continuing efforts by personnel psychologists to improve the reliability and validity of their instruments of *all* kinds represent attempts to reduce the proportion of "unfair" rejections. These attempts have been much more successful for tests than for more subjective devices.

Selecting "Conformists?" The mere fact that management employs only persons who have passed a battery of preemployment measures does not imply that all persons thus selected will be cut from the same cloth.

Some selection programs deliberately seek to identify for employment those persons who are "innovative," "original," "experimental," and "creative." The only kind of conformity displayed by persons so selected is that they are intolerant of traditional solutions and of doing things in the usual way solely because of tradition.

But what happens in the more usual case; that is, when management is not deliberately seeking to identify nonconformists? Brief reflection should prove reassuring in this circumstance also. Psychologists and management agree with the commonsense idea of compensating skills—of strengths offsetting weaknesses. Everyone has some of each. The purpose of selection is to identify those persons for whom their own unique combination of strengths and weaknesses will permit satisfactory job performance and personal satisfaction. The variety of such combinations for any job is enormous and is reflected in the way in which proper use is made of test information.

Ethical-Moral-Legal Considerations

There are two fundamental questions involved here:

1. Do psychological tests constitute an unwarranted invasion of the individual's right to privacy?

2. Do tests unfairly discriminate against culturally and educationally deprived persons?

Invasion of Privacy? This is clearly not an issue when tests are used in the context of psychological treatment. However, there has been much consideration, both professional and public, of whether *preemployment* testing constitutes an invasion of the individual's right to privacy.[27] The issue here is a complex one compounded by the fact that preemployment testing is involuntary for the applicant if he is to be considered for employment. Furthermore, some tests of doubtful validity are occasionally included in the preemployment battery.[28]

The use of tests with doubtful validity can never be condoned. When such tests involve personality assessments more appropriate to the clinic than to industry and inquire into matters irrelevant to job success, they constitute an unwarranted invasion of privacy. Such an invasion of privacy constitutes unethical practice.

However, the presumably involuntary aspect of preemployment testing is really irrelevant to the issue of invasion of privacy. Employers always make *some* kind of preemployment assessment, and the applicant is always an involuntary party to this assessment. It is generally agreed that this is the employer's right. Indeed, there is little quarrel with the view that it is the employer's particular responsibility to identify and select only the most able of the available applicants. As long as the employer's decision rests upon matters like capability and the applicant's job knowledge, tests are fairer to the applicant than all other assessment techniques.

The key issue when considering "invasion of privacy" is the *relevance* of whatever is tested to eventual job success. Testing of relevant skills and abilities is clearly defensible, and not really in question. Testing of irrelevant skills or snooping into irrelevant (as far as job performance) personal characteristics or behavior is regarded as an unwarranted invasion of privacy, and therefore is avoided by industrial psychologists.

Civil Rights and Discrimination. The *Civil Rights Act of 1964* makes it illegal when hiring to discriminate on the basis either of ethnic background or sex. The charge is sometimes made that preemployment screening procedures unfairly discriminate against culturally and educationally deprived groups because such procedures do not lead to proportional representation of these group members in the employees so selected. This charge is most evident, of course, for Negroes and Mexican-Americans. As groups, their absolute educational levels and relative educational attainment levels are below those of white Americans. Hence, proportionately

---

[27] This issue is discussed in considerable detail in the *American Psychologist*, Vol. 20 (1965).

[28] M. H. Freedman, "A Plea to Professional Psychologists," *ibid.*, pp. 877–79.

fewer "survive" a preemployment requirement of, say, high school graduation. Likewise, proportionately fewer are able to satisfy the requirements imposed by a test of 10th-grade arithmetic or verbal fluency.

One solution sometimes advocated is to use different selection standards in order to compensate for socially imposed educational deficiencies. This is not to be confused with "lowering" standards; and it is not defensible in the absence of supporting data.

In essence, the effective use of differential selection standards by ethnic origin rests upon a moderator-variable analysis. Such an analysis requires that predictor and criterion scores be separately correlated for each ethnic subgroup (see Chapter 6). If the resultant correlations are similar, there is no empirical justification for applying different selection standards in the subgroups.

However, as often happens, the resultant correlations are dissimilar. Here, the probability of success differs for each raw predictor score depending upon the person's subgroup (for example, Negro or white); and it therefore makes sense to use different selection standards for applicants from each subgroup. As one illustration contrary to the usually assumed pattern, test-criterion correlations were found to be 0.39 for Negro toll collectors and −0.24 for white toll collectors. In order to avoid discriminating against *white* applicants for this job, it is proper to accept as "passing" much lower test scores for them than for Negro applicants.[29]

An excellent definition of employment discrimination, consistent with the above-described moderator-variable analysis is that ". . . unfair discrimination exists when persons with equal probabilities of success on the job have unequal probabilities of being hired for the job."[30] In addition to supporting validity studies by subgroups, this also calls the attention of companies seriously interested in hiring qualified minority group members to the necessity for actively recruiting them. The federal government and the military services have obviously recognized the importance of recruiting for attracting qualified but reluctant job applicants.

The government, military, and private industry are all cognizant of yet another factor bearing upon this issue. Social responsibility

---

[29] F. M. Lopez, Jr., "Current Problems in Test Performance of Job Applicants: I," *Personnel Psychology*, Vol. 19 (1966), pp. 10–18.

[30] R. M. Guion, "Employment Tests and Discriminatory Hiring," *Industrial Relations*, Vol. 5 (1966), p. 26.

requires the development and implementation of training programs to compensate for heretofore socially imposed educational deprivation. The definition of "discrimination" cited above contains within it, at least implicitly, the moral responsibility to provide opportunities for *all* persons to develop those abilities and skills contributing to probable job success.

SUMMARY

This chapter explored the range of standardized and commercially published psychological tests available for industrial application. The outstanding advantages of standardized tests include economy, immediate availability, and accessibility to norms. In spite of these advantages, the validity of such tests cannot be assumed; it must be established under the particular circumstance in which the test is to be used.

Psychological tests differ from one another in the way in which they are structured, administered, and scored. In addition to the frequently mentioned differentiation between subjective and objective tests, some tests have a time limit (speed tests) while others do not (power tests) ; some are suitable for administration to groups while others are designed for administration to one person at a time; and some require the respondent to perform on some kind of apparatus or equipment while others require him to reply by marking an answer to a written question.

In addition to differences in format, psychological tests are differentiated from one another on the basis of the functions they measure. These functions are identified as intelligence, aptitude, achievement, interest, and personality.

All tests of ability, including intelligence, aptitude, and achievement, measure the present level of cognitive performance. However, intelligence and aptitude tests are regarded as tests of "capacity" or "potential" because of their demonstrated success in predicting future cognitive accomplishments. Thus, these two types of test are most appropriate in situations wherein the job to be filled requires unique skills or knowledges which the company expects to teach its new employees. Most often, however, the employment office will seek employees who now know how to do certain kinds of work. In such cases the selection tests will measure achievement, knowledge, or proficiency.

Measures of "capacity," like intelligence and aptitude tests, and of achievement are fundamental to a personnel testing program. They are sometimes supplemented by devices to assess interests and personality. The primary objection to the use of interest and personality inventories for personnel selection is that these devices tend to be transparent. The respondent can often determine by reading the items which response will portray his personality most favorably for the job in question.

This chapter was ended by discussing several critical issues related to personnel testing. The conclusions with respect to these matters were:

1. Although usually paid for by management, preemployment testing benefits job applicants as well as employers.

2. Whereas preemployment tests are fallible, they are more fair to job applicants than are more subjective preemployment assessments.

3. Properly used preemployment tests do not select only "conformists."

4. Testing of irrelevant skills or snooping into irrelevant (as far as job performance) personal characteristics is an unwarranted invasion of privacy.

5. Properly used preemployment tests do not violate either the provisions or the spirit of the *Civil Rights Act of 1964.*

8. Employee Training

Learning is a key factor in the development and modification of behavior, including those activities related to job performance. Behavior is learned as a consequence of certain kinds of experiences. *Training* refers to industrial efforts to provide those experiences calculated to facilitate the development of attitudes, skills, and knowledges most germane to satisfactory job performance.

The value both to management and employees of training for job-related behavior is self-evident. An effective training program may increase productivity, generate increased job satisfaction, decrease turnover and accidents, and so on. In one way or another, all of these desirable ends improve the quality of the product or service and reduce operating costs.

In addition, employee training has become a concern of great social importance. Educationally and socially deprived persons must through training be provided opportunities for productive citizenship. Likewise, automation makes imperative the provision of opportunities for retraining persons whose present skills are inappropriate to contemporary industrial technology.

Although automation and the social milieu have called attention to industry's need and responsibility for training in a dramatic way, this need has always existed, and industry has for a long time accepted the responsibility. An early form of on-the-job training, for example, is represented in the following agreement:

Know all men that I, Thomas Millard, with the Consent of Henry Wolcott of Windsor unto whose custody & care at whose charge I was brought over out of England into New England, doe bynd myself as an apprentise for eight yeeres to serve William Pynchon of Springfield, his heires & assigns in all manner of lawful employmt unto the full ext of eight yeeres beginninge the 29 day of Sept 1640 & the said William doth condition to find the said Thomas meat, drinke & clothing fitting such an apprentise

& at the end of his tyme one new sute of apparell & forty shillings in mony: subscribed this 28 October 1640.[1]

The kind of "on-the-job training" promised Thomas Millard was typical of New England apprenticeship in Colonial days. The employer's commitments were minimal. In return for receiving devoted service for "eight yeeres," he was to provide merely "meat, drinke and clothing" and, at the end of the period, "one new sute of apparell & forty shillings in mony." Little enough perhaps, but even the full extent of the generosity provided by this indenture was not realized. Apparently, Millard became itchy to strike out on his own before completing the full term of his apprenticeship. The following statement appears at the foot of the indenture:

> Tho Millard by his owne consent is released & discharged of Mr. Pynchon service this 22. of May 1648 being 4 months before his tyme comes out, in Consideration whereoff he looses the 40 *s* in mony wch should have bin pd him, but Mr. Pynchon giveth him one New sute of Apparell he hath at present.[2]

It is apparent from the foregoing indenture agreement that industrial training is far from a new concept. However, both the scope and methods of present-day industrial training differ considerably from Colonial apprenticeship. Although development of job-related knowledges and skills has always been a fundamental objective of training, this objective has been considerably broadened, particularly since World War II.

One assumption underlying apprenticeship training which is particularly called into question is that experienced employees with job skills are automatically thereby qualified to teach these skills to novices. Whereas training can be conducted in this way, it is often inefficient; that is, it takes longer than necessary and generally does not allow the trainee to make maximum use of his potential for development and job performance. Thus, the position taken in this chapter is that industrial training is most effectively conducted by capitalizing upon sound principles of human learning developed both in industry and in psychological laboratories.

Although training programs of various kinds permeate virtually all levels of the company, the present discussion is restricted to employee training. Special consideration is given to management

---

[1] United States Department of Labor, Bureau of Apprenticeship, *Apprenticeship Past and Present*, 1952.

[2] *Ibid.*

and supervisory training in Chapter 17. The present chapter treats five main topics: (1) the scientific foundations of training programs in terms of principles of learning, (2) preliminary considerations in developing training programs, (3) implementing training programs, (4) evaluating training outcomes and procedures, and (5) training the trainer.

LEARNING PRINCIPLES UNDERLYING INDUSTRIAL TRAINING

Industrial training is a learning situation fundamentally similar to formal kinds of schoolroom learning. To be conducted successfully, a training program must take into account certain basic psychological principles of learning and forgetting. We cannot here review the very substantial body of evidence on learning theory. Rather, we will merely summarize some of the highlights.

What happens when a person learns? Attempts to describe and guide this experience must take into account something like the following sequence of events:[3]

1. The learner is motivated; he wants to attain some goal or goals.

2. The learner responds in ways calculated to attain these goals. However, his initial responses are limited by the "givens" which he brings with him into the learning situation. These initial "givens" include:

    a) The sum total of his past learning and abilities;

    b) The way in which he interprets the goal.

3. The learner practices behavior for goal attainment.

4. As he does so, the consequences of his responses are continuously fed back to him. He assesses these responses with respect to their adequacy for goal attainment.

5. Learning has occurred when the learner can attain his goal (s) using responses not formerly in his behavior repertoire.

Motivation

Repetitive practice or exposure is not by itself a sufficient condition for learning. A person learns only when he is motivated to do

---

[3] Modified from W. McGehee, "Are We Using What We Know about Training?—Learning Theory and Training," *Personnel Psychology*, Vol. 11 (1958), pp. 1–12.

so. The importance of motivation as a precondition for learning has two major implications. First, any training program should be preceded by an orientation session (or sessions) to discuss and clarify the need for the program. Second, the program itself must provide continuing motivation during the course of training.

Clarifying the Need for the Program. Both new and experienced employees sometimes resent training. Such resentment may be based upon the feeling that the program really betrays a lack of confidence in their ability to do the work. Experienced supervisors likewise may object to the introduction of "newfangled" working procedures which are at variance with their familiar and accustomed ways of doing the job. Thus, one objective of the orientation to training is to attempt to forestall such resentments.

Another objective is to clarify the goals and the reasons for seeking to attain these goals. It is naïve to believe that work goals are self-evident for everyone alike. Whereas management, for example, may seek maximally efficient high-quality production, the employees may be influenced by work group goals established to maintain only whatever level of productivity will pacify the supervisor. Likewise, whereas a training program may be designed to teach a specific method of task performance, this method will not be perceived as desirable by those trainees who fail to understand its superiority to alternative procedures.

As a case in point, a company specializing in the manufacture of miniature motors for guidance systems in aircraft was disturbed by an unduly high rate of rejections during final inspection. The defects were attributable to poorly soldered connections. Further checking indicated that conditions caused by rapid expansion in the labor force had led management to utilize a kind of on-the-job training in which experienced solderers were teaching new employees how to do the work. None of these teachers was able, however, to explain the reason for using flux prior to applying the solder. As a result, new operators often regarded this as an unnecessary step in the soldering process. The simple expedient of explaining some elementary principles of soldering to the employees and to the new trainees led to an appreciable decrease in the rate of rejections.

Short-Term Goals. It has been found desirable to establish a number of readily attainable short-term subgoals throughout the learning sequence in addition to the fundamental long-term goal of "completion of training" or a "certificate" or achievement of "regular salary status." It would be difficult for most university students, for example, to attend school with a high level of motivation for the full four years if the only goal was eventual employment within a selected occupation. This goal is, to be sure, extremely important. Fortunately, from a motivational standpoint, it is supplemented by such subgoals as obtaining the diploma, earning satisfactory course grades, performing well on a specific final examination, and doing well on hourly examinations and even on 10-minute quizzes in any one course. In addition, the learner may derive considerable satisfaction from having grasped a difficult concept or gaining insight into a hitherto unknown process.

Individual Differences

We have said that once training begins, the trainee's initial responses are limited by the "givens" he brings with him. One of these givens is his idiosyncratic interpretation of the training goal. Another is the sum total of his past learning and of his abilities.

Idiosyncratic Goals. In spite of pretraining orientation some trainees may fail to understand the type of behavior finally desired. This failure may occur because the desired behavior is not in the response repertoire of the trainee. He therefore interprets what he is supposed to do in terms of whatever behavior *is* available in his repertoire.

For example, management may institute training for job rotation, anticipating that this will enable employees to cover for each other during vacation periods. However, unless this is clear to the trainees, they may simply view the training as an opportunity to appreciate something of the diversity of tasks performed by company employees. Such appreciation alone is not enough to insure satisfactory performance when jobs are actually rotated.

Past Learning and Abilities. Recognition of the existence of differences in capabilities, interests, attitudes, and so on between persons is fundamental to psychological testing programs. All men are *not* equal. Some are more capable than others of learning particular types of tasks. Contrary to popular belief, the effect of training is often to accentuate such differences rather than to cancel or reduce them. Thus, the spread between the best and poorest trainees in initial level of performance usually becomes progressively greater as the training program progresses. This is particularly noted when the task being learned is relatively complex or difficult, although it has even been reported when training was deliberately structured into a series of small, simple steps, one building upon the other.[4]

The effect of individual differences upon subsequent performance in a training program is evident from the following study. Four groups of soldiers, classified on the basis of their scores on the Army

FIGURE 8-1

Radiotelegrahic Code Learning as a Function of Trainee Aptitude

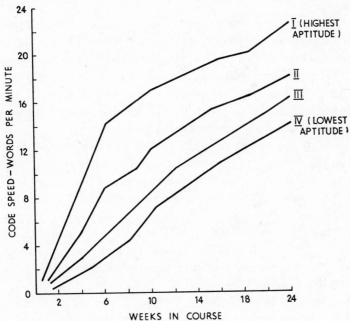

Radiotelegraph Operator Aptitude Tests, received radiotelegraphic code instruction. The aptitude classifications ranged from I (highest) to IV (lowest). The rate of learning plotted for these four groups at two-week intervals during the training program is shown in Figure 8-1.[5] Note that the early differences between these groups, which were pronounced even at two weeks, became even more accentuated as training progressed.

---

[4] P. Welsh, J. A. Antoinetti, and P. W. Thayer, "An Industrywide Study of Programed Instruction," *Journal of Applied Psychology,* Vol. 49 (1965), pp. 61–73.

[5] E. G. Boring, *Psychology for the Armed Services* (Washington, D.C.: Infantry Journal, 1945), p. 244.

Practice

It is fairly obvious that trainees must actually practice a skill if they are to learn it. Even a highly motivated student attending lectures and seeing demonstrations of automobile driving, for example, is poorly trained to drive until after he has received supervised driving practice. Similarly, the foreman who merely attends lectures on "how to train" or "how to lead" is trained incompletely either as a trainer or as a leader. The essential element of supervised practice is lacking.

Thus, a training program must make provision for the trainees actually to practice their job in the way in which they ultimately will be expected to perform it. If a motor skill, like operation of a piece of equipment, is being taught, the trainees must have an opportunity to practice the operation of the equipment. The supervisor who is learning to train, in like fashion, must receive supervised practice in actually training employees.

In spite of the widely quoted maxim, practice may make imperfect. Improper or inappropriate behaviors which are practiced will be learned as effectively as correct behaviors. Thus, a key feature of the practice phase is that the trainees must be very carefully supervised. Mistakes must be corrected as soon as they occur. Anyone who has attempted to teach himself to play golf, for example, and then consults a professional is well aware of the fact that he must unlearn a number of bad habits that have become established as a result of unsupervised practice.

Whole versus Part Learning.   One of the implications of the desirability of short-term goals for industrial training is that complex tasks should wherever possible be divided into their significant component parts for teaching purposes. The trainee is enabled thereby to attain a measure of satisfaction from successfully learning portions of the task even though he is not yet able to perform the entire task.

The nature of the parts to be learned and the sequence in which they are taught varies from one task to another. The disassembly of a weapon, for example, requires trainees first to learn to handle various subassemblies. Similarly, a typist must learn various subskills, including proper fingering and spacing, which she then integrates into a total behavior pattern.

The entire matter of the feasibility of teaching segments of the total task and, if this is done, of the optimal decomposition of the task and sequence for presenting its constituent parts requires examination in each specific training situation. In a general way, it has been shown that these matters depend upon two aspects of the task's components: complexity and organization.[6] "Complexity" refers to the difficulty of each of the separate components of the overall task; "organization" refers to the interrelationships among task components.

When a task is highly organized, it has an essential cohesiveness the integrity of which would be destroyed by decomposing it into parts or subtasks. Thus, the whole method of training is particulary appropriate. Furthermore, its superiority to part training for such tasks increases as the difficulty of the constituent components of the overall task increases.

Part training, on the other hand, is particularly efficient when the constituent responses are not closely interrelated (that is, low task organization). The superiority of part over whole training for such tasks is increased when certain portions of the total task are much more difficult than others.

Massed versus Spaced Learning. Another aspect of the arrangement of training sessions is the matter of the optimal length of each session. Practice periods may be *massed*, in which case training consists of relatively few but long sessions, or they may be *spaced* so that there are more sessions, each of shorter duration. Five hours of training may be massed, for example, in a single session starting at 8:00 A.M. and continuing until 1:00 P.M. The same five hours may be spaced by setting up a 2½-hour session in the morning and another in the afternoon, or by establishing five one-hour sessions, or 10 half-hour sessions, and so on.

The primary advantage of spaced training is that it is generally easier to maintain a high level of trainee interest and to avoid fatigue during several sessions of shorter duration than during a few very long sessions. Spaced training has in general been demonstrated to produce more rapid learning and more permanent retention. Exceptions to this generalization occur in instances in which the skills or concepts to be learned are so simple that even massed practice periods will be of relatively brief duration.

---

[6] J. C. Naylor and G. E. Briggs, "The Effect of Task Complexity and Task Organization on the Relative Efficiency of Part and Whole Training Methods," *Journal of Experimental Psychology*, Vol. 65 (1963), pp. 217–24.

The optimal spacing of training sessions must be determined for each task to be taught. If the time intervals between spaced practice periods are too long, the advantages of spaced practice may be more than offset by the amount of forgetting transpiring during the time interval. Similarly, if the individual practice periods are too brief in duration, they may be filled almost entirely by having the trainees check out tools and materials and receive instructions. Such periods will end just as the trainees are about to move into the task itself!

Transfer of Training.   Most training takes place in settings which are artificial in some degree. This is most obvious for training physically removed from the actual work site. However, it is true to some extent also even of training at the site because of subtle variations between training and working conditions. In the former, for example, the supervisor may tend to be more helpful than usual, and the wage may be independent of output.

Irrespective of *where* training takes place, the objective is to have the trainee learn to perform satisfactorily on the job. Thus, there must be some carryover, or transfer, from what is learned during training to actual job performance. This transfer may be either *positive,* in which case learning during training facilitates job performance, or *negative,* where training is actually an initial hinderance to job performance.

Positive transfer between two situations is encouraged when the stimulus-response requirements in those situations are similar. Furthermore, the more nearly similar these requirements, the greater will be the amount of positive transfer. Thus, it is clear that the more nearly the required behavior during training approximates the behavior required on the job, the greater will be the amount of positive transfer. If, for example, both speed and accuracy are required for satisfactory job performance, both of these response characteristics ought to be encouraged also during training.

Concern for transfer must also guide the way in which the training program itself is internally constituted and sequenced.[7] Virtually any human task may be analyzed into subtasks, each critical to final performance. Consider, for example, a complex task like troubleshooting a radio. The mechanic is required, first, to know the rules of signal flow through each component. Second, he must know the proper use of electronic test instruments. Each of these subtasks can

---

[7] R. M. Gagné, "Military Training and Principles of Learning," *American Psychologist,* Vol. 17 (1962), pp. 83–91.

be further analyzed into subordinate subtasks. For example, proper instrument usage requires the mechanic to know which instrument to use for which kind of check, how to set up the test instrument, how to interpret the instrument reading, and so on.

Proceeding from a detailed analysis of the subtasks constituting final performance (*task analysis*), the training program must be designed to insure that each subtask is fully learned. To accomplish this, the program must present the component subtasks in a sequence which maximizes the likelihood of positive transfer from learning one component to another.

Knowledge of Results

Trainees must be given a stream of information (or "feedback") about their performance if they are to maintain a high level of interest in the training program. The importance of feedback is evident from an investigation in which two groups of subjects were trained to aim a rifle at an unseen moving target.[8] One group was given information indicating whether or not they were aiming in the vicinity of the target. The other group received no information of this kind. At the end of the 400th practice trial, the dissemination of information to the "knowledge" group was terminated, and both groups operated under conditions of "no knowledge" for 400 additional trials.

The results for these two groups of subjects expressed in terms of the mean number of seconds the rifle was actually aimed on the target are shown graphically in Figure 8–2. Knowledge of results produced a more rapid increment in performance than did the control condition during the original 400 trials. Furthermore, additional learning in the "knowledge" group ceased after the 400th trial paralleling the cessation of information about performance. The "no knowledge" group eventually performed essentially as well as the "knowledge" group, but it required about twice as long for them to do so.

The incentive effect of knowledge of results is generally more important in the later stages of practice than during the initial stages. In the earlier stages, most trainees have a degree of enthusiasm tending to carry them forward. Later on as this intrinsic enthu-

---

[8] H. C. W. Stockbridge and B. Chambers, "Aiming, Transfer of Training and Knowledge of Results," *Journal of Applied Psychology*, Vol. 42 (1958), pp. 148–53.

siasm diminishes, it must be rekindled by such externally imposed factors as proof of progress.[9]

The provision of feedback information ought to follow the trainee's performance with as little time lapse as possible. You are aware in your own case of the instructional value of rapid feedback by the teacher of the correct answers to an examination. Similarly, the industrial trainee benefits most from a training environment permitting for frequent and rapid performance evaluations.

In spite of the clear necessity for feedback during training, it is possible for such feedback to be either too general or too specific to be helpful. Feedback that is too general fails to provide the learner

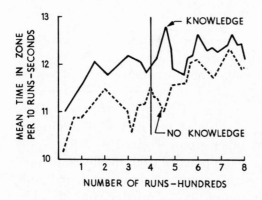

FIGURE 8–2

Effect of Knowledge of Results upon Accuracy of Rifle Aiming

with sufficient information by which he can improve his performance. However, overly specific feedback providing more detailed information than the trainee can use at his present level of sophistication may actually retard his learning. The latter situation is analogous to "overloading" the system.

PRELIMINARY CONSIDERATIONS IN DEVELOPING TRAINING PROGRAMS

Granting the importance of the foregoing conditions of effective learning, these conditions alone do not specify the optimal nature of the training program. Training can take many forms, each incorporating appropriate learning principles. What, then, determines how the training program ought actually to be structured? And is there

---

[9] J. N. Mosel, "How to Feed Back Performance Results to Trainees," *Journal of American Society of Training Directors* (February, 1958).

any evidence that certain kinds of instructional formats are more efficient than others?

Determining Training Needs and Objectives

A properly structured training program has certain well-defined objectives. These objectives follow logically from a systematic determination of training needs within the company and in turn suggest the ways in which training will be conducted, the persons who will be trained, and a scheme for evaluating the effectiveness of the program.

Often the need for some kind of training becomes evident because of the existence of a problem. Automation, for example, may be accompanied by layoffs and a consequent need to train displaced workers for other jobs. Rapid expansion of production or changes in the labor market may necessitate training designed to teach requisite job knowledges or skills to relatively inexperienced workers. Sometimes a company suddenly discovers a rather marked increase in accidents accompanying the introduction of new equipment and needs to institute a safety training program. Or, in anticipation of the retirement of a number of supervisory persons, the company may need to train replacements as effective leaders.

The foregoing problems merely suggest the kinds of situations that may create a need for training. The program begins with certain questions related to need: In what areas (safety, skills, supervision, and so on) is training needed? Which workers need to be trained? What are the specific training needs of these workers? Only after questions like these are answered, can the company begin to think in terms of the kind of program that will be appropriate to its needs.

Discovering Training Needs. Analyses of training needs typically begin with an overview of the entire company in an attempt to identify areas of relatively inefficient operation. Interviews, studies of company records concerning turnover, accidents and customer complaints, and observations by the training analyst may all be suggestive.[10]

Although this overview can suggest *general* areas of training need, it must be supplemented by studies to determine specific groups of

[10] D. H. Fryer, M. R. Feinberg, and S. S. Zalkind, *Developing People in Industry* (New York: Harper & Bros., 1956).

workers in need of training. For example, safety training may be indicated for a company, but it is unlikely that all groups of workers will need such training. The analyst's focus narrows during this phase of training need determination as he studies the workers in particular departments. He may consult existing job analyses or make new ones of his own; he makes systematic observations; and he interviews.

Finally, the analysis of training needs gets down to the level of individual workers. Training may be necessary only for certain workers within a department; or differential amounts and types of training may be indicated for the various department members. Various tests of ability, skill, or job knowledge may be administered if these are appropriate to the identified areas of training need. Supervisory ratings may help identify particular workers most in need of training and indicate the kinds of training they ought to receive. Company records of individual productivity, accident frequency, and so on may provide further clues.

Training Objectives.   A training program properly conceived permeates all levels and activities of an industrial organization. Its impact is felt by workers with varying amounts of experience and at various levels or classifications.

The diversity of training needs makes it impossible to present a really comprehensive list of the objectives that can be realized as a result of training. We will consider only some that are most generally applicable.

1. Orientation and Indoctrination. This kind of training is designed for newly hired personnel regardless of whether these workers have had prior experience. It serves primarily to explain the company's politicies and practices. Secondarily, it may seek to develop attitudes of pride in the company and personal identification of the employee with it.

2. Job-Related Skills and Knowledges. Such training is mandatory when a company is compelled to hire relatively inexperienced employees either because of conditions of the labor market or because the job to be filled is novel or unique to the particular company. A continuous program of skills-and-knowledges training for in-service personnel may be necessary also to upgrade present levels of employee performance.

3. Personal Improvement and Enrichment. This objective extends the impact of training considerably beyond the confines of the

worker's job. It is based on the assumption that more broadly educated employees handle their work more efficiently. In addition, programs with more general educational objectives lay the groundwork for teaching new skills and knowledges demanded of workers by an ever expanding technocracy. Thus, an organization like the National Secretaries Association has considered it desirable to sponsor courses for its members in such areas as Art Appreciation and Human Relations. Individual companies, likewise, provide opportunities for employees at various levels to take such courses as Speed Reading, Blueprint Reading, Speech, and Written Communication.

4. Management Development. The executive, administrative, and human-relations skills required for effective leadership are not acquired by virtue of seniority or demonstrated job performance. As men progress to increasingly higher management positions, their responsibilities shift from the specific to the general; they must make decisions having broad impact and affecting many other persons.

5. Technological and Scientific Information. Rapid technological and scientific advances have necessitated special programs designed to keep employees abreast of the most recent developments. Many accounting procedures utilizing punched-card equipment "brand new" only 20 years ago, for example, have been superseded by the development of relatively inexpensive data-processing machines capable of storing and providing ready access to vast amounts of information. In a competitive society it is imperative that industrial organizations avail themselves of all pertinent technological advances. To do so requires that scientific and professional employees be provided the opportunity and incentive to learn about such advances.

Training and Personnel Selection. It should be evident from the foregoing discussion that selection procedures and training goals for new employees are interdependent. The more qualified the selected employee, the less likely he is to require elaborate and lengthy job training. Conversely, the more comprehensive and effective the company's training program, the less elaborate need be its selection program.

This interaction between selection and training procedures must finally be interpreted in terms of cost. Both procedures require expenditures. Therefore, in the interest of economy, management must optimize the relationship between these two elements of its personnel program. Clearly, when selection test scores correlate positively with training success, acceptance of those applicants with the highest test scores is justified. They are the ones most likely to complete satisfactorily the training program. And by reducing the number of unsuccessful trainees, the overall cost of the training program is also thereby reduced. However, selection programs cost money too. If many applicants must be tested to identify a relatively small number with sufficiently high scores for training purposes, it may prove more efficient to modify the training program at some additional cost in order to effect more substantial economies in the selection program itself.

A cost analysis suggesting the optimum balance between selection and training expenditures is therefore dependent upon the (a) number of job applicants available, (b) validity of selection procedures for predicting success in training, (c) cost per man of selection, and (d) cost per man of training.

Retraining. Retraining programs are developed in two kinds of situations. First, the retraining program may provide refresher instruction for present employees. Such refresher training may be required because of the introduction of new work methods and/or equipment, employee reassignment, or because a periodic performance review has indicated that the employee needs additional instruction in order more effectively to handle his present assignment.

Second, retraining may be necessitated by displacement. Retraining for displaced workers has become an increasingly important social concern because of automation and the changing nature of jobs away from repetitive short-cycle work. The area is a new one for psychological investigation; the meager results thus far available point to the importance of attitudinal factors to the success of this type of retraining.

A study of the feasibility of retraining factory employees for work as technicians concluded that only 15 percent were completely ineligible for such retraining. The primary limiting psychological factor was deficient educational background rather than a low level of learning ability. However, this is compounded by the increased cost of retraining men with minimally sufficient aptitude.[11]

Even when companies are willing to defray the cost of retraining persons with requisite abilities, there is likely to be a certain amount

---

[11] W. J. McNamara, "Retraining of Industrial Personnel," *Personnel Psychology,* Vol. 16 (1963) , pp. 233–47.

of initial employee resistance to change in work role.[12] Retrainees, for example, were found to be much less satisfied with the company immediately following a retraining program than formerly. However, three years later, the level of job satisfaction returned to about the pretraining level.[13]

One particularly disturbing factor is the reluctance of older adults to seek retraining because of their conviction, or industry's, that they are too old to learn something new. To be sure, age is accompanied by some decrement in certain kinds of cognitive functions and abilities. However, in the age range of most employees eligible for retraining, the actual decrement is much less serious than the attitude of resistance.

The challenge to psychologists engaged in retraining is thus that of designing programs that effectively overcome such resistance by facilitating successful experiences by middle-aged trainees. That this is possible was demonstrated with inspection trainees for whom the training method emphasized active responses and minimized the possibility of making errors.[14]

Considerations in Training Design

In many ways industrial training is essentially like other kinds of formal education. Neither training nor education should be permitted to evolve by happenstance. Both must be carefully designed most efficiently to implement the learner's attainment of the desired goals.

Terminal Behavior Desired. The initial consideration in formulating any educational program is to specify the behavior ultimately desired. Broadly speaking, the goals of industrial training may be to convey knowledge (for example, orientation training), develop skills, or modify attitudes (for example, concerning accident hazards). Within each of these broad areas the training director must specify the training goals as precisely as possible. Clearly specified objectives serve two purposes. First, they guide the formulation of a training program that is calculated to implement goal attainment.

---

[12] E. A. Fleishman, "Attitude versus Skill Factors in Work Group Productivity," *Personnel Psychology*, Vol. 17 (1965), pp. 253–66.

[13] N. A. Rosen, L. K. Williams, and F. F. Foltman, "Motivational Constraints in an Industrial Retraining Program," *Personnel Psychology*, Vol. 18 (1965), pp. 65–79.

[14] E. Belbin and S. Shimmin, "Training the Middle Aged for Inspection Work," *Occupational Psychology*, Vol. 38 (1964), pp. 49–57.

Second, they suggest criterion measures which when applied to training program graduates permit evaluation of the effectiveness of the program for generating the desired terminal behavior.[15]

Trainee Characteristics. It is doubtful, even for a specified objective, that a single training format is appropriate for all learners. Instead, it is likely that the appropriateness of any training procedure depends both upon the objectives sought and the characteristics of the learner.[16] The kinds of trainee characteristics that will most obviously concern the training director as he designs his program are ability or aptitude and previous job-related experience. If the trainees constitute a heterogeneous group with respect to these qualifications, he may well find it necessary to develop parallel programs for subsets of trainees. Each program, although designed to generate the same terminal behavior, may differ with respect to content, sequence in which the content is presented, instructional materials and methods used, and so on.

An Overview of the System. The activities of training program graduates must mesh well with those of workers on related jobs. Otherwise, there is a danger that newly trained employees will either take over work responsibilities of other employees with a consequent duplication of effort and cost or that certain task elements will not be performed either by the newly trained or experienced employees. To prevent either occurrence, the training director must have a clear notion of the interdependence of related jobs within the overall company system.

IMPLEMENTING TRAINING PROGRAMS

Given an analysis of the terminal behavior desired, trainee characteristics, and the interdependence of work roles within the system, the training director may structure his program to be conducted at various sites and in various ways. The primary considerations in selecting a training site are (a) the appropriateness of the site for the attainment of the desired objectives and (b) economy, including the speed with which training is completed.

Two self-evident training sites are the classroom and some other

---

[15] G. A. Eckstrand, "Current Status of the Technology of Training," *AMRL Document Technical Report 64–86*, September, 1964.

[16] L. Siegel and L. C. Siegel, "A Multivariate Paradigm for Educational Research," *Psychological Bulletin*, Vol. 68 (1967), pp. 306–26.

unspecified location away from the company (for example, studying at home). Both of these settings are commonly used for training which involves acquisition of knowledge and/or attitude change.

Skills Training

Skills training may be contrasted with other kinds of training in that it requires some provision for actually performing the task under supervision. Such training may be conducted on the job, in a vestibule school simulating the work environment, in an apprenticeship program, or in a vocational school.

On-the-Job Training. The oldest and simplest approach to training a new employee is to orient him directly on the job under the close supervision of a foreman, a trained instructor, or an experienced operator. Ideally, on-the-job training should involve a systematic program of instruction, supervision, and evaluation of trainee progress. Too often, however, this type of training is conducted unsystematically.

The defects in unsystematic on-the-job training are all too obvious. Although the trainer is a skilled and experienced operator, he may be unable to teach this skill to others. Many husbands, for example, are excellent automobile drivers but are utterly incapable of teaching this skill to their wives.

Furthermore, the skilled employee who is supposed to act as the trainer may perceive the training situation as an opportunity to enjoy a vacation with pay. He may relax, read the paper, socialize with other on-the-job "trainers" while the trainee gains experience. Thus, the learner does not get the close supervision he needs and may require an unduly long period of time to become proficient at the job. He may, in addition, practice improper work habits leading to undue spoilage, and perhaps to unnecessary injury as well as to poor productivity.

Another difficulty sometimes encountered with on-the-job training results from the fact that the employee-trainer may actually resent the presence of the trainee. Such resentment, when it occurs, often reflects insecurity. Skilled employees may, for example, fear displacement by younger men and object to teaching skills and shortcuts developed through years of experience.

The aforementioned criticisms of on-the-job training apply, of course, only to such training at its worst. At its best, when the trainer has been taught how to teach, when he is made to feel secure and needed so that he does not fear displacement, and when he is made to realize the importance of maintaining vigilant supervision, this approach to training can be exceedingly valuable.

Vestibule Training. A vestibule school is a separate room or building within a company that is equipped with production equipment and staffed by full-time instructors. It is an industrial plant in miniature in which trainees learn their jobs under conditions like those found in the working environment except that close supervision by skilled trainers is assured and production pressures are not present.

In spite of the relatively high expense of vestibule training, it offers certain rather distinct advantages. Since the focus in vestibule training is learning rather than production, a greater amount of individualized attention can be given to the trainee's problems than is possible when he is trained on the job. Furthermore, whenever there are several openings, the vestibule school can allow the trainee to try out for various jobs rather than assuming a specific job assignment right from the beginning.

The advantages of vestibule training predicated upon provision of optimal learning conditions are, of course, immediately diminished whenever the vestibule school becomes a repository for obsolete equipment. Whatever economies management may seek to effect in this fashion are countermanded by the consequence that employees are trained to do a job with equipment they will not find in the plant.

Apprenticeship. Apprenticeship training is utilized to prepare journeymen in skilled trade areas requiring relatively prolonged preparation. The period of apprenticeship varies from one to seven years, four years being quite typical.

Modern apprenticeship practices are quite different from the early practice described at the beginning of this chapter. Today's apprentice proceeds through a formal program of training, spending specified periods of time working at various kinds of jobs and taking certain courses. His hours of work are generally the same as those of employees within the department in which he is being trained, and he is paid a salary with provision for a systematic wage increase.

Satisfactory completion of apprenticeship makes the trainee eligible for admission to his trade union. Thus, apprenticeship training programs represent joint efforts of trade unions and industrial organizations to maintain a high level of preparation for certain skilled trades like carpentry and tool and die making.

Outside Training. A good deal of vocational training is given outside of industry in trade and vocational high schools and in colleges and universities. Many schools offer shop training, specific vocational preparation in fields like automotive repair, and courses in clerical skills including typing and shorthand. The danger in such training is that it may tend to emphasize outmoded practices and obsolete equipment. It is an unusual publicly supported school, indeed, which can furnish its vocational shops with the most modern equipment and staff them with personnel familiar with current vocational practices.

Programed Self-Instruction

The armamentarium of training techniques available to an industrial trainer is essentially like that available to any vocational teacher. These include such familiar techniques as lecture, discussion, demonstration, films and television, simulators, and so on. In addition, the training director has available to him such less familiar techniques as programed instruction, sensitivity training, role playing, and case conferences. Since the three latter techniques are especially appropriate to supervisory and management training, their discussion is deferred until Chapter 18. We will consider programed instruction in the remainder of this section.

All *good* instruction, regardless of the manner of presentation, is "programed" in the sense that the material to be taught is organized, sequenced, and presented in steps calculated to maximize learning efficiency. Thus, although widely used as a designation for a particular instructional technique, the term *programed instruction* does not fully convey the other essential components of the technique. These include: (*a*) self-pacing whereby the rate at which the learner masters the material determines the rate at which new material is presented; (*b*) active participation by the learner; and (*c*) immediate feedback to the learner about the correctness or incorrectness of his response. The designation *auto-instructional procedure* is sometimes used interchangeably with "programed instruction." Another frequently used synonym, *teaching machines*, implies that programed instruction entails the use of some sort of hardware. Although in fact it often does, programed material can be presented in other ways including books, films, computers, and sheets of questions. The essence of programed instruction, regardless of how the materials are presented, is the program itself; that is, the sequence and organization of the informational bits contributing to the development of the desired terminal behavior.[17]

Programed self-instruction is not a new concept. The original "teaching machine" was invented in the mid-twenties as an elaboration of a device permitting students to score their own objective tests.[18] The rationale was that this machine would facilitate learning in two ways. First, by scoring his own test and *immediately* learning the right answer, the student learns from the test itself. Second, by including diagnostic self-testing along with other traditional forms of instruction, the student is encouraged to identify for himself those areas requiring further study. Thus, programed self-instruction was originally conceived as a supplement to more traditional teaching procedures. The technique gained few adherents until the mid-fifties when the procedure was elaborated for complete rather than supplemental instruction and given support grounded in reinforcement learning theory.[19]

Programing.   The teaching materials for programed self-instruction are presented in small units or "frames." Each frame presents or reviews a bit of information building upon previously presented frames and requires the learner to respond. Immediately following his response, the learner is given feedback about its correctness or incorrectness.

These qualities are illustrated by the programed segment shown in Figure 8–3. This segment is taken from a programed booklet describing the nature of programed instruction.[20] The frames preceding the ones selected for this illustration introduce the learner to the fundamental notions of stimulus, response, and association. Those following this segment apprise the learner of other elements

---

[17] The interested reader is referred to the following sources for a more complete discussion of programing: A. A. Lumsdaine and R. Glaser (eds.), *Teaching Machines and Programed Learning. A Source Book* (Washington, D.C.: National Educational Association, 1960) ; and J. L. Hughes (ed.), *Programed Learning: A Critical Evaluation* (Chicago: Educational Methods, Inc., 1964).

[18] S. L. Pressey, "A Simple Apparatus Which Gives Tests and Scores—and Teaches," *School and Society*, Vol. 13 (1926), pp. 373–76.

[19] B. F. Skinner, "The Science of Learning and the Art of Teaching," *Harvard Educational Review*, Vol. 24 (1954), pp. 86–97.

[20] O. Milton and L. J. West, *Programed Instruction: What It Is and How It Works* (New York: Harcourt, Brace, & World, Inc., 1961).

of programing: frames structured with small, logical steps; presented at a rate appropriate to each learner; and provision of immediate knowledge of results following an active response by the learner.

The program illustrated in Figure 8–3 is *linear;* that is, each learner proceeds in sequence through every frame. The steps presented in each frame are very small ones calculated to generate a high proportion of correct response and, hence, of positive reinforcement.

FIGURE 8–3

A Segment of a Program concerning Programed Instruction

Instructions: Read each frame carefully and fill in the blank(s). Verify the accuracy of your response against the answers provided in parentheses.

13. One important condition for effective learning is suggested by the phrase "learning by doing." The learner should not be passive. Instead, he should make an active _____ to each stimulus.   (Response)

14. The piano student does not learn a new "piece" just by silently reading the music; he plays it. He makes active responses to the printed notes which serve as _____.   (Stimuli)

15. Few of us are aware, however, that in *all* learning—not just in physical skills—it is preferable that the learner not be passive. On the contrary, he should make _____ responses to _____.   (Active; Stimuli)

16. Much of instruction consists of a teacher talking and students (sometimes!) listening. Stimuli are presented, but active _____ are not made to them.   (Responses)

17. Textbooks resemble lectures in that, although they present _____, readers rarely make _____ responses to them.   (Stimuli; Active)

18. Contrast the steps or statements you are reading here with those in an ordinary textbook. Here you not only read; you also fill in blanks. This is to insure that your responses are _____ ones.   (Active)

In contrast, a *branched* (or "intrinsic") program provides remedial material when the learner responds to a frame incorrectly. These remedial frames may differ depending upon the type of error made by the respondent.[21]

Research on Programed Instruction. The evidence concerning the relative effectiveness of programed instruction in comparison with other training methods is equivocal. Savings in training time (and hence in cost) have, for example, been reported when programed instruction was substituted for the original training pro-

---

[21] N. A. Crowder, "Automatic Tutoring by Means of Intrinsic Programing," in Lumsdaine and Glaser (eds.) , *op. cit.*

gram for mail-order employees and telephone relay adjustors.[22] However, programed instruction was not found to be superior to conventional lecture-discussion instruction for teaching statistics to clerical employees. In fact, in the latter study, a retention test six months after training showed the smallest loss of information by the conventionally taught trainees.[23] Similarly, a programed text was not found to be superior to a traditional text for teaching insurance fundamentals.[24]

The issue of the superiority of linear versus branched programs is also not resolved.[25] Here, as with other issues related to educational procedure, there is unlikely ever to be clear-cut evidence favoring one over the other under all circumstances. Research on this matter must take into account the nature of the material to be taught, the terminal behavior desired, and pertinent learner characteristics.

Although, as discussed in the ensuing section on "evaluating training outcomes and procedures," the assessment of any training method poses difficult problems, programed self-instruction does seem to have unique strengths for certain purposes. Since it is individually paced, it may be more efficient than instruction geared to the "average" learner. And since programing by its very nature compels close attention to training objectives and the sequencing of information, well-designed programed materials are likely to be well organized and free from extraneous details.

However, programed self-instruction is not a panacea either for training or education. The development and pretesting of effective programs is costly. Whether or not the gain in training economy (when there is one) warrants the cost must be assessed in each instance. Furthermore, since the program is self-contained, it must provide a complete learning experience.

The sensible alternative to an all-inclusive, self-contained program is to combine programed instruction with other procedures permitting the learner to obtain whatever clarification he needs.

[22] A. E. Hickey, "Programed Instruction in Business and Industry," in S. Margulies and L. D. Eigen (eds.), *Applied Programed Instruction* (New York: John Wiley & Sons, Inc., 1961).

[23] M. H. Goldberg and R. I. Dawson, "Comparisons of Programed and Conventional Instruction Methods," *Journal of Applied Psychology*, Vol. 48 (1964), pp. 110–14.

[24] R. Hedberg, H. Steffan, and B. Baxter, "Insurance Fundamentals—A Programed Text versus a Conventional Text," *Personnel Psychology*, Vol. 18 (1965), pp. 165–71.

[25] R. J. Senter, A. Neibert, J. S. Abma, and R. L. Morgan, "An Evaluation of Branching and Motivational Phrases in a Scrambled Book," *Technical Document Rep. No. AMRL–TRD–63–122*, 6570 Aerospace Medical Research Laboratories, Wright-Patterson A.F.B., Ohio, November, 1963.

Otherwise, the necessity for comprehensiveness in structuring the program tends to lead to undue repetitiveness and miniscule incre- ments of information from frame to frame. A consequent decline in motivation when the program is a lengthy one is almost inevitable.

EVALUATING TRAINING OUTCOMES AND PROCEDURES

The evaluation of a training program rests in large measure upon the adequacy of the criteria of training effectiveness. Lawshe[26] has listed a number of such criteria, including:

1. The number of man-hours per unit of product.
2. The amount of time required to bring a new employee up to a specified quantity or quality performance level.
3. The average production per unit of time after a specified number of hours or days on the job.
4. The average production performance of employees with vary- ing amounts of training when length of the training period is not standardized.
5. The number of employees required to do a job or to produce a specified number of units.
6. The average straight time hourly earnings when piecework or a bonus plan is in use.
7. The average amount of merit increase received after a specific period of time on the job.
8. The average merit rating score.
9. The average quantity or value of scrap produced.
10. The average number of "reworks."
11. The accident frequency rate.
12. The number of man-hours of lost time from accidents.
13. The number of hospital visitations.

The assessment of training programs is often facilitated by sup- plementing these kinds of criterion data with information about the course of learning during the training period. Such information is made accessible by plotting learning curves.

Learning Curve Analysis

A learning curve is a graph showing the relationship between amount of practice and level of performance. The amount of prac-

---

[26] C. H. Lawshe, Jr., "Training Operative Personnel," *Journal of Consulting Psy- chology*, Vol. 8 (1944), pp. 154–59.

tice may be expressed in terms of the number of hours of training received, the number of training periods completed, or the length of time on the job. Performance may be measured in terms of criteria like those cited by Lawshe.

A classic study involving learning curve analysis was the one performed in 1899 by Bryan and Harter upon telegraphic transmission and reception.[27] The number of letters which could be sent and received in a one-minute period by apprentice telegraphic operators was determined at weekly intervals. The learning curves for one of the operators is shown in Figure 8–4.

FIGURE 8–4

Learning Curves for Sending and Receiving Telegraphic Code

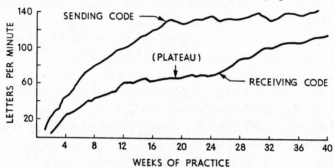

Several of the features apparent in these learning curves are of particular interest. It was obviously easier for this subject to learn to send code than to receive it. He reached an acceptable level of performance for sending much earlier than he did for receiving. Secondly, both curves indicate that learning proceeded more rapidly during the initial training periods than during the subsequent periods. This is characteristic of most but not all industrial training. Thirdly, the curves are jagged rather than smoothly contoured. Minor recessions and advances are always found in learning curves plotted for individual performance. Finally, a period of virtual lack of progress (*plateau*) is indicated on the curve for receiving. Plateaus do not occur in every learning curve, but when they do appear they are worthy of study. The temporary cessation of progress may

[27] W. L. Bryan and N. Harter, "Studies in the Telegraphic Language," *Psychological Review*, Vol. 6 (1899), pp. 346–76.

be attributable to diminished motivation, fatigue, or the necessity for integrating previously learned habits.

Thus, the learning curve is a visual display of the effects of training upon performance at every point in the training sequence. Learning curves may be plotted for groups of trainees as well as for individuals. The points to be plotted for group curves would be determined by averaging the performance at every trial in the training sequence. Such curves may then be compared for various kinds

FIGURE 8–5

Performance Curves of Trained and Untrained Cork Sorters

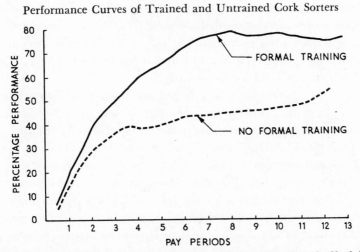

Source: W. R. Mahler and W. H. Monroe, *How Industry Determines the Need for and Effectiveness of Training;* Contract Research Report to Personnel Research Section, Adjutant General's Office, Department of the Army (New York: The Psychological Corp., 1952), p. 77.

of training (for example, on-the-job training versus vestibule training), various instructors, various training methods (for example; lecture versus demonstration versus practice), and various kinds of incentives. Figure 8–5 shows learning curves plotted for two groups of cork sorters. One of these groups had been formally trained, while the other had received no formal training.

Procedural Comparisons

The time-honored research design for investigating the relative effectiveness of alternative training procedures (for example, classroom versus programed instruction) is to compare post-training criterion scores for groups trained by each of the procedures under consideration. The overwhelming finding following this design, both for assessing formal educational procedures and industrial training procedures, is that of "no significant difference"; that is, groups of learners do about as well regardless of how they are taught.

However, it has been suggested that this finding is frequently an artifact of an inappropriate research design which fails to take into account the interactions between the instructional procedure and other pertinent elements of the teaching-learning configuration.[28]

Clearly, one such element is the learner. The finding that mean criterion scores are not significantly different for two groups trained in two different ways may mask the fact that procedure A is actually superior for learner type X and inferior for learner type Y, whereas the converse may hold for procedure B.

When this rationale was applied to learners differentiated by level of academic ability, for example, it was discovered that the conditions facilitating learning were quite different for "low-ability" and "high-ability" undergraduate students. The facilitating learning environment for *low-ability* students was the one that reduced their perception of the likelihood of failure and directed their attention to the material to be learned. Their performance was adversely affected by circumstances increasing their perception of the likelihood of failure and/or directing their attention away from the content to be learned. The facilitating learning environment for *high-ability* students was one providing an intellectual challenge appropriate to their level of ability. Again, the converse of this condition (that is, a perception that the material was too easy) adversely affected performance by high-ability students.

The implications of generalizations like the foregoing for training are relatively clear. Linear programing with small steps and considerable repetition is likely to be more appropriate for low- than for high-ability trainees. Likewise, classroom instruction to large groups wherein the students are relatively anonymous and therefore free from the likelihood of educational threat (for example, televised instruction) is more likely to satisfy the needs of low- than high-ability learners.

The implication of this emphasis upon studying interactions be-

---

[28] Siegel and Siegel, *op. cit.*

tween features of the training procedure and other aspects of the teaching-learning complex rather than making control-group comparisons is also clear. It is relatively inappropriate to inquire whether one training procedure is "as good as" or "better than" another. The more significant question requires much more specificity; that is, for what kinds of learners, under what kinds of conditions, and for the attainment of what objectives does a given training procedure optimize learning?

Such a question recognizes the idiosyncratic nature of learning. When properly answered, it will lead to one of two alternatives. First, it can specify a very carefully designed program for selecting trainees who are sufficiently homogeneous with respect to the critical learner characteristics required by the training procedure in use. Alternatively, if such selection is infeasible, it must lead to the development of multiple parallel training programs each calculated to optimize training outcomes for homogeneous subgroups of trainees.

TRAINING THE TRAINER

The success or failure of a training program depends in large measure upon the quality of instruction given to the trainees. A criticism, mentioned earlier, of many training programs is that they are founded upon the erroneous premise that men who know how to do a job are automatically qualified to teach others how to do it.

The value of training the trainer is illustrated by a study conducted by Bavelas.[29] Learning curves were plotted for three groups of trainees, all taught by the same instructor. At the time he trained the first group, the instructor had received no training in teaching methods; he had received partial instructor training in the second group; and in the third, he had completed the training program. The extent of instructor training is reflected in the performance of the trainees being taught by him as shown in Figure 8–6.

Granting the necessity for training the trainer, there remains the fundamental question of who should conduct the training of line personnel.

---

[29] A. Bavelas in N. R. F. Maier, *Psychology in Industry* (Boston: Houghton Mifflin Co., 1946), p. 227.

FIGURE 8–6

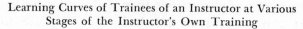

Learning Curves of Trainees of an Instructor at Various
Stages of the Instructor's Own Training

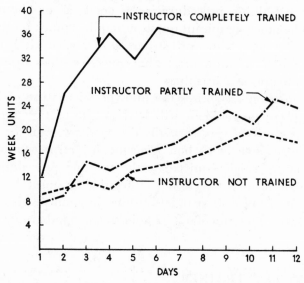

Who Should Train?

Industrial training may be regarded either as a line function or as a staff function. In the former instance, the employees are trained by their immediate supervisor. In the latter, training is administered either by a separate training department or by an outside consultant.

Although there may be certain circumstances in which training must be administered by the training department or by an outside consultant, this type of administrative arrangement is less satisfactory than is training by immediate supervisors and foremen. The danger inherent in classifying training as a staff function is that this arrangement may lead to behavioral change in the classroom but not in the working environment. The trainee learns to give the correct responses in the presence of the "expert" but does not transfer these responses to the job itself.

The immediate supervisor is in the final analysis the person who determines how employees will behave. He enforces certain standards of satisfactory performance and is most immediately responsible for the employee's success and job satisfaction. He is, in consequence, the most appropriate trainer.

The desirability of having the supervisor conduct training for his immediate subordinates is evident throughout the entire organizational framework. This kind of arrangement does, however, become increasingly difficult to implement as we progress up the management hierarchy. It may be difficult to convince busy executives of the necessity for their active participation in training their immediate subordinates.

Where does the staff training expert or industrial training department fit into the picture if training is to be given at each supervisory level to the immediately subordinate level? The staff training department performs two vital and related functions. First, it is responsible for training the trainers. Secondly, the training department consults with the persons doing the training in order to develop, evaluate, and improve the quality of ongoing training programs.

SUMMARY

Training objectives follow logically from a systematic determination of training needs. These objectives, in turn, suggest the ways in which training will be conducted, the persons who will be trained, and a scheme for evaluating the effectiveness of the program.

A properly conceived training program permeates all levels of an industrial organization. The need for management and supervisory development programs has been increasingly recognized in recent years.

Successful training programs are predicated upon certain basic psychological principles of learning. The most important of these principles is that a person learns only when he *wants* to learn. Motivation for learning requires that the trainee understand the reasons for training requirements, be provided with knowledge about his progress during the program, and be permitted to achieve short-term intermediate subgoals.

Motivation is enhanced also by the proper decomposition of a task into its meaningful parts for training purposes, the presentation of these parts in an appropriate sequence, and by training sessions that are of optimal length. These matters require that research be conducted in each instance to define the parts to be taught, the sequence in which these parts are to be presented, and the most appropriate spacing of training sessions.

In addition to providing for trainee motivation, the program must include provisions for selecting trainees. Marked differences exist in the ability of individuals to profit from industrial training.

Finally, skills training is sterile unless it contains the element of closely supervised practice. The reason for requiring very careful supervision during this phase of the program is that improper or inappropriate behaviors which are practiced may be learned quite as efficiently as correct behaviors. Mistakes must therefore be corrected as soon as they occur.

The training program must be internally constituted and sequenced to encourage positive transfer both within the program itself and from the program to actual job performance.

In many ways, industrial training is similar to other kinds of formal education. Neither should be permitted to evolve by happenstance. Both must be carefully designed most efficiently to implement the learner's attainment of the desired goals. This means that training programs must take into account the terminal behavior desired, the characteristics of trainees admissable to the program, and the interdependence of work roles within the entire system.

Training may be conducted in any number of sites including, in addition to the classroom and home study, training on the job and in a vestibule school. Likewise, the instructional procedures for training are diverse including lectures, discussions, demonstrations, simulation, and so on.

One technique that has gained recent attention is programed instruction characterized by self-pacing, active learner participation, and immediate reinforcement. Programed instruction is not a panacea either for education or training. The evidence concerning its effectiveness is conflictual. Furthermore, the cost of program development may mitigate against its use except when relatively large numbers of persons are to be trained.

In addition to various kinds of tests and ratings, evaluation of training outcomes may require an analysis of learning curves. Such curves are graphs showing the relationship between amount of practice and level of performance. Learning curves may be plotted for individual trainees or for groups of trainees. They are diagnostic aids in the sense that they provide a visual display of the effects of training upon performance at every point in the training sequence.

The evaluation of alternative training procedures has generally not been fruitful. The typical research finding is that learners profit about equally irrespective of the instructional procedure. This chapter suggests that such findings may be artifactual, resulting from the application of an inappropriate research design to an inappropriate question. It suggests further that such evaluations are most meaningful when they delineate those interactions between learners, instructional conditions, and training objectives that optimize learning.

Retraining has become an increasingly important social problem. The evidence thus far available points to the greater importance of attitude over ability as a determinant of acceptance of new work roles and retraining programs.

A key feature of any training program, regardless of its nature, is the trainer himself. He must be capable of teaching his knowledges and skills to the trainee and be willing to do so. Many training programs are open to criticism because they are founded on the erroneous premise that men who know how to do a job are automatically qualified by virtue of this knowledge to teach others how to do it. Nothing could be farther from the truth. It requires the possession of skill as a trainer to be an effective teacher.

However, this does not imply that industrial training should be conducted only by training specialists; that is, consultants or the staff training department. The immediate supervisor is in the final analysis the person who determines how employees will behave. He enforces performance standards and is most immediately responsible for the employee's success and job satisfaction. He is, in consequence, the most appropriate trainer. The role of the staff training department is to teach the supervisor how to train and to consult with supervisors in order to develop, evaluate, and improve the quality of ongoing training programs.

9. Performance Rating

Performance rating is a special case of performance appraisal. It is distinguished from other forms of appraisal by its subjectivity. Why should we be interested in a subjectively derived criterion when the preceding chapters have referred frequently to such objective indicators of worker efficiency as output, spoilage, absenteeism, turnover, and accident rate? The point was made in Chapter 4, concerning criteria, that objective indices of proficiency sometimes are unobtainable or insufficient. There are some jobs for which it is impossible to count units of production or for which the units when counted reveal relatively little about job performance. In such instances the assessment of performance must rest upon some kind of subjectively made estimate of employee proficiency. These opinions may be rendered by supervisors, managers, or co-workers, and take the form of some kind of rating. Such ratings order employees along subjective continua of overall performance or of selected aspects of overall performance. When the results of a performance rating are properly interpreted to and discussed with the employee, he can be materially aided in improving his performance.

The element of subjectivity is at once the peculiar weakness and strength of rating techniques. Rating procedures tend to be much less reliable than psychological tests or objective performance criteria. Thus, if a supervisor wished to obtain a meaningful index of efficiency for factory assemblers, he might do better to utilize an output measure involving a count of production per unit of time adjusted for spoilage than to trust his personal opinion about employee efficiency.

There are circumstances, however, when a reliable criterion measure is not available. The decision must be made in such instances either to measure with a relatively subjective device or to forego measurement entirely. What can the office supervisor count, for example, when she wishes to appraise the overall efficiency of a statistical clerk in her section? Similarly, what objective measures can be applied to assessing the efficiency of office receptionists or Army officers? The diversity and nature of tasks performed by such workers prevents their assessment by objective indicators. Rating procedures must of necessity be used to provide assessments of performance.

USES OF PERFORMANCE APPRAISAL

In order to place performance ratings in context, it is helpful at the outset to consider the range of applications of performance appraisal in general—both objective and subjective. The necessity for multiple approaches to assessing job proficiency is evident for all of these applications in order to obtain the best possible picture of the employee's performance. Given a choice between a more objective and a more subjective form of appraisal, the former will, of course, be selected on the grounds of superior reliability and validity.

Wages

Since it is generally assumed that efficiency ought to be rewarded financially, performance appraisal may be used as a partial determinant of wages. This use of performance appraisal supplements, but does not vitiate, periodic wage increments based upon such things as seniority or changes in the cost-of-living index. Most employees want to feel that their own personal efforts are recognized and rewarded by management. A lockstep wage system in which all employees on a particular job or in a particular level are paid essentially the same wage reduces individual initiative.

Promotions

The identification of employees who ought to be advanced to a supervisory position or to a higher job classification is a management problem of considerable significance. Union contracts often specify consideration of seniority as a criterion for promotion. However, prolonged experience does not by itself guarantee the employee's readiness for a more responsible position. The most experienced welder in the world may be totally unqualified for promotion to a position in which he is required to direct the activities of other welders.

Most union contracts recognize this fact and specify that seniority should be the deciding factor in promotion only when such things as skill and the job proficiency of the eligible employees are equal. Performance appraisal can be helpful in deciding whether the applicants for promotion are equally qualified on grounds other than seniority. Where this appraisal takes the form of ratings, it must where appropriate be supplemented by consideration of factors like ability as measured by psychological tests, age, physical health, and formal education.

Layoffs

The use of information from performance appraisal during periods when personnel must be dismissed, either temporarily or permanently, parallels its use for employee promotions. If the labor force must be reduced, management benefits most by retaining only those employees who have demonstrated a satisfactory level of proficiency. Although seniority must be considered during layoffs, some union contracts recognize management's prerogative to weight skill and ability more heavily than mere tenure on the job.

Employee Transfer

Management has two alternatives in the case of dissatisfied or inefficient personnel. Such employees may either be dismissed or transferred to another job within the organization. If a transfer is to be effective, the employee must be moved to a job which is more congruent with his abilities and hence more conducive to job satisfaction. Performance appraisal may reveal certain of the worker's strengths that can be utilized more effectively in another position within the company.

Employee transfers sometimes are necessitated by the creation of new positions within the company or by the development of critical vacancies on other jobs or in other departments. Screening by management of all employees in a given grade or classification may be desirable under these circumstances in order to identify persons who have the requisite skills and abilities to fill these positions. Performance appraisal can help management match present personnel with positions requiring transferees.

Knowledge of Progress

Most of us are interested in knowing how our supervisor appraises our performance. A student, for example, is understandably distressed if he attends an entire course believing that he is doing satisfactory work only to learn after the final examination that he has failed the course. Similarly, employees cannot be expected to perform at maximum efficiency and high plant morale cannot be maintained unless the workers are systematically informed about their supervisors' opinions. In the absence of knowledge of progress or standing, the employees may feel considerable tension disruptive of industrial efficiency. The fact that performance is appraised and the results discussed with individual employees can do much to quell unfounded rumors of dismissal or transfer. Furthermore, a wisely conducted systematic program of employee appraisal injects the very important element of personal recognition into the industrial situation.

Diagnostic Applications

The use of performance appraisal for diagnostic purposes is closely related to its use for informing workers about their supervisors' perceptions of them. The company stands to benefit whenever an employee is made aware of his own particular strengths and weaknesses in a constructive manner. Tactful criticism can alert the employee to previously unrecognized deficiencies. Unfortunately it is very difficult to implement this particular use of performance appraisal. When feedback about performance is attempted, its value depends upon the supervisor's skill and understanding.

In-Service Training

Extending the type of diagnostic application mentioned above, performance appraisal may reveal deficiencies of skill, knowledge, or attitude which can be remedied by providing the employee with additional training. Furthermore, when ratings or other performance measures are collated for an entire unit, section, or department, the summary may occasionally reveal a rather prevalent area of employee deficiency. Entire groups of workers responsible for handling small and delicate subassemblies, for example, may receive low ratings on such an important characteristic as *carefulness*. In this instance, the prevalence of low ratings might suggest modifications in the training program for such employees. Thus, it may be advisable to institute a program of in-service training concerning the extent, type, and consequences of damage caused by improper handling of the subassemblies. The training program for newly hired employees would, of course, also have to be bolstered in this regard.

Validation Criteria

You will recall that validation is the most critical phase in the construction of tests or batteries for personnel selection and placement. Management must have adequate assurance that its selection procedures do in reality lead to the rejection of applicants for whom the probability of unsuccessful job performance is high.

The usual procedure in validating a test is to try it out on the present group of employees and to compare the test performance with some criterion of employee efficiency. A better procedure requires the administration of the test to applicants, all of whom are hired, and the correlation of test scores with a criterion measure subsequently obtained.

In either case, the validation procedure rests upon the availability of some criterion of employee efficiency.

PRELIMINARY PLANNING

Regardless of its objectives, a rating program cannot be instituted within a company without considerable preliminary planning. Decisions must be made about who is to rate and be rated, what traits to evaluate, when and how often ratings will be made, and the procedures for making the ratings and feeding back the results to the ratees.

Many employees and employee organizations are strenuously opposed to rating, particularly when used for the purposes of wage and promotional determination. Hence, preliminary decisions about the mechanics of a rating program must be accompanied by a concerted effort to "sell" the program, both to the prospective ratees and raters. The specific way in which the program is sold will vary with the particular situation encountered in a given company. As generalizations, the following points have been suggested as helpful:

1. Merit ratings should be sold first at the top levels of supervision. The lower supervisory levels, comprised of the majority of raters, should be approached only after the top levels have endorsed the program.
2. The raters ought to be involved as early as possible in developing the rating procedure. Such participation encourages identification with the program and its success.
3. Delegations of raters might be sent to other companies to investigate their rating programs and report back to a meeting of all supervisors.
4. The program should not be started prematurely: that is, until the groundwork has been properly laid.[1]

RATING PROCEDURES

All of us constantly evaluate the persons with whom we come in contact. We form first impressions often based upon physical appearance, dress, personal mannerisms, and speech. Subsequent contacts may either reinforce our original impression or cause us to change it. In any event, we continually appraise others and are in turn ourselves appraised in a highly subjective and uncontrolled fashion.

Figure 9–1 shows a "horrible" but historically interesting example of unsystematic efficiency rating. It is difficult to ascertain the bases that were used by General Cass in forming his judgments, but it is apparent that he was responding to certain factors extraneous to "efficiency."

Fortunately, we have come a considerable distance in the application of rating procedures during the past 150 years. Rather than permitting the rater to use his own idiosyncratic standards of judgment, the present application of performance rating attempts to impose a degree of uniformity on these standards. To the extent that

---

[1] R. Bittner, "Developing an Employee Merit Rating Procedure," *Personnel Psychology,* Vol. 1 (1948) , pp. 403–32.

FIGURE 9–1

The First Recorded Efficiency Report in the Files of the War Department

```
                                                           Lower Senaca Town
        Sir:                                               August 15, 1813

               I forward a list of the officers of the 27th Regt. of Infty. arranged agreeably to rank.  An-
        nexed thereto you will find all the observations I deem necessary to make.

                                                      Respectfully,
                                                      I am, Sir,
                                                      Yo. Obt. Servt.

                                                      Lewis Cass
                                                      Brig. Gen.


                                    *******************

                                     27th Infantry Regiment
```

Name	Rank	Observation
Alex Denniston	- Lieut. Col., Comdg.	- A good natured man.
Clarkson Crolins	- First Major	- a good man, but no officer.
Jesse D. Wadsworth	- 2nd Major	- an excellent officer.
Captain Christian Martel) " Aaron T. Crane) " Benj. Wood) " Maxwell)		- all good officers.
" Shotwell		- a man of whom all unite in speaking ill. a knave despised by all.
" Allen Reynolds		- An officer of capacity, but imprudent and a man of most violent passions.
" Danl. Warren Porter		- Stranger but little known in the regiment.
First Lieut. Jas. Kerr) " " Thos. Darling)		- Merely good, nothing promising.
" " Wm. Perrin) " " Danl. Scott) " " Jas. I. Ryan) " " Robt. McElwrath)		- Low vulgar men, with exception of Perrin, Irish and from the meanest walks of life -- Possessing nothing of character of officers or gentlemen.
" " Robt P. Ross		- Willing enough - has much to learn -- with small capacity.
" " Hall		- Not joined the regiment.
2nd Lieut. Nicholas G. Carner		- a good officer but drinks hard and disgraces himself and the service.
" " Stewart Elder		- An ignorant unoffending irishman.
" " McConkey		- Raised from the ranks, ignorant, vulgar and incompetent.

rating procedures are successful in accomplishing this end, the rater is provided with a yardstick for appraisal that is appropriate to the particular characteristics he is attempting to describe. In short, effective rating procedures encourage an increased degree of objectivity, reliability, and validity in appraising human behavior.

FIGURE 9–1—*Continued*

2nd Lieut.	Piercy)	- Come from the ranks, but all behave
" "	Jacob J. Brown)	well and promise to make excell
" "	Thos. G. Spicer)	officer
" "	Oliver Vance)	
" "	James Garry	- A stranger in the regiment.
Third Lieut.	Royal Geer)	- All irish, promoted from the ranks.
" "	Mears)	low vulgar men, without any one qualifi-
" "	Clifford)	cation to recommend them, more fit to
" "	Crawford)	carry the hod than the epaulette.
" "	McKeon)	
" "	John G. Scholtz)	- Promoted from the ranks, behave well
" "	Francis T. Wheeler)	and will make good officers.
	Darrow	- Just joined the regiment - of fine appear-
		ance.
Ensign	Behan	- The very dregs of the earth, Unfit for
		anything under heaven. God only knows
		how the poor thing got an appointment.
"	John Brown)	- Promoted from the ranks - men of no
	Bryan)	manner and no promise.
"	Charles West	- From the ranks. a good young man who
		does well.

****

The Ranking Method

The rater using this technique merely orders the ratees from best to worst, generally assigning a rank of 1 to the person he judges to be highest or best, a rank of 2 to the second best, and so on. The method is a simple one and may be applied either by assigning "man-as-a-whole" ratings or "trait" ratings. In the former case, the employee is assigned a rank on the basis of the supervisor's overall impression about his efficiency. Ratings of traits, on the other hand, may require the supervisor to rank his employees on several specific characteristics like "cooperativeness," "initiative," or "versatility." Such trait ratings are sometimes averaged to yield a composite index of the supervisor's opinions.

Appraisal of the Ranking Method. The ranking method is susceptible to two deficiencies that may have deleterious effects upon the validity of the resultant information: (1) the hair splitting necessitated by differentiating between adjacent ranks in the middle of the continuum and (2) the fallacious appearance of equal intervals along a scale of ranks. Thus, if 50 employees are to be ranked, the supervisor very likely will experience difficulty in differentiating between the one who should be ranked 23 and the one who should be ranked 24. Furthermore, it is unlikely that the magnitude of the difference between employees ranked 2 and 3 is of the same order as the difference between the employees ranked 26 and 27, even though only one rank separates each of these pairs.

Certain procedures for minimizing these deficiencies have been suggested. It often is desirable, for instance, to differentiate ranks only for persons in the upper and lower quarter of the total group, assigning a common middle rank to the remaining 50 percent of the group. This modification of the ranking procedure obviates the necessity for making impossibly fine discriminations between persons in the middle of the range.

It should be apparent, however, that the ranking method is a crude one. Its usefulness is limited to situations in which relatively few employees are to be rated. Furthermore, it is applicable only when rating is intended to order employees from best to worst without providing an indication of *how much* better or worse one employee is than another.

Paired Comparisons Method

This procedure for making and summarizing judgments has numerous psychological applications. Fundamentally, the procedure requires the evaluator to compare two objects or events and to judge which is the heavier, rounder, sharper, louder, and so on. The paired comparisons method has enjoyed extensive use in studies of sensation and perception.

The application of the paired comparisons method to rating leads to a certain degree of systematization in the assignment of ranks to employees.[2] Every employee to be rated is compared with every other employee, and the rater judges which member of the pair is the better. The supervisor generally predicates this judgment upon his overall impression of the employees' efficiency, but the method may be used also in a more analytical fashion by requiring the rater to consider specific traits one at a time.

To illustrate this procedure, let us assume that five employees (designated A, B, C, D, E) are to be rated relative to "overall performance." The supervisor would compare each employee with every other employee and check the name of the member of each pair judged to be superior. The comparisons required and a hypothetical set of judgments are shown below.

A with B✓	✓B with C	✓C with D	D with E✓
A with C✓	✓B with D	C with E✓	
✓A with D	✓B with E		
A with E✓			

It is a rather simple matter to transmute these judgments to ranks for the purpose of summary. In the illustration above, the best worker is judged to be B, the second best is E, and so on. Thus, the resultant rank order for these employees would be B = 1, E = 2, C = 3, A = 4, and D = 5.

Appraisal of the Paired Comparisons Method. The fundamental advantage of this method over the ranking procedure is that it simplifies the kind of judgment required of the rater. Instead of necessitating simultaneous consideration of all members of the group, the paired comparisons method narrows the field for consideration by the supervisor to just two workers at a time.

A very important practical objection to the procedure, however, is that it is quite unwieldy. The number of pairs of employees to be

---

[2] C. H. Lawshe, Jr., N. C. Kephart, and E. J. McCormick, "The Paired Comparisons Technique for Rating Performance of Industrial Employees," *Journal of Applied Psychology*, Vol. 33 (1949) , pp. 69–77.

considered is given by the general formula N $(N - 1)$ $/2$, where N is the number of workers included in the evaluation. Thus, if a supervisor applies the paired comparisons method to 20 employees, he must make 20 (19) $/2$ or 190 comparisons. It is not surprising that the use of this procedure is generally limited to assignment of man-as-a-whole ratings rather than analytical or trait ratings. The latter application in a 20-man department would, of course, require the supervisor to make 190 comparisons for each of the several traits or dimensions of behavior being appraised.

Man-to-Man Rating

Although this procedure is no longer used very extensively, it is of interest both from an historical standpoint and because it further clarifies some of the difficulties experienced in attempts to objectify merit ratings.

With man-to-man ratings, subjective judgments are recorded on a scale consisting of something like equal units. In this respect the procedure is superior to techniques converting judgments to ranks. Unfortunately, however, the man-to-man rating method has some unique deficiencies of its own that diminish its value considerably.

The procedure can be easily illustrated by assuming that you are required for some reason to evaluate the teaching effectiveness of each of your present instructors. Once general agreement is reached on a definition of "teaching effectiveness," you would proceed to establish and differentiate between several levels (generally five) of teaching effectiveness. These levels might be identified as follows:

1. The very best college teacher you have ever known.
2. A good college teacher.
3. An average or run-of-the-mill college teacher.
4. A poor college teacher.
5. The worst college teacher you have ever known.

Next to each of these descriptive levels, write in the name of a particular teacher. In doing this, you are to draw from the entire pool of college teachers you have known, selecting one as typical of each level. The five names you have written constitute a kind of master scale which can serve as a yardstick for evaluating the teachers you have during the present term. You need simply compare each of the teachers you are rating with the five teachers in your master scale, and decide where on the master scale he fits. You can assign the ratee the corresponding classification level (1, 2, 3, 4, 5), or you can convert these levels to points (for example, 15 points for level 1, 12 points for level 2, and so on). In any event, the master scale provides you with a standard for ordering your present teachers along a continuum of effectiveness.

The procedure, as we have illustrated it, involved an overall efficiency rating. It would, however, be perfectly possible to use the method in similar fashion to provide ratings of particular traits or specific characteristics. One of the earliest applications of man-to-man rating, for example, required that U.S. Army officers and prospective officers be rated separately in this manner on physical qualities, intelligence, leadership, personal qualities, and general value to the service. A composite rating was derived by adding the weights received by a particular ratee for each of these five characteristics.[3]

Appraisal of Man-to-Man Rating. The primary objection to this procedure is that although the scheme helps to objectify supervisory judgments, it does so in a way that prevents comparisons between the ratings assigned by different raters. To clarify this point, let us return to the earlier illustration in which you were rating college teachers. If you compare the master scale that you developed with the master scales developed by any of your classmates, you will undoubtedly find some startling discrepancies. The teacher that you have named as typical of level 2 of your master scale, for example, may not appear at all on your classmate's scale; or if he does appear, he may have been cited as typifying a level either above or below level 2. Since the master scales from which various raters operate are not comparable, the resultant ratings cannot be collated.

The reasons for the lack of uniformity in the master scales constructed by different raters are simple to comprehend. First, every rater has his own unique perception of what constitutes a high, intermediate, or low level of almost any kind of human behavior. These differential perceptions may lead him to interpret the definitions of the various levels for the master scale differently from the interpretations made by some other rater.

Secondly, all raters do not share a common base of experience from which to identify persons for inclusion in their master scale.

---

[3] Committee on Classification of Personnel, Adjutant General's Department, *Personnel Manual* (Washington, D.C.: U.S. Government Printing Office, 1919).

Just as you have received instruction from a different set of teachers than any of your classmates, industrial supervisors have each been exposed to different sets of workers. This experiential factor causes some supervisors to be acquainted with workers who are either markedly superior or inferior to those known by other supervisors. As a result, the master scales constructed by different supervisors may differ considerably in the amount of "top" or "bottom" contained in them.

Graphic Rating Scales

This approach to merit rating is very widely used in one form or another. The procedure for constructing graphic rating scales requires that levels or degrees of trait possession be established and defined as unambiguously as possible.

There are so many variations of this procedure now in use that it is possible only to indicate something of the diversity of graphic formats. These formats can be conveniently grouped into two classes: continuous scales and discontinuous scales. *Continuous scales* require the supervisor to inspect a rating continuum and to indicate his evaluation of the employee by making a mark somewhere along that continuum. *Discontinuous scales* require the rater to consider only selected points on the rating continuum. A few illustrations of each type of format are shown in Table 9–1.

Appraisal of Graphic Rating. All rating procedures, including graphic scales, have certain deficiencies. In spite of these deficiencies, the graphic scale approach to rating has much to recommend it. Its use entails consideration of scale units that can be made more or less comparable across raters if the supervisors are adequately trained. Furthermore, graphic rating scales are easily understood by all persons within the company.

A major source of unreliability in graphic ratings is halo effect. This, you will recall, is the tendency for a ratee to receive consistently high or low ratings as a result of generalization by the rater.

This phenomenon operates in many kinds of situations requiring subjective appraisal. We have already discussed its potential influence during job interviews (Chapter 5) and grading of subjective examinations (Chapter 6). Halo effects may operate in any kind of rating scheme including, but not limited to, graphic procedures. Hence, we will reserve a more extensive discussion of this source of

TABLE 9–1

Illustrative Formats for Graphic Scales Requiring Ratings of "Dependability"

Instructions to the rater: Consider the manner and extent to which the employee is "dependable," using the definition given below, and place a check mark indicating your opinion at the appropriate point (or in the appropriate box) of the scale.

Dependability is evidenced by the following behaviors: (1) follows instructions, (2) completes job on time, (3) is punctual and regular in attendance, (4) does not require excessive supervision.

Illustrative Continuous Scales

```
 |---------|---------|
 0         5         10

 |---------|---------|
 A         F         K

 |              |              |
Extremely     About        Extremely
Dependable    Average      Undependable
```

Illustrative Discontinuous Scales

In the highest 10% of workers.	In the next 20% of workers.	In the middle 40% of workers.	In the next 20% of workers.	In the lowest 10% of workers.
□	□	□	□	□

Exceedingly dependable; follows instructions with only minimal supervision.	Generally dependable but sometimes needs supervision.	About average.	Usually undependable. Needs more than average supervision.	Exceedingly undependable, requires continual supervision.

unreliability for a later section in which we will consider the short-comings of merit rating procedures in general.

The Weighted Checklist

It has been suggested that the Thurstone scaling procedure for measuring attitudes can be adapted to provide a scheme for rating.[4] This scaling procedure assigns differential weights to statements of opinion. The respondent's attitude is converted to a numerical value by averaging or summing the weights of the statements with which he agrees.[5]

The procedure for deriving weights requires that a large number of statements describing work behavior be prepared and submitted to "expert" judges. Illustrative statements used in one such study for rating bake shop managers included: "he seldom forgets what he has once been told"; "his weekly and monthly reports are sometimes inaccurate"; "he often has vermin and insects in his shop."[6]

Each judge independently places every statement somewhere along a continuum (usually of 7, 9, or 11 categories) ranging from extremely desirable (or favorable) behavior to extremely undesirable (or unfavorable) behavior. The summarized pattern of judgments permits identification and rejection of those statements which are "ambiguous"; that is, yielding considerable variability in the distribution of judgments indicating that the judges failed to agree on the relative desirability or undesirability of the behavior described in the statement.

The remaining statements are assigned weights reflecting the "average" judgment of their positions on the desirability-undesirability scale. The statement's weight may be the median of the distribution of judgments assigned to it, or some transformation of this value.

After the appropriate weights for relatively unambiguous statements are calculated, the statements are arranged as a checklist. The rater, of course, sees only the statements; he is not informed of the weights to be used in scoring. The rater is instructed merely to check

---

[4] M. W. Richardson and G. F. Kuder, "Making a Rating Scale That Measures," *Personal Journal*, Vol. 12 (1933), pp. 36–40.

[5] L. L. Thurstone and E. J. Chave, *The Measurement of Attitude* (Chicago: University of Chicago Press, 1929).

[6] E. B. Knauft, "Construction and Use of Weighted Check-List Rating Scales for Two Industrial Situations," *Journal of Applied Psychology*, Vol. 32 (1948), pp. 63–70.

those statements most descriptive of the employee's behavior. The weighted checklist is scored by summing or averaging the weights of the checked statements.

A checklist was developed using this procedure, for example, to rate salesmen. The scale underlying the assignment of weights to each descriptive statement was based upon a seven-point continuum ranging from "extremely undesirable" at 1 to "extremely desirable" at 7. A few of the items included in this checklist are reproduced below. The weights in parentheses are median values with the decimal eliminated for convenience.

Is weak on planning (29)
Is a good worker (46)
Is making exceptional progress (69) [7]

More recently, a comprehensive set of 2,000 statements concerning worker behavior has been scaled in this fashion.[8] It is possible from these 2,000 items to select a number at various points on the judgmental continuum and appropriate to many different kinds of jobs.

Forced-Choice Ratings

This procedure evolved in the main from research conducted for the military services during World War II. The forced-choice procedure was specifically designed to overcome a major deficiency inherent in all of the other rating techniques; that is, the fact that the rater knows whether he is giving either a high or low rating. This kind of awareness permits the rater to slant his recorded judgment in any direction he chooses. The effects of personal biases and favoritism can be only partly eliminated from rating procedures by a training program for supervisors. The forced-choice procedure is an attempt to increase the objectivity of ratings by preventing the rater from knowing whether he is assigning a favorable or an unfavorable rating.

In its simplest form, a forced-choice format requires the rater to select the one statement from a pair that is either most or least descriptive of the person he is rating. A supervisor might, for exam-

---

[7] Richardson and Kuder, *op. cit.*

[8] R. S. Uhrbrock, "2000 Scaled Items," *Personnel Psychology*, Vol. 14 (1961), pp. 375–420.

ple, be required to select the statement from each of the following pairs that he feels best describes the employee he is rating.

1. *a)* Is punctual.
   b) Is careful.
2. *a)* Hard worker.
   b) Cooperative worker.

Similarly, he may be required to select the least descriptive statements from pairs of undesirable behaviors like the following:

3. *a)* Is dishonest.
   b) Is disloyal.
4. *a)* Is overbearing.
   b) Is disinterested in his work.

Alternative arrangements for forced-choice items may consist of groupings of three or four statements with instructions to the rater to mark the one least descriptive and the one most descriptive statement from each triad or tetrad.

The key to the development of forced-choice scales is that the statements within any item are equally attractive or unattractive but differ in discriminative power. In the preceding illustrations, for example, the two statements constituting each pair are grouped together partly because the results of a preliminary investigation have indicated that these statements have similar *preference values;* that is, raters tend to interpret these behaviors as being about equally desirable or undesirable. A second basis for pairing alternatives is that they have been demonstrated to have different *discriminative power;* that is, only one of the alternatives differentiates between efficient and inefficient employees. Each of the alternatives in a forced-choice scale is weighted in terms of its discriminative power, and the entire rating form can thus be scored by summing the weights of the statements marked by the supervisor.

The supervisor who deliberately attempts to overrate or underrate an employee is likely to find that it is very difficult to display intentional bias on a forced-choice scale. The format compels him to choose between alternatives that look equally attractive or unattractive; the rater does not, of course, know which of the alternatives contribute positively or negatively to the scale score. Thus, in theory at least, it would be quite possible for a supervisor to mark only desirable behaviors for a ratee without assigning a favorable rating to him.

Appraisal of the Forced-Choice Technique. The rationale underlying forced-choice procedures is rather ingenious. The available evidence supports the particular usefulness of this technique for developing personality inventories. Studies conducted by the Personnel Research Section of the Adjutant General's Office indicate also that the application of forced-choice procedures to merit rating tends to reduce halo and bias and to yield improved validity and reliability.[9]

The forced-choice method has been used for rating in many different occupations and professions including highway patrolmen, engineers, teachers, and physicians.[10] Nevertheless, it is not as extensively used in industry as the methods described earlier in this chapter. A primary reason for some reluctance to use this procedure is that the development of forced-choice scales is relatively time consuming and costly.

Raters sometimes express objections to the procedure because it compels them to select a descriptive statement from a limited number of alternatives. The supervisor responding to such a scale sometimes feels that he is being forced to choose between alternatives, none of which are applicable. This kind of objection is a relatively superficial one. It can usually be overcome by care in pairing alternatives and training raters.

It has been suggested that one of the major limitations of forced-choice rating is its failure to provide the kind of information that can be used for diagnostic feedback to the employee.[11] This can be a serious objection to the procedure if the rating is to be used for informing individual employees about their own particular strengths and weaknesses.

Forced-choice rating should not be regarded as a panacea. The primary advantages of the technique involve possible reductions in the influence of rater bias and halo. The operation of these undesirable factors can, however, be reduced also for the more usual and

---

[9] D. E. Baier, "Reply to Travers' 'A Critical Review of the Validity and Rationale of the Forced-Choice Technique,' " *Psychological Bulletin*, Vol. 48 (1951), pp. 421–34.

[10] An excellent summary of research using the forced choice technique has been prepared by A. Zavala, "Development of the Forced-Choice Rating Scale Technique," *Psychological Bulletin*, Vol. 63 (1965), pp. 117–24.

[11] J. A. Patton and C. L. Littlefield, *Job Evaluation* (Homewood, Ill.: Richard D. Irwin, Inc., 1957), p. 306.

less expensive graphic rating procedures. Thus, it is appropriate to consider some of the major sources of unreliability in rating procedures, with particular reference to graphic scales, and some of the steps leading to improved reliability.

SOURCES OF ERROR IN PERFORMANCE RATING

Rating procedures are subjective and hence unreliable by the standards applied to psychological tests. The reliability of a composite rating derived for a 12-item scale completed by different raters, for example, was estimated at 0.55.[12] This value is far different from the reliability coefficients usually required for standardized tests and suggests that different raters really use different subjective yardsticks for appraising human behavior. A fundamental problem, then, in improving rating procedures is to increase the uniformity with which subjective evaluations are made. To the extent that this is accomplished, the agreement between raters (reliability) will be increased and the correlations between ratings and other industrial criteria will be improved. We will focus in this section upon the major sources of unreliability in rating and suggest the importance both of training raters and of modifying the techniques themselves to overcome this difficulty.

Format of the Rating Scale

In appraising each of the performance rating procedures, we have observed that some procedures tend to be more reliable than others. This is partly a function of the format employed for rating.[13] The paired comparisons method, for example, was found in one study to yield an average reliability coefficient across three pairs of raters of 0.83.[14] Whereas this value compares favorably with those obtained with more objective assessment procedures, it is unusually high for rating procedures.

One aspect of format clearly influencing the reliability of ratings is ambiguity in the scale itself. If the trait descriptions or guideposts along the continuum are ambiguous, various raters cannot possibly

---

[12] J. Tiffin and E. J. McCormick, *Industrial Psychology* (Englewood Cliffs, N.J.: Prentice-Hall, Inc., 1965) , p. 256.

[13] J. M. Madden and R. D. Bourdon, "Effects of Variations in Rating Scale Format on Judgment," *Journal of Applied Psychology*, Vol. 48 (1964) , pp. 147–51.

[14] Lawshe, Kephart, McCormick, *op. cit.*

respond to them uniformly. A trait designation like "cooperativeness," for example, may mean quite different things to different raters. Hence, it is imperative that the characteristics to be rated be defined with extreme care and that the raters themselves be trained to interpret these definitions in the intended manner.

Halo Effect

You are well aware of the lasting consequences of first impressions because of the halo effect. We tend to generalize from our present experiences to our subsequent experiences. This kind of generalization may exert a pronounced effect upon performance ratings. Thus, although a rating form may contain 10 or 15 separate scales, the supervisor may respond carefully only to the first one or two of these, marking the remaining ones on the basis of the impressions he has recorded earlier.

Reversal of the Poles. One solution to this problem is to randomize the location of the favorable and unfavorable ends of each scale. By designating the left end of some scales as the "high" or "favorable" pole and of others as the "low" or "unfavorable" pole, the rater is at least compelled to examine each scale carefully enough to determine which end is favorable.

Horizontal Rating. Although reversal of the poles probably reduces the operation of halo effects somewhat, it is not as effective as horizontal rating. Horizontal rating requires that all employees be rated on a single trait or characteristic at a time.[15] Thus, if employees were to be rated on 10 different graphic scales, the supervisor would be asked to rate every one of the employees on the first scale before moving on to the subsequent ones. This procedure is superior to "vertical rating" in which all trait ratings are assigned in immediate succession to one employee, then to a second employee, and so on.

Systematic Bias

Specific raters sometimes exhibit consistently favorable or unfavorable biases in appraising the performance of virtually all of their subordinates. Such a predilection for using either the high or the

---

[15] S. N. Stevens and E. F. Wonderlic, "An Effective Revision of the Rating Technique," *Personnel Journal,* Vol. 13 (1934), pp. 125–34.

low end of the rating continuum defeats the fundamental purpose of performance rating by making it virtually impossible to differentiate between the ratees.

Forcing the Distribution. If a relatively large number of persons are to be rated by a particular supervisor, we might expect the distribution of the ratings he assigns to approximate a normal distribution. If a five-point graphic scale is used, for example, rather few employees ought to be assigned ratings at either the top or bottom pole. Assuming a perfectly normal distribution, we would anticipate that about 7 percent would receive ratings at each of the poles, 38 percent in the middle or "average" category, and 24 percent in each of the remaining categories.

Supervisors can be forced to adhere to a normal distribution when making their ratings. Such forcing will, of course, overcome any systematic rating bias that the supervisor may have. There is the danger, however, that forced distributions of ratings may actually produce some unfairly harsh appraisals when the department as a whole is better than average. Similarly, a forced distribution will produce a number of overly lenient ratings in departments with a large number of inefficient employees.

The dilemma of forced distributions for ratings is quite analagous to "curved" grades. It is advisable to make a study of the legitimacy of requiring a normal distribution before deciding to force either merit ratings or course grades to such a distribution. How can we know whether or not it is legitimate to impose a normal distribution upon merit ratings? We would have to examine both the personnel selection program and the training program before answering this question. If employees were carefully selected through the application of rather rigorous standards and if they were carefully trained, it would be erroneous to require the supervisor's appraisals of their performance to conform to a normal distribution. The anticipated distribution under these circumstances should contain a relatively large proportion of favorable ratings. Conversely, if the selection and training programs were relatively weak, we should anticipate a skew in the opposite direction.

Ratings Based upon Inadequate Information

Supervisors often feel compelled to assign ratings even though they have not had an adequate opportunity to observe the employee relative to the particular characteristic in question. In many instances, this feeling probably reflects the supervisor's own insecurity. He may be concerned lest an admission that he is not sufficiently familiar with one of his subordinates be interpreted by management as an indication of his inadequacy as a supervisor.

Ratings made on the basis of inadequate information are relatively valueless to management and may do considerable harm to the employee so rated. Thus, it is advisable for the rating scheme to embody a provision whereby the supervisor can refuse to rate any subordinate if he feels that he possesses insufficient or inadequate information to make a valid rating. This provision must be accompanied by a program of management education and supervisory training, however, if it is to work effectively. Management must not impose the impossible demand that supervisors know enough about every salient characteristic of every employee to rate him; supervisors must be informed about the deleterious effects of assigning ratings predicated upon inadequate information and reassured that their unwillingness to rate under such circumstances will not reflect unfavorably upon them.

Ratings Reflecting Uncontrolled Factors

Assuming that the rating procedures have been developed to maximize their reliability and validity and that the raters are carefully trained to make their ratings as objective and useful as possible, the interpretation of the ratings may be confounded by a variety of uncontrolled factors. The rater is required to appraise certain of the employee's behaviors. Unfortunately, this appraisal may reflect the influence of factors that really are unrelated to the dimensions supposedly under consideration. The supervisor may be unduly influenced, for example, by such things as the employee's job level or classification, the department within which he works, his age and seniority, and even by the employee's sex.

It is generally desirable, therefore, to interpret the merit ratings received by an employee in relation to those received by others in his own reference group; that is, other employees in similar departments, on similar jobs who are of about the same age, and so on.

FEEDBACK TO THE RATEE

In introducing this chapter, three general uses for performance appraisal, including ratings, were specified: (*a*) as criteria for validation studies, (*b*) as partial bases for such management actions as promotions and salary increases, and (*c*) as sources of information aiding the employee in improving his performance. The latter implies provision for feedback to the ratee of the performance evaluations made by his supervisor. However, as will be discussed subsequently, there is a certain degree of incompatibility between the intended "helpful" aspect of feedback of rating results and the use of such information for management actions which may adversely affect the employee.

The Need for Feedback

Lack of information about one's job-related weaknesses can contribute to one's ineffectiveness. This was demonstrated by comparing the performance ratings assigned to dental supply salesmen known to be "effective" and "ineffective." The criterion of effectiveness was based upon actual sales records. Each salesman rated himself and was rated by his branch manager on such characteristics as overall job performance, job knowledge, and organization and planning.

Whereas some branch managers were clearly aware of deficiencies contributing to employee ineffectiveness, as evidenced by lower ratings assigned to "ineffective" salesmen, the self-ratings of both criterion groups were almost identical! Because these criterion groups were similar with respect to aptitude, age, and training or experience, the investigators concluded that the failure of branch managers to apprise ineffective salesmen of their weaknesses was itself largely responsible for their ineffective performance.[16]

Kinds of Feedback

In spite of the apparent desirability of providing employees with a periodic review of their performance, such feedback is not always helpful, well received, or followed by constructive action. This statement is made notwithstanding the fact that employees tend to reply favorably to a question like: "Should performance appraisal discussions be continued?"[17] An employee would have to be hard pressed,

---

[16] L. Huttner and T. R. O'Malley, "Let Them Know!", *Personnel Psychology*, Vol. 15 (1962), pp. 179–86.

[17] H. Mayfield, "In Defense of Performance Appraisal," *Harvard Business Review*, Vol. 38 (1960), pp. 81–87.

indeed, to indicate that he was not interested in a periodic perform-ance review. The fact remains that there is a clear discrepancy between employees' verbalizations about the helpfulness of such reviews and the actual impact of these reviews upon subsequent work behavior.

The typical performance appraisal is made annually or semian-nually by a supervisor who is then placed in the untenable position of judging the subordinate and acting upon this judgment.[18] The usual feedback interview largely involves one-way communication; that is, the supervisor informs the employee of the latter's strengths and weaknesses.

Employees, naturally enough, tend to resist suggestions offered during such appraisal interviews for at least three reasons: (*a*) their infrequency, (*b*) the supervisor's conflicting roles as judge and helper, leading to (*c*) the clearly subordinate nature of employee participation during the interview. The dubious value of such infre-quent (annual) and nonparticipative performance appraisals was clearly demonstrated in a study conducted at the General Electric Company.[19] Praise offered during the appraisal interview was found to have virtually no effect in further motivating the employee, perhaps because it was perceived as a buffer between criticisms. And criticism by the supervisor tended to evoke defensive reactions that were essentially denials of responsibility for poor performance rather than stimulating the intended constructive search by the employee for ways of improving his performance.

What is required to increase the likelihood of constructive action following performance appraisal is greater involvement of the em-ployee in setting his performance goals and more of a daily ap-praisal-type interaction between employee and supervisor.

The advantages of continuous, less formal feedback over infre-quent and more formal feedback include the likelihood that criti-cism will be less concentrated and ineffective performance will be discussed soon after it is displayed. Furthermore, by having the employee participate in setting goals for overcoming his deficiencies, the supervisor is likely to evoke enthusiasm and interest rather than defensiveness.[20]

---

[18] D. McGregor, "An Uneasy Look at Performance Appraisal," *Harvard Business Review*, Vol. 35 (1957) , pp. 89–94.

[19] H. H. Meyer, E. Kay, and J. R. P. French, Jr., "Split Roles in Performance Appraisal," *Harvard Business Review*, Vol. 43 (1964) , pp. 124–29.

[20] *Ibid.*

Finally, if performance appraisals are truly to be interpreted helpfully to employees, it seems imperative that this function of the appraisal be separated from the judgmental function. Appraisals for the latter purpose may be made as needed, annually or semiannually, and followed by a discussion with the employee of the resultant salary action. However, the occasion of this feedback should not also be expected to provide the employee with the information he needs to establish new, more desirable, and appropriate work goals.

SUMMARY

Performance ratings are designed to summarize and systematize subjectively held opinions about employees. As one of several forms of performance appraisal, they may supplement more objective measures of job proficiency like output or absenteeism. Such appraisals have a wide range of possible administrative applications in the areas of wages, promotions, layoffs, transfers, and training. In addition, feedback of information from performance appraisal can provide employees with an indication of their job-related competencies and deficiencies. Finally, such appraisals are often used as criteria against which to validate selection and placement procedures.

Several different rating techniques were described in this chapter, which emphasized subjectively derived performance appraisals. The weighted checklist and the forced-choice approach to rating have special advantages, but these are often offset by the relatively high cost involved in developing such scales.

The fundamental problem in improving rating procedures is to effect a higher level of reliability. Various sources of unreliability including halo effect, bias, ambiguity, and others were discussed. It is imperative that the scales be properly structured and the raters trained in their use of the reliability of rating procedures in order to approach satisfactory levels.

The diagnostic value of performance ratings for guiding employees in improving their proficiency rests upon properly conducted appraisal feedback interviews. To be most effective, these interviews must be separated from reviews of management decisions involving such things as salary or promotion, and must actively involve the employee in establishing goals designed to overcome his deficiencies.

III.

Worker Efficiency

We turn now from concern with preemployment and training practices to consideration of some job-related factors influencing the employee's performance after he is hired. Appropriate selection, placement, and training procedures themselves contribute to facilitating job performance by increasing the likelihood of matching job requirements with abilities and interests. A further contribution is made by arranging working conditions, including equipment, to capitalize upon the strengths and to minimize the influence of the limitations of the human organism.

Chapter 10 considers the effect upon performance and attitudes of certain aspects of the physical work environment. In particular, attention is given to the relationship between work behavior and industrial illumination (including color), noise, music, and ventilation. In addition to summarizing information about the influence of these environmental conditions, this chapter discusses two methodological problems associated with investigations in this and other areas. One of these is the "Hawthorne Effect"; that is, performance improvements attributable to improved motivation ancillary to changed environmental conditions rather than to the actual nature of the change. The other methodological problem is the discrepancy sometimes evident between findings from laboratory and field studies.

Even a well-trained employee working under optimal environmental conditions may experience fatigue as a consequence of prolonged work, or boredom as a result of monotonous work. Since both of these conditions interfere with effective performance, their assessment, nature, and procedures for their alleviation are also discussed in Chapter 10.

Another condition of efficient industrial performance is safety (Chapter 11). Accidents are here regarded as a kind of undesirable behavior due in part to correctable deficiencies in the working situation and in part to improper but correctable employee attitudes. The fact that proportionately few accidents can be attributed to equipment malfunctions seems to indicate that engineering principles related to safety have been relatively well developed and widely accepted. Thus, in this chapter, we are concerned primarily with the human factors responsible for accidents and with procedures for preventing their occurrence.

This part is terminated with a discussion of engineering psychology (Chapter 12). This is a fairly recent area of concern for industrial psychologists. Machine and plant design had traditionally been regarded as the province of the engineer. However, technological advances and man's activities in new environments, including space and ocean depths, made imperative an increased concern for planning and designing equipment in the light of the capabilities and limitations of prospective human operators. The engineering psychologist seeks to develop an optimally functioning unit of man and machine, that is, a man-machine system.

10. Working Conditions and Environments

This chapter concerns two sets of factors potentially affecting job performance. One of these is the provision of appropriate working conditions, like rest periods and job rotation, to minimize the deleterious effects of fatigue and boredom. The other is the arrangement of the physical working environment in those ways calculated to make it easier for employees to do their work.

The physical working environment has probably been manipulated and studied by more legitimate professionals and self-styled "experts" than any other aspect of business and industry. Management is bombarded by literature describing the beneficial effects of certain color schemes and of "piped" music and is led sometimes to expect a tremendous increase in productivity if the water cooler is moved to a different location or if bowling alleys are installed for employee recreation.

There is no doubt that an uncomfortable or unpleasant working environment may be partially responsible for lowered productivity, increased spoilage, and unnecessary accidents. Furthermore, work may be made less fatiguing and employee morale improved by creating a more pleasant and efficient work environment. The thing that must be remembered, however, is that often a change in the physical working environment is paralleled by a temporary increase in industrial productivity because of improved morale rather than a real improvement in conditions of work. It is imperative that environmental manipulations producing only transitory effects be distinguished from environmental changes having lasting beneficial effects.

The phenomenon whereby environmental alterations lead to temporary improvements in productivity attributable to morale improvement is sometimes referred to as the "Hawthorne effect" because of the studies conducted in the Hawthorne Works of the Western Electric Company which called particular attention to it. This series of studies, begun in 1924 and spanning a 15-year period, has been reported in what is now regarded as a classic reference for industrial psychologists.[1] We will not attempt to summarize the entire set of investigations. Rather, our concern at the present time is only with the first three experiments on illumination which serve to illustrate the "Hawthorne effect."

THE HAWTHORNE STUDIES OF ILLUMINATION

The fundamental purpose of the three studies to be described was to investigate the "relation of quality and quantity of illumination to efficiency in industry." It soon became apparent, however, that implementing this objective was not as simple as one might suppose. The studies, themselves, had implications extending far beyond the matter of the relationship between illumination and industrial efficiency.

The First Study

The first experiment on illumination involved workers in three different departments of the Hawthorne Works: small parts inspection, relay assembly, and coil winding. The first step in the procedure involved establishment of a base or control rate of production within each department. Thus, the employees worked initially under the existing lighting installation.

After the base rate of productivity was established for each department, the intensity of the illumination was increased in graduated steps, and the corresponding changes in production efficiency were noted. No clear-cut relationship between productivity and intensity of illumination was evident. The report of this study concludes that the results

. . . brought out very forcibly the necessity of controlling or eliminating the various additional factors which affected production output in either

---

[1] F. J. Roethlisberger and W. J. Dickson, *Management and the Worker—An Account of a Research Program Conducted by the Western Electric Company, Chicago* (Cambridge: Harvard University Press, 1939).

the same or opposing directions to that which we can ascribe to illumination.[2]

The Second Study

This experiment, conducted only with operators in the coil winding department, was designed to overcome some of the deficiencies apparent in the first study. The workers were divided into two groups which were equated for experience and average output. The groups were housed in different buildings in order to reduce the possible effects of competition upon productivity.

One of the groups, the "test group," worked under three different illumination intensities (24, 46, and 70 footcandles). The other group ("control") worked under a more or less constant illumination level of 16–28 footcandles. The variations in the intensity of illumination for the control group resulted from variations in the amount of daylight which supplemented the artificial light.

Although this seemed like an excellent research design for comparing the effect of varying illumination intensities, the results were somewhat surprising. The report of the findings states:

> This test resulted in very appreciable production increases in both groups and of almost identical magnitude. The difference in efficiency of the two groups was so small as to be less than the probable error of the values. Consequently, we were again unable to determine what definite part of the improvement in performance should be ascribed to improved illumination.[3]

The Third Study

The third study involved the same test and control groups but further refinements were made in the experimental design. The control group now worked under a constant illumination of 10 footcandles of purely artificial light. The test group was provided with intensity levels from 10 to 3 footcandles in steps decreasing 1 footcandle at a time. Again, quoting from the summary of findings:

> After the level of illumination in the test group enclosure changed to a lower value, the efficiencies of both the test and control groups in-

[2] C. E. Snow, "A Discussion of the Relation of Illumination Intensity to Productive Efficiency," *The Tech Engineering News*, November, 1927.
[3] *Ibid.*

creased slowly but steadily. When the level of illumination for the test group finally reached 3 footcandles, the operatives protested, saying that they were hardly able to see what they were doing, and the production rate decreased. The operatives could and did maintain their efficiency to this point in spite of the discomfort and handicap of insufficient illumination.[4]

Implications of the Hawthorne Studies

It was apparent from the three studies cited above and the others that followed that something other than illumination was acting to affect employee performance. This "other" factor is clarified by referring again to the *S-I-R* scheme discussed in Chapter 1. You will recall that our behavior is a function not only of the stimulus condition (amount of illumination, in the case of the Hawthorne studies) but also of our interpretation of this stimulus condition. The Hawthorne employees interpreted the experimentation with illumination as evidence for the fact that management was interested in them and their welfare. This interpretation was responsible for the development of favorable attitudes and the consequent desire to perform at maximum capacity even when the illumination was reduced to very low levels.

There is, then, an important caution to be observed on the basis of the Hawthorne findings. One must be careful to separate out the effects attributable to the environmental change itself from the effects attributable to employee predispositions toward that change. Furthermore, short-term production or efficiency increments following the manipulation of environmental conditions are not very convincing. A valid test of such manipulation requires that the effects of environmental changes be studied over a relatively long period of time.

FATIGUE AND BOREDOM DIFFERENTIATED

Fatigue and boredom are factors of considerable consequence in industry. The most apparent indicators of either of these conditions is diminished output and increased spoilage. Secondary effects in-

---

[4] *Ibid.*

clude increased turnover and accident rate. Although the correlates of fatigue and boredom are on the whole somewhat similar, the nature of these conditions and the factors responsible for them are quite different.

The Nature of Fatigue

Fatigue is a complex phenomenon from both a physiological and a psychological standpoint. Prolonged muscular activity eventually produces physiological changes, including the accumulation of waste products resulting from the activity of the muscles and depletion of the reserve of carbohydrates which serve as fuel for such activity. In addition, the continuation of activity ultimately leads to unpleasant subjective feelings of strain or tension. These two types of change, the physiological and the subjective, do not, however, parallel each other very closely. Furthermore, the time at which either of these changes occurs and the intensity of their occurrence correlates only imperfectly with a measurable decrement in productivity.

The absence of a close relationship between the physiological changes, the subjective experiences, and productivity are evident in situations in which persons fatigued from a physiological standpoint may continue to maintain a high level of productivity and may not report feelings of "tiredness." It is apparent that strong motivation, like that encountered during athletic contests or in defense plants engaged in wartime production, may reduce or almost obliterate any noticeable deterioration in performance. Conversely, poorly motivated persons may experience subjective feelings of fatigue, and their output may decline, some time in advance of the physiological changes associated with fatigue.

It is difficult to formulate a definition of fatigue because of the imperfect relationship between its physiological and subjective components. The formulation of a definition is further complicated by the fact that the relationship between the physiological and subjective changes accompanying fatigue may be either reduced or accentuated by motivational factors. It will be satisfactory for our purposes to define fatigue in terms of its practical implications in the industrial setting. It is a temporary condition resulting from prolonged muscular activity and is manifest in a declining capacity for continued work.

The Nature of Boredom

Boredom is sometimes thought of as a kind of "mental fatigue," implying that it results from a psychological rather than a physiological cause. This distinction considerably oversimplifies the situation since, as we have already said, fatigue also entails a psychological or subjective component.

It is, perhaps, most meaningful to distinguish between fatigue and boredom on the basis of the kind of activity that generates these experiences. Fatigue results only when the person is engaged in prolonged muscular activity. Boredom results when the activity is regarded as monotonous or uninteresting. Prolonged muscular activity is not a necessary precursor to boredom. We may be bored, for example, when we read an uninteresting book, listen to a dull lecture, or watch a trite television program.

A further distinction between fatigue and boredom is predicated upon the fact that the former tends to generalize, while the latter is highly specific. When we are fatigued, we seek rest from all activity. When we are bored, we seek relief only from the monotonous activity. This fact should not be taken as an indication that boredom is somehow less significant or less important than fatigue. The production decrement for tasks regarded as monotonous is quite as real and as serious as that which accompanies the performance of fatigue-producing tasks.

FATIGUE

The fact that fatigue reduces the capacity for further work is amply illustrated by studies of industrial productivity or output during the course of a typical working day. A schematic plot of average hourly output for an industrial task involving motor activity is shown in Figure 10–1. The irregularities which are always apparent when such a curve is plotted have been smoothed in order to make the fundamental trends more apparent. Note that prolonged motor activity is characterized by an initial period of "warm-up" followed by a decline in output during the latter hours of the morning, and again toward the end of the work period.

Such a graph suggests that the examination of production records throughout the course of the workday may serve to identify the existence of fatigue. Furthermore, the comparative analysis of such records obtained under varying circumstances probably indicates something about the relative amount of fatigue experienced under these circumstances. Although output curves can be used in this way, they are not entirely satisfactory as indices of the existence of fatigue or as measures of the amount of fatigue generated by particular

FIGURE 10–1

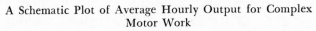

A Schematic Plot of Average Hourly Output for Complex Motor Work

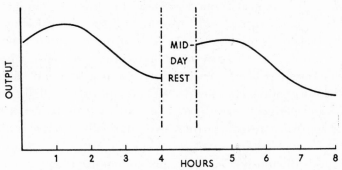

Source: R. A. Katzell, "Fatigue and Its Alleviation," in D. H. Fryer and E. R. Henry, *Handbook of Applied Psychology* (New York: Holt, Rinehart & Winston, Inc., 1950), p. 75.

tasks. Any record of employee performance reflects the factor of motivation in addition to the effects of fatigue. Thus, a decline in output may be erroneously attributed to fatigue when in fact it may result from a progressive decline in interest. Conversely, of course, the output rate may remain high in spite of fatigue because of a high motivational level.

It is obvious, also, that many kinds of jobs do not lend themselves to work-curve analyses. It is possible to graph output only when the work is repetitive and when some kind of production unit can be counted. Work which varies in nature, like that of an office secretary, does not provide equivalent units which can be summated and graphed. Under such circumstances, the existence of fatigue must be verified by some other method.

Measurement of Fatigue

One of the first things to suffer as a person becomes fatigued is his "timing."[5] This calls for precise receptor-effector coordination in order to produce the smooth patterns required for such skilled activities as hitting a baseball or flying an airplane.

Clearly related to the matter of timing is *vigilance;* that is, alertness in monitoring and responding to critical stimuli. The automobile driver, for example, must be continuously aware of and responsive to road conditions, other traffic, pedestrians, highway signs and signals, the "feel" of the car, and information provided by his instruments. A typical laboratory task for assessing vigilance requires the subject to respond in some way (say, by pressing a button) when a slowly moving light intersects the crosshairs marked on an oscilloscope. The variance of an individual's responses about his mean response has been found to increase as a function of fatigue. Thus, whereas pilots completing this task prior to a flight mission exhibited a relatively narrow range of response times, the variability of their vigilance responses increased markedly after a prolonged flight.[6]

Fatigue is obviously a complex phenomenon. There are individual differences in susceptibility to fatigue under similar circumstances and intraindividual differences in susceptibility on different occasions. We have previously alluded to one of the reasons for the complex nature of fatigue; it is both a physiological and a psychological phenomenon. The intimate relationship of these two components of fatigue has been clearly demonstrated in an investigation wherein the actual work load was increased without the subjects' knowledge. In spite of the fact that they believed the physical demands of the experimental task to be constant, the subjects reported increased feelings of fatigue paralleling actual increases in the work load.[7]

Some attempts separately to measure the physiological and subjective components of fatigue are described below.

Physiological Components. Some of the very early studies of

---

[5] D. C. Fraser, "Recent Experimental Work in the Study of Fatigue," *Occupational Psychology*, Vol. 32 (1958) , pp. 258–63.

[6] *Ibid.*

[7] J. E. Hueting and H. R. Sarphati, "Measuring Fatigue," *Journal of Applied Psychology*, Vol. 50 (1966) , pp. 535–38.

fatigue were directed toward the measurement of the limitations upon prolonged work imposed by the musculature. The device used for such studies, known as an *ergograph,* permits for the conduct of fatigue experiments involving specific muscles or muscle groups. A weight is attached by a cord to an extremity of the body (for example, the fingertip or the hand) and the rest of the limb is strapped in order to inhibit movements of the muscles that are not under investigation. The subject is required to raise the weight periodically at a signal, and the height of each lift is automatically recorded. This recording, called an *ergogram,* is really a plot of the work decrement accompanying prolonged activity of the muscle or muscle group being studied. An ergogram produced by a subject required to lift a weight using one finger is illustrated in Figure 10–2. Note the progressive deterioration in his performance.

Ergographic studies clearly demonstrate that there is a considerable range of individual differences in the amount of prolonged muscular work that can be performed. The tracings obtained from different subjects vary tremendously with respect to the maximum level of performance, the length of the period during which near-maximum performance is maintained, and the rate at which performance deteriorates. This suggests, of course, that there are individual variations in susceptibility to the physiological components of fatigue. Again, however, it is important to realize that some portion of the differences obtained from ergographic studies must properly be attributed to variations in the motivational levels of the subjects rather than to variations in susceptibility to physiological fatigue.

A more direct approach to the measurement of the physiological aspects of fatigue requires a study of the involuntary physiological processes themselves while work is being performed. Such factors as oxygen consumption, muscular tension, and circulatory activity have been found to be related to fatigue and are relatively, although not completely, independent of motivational factors. This approach to the measurement of fatigue is, however, generally too unwieldy for use in industry.

Subjective Components. The subjective component of fatigue (that is, feelings of strain or tiredness) have also been explored. It has been found, for example, that feelings of weariness generally occur prior to a noticeable decrement in actual performance.[8] Such

---

[8] A. T. Poffenberger, "Effects of Continuous Work upon Output and Feelings," *Journal of Applied Psychology,* Vol. 12 (1928), pp. 459–67.

FIGURE 10-2

An Ergogram

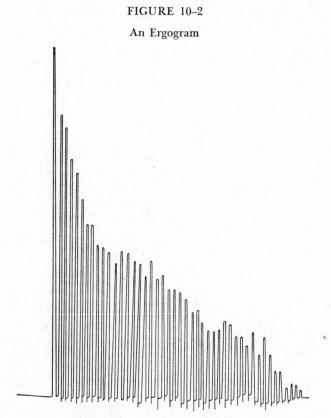

Each stroke represents a complete cycle of lifting and drop-
ping the weight. The temporal sequence is from left to right.
Source: T. A. Ryan, *Work and Effort* (New York: The Ronald
Press Co., 1947), p. 50.

subjective fatigue does, however, tend to parallel production curves
even though it anticipates them. Workers report the greatest feelings
of tiredness when they begin work in the morning, immediately
prior to lunch, and again immediately prior to the time that their
shift ends (see Figure 10-3). You will recall that the typical curve of
industrial productivity exhibits declining output also at these three
periods.

Perhaps the most surprising aspect of industrial fatigue, defined
either in terms of subjective feeling or in terms of output, is that it
does not appear to accumulate continuously throughout the workday. Workers neither produce less nor do they feel more weary in the

FIGURE 10–3

Percent of Employees Reporting Maximal Feelings of Tiredness at Each Hour of an Eight-Hour Work Shift

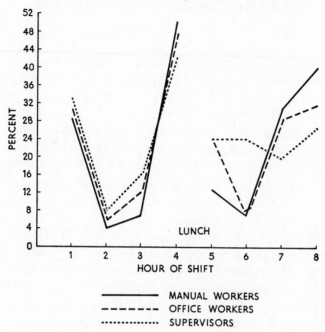

Source: J. W. Griffith, W. A. Kerr, T. B. Mayo, Jr., and J. R.
Topal, "Changes in Subjective Fatigue and Readiness for Work during the Eight-Hour Shift," *Journal of Applied Psychology,* Vol. 34
(1950), pp. 163–66.

midafternoon than in the midmorning. Furthermore, both productivity and feelings of tiredness at the end of the shift are about the
same as they are immediately prior to lunch. It is certain that a
45-minute or one-hour lunch period is not, itself, sufficiently long to
dissipate completely the physiological component of fatigue. These
findings again reinforce the importance of motivational factors in
offsetting at least partially both feelings of fatigue and the concomitant work decrement associated with it.

Alleviation of Fatigue

It is apparent that certain difficulties are encountered when the
psychologist studies fatigue. These difficulties are inherent in the

formulation of a definition of fatigue, in measuring it, in reconciling discrepancies between its physiological and subjective components, and in separating out the effects of fatigue from those attributable to declining interest and motivation. In spite of these problems, however, the reduction of industrial fatigue is of extreme practical importance.

The findings of ergographic studies and of other types of observations relative to the widespread individual differences in susceptibility to fatigue suggest that appropriate selection and placement procedures can serve as a partial solution to the problem. The assignment of employees to jobs should not be predicated solely on the fulfillment by them of the necessary experiential and educational requirements. The state of their physical health and the likelihood that they will experience real satisfaction from their work are factors that must be considered also in order to minimize susceptibility to fatigue.

The attempts of the psychologist to reduce the fatigue experienced by employees presently on the job are, in general, directed toward the maintenance of productivity or output while simultaneously reducing the effort or input required of the employee. Thus, the alleviation of fatigue involves for the most part the manipulation of certain features of the physical working environment. It is imperative that the beneficial effects accruing from the actual reduction of effort be sorted out from those effects attributable to the improved employee motivation which often accompanies the conduct of this type of investigation. You will undoubtedly recall the implications of the Hawthorne Studies in this regard.

Length of the Work Period. Since fatigue is generated by prolonged activity, one avenue to its alleviation is the reduction of the length of the working period. The length of the typical working day and workweek has been progressively shortened during the past several years and in all likelihood will be further shortened within the next few years.

Unfortunately, the matter of the optimal length of the work period is too often approached with a background of misconceptions that appear on the surface to be reasonable. Management, for example, often expresses the view that the way to increase productivity is simply to increase the length of the workday or workweek. Representatives of management are sometimes heard to express concern about reduction in the length of the work period on the grounds that this will force an undue decline in productivity and create certain social problems related to the increase in available leisure time. Union representatives, on the other hand, may perceive reductions in the length of the workweek as an indirect device for increasing employee salaries and as a means by which the number of available jobs may be increased.

Both of these points of view stem from the erroneous assumption that productivity is directly related to the amount of time spent at work. The fact of the matter, however, is that changes in the length of the work period do not yield proportional changes in productivity. It is helpful, in this regard, to differentiate between *nominal* and *actual* hours worked. The "nominal" hours of work are defined by the clock; that is, the employee checks in and out at specified times and is nominally on the job for the number of hours elapsing between his check-in and check-out times. It is apparent, however, that he does not actually produce during this entire period. Virtually every job entails a certain amount of unproductive time, some of which is scheduled (for example, formally recognized rest periods) and some of which is not scheduled. We are dealing, after all, with a human being rather than with a machine. He alters his work pace, he has "good" days and "bad" days, he becomes tired and must rest, he experiences boredom and takes a "break," and so on. Thus, the critical factor affecting productivity is actual rather than nominal hours worked. It has been found in general that increases in nominal hours decrease actual hours worked and conversely that decreases in nominal hours tend to be accompanied by increases in actual hours worked. Employees for whom the workday is lengthened spend on the average proportionately less time each hour in productive work.

This generalization holds within certain limits even for highly motivated employees engaged in wartime production. One of the earliest series of studies of the effect of the length of the work period was conducted in Great Britain during World War I. The hourly output of women engaged in munitions work during 12- and 8-hour shifts, for example, was 19½ percent higher during the short shift. Furthermore, when the nominal hours of weekly work by women who turned fuse bodies were reduced from 63½ to 47½ hours, their total weekly output increased by 13 percent.[9]

---

[9] Industrial Fatigue Research Board, Great Britain, *Report No. 2.*

Decisions about the optimal length of the work period are in practice somewhat influenced by economic factors. Although there is ample evidence for the fact that hourly productivity tends to increase when nominal hours are reduced, the two factors do not balance each other entirely with respect to total productivity. A 25 percent reduction in nominal hours, for example, leading to a 15 percent increase in hourly productivity will yield a net loss in plant production unless additional employees are hired or extra shifts are run. This may be entirely feasible from an economic standpoint because of the savings resulting from the higher proportion of actual to nominal hours of work. It is a matter that must be studied, however, by each company contemplating a reduction in nominal hours.

Factors other than economic considerations also enter into decisions about the optimal length of the work period. The type of work being performed and employee reaction to altered periods of work may have considerable bearing upon the matter.

The relationship between the characteristics of the job and the actual amount of work performed is clearly apparent from a study conducted by the U.S. Department of Labor.[10] The hourly productivity of employees in the metalworking industry was compared for persons doing light work under wage incentive systems and those engaged in heavy labor. These employees worked nominally between 55 and 58 hours a week. Those doing light work averaged approximately two hours' output for every three hours worked in excess of 48. Employees engaged in heavy work, however, only averaged about one hour's output for every two hours worked in excess of 48.

The 8-hour day and the 40-hour week are generally regarded as optimal for striking a balance that maximizes industrial efficiency under normal (nonemergency) conditions. Hourly productivity in a box factory was found, for example, to be highest when the employees worked a 40-hour week, slightly reduced when they worked either a 36- or a 44-hour week, and considerably reduced when they worked a 48-hour week.[11] Another study, contrasting a 7½-hour day

---

[10] U.S. Department of Labor, "Hours of Work and Production," *Labor Information Bulletin*, No. 2, 1944, pp. 4–7.

[11] S. L. Pressey *et al.*, *Life: A Psychological Survey* (New York: Harper & Bros., 1939), p. 524.

and a 9½-hour day, found that the former condition led to higher productivity and lowered absenteeism.[12]

The desirability of decreasing the length of the working day below 8 hours and that of the workweek below 40 hours is still an open issue. A certain amount of resistance to further reductions can undoubtedly be attributed to a prevailing conservatism relative to any kind of a change in the established way of doing things. It is likely, for some jobs requiring a lengthy "warm-up" building slowly to maximum output each day, that the eight-hour day is indeed optimal. Other kinds of work, particularly those generating extreme fatigue or boredom, however, will be performed most efficiently when the nominal hours are reduced below eight each day.

Rest Periods. The effect of authorized rest pauses during the day has been investigated rather extensively. It has been demonstrated that employees will rest regardless of whether or not rest periods are scheduled. A careful study of unauthorized breaks taken when formal rest periods were introduced into the work schedule of comptometer operators indicated that the effect of the authorized rest periods was to produce a sharp decline in unauthorized breaks and an increase in productivity.[13]

The beneficial effects of scheduled rest pauses accrue from the fact that such pauses provide opportunities for a partial recovery from fatigue and for a change of pace which undoubtedly helps to relieve boredom. The mere fact of a scheduled rest period is, however, an insufficient guarantee of its effectiveness. The time of the day at which such breaks are scheduled, their frequency and duration, and the employee activity during the rest period may all be of considerable importance.

There is considerable variation between companies in the number and length of scheduled rest periods, even for jobs essentially similar. The typical procedure is to schedule one rest around mid-morning and another around midafternoon, each period being 10 to 15 minutes in length. The ideal schedule for rest pauses is something that must be determined for each kind of work. It is likely that each rest period ought to be somewhat longer for very strenuous tasks

---

[12] M. D. Kossoris, "Studies in the Effects of Long Working Hours," *Bureau of Labor Statistics, Bulletin No. 791,* 1944.

[13] W. McGehee and E. B. Owen, "Authorized and Unauthorized Rest Pauses in Clerical Work," *Journal of Applied Psychology,* Vol. 24 (1940), pp. 604–13.

than for light work. It is probable, also, that rest periods should be scheduled with greater frequency when the task is monotonous or physically taxing than when it is interesting or relatively sedentary.

An examination of the production curve during the course of the day can furnish very helpful clues about the specific times at which

FIGURE 10–4

Effects of Authorized Rest on Production
during the Morning Hours

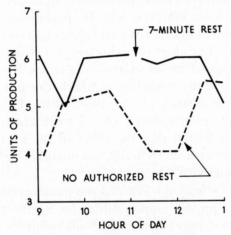

Source: J. Tiffin and E. J. McCormick, *In-dustrial Psychology* (New York: Prentice-Hall, Inc., 1965), p. 489, drawn from data by E. Farmer and S. M. Bevington, an experiment in the introduction of rest pauses, *Journal of National Institutional and Industrial Psychology*, 1922, pp. 89–92.

rest periods should be introduced if they are to be most beneficial. You will recall that the typical output curve for fatiguing work (Figure 10–1) indicates that productivity declines sometime after midmorning and again sometime after midafternoon. The usual practice is to schedule rest periods immediately prior to these declines in productivity in order to forestall their occurence (see Figure 10–4).

The time scheduled for rest must be used wisely if the break is to be most beneficial. Employees engaged in heavy labor should relax; employees engaged in sedentary activity should move about and experience a change of scene. The rest period should provide a variation in pace and an opportunity for fatigue to be dissipated.

Miscellaneous Environmental Factors. Many of the environmental conditions that serve to accelerate or retard the development of fatigue are discussed later in this chapter. Reduction in the prevailing noise or vibration level and improvements in illumination and ventilation may lead to both improved output and diminution in subjective feelings of tiredness. Changes in work methods or in equipment design may materially decrease industrial fatigue by making it easier for the employee to do his work.

BOREDOM

We have already mentioned that the effects of boredom and of fatigue have much in common. Both may lead to increased turnover, spoilage and accidents, lowered morale, and subjective feelings of strain or discontent. Both factors also affect productivity. The output curve for monotonous work, however, is sometime differentiated from that resulting from fatiguing work by the appearance of an "end-spurt" in anticipation of release from the task (see Figure 10–5).

Whereas it was once believed that such an end-spurt output curve was invariably associated with monotonous work, there is evidence to the contrary. For example, one investigator plotted the output of piece-rate operators in a knitwear mill against time of day and correlated these factors with self-reports of boredom.[14] It was noted here that the shape of the output curves for any operator varied markedly from day to day. Also, there was no noticeable trend toward end-spurt curves for those operators reporting the most boredom.

In interpreting her findings, this investigator makes the important point that production curves are sensitive to factors other than the simple one of subjectively experienced boredom. An important such factor is self-pacing. Employees engaged in repetitive work often develop an output standard for themselves. If near the end of the day, they are behind schedule in terms of this standard, they tend to rush in order to catch up. Likewise, if they are ahead of this self-imposed schedule, they tend to slow down. The former would be

---

[14] P. C. Smith, "The Curve of Output as a Criterion of Boredom," *Journal of Applied Psychology*, Vol. 37 (1953), pp. 69–74.

FIGURE 10–5

Schematic Plot of Average Hourly Output for Monotonous
Work

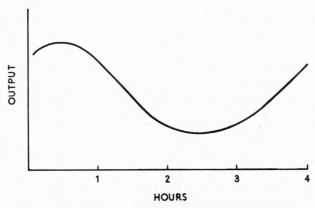

Source: R. A. Katzell, "Fatigue and Its Alleviation," in D. H.
Fryer and E. R. Henry, *Handbook of Applied Psychology* (New York:
Holt, Rinehart & Winston, Inc., 1950), p. 75.

reflected in an end-spurt, whereas the latter would, of course, have
the opposite effect.

Personal Characteristics Related to Boredom

Monotonous tasks are thought of typically as being rather routine
and highly repetitive. The relationship between the nature of the
task and the experience of boredom is not nearly as direct, however,
as the relationship between the kind of work performed and the
experience of fatigue. Tasks that are monotonous for some workers
may be rather interesting and challenging for others. Thus, boredom results from a lack of interest in the work. The experience of
boredom is dependent upon the character of the work *as it is perceived by the worker* rather than upon the character of the work as
it may be described objectively.

Remedies for boredom are predicated upon an understanding of
the factors that lead workers to regard their jobs as monotonous.
The factors which have been explored in this regard include intelligence, interest, and personality.

Intelligence of the Employee. It is reasonable to anticipate that
jobs requiring either more or less intellectual capability than the

worker possesses will prove to be monotonous. It is difficult for workers who are too intelligent for their task to maintain a continuing interest in it. The job does not challenge them sufficiently and therefore does not provide them with a feeling of satisfaction and accomplishment. Conversely, workers placed on jobs requiring more intellectual capability than they possess may also be expected to lose interest in their work because of the frustration of continual failure. It is not gratifying to be confronted continually by one's shortcomings.

It has been found, for example, that highly intelligent employees performing simple clerical tasks had a much higher turnover rate than did less intelligent employees on the same job.[15] Turnover may be regarded as a partial indication of boredom since some employees undoubtedly terminate their employment in order to accept a more interesting job. It is likely, however, that many workers leave their present employment in order to accept a higher paying but not necessarily more interesting position. This factor confounds the utilization of turnover as a criterion of boredom.

The relationship between intelligence and boredom has been studied more directly by comparing the average intelligence test scores of workers who completed a questionnaire appraising the degree of boredom they experienced on the job. The average intelligence of the groups of workers reporting the most boredom tended to be higher than that of workers reporting the least boredom. The differences between the mean test scores of these groups did not, however, always meet the requirements for statistical significance, and the groups utilized for the study were very small in size (four to 10 persons each) .[16]

Although there is some evidence in support of a relationship between employee intelligence and boredom, this relationship is by no means as strong as one might suppose. It is apparent that other factors, including interest and personal adjustment, may operate to counteract or minimize this relationship.

Employee Interests. The kinds of activities that interest us are determined in part by our intellectual capacity and to a large extent by our past experiences. We develop our own unique pattern of

---

[15] M. A. Bills, "Relation of Mental Alertness Test Score to Position and Permanency in Company," *Journal of Applied Psychology*, Vol. 7 (1923), pp. 154–56.

[16] S. Wyatt, J. N. Langdon, and F. G. L. Stock, "Fatigue and Boredom in Repetitive Work," *Industrial Health Research Board, Great Britain, Report No. 77, 1937.*

interests on the basis of the successes which we have experienced in the past and the environment to which we have been exposed. Thus, we each have proclivities toward certain kinds of industrial activities and away from other kinds of activities.

Individual differences with respect to interest were demonstrated by having workers in a candy packing department alternate on five different jobs for one month each. The employees were questioned about the amount of boredom they experienced on each of the five jobs, and highly individual patterns of boredom were discovered. A job that was the least interesting for one worker often proved to be the most interesting for another.[17]

Personality. Attempts to establish a "personality pattern" characteristic of workers who are easily bored as differentiated from those who withstand boredom have not been outstandingly successful. One investigation of the problem led to the conclusion that extroverted persons tend to experience boredom more readily that introverted persons.[18] Presumably, this relationship exists because introverted workers are less dependent upon social stimulation for personal gratification and are therefore better able to function under conditions involving repetitive activity and relative isolation. It has been found, also, that older employees and those who prefer a degree of regularity in their daily activities are least susceptible to boredom during repetitious work.[19]

These bits of evidence provide meager clues to the relationship between personality patterns and susceptibility to boredom. The relationships are neither sufficiently strong nor sufficiently consistent to permit the utilization of such measures for predictive purposes.

A more promising approach to this problem focuses upon employee needs and personal adjustment as the critical factors rather than upon identification of a personality pattern associated with boredom. A job which is satisfying to the employee and provides him with a feeling of accomplishment and a sense of personal worth is rarely regarded as monotonous. Work, on the other hand, that does not provide the employee with a degree of job satisfaction is often boring regardless of the nature of the activity performed. In many ways, the factors responsible for job satisfaction are quite

---

[17] *Ibid.*

[18] *Ibid.*

[19] P. C. Smith, "The Prediction of Individual Differences in Susceptibility to Industrial Monotony," *Journal of Applied Psychology,* Vol. 39 (1955) , pp. 322–29.

similar to those responsible for deriving satisfaction from life in general. Employees who seek variation in activities after working hours tend also to derive the greatest amount of job satisfaction when their work is varied in nature. Similarly, employees who are dissatisfied with life in general and who are poorly adjusted in their familial and home relationships tend to be dissatisfied with their work and to be most susceptible to boredom.[20]

Alleviation of Boredom

Industrial automation has made it possible within certain limits to eliminate many routine and highly repetitive jobs. Automated equipment cannot, however, relieve workers from all such tasks. The equipment itself generates some new jobs of a repetitive nature and many rather routine industrial activities are not amenable to automation. In addition, the fact that boredom is a function of the worker's perception of the job rather than of the characteristics of the job as objectively defined implies that a certain amount of monotonous activity will always be present in industry.

Personnel Selection and Placement. One solution to the problem of boredom entails the utilization of appropriate personnel selection and placement procedures. A gross mismatching of the job and the worker relative to such factors as his intelligence, interests, and other personal characteristics should be avoided. Even the most careful selection and placement program will not, however, be a full solution to the problem. Selection and placement procedures must be supplemented by measures designed to reduce the boredom that is an inevitable consequence of certain kinds of work for some employees.

Motivation. The fundamental consideration in alleviating boredom is, of course, that of increasing the employee's interest and involvement in his work. This can be accomplished in a number of ways. Almost any job assumes additional significance for the employee when he is informed about the relationship between what he is doing and the end product being produced. It is imperative that the training program for new employees include some kind of an

---

[20] P. A. Cain, "Individual Differences in Susceptibility to Monotony" (Ph.D. dissertation, Cornell University, 1942). Cited in R. A. Ryan, *Work and Effort* (New York: Ronald Press Co., 1947), pp. 199 ff.

overview of the entire industrial operation and an indication of the role played in this operation by the individual worker.

Typically, employees are presumed to be motivated by instructions to do their "best." However, laboratory findings confirm the superiority of a specific assigned work goal over this kind of abstract instruction. This superiority is evident both in terms of actual output and subjective reports of freedom from boredom. Subjects for this study had to perform a complex psychomotor task requiring them to match patterns of lights shown on a display panel by manipulating controls consisting of foot pedals and a joy stick. Half the subjects were instructed to do their "best"; the other half were assigned a goal specifying the number of correct matches they were to attempt to make. For these latter subjects, the goal for each trial was always set above the number of matches successfully made during the previous trial. Figure 10–6 shows the superiority of establishing specific and relatively difficult performance goals for maintaining a reasonably high level of interest in an essentially monotonous task.[21]

These findings suggest that it may be possible to reduce boredom on many repetitive tasks by having the worker periodically (each day or hour) set determinate goals. Further research is needed both to test the applicability of this laboratory finding in the field and to determine the optimal level of difficulty at which goals should be set.

Other Factors.   It is often possible to permit employees engaged in fragmented work a greater amount of responsibility for planning and organizing their activities. Such enlargement of the scope of the work provides the worker with a degree of variety which can be very helpful in counteracting boredom.

When job enlargement is not feasible, variety may be introduced by means of job rotation. Several employees, each performing a different monotonous task, may be permitted to change jobs with each other every two hours or so. The actual change in activity combined with a change in the physical and social environment relieves the routine and enhances the maintenance of a level of interest. This may well justify the added costs incurred by job rotation.

Certain other approaches to the alleviation of boredom are based

---

[21] E. A. Locke and J. F. Bryan, "Performance Goals as Determinants of Level of Performance and Boredom," *Journal of Applied Psychology*, Vol. 51 (1967), pp. 120–30.

FIGURE 10–6

Effect of Performance Instructions upon Boredom Ratings
(higher scores indicate greater interest and less boredom)

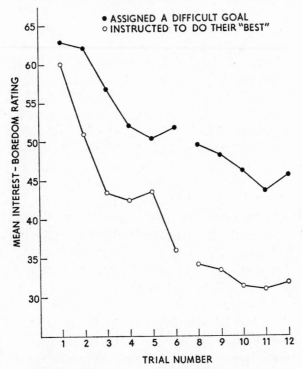

Source: E. A. Locke and J. F. Bryan, "Performance Goals as
Determinants of Level of Performance and Boredom," *Journal
of Applied Psychology*, Vol. 51 (1967), p. 127.

upon factors other than that of increasing the employee's interest in
his work. Strategically placed rest pauses, for example, are very
helpful in forestalling the experience of boredom. Similarly, music
may serve as a mild diversion acting to make time seem to pass more
quickly and the job itself to seem more pleasant. Finally, bonus
payments for productivity in excess of some established minimum
may reduce the deleterious effects of boredom upon output.

THE WORK ENVIRONMENT

In addition to the job task itself, the physical environment in
which work is performed may contribute to undue fatigue and have

other deleterious industrial consequences. The sections that follow discuss selected aspects of the visual, auditory, and atmospheric surroundings in which work is done.

Illumination

The prevalence of visual defects among industrial employees is somewhat surprising. A company program to detect and correct such defects is likely to improve efficiency markedly. Motorola, Inc., for example, found that about 30 percent of the workers in one of its inspection departments had faulty vision.[22] Correction of these defects led to decreased absenteeism, diminution in complaints about the product from the field, and a lower turnover and accident rate. Thus, the relatively small expenditure by a company to check upon and correct visual defects would seem to be extremely worthwhile.

Although the Hawthorne experiments described previously were concerned solely with the intensity of illumination, this aspect of light is by no means the only factor of importance in the visual environment. Other aspects of illumination, including the distribution and reflection of light and its hue or color, are of concern in industry.

Intensity. Industrial requirements in terms of the amount of light on a work surface vary considerably with the nature of the task to be performed. In general, work involving precise manipulation of small objects requires more intense illumination than does work involving the manipulation of large objects for which precision is not a critical requirement.

Although illumination intensity requirements increase as the task makes increased visual demands, attempts to formulate generally useful sets of intensity recommendations have generated considerable controversy. While one investigator concluded that 40–50 footcandles is sufficient illumination for even the most severe industrial tasks,[23] others have recommended minimum intensities as high as 200 footcandles for automotive final assembly and inspection, and 2,000 footcandles for cloth inspection.[24]

---

[22] Kenneth Piper, "Motorola's Vision Program Pays Off," *Advanced Management,* September, 1951, pp. 24–25.

[23] M. A. Tinker, "Illumination Standards for Effective and Easy Seeing." *Psychological Bulletin,* Vol. 44 (1947) , pp. 435–50.

[24] *Footcandles in Modern Lighting,* Technical Publication LS–119, General Electric Co. (Nela Park, Cleveland, 1960) .

Such divergent recommendations result in part from differing definitions of criteria of "effective seeing." The criterion problem aside, however, it is evident that any set of intensity recommendations must properly be considered rough guides rather than definitive statements of illumination requirements for specific tasks in particular work settings. It is impossible accurately to generalize about intensity requirements alone, without regard for the factors that may interact with intensity. These potentially interactive variables include: (*a*) such other characteristics of illumination as glare, spectral composition, and amount of reflected light; (*b*) characteristics of the visual task, including the nature of the work, and the contrast between the work object and the background against which it is seen;[25] and (*c*) the entire range of physical, social, and personal factors influencing job performance. Once these factors are specified for a particular job, it is a relatively simple matter to determine optimal illumination requirements for that job by empirical test.

Distribution and Reflection of Light. Virtually everyone is acquainted with the visual discomfort experienced when reading directly under a lamp that is the sole source of illumination in the room. Whenever the visual field is shifted from the well-illuminated page to the poorly illuminated surroundings, the pupil of the eye dilates. Similarly, the pupil contracts when shifting from low to high illumination. Excesses of pupillary activity are fatiguing; they cause eyestrain. Consequently, it is advisable to have the light well distributed throughout the visual field. It is for precisely this reason that television viewing in a moderately lit room is preferable to viewing in a totally darkened room.

Solutions to the problem of glare are relatively simple. They include the proper shading of lamps, the elimination of highly reflective surfaces from the visual field, and the diffusion of light at its source.

Color

Many extravagant claims have been made about the beneficial effects of using certain colors or color combinations in industry and in the home. Not all of these claims, however, are supported by valid

----

[25] H. R. Blackwell, "Development and Use of a Quantitative Method for Specification of Interior Illumination Levels," *Illuminating Engineering*, Vol. 54 (1959), pp. 317–53.

evidence. It is quite true that the appropriate use of color can do much to provide a safer, more pleasant, and more efficient working atmosphere. Such benefits result from painting the equipment and background in such a way as to: (1) indicate danger zones, traffic patterns, fire and safety equipment, and so on; (2) focus attention upon the critical elements in the visual field; (3) provide ample reflection without glare; and (4) provide a restful visual relief when the employee turns momentarily from his work. About the only thing that can be said about the overall color scheme or *decor*, however, is that it should be one that is not regarded by employees as unpleasant.

Color as a Focusing Agent.   The color coding of fire protection equipment (red), first-aid and safety facilities (green), and danger zones (yellow) can make a valuable contribution to safety practices throughout the plant. Awareness of danger zones reduces accident frequency; facile identification of fire and first-aid equipment reduces the severity of mishaps once they occur.

The equipment with which an employee works may also be painted in a way calculated to improve safety and increase productivity. The suggestion has been made that color be used to differentiate between three areas of machinery or equipment: the moving, working, or critical area; the body of the machine or noncritical area; and the controls, including buttons, levers, handles, and so on.[26] The *working area* consisting of operating parts of the machine should be painted in a color which contrasts strongly with the noncritical portion of the machine and with the material being worked on. Danger areas (moving and cutting parts) should be further spotlighted by using strips of bright color like orange or yellow. The *body* of the machine, it is suggested, ought to blend into the background wall and ceiling color. This will prevent visual attention from being directed toward it. *Controls* should be painted to contrast sharply with the body of the machine so the worker can locate and use them with a minimum of difficulty.

Walls and Ceilings.   The color of the walls and ceilings surrounding the immediate work area can do much to produce either visual comfort or discomfort. These surfaces must reflect an adequate amount of light without either producing glare or an undue contrast

---

[26] Robert B. Fetter, *How Color Can Increase Your Productivity*, Business Information Bulletin No. 8, Bureau of Business Research, Indiana University (Bloomington, Ind., 1950).

in brightness with the working area. Surfaces painted white, cream, or ivory reflect a considerable amount of light; pastel shades have intermediate reflectance values; and shades of brown, dark red, dark green, or dark blue have low reflective values. The appropriate wall and ceiling color will depend, quite obviously, upon the adequacy of the lighting and the specific type of work being performed.

Another factor that may affect decisions about the wall color to be used is the color of the material upon which work is being performed. All of us rest our eyes momentarily by looking away from the work surface. You look away from the textbook occasionally, for example, when you are reading; and your eyes wander away from the instructor or demonstration during a class period. Similarly, the industrial employee looks up from his work periodically.

An interesting illustration of the relationship between these brief visual rest periods and the optimal color for painting the surrounding surfaces occurred in the inspection room of a textile mill. The inspectors were scanning bluish denim, searching for defects. The walls were painted white to provide high reflectance on the assumption that the high illumination level would facilitate the inspection process. This assumption was entirely correct, but it neglected one important feature of the job. Since the employees were staring at the denim for relatively long periods of time, they reported a disturbing visual "afterimage" (peach color, in this instance) when they looked up from their work to rest their eyes momentarily. This negative afterimage, which is always the complement of the color to which the eye has been exposed for a prolonged period, interfered with normal vision for a while after the inspectors returned to their task. The simple solution in this case was to paint the walls in the color demanded by the eyes—that is, peach.[27]

The aesthetic value of particular hues and their influence upon behavior has been the subject of some investigation and considerable discussion. Darker hues create the illusion of pulling walls in or ceilings down; lighter hues create the visual impression of added spaciousness and airiness.

Colors on the red side of the spectrum are regarded as *warm,* exciting colors; those on the green and blue end of the spectrum are regarded as *cool,* tranquilizing colors. The distinction between

---

[27] "Color Punches the Time Clock," *The Management Review,* American Management Association, September, 1947, p. 452; and after Lloyd Stauffer, *Popular Science,* June, 1947, pp. 124–26.

warm and cool colors is regarded as extremely important by most interior decorators and color consultants and is exploited in a variety of ways. Persons are presumed to move more rapidly, to talk with greater animation, and generally to maintain a higher level of excitation in a predominantly red-orange environment than in a blue-green environment. Thus, an environment that is meant to be relaxing and calming ought to be painted in cool colors. The suggestion is sometimes made that work involving the generation of considerable heat should be performed in a room painted in cool colors, while large, vaulty work areas should be painted in warm colors.[28]

Such generalizations about the effect of color upon mood or subjective experiences of warmth and coolness are not well documented. We learn to make associations relative to particular colors and attach our own personal significances to particular hues. The range of such associations is tremendous, and generalizations about them are quite tenuous.

Noise

In assessing the industrial effect of noise, we must be concerned both with employee output (productivity) and with the input (or energy) necessary to achieve or maintain a given level of productivity. The finding, for example, that employees can adjust to noisy conditions without a production decrement would in itself be rather unimportant if this adjustment required them to expend considerable additional effort in order to maintain their productivity. Such additional effort would be reflected in undue fatigue, leading, perhaps, to job dissatisfaction and consequent personnel turnover and to an increased accident rate.

The interpretation of the effects of any environmental condition is complicated by differences in investigatory procedure. It is convenient in this regard to distinguish between "laboratory" and "field" studies. The former kind of investigation requires that groups of persons (either employees or persons assumed to be like employees) be removed from their actual working environment and required to perform in an artificially created environment. The task they perform for experimental purposes may be identical to the one they do on the job, or it may be a special task designed to incorporate the major elements of their job task.

---

[28] Fetter, *op. cit.* p. 4.

"Field" studies, on the other hand, are performed in the working environment. It is possible within certain limits to manipulate the environmental conditions in an office or a factory. It is also possible on occasion to study groups of employees performing essentially the same job but working in different environments.

The fundamental difference between these experimental procedures is an important one. The "Hawthorne effect," noted earlier, may be confounded in laboratory investigations by the fact that the entire setting is artificial. Thus, the discrepancy in experimental procedure (that is, laboratory versus field investigations) may account in part for discrepancies in the outcomes of studies concerned with noise and music. The amount of agreement based upon solid evidence concerning these variables is not outstanding.

Psychological Studies of Noise. Sounds differ with respect to loudness, pitch, and quality. Furthermore, a given sound may be continuous or, as most often the case in industry, intermittent. Considered together, these variables serve to distinguish between "pleasant" or "desired" and "unpleasant" or "unwanted" sounds. For practical purposes, the latter is what is meant by noise. Virtually all studies of industrial noise have been concerned with sounds that are reasonably loud, unpleasant in pitch and quality, and varying in continuity. There is, however, another aspect of sound having some bearing upon work efficiency, that is, its meaningfulness. It is considerably easier to disregard meaningless extraneous sounds (like the clatter of a typewriter) than it is to disregard meaningful sounds (like the conversation of other students in the study hall).

Several of the early laboratory investigations indicated that following the onset of noise, there is a minor decrease in productivity after which productivity increases above the level attained when the environment was relatively quiet. The maintenance of productivity is accomplished, however, at the worker's expense. He must exert additional effort to maintain his output. It has been found, for example, that noise leads to increases in muscle tension and metabolic rate.[29] These physiological changes are noted most immediately

[29] F. L. Harmon, "The Effects of Noise upon Certain Psychological and Physiological Processes," *Archives of Psychology*, Vol. 23, No. 147 (1933); D. A. Laird, "The Measurement of the Effects of Noise upon Working Efficiency," *Journal of Industrial Hygiene*, Vol. 9 (1927), pp. 431–34; J. J. B. Morgan, "The Overcoming of Distraction and Other Resistances," *Archives of Psychology*, Vol. 5, No. 35 (1916); and H. M. Vernon and C. G. Warner, "Objective and Subjective Tests for Noise," *Personnel Journal*, Vol. 11 (1932–33), pp. 141–49.

after the onset of noise. They decline, indicating diminished exertion, after a period of time during which the employee adapts to the noise.

The generalization that workers can adapt to noise and equal or surpass their former production level is, however, an artificial one. This generalization is founded upon laboratory investigations in which the participants were highly motivated and performed tasks requiring the exertion of short spurt-like efforts. These conditions are unlike those found in many industrial settings.

A more recent study examined the effects of noise upon sustained performance, leading to boredom and fatigue.[30] Groups of subjects were required to monitor a panel of dials under conditions of "relative quiet" and "noise." The former condition consisted of a background sound of approximately 80 decibel intensity (about as loud as the noise present in a typical office). The "noisy" condition consisted of sound intensity in excess of 110 decibels (about as loud as the sound of thunder).

The subjects were required to "work" for periods of two hours. Under the control condition, the laboratory was relatively quiet for the full time; under the experimental condition, the laboratory was relatively quiet for one half hour and noisy for the remaining $1\frac{1}{2}$ hours. The results, showing the average performance at the end of each half hour under these conditions, are shown in Figure 10–7. It is evident that the deleterious effects of noise upon the performance of this task (which required the maintenance of vigilance) became evident only after a relatively long period of time.

We will consider the results of one additional investigation of particular interest for three reasons: (1) it was a field rather than a laboratory study, (2) the performance investigated was manual rather than mental work, (3) a deliberate attempt was made to control for the Hawthorne effect.[31] The latter was accomplished by having the same subjects work under noisy and "quiet" conditions.

The investigators studied the output and other measures of efficiency for groups of employees working for periods under pre- and postnoise reduction conditions. These workers operated equipment perforating the side of movie film. Since they normally shifted

[30] H. J. Jerison, "Effects of Noise on Human Performance *Journal of Applied Psychology*, Vol. 42, No. 2 (1959), pp. 96–101.

[31] D. E. Broadbent and E. A. J. Little, "Effects of Noise Reduction in a Work Situation," *Occupational Psychology*, Vol. 34 (1960), pp. 133–40.

from one room to another in a systematic cycle of six weeks, this was chosen as the length for experimental and control periods. Noise reduction in one of the workrooms was accomplished by baffling between rows of machines and acoustic treatment of the walls and ceilings.

The outstanding finding was that although noise reduction did

FIGURE 10–7

Average Performance under Conditions of Relative Quiet and Noise

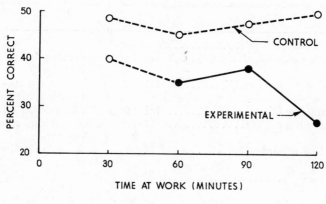

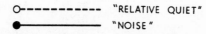 "RELATIVE QUIET"
"NOISE"

Note that the initial discrepancy between the experimental and control groups was maintained at a constant level for the first hour and a half. The deleterious effects of noise were apparent only after two hours.

not improve the rate of work, it significantly reduced shutdowns due to operator error and calls for maintenance. The magnitude of reduction in human errors following noise reduction led the investigators to hypothesize an interaction between noise and other features of this particular job, including the low illumination levels required for handling film. If such an interaction existed it might have acted to magnify the effects of noise reduction beyond what would be observed in other work conditions.

Nevertheless, the conclusions from this field study are consistent with those derived from laboratory investigations of high intensity, meaningless, and continuous noise upon tasks requiring continuous attention. Noise does not markedly affect productivity defined by work rate. It does, however, increase the frequency of momentary lapses in attention and is thereby responsible for some kinds of "human error."[32]

As with other factors in the work environment, it is impossible to formulate a generalization about the psychological effects of noise

TABLE 10–1

Typical Sound Levels for Selected Noise Sources and Environments
(distances are indicated in feet where appropriate)

Noise Source	Decibel Level	Environment
Hydraulic press (3′)	Above 130	
Large pneumatic riveter (4′)	121–130	Boiler shop (maximum level)
Trumpet auto horn (3′)	111–120	Jet engine test control room
Cutoff saw (2′)	101–110	Inside DC-6 airliner
Heavy trucks (20′)	91–100	Inside Chicago subway car
10 hp outboard	81–90	Inside sedan in city traffic
Autos (20′)	71–80	Office with tabulating machines
Conversational speech (3′)	61–70	Average traffic (100′)
	51–60	
	41–50	Average residence
	31–40	
	21–30	Broadcasting studio (music)

Adapted from A. P. G. Peterson and E. E. Gross, Jr. *Handbook of Noise Measurement* (New Concord, Mass.: General Radio Co., 1963), p. 4.

applicable in all circumstances. Whether or not the potential of noise for increasing human errors is of practical importance depends upon such things as the kind of work being done, the characteristics of the noise, and other aspects of the physical and social working environment.

Physiological Damage. Noise can have serious consequences apart from those regarded as fundamentally psychological in nature. Workmen's compensation is provided persons with hearing loss at-

---

[32] D. E. Broadbent, "Effects of Noise on Behavior," C. M. Harris (ed.), *Handbook of Noise Control* (New York: McGraw-Hill Book Co., Inc., 1957).

tributable to industrial noise. Legal proof of auditory damage is typically based upon the factors of intensity and length of time the worker is exposed to the noise. The New York State Workmen's Compensation Board, for example, uses the following standards in evaluating claims: (1) most persons will suffer permanent damage in a matter of months if exposed to over 120 decibels of noise for several hours daily; (2) a considerable portion of workers can suffer permanent hearing damage from exposure to 100–120 decibels for several hours daily; (3) a few persons may be permanently damaged by exposure for many years to noise between 90 and 100 decibels.[33]

The meaning of these decibel levels is clarified in Table 10–1.

Other factors interact with noise intensity and duration of exposure to cause permanent hearing loss. These include the continuity and pitch of the noise, and the health, age, and susceptibility of the listener.[34]

Music

You undoubtedly have certain personal feelings about the desirability or undesirability of having a radio or a record player operating while you are studying. It is likely, also, that you know someone (perhaps your room-mate) who feels quite differently from you about this matter. The interesting thing about this kind of discrepancy in attitude toward music as a facilitator or inhibitor of work is that there is a direct relationship between attitudes toward music and productivity during music periods.

This relationship has been investigated in the following way. Two groups of subjects were each required to do arithmetic calculations during a sequence of music periods and nonmusic periods. The groups were each given a different *set* or expectation regarding the effects of music. One of the groups was informed at the beginning of the experiment that the music would probably interfere with its ability to do mental arithmetic. This expectation was reinforced by the presentation of "data" allegedly showing that this finding had resulted from a previously conducted experiment. The other group was told that previous research had indicated that music facilitates

[33] John F. Goldsmith, "New and Noteworthy," *Factory Management and Maintenance,* February, 1954, p. 132.

[34] L. J. Williams, "Some Industrial Noise Problems and Their Solution," *Noise Control,* Vol. 5 (1959), pp. 36–43.

FIGURE 10–8

The Effect of Expectation about the Effects of Music upon Actual Performance

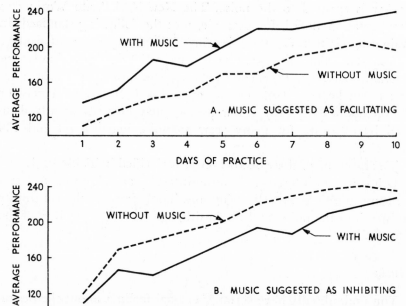

The performance of subjects during music and nonmusic sessions was compared for two groups:
A. Music was suggested as facilitating performance.
B. Music was suggested as inhibiting performance.

mental arithmetic, and appropriate "documentation" was presented to this group also. The actual arithmetic performance of the subjects in these groups indicated that their productivity was directly related to their expectations concerning the effects of the music (see Figure 10–8).[35]

From these and other findings, it is evident that unqualified claims for increased production resulting from the introduction of music at work are not proven.[36] Some of the factors influencing the effect of music upon productivity, aside from the individual's expectations, are the kind of work being done and his preferences con-

---

[35] K. H. Baker, "Pre-experimental Set in Distraction Experiments," *Journal of General Psychology*, Vol. 16 (1937), pp. 471–86.

[36] R. S. Uhrbrock, "Music on the Job: Its Influence on Worker Morale and Production," *Personnel Psychology*, Vol. 14 (1961), pp. 9–38.

cerning music. Not all workers, in fact, like music. It is estimated that from 1 to 10 percent are annoyed by it.

Nature of the Work. Music is most likely to be beneficial for work that is of a short-cycle and highly repetitive nature. Such work often does not utilize enough of the employee's abilities. His attention is not absorbed by the task, and he regards the work as monotonous. The hours of the day tend to move slowly, and the employee may experience very little personal satisfaction. In such circumstances, music may increase productivity and worker satisfaction. It is pleasantly diverting and may make time appear to move more rapidly.

The beneficial effects of music under such circumstances were demonstrated quite clearly by a very careful investigation involving a large number of employees engaged in radio assembly.[37] It was found that a production increase attributable to music was considerably more marked during the night shift than during the day shift, although music was beneficial also during the day. Employee reaction to the music was extremely favorable; only 2 percent of the workers indicated that they did not care at all for it.

The effect of music is, of course, to distract the worker. Music is beneficial both to productivity and morale only when such distraction is desirable. Thus, it must be emphasized that results favorable to music are generally obtained only for employees performing routine, repetitive jobs. More complex jobs requiring a greater amount of employee attentiveness generally are performed better in the absence of any distracting influence.

Kinds of Music. It is not clear whether output is affected by the type of music played, in spite of employee preferences for certain types of music. Factory operators participating in one study, for example, were found to prefer popular and march-polka music over waltz-Hawaiian music. Furthermore, output and quality were lowest on days when the latter kind of music was played.[38] However, comparable results were not obtained in a more recent study with assembly line workers. Here, performance was compared for four kinds of music conditions and a control (no music) condition. The types of music were: show (Broadway musical numbers, both instru-

---

[37] H. C. Smith, *Music in Relation to Employee Attitudes, Work Production and Industrial Accidents,* Applied Psychology Monographs, No. 14, 1947.

[38] W. A. Kerr, *Experiments on the Effects of Music on Factory Production,* Applied Psychology Monograph, No. 5, 1945.

mental and vocal) ; dance (instrumental arrangements of old favor-
ites and current songs) ; folk (vocal selections by Joan Baez, Peter,
Paul, and Mary, and so on) ; popular (largely vocal selections by the
Beatles, the Brothers Four, and similar groups) . Although the latter
music was the most preferred, this preference was not reflected in the
quantity or quality of output.[39]

Because no simple generalization is possible about the effects of
different kinds of music, this variable should be treated experimentally in each work setting without making prior assumptions about
the likely impact of different types of music.

The typical practice when making use of music in an industrial
setting is to restrict each music session to a 20- to 40-minute period.
These periods are generally inserted into the midmorning and midafternoon schedule at about the time when monotony and fatigue
reach a maximum. Some companies make a practice also of scheduling music periods at the beginning and at the end of the shift. This
procedure is presumed to create a pleasant working environment
when the employees begin and terminate the day's work.

Temperature and Ventilation

Industrial ventilation is of considerable interest because of the
demonstrated relationship between this environmental factor and
such criteria as productivity, spoilage, and accident rate. A substantial body of research has been conducted relative to the three essential components of ventilation: temperature, humidity, and air
movement. It has been found that control of any one of these factors
is by itself relatively valueless unless the others are controlled also. A
temperature of 90° F, for example, is much less comfortable when
the humidity is high and the air relatively stationary than it is when
the humidity is low and the air is in motion.

Thus, it is much more meaningful to consider *effective temperature* than it is to consider absolute temperature (as measured by a
dry-bulb thermometer) . The effective temperature scale combines
the subjective effects of temperature, humidity, and air movement.
When air movement is at a minimum, a dry bulb temperature of
90 F at 10 percent humidity constitutes the same effective tempera-

---

[39] R. I. Newman, Jr., D. L. Hunt, and F. Rhodes, "Effects of Music on Employee
Attitudes and Productivity in a Skateboard Factory," *Journal of Applied Psychology*,
Vol. 50 (1966) , pp. 493–96.

ture (that is, is as comfortable as) a temperature reading of 75° F at 100 percent humidity or a reading of 80° F at 60 percent humidity.[40]

The relative comfort or discomfort experienced in a particular effective temperature is, of course, partially a function of the kind of work being performed. One reviewer concluded, as a cautious generalization, that the maximum effective temperature for the performance of simple sedentary tasks without serious impairment is 85° F.[41] Tolerance limits for heavy physical labor are, of course, much lower.

SUMMARY

The effects of changes in the physical working environment must be interpreted cautiously for a number of reasons. First, employees respond not only to an objectively definable change in illumination or noise level but also to their attitudes concerning such changes. If they interpret a change as evidence for the fact that management is interested in their welfare, they will respond positively and their productivity may increase. If, however, the employees interpret the change solely as an economy measure designed by management to "get more for its money," actual productivity may decline.

Related to the matter of employee attitudes are the facts that short-term effects of environmental changes are insufficient as a basis for determining the true worth of such changes, and that the results of laboratory investigations are not always verified when similar changes are instituted in the field.

Finally, environmental changes which lead to a production increase are not always desirable. It would be unwise to institute any such change, even if it increased productivity and reduced expenses, if these outcomes were accomplished by forcing a considerable increase in employee input or effort. Such additional effort may lead to job dissatisfaction, increased spoilage, and accidents, all of which may well offset the advantages relative to improved productivity and economy.

Fatigue and boredom are both undesirable consequences of industrial activity. These conditions lead to diminished output and subjective feelings of strain and tension. Although the effects of

---

[40] *Heating, Ventilating, Air Conditioning Guide,* American Society of Heating and Ventilating Engineers Comfort Chart for Still Air, 1947.

[41] L. Connell, "The Effect of Heat Upon the Performance of Men in High Speed Aircraft: A Critical Review," *USN, Special Devices Center Report* 151–1–17, 1948.

fatigue and boredom are somewhat similar, the factors responsible for these conditions are quite different.

Fatigue is a temporary experience resulting from prolonged muscular activity, and it is characterized by a declining capacity for continued work. Boredom is differentiated from fatigue by the kind of activity that generates it and its rather high degree of specificity. Monotonous work is uninteresting to the employee. Furthermore, the bored worker seeks relief only from the activity he regards as monotonous, while the fatigued worker seeks rest from all activity.

The alleviation of fatigue may be approached in several ways including: (a) the use of appropriate personnel selection and placement procedures; (b) modifications in the length of the work period and the insertion of authorized rest pauses into the schedule; (c) improvements in certain environmental conditions including illumination and ventilation, and the reduction of undue noise and vibration; (d) changes in work methods and equipment.

Because of the different nature and consequences of monotonous activity, remediational measures for boredom differ from those for fatigue. Boredom may be somewhat reduced by assigning employees to jobs that are congruent with their interests and capabilities. In addition, provision should be made in the training program for informing employees about the relationship between their particular job and the total industrial operation. Other approaches to alleviating boredom include job enlargement, job rotation, authorized rest pauses, music, and bonus payments for high productivity.

Studies of industrial illumination have indicated that the critical requirements for light intensity vary with the nature of the task being performed. Work involving the manipulation of small objects with great precision requires more intense illumination than does work involving the manipulation of large objects for which precision is not a critical feature. Light distribution and reflection are also important aspects of the visual environment. The entire visual field must be relatively evenly illuminated and glare must be eliminated if visual comfort is to be maximized.

The use of color in the working environment has been the subject of many extravagant claims, not all of which can be documented. The appropriate use of color can contribute to the safety and efficiency of the work environment. About the only thing that can be said about the overall color scheme or decor, however, is that it should not be regarded by the employees as unpleasant.

Noise may, but need not, impede industrial efficiency. Whether or not the potential of noise for increasing "human error" is of practical importance depends upon such factors as the characteristics of the noise, the kind of work being done, and other aspects of the physical and social working environment. Aside from the possibility of undesirable psychological consequences, certain kinds of noises are clearly responsible for auditory damage.

Music is a distracting factor and is thus most likely to be beneficial for work that is of a short-cycle and highly repetitive nature. More complex tasks requiring a greater amount of employee attentiveness generally are performed better in the absence of any distracting influence.

Psychologists and engineers have been concerned with three essential and interdependent components of ventilation: temperature, humidity, and air movement. These components, considered together, constitute the subjective factor of "effective temperature." The worker's tolerance for a relatively high effective temperature is greatest if he is engaged in simple sedentary tasks and lowest if he is engaged in heavy physical labor.

11. Safety and Accident Control

Everyone regards war as a cause of extensive devastation, death, and injury. The weapons recently developed by man for destroying the enemy are horribly effective. Even during World War II, fought with much more rudimentary weapons, our own casualties between the start of the war and the surrender of Japan numbered in excess of 900,000 persons, almost one third of whom were killed.[1] Thus, war injuries and deaths affected a group of persons comparable to the entire population of a fair-size city.

The destructiveness of a war, however, is exceeded by the sheer waste of human resources attributable to civilian accidents. The number of deaths and injuries from civilian accidents during the period of World War II exceeded those classified as war casualties. Accidental civilian deaths during this period numbered approximately 350,000, and injuries numbered 36,000,000.[2] Accidents in the home were responsible for the greatest proportion of these injuries and deaths, but occupational and automotive accidents also contributed substantially to this enormous waste of manpower.

One other alarming statistic will suffice to set the stage for this chapter. Although we will be concerned most specifically with the matter of occupational safety, much of the discussion will be sufficiently general to apply with equal facility to nonoccupational accidents. The data relative to injuries and deaths resulting from automobile accidents provide convincing evidence for the fact that the improperly handled automobile is a lethal weapon that rivals those

---

[1] National Safety Council, Inc., *Accident Facts* (Chicago, 1946), p. 17.
[2] *Ibid.*

deliberately developed for combative purposes. Vehicular accidents alone in the United States during 1966 were responsible for about 52,000 deaths and 1,900,000 nonfatal injuries.[3]

We cannot, as a society, afford to neglect the matter of accident prevention. Research and the application of knowledge in this area is as critical as it is in combating such medical scourges as cancer and heart disease. The fatalistic notion that accidents cannot happen to us or that they will occur because of "bad luck" regardless of our efforts to prevent them is contrary to the facts. The role of luck (including such things as unavoidable equipment malfunction) as a cause of accidents has been the subject of considerable study. Estimates of the percentage of accidents due to such causes, and therefore unpreventable, vary between 10 and 20 percent. The large majority of accidents are clearly due to human factors rather than to "fate." The most efficient eyeshield in the world is valueless, for example, if an employee refuses to use it. And even a smoothly functioning aircraft is subject to pilot error involving misinterpretation of its instrumentation or poor judgment relative to landing conditions.

Accident prevention requires the joint efforts of engineers and psychologists. The fact that proportionately few accidents are attributable to equipment malfunction would seem to indicate that engineering principles related to safety have been well-developed and widely accepted. The psychological factors responsible for accidents have been studied also, but there is some reticence about applying the knowledge now available in this area.

This chapter is concerned primarily with the human factors responsible for accidents and with certain procedures for preventing their occurrence. The fact that relatively little attention is given to many of the engineering problems related to safety should not be taken as an indication that these factors are unimportant. Rather, this emphasis reflects the fact that the majority of accidents are due to human factors rather than to equipment malfunction.

CAUSES OF ACCIDENTS

It is not difficult to understand management's concern for employee safety. Accidents are expensive. They are responsible for a direct cost in terms of diminished productivity, as well as for the

---

[3] *Automobile Facts and Figures* (Automobile Manufacturer's Association, 1966–67).

related costs of providing medical attention and compensation. For 1963, the National Safety Council estimated the economic loss attributable to industrial accidents as $5,300,000,000. This figure is certainly higher now. Accidents, furthermore, may have a deleterious effect upon plant morale. It is understandably disturbing to employees, for example, to know that they are working at a job that has led in the past to a substantial number of injuries.

Work in certain industries is more hazardous than in others. The lumber, mining, and construction industries characteristically rank higher with respect to accident frequency than do communications and electrical equipment.[4] This discrepancy in safety record as a function of the industry suggests at least three general factors which are potential causes of accidents. The first, and most obvious, of these is the *physical working environment*. The greater the exposure of an employee to dangerous equipment and to unfavorable working circumstances, the greater is his liability to accidents. A second causal factor suggested by interindustry differences in accident frequency is *personal* in nature. Certain industries are more selective than others in hiring and retaining employees on the basis of such personal variables as age, prior experience, and physical health. Finally, industries (and individual companies within an industry) may differ markedly in the extent of their concern about employee *attitudes* relative to safety. Workers who are unimpressed by the potential of their surroundings and job activities for causing accidents are more likely to be injured than those who have developed attitudes of appropriate caution.

The Physical Work Environment

A good deal has already been said about the working environment in Chapter 10. Unfavorable or unpleasant environments are responsible for diminishing productivity and lowering morale. It should be readily apparent also that certain environmental conditions may be either direct or indirect causes of accidents. Improperly anchored equipment, for example, would be regarded as a direct causal agent. Such factors as improper illumination or ventilation may either act directly as causes of accidents by making it virtually impossible for the worker to perform with safety, or may act indirectly by making the job unpleasant and the worker incautious.

---

[4] National Safety Council, Inc., *Accident Facts* (Chicago, 1955).

Ventilation. The component of ventilation usually explored with reference to accidents is temperature. The relationship between accident frequency and temperature is shown clearly in Figure 11–1. The employees upon whom these data were based were all engaged in factory work. Fewest accidents occurred when the temperature was about 68 to 70°; a noticeable increase in accident

FIGURE 11–1

Accident Frequency in Relation to Temperature

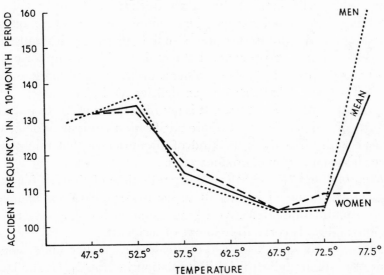

Source: E. E. Osborne and H. M. Vernon, *The Influence of Temperature and Other Conditions on the Frequency of Industrial Accidents,* Industrial Fatigue Research Board, No. 19 (London: H. M. Stationery Office, 1922).

frequency was observed when temperatures declined. The discrepancy between the accident rates noted for men and women as the temperature increased above 70° is of some interest. It suggests the possibility that the adverse effects of high temperatures may be sex-linked. This conclusion is confounded, however, by the fact that men are generally assigned to jobs requiring a greater amount of physical exertion and hence may be more vulnerable to accidents as temperature increases.

The results discussed above were based upon records of relatively minor accidents. When coal mine accidents were classified according to severity (i.e., length of time absent from work), it was found that rising temperature increased the rate of minor accidents to a much greater extent than that of major accidents.[5] The discomfort associated with higher temperature probably leads to the kind of carelessness or indisposition toward work that is particularly responsible for minor accidents. The suggestion has been made, also, that workers may be more likely to use a minor injury as an excuse to take time off when the working environment becomes unpleasant.

One aspect of ventilation that may on occasion be a very direct cause of accidental injury is oxygen deprivation and the accumulation of noxious fumes. Flights at an altitude of about 14,000 feet without supplemental oxygen, for example, will produce oxygen starvation. The pilot may suffer visual impairment, his muscular coordination will be poor, and he may feel giddy or euphoric. His ability to reason and to solve problems under such circumstances is affected seriously. Anoxia (oxygen deficiency) is, of course, a rare occurrence at the present time. It is not of major concern to industry because of the development of air purification equipment sufficient to cope with virtually every kind of circumstance that might produce an accumulation of noxious gases.

Illumination. Twilight is a dangerous time of the day for driving simply because it is difficult to see under conditions of inadequate illumination. Defective illumination in industry is a rather obvious and easily correctible source of accidents.

Studies made some years ago of accident frequency under conditions of daylight and artificial illumination indicated that the latter circumstance produced a considerable increase in accident rate. Enormous improvements have been made by lighting engineers, however, since these investigations were conducted. The unshielded, low intensity incandescent lamp should by now be a relic of the past. Proper artificial lighting still provides illumination that is somewhat inferior to daylight, but the differences are not great.

Equipment Design. The newspapers occasionally report an automobile accident occurring at night because the driver erroneously depressed his headlight button instead of his cigarette lighter. This kind of accident reflects the folly of poor equipment design and the sacrifice of safety in the interest of the aesthetics of dashboard arrangement. Many accidents can be avoided in circumstances in which rapid judgments are necessary by utilizing knobs of appropri-

---

[5] H. M. Vernon, *Accidents and Their Prevention* (Cambridge, Eng., and New York: The University Press and The Macmillan Co., 1936) , p. 80.

ate shapes and dials that are amenable to accurate interpretation. It is apparent that some automobile manufacturers are less impressed than they should be with the importance of proper equipment.

The design of manufacturing equipment with built-in safety devices and power cutoffs, and of special clothing that does not itself interfere with productivity, is a matter of very direct concern to industry. This is a particularly critical problem in circumstances in which the operation of the equipment demands continual exposure of the employee to moving parts, cutting edges, and flying debris.

This entire matter of the relationship between equipment design, intended function, and the capabilities and limitations of human operators is discussed in detail in the next chapter. As it relates to safety, proper equipment design requires a rather precise understanding of the sources of particular kinds of accidents.

This line of reasoning provided the rationale for a study of taxicab drivers with an abnormal number of accidents in which they were struck from behind. These drivers were found to have a reaction pattern made up of slow initiation time and compensatingly fast movement time. Thus, they probably stopped their vehicles abruptly in a way that cannot be duplicated by a following driver. The two solutions proposed by the investigator are retraining and/or human engineering. The latter would call for changes in the braking system, perhaps adjusting it to the driver as one adjusts the seat.[6]

Personal Characteristics of the Employee

The Metropolitan Life Insurance Company classified the causes of accidents experienced by employees of a railway company with the results noted in Table 11–1.[7] About 20 percent of the accidents were attributed to physical and personal disability (including defective vision, organic disease, worry and depression, and so on) ; the remainder were caused primarily by attitudinal factors.

Health. It is unnecessary to belabor the importance of physical health to safe industrial operation. An employee who is ill cannot devote the required amount of attention to his job and is likely to be somewhat careless.

The relationship between physical disability and accident liabil-

---

[6] P. Babarik, "Automobile Accidents and Driver Reaction Pattern," *Journal of Applied Psychology*, Vol. 52 (1968) , pp. 49–54.

[7] *The Accident Prone Employee* (New York Metropolitan Life Insurance Co., 1930).

ity is, however, a somewhat different matter. If the disability inter-feres with satisfactory job performance, the employee may experi-ence an accident because of his defect rather than carelessness. One of the sources of accidents that can be most readily identified and easily corrected is defective vision. A comparison between the preva-lence of visual defects among good and poor drivers, for example, indicated that accident-free drivers were significantly less susceptible

TABLE 11-1

Causes of Accidents in the Cleveland Street
Railway Company

Faulty attitude.............................14%
Failure to recognize potential hazards.......12
Faulty judgment of speed or distance........12
Impulsiveness.............................10
Irresponsibility........................... 8
Failing to keep attention constant........... 8
Nervousness and fear...................... 6
Defective vision.......................... 4
Organic disease.......................... 4
Slow reaction............................ 4
High blood pressure...................... 2
Senility................................. 2
Worry and depression..................... 2
Fatigue................................. 2
Improper distribution of attention.......... 2
Inexperience............................ 2
Miscellaneous........................... 6

to glare sensitivity, relatively free from astigmatism, and more likely to have adequate visual acuity.[8]

Many companies have drawn up rather elaborate sets of physical specifications for various jobs in recognition of the fact that it would be utter foolishness to assign persons with certain disabilities to certain kinds of jobs. It is important to bear in mind, however, that the mere fact of the existence of a physical disability should not be construed as a contraindication for employment unless it is clear that the disability will interfere with satisfactory job performance. Quite often the handicapped worker, once aware of his limitations, can learn to compensate for a disability effectively. Thus, when

---

[8] E. D. Fletcher, *Capacity of Special Tests to Measure Driving Ability,* State of California, Department of Motor Vehicles.

handicapped workers are properly placed, employers report lower absenteeism and termination as well as accident rates than for able-bodied persons employed on similar jobs.[9]

Age and Experience. The relationship between age and accident frequency reflects the operation of at least three variables which underlie the age factor: health, experience, and attitude. Younger employees as a group may be in better physical health than older workers, but they are more likely to be relatively inexperienced and somewhat more irresponsible. Studies of age as a cause of accidents

TABLE 11–2

Tabulation of Accident Frequency
at an Ordinance Depot

Age Group	Male Rate per Hundred	Female Rate per Hundred
17–21. 172		41
21–28. 75		36
28–35. 65		17
35–45. 50		26
45–60. 42		37
60+. 35		0

Source: J. Mann, "Analysis of 1,009 Consecutive Accidents at One Ordinance Depot," *Industrial Medicine,* Vol. 13 (1944), pp. 368–74.

are further complicated by the selective factors sometimes applied to older employees. Advancing age may be used by management as a reason for discharging an employee, particularly if he has a history of high accident frequency, or for reassigning him to less hazardous work.

The effect of this constellation of factors associated with aging is to produce consistent findings indicative of a lower accident rate for older than for younger employees. The data for workers in an ordinance depot, shown in Table 11–2, are typical of such studies. The incidental evidence apparent in this table, that men are more likely to have accidents than are women, is also a persistently recurring finding.

A similar pattern of accident frequency is discovered when acci-

---

[9] C. H. Stone and W. E. Kendall, *Effective Personnel Selection Procedures* (Englewood Cliffs, N. J.: Prentice-Hall, Inc., 1956) .

dents are plotted as a function of length of service or experience rather than of age. The more experienced employees (generally the older employees) have considerably fewer accidents than do the relatively inexperienced employees. That this is due to experience and is not merely an artifact of increased maturity is confirmed by two studies: one with youthful employees (see Figure 11–2) and one with older employees (see Figure 11–3).

In spite of the favorable safety record accumulated by older

FIGURE 11–2

Accidents Incurred by Young Employees as a Function of Years of Experience

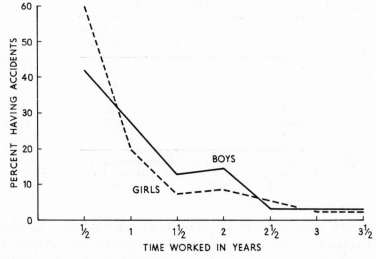

Source: H. M. Vernon, "Prevention of Accidents," *British Journal of Industrial Medicine*, Vol. 2 (1945), p. 3.

employees by virtue of experiential and attitudinal factors, there is a particular set of circumstances in which age must be regarded as a detrimental factor. Whenever the job makes physical demands upon the employee which are more readily satisfied by younger workers, the older employee is likely to be particularly susceptible to accidents. Thus, as shown in Figure 11–4, age is positively correlated with accident frequency under adverse temperature conditions when the work is strenuous.

The entire matter of the employment of older personnel is one that requires serious consideration by management because medical

FIGURE 11–3

Accidents by Older Employees as a Function of Experience on the Job

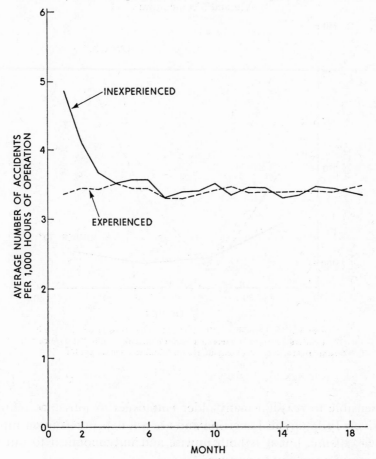

Source: R. H. Van Zelst, "The Effect of Age and Experience on Accident Rate," *Journal of Applied Psychology*, Vol. 38 (1954), pp. 313–17.

advances have increased our span of active, healthy years. There is no magic inherent in the number "65" dictating this as an age for mandatory retirement. Certain physical abilities, including vision and speed of reaction, are known to decrease with advancing age. There are, however, widespread individual differences in the rate and severity of such impairments. Furthermore, the depth of job knowledge accumulated by virtue of experience may act in many instances to offset the physical accompaniments of aging. It is proba-

FIGURE 11–4

Accident Frequency of Coal Face Workers in Relation to
Age and Temperature

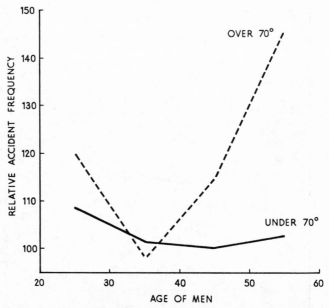

Source: H. M. Vernon and T. Bedford, *The Absenteeism of Min-
ers in Relation to Short Time and Other Conditions*, Industrial Health
Research Board, No. 62 (London: H. M. Stationery Office, 1931).

bly sensible to reassign many older employees to jobs that require
relatively little physical exertion and are not dependent upon rapidity of response, but it is both unwise and uneconomical to put all
older employees "out to pasture."

Fatigue. You will recall from the discussion in Chapter 10 that
one of the effects of fatigue is to decrease productivity. This decline
in the output curve typically is observed during the periods immediately preceding lunch and the termination of the workday. The
same general kind of curve has been found to result when accidents
(rather than output) are plotted as a function of time of the day.[10]
Thus, there appears to be a relationship between production rate
and accident frequency.

It is necessary, therefore, in investigating the relationship be-

---

[10] Vernon, *op. cit.*

tween fatigue and accident rate, to somehow separate out the influence of output which is related both to fatigue and to accident
frequency. This has been done by utilizing a simple index of accident frequency per unit of production. The resultant data, obtained
over a relatively long period of time in plants working 8- and
10-hour shifts, are exhibited in Figure 11–5. The accident index was
found to parallel the output curve very closely during the 8-hour
shift, indicating that production increases tend to be accompanied

FIGURE 11–5

Accident Ratio for 8-Hour and 10-Hour Day with Production Rate Constant

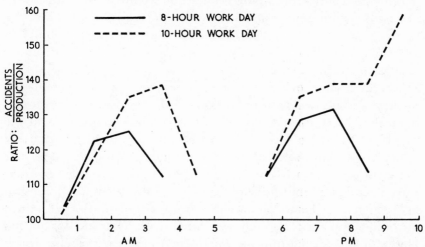

by an increment in accident frequency. The 10-hour shift, however,
provided for the development of considerable fatigue leading to a
rise in the accident index during the last two hours of the shift in
spite of declining productivity.[11]

Evidence of this sort leads to the conclusion that although fatigue
can be rather directly responsible for accidents, it is not a causal
factor of significant concern in most industrial settings. The 8-hour
workday, which tends to prevent the occurrence of the kind of

---

[11] J. Goldmark, M. D. Hopkins, P. S. Florence, and F. S. Lee, "Studies in Industrial
Physiology: Fatigue in Relation to Working Capacity, No. 1 (Comparison of an
Eight-Hour Plant and a Ten-Hour Plant)," *Public Health Bulletin No. 106,* U.S.
Public Health Service, 1920.

extreme fatigue associated with accidental injury, is fairly well standardized.

Attitudes, Adjustment, and Emotional Factors

An employee who is free from debilitating physical characteristics, who works under optimal environmental conditions, and who is aware of the limitations of his equipment is still quite likely to have an accident if his attitudinal pattern is one of recklessness, irresponsibility, or uncooperativeness. Such attitudes are, of course, symptomatic of more fundamental kinds of personal maladjustment. A mature, well-adjusted employee does not regard it as "sissified" to observe safety precautions and to avoid unnecessary risks. Thus, the entire matter of the relationship between attitudes and liability to accidents has generally been investigated within the broader context of adjustmental and emotional factors.

There is some evidence, for example, that high accident frequency is associated with neuroticism. This evidence is predicated upon the observed correlation between accident frequency and the number of visits to the dispensary for the treatment of relatively minor conditions. Since absences for reasons of sickness were not found to correlate with accident frequency, the investigator interpreted his data as indicative of something other than a relationship between general health and accidents. A continual history of minor medical complaints is often associated with neurotic instability. Hence, it appears that this underlying personality pattern is a factor of some importance in causing accidents.[12]

More concrete evidence relative to the relationship between personal maladjustment and susceptibility to accidents was provided by a study of over 100 workers who had experienced more than 400 minor accidents. More than half of these accidents occurred when the worker was emotionally disturbed, that is, worried, apprehensive, and so on. Such emotional states resulted either from concerns about the job or represented a transference of difficulties being experienced in the home. Some of the workers who experienced accidents were found also to be susceptible to rather regular periodic fluctuations in mood or emotional tone.[13]

---

[12] Vernon, *op. cit.*

[13] R. B. Hersey, "Emotional Factors in Accidents," *Personnel Journal,* Vol. 15 (1936), pp. 59–65.

The picture that emerges of the person who is a high accident risk is that of one given to transitory and situational rather than more pervasive and basic emotional upset. Note, for example, in Table 11–3 that the distribution of automobile accident frequencies for neuropsychiatric patients admitted to a California Veterans Administration hospital closely approximates the distribution for a random sample of all California drivers.

TABLE 11–3

Distribution of Accident Frequencies for Patient
Sample and Random Sample of California Drivers

Accidents	California Drivers' Percentages	Patient Frequencies	Expected Patient Frequencies
None	78.66	133	129.79
1	17.49	31	28.85
2	3.20	1	5.28
3	0.53	0	0.87
4	0.10	0	0.17
5	0.01	0	0.02
6 or more	0.01	0	0.02
Total	100%	165	165.00

Source: M. W. Buttiglieri and M. Guenette, "Driving Records of Neuropsychiatric Patients," *Journal of Applied Psychology*, Vol. 51 (1967), p. 97.

Efforts to identify a "personality type" or a constellation of personality traits associated with high accident liability have not been particularly successful. Although the data from such studies have not proven to be especially useful for predictive purposes, they have provided some important clues about the personalities of individuals who have repetitive accidents. Accident repeaters were found in one study to be differentiated from other workers by being overly fearful, fatalistic (feeling that they were unlucky), overly ambitious, revengeful, and desirous of pampering.[14] A similarly unhealthy emotional pattern involving feelings of hostility and lack of concern for the social consequences of actions was discovered as a

[14] A. Adler, "The Psychology of Repeated Accidents in Industry," *American Journal of Psychiatry*, Vol. 98 (1941), pp. 99–101.

correlate of automotive accidents.[15] Emotional immaturity as evidenced by a tendency to become easily disturbed by minor irritations, to "blow off steam" in excess of that required by the situation, and by a kind of general irresponsibility and lack of considerateness, was found to be related to accident frequency for route salesmen.[16]

It must be reiterated that the above noted relationships between personality and accident frequency are not strong. Were they more potent, we should have some basis for a statement to the effect that certain kinds of persons are "accident-prone"; that is, that their personality is such that we would expect them to have accidents with considerably greater frequency than dictated solely on the basis of chance. The issue of accident-proneness has received considerable attention in the professional literature, and it is appropriate that we direct our attention next to this matter.

ACCIDENT-PRONENESS

The reasons for interest in, and even excitement about, the possibility of demonstrating the existence of an accident-prone personality are relatively apparent. If it could be demonstrated that certain kinds of persons are much more susceptible than others to accidents, we would be provided with a powerful tool for the prevention of accidents. Accident-prone employees could presumably be identified and assigned to nonhazardous jobs.

The tenability of the principle of accident-proneness hinges upon the demonstration that some persons have many more accidents than one would forecast for them on the basis of chance, while others have many fewer accidents than one would expect if chance factors alone were operative. The typical evidence in support of the principle is based upon the demonstration that a relatively small percentage of employees have a disproportionately large percentage of accidents. One study of accidents in which taxicab drivers were involved, for example, found that 40 percent of the drivers had 70 percent of the accidents.[17] Thus, the argument was made that since some drivers never had an accident while others had several accidents, the latter must be accident-prone.

---

[15] P. L. Brown and R. P. Berdie, "Driver Behavior and Scores on the MMPI," *Journal of Applied Psychology*, Vol. 44 (1960) , pp. 18–21.

[16] A. H. Malo, "New Light on the Accident Prone," *Personnel*, July, 1954, p. 65.

[17] *Preventing Taxicab Accidents* (New York: Metropolitan Life Insurance Company, 1931) .

The critical feature overlooked in such "demonstrations" of accident-proneness is the proper definition of chance. The question of the number of accidents to be expected solely on the basis of chance is a little like asking how many heads in a row would result from flipping a coin. Assuming no bias in the coin or in the flipping procedure, we would expect to observe 50 percent heads and 50 percent tails *in the long run.* You are well aware, however, that it would be possible to observe five heads in a row on five consecutive flips just by chance. The odds against this occurring are high, but it can happen! The fact that it does happen occasionally is what tempts the inveterate gambler to try the "long shots."

Mintz and Blum have been most articulate in pointing out the defect inherent in the interpretation of accident data like those cited for taxicab drivers as supportive of the principle of proneness. They write:

The method of percentages of people and accidents implies an incorrect assumption, *viz.,* that chance expectation requires that all people in a population should have the same number of accidents. This is not the case. An obvious limitation that has often been overlooked is the fact that very often the reported total number of accidents in a population is smaller than the number of people in the population. For example, if a group of one hundred factory workers had fifty accidents in one year, then a maximum of fifty people could have contributed to the accident record and accordingly a maximum of 50% of the population would have contributed to 100% of the accidents. Obviously, a small percentage of the population in this case does not establish the principle of accident proneness.[18]

They follow this argument with another: there is no reason to assume that one accident immunizes the victim against the possibility of having other accidents. It is perfectly plausible to expect that some persons will just by chance have several accidents while others may not have any. The application of these arguments was used to develop an appropriate chance distribution of accident frequency for the taxicab accidents cited earlier, with the result shown in Figure 11–6. You will note that the obtained accident frequency and the chance expectancies are very similar in shape. There is some evidence for the fact that something other than chance was operating to produce the observed distribution of accidents because the discrepancy between the obtained and chance distributions is statis-

[18] A Mintz and M. L. Blum, "A Reexamination of the Accident Proneness Concept," *Journal of Applied Psychology,* Vol. 33 (1949), p. 196.

tically significant. It is quite clear, however, that the principle of accident-proneness is not nearly as formidable as it was once thought to be. Mintz and Blum concluded, from the examination of these and similar sets of data, that the variance attributable to differences in accident liability is about 20 to 40 percent. The effect of this factor is small when compared with the estimated 60 to 80 percent attributable to other factors.

FIGURE 11–6

Obtained and Expected Distributions of Accidents by
Taxicab Drivers

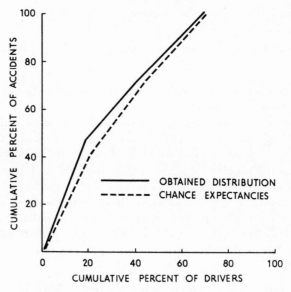

A somewhat lower estimate of the accident variance attributable to a constitutional or permanent predisposition is arrived at in another way. If a person were accident-prone, he ought to experience an abnormally high accident rate over two different periods of time.[19] It has been estimated from collating such correlations of accident frequency over time that constitutional predisposition accounts for a *maximum* of 15 percent of accidents.[20] Actually, since certain factors, like exposure to hazard, are uncontrolled in such

---

[19] J. S. Maritz, "On the Validity of Inference Drawn from the Fitting of Poisson and Negative Bionomial Distributions to Observed Accident Data," *Psychological Bulletin,* Vol. 47 (1946), pp. 434–43.

[20] W. Kerr, "Complementary Theories of Safety Psychology," *Journal of Social Psychology,* Vol. 45 (1957), pp. 3–9.

studies and therefore may be systematic sources of error spuriously raising the correlations, the actual importance of accident-proneness may be even less.

Thus, the accident-proneness hypothesis has been placed in perspective. It was thought at one time that the primary route to the prevention of accidents was the utilization of appropriate personnel selection procedures designed to identify and eliminate those applicants who would tend to be accident-prone under virtually all circumstances. The most recent evidence, however, supports the contention that an individual's liability to accidents is highly specific. The fact that he is accident-prone under a given set of circumstances does not mean that he will be accident-prone under other circumstances. And the role of constitutional tendencies toward unsafe behavior is regarded as much less important than originally believed.

Two other concepts have been proposed as more powerful explanatory hypotheses than accident-proneness: (a) goals-freedom-alertness and (b) adjustment-stress.[21]

In terms of the "goals-freedom-alertness" hypothesis, the greater the worker's freedom to establish goals with a reasonable probability of attainment (that is, the greater his involvement in the task), the greater will be his alertness and work quality. Since an accident may be regarded as a variety of low-quality work, a participative and involving psychological climate may reduce accident frequency.

The "adjustment-stress" hypothesis holds that any adverse stress increases the organism's liability to accidents. Such stresses are temporary and may be internal to the organism (for example, disease) or external (for example, excessive temperature or noise).

All three hypotheses (accident-proneness, goals-freedom-alertness, and adjustment-stress) are complementary. Therefore, the focus of activity in the area of industrial safety has changed from that of a fundamental emphasis upon the identification of potential accident victims to a multidimensional approach emphasizing accident prevention.

ACCIDENT CONTROL

An industrial safety program must contain at least three elements in order to be of maximum effectiveness. Such a program must

---

[21] *Ibid.*

include provisions for (1) the identification and correction of unsafe working practices and conditions; (2) the specification of employee characteristics required for safe performance on certain jobs, and the consequent implementation of these specifications by means of appropriate selection procedures; and (3) a continuing program of pre-service and in-service training.

Eliminating Unsafe Practices and Environmental Conditions

Certain environmental conditions which are potential sources of accidents are controlled by state regulations of various kinds. The placement of fire extinguishers and mandatory inspections of elevators and other moving equipment are illustrative of this kind of control. Ultimately, however, the responsibility for identifying and eliminating unsafe work practices rests with management and with every employee. It is management's responsibility to arrange the physical working environment in such a way that it provides adequate ventilation and illumination and the safest possible equipment. Management must arrange also to staff and equip a maintenance department adequate to the task of keeping the plant and its equipment in excellent working order. The fact that maintenance was too overworked to repair a defective rung on a ladder is small consolation to the painter who falls when the rung gives way.

The entire burden of accident prevention cannot, however, be placed upon management alone. Each employee must assume responsibility for reporting defective equipment or unsafe practices. In addition, every worker must appreciate and implement his own personal stake in a safe environment by observing certain rudimentary principles of industrial housekeeping, including mopping floors to prevent the accumulation of water or grease, piling materials properly, and removing loose objects from floors, stairs, and platforms.

There is some evidence for the fact that the psychological environment in which work is performed may be as important a consideration in accident prevention as is the physical environment. A comparison between employees in factory departments who had variable safety records indicated that accidents tended to occur with the greatest frequency in those departments with the lowest intracompany transfer mobility rates and the least promotion possibility for the typical employee. These factors are interpreted as symptomatic of an unwholesome psychological work environment. The lack of intracompany mobility and of promotional opportunities may lead to the development of attitudes of indifference toward the work. A more favorable psychological climate can provide incentives which act to raise the general level of alertness to potential hazards and to promote a desire to cooperate with safety personnel.[22]

Appropriate Personnel Selection Procedures

A comprehensive job analysis leading to an adequate set of worker specifications can quite often suggest certain of the physical or personal employee characteristics which are associated with accidents. Some of these kinds of characteristics, like defective vision or health, are self-evident. Others are a little more obscure but may nevertheless be of considerable importance. It has been suggested, for example, that accidents in certain kinds of activities are especially likely when the employee's perceptual speed is slow in relation to his motor speed.[23] Since both of these factors appear to represent inherited capacities or limitations and are not amenable to training, they can be controlled only by the utilization of appropriate selection procedures.

Training

The discussion earlier in this chapter of the causes of accidents indicated that the majority of accidents are attributable to "faulty attitude." Although this is a rather vague classification, it implies that the utilization of selection procedures and the modification of the working environment can, at best, prevent only a relatively small proportion of industrial accidents. The most fundamental cause of accidents appears to be attitudinal in nature. Consequently, workers, and supervisors must be taught to be safety-minded.

Such safety-mindedness does not always accompany the acquisition of skill or knowledge about equipment operation. Most persons learn how to drive an automobile, for example, with relatively little difficulty. An attitude of maturity in its operation, however, is quite

---

[22] W. A. Kerr, "Accident Proneness of Factory Departments," *Journal of Applied Psychology*, Vol. 34 (1950), pp. 167–70.

[23] C. A. Drake, "Accident Proneness: A Hypothesis," *Character and Personality*, Vol. 8 (1940), pp. 335–41.

TABLE 11–4

Motor Vehicle Violations Recorded for Driver Samples

	Number of Drivers	
	Accident Free (N = 59)	Accident Repeater (N = 88)
Minor Offenses		
Leaving vehicle running and unattended	1	1
Driving within 8 feet of streetcar stopped for passengers	7	20
Not reasonably right for vehicle coming from opposite direction	4	15
Not keeping to right half of road when view is obstructed	2	5
Crossing throughway without stopping	7	16
Failure to obey traffic signal	1	11
Speeding	24	50
Left of streetcar	0	2
Violation of traffic rules	6	8
Mechanical defect	0	1
Without proper lights	1	5
Without proper brakes	0	2
Without proper muffler	0	1
No vehicle inspection sticker	4	19
Improper operation	5	7
Negligent collision	3	5
Serious Offenses		
Operating under influence of liquor	8	13
Operating so as to endanger lives and safety	8	15
Going away after injury to property	1	7
Going away after injury to persons	0	1
Operating after license suspension	0	7
Operating without proper registration	0	10
Operating without being properly licensed	4	9
Violation of compulsory insurance law	0	6
Operating without authority	0	4

Source: R. A. McFarland and A. L. Moseley, *Human Factors in Highway Transport Safety* (Cambridge, Mass.: Harvard University Press, 1954).

a different matter as shown by the comparison in Table 11–4 between the violations recorded for samples of accident-free and accident-repeater drivers.

Virtually all of the accumulated evidence about automobile accidents indicates that the safe driver is one who is skillful, knows the limitations of his equipment, and has a high degree of social awareness, including consideration for others. Safe drivers are neither resentful of authority nor do they regard the automobile as a tool for the extension of their own power. The National Safety Council's admonition that we reveal a good deal about our level of maturity by the way in which we drive is based upon solid evidence. It is likely that the relatively low proportion of accidents among drivers who are trained in a high school driver-training program can be

FIGURE 11-7

Monthly Accident Frequency When Foremen Are Trained

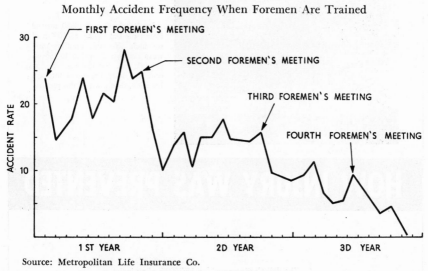

Source: Metropolitan Life Insurance Co.

attributed to the fact that such training emphasizes the acquisition of appropriate attitudes as well as of driving skills.

Since accident prevention is largely dependent upon the development of appropriate attitudes, industrial safety requires a continuing program designed to alert all personnel to the potential sources of accidents and to reinforce safe practices. The safety program must make provision for the systematic study of accident reports and regular inspections to detect unsafe procedures. The findings from such reports and inspections provide a firm base for the development of safety training programs.

Training of foremen relative to accident prevention has been shown to be highly effective (see Figure 11-7). The foreman, after all, is the person who is in the best possible position to see to it that safety precautions are observed.

FIGURE 11-8

"What Happened?" A Near-Accident Report

WHAT HAPPENED?
NEAR-ACCIDENT REPORT – INDIANA HARBOR WORKS

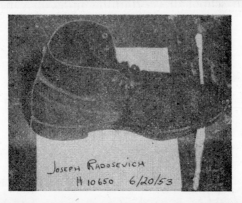

Joe Radosevich, #10650, missed losing his big toe by 55/1000th of an inch. He and another man were using a dolly bar to loosen a work roll. Joe lost his balance and the dolly bar went through his shoe, as shown in the picture.

JOSEPH RADOSEVICH
H 10650 6/20/53

HOW INJURY WAS PREVENTED

The dolly bar came within 55/1000th of an inch of Joe's big toe. This is the thickness of the safety cap in his shoe. The steel bar went between the leather and the safety cap. Wearing of safety shoes saved a toe or more for Joe.

76" Hot Strip Mechanical
Bulletin #35
July 1953

 Issued by . . . SAFETY DEPARTMENT

The training of foremen alone, however, is not sufficient. It is important also that a continuing program of in-service training be directed toward the workers. Such a program typically consists of several elements, all of which are designed to impress constantly the matter of industrial safety upon the individual employee. Publicity including safety bulletins, payroll envelope inserts, charts, displays, and articles in the house organ can be highly effective in this regard. It is difficult to remain callous to the kind of evidence contained in the bulletin shown in Figure 11–8, for example. Other devices for encouraging safe work practices include the conduct of contests and the provision of awards to personnel or departments with outstanding safety records.

These apparently simple devices should not be dismissed lightly. The data on the effectiveness of organized safety programs are extremely impressive. Proctor and Gamble, for example, was able to reduce the frequency of disabling injuries from 36 per million man-hours in 1930 to 1 per million man-hours in 1955 by means of a program in which everyone was encouraged to "think" and "work" safety.[24] This kind of record is quite typical. The essence of successful safety training is the philosophy underlying the program rather than the specific methods whereby the program is implemented. Some companies with successful programs favor contests, others favor bulletin bombardments, and still others lean toward the use of the house organ for this purpose. All programs that work, however, are directed toward the fundamental objective of creating an attitude of pride in individual and company safety records, and of consideration and respect for one's fellow employees.

SUMMARY

The majority of accidents are attributable to three factors: (1) defective working environment and equipment design; (2) human limitations in the operation of equipment; and (3) improper worker attitudes relative to safety, including carelessness.

The role of the physical environment, including such factors as illumination, ventilation, and equipment malfunction, has been the subject of considerable study by engineers and psychologists. Although there is still room for further improvements in this area, it cannot be regarded any longer as a primary cause of accidents. The more fundamental problem in accident prevention is a human one and requires the application of appropriate selection and training procedures.

---

[24] J. M. Ewell, *Safety Bulletin* (Cincinnati, Ohio: Proctor and Gamble, January, 1956).

Efforts to identify a personality type associated with high accident liability have not been outstandingly successful. There is some evidence that the accident-repeater tends to be emotionally immature, somewhat hostile, and socially irresponsible. This pattern is not sufficiently consistent, however, to support the principle of accident proneness as the basic factor underlying accidents.

The importance of accident-proneness has quite often been overstated because of misinterpretations of studies, indicating that a relatively small percentage of employees have a relatively large proportion of the accidents. The proper application of chance expectancies to observed distributions of accident frequency leads to the conclusion that accident-proneness accounts for about 20 percent or less of the total accident variance. Thus, although of some consequence, this factor must be placed in proper perspective.

The most satisfactory approach to industrial safety involves the development of a comprehensive program of pre-service training and in-service education relative to accident prevention. Such a program must place a continuing emphasis upon the study of the causes of accidents and near-accidents, the identification and correction of unsafe working procedures, and the development of an employee attitude best described as "safety-mindedness."

12. Engineering Psychology

Until fairly recently, machine and plant design were regarded pretty much as the province of the engineer. The comfort of the person operating the machine and indeed his capability for operating various kinds of "mechanical monsters" was considered (if at all) almost as an afterthought.

With the equipment as a "given," early attempts to improve worker efficiency had to rest upon an analysis of the job with a view toward task simplification. In this approach, tasks were reduced to their essential components and these components were arranged or sequenced so each could be performed in minimum time with the least wasted or fatiguing motion.

This rather one-sided regard for the machine could not continue indefinitely. Technological advancements made possible the design of even more powerful machines capable of performing previously unimagined tasks with staggering speed and precision *provided they could be operated effectively*. Such a provision removes the human operator from the realm of afterthought and makes his limitations and strengths essential considerations in machine and equipment design.

The urgent military requirements of World War II focused particular attention upon the necessity for merging the talents of engineers, psychologists, physiologists, physicians, and others in designing equipment (aircraft instrument panels, submarine diving controls) and structuring working conditions. This represented the beginning of the field designated "human engineering" or "engineering psychology." Alternative designations sometimes used include "Biotechnology" and "Ergonomics."

The point of departure for engineering psychology is information about man's capabilities and limitations. Utilizing such informa-

307

tion, the engineering psychologist seeks to develop an optimally functioning unit of man and machine—a *man-machine system*. Virtually every major type of military equipment has, at least since Word War II, received some attention from engineering psychologists. Nonmilitary applications have included such diverse products as aircraft and space vehicle instruments and cabins, artificial limbs, semiautomatic post-office sorting equipment, control panels for atomic reactors, telephone sets, and industrial machines of various kinds.[1]

Whereas this chapter is concerned primarily with engineering psychology, it is appropriate to begin by briefly considering its historical precursor: task simplification.

TASK SIMPLIFICATION

Task simplification entails a critical study of work activities with a view to revealing inefficient operations and working techniques. It may be discovered, for example, that employees are making unnecessarily fatiguing movements or that the sequence of operations is not conducive to expeditious job performance.

Time Study "Speedup"

Certainly there can be no quarrel with attempts to improve plant efficiency by eliminating unnecessary motions and reducing employee fatigue. However, the time-and-motion studies of some of the early "efficiency experts" were sometimes misapplied. They rested upon the erroneously simplistic view that employees want only high wages, employers want only low labor costs, and that both objectives can be attained by having employees accomplish more in less time.[2]

Attempts simply to speed up employee activity without regard for the consequent toll in human resources have always been repugnant to workers, psychologists, and many managers. The employees' primary defense against such speedup programs is to maintain social pressures which prevent exceeding what they consider to be a fair

---

[1] F. V. Taylor, "Psychology and the Design of Machines," *American Psychologist,* Vol. 12 (1957) , pp. 249–56.

[2] F. W. Taylor, *Principles of Scientific Management* (New York: Harper & Row, 1947) .

level of production. "Rate busters" who violate tacit agreements about production level are likely to find themselves ostracized by their fellow employees.

The usual procedure for such studies is to observe and time a relative brief sample of cycles of a repetitive task. Time standards for performing the constituents of the cycles are then established from averages based upon these limited observations.

Psychologists reject the utilization of time study data to set absolute performance standards because of the fallibility of certain assumption underlying this application.

If the average times are to be used for setting standards, we must assume that the observed performances are sufficiently consistent and have been adequately sampled to produce reliable means. This assumption fails on two counts. First, only rarely is an adequate sample of observations recorded across employees, segments of the workday, days of the week, and so on. Second, times recorded for performance of various components of a total work cycle by individual employees tend to be characterized by a high degree of inconsistency. In view of the failure of these assumptions, we must conclude that average performance time calculated from observations is not a sufficiently reliable criterion for establishing normative performance rates.

A second psychologically fallible assumption is that there is one best way for doing a task regardless of who is doing it. This assumption disregards the body of evidence concerning individual differences. Although a sequence of motions or activities proving satisfactory for many persons may be discovered, it is likely that some persons will remain who could better perform the task using a different sequence or different motions. This realization has even permeated some of the aircrew training in the Strategic Air Command in which "Standard Operating Procedures" for particular elements of a mission have given way to "Crew Operating Procedures" which, although unstandardized, work best for the particular crews in question.[3]

Thirdly, it is psychologically unsound to conceive of *rate* of production as the sole important criterion of industrial effectiveness.

---

[3] P. D. Hood, A. W. Halpin, J. J. Hanitchak, L. Siegel, and J. K. Hemphill, "Crew Member Agreement on RB-47 Crew Operating Procedure," Research Report AFPTRC–TN–57–64, ASTIA Document No. 126395 (Lackland Air Force Base, Texas: Air Force Personnel and Training Research Center, May, 1957).

Increased productivity is undoubtedly extremely *inefficient* when it is accompanied by such things as heightened fatigue, worker dissatisfaction, and increased accident frequency.

Motion Simplification

Task simplification based upon the elimination of unnecessary motions and otherwise facilitating job performance is markedly different from the kind of "speedup" described above. Its emphasis is upon the individual and the effective utilization of his capacities rather than upon the job without regard for the characteristics of the worker. In jointly considering the nature of the work to be done and the person who is to do it, task simplification was a forerunner —and to some extent is still a component—of present-day engineering psychology.

Therblig Analysis. The primary principle of task simplification, as advocated and practiced by Frank and Lillian Gilbreth, is that tasks can be modified to suit individuals rather than forcing individuals to comply with the requirements of the task.[4] Thus, in an early study of bricklaying, Gilbreth was able to reduce the motions from 18 to 5, thereby increasing production from 120 to 350 bricks per man-hour without speeding up the work pace.[5]

As practiced by the Gilbreths, task simplification entailed first a detailed analysis of each task into its constituent motions and activities. These constituents, termed "therbligs"—you can figure out why —included such activities as searching, finding, positioning, assembling, and so on. After identifying the therbligs, the task was simplified by eliminating those activities that were unnecessary, combining steps in task performance, and altering the sequence of activities.

Some Principles of Efficient Movement. A body of lore, based primarily upon experience rather than empirical evidence, supports the relative superiority of certain kinds of motions over others.

1. Symmetrical movements are more efficient than asymmetrical movements. It is preferable, for example, to have an assembler simultaneously reach for a bolt with his left hand and a nut with his right hand than to have him use the same hand to collect both components.

---

[4] F. B. Gilbreth and L. M. Gilbreth, *Applied Motion Study* (New York: The Macmillan Co., 1917).

[5] F. B. Gilbreth, *Brick Laying System* (New York: Clark Publishing Co., 1911).

2. Parts, tools, and so on should be within easy reach. The region of most comfortable reach by a seated employee is defined by an arc circumscribed on the work surface by his hands extended to the length of his forearms. Next in comfort is a region defined by arcs similarly drawn when his arms are fully extended. These areas of most comfortable reach without disturbing the worker's posture are sometimes referred to as "semicircular workpits" (see Figure 12–1).

FIGURE 12–1

Semicircular Work Pits

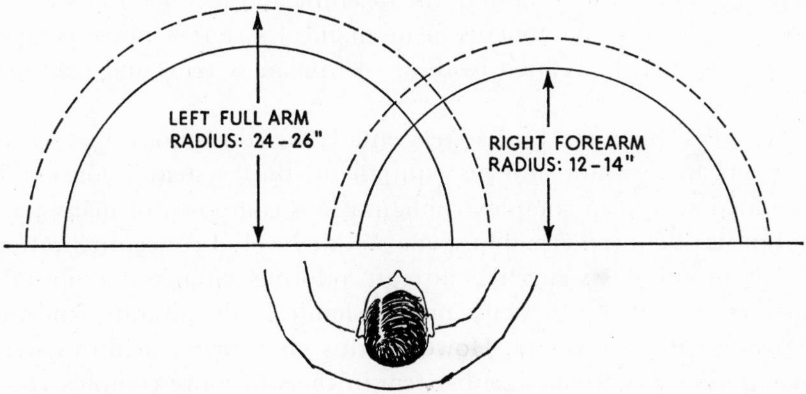

The semicircles delimit the areas of comfortable reach for each arm. The overlapping area is accessible to both hands.

3. Circular movements are more efficient than straight line movements.

4. Tasks that can be arranged in terms of rhythmic patterns are easier to perform than tasks requiring jerky or irregular movements.

5. Holding and carrying operations are more efficiently handled by equipment than by human operators. Unnecessary fatigue is generated by requiring an employee, for example, to hold a part while he works on it instead of clamping the part in a vise. Likewise, many part transport operations can be simply replaced by a "drop delivery" whereby the finished work is dropped down a hole leading to a chute and carrying it away from the work area.

6. Demands made upon the limbs and fingers should be proportional to their strength and dexterity. An outstanding and long

recognized illustration of poor design in this regard is the typewriter keyboard. However, with the advent of electric typewriters the work load for the fingers has been so minimized that differences in finger strength and dexterity have become relatively unimportant in spite of poor keyboard design.

MAN-MACHINE SYSTEMS

We have said that more recent psychological activity in the area of equipment design is founded on the *system* concept. To clarify the meaning of a man-machine system, which is an optimally functioning unit consisting both of the machine and its operator, we will first consider the components of mechanical systems. These components will then be related to those of human systems and man-machine systems.

Whereas a man-machine system entails the continuous interaction between an operator and his equipment, the "systems" concept is extended as well to complex configurations composed of many men and units of equipment. Thus, at a simple level of conceptualization a man-machine system like aircraft piloting entails the optimal interaction of two subsystems, one mechanical (the aircraft) and the other human (the pilot). However, this same man-machine system functions as a component subsystem in the still more complex coordination of several aircraft, each with its pilot and ground facilities, including their operators, comprising an air traffic control system.

Mechanical Systems

The simplest kind of system is designed to perform a specific function or group of functions indefinitely (or until it wears out) once it is triggered. This is an *open-loop* system. *Closed-loop* systems are ones in which the performance of a function by the equipment is sensed or fed back into the machine, making it self-regulating.

Open-Loop Systems. Many commercial buildings are equipped with sprinkler systems for fire control. The overhead sprinklers automatically spray water when there is a fire. The system is *controlled* by metal plugs which melt at a critical temperature. When the heat (the *input*) causes these plugs to melt, a water spray is released (the *output*).

This system is not self-regulating. It will continue to spray water as long as it is functional until it is shut down by some force external to the system itself. Figure 12–2 shows the system diagrammatically.

Closed-Loop Systems. A thermostatically controlled home freezer is a closed-loop system because it is self-regulating (see Figure 12–2). Once the thermostat is set for a particular temperature (say, 10° F),

FIGURE 12–2

Mechanical Systems

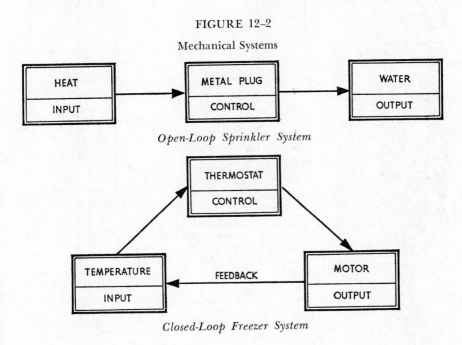

Open-Loop Sprinkler System

Closed-Loop Freezer System

the refrigerating motor will operate whenever the temperature rises above that level. However, the output itself serves to change the input, in turn signaling to the control when the temperature again drops to 10° F and motor operation ceases.

Human Systems

We may consider man also as a closed-loop system. This analogy is not difficult if we substitute for the terms Stimulus-Interpretation-Response, the mechanical concepts Input-Control-Output. Viewed as a system, man receives information, somehow processes it, and reacts to it.

Inputs for the human system take the form of receptor organ

FIGURE 12–3

A Human System: Maintaining Driving Speed at 55 Miles per Hour

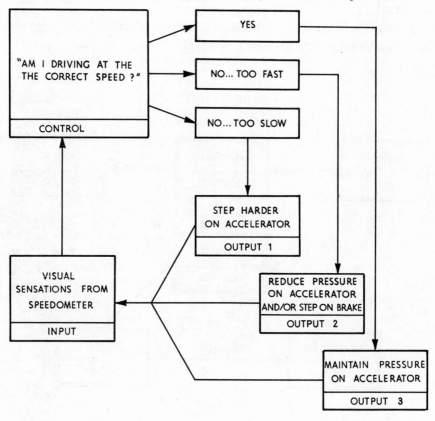

activity. These sensations are processed by such interpretive control functions as thinking, reasoning, deciding, and so on. The output, of course, is some kind of behavior. This response in turn affects the input and the cycle continues.

Consider the operation of a human system performing a relatively simple task like maintaining a constant driving speed of 55 miles per hour (see Figure 12–3). The basic input is a set of visual sensations from the speedometer. These are supplemented by other inputs not considered in Figure 12–3, including the sound of wind rushing past the car, the "feel of the wheel," or the sound of certain squeaks or rattles we have learned to associate with certain speeds. The visual sensations from the speedometer are processed, and an appropriate response is made, depending upon the interpretation.

Note that the situation described and diagrammed in Figure 12–3 provides for *branching*. Instead of a system limited to a single control action and a single output, we have a variety of control decisions each eliciting a different output. Branching is not limited to human systems. Electronic computers, for example, are often controlled by branching programs permitting specified operations to occur under specified circumstances.

A Man-Machine System

It has undoubtedly occurred to you that the human system we have just described is only a part of the total system involving both the man and the machine. A portion of this man-machine system is shown diagrammatically in Figure 12–4 (see p. 316).

The essence of this system is that the human portion with its inputs, controls, and outputs constitutes an overall control system for the mechanical portion of the system. The entire man-machine system thus is mediated by the human operator. Should he fall asleep at the wheel, the mechanical controls become useless.

This suggests what is at once the strength and weakness of man-machine systems compared with systems that are entirely mechanical. The latter are foolproof except for mechanical breakdown. However, they lack the precision of control and flexibility of output that can be exerted only when the higher cognitive processes of a human being are incorporated within the system. In order for man to function as part of the system, there must be an optimal rapprochement between the human being and the machine. The inputs, controls, and outputs required of him must be facilitated by the machine's design and within the range of human capability.

Allocation of Functions between Men and Machines

Any man-machine system can be designed in alternative ways. Variations are possible in the numbers and complexity of machine components, the number of people in the system, and the functions performed by these people. Since the proportional work load assigned to machines and people comprising the system can be varied,

FIGURE 12–4

A Man-Machine System

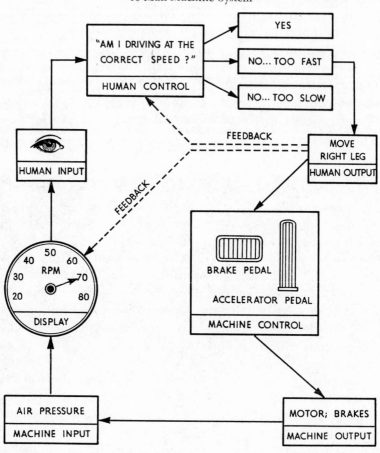

it is important to consider the kinds of things best done by men and those best handled by machine.[6]

Several attempts have been made to list the relative advantages of people and machines for various kinds of functions.[7] These lists include such things as the superior flexibility of man, superior computational speed of machines, and so on. However, such compari-

[6] A. Chapanis, "On the Allocation of Functions between Men and Machines," *Occupational Psychology*, Vol. 39 (1965), pp. 1–11.

[7] A. Chapanis, "Human Engineering," in C. D. Flagle, W. H. Huggins, and R. H. Roy (eds.), *Operations Research and Systems Engineering* (Baltimore, Maryland: Johns Hopkins Press, 1960), chap. xix, pp. 534–82.

FIGURE 12–5

The Reliability of a Double Redundant Navigation System
in Which One of the Redundant Components Is Man
(Dashed Line) as Compared with the Reliability of Systems
with Various Orders of Redundancy in Which All Components Are Machines (Solid Lines)

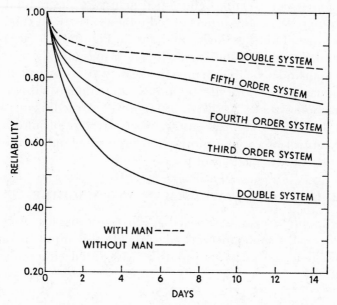

Source: M. A. Grodsky, "Risk and Reliability," *Aerospace Engineering,* Vol. 21, No. 1 (1962), pp. 28–33.

sons have not themselves proven helpful in designing man-machine
systems. Such lists neglect two important principles of man-machine
design.[8]

First, social, economic, and political values partially determine
the allocation of functions. The technology of automation cannot be
applied irrespective of its broad social ramifications including employee displacement, job retraining, and unemployment.

Second, assignment of functions must be continuously reeval-
uated. As technology advances, machines are made capable of performing functions not contemplated when the system was instituted.
Post-office mail sorting for destination using machines to read zip
codes is a case in point. In this instance, the development of a

[8] Chapanis (1965) , *op. cit.*

machine to "read" has caused the entire system to be redesigned.

Although the initial allocations of functions to men and machines are often based upon the judgments of the systems designers, these judgments are usually amenable to empirical test. Such a test, for example, has confirmed the superior reliability of a space vehicle navigation system when a well-trained man provides redundancy in the system, over various orders of redundancy where all components are machines. This superiority, as shown in Figure 12–5 (see p. 317), is attributed to the flexibility which man brings into the system.

The remainder of this chapter is devoted to a discussion of various human factors (or if you prefer, the human subsystem) in man-machine systems. As shown in Figure 12–3, the linkage between man and machine requires sensory inputs (receipt of information), central control processes (information processing and decision making), and outputs (actions of various kinds).

INPUT LINKAGE BETWEEN MAN AND MACHINE

The input to man is received by his sense organs. Any of the receptor organs could theoretically provide this input linkage, but for most practical purposes inputs are presented either visually or auditorially.

Choice of Input Modality

Four factors influence the choice of sense channel for presenting information to the human operator and qualify the nature of the input itself: appropriateness, precision, present load on the input channel, and efficiency.

With respect to appropriateness, it makes more sense to provide input by sound rather than light when the operator is sometimes absent from the input source. For example, we rely upon the telephone ring to signal us from any location in home or office. Visual inputs, on the other hand, are most appropriate when an auditory signal would interfere with other listening activities.

Other things being equal, inputs *not* providing precise information can be presented either by light or sound. Thus, low engine oil pressure can be signaled either by a warning light on the dashboard or by a warning buzzer. Such inputs have an "all-or-none" character; they provide information that a mechanical system either is or is not working properly, that some critical point has or has not been reached, and so on. Although such gross inputs frequently are satisfactory, there are many circumstances wherein the operator must be provided with more precise information about machine function. Here, the input must indicate quantitative variations in function on some kind of dial or scale. A pilot, for example, needs accurately to know his altitude and rate of climb. Generally, such information is provided visually; auditory discrimination along a graduated scale is difficult.

If there is a choice of sense modality for providing inputs, the systems designer will take into account the demands already being made upon the various receptor channels. When the operator is already much occupied with visual inputs, the designer will seek to provide any needed additional inputs by sound or touch.

Finally, the efficiency of the input modality must be considered. Whereas all receptor systems usually considered for input linkage have about equally fast response times, some are more efficient for certain purposes than others. Comparing the efficiency of the two most frequently used receptor systems, sight and hearing, the latter is generally superior for simple, brief messages calling for immediate action. The converse conditions favor visual input. Furthermore, visual input is obviously more efficient than auditory input when the receiving environment is noisy. And, auditory input would be required when dark adaptation integrity must be maintained.[9]

Visual Displays

Matters of display design have received considerable attention by engineering psychologists. Studies of the readability of different kinds of dials, like those shown in Figure 12–6, indicate that vertical scales are read less accurately than horizontal or circular scales.[10]

Another problem related to the display components of man-machine systems concerns the arrangement of display clusters like those

---

[9] C. T. Morgan, J. S. Cook, III, A. Chapanis, and M. W. Lund, *Human Engineering Guide to Equipment Design* (N.Y.: McGraw-Hill Book Co., Inc., 1963) , p. 125.

[10] R. B. Sleight, "The Effect of Instrument Dial Shape upon Legibility," *Journal of Applied Psychology*, Vol. 32 (1948) , pp. 170–88; and Norah E. Graham, "The Speed and Accuracy of Reading Horizontal, Vertical and Circular Scales," *Journal of Applied Psychology*, Vol. 40 (1956) , pp. 228–32.

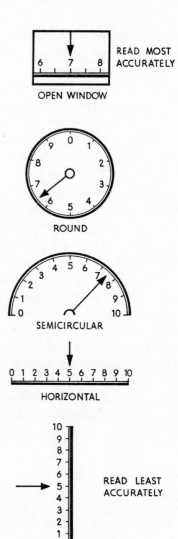

FIGURE 12–6

Dial Shapes in the Order in
Which They Are Read Most
Accurately

on automobile dashboards and in airplane cockpits. Whenever the
operator must keep abreast of information conveyed simultaneously
by several different dials, his task can be simplified by patterning the
dial display.[11] This is done by orienting each dial so the "normal"
position of the pointer is the same for every one. Thus, the operator

[11] W. E. Woodson, *Human Engineering Guide for Equipment Designers* (Berkeley,
Calif.: University of California Press, 1954).

can quickly spot and identify a dial pointer indicating an abnormal condition.

Vigilance

Monitoring mechanical equipment requires a particular type of attentiveness termed "vigilance." The characteristics of vigilance include prolonged attention to infrequently occurring stimuli which signal the necessity for some kind of action. This describes the fundamental activity of such diverse tasks as monitoring a radar scanning device for detecting approaching aircraft and monitoring electronic telescopes for extraterrestrial sounds. In both instances the "normal" condition, requiring no response, is the *absence* of a critical stimulus. The "critical" condition, requiring a response, is the occurrence of some kind of visual or auditory signal.

There appear to be two principal determinants of vigilance performance: expectancy and level of arousal.[12] Both factors are probably related to the monotonous nature of monitoring tasks.

Expectancy. The most frequently occurring vigilance error is an error of omission; that is, failure to respond appropriately to an infrequently occurring signal. Laboratory studies have confirmed that this error can be reduced by familiarizing subjects with the approximate frequency with which they can expect to receive critical signals. Thus, the accuracy of infrequent signal detection during a test period was found to be affected by the rate at which these signals were presented during the pretest orientation period. Vigilance performance over a prolonged period was best when the pretest orientation presented signals with about the same frequency as presented during the vigilance test itself.[13] The implication is, of course, that vigilance training must be realistic in the sense that trainees should develop an awareness of the likelihood of occurrence of critical signals during a finite time period.

Arousal. Since the normal condition in vigilance tasks is absence of the critical stimulus and since the abnormal condition requiring a response occurs infrequently, it is essential to maintain a satisfactory level of operator alertness or arousal.

---

[12] E. C. Poulton, "Engineering Psychology," *Annual Review of Psychology*, Vol. 17 (1966), p. 184.

[13] W. P. Colquhoun and A. D. Baddeley, "Role of Pretest Expectancy in Vigilance Decrement," *Journal of Experimental Psychology*, Vol. 68 (1964), pp. 156–60.

The importance of this factor was clearly demonstrated in an investigation of the percentage of signals detected when varying numbers of signals were presented each hour. Whereas almost 90 percent of the signals presented at a rate of 40 per hour were detected, this percentage declined to about 65 percent when the rate was 20 per hour, and dropped below 50 percent when the rate was 10 per hour.[14]

There are limits, of course, to this relationship between signal rate and arousal. Signals which come too frequently can also produce a performance decrement, perhaps because of a perceptual "overload."[15] Given this U-shaped function between signal frequency and accuracy of identification, there is probably an optimum frequency for maximizing arousal and minimizing perceptual overload which varies with the nature of the signal.

To maintain a proper state of arousal when critical stimuli occur rarely, it has been helpful sporadically to present "artificial signals." These artificial signals should be identical to the real signals[16] (but presented only for arousal purposes) and followed by feedback to the operator concerning the adequacy of his response.[17] The rationale for artificial signals is clearly similar to the intended arousal function of an unanticipated question suddenly asked of you during class by the lecturer.

Other ways to maintain a satisfactory level of arousal have been suggested. These include making the signals as obvious as possible (for example, by signaling with very bright, large lights); allowing operators to work in pairs and when possible permitting conversation; providing ample rest and brief work periods (up to 10 minutes rest after every 30-minute work period); and observations by a supervisor on a random interval schedule.[18]

---

[14] J. Deese, *Changes in Visual Performance after Visual Work*, USAF, Wright Air Development Center, Tech. Rept. 57–285, 1957.

[15] E. C. Poulton, "The Optimal Perceptual Load in a Paced Auditory Inspection Task," *British Journal of Psychology*, Vol. 51 (1960), pp. 127–39.

[16] R. T. Wilkinson, "Artificial 'Signals' as an Aid to an Inspection Task," *Ergonomics*, Vol. 7 (1964), pp. 63–72.

[17] C. H. Baker, "Maintaining the Level of Vigilance by Means of Artificial Signals," *Journal of Applied Psychology*, Vol. 44 (1960), pp. 336–38.

[18] B. O. Bergum and D. J. Lehr, *Vigilance Performance as a Function of Task and Environmental Variables*, Report 11 (Fort Bliss, Texas: U.S. Army Air Defense Human Resources Unit, 1962).

CENTRAL CONTROL PROCESSES

Once an input linkage between man and machine is established, the operator must identify and process the information he has been provided and decide upon an appropriate course of action. This is shown as the controlling aspect of Figure 12–3. Information processing may involve any one or combination of such processes as evaluation, comparison, computation, judgment, reasoning, and so on. These processes eventuate in a decision about the type of action to be taken.

The one outstanding characteristic of human information processing functions is that they involve "recoding." The input data are manipulated and interpreted in some fashion. Such recoding is man's unique contribution to a man-machine system. When recoding is unnecessary, that is, when each input uniformly predetermines a specific output, the system can be automated.

Most kinds of decision making have three components: information collection, subjective assessments of this information, and some sort of appreciation of the overall pattern of evidence.[19] The two latter components are involved in recoding.

All of the components of decision making are enormously compounded and the resultant decision made more difficult as the inputs become more numerous and complex. Too much informational input may hinder rather than facilitate decision making. This was demonstrated in an investigation of the quality of decisions concerning the allocation of aircraft to search for a reported submarine.[20] The subjects (Naval enlisted men) could choose up to eight aircraft and could use up to eight characteristics (distance and speed of the aircraft, fuel carried, and so on) in making their choices. Decision-making time was found to increase both with the number of aircraft available as alternatives and the number of characteristics to be considered. The increase in decision quality gained by additional information input did not always offset the resultant increase in decision-making time. In other words, although decisions were improved *to a point* by providing more information, the time required

---

[19] Poulton (1966), *op. cit.*, p. 190.

[20] J. R. Hayes, *Human Data Processing Limits in Decision Making*, ESD–TDR–62–48 (Bedford, Mass.: USAF Electronic Systems Division, 1962).

to reach a decision was thereby increased. Thus, it is possible to present too much information for efficient decision making.

Aside from such input overload, another condition adversely affecting decision-making time is an overload in the variety of decisions that may be potential alternatives. This was demonstrated in the above-mentioned investigation. It was also demonstrated in another study wherein subjects had to respond by using a particular finger assigned to a particular signal.[21] The fewer the number of signals used and hence the fewer the number of response alternatives, the more rapid was the decision or response time.

The interaction between number and quality of inputs with number and variety of decisions required as joint determinants of decision-making time and decision quality is compounded by still other conditions of the system. One of these is the amount and quality of other simultaneous inputs which are extraneous to the particular decision in question. This is a realistic consideration since decision processes rarely interrupt the flow of information related to potential decisions about other matters. For example, while deciding whether or not to pass the car ahead of you, you must still remain attentive to the possibility of a blowout or an overheating motor.

From the above, it follows that information processing and decision making is facilitated by three conditions:

1. Input should consist of the minimum number and variety of information required to make the decision. Where possible, inputs which otherwise might have been separately presented may effectively be combined as an integrated signal. Thus, an efficient way to present information about an aircraft's turn, bank, and airspeed is by a combination auditory signal to both ears with variations in steadiness, frequency, and modulation of the tone.[22]

2. Decision alternatives should be limited to the smallest number possible to accomplish the objectives of the system.

3. When attention is divided, input stimuli must be more intense (louder, brighter) than when attention is undivided. This was demonstrated by presenting bursts of noise, some of which contained a barely audible tone, to one ear. Simultaneously, a six-digit number was sounded in the other ear. The subjects were instructed to rate

[21] W. E. Hick, "On the Rate of Gain of Information," *Journal of Experimental Psychology*, Vol. 4 (1952), pp. 11–26.

[22] J. W. Forbes, "Auditory Signals for Instrument Flying," *Journal of the Aeronautical Sciences*, Vol. 13 (1946), pp. 255–58.

the certainty with which they were able to discriminate the tone from the noise under two conditions: while listening to the six-digit number and while ignoring it. Discriminability was superior under the latter condition; that is, when attention was undivided.[23]

OUTPUT LINKAGE BETWEEN MAN AND MACHINE

Man's output affecting machine function can be mediated by a wide assortment of equipment controls including levers, knobs, buttons, pedals, and so on. At least three factors must be considered in designing any control: (1) its operation must not require undue force; (2) it must be easily distinguished from other controls for different functions; and (3) it must be as conceptually simple as possible.

The first of these requirements is self-evident and need not be discussed further.

Distinguishability is a particularly important consideration when the operator is confronted by an array of controls in close proximity and must select the appropriate one very quickly. This situation is typical in high-speed aircraft. One study of aircraft controls found that certain shapes are more readily identifiable by touch than others even when gloves are worn (see Figure 12–7).[24]

Conceptual simplicity is sometimes facilitated by the shape and direction of movement of the control. Controls shaped as reminders of their function and moving in the same direction as the resultant machine operation tend to facilitate man-machine linkage. The automobile steering wheel is a realistic control. You turn it to the right to move the vehicle to the right. It would be confusing indeed if the control and resultant operation were to act in opposite directions.

Another approach to conceptual simplicity is that of reducing the number of alternative controls and arranging them in meaningful patterns.

The usual typewriter keyboard illustrates conceptual *complexity*. It consists of approximately 45 different keys arranged in illogical fashion and operated by 10 fingers. An alternative arrangement is a

[23] D. E. Broadbent and M. Gregory, "Division of Attention and the Decision Theory of Signal Detection," *Proceedings of the Royal Society* (London), B, Vol. 158 (1963), pp. 222–31.

[24] W. O. Jenkins, "Tactual Discrimination of Shapes for Coding Aircraft-type Controls," in P. M. Fitts, *Psychological Research on Equipment Design* (Washington, D.C.: U.S. Government Printing Office, 1947).

chord keyboard whereby letters are signaled by pressing a pair of keys, one with each hand. With this arrangement the fingers remain poised above their own keys (except for numerals) and the correspondence between pairs of keys and the letters is logical. Postal workers learned to operate this chord keyboard two weeks sooner than did a matched group learning to type on a conventional keyboard. Furthermore, even after seven weeks of training, the group

FIGURE 12–7

Knob Shapes That Are Readily Identified by Touch

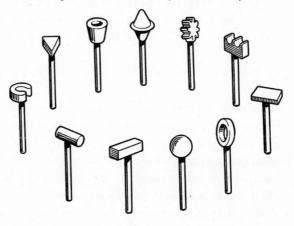

on the chord keyboard was about four days ahead of the group practicing on the typewriter keyboard.[25]

Although it is doubtful that the results of studies like this one will lead to significant changes in the typewriter keyboard for ordinary secretarial work, they suggest the importance of conceptual simplicity in arranging keyboard controls.

SUMMARY

Engineering psychologists seek to develop an optimally functioning unit of man and machine, that is, a man-machine system. Such systems capitalize upon man's unique capabilities and minimize the effects of his limitations.

---

[25] R. Conrad and D. J. Longman, "A Standard Typewriter Versus Chord Keyboard —An Experimental Comparison," *Ergonomics*, Vol. 8 (1965), pp. 77–88.

Previous to World War II and the beginnings of engineering psychology, attempts to improve employee efficiency emphasized time study and motion analysis. The most salutary applications of these approaches were directed towards task simplification rather than merely to performance speedup. In task simplification, the constituent motions and activities of each task are analyzed with a view toward eliminating those that are unnecessary, combining those that can be more effectively performed jointly, and altering the sequence in which the constituent activities are performed.

With an accelerated pace of technological development, it became increasingly necessary to consider the characteristics of potential human operators while machines were being designed rather than as an afterthought. From the human engineering point of view, man operates as a subsystem within the total man-machine configuration. Viewed in this way, man receives information (inputs), somehow processes this information and makes appropriate decisions, and takes action (outputs).

The inputs from machine to man are transmitted through the sense modalities, particularly vision and audition. Hence, the engineering psychologist is much concerned with optimal arrangements of input displays. A particular input problem area of considerable concern is that of vigilance; that is, prolonged attentiveness to infrequently occurring stimuli which signal the necessity for some kind of action. Vigilance is required whenever the task is characterized by monitoring. The two principal determinants of vigilance performance are expectancy and the level of arousal.

Once an input linkage between man and machine is established, the operator must process the information he has been provided. Information processing (or recoding of the inputs) may involve any one or combination of such processes as evaluation, comparison, computation, judgment, reasoning, and so on. These processes eventuate in a decision about the type of action to be taken.

The action, itself, can be mediated by a wide assortment of equipment controls including levers, knobs, buttons, and pedals. At least three factors influence the design of controls: ease of operation, distinguishability from other controls, and conceptual simplicity.

IV.

Motivation for Work

One of the questions most frequently asked by management is: "How can employees be motivated to do their best work?" Ability, aptitude, and knowledge are clearly important prerequisites for satisfactory job performance. Likewise, proper placement, training, job and equipment design facilitate satisfactory performance, but these alone are of little avail unless the employee is motivated.

Among the various sources of motivation, one is related to work itself. Employees are engaged in company activities for more than a third of their waking hours each week. As an important aspect of life in our culture, satisfying work contributes to man's sense of general well-being and feeling of personal worth. Work that is not personally satisfying tends to have the opposite effects. The conditions and effects of job satisfaction or dissatisfaction are considered in Chapter 13.

In the constellation of gratifications provided by work, the importance of wage or salary is frequently overestimated. Neverthe-

less, it would be absurd to move to the other extreme by denying the incentive value of money. Thus Chapter 14 discusses the importance of wages and describes job evaluation procedures for establishing equitable salaries.

13. Job Satisfaction

It was stated earlier, when defining the role of the industrial psychologist, that ". . . the psychologist is interested in maximizing the realization of the employee's and employer's potential for accomplishment and personal satisfaction." Appropriate training procedures and a favorable work environment may contribute positively to employee efficiency by increasing output and diminishing fatigue, accidents, turnover, spoilage, and absenteeism. Reference has been made from time to time to the relationship also between such factors and job satisfaction. We will now bring this matter into somewhat sharper focus. Just what is it that employees seek from their work, and how can the realization of personal satisfactions be facilitated? This important question requires that we first discuss some general principles of human motivation and then apply these principles to the matter of job satisfaction.

MOTIVATION

Motivation is a fundamental explanatory concept related to the *why* of behavior. Organisms continually experience needs or wants which impel them to action. When the individual is driven either to attain some goal or to avoid some undesirable consequence, we have evidence for motivation. A simple illustration will serve to clarify the semantics of motivation. A hungry person *needs* food, he is *driven* by hunger, and *motivated* by a desire to obtain food in order to satisfy his need.

Differences in motivation often account for the fact that various persons may react quite differently when confronted by the same set of circumstances and, indeed, a given person may behave differently when confronted by a particular set of circumstances on different occasions. You will recall the *S-I-R* scheme introduced in Chapter 1. We stated then that in order to understand behavior, we had to know something about the determinants of the way in which a respondent interprets and perceives a particular stimulus condition. Motivation is, of course, one of the keys to such understanding.

Motives related to work have quite generally been oversimplified. The typical response of uninformed management to the question, "Why do employees work?" is "To earn money." If this were correct, it would be a relatively simple matter to increase job satisfaction by raising salaries. The fact that this approach does not work in the long run is indicative of the complexity of industrial motivation.

Motives have often been classified on the basis of the need or want that generates activity. *Primary drives* are linked to physiological imbalance and are responsible for motives in the direction of such incentives as food, water, and sleep. These drives can be extremely powerful as determinants of behavior, but they generally are easily satisfied under normal conditions of life in our society. The *secondary drives* are socially derived (that is, learned) and include such things as the desire for acceptance by the group, status, and personal recognition. The fact that these drives are learned and that their satisfaction is not a requirement for survival in the physiological sense does not diminish their importance as determinants of behavior.

Since social motives are not a product of the physiology of the organism, it is reasonable to anticipate considerable diversity among them. We each have a somewhat unique environmental history which has led us to develop our own special and particular pattern of secondary drives. Certain patterns of socially derived motives do, however, appear to occur with a high degree of consistency because of gross similarities in environmental patterns within a culture. Almost everyone, for example, has learned needs for some kind of social approval. Persons who do not respond in terms of such needs (that is, who flout society) are in fact generally regarded as deviant.

Job Involvement

Work can be a very important source of satisfaction for socially derived needs and, in consequence, a means toward the realization of satisfaction with life in general.[1] The job is not, however, the only means by which such needs can be satisfied. Other sources of gratification of these needs may include the family, church, fraternal lodge, and so on.

The importance of work to a person's self-esteem or sense of worth is termed "job involvement." The job-involved person is one for whom work is a very important part of life; therefore, he is very much affected by what transpires at work. In contrast, the nonjob-involved worker does a major share of his living away from the job. His self-image is not greatly affected by the kind of work he does or how well he does it. Differences in job involvement can probably be traced back to value orientations toward work learned early in the course of socialization[2] and internalized as determinants of behavior.[3]

The importance of the socialization process as a determinant of job involvement is evident from observed differences in the meaning of work as a function of sex. As a group, men are more likely than women to value work aside from its importance to earning a livelihood. The producing role is important to them for maintaining their sense of general well-being.[4] Most women have other roles to fulfill besides that of breadwinner, and other important routes to deriving personal satisfactions outside of the work environment.

Persons characterized by high job involvement tend also to be organizationally involved; that is, they are ambitious, more satisfied with the work, supervisors, and fellow workers, and are optimistic about being promoted.[5] This relationship poses an unresolved question of causality. It can be argued that ambition, job satisfaction, and upward mobility are corollaries of job involvement, with this entire constellation of personal characteristics grounded in early socialization. Alternatively, a case can be made for the effect of local

---

[1] F. Friedlander, "Importance of Work versus Nonwork among Socially and Occupationally Stratified Groups," *Journal of Applied Psychology*, Vol. 50 (1966), pp. 437–41.

[2] T. M. Lobdahl, "Patterns of Job Attitudes in Two Assembly Technologies," *Administrative Science Quarterly*, Vol. 8 (1964), pp. 482–519.

[3] R. Dubin, *Human Relations in Administration* (Englewood Cliffs, N.J.: Prentice-Hall, Inc., 1961), pp. 51–53.

[4] Nancy Morse and R. S. Weiss, "The Function and Meaning of Work and the Job," *American Sociological Review*, Vol. 20 (1955), p. 198.

[5] T. M. Lobdahl and M. Keyner, "The Definition and Measurement of Job Involvement," *Journal of Applied Psychology*, Vol. 49 (1965), pp. 24–33.

organizational conditions (such as opportunity for advancement, and personal recognition) in heightening or diminishing the level of involvement which the employee initially brings to the job. It seems likely that both of these positions are correct—that job involvement reflects the interaction of early and current experiences and in turn exerts an effect upon the employee's performance within the organization.

Socially Derived Motives

The assumption that employees can best be motivated to produce by financial incentives disregards the complexity of human motivation. It is predicated in part upon the erroneous belief that whatever goals we seek can be bought or at least are attainable by means of increased income. It is founded also on the untenable notion that the needs of employees and employers coincide. These assumptions have been evaluated critically in an excellent article by Brayfield and Crockett.[6] The authors discuss motivation as a function of three social systems within which virtually every employee operates: (1) fellow workers, (2) the company, and (3) the community.

Relations with Other Workers. There is considerable evidence for the fact that an individual's productivity tends to conform to a group norm. Standards of output once established by the work group are often imposed upon new employees. The individual who attempts to deviate from the group norm of a "fair day's work" by overproducing may be ostracized by his fellow employees.

When it exists, this situation represents a conflict of interests between employees and employers. The latter may wish to increase productivity in order to improve the economic position of the company and, parenthetically, to improve the wage schedule. The employees, however, may perceive such increased productivity as a threat to full employment. Social acceptance by fellow workers often proves to be a more powerful incentive for maintaining the present level of production than does the promise of increased wages for improving productivity.

Relations within the Company Structure. Improved productivity is perceived by some employees to be a path leading to promotion

---

[6] A. H. Brayfield and W. H. Crockett, "Employee Attitudes and Employee Performance," *Psychological Bulletin,* Vol. 52 (1955), pp. 396–424.

and improvement of status within the company structure. Not all employees, however, are motivated by the incentive of promotion within the company. Workers who are reasonably well-satisfied with their present position and earnings are not likely to respond by increasing production in order to improve their salary or to gain a promotion.

An additional factor that diminishes the effectiveness of financial or status incentives is sometimes operative in unionized plants. The worker may be oriented more toward advancement within the framework of the union hierarchy than the company hierarchy. There is no evidence that the realization of this objective is dependent upon high productivity. Financial incentives provided to such employees by management do not bear upon the goals which they have elected to pursue.

Relations outside of the Company. The generalization is sometimes made that all employees desire to improve their status in the community. Since community status is somewhat dependent upon the possession of tangible wealth (house, car, clothes, furniture), it follows that the desire for status ought to lead the employee to increase his output in order to reap financial gain.

This line of reasoning is erroneous on two counts. First, many employees do not desire to improve their position in the community. Unless the employee is upwardly mobile, he probably evaluates his status in terms of some segment of the community rather than in the light of the total community. Thus, an individual may compare himself with others in his neighborhood, his religious or ethnic group, his occupational classification, his high school graduating class, or from his own particular environmental background and conclude that he has done quite well indeed. Furthermore, an improvement in his wage leading to the acquisition of additional tangible wealth may actually be regarded as undesirable because it may lead to his exclusion from the social group with which he chooses to identify.

Secondly, it is incorrect to assume that the attainment of socially rewarding goals outside of the plant is necessarily dependent upon financial or status gains within the company. Individuals who are active participants in community activities may have their needs fulfilled by such activities regardless of their income level or their position within the company.

Two Theories of Motivation

An overall view of motivation is that it directs behavior in two ways: (1) by causing the individual to seek one of several available goals and (2) by causing him to seek certain goals not present at the moment.

The former is illustrated by an employee who must choose between remaining in his present position or accepting advancement within the company entailing greater income but less security than he presently enjoys. Other things being equal, the choice he makes will reflect a discrepancy in the value he places upon income and security. Similarly, an employee dissatisfied with his present position because it provides little opportunity for advancement may be motivated to seek a job with another company providing greater opportunities.

The "needs-hierarchy" theory and the "valence-expectancy" theory are two attempts to explain the goal choice and goal search aspects of motivation. Each of these theories is considered separately below.

Needs-Hierarchy Theory.   It is evident that needs, and hence the goals we seek, are arranged in a hierarchy of importance. At any given time certain needs are stronger than others.[7] However, this hierarchy is flexible rather than static because of the interdependence of needs. Relatively less important goals may assume real importance after previously more basic ones have been satisfied.[8]

We will have occasion to invoke the notion of interdependence of needs throughout the ensuing discussion of job satisfaction.

The needs-hierarchy operative at a given time for any employee reflects the interaction of two sets of factors: his personal history and the immediate situation. The situational determinants of the needs hierarchy are provided by the organizational environment which rewards certain kinds of behavior and discourages others. Thus, attempts to generalize about the perceived importance of specific job factors must take into account the overall job picture.[9] As an illustration, in certain job situations pay and security may be reasonably satisfactory while working conditions are poor; in others working

---

[7] A. H. Maslow, "A Theory of Human Motivation," *Psychological Review,* Vol. 50 (1943), pp. 370–96.

[8] M. Haire and J. S. Gottsdanker, "Factors Influencing Industrial Morale," *Personnel,* Vol. 27 (1951), pp. 445–54.

[9] F. Herzberg, B. Mausner, R. O. Peterson, and D. F. Capwell, *Job Attitudes: Review of Research and Opinion* (Pittsburgh: Psychological Service of Pittsburgh, 1957).

conditions may be good but pay and security are unsatisfactory. Workers in the former situation would probably perceive working conditions as more important than pay and security while the converse would be characteristic of workers in the latter.

The importance of the interaction between personal and situational factors as joint determinants of needs hierarchies has been clearly demonstrated for technical personnel engaged in governmental research and development work.[10] The relative importance assigned by these employees to three areas of need was investigated: (*a*) social environment (for example, working relationship with supervisor, relationship with co-workers) ; (*b*) intrinsic self-actualizing work (challenging assignments, a feeling of achievement) ; and (*c*) recognition through advancement (increased salary, promotion) . When these employees were separated into "high" and "low" performers based upon salary controlling for age and tenure, the results were as shown in Figure 13–1.

For high performing employees, irrespective of age, the needs hierarchy was: intrinsic work most important, recognition second, and social environment valued least. For low performers, irrespective of age, the hierarchy was: social environment valued most, intrinsic work second, and recognition was least important.

The interesting thing about the findings shown in Figure 13–1 is that the hierarchies in the two performance subgroups are affected in important ways by age, which is a personal factor.

For all younger employees—both high and low performers—the greatest importance is assigned to intrinsic, self-actualizing work. But whereas this emphasis is maintained by high performers, it soon shifts for low performers in favor of the social environment. Conversely, whereas the discrepancy in the importance of the social environment is very evident when employees are young (with high performing employees ranking it at the bottom of their needs hierarchy) , this factor assumes increasing importance for them over the years.

This finding cannot be attributed *solely* to the personal factor of age and therefore cannot be generalized to other organizations. It reflects also situational factors unique to this particular organization. The investigator describes this organization as one discouraging promotion based upon individual effectiveness. Instead, the system provides some rewards which become increasingly attractive

---

[10] F. Friedlander, "Motivation to Work and Organizational Performance," *Journal of Applied Psychology*, Vol. 50 (1966) , pp. 143–52.

FIGURE 13–1

Differences in Expressed Needs as a Function of Age and Performance

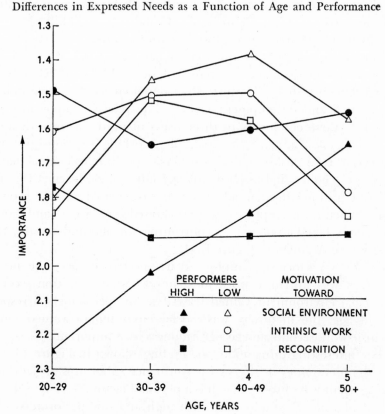

Source: F. Friedlander, "Motivation to Work and Organizational Performance," *Journal of Applied Psychology*, Vol. 50 (1966), p. 148.

with seniority, including comradeship with one's fellows and the
satisfaction of group membership. In other words, the situation in
which these employees work rewards a kind of behavior that sooner
or later is regarded as important by all employees who elect to
remain with the organization.

Valence-Expectancy Theory. Further clarification of motivation,
particularly with reference to work, is provided by the valence-expectancy theory.[11] This theory is similar to the needs-hierarchy concept in that both emphasize the idiosyncratic nature of motivation.
Since motivation is regarded as specific to the individual, motiva-

---

[11] V. Vroom, *Work and Motivation* (New York: John Wiley & Sons, Inc., 1964).

TABLE 13-1

A Hypothetical Decision Using Value-Expectancy Theory

Alternatives	Expected Consequences (and Valences)				Total Valence
	Immediate Income	Opportunity for Advancement	Nature of Work	Hours of Work	
Remain on present job............	Present level (0.00)	Fair (0.25)	(0.00)	Convenient (0.50)	0.75
Change to job A.................	Slightly above present level (0.25)	Good (0.50)	More interest-ing than present work (0.75)	Very incon-venient (−0.50)	1.00
Change to job B.................	Slightly above present level (0.25)	Excellent (0.75)	More interest-ing than present work (0.75)	Moderately inconvenient (−0.25)	1.50

tional patterns cannot easily be generalized to *groups* of workers. Hence, both theories predict a finding which we will discuss subsequently: the correlations between satisfaction or dissatisfaction with work and such behavioral criteria as productivity are weak.

A second similarity follows from the above. Both concepts seek to explain the origins of idiosyncratic motivational patterns evident at any point in time. In other words, instead of asking whether job dissatisfaction is related to a criterion like turnover, both emphasize the question: "Why does this dissatisfied employee leave his job whereas that equally dissatisfied employee elects to remain?"

The two approaches provide complementary answers to this question. The needs-hierarchy theory says, in essence, that behavior is dictated by those needs with greatest primacy. The valence-expectancy theory attempts to explain how such primacy develops among several competing needs.

The term "valence" refers to the attractiveness of any goal or outcome. Before following a course of action, we assign valences (consciously or unconsciously) reflecting our expectations about the consequences of each alternative open to us. We behave in the direction of the strongest or most positive valence.[12]

To illustrate, let us consider a hypothetical employee's drive for changing jobs. As shown in the top row of Table 13–1, he assigns a valence of 0.75 to his present job. This valence is compounded of the importance to him of present salary, opportunity for advancement, the nature of the work he does, and the hours of work. (Although other factors will also enter into this decision, we have limited the number for the purpose of illustration.)

His expectations concerning these same factors are also shown in Table 13–1. The valence-expectancy theory predicts that this employee is predisposed to move from his present job to job B. If the valence for job B were higher than 1.50, the likelihood of his actually making the move would be even greater.

JOB SATISFACTION AND JOB PERFORMANCE

We have already mentioned that the correlation between job satisfaction and such performance criteria as productivity, accident

---

[12] The psychologically sophisticated reader will note the origins of this concept in "field theory."

rate, absenteeism, and turnover tends to be weak. This finding is contrary to what common sense leads us to anticipate.

Productivity

Quite a number of investigators have correlated a measure of job satisfaction with supervisory ratings of employee performance and been forced to the conclusion that these two factors are not particularly related. The correlations actually obtained for groups of office clerical workers, for example, ranged between −0.06 and +0.13.[13] Similarly low values have been reported for plumber apprentices, farmers, IBM operators,[14] retail salesclerks,[15] and other employee groups. The median correlation reported in a recent summary of various studies across many occupational groups was only 0.14.[16]

Such studies are open to a certain amount of criticism because of the subjective nature of the criterion of employee performance. Supervisory ratings of performance leave much to be desired in the way of reliability and validity. An objective criterion, sales volume, was correlated with an index of job satisfaction for insurance agents with positive results. The two measures yielded a correlation coefficient of 0.26.[17] Although this correlation is not high, it provides some support for the contention that there is a slight tendency for satisfied employees to be more productive than dissatisfied employees. However, even such a slight positive relationship is not uniformly obtained where an objective performance criterion is used. For example, a correlation of only 0.22 has been reported between job satisfaction and performance of positioners.[18]

---

[13] Brayfield and Crockett, *op. cit.*

[14] M. S. Gadel and P. H. Kriedt, "Relationships of Aptitude, Interest, Performance and Job Satisfaction of IBM Operators," *Personnel Psychology,* Vol. 5 (1952), pp. 207–12.

[15] A. C. Mossin, *Selling Performance and Contentment in Relation to School Background* (New York: Bureau of Publications, Teachers' College, Columbia University, 1949).

[16] Vroom, *op. cit.*

[17] B. Baxter, A. A. Taaffe, and J. F. Hughes, "A Training Evaluation Study," *Personnel Psychology,* Vol. 6 (1953), pp. 403–17.

[18] F. C. Mann, B. P. Indik, and C. H. Vroom. *The Productivity of Work Groups* (Ann Arbor, Mich.: University of Michigan, Institute for Social Research, Survey Research Center, 1963).

Turnover

Another plausible, but often unsubstantiated, hypothesis is that job satisfaction ought to be related to such criteria as absenteeism and turnover. It seems reasonable to anticipate that employees who are for some reason unhappy with their job will seek other employment when possible. Although this expectation has been supported in several studies,[19] the evidence for it is not very strong. Furthermore, contrary findings showing no relationship between job dissatisfaction and turnover have also been reported in the literature.[20]

Job satisfaction is clearly only one part of the answer to turnover. Again, we must invoke the notion of individual needs herarchies and the susceptibility of these hierarchies to personal factors (like sex, age, and education) and situational factors (including the availability of other jobs and economic obligations). Taken together, these conditions influence the worker's propensity to leave if dissatisfied with his job.

It has been hypothesized that those workers with a high propensity to leave if dissatisfied tend to be young, highly skilled employees with few economic obligations who live in an area where there is a demand for their skills. The opposite conditions generate a low propensity to leave if dissatisfied.[21] This interpretation fits nicely into the valence-expectancy theory of motivation discussed earlier.

Factors Influencing the Relationship

It would be erroneous to conclude from the foregoing discussion that job satisfaction is an unimportant consideration in industry or that it cannot be improved regardless of management's efforts to do so. The point is simply that human motivation is complex. This complexity makes it difficult to generalize about the factors contributing to job satisfaction and dissatisfaction and about the influence of these attitudes upon job performance.

---

[19] I. C. Ross and A. F. Zander, "Need Satisfactions and Employee Turnover," *Personnel Psychology*, Vol. 10 (1957), pp. 327–38; and C. L. Hulen, "Job Satisfaction and Turnover in a Female Clerical Population," *Journal of Applied Psychology*, Vol. 50 (1966), pp. 280–85.

[20] W. J. Giese and H. W. Ruter, "An Objective Analysis of Morale," *Journal of Applied Psychology*, Vol. 33 (1949), pp. 421–27.

[21] Hulen, *op. cit.*

Individual Differences in Motivation. There are widespread individual differences between employees in the goals which they seek (individual needs hierarchies) and hence in the effectiveness of specific factors as determinants of job satisfaction and behavior. Furthermore, as we have already pointed out, needs hierarchies are exceedingly flexible since they reflect the valences currently attached to potential outcomes.

This situation is quite analagous to your own experience in school. It is unlikely that the amount of effort you expend in a particular course is affected solely by your feelings about that course. Regardless of whether you are happy or unhappy in it, and whether you have elected to take it or have been compelled to take it in order to fulfill a university requirement, you are under a certain amount of pressure to produce (that is, to earn a passing grade) in order to be graduated.

Employees also function under conditions of constraint. Productivity or job stability may be no more of an ultimate goal for them than earning a satisfactory grade is for you. High productivity or job stability may for some employees be a means toward the realization of certain other goals like status or ownership of a new car. When the pressure for productivity is high, the employee may perform efficiently either in the absence of any real job satisfaction or even when he is quite dissatisfied.[22]

Furthermore, it is naïve to assume that management's goals and the employee's goals always coincide. Whereas management may value efficient productivity, at least some employees are more intensely driven toward other ends also satisfied in work settings. For example, the worker who is highly motivated by a desire for social acceptance by his fellow employees may actually derive increased satisfactions from limiting his productivity and thereby gaining group acceptance.

Methodological Factors. The reported correlations between measures of job satisfaction and job performance are undoubtedly underestimates resulting from certain procedural difficulties adversely affecting the reliability and validity of both measures. To some extent this is a function of the subjectivity inherent in certain of the satisfaction and performance criteria. In addition, it results

---

[22] H. C. Triandis, "A Critique and Experimental Design for the Study of the Relationship between Productivity and Job Satisfaction," *Psychological Bulletin*, Vol. 56 (1959), pp. 309–12.

from such things as inadequate record keeping and certain evaluative problems inherent in assessing attitudes.

PERSONAL CHARACTERISTICS RELATED TO JOB SATISFACTION

The emphasis in the remainder of this chapter is upon the factors or conditions associated with employee attitudes of satisfaction or dissatisfaction with the job. It is convenient for this discussion to separate the personal from the situational components of job satisfaction.

That certain personal characteristics like sex, age, intelligence, and mental health or adjustment should be related to job satisfaction is not surprising. Work is an aspect of the total life experience. To some extent, our attitudes toward work reflect our personal history.

Sex

A higher overall level of job satisfaction has been reported for women than for men.[23] Work is generally a less consuming element in the lives of women and hence of somewhat lesser importance to their status in the community.

Differences in the relative importance attached by men and women to specific aspects of the job have also been investigated. A sample of workers completed a questionnaire in which the following five factors were presented in various combinations as pairs: advancement, hours of work, salary, security, and supervisor. The respondent was required to check the item in each pair of statements that he (or she) regarded as most important in a job.[24] The choices, expressed as percentages of the total number of choices attainable, are summarized by sex and by marital status in Table 13–2.

Men attached considerably more importance than women to advancement possibilities and somewhat greater importance to salary. The women, on the other hand, regarded the supervisor as a more potent determinant of job satisfaction than did the men.

---

[23] N. C. Morse, *Satisfactions in the White Collar Job* (Ann Arbor, Mich.: Institute for Social Research, University of Michigan, 1953), p. 72.

[24] M. L. Blum and J. Russ, "A Study of Employee Attitudes towards Various Incentives," *Personnel*, Vol. 19 (1942), pp. 438–44.

The replies of unmarried female workers corresponded in some ways more closely to those of men than to those of married women. This is particularly apparent for the ratings assigned to the supervisor, hours of work, and advancement. Thus, these data are suggestive of some fundamental differences in the gratifications which employees seek from their job and of the role of work in overall life adjustment as a function of sex and marital status.

TABLE 13–2

Attitude toward Various Incentives by Sex and Marital Status

	Men			Women		
	Married	*Single*	*Total*	*Married*	*Single*	*Total*
Salary................	46%	46%	46%	34%	36%	39%
Security...............	76	65	69	65	73	72
Supervisor.............	32	34	33	51	45	45
Hours of work..........	13	16	15	29	18	21
Advancement...........	83	89	87	71	78	76

Age

There is some evidence indicative of increased job satisfaction with increased employee age.[25] This relationship has been attributed to a combination of factors, including the termination of employment by dissatisfied older personnel and a kind of conservatism or resignation with advancing age to the realities of life and the job. In addition, some of the factors responsible for job dissatisfaction, like lack of opportunity for advancement and low salary, are of somewhat lesser importance to older workers than to younger employees who are in the midst of raising a family.

Intelligence

The level of intelligence does not itself appear to be a determinant of job satisfaction or dissatisfaction. The employee's intelligence in relation to the nature of the job he performs is, however, a factor of considerable consequence. Employees who are either insuf-

---

[25] Morse, *op. cit.*; and R. Hoppock, "Age and Job Satisfaction," *Psychological Monographs*, Vol. 47, No. 212 (1936).

ficiently challenged by their work or who are engaged in activities that are too demanding relative to their intellectual capabilities are often dissatisfied with their job. The implication of this relationship for the implementation of adequate personnel selection procedures is self-evident.

Experience

Job experience is related to satisfaction in a rather interesting fashion. As one might expect, new employees tend to be relatively well satisfied with their jobs. This "honeymoon" terminates after a period of time, however, unless the worker feels that he is making rather steady progress toward the satisfaction of his occupational and social needs.

Almost every company employs a number of persons who after several years with the company feel that advancement or salary increases have not been forthcoming with sufficient regularity and that they are working at a dead-end job. The effect of this is to cause a perceptible decline in the prevailing level of job satisfaction during the several years following the start of employment. The level of job satisfaction appears to increase again after six or seven years and reaches a maximum for workers who have remained with a company for about 20 years.[26] This is undoubtedly due to the fact that the most dissatisfied employees have sought other employment either voluntarily or involuntarily. In addition, employees who have been encouraged to remain with the company for as long a period as 20 years have probably been provided with the kind of incentives that lead to feelings of job satisfaction.

Personal Adjustment

"Adjustment" is a word that is bandied about a good deal in Sunday Supplements and popular magazines. Writers of such articles sometimes erroneously equate it with conformity. This equation implies that the well-adjusted person is one who submerges his own individuality, often disregarding the fulfillment of his own needs in order to gain or maintain acceptance by some group.

There is no doubt that well-adjusted individuals often do con-

---

[26] R. L. Hull and A. Kolstad, "Morale on the Job," in W. Goodwin (ed.), *Civilian Morale* (New York: Reynal & Hitchcock, Inc., 1942).

form to societal and group pressures. Their conformity is, however, to be regarded as evidence for, but not as identical with, personal adjustment. The well-adjusted person is one who after weighing the issues may feel quite free to be a nonconformist if such behavior best satisfies his fundamental needs and does not deprive others of the right to satisfy their needs. Thus, from a psychological standpoint, adjustment is more nearly equated with personal satisfaction than it is with conformity.

The existence of a relationship between job satisfaction and adjustment to, or satisfaction with, life in general has been implied throughout the preceding sections of this chapter. One study concerning this relationship compared employees in a paper converting company who regarded work as one of their outstandingly pleasant experiences, and therefore were presumably satisfied with it, with a matched group not regarding work as an outstandingly pleasant experience. The former, "work-motivated" group was found to rate more highly on the adequacy of their job performance. In addition, employees in this group tended to report their life experiences as being predominantly pleasant and to give more evidence of autonomy and competence in interacting with people. These are regarded as signs of general adjustment.[27]

The interpretation of a relationship between job satisfaction and life adjustment is somewhat risky as regards cause and effect. It might be assumed that a worker who is personally maladjusted and unhappy about circumstances outside of the plant will generalize this attitude to include dissatisfaction with his company and job. There is some evidence, however, that the relationship may also work the other way; that is, job satisfaction is partly responsible for a general feeling of well-being and satisfaction with life.[28] In any event, either as cause or effect or as some combination of the two, management has reason to be concerned with the worker's adjustment to the job itself and, in a larger sense, to life.

Almost any industrial organization will occasionally hire an employee who is seriously maladjusted. The treatment of such persons is a matter that extends considerably beyond the scope of the present

---

[27] H. Meltzer and D. Ludwig, "Memory Dynamics and Work Motivation," *Journal of Applied Psychology*, Vol. 52 (1968), pp. 184–87.

[28] A. H. Brayfield, R. V. Wells, and M. W. Strate, "Interrelationships among Measures of Job Satisfaction and General Satisfaction," *Journal of Applied Psychology*, Vol. 41 (1957), pp. 201–5.

discussion and, in fact, beyond the limits of the counseling activities usually undertaken by the company. Employees who suffer from major personality disturbances are generally referred to more appropriate agencies for treatment.

However, even reasonably well-adjusted persons may experience a certain amount of job dissatisfaction generalized from situational factors in the environment outside of work. Since it is not always possible for an individual to achieve his goals or to satisfy his needs, most employees are occasionally confronted by circumstances which temporarily produce tension and feelings of dissatisfaction.

SITUATIONAL FACTORS RELATED TO JOB SATISFACTION

Turning our attention now to aspects of the job and work environment, we ask, "How do workers in general feel about various aspects of their work? What do employees want from their jobs?"

A procedure often used to answer questions like these requires employees to consider a list of job characteristics and to rank or rate them in order of their perceived importance. The 10 factors ranked as most important by employees in six companies is shown in Table 13–3. This table also shows the expectations of executives in these companies and labor leaders about the ranks that the employees would assign to these factors.

One very important conclusion from such studies is that the needs of employees often are not well understood either by executives or by labor leaders. A factor, for example, like "information on success or failure at the job," was ranked as quite important by workers but excluded from the top 10 ranks expected by executives and labor leaders. The latter group, in particular, tended to overestimate the extent of employee concern about union matters.

The rank assigned by employee groups to any job factor is, of course, a function of the specific factors that employees are asked to consider. It is a function also of the employee's position and job context. Thus, a rank ordering of the importance to industrial supervisors of various job characteristics[29] differed in important ways from the ranks shown for line employees in the first column of Table 13–3. The supervisors included as important several characteristics

---

[29] L. W. Gruenfield, "A Study of Motivation of Industrial Supervisors," *Personnel Psychology*, Vol. 15 (1962), pp. 303–14.

that did not enter into the ranking by line employees; for example, increased personal responsibility and greater opportunity for independent action. The supervisors also assigned lower ranks to some characteristics, like fringe benefits, than did line employees. However, for both groups of workers, working conditions were ranked as least important and security and opportunity for advancement were ranked as most important.

TABLE 13–3

The 10 Most Important Factors Contributing to Job Satisfaction as Ranked by Employees, Executives, and Labor Leaders

Rank	By Employees	Expected by Executives	Expected by Labor Leaders
1......Security		Pay	Pay
2......Advancement		Security	Security
3......Pay		Vacations	Hours
4......Benefits		Advancement	Working conditions
5......Information on success or failure at job		Working conditions	Unions
6......Type of work		Company attitude	Company attitude
7......Vacation and holiday practices		Type of work	Handling of grievances
8......Supervisor		Benefits	Vacations
9......Profit sharing		Supervisor	Union-management relations
10......Working conditions		Hours	Job evaluation programs

Source: National Industrial Conference Board, *Factors Affecting Employee Morale,* Studies in Personnel Policy No. 85 (1947), p. 21.

In the remainder of this section we will focus upon *employee* perceptions. We consider first the relationship between job satisfaction and selected situational factors. Following this, we discuss the two-factor theory of job satisfaction as an attempt to organize information about the situational sources of job satisfaction and dissatisfaction.

Specific Situational Factors

We are here concerned with employee attitudes about the following aspects of the job and work setting: pay, security, opportunity for participation and personal recognition, hours and working conditions, occupational level and status, and supervision.

Pay. It is evident in Table 13–3 that management tends to overemphasize the importance of pay as a determinant of job satisfaction. Quite elaborate incentive pay systems have been developed to recompense employees on the basis of productivity (either as individuals or in groups) or some related criterion. Employees rarely, however, rank pay as the most important determinant of their satisfaction with the job.

TABLE 13–4

Importance of Various Job Factors as Rated by Workers

	Percentage of 7,000 Workers Including This Item in the First Five	Percent Assigning It First Choice
A steady job	61.9%	36.1%
Pay rate	52.6	7.2
A chance to get ahead	41.9	6.9
A square boss	39.6	4.8
Working on the job you prefer	35.3	15.2
Credit for the job you do	29.6	2.2
Vacations and holidays	21.5	0.4
Friendly working companions	21.3	0.7
Medical and health facilities	20.8	0.6
Pension	9.7	7.1

Source: R. Stagner, "Psychological Aspects of Industrial Conflict, II: Motivation," *Personnel Psychology*, Vol. 3 (1950), pp. 1–16.

The relative importance attached to this factor by workers is undoubtedly a function of the wage currently being received in relation to that being paid to other employees in similar jobs or requiring similar training and experience. Its perceived importance is also a function of the employee's needs relative to what he can purchase with the wage he is receiving.

The fact that employees quite often rate factors related to ego-satisfaction and personal recognition as more important than salary is apparent from the results obtained from a large group of workers and shown in Table 13–4.

It would be incorrect, of course, to maintain that rate of pay is unrelated to job satisfaction. The point, however, is that once the employee surpasses some minimum income, his feelings about the job tend to reflect the extent to which it satisfies certain of his socially derived needs. Thus, financial rewards cannot be regarded as a panacea or even as the most important incentive governing employee motivation.

Job Security. The importance attached by workers to the factor of security is clearly evident in Table 13-4 and substantiated by other investigations of a similar nature.[30]

The relative importance of security in comparison with other aspects of the job, such as pay or personal recognition, varies as a function of the job classification and the extent to which the workers actually do feel secure in their job. It is likely that workers who are not confronted by the possibility of precipitous dismissal will regard factors other than security as being of primary importance. Many employees, however, remember the widespread unemployment and the real economic pinch of the depression and, in consequence, place a very high value upon job security.

Participation and Personal Recognition. Improvements in industrial efficiency are often accompanied by fragmentation of the task performed by each employee. The craftsman's feeling of satisfaction and personal pride derived from his ability to transform raw materials into a finished product is rarely experienced within our present factory structure. The employee today has the same needs for a feeling of accomplishment, pride, and personal worth as did his artisan predecessor. The importance of these factors is evident from the high ratings consistently assigned by workers to such questionnaire items as "opportunity to use own ideas" and "credit for the job you do."

Although it is often impossible to enable each employee to experience the pride of a craftsman, it is both possible and necessary to provide the kind of training that will enable each worker to see how his sometimes miniscule task fits into the manufacture of the total product. This kind of training has been found, by way of illustration, to improve materially the net good yield produced by a manufacturer of miniature motors utilized in guidance systems and on space satellites. Prior to training, the assemblers tended to be somewhat careless in handling components. This lack of caution often

---

[30] R. Hersey, "Psychology of Workers," *The Personnel Journal*, Vol. 14 (1936), pp. 291–96; and S. Wyatt and J. N. Langdon, "Fatigue and Boredom in Repetitive Work," *Industrial Health Research Board, No. 77* (London: H. M. Stationery Office, 1937).

produced microscopic chips which were ultimately responsible for motor malfunctions. The solution developed by the company was to organize a training program in which all employees became aware of the importance of their motor to the successful performance of the satellite and of the importance of their own job to the proper functioning of the motor.

Hours and Working Conditions. It is of some interest to note that the hours worked and the physical conditions under which work is performed are generally not regarded by employees as very

TABLE 13–5

Job Satisfaction as a Function of Occupational Classification

Classification	Number of Cases	Range of Indices	Mean Index
Unskilled manual..........................	55	100–650	401
Semiskilled.............................	74	125–650	483
Skilled manual and white collar.............	84	125–675	510
Subprofessional, business, and minor supervisory...........................	32	250–700	548
Professional, management, and executive........	23	300–700	560

Source: R. Hoppock, *Job Satisfaction* (New York: Harper & Bros., 1935).

important determinants of job satisfaction. The consistently low ratings assigned to these factors probably indicates that most jobs are performed on a tolerable work schedule and under at least minimally adequate working conditions.

Occupational Status. It has been estimated that approximately 13 percent of employees are dissatisfied with their jobs. This percentage is a median value based upon the results of a large number of job satisfaction studies spanning many years.[31]

Although most employees either are satisfied with their jobs or else maintain a feeling of relative neutrality toward them, the degree of job satisfaction reported varies with the worker's occupational status. The higher his position in the job hierarchy, the more likely he is to report satisfaction with his job. This generalization is evident from the results of studies like the one reported in Table 13–5. The index of job satisfaction utilized in this investigation

---

[31] H. A. Robinson, "Job Satisfaction Researches of 1958," *Personnel and Guidance Journal,* Vol. 37 (1959), pp. 669–73.

extends from a low of 100 (extreme dissatisfaction) to a high of 700 (extreme satisfaction) with a neutral or indifference point at 400. The progression of satisfaction indices as a function of occupational classification is self-evident.

This kind of finding tends to substantiate the point made earlier that ego-satisfaction is an important contributor to job satisfaction. The occupational levels delineated in this study represent a hierarchy with respect to social prestige and status. It is quite likely that the worker's reported level of satisfaction with his job is related to the value placed upon his services by the community at large.

Occupational differences have been found also in the priority assigned by workers to the importance of specific factors as determinants of job satisfaction. Security, for example, is of much greater concern to unskilled and semiskilled employees than it is to personnel at the higher end of the occupational scale. Conversely, the opportunity for self-expression is weighted more heavily by professionals and business personnel than by laborers.[32] In another study, college graduates ranked both pay and opportunity for advancement above security in importance to job satisfaction.[33] It is quite likely that such findings reflect both the fact that highly trained persons are less susceptible to precipitous job termination and the likelihood that should their employment be terminated, they anticipate relatively little difficulty in obtaining other employment.

Supervision. One of the significant findings of the Hawthorne study was that it was possible to change the attitudes of the employees by developing a cooperative spirit between workers and supervisors.[34] A friendly supervisory-subordinate relationship appeared to generalize to a favorable work climate. The importance attached by workers to the quality of supervision probably results from the fact that the supervisor is in a way a representative of the company. When perceived in this light, he is a primary force facilitating or inhibiting the satisfaction by the employee of his needs for personal recognition.

A strong relationship has been found, for example, between dis-

[32] R. Centers, "Motivational Aspects of Occupational Stratification," *Journal of Social Psychology*, Vol. 28 (1948), pp. 187–217.

[33] Stanford Research Institute, "Tomorrow's Manpower," *Research for Industry News Bulletin*, May, 1955, pp. 8–9.

[34] F. W. Roethlisberger and W. J. Dickson, *Management and the Worker* (Cambridge, Mass.: Harvard University Press, 1939).

satisfaction with certain aspects of supervision and the subsequent termination of employment by life insurance salesmen. Two groups of salesmen, equated for length of service, age, and company for which they worked, were differentiated on the basis of survival or termination of employment during the year subsequent to completion of a job satisfaction questionnaire. The comparison between the responses made by these groups relative to certain supervisory matters is shown in Table 13–6.[35]

TABLE 13–6

Responses of Groups of Insurance Salesmen to Selected Items concerning Supervision

	Percent of Survivors	Percent of Terminators
Like freedom from supervision	56	34
Like helpfulness of supervision	62	41
Like personal friendship with the manager	70	53
Dislike manager misrepresenting or failing to explain all provisions of the contract	6	16
Manager doesn't devote enough time to the agent's problems	4	12
My job was misrepresented by the manager during the hiring interview	9	19
Feel free to talk over personal problems with the manager	94	74
Feel free to discuss selling problems with the manager	99	90
Manager makes you feel you are doing a worthwhile job	90	78
Enjoy manager socially	92	83
Manager spends part of his time handling agents' personal problems and grievances	83	64
Manager gives each agent a detailed explanation of changes in company policy or procedure	88	73

The "Two-Factor" Theory

About 10 years ago, an attractively simple theory of job satisfaction was proposed by Herzberg and his colleagues.[36] This theory made a concise statement about the conditions contributing to job satisfaction and dissatisfaction and has been responsible for giving direction to a tremendous amount of research in the general area.

---

[35] J. Weitz and R. C. Nuckols, "Job Satisfaction and Job Survival," *Journal of Applied Psychology*, Vol. 39 (1955), pp. 294–300.

[36] F. Herzberg, B. Mausner, and B. B. Snyderman, *The Motivation to Work* (New York: John Wiley & Sons, Inc., 1959).

The evidence has been contradictory, sometimes supporting and sometimes refuting the theoretical propositions. Therefore, several reviewers have concluded that the theory is *over*simplified and does violence to the richness of the motivational milieu.[37]

Although the position taken here is that the two-factor theory is indeed an oversimplification of the complexities of work motivation, consideration of its propositions and some of the related evidence is instructive.

The Propositions. The theory distinguishes between job factors which are "satisfiers" and those that are "dissatisfiers." The former are effective in motivating the employee to superior performance and effort *but play an extremely small part in producing job dissatisfaction.* Therefore, these factors with potential for generating satisfaction are termed "motivators." In contrast, the dissatisfiers have high potential for producing job dissatisfaction *but are relatively inconsequential as positive determinants of satisfaction.* Thus, they operate in preventative fashion as "hygiene" factors.

The two-factor theory states that those factors which are intrinsic to the job (that is, are part of the job task) are "motivators"; those that are extrinsic to the job (that is, are related to the job environment) are "hygiene factors."[38] Thus, according to this theory, "motivators" include such things as the nature of the task, the extent of employee responsibility for task performance, and the employee's sense of achievement from doing the task. In contrast, such things as company policy, administrative practice, type of supervision, quality of working conditions, and pay (all extrinsic to the task itself) operate as "hygiene factors."

The predicted effects of the "motivator" and "hygiene" factors are shown schematically in Figure 13–2.

Some Evidence. Because of the large volume of research testing this theory, we will consider only some representative findings.

The original study leading to the formulation of the theory[39] was based upon the results of interviews with samples of engineers and accountants. They were asked to describe events in their job experi-

---

[37] M. D. Dunnette, *Factor Structures of Unusually Satisfying and Unusually Dissatisfying Job Situations for Six Occupational Groups* (speech to the meeting of the Midwestern Psychological Association, Chicago, 1965); and L. W. Porter, "Personnel Management," *Annual Review of Psychology,* Vol. 17 (1966), p. 411.

[38] F. Herzberg, "New Approaches in Management Organization and Job Design —1," *Industrial Medicine and Surgery,* Vol. 31 (1962), pp. 477–81.

[39] Herzberg, Mausner, Snyderman, *op. cit.*

ence resulting either in a marked improvement or deterioration in job satisfaction. The analysis of their replies led to identification of the two classes of job factors, each with its postulated effects. Using essentially this procedure, similar results have been reported for manufacturing company employees,[40] lower level supervisors,[41] assembly workers,[42] and others.

Several other studies have failed to support the two-factor theory. Generally, the explanation is to be found in methodological differ-

FIGURE 13–2

Schematic Representation of the Two-Factor Theory of Job Satisfaction*

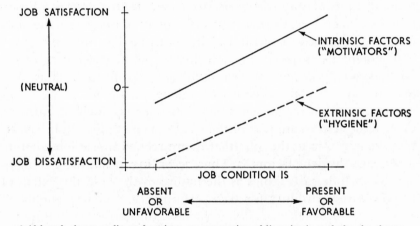

* Although shown as linear functions, no assumption of linearity is made by the theory.

ences. In particular, the use of interviews for generating information about job satisfaction and dissatisfaction has been questioned because of their introspective nature. It has been argued that when people are asked the sources of their satisfaction and dissatisfaction, they may respond defensively. Such defensiveness could lead them to attribute the former to their personal accomplishments (which would include intrinsic job factors) and the latter to factors beyond their control (including extrinsic job factors).[43]

[40] M. S. Myers, "Who Are Your Motivated Workers?" *Harvard Business Review*, Vol. 42 (1954), pp. 73–88.

[41] M. M. Schwartz, E. Jenusaitis, and H. Stark, "Motivational Factors among Supervisors in the Utility Industry," *Personnel Psychology*, Vol. 16 (1963), pp. 45–53.

[42] T. M. Lobdahl, "Patterns of Job Attitudes in Two Assembly Technologies," *Administrative Science Quarterly*, Vol. 8 (1964), pp. 482–519.

[43] G. Gurin, J. Veroff, and S. Feld, *Americans View Their Mental Health* (New York: Basic Books, Inc., 1960).

Attempts to analyze other criteria of job satisfaction to determine whether their components are organized into the two factors or classes predicted by the theory have been unsuccessful.[44] Also, by varying the procedure for recalling satisfying and dissatisfying incidents, several investigators have found that both intrinsic and extrinsic factors could produce either satisfaction or dissatisfaction.[45]

An Assessment. Taken together, the evidence concerning the two-factor theory of job satisfaction seems to support two conclusions:

1. Although the older distinction between intrinsic and extrinsic factors in job satisfaction is still a meaningful one, the former are not uniformly satisfiers only and the latter are not uniformly only dissatisfiers. Either type of factor, intrinsic or extrinsic, may operate as a source of either job satisfaction or dissatisfaction.

2. There is a growing body of evidence that intrinsic factors are more powerful than extrinsic factors for generating satisfaction and dissatisfaction.[46]

The latter conclusion is an interesting one from the standpoint of improving the motivational milieu. It suggests that greater improvements in job satisfaction will follow from altering the relationship between the worker and his job task than from modifying the job environment. This same suggestion follows, but for a different reason, from the two-factor theory!

INCREASING JOB SATISFACTION

The preceding discussion has been descriptive of the importance attached by employees to various incentives and job conditions. Although a comprehensive consideration of organizational management, including the management of employee motivation, is deferred until Part V, it is appropriate to introduce this matter briefly here.

To increase job satisfaction and facilitate personal adjustment

---

[44] R. B. Ewen, "Some Determinants of Job Satisfaction: A Study of the Generality of Herzberg's Theory," *Journal of Applied Psychology,* Vol. 48 (1964), pp. 161–63.

[45] P. F. Wernimont and M. D. Dunnette, "Intrinsic and Extrinsic Factors in Job Satisfaction" (paper read at Midwestern Psychological Association, St. Louis, 1964); R. B. Ewen, C. L. Hulin, P. C. Smith, and E. A. Locke, "An Empirical Test of the Two Factory Theory," *Journal of Applied Psychology,* Vol. 50 (1966), pp. 544–50; and F. Friedlander, "Job Characteristics as Satisfiers and Dissatisfiers," *Journal of Applied Psychology,* Vol. 48 (1964), pp. 388–92.

[46] G. B. Green, "Addendum to 'An Empirical Test of the Two-Factor Theory,'" *Journal of Applied Psychology,* Vol. 50 (1966), pp. 551–55.

requires that the employee be recognized and accepted as an individual with his own unique pattern of needs, strengths, and weaknesses. He cannot be expected to compartmentalize and separate his "job life" from his "home life"; and he cannot be regarded by management at any level solely as a statistic or as an organizational cog.

A traditional approach has been to assume employees are satisfied until such time as they express a grievance of some kind and then to cope specifically with the expressed dissatisfactions. This approach is unsatisfactory on two counts. First, it is probably less efficient from management's standpoint to cope with grievances than to prevent their occurrence. Second, the grievance presented to management may not truly reflect the underlying sources of dissatisfaction. In the latter regard, complaints about such things as wages or working conditions cannot always be accepted at face value. Unless the fundamental sources of dissatisfaction are corrected, wage increases or modifications in the work environment will improve job satisfaction only temporarily.

Communication and Participation

Many potential sources of grievance can be avoided by adequate communication throughout the entire company structure. If the employee is made aware of the reasons for certain company policies, practices, and decisions, he is more likely to accept them. Similarly when management is receptive to expressions of employee feeling and attitude, appropriate measures can be taken to prevent the explosion of potential sources of dissatisfaction.

Actual employee participation in programs of industrial change goes one step beyond such communication. The workers do not merely learn of an impending change and the reasons for it; they may actually participate in working out some of the details of the program. In addition to the positive effects upon job satisfaction, employee participation tends to produce feelings of group solidarity and personal identification with the program.

The conduct and effects of one such employee participation program have been described for workers engaged in manufacturing men's apparel.[47] Management had decided to make major changes in

---

[47] J. R. P. French, Jr., I. C. Ross, S. Kirby, J. R. Nelson, and P. Smyth, "Employee Participation in a Program of Industrial Change," *Personnel*, Vol. 135 (1958), pp. 16–29.

production methods in order to (1) reduce the in-process inventory and shorten the time required to produce a given garment, (2) attain more flexible control of production, (3) reduce manufacturing costs, and (4) improve the quality of the garments.

Although a general plan had been evolved for re-engineering the production lines in order to accomplish these objectives, the precise changes to be made were not known at the outset. The program was introduced to the workers in two smaller plants in a series of meetings conducted by local plant management. Following the initial meeting, changes were gradually introduced on the production floor.

After the new system had been in effect long enough to be stable, another series of meetings was called to discuss revised wage rates. Care was taken to protect earning opportunities and compensate for any economic loss brought about by the new methods. At these meetings, the workers also raised a number of complaints about equipment and mechanical difficulties. These were investigated and remedied. After the new system had been developed and refined in the smaller plants, the change was successfully introduced into the third and largest plant.

The economic goals anticipated by management at the beginning of the program were realized with minimal expressions of employee dissatisfaction. Throughout the process of change, management did not forego its right to make the changes it contemplated, but it also remained aware of what the changes meant to the employees.

Job Design

Job design specifies the individual tasks assigned to individual workers and the method by which these tasks are to be performed. Typically the criteria for job design are consistent with specialization; that is, minimizing immediate cost and maximizing immediate productivity.

These criteria have been criticized on the ground that "minimum *immediate* cost" is not the same as minimum *economic* cost. The latter includes social costs attendant upon depersonalization of the job and enforcement of worker anonymity. These social costs attributable to overfractionalization in job design are reflected in worker dissatisfaction. Hence, there is a growing emphasis upon what has been termed a *job-centered approach* to job design taking into account (1) the processes to be accomplished, (2) the unique capacity of human beings to make decisions, and (3) optimal organizational groupings of workers to maintain continuity of production.[48]

Miscellaneous Solutions

At least three additional practices bear upon job satisfaction: initial employee selection and placement; provision of evidence to the employee that management recognizes and appreciates his contribution to the company; and provision of opportunities for industrial counseling. Counseling in industry is not geared to treating serious psychological disorders. It is intended rather to help employees cope with the less severe kinds of emotional problems that may interfere with his behavioral effectiveness in the company, family, and community.

SUMMARY

Motivation is a fundamental explanatory concept underlying the understanding of behavior. A person's needs or wants and the drives generated by them sensitize him to awareness of particular stimulus conditions and influence the way in which he perceives and responds to these conditions.

Motives related to work have generally been oversimplified. Employees do not work solely, or, in most instances, even primarily to earn money. The work role is for many people central to the maintenance of a sense of general well-being. The origins of attitudes toward work are learned early in the course of socialization and internalized as determinants of adult behavior.

Two complementary views about motivation are presented in this chapter: needs hierarchies and valence expectancy.

The needs-hierarchy concept refers to the arrangement of our needs, and hence the goals we seek, in a hierarchy of importance. Certain needs are stronger than others at a given time. The relative strength of any need at a particular time depends upon the interaction of both personal and situational factors.

The valence-expectancy concept further clarifies the organization

---

[48] L. E. Davis, "Job Design and Productivity: A New Approach," *Personnel*, Vol. 33 (1957), pp. 418–30.

of idiosyncratic needs hierarchies. It regards the predilection for a course of action as dependent upon our expectations about the consequences of that action. In these terms, behavior is directed toward the outcome from which we anticipate the strongest and most positive consequence.

Because of the complexity of motivation and its highly individualized nature, measures of job satisfaction do not correlate substantially with such criteria as productivity, absenteeism, and turnover.

The overall level of job satisfaction varies with such personal characteristics as sex, age, intelligence, and personal adjustment. Intelligence per se is not related to job satisfaction except as level of intelligence is considered in relation to the nature and demands of the job. Employees who are either insufficiently challenged by their work or who are engaged in activities that are too demanding tend to feel dissatisfied. The relationship between job adjustment and life adjustment is a strong one, probably operating in two directions: job satisfaction contributes positively to satisfaction with life; and adjustment to factors outside of the work environment reinforces the employee's adjustment to his job.

Situational factors associated with job satisfaction are conveniently separated into those intrinsic to the job and those related to the job context or work environment (extrinsic).

The two-factor theory of job satisfaction developed about 10 years ago hypothesized that intrinsic factors are potential satisfiers but play an extremely small part in producing dissatisfaction. Conversely, this theory also hypothesized that extrinsic factors are potential dissatisfiers but are relatively inconsequential as positive determinants of satisfaction. This theory has generated a temendous amount of research on job satisfaction. The evidence supporting the theory tends to be derived from a particular methodological approach relying upon recall during an interview of job events producing feelings of satisfaction or dissatisfaction. Contradictory evidence tends to follow when other investigative procedures are used. Overall, the data seem to support a different view of job satisfaction; that is, either type of factor, intrinsic or extrinsic, may operate as a source of either satisfaction or dissatisfaction. Furthermore, there is growing support for the contention that intrinsic factors are more powerful determinants of satisfaction or dissatisfaction than are extrinsic factors.

The needs of employees are generally not well understood, either by executives or labor leaders. The latter group tends to overestimate the extent or employee concern about union matters. Executives, on the other hand, often overestimate the importance attached by workers to such factors as pay and working conditions.

14. Wages and Job Evaluation

It was pointed out in the previous chapter that management often overestimates the importance of wage or salary to job satisfaction. This is not totally to deny the importance of pay. However, compensation must be viewed in perspective as only one aspect of the job. This, in interaction with other job characteristics, is viewed somewhat idiosyncratically by each employee. After exploring the psychological evidence concerning financial incentives, this chapter describes job evaluation procedures. The purpose of job evaluation is to assist management in establishing internally equitable rates of pay.

PAY AS AN INCENTIVE

Given the close link between financial incentives and work, it is surprising that this matter had until recently hardly been the subject of psychological investigation. Of course, there has always been much speculation about the importance and proper distribution of pay. And there has been no shortage of incentive pay schemes assuming that compensation is the keystone to employee motivation. However, in recent reviews[1] of the status of our knowledge about financial incentives, the authors note the paucity of information about even very basic issues. For example, we do not know the

---

[1] R. L. Opsahl and M. D. Dunnette, "The Role of Financial Compensation in Industrial Motivation," *Psychological Bulletin*, Vol. 66 (1966), pp. 94–118; and M. Haire, E. E. Ghiselli, and L. W. Porter, "Psychological Research on Pay: An Overview," *Industrial Relations*, Vol. 3 (1963), pp. 3–8.

nature of the effect of a pay raise or the length of time that must elapse before that effect occurs. Likewise, we do not know how long the effects of a pay raise endure or the optimal frequency for increasing salary in order to encourage the desired job behavior.

Perceived Importance of Money

The amount of money needed by persons is relative rather than absolute. Living standards and habits are highly individualized; so, too, is the cost of living defined both by the acquisition of basic necessities and expenditures for discretionary items. Although it is impossible to define the amount of money required by any person, considerable insight into the role of money as an incentive is available by drawing upon the two theories of motivation introduced in the previous chapter: needs hierarchies and valence expectancy.

Need for Money. In terms of the needs-hierarchy concept, the degree to which financial incentives influence job satisfaction and/or performance depends upon the placement of the need for money in the employee's need hierarchy. The fact that some employees value money highly enough to change jobs primarily for this reason alone is evidence that for these employees at least the need for money stands in superordinate position to many other needs.

In rare instances this high value placed upon money may result from its utility for satisfying basic needs like food and shelter. However, it is impossible to account for the importance attached to money by some persons solely in terms of such basic needs. These needs are satisfied, at least beyond the "survival level," for the majority of workers in contemporary society.

The strength of the need for money, and hence its superordinate placement in the hierarchy for such employees, must be derived from its association with other, more basic, needs. Money, which originally is seen as instrumental for satisfying primary needs, may assume value for satisfying such secondary needs as the desire for security, status, recognition, power, and so on. To the extent that an employee places such social needs near the top of his needs hierarchy and to the extent that he has learned to associate money with the realization of such secondary goals, the need for money itself becomes a powerful incentive.

Valence-Expectancy Theory. In terms of the valence-expectancy concept, the incentive value of money derives from its perceived instrumentality for attaining desired goals. Thus, if the goal is status and the employee perceives income as associated with attainment of this goal, he attaches a positive valence to income. The extent to which his job behavior is influenced by financial incentives will depend upon the strength of the need (status, in this case) and the strength of the valence attached to money (that is, the strength of the expectation that money will contribute to need satisfaction).

Equity Theory

Much of the recent research concerning the relationship between pay and employee attitudes and performance has been conducted in the framework of equity theory.[2] As applied to wages, this theory hypothesizes that satisfaction is associated with the perception that the pay received is equitable or fair. Deviations either above or below this equitable point result in dissonant perceptions and consequent changes in attitude or performance.[3]

The Meaning of Equity. Pay is perceived as equitable when the job provides a balance between the inputs required and the outcomes provided. The inputs include how hard the person works as well as certain personal characteristics, like education and skill, brought by him to the work. The outcomes provided by a job include pay, fringe benefits, and such nonmonetary consequences as interesting work, status, and so on. For equity to exist, the employee must perceive a balance between what he gives to the job and what he receives from it. In this regard, other people's perceptions are immaterial; equity is a function of the perceptions of the individual in question.

The frame of reference for the perception of an equitable or inequitable balance between input and outcome is the individual's comparison between this ratio for himself and for some other significant person. This other person serving as the frame of reference may either interact directly with the person in question or may join this individual in interacting with some third party.[4] Thus, in an office,

[2] J. S. Adams, "Inequity in Social Exchange," in L. Berkowitz (ed.), *Advances in Experimental Social Psychology,* Vol. 2 (New York: Academic Press, 1965), pp. 267–99.

[3] P. C. Smith and C. J. Cranny, "Psychology of Men at Work," *Annual Review of Psychology,* Vol. 19 (1968), p. 475.

[4] Adams, *op. cit.,* p. 280.

the frame of reference for a secretary may be either her supervisor (with whom she interacts directly) or another secretary who is a co-worker also responsible to the same supervisor.

The Effect of Inequity. When the comparison described above leads an employee to perceive inequity in his input-outcome ratio, he

FIGURE 14–1

Corrective Actions Predicted from Equity Theory

Perceived Condition   *Corrective Action*

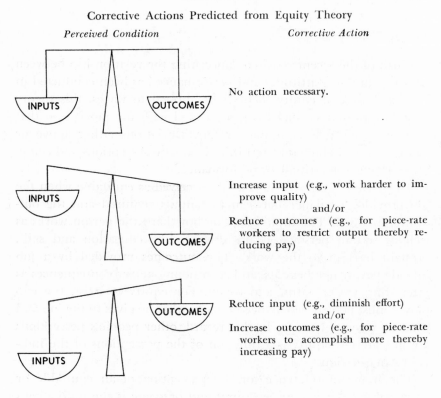

No action necessary.

Increase input (e.g., work harder to improve quality)
                and/or
Reduce outcomes (e.g., for piece-rate
workers to restrict output thereby reducing pay)

Reduce input (e.g., diminish effort)
                and/or
Increase outcomes (e.g., for piece-rate
workers to accomplish more thereby
increasing pay)

will take corrective action designed to achieve balance. Such corrective action may involve increasing or decreasing his inputs and/or
increasing or decreasing the outcomes (see Figure 14–1).

Let's consider first inequity created by the perception that outcomes are disproportionately high relative to inputs. This situation
was created for one study[5] by giving the subjects the impression that
they were unqualified for the job. In consequence, these subjects

---

[5] J. S. Adams, "Wage Inequities, Productivity, and Work Quality," *Industrial Relations*, Vol. 3 (1963), pp. 9–16.

worked harder and produced more than did the subjects who were led to believe that they were qualified for the job.

In another investigation of the same inbalance (perceived excess of outcome over input) subjects paid on a piece-rate basis were made to feel that they were being overpaid. These subjects reduced their output, thereby decreasing the amount of their pay, while simultaneously improving the quality of their performance.[6] These modifications in their behavior were interpreted as attempts to attain equity.

As shown in Figure 14–1, inequity may also result from an excess of input over outcome. To test the hypothesized consequences, undergraduate interviewers were paid either 10 cents or 25 cents for each completed interview. These amounts were determined by a preliminary study as constituting underpayment and equitable payment, respectively, in terms of the going hourly rate for campus employees. The underpaid interviewers produced more interviews during the two-hour test period than did the equitably paid interviewers. Furthermore, the quality of the interviews by underpaid employees was judged to be poorer.[7] Again, these findings are predicted by equity theory.

An Assessment. It seems evident that equity theory is helpful in understanding the dynamics of employee perceptions concerning pay and in predicting certain behavioral consequences of these perceptions. However, the theory needs additional refinement through research to answer a number of important questions.

One such question concerns the threshold for equity. How much inbalance can be tolerated without generating a perception of inequity? There is some evidence that thresholds above equity are larger than those below; that is, people are more sensitive to underpayment than to overpayment.[8] However, the influence upon equity thresholds of factors like previous wage experience and properties of the organization itself are not well understood.[9]

Additional evidence is required also on the specific inequity re-

---

[6] I. R. Andrews, "Wage Inequity and Job Performance: An Experimental Study," *Journal of Applied Psychology*, Vol. 51 (1967), pp. 39–45.

[7] E. E. Lawler, III, and P. W. O'Gara, "Effects of Inequity Produced by Underpayment on Work Output, Work Quality, and Attitudes Toward Work," *Journal of Applied Psychology*, Vol. 51 (1967), pp. 403–10.

[8] Adams (1963), *op. cit.*

[9] K. E. Weick, "The Concept of Equity in the Perception of Pay," *Administrative Science Quarterly*, Vol. 11 (1966), pp. 414–39.

duction methods chosen by an individual. This will entail investigations of individual differences in reactions to inequity as a manifestation of more basic personality characteristics.[10]

Finally, both issues, equity threshold and inequity reduction method, are undoubtedly related to the placement of monetary compensation in the individual's needs hierarchy and his expectations about the utility of money as an instrument for attaining desired secondary goals. Money cannot operate as an incentive and hence cannot enter into the input-outcome balance, unless it exerts an effect upon the employee's goals and his intention to pursue those goals. In other words, money or any other proposed reward has no incentive value unless it is perceived either as an end worth obtaining for its own sake or as a means to attainment of some other end.[11]

Attitudes Toward Pay Determination

Following equity theory, one determinant of whether an employee feels he is being paid "enough" is his perception about the input-outcome balance. This perception in turn is influenced on the outcome side by the psychological value he places upon money and its absolute magnitude relative to his needs.

But satisfaction or dissatisfaction with pay reflects something in addition to whether or not the employee feels he is being paid "enough." This additional factor is the congruence, or lack thereof, between how he feels his pay should be determined and how it is, in fact, determined. It has been suggested that satisfaction with pay exists only when these conditions are congruent.[12]

Pay must be linked with performance if it is to have maximum potential incentive value. Thus, in evaluating their preferred method of pay determination, industrial managers generally agreed that the most important determinant of their own pay ought to be merit.[13] Whether or not merit is similarly important as a determi-

---

[10] Lawler and O'Gara, *op. cit.*

[11] E. A. Locke, J. F. Bryan, and L. M. Kendall, "Goals and Intentions as Mediators of the Effects of Monetary Incentives on Behavior," *Journal of Applied Psychology*, Vol. 52 (1968), pp. 104–21.

[12] S. M. Klein, "Pay for Performance: A Research Report" (paper read at meetings of the Midwestern Psychological Association, Chicago, April, 1965).

[13] E. E. Lawler, III, "Manager's Attitudes Toward How Their Pay Is and Should Be Determined," *Journal of Applied Psychology*, Vol. 50 (1966), pp. 273–79.

nant of pay for lower level employees is somewhat, but not entirely, an academic matter because of the provisions in most union contracts which emphasize other factors, like seniority. There is usually some latitude in union contracts for recognizing merit monetarily, although there clearly is less latitude for unionized workers than there is for managers and sales personnel.

COMPANY SIZE AND WAGE PRACTICES

The typical wage practice in small business organizations employing relatively few workers tends to be a simple one. The basic wage is often determined by the "going rate" for similar jobs in comparable businesses operating in the same general locale. Although this basic wage may be increased periodically in the case of employees whom management wishes to retain, the matter of wage determination in small business often rests upon the relationship between the available supply of workers and the demand exerted by competitive employers.

The salary structure within a company becomes increasingly complex as the industrial organization increases in size. This added complexity is due in part to the fact that a larger number of workers will be affected by any revision in salary policy. Furthermore, the direct relationship between wages and the supply and demand of workers breaks down in large organizations because of the unions' attempts to stabilize base wage levels. Such wage stabilization tends to prevent salary reduction when labor is in overabundant supply and to inhibit the release of highly paid employees when cheaper labor becomes available.

Diversity of Jobs

Another difference between large and small companies contributing to the added complexity of the salary structure in larger organizations is the relative diversity of the jobs performed in such organizations. A small business may, for example, employ two or three salesclerks, each of whom has essentially the same qualifications for his work and performs essentially similar tasks. The matter of maintaining internally equitable wage scales is not a serious one in this type of organization.

As companies become larger, however, the work performed by the individual employees tends to become increasingly diverse. This diversity of tasks and the consequent diversity in experiential and educational requirements for satisfactory job performance create certain rather serious problems. To illustrate: what salaries should be established within a given company for chemists on the research staff, plumbers on the maintenance staff, and line personnel engaged in assembly? Certain of the jobs within almost any company will require a high level of formal education or training, while others may expose employees to unusual physical hazards or unpleasant working conditions. If industrial harmony is to be maintained, it is imperative that salary schedules be established in a manner that takes account of the unique requirements of each of the jobs within the company.

RELATIONSHIP BETWEEN JOB EVALUATION AND PERFORMANCE RATING

The primary function of job evaluation is to provide a systematic study of all jobs within the company with a view toward establishing equitable salary ranges or pay rates. The assumption underlying all job evaluation procedures is that it is possible to determine the relative worth of the various jobs within a company and to translate job worth into a monetary value.

It is important to recognize that job evaluation is concerned with the job or position rather than with the relative level of efficiency or inefficiency of the individual workers filling this position. The evaluative scheme makes it possible to consider every job in relation to every other job and to arrange the various jobs in some kind of hierarchy of overall worth to the company. Thus, the results of a job evaluation typically indicate a range of salaries for all employees filling a particular position.

The determination of the particular salary to be paid to an individual worker requires an analysis beyond the job evaluation itself. Let us assume that a job evaluation has been performed, leading to the establishment of a base weekly wage range for bookkeepers between $85 and $112. What specific salary should be paid to any bookkeeper in this particular company? Should he receive $85 a week, $112 a week, or some rate between these extremes?

The particular base wage paid to an individual employee is often determined by considering his seniority and his efficiency as an employee. Other things being equal, a newer and less experienced employee will be paid at a lower base rate than one who has been with the company for a period of time. Similarly, a less efficient employee will be paid less than a more efficient one. Although it is a relatively simple matter to determine seniority, as we discussed in Chapter 9, the appraisal of employee efficiency can be a difficult matter. This appraisal often requires some kind of quantification of the supervisor's opinion about the employee in the form of a performance rating. Thus, job evaluation is an aid to determining the range of base salaries to be paid to employees filling a particular position; performance rating, on the other hand, may aid in determining the particular base rate within this range to be paid to each employee within a job classification.

Quite often the base rate, reflecting the results both of job evaluation and performance rating, is supplemented by incentive earnings based upon actual productivity in relation to some standard of productivity. This standard may be established by a motion-and-time study. The amount of additional payment for "overproduction" relative to the standard will reflect various factors, including the results of labor-management negotiations on this matter as well as the outcomes of the job evaluation and performance rating procedures.

The remainder of this chapter describes the techniques for assembling one of the fundamental kinds of information critical to the establishment of equitable rates of pay: that is, job evaluation. It is well to emphasize at the outset that job evaluation procedures are exceedingly subjective; they rest entirely upon the rather frail foundation of human judgment. The discussion that follows will call attention to some of the major pitfalls in these procedures and will describe certain techniques for reducing some of the undesirable consequences of their inherent subjectivity.

JOB EVALUATION IN PERSPECTIVE

Job evaluation has not been embraced wholeheartedly either by management or by the unions, although there has been a growing realization of its value, particularly since World War II. As is the case with many other techniques, job evaluation too often has been oversold by some of its well-meaning enthusiastic advocates. Its fundamental value inheres in the fact that it provides a systematic approach to the development of a wage yardstick applicable throughout the range of diverse jobs within a sizable company. It has value also in pegging wages for newly created positions because the evaluative scheme provides a standard against which the value of a new position can be appraised. If the job evaluation is accepted by both management and employees, grievances about wages may be materially reduced. However, management and the union may have legitimate reservations about the desirability of performing a job evaluation.

Reservations by Management and Unions

Management's reluctance to engage in job evaluation is often explicable in part by lethargy and a reluctance to "rock the boat" of existing salary structure. In addition, complacency about the present salary scheme may make the cost of performing a job evaluation seem unduly high.

Much union opposition to job evaluation is founded upon the suspicion that it will lead to a certain amount of wage cutting. The union may be concerned, for example, about what will happen to the salaries of employees who are presently being "overpaid" in the light of the results of an evaluation. Furthermore, unions often are reluctant to embrace or endorse any procedure that appears to interfere with their prerogatives in collective bargaining.

The concerns expressed both by management and the unions are legitimate ones. Job evaluation cannot be sold to a company as a replacement for wage negotiation because in fact it cannot be substituted for such negotiation. Provision must be made in the evaluative scheme to protect the salaries of employees now on the job whose earnings exceed the standards established by the job evaluation. Finally, management must be sensitized to the deleterious effects of an inequitable wage structure upon job satisfaction and morale before it will be ready to accept and implement a companywide job evaluation.

Job Evaluation Not a Panacea

Even when the performance of a job evaluation gains company-wide acceptance, the results of the evaluation must not be expected to resolve all industrial wage problems. Job evaluation procedures are founded upon subjective judgments which sometimes neglect consideration of a number of factors related to wage rate.

The fact that evaluative procedures do not resolve all wage problems is illustrated in the following case. A job requiring only a moderate amount of skills, training, and prior experience will generally show up in the evaluation as being of less worth to the company than one requiring a high level of professional or technical competence. This discrepancy will, of course, be translated into differential salary schedules for the two positions. It may be necessary, however, to deviate from the established wage plan for these jobs because of the supply of workers relative to the demand for their services. Relatively unskilled employees in a plant devoted to the separation of radioactive metals from the raw ore, for example, may have to be highly paid because of the unattractive working conditions to which they are subjected. Although the work itself does not require particularly valuable skills or abilities, the shortage of workers willing to undertake this activity may necessitate the payment of wages which are disproportionate to the job's experiential and skills requirements.

Another factor generally neglected by job evaluation schemes is the possibility for employees on particular jobs to advance within the company. Assume, for example, that a company has two positions which have very similar requirements and make similar demands upon the workers. Such positions would be assigned essentially similar base rates by the job evaluation. If, however, one of these jobs presented substantial opportunities for advancement within the company while the other was regarded as a "dead-end" position, they would prove to be unequally attractive to employees. It might be necessary under such circumstances to adjust the base rate for the less attractive position.

PRELIMINARIES TO PERFORMING A JOB EVALUATION

Before considering the specific procedures for conducting a job evaluation, it will be helpful to discuss some of the general principles and approaches held in common by all of the procedures. Job evaluation can be a touchy area of management activity. Certain preliminaries to the institution of the evaluative program are critical to its acceptance by the employees.

Introducing the Job Evaluation

Considerable spadework must be done within the company to prepare both management and employees for the installation of a job evaluation plan. This preparatory groundwork prior to the actual conduct of the evaluation will require joint meetings of labor and management representatives directed toward the formulation and dissemination of a clear-cut policy statement concerning the way in which the evaluation is to be conducted, and the uses to be made of the findings. This statement of policy will vary somewhat from one company to another but should generally contain information of the type listed below.

1. *The Fundamental Objective of Job Evaluation and the Critical Assumption Underlying It.* The objective, of course, is to appraise the relative worth of the jobs within the company. The underlying assumption is that the worth of a job, and hence the pay for it, should be a function of the requirements for satisfactory job performance.

2. *The Company's Stake in the Plan.* The company, particularly top management, must make explicit its endorsement of the plan and its willingness to abide by the results of the evaluation. Furthermore, provisions must be made for periodic reappraisal and appropriate revision of wage policies.

3. *Labor's Stake in the Plan.* The policy statement should define labor's role in the conduct of the job evaluation. Representatives of labor should, ideally, become sufficiently involved in the plan to function as effective partners along with management.

4. *The Effects of the Plan upon Individual Employees.* This section of the policy statement will be particularly critical to acceptance of the job evaluation plan and implementation of its findings. There must be a clear-cut agreement between management and labor on the following points, and the implications of this agreement must be understood by the employees.

a) The policy statement should contain assurance that although the job evaluation will establish maximum and minimum rate ranges for the job classifications, adequate provisions will be made also for rewarding both seniority and merit.

b) The employees now on the job must be assured that no worker's base rate will be reduced because of the results of the evaluation. If an employee is found to be overpaid, he may be transferred or promoted to a new position in conformance with his present salary, or else he will be retained on his present job at his current base rate.

c) If the results of the job evaluation indicate that an employee is being underpaid for the work he does, his salary will be adjusted upward.

d) The effect of the job evaluation will not be to reduce the general level of company rates below that currently being paid within the community and the industry in general.

5. *The Constituency of the Committee and the Nature of the Plan.* The policy statement should describe the procedures to be used in implementing the job evaluation plan and specify the persons who are to be responsible for the conduct of the evaluation (that is, the committee) .

The Job Evaluation Committee

The committee is the heart of any job evaluation scheme. It is the combined judgment of the members of this committee that will decide the relative worth of each job, and hence determine the appropriate rate schedules to be applied to it. A typical arrangement is to constitute the committee of company representatives, union, or labor representatives, and an outside consultant specializing in job evaluation procedures. Resource persons (for example, departmental supervisors) familiar with a particular job or a group of jobs can be consulted by the committee as it engages in deliberations about jobs within particular departments or sections. The entire committee must recognize and accept each other's stake in the evaluation. It cannot function well if it is loaded by members representing either management or labor, since satisfactory implementation of the job evaluation plan will require a truly cooperative endeavor by all of the committee members.

Regardless of the specific technique of job evaluation finally accepted by the committee, it must understand and accept the following assumptions about the relationship between work performed and the base rate justified by that work:

1. The salary schedule for a particular job should reflect the effort expended by employees and the nature of the work performed.

2. All jobs being evaluated can be reduced to certain elements (like Skill, Responsibility, and so on) which are held in common but to varying degrees.

3. The degree to which a job is characterized by these elements should be correlated with the salaries paid to employees on the job.

4. The results of the job evaluation should lead, ultimately, to the establishment of a maximum and minimum rate for every job. The establishment of such rate ranges recognizes the existence of individual differences in the efficiency with which the same job is performed by different employees, and makes it possible to provide additional rewards to particular employees deserving them. Thus, an equitable wage structure requires that job evaluation be supplemented by performance rating.[14]

The committee must be trained both in the conduct of the specific evaluative scheme they are going to use and in the fundamental intent of job evaluation in general. One of the most prevalent kinds of error unintentionally committed during the course of job evaluation can be attributed to halo effect. Unless the members of the committee are specifically trained to eliminate this factor, they will exhibit a tendency to appraise the job's worth in terms of the salary now being paid to employees on that job.[15] Such a basis for judgment, of course, obviates the intent of the evaluation. The committee members must be trained, therefore, to discard their prior conceptions about particular jobs based upon present wage rate, and to approach the appraisal of every job with completely open minds.

The Job Description and Job Specification

The committee members must be provided with accurate and complete information about each of the jobs they are evaluating. It has already been suggested that the committee may wish to consult with departmental supervisors in order to clarify the requirements of particular jobs. The fundamental sources of information about each job included in the evaluation, however, are the job description and job specification. The former, you will recall from the discussion in Chapter 3, outlines the duties involved in the perform-

---

[14] H. Moore, "Problems and Methods of Job Evaluation," *Journal of Consulting Psychology*, Vol. 8 (1944), pp. 90–99.

[15] E. P. Prien and S. D. Saleh, "A Study of Bias in Job Analysis and Evaluation," *Journal of Industrial Psychology*, Vol. 1 (1963), pp. 113–17.

ance of the job; the latter specifies the worker requirements for satisfactory job performance. It is virtually impossible for any job evaluation plan to proceed satisfactorily if it is built upon sketchy or inaccurate job descriptions and specifications. The evaluator's degree of differential familiarity with the various jobs may contaminate the required judgments.[16]

TECHNIQUES OF JOB EVALUATION

The purpose of job evaluation is to order or scale the jobs within the company along a continuum of overall worth. The translation of this rating of job worth into a monetary value cannot be undertaken until the entire job evaluation is completed. These two phases of wage determination, the job evaluation and the translation to base rates, are separated with good reason. The committee members can generally appraise jobs with less partiality when they are dealing with numerical values like points or ratings than when they are dealing with actual monetary values. Personal biases, intentional and otherwise, are somewhat less likely to influence a decision about whether a job is worth 300 or 320 points than they are to influence a decision about whether employees on the job ought to be started at a base rate of $2.60 or $2.70 an hour. Thus, the ensuing discussion of the techniques for performing a job evaluation makes only occasional reference to wages. The procedures for translating the numerical index of job worth derived from the evaluation to dollars and cents are discussed in a subsequent section.

Four basic methods of job evaluation are now in use: the ranking method, classification method, factor comparison method, and points method.[17]

The Ranking Method

This is the simplest and poorest method for ordering jobs along a continuum of worth. The general procedure, without going into its many possible variations, is to require the committee members to rank the jobs under consideration in order from most to least impor-

---

[16] J. M. Madden, "A Further Note on the Familiarity Effect in Job Evaluation," *Personnel Administration*, Vol. 26 (1963), pp. 52–54.

[17] L. C. Pigage and J. L. Tucker, *Job Evaluation*, University of Illinois Bulletin, No. 49, No. 36 (January, 1952), 43 pp.

tant. Thus, if 30 jobs were included in the plan, the most important job would be assigned a rank of 1 and the least important a rank of 30. This ranking may be accomplished by the committee as a whole engaging in a group discussion of each job, or it may be done independently by each committee member. In the latter case, the rankings by each member must be collated and the discrepancies arbitrated to arrive at a consensus of opinion about each job.

Appraisal of the Ranking Method.   The ranking approach to job evaluation is subject to many kinds of error. Its usefulness, to the extent that it is at all useful, is limited to the situation in which relatively few jobs are to be evaluated. The primary reason for this limitation upon the usefulness of the ranking method is that it is exceedingly difficult to differentiate between adjacent ranks in the middle of the continuum when a large number of jobs are being simultaneously evaluated. The differences between jobs relative to their overall worth requires considerable hairsplitting when the committee is attempting to decide, for example, which of 70 jobs ought to be assigned a rank of 31 and which deserves a rank of 32.

A further limitation of this procedure results from the fact that the committee is attempting to rank the jobs in terms of their *overall* worth rather than on the basis of more specific critical elements like the skill or experiential requirements of the job. The necessity for making gross judgments about each job often leads the committee to the assignment of ranks based, at least in part, upon the salaries currently being paid or upon the level of performance of the persons presently employed in these positions. The utilization of these factors, even as partial determinants of the assigned ranks, contradicts the intent of the job evaluation plan.

A final deficiency of the ranking method is related to the fact that adjacent ranks are not spaced equidistantly along a scale. The actual difference in overall worth between the jobs ranked 3 and 4, for example, may be either considerably greater or less than the actual difference in worth between the jobs ranked 4 and 5. The absence of equal scale units along the rank continuum can create rather serious problems when the attempt is made to convert job ranks to monetary values.

The Classification Method

This procedure is also a very simple one and overcomes the necessity, sometimes present when the ranking method is used, for making overly fine discriminations between jobs. The classification method is rather widely used, particularly for Civil Service jobs.

The committee using this method begins by establishing a master rating scale consisting of broad labor grades or job classifications. The number of classifications or grades is not of particular consequence as long as the number of levels is sufficient to permit the assignment of all jobs under consideration. To illustrate, The Classification Act of 1949 established 18 levels of Federal Civil Service positions in a General Schedule covering professional and scientific service, clerical, and administrative positions. The range of levels embodied within this classification is evident in Table 14–1.

The committee matches each of the jobs included within the evaluation against the classification scheme and assigns it to the particular classification with which it corresponds most closely. In effect, this procedure leads to an ordering of jobs along a continuum consisting of as many units as there are levels or classifications in the master rating scale.

Appraisal of the Classification Method. This method is similar to the ranking method in that the committee in both instances evaluates the jobs in terms of their overall worth rather than in terms of the specific factors that contribute to overall worth. Thus, the classification method and the ranking method share a common deficiency; that is, committee judgment of job worth may be based, at least in part, upon the performance of incumbents and the salaries they are receiving.

The factor comparison method and the points method, discussed in the following sections, attempt to circumvent this difficulty by starting from the assumption that certain common factors are present in varying degrees in all jobs. Thus, instead of requiring the committee to rank or classify jobs on the basis of "overall worth," these methods require consideration of each of the jobs relative to these commonly held factors. The composite appraisal of the factorial components of each job serves as the basis for differentiation between the "overall worth" of the jobs. The specific ways in which this composite may be effected are clarified in the discussion that follows.

The Factor Comparison Method

In broad outline, this method requires the committee to identify the factors or elements common to all of the jobs included within

TABLE 14-1

Selected Federal General Schedule Classification Levels

Grade GS-1 includes all classes of positions the duties of which are to perform, under immediate supervision, with little or no latitude for the exercise of independent judgment, (1) the simplest routine work in office, business, or fiscal operations, or (2) elementary work of a subordinate technical character in a professional, scientific, or technical field.

Grade GS-2 includes all classes of positions the duties of which are (1) to perform, under immediate supervision, with limited latitude for the exercise of independent judgment, routine work in office, business, or fiscal operations, or comparable subordinate technical work of limited scope in a professional, scientific, or technical field, requiring some training or experience, or (2) to perform other work of equal importance, difficulty, and responsibility, and requiring comparable qualifications.

Grade GS-8 includes all classes of positions the duties of which are (1) to perform, under general supervision, very difficult and responsible work along special technical or supervisor lines in office, business, or fiscal administration, requiring (*a*) considerable specialized or supervisory training and experience, (*b*) comprehensive and thorough working knowledge of a specialized and complex subject matter, procedure, or practice, or of the principles of the profession, art, or science involved, and (*c*) to a considerable extent the exercise of independent judgment; or (2) to perform other work of equal importance, difficulty, and responsibility, and requiring comparable qualifications.

Grade GS-13 includes all classes of positions the duties of which are (1) to perform, under administrative direction, with wide latitude for the exercise of independent judgment, work of unusual difficulty and responsibility along special technical, supervisory, or administrative lines, requiring extended specialized, supervisory, or administrative training and experience which has demonstrated leadership and marked attainments; (2) to serve as assistant head of a major organization involving work of comparable level within a bureau; (3) to perform, under administrative direction, with wide latitude for the exercise of independent judgment, work of unusual difficulty and responsibility requiring extended professional, scientific, or technical training and experience which has demonstrated leadership and marked attainments in professional, scientific, or technical research, practice, or administration; or (4) to perform other work of equal importance, difficulty, and responsibility, and requiring comparable qualifications.

Grade GS-18 includes all classes of positions the duties of which are (1) to serve as the head of a bureau where the position, considering the kind and extent of the authorities and responsibilities vested in it, and the scope, complexity, and degree of difficulty of the activities carried on, is exceptional and outstanding among the whole group of positions of heads of bureaus; (2) to plan and direct or to plan and execute frontier or unprecedented professional, scientific technical, administrative, fiscal, or other specialized programs of outstanding difficulty, responsibility, and national significance, requiring extended training and experience which has demonstrated outstanding leadership and attainments in professional, scientific, or technical research, practice, or administration, or in administrative, fiscal, or other specialized activities; or (3) to perform consulting or other professional, scientific, technical, administrative, fiscal, or other specialized work of equal importance, difficulty, and responsibility, and requiring comparable qualifications.

the evaluation, to rank the jobs relative to each of these factors, and to apportion wages on the basis of this ranking.

Selection of the Factors. It has been suggested that five factors are applicable to the evaluation of a diversity of jobs by means of the factor comparison method. These factors, which thread their way in varying degrees through almost every job, have been identified as:

1. Mental requirements.
2. Skill requirements.
3. Physical requirements.
4. Responsibility.
5. Working conditions.[18]

The five factors are intentionally broad in order to permit for their adaptation to a diversity of companies and industrial situations. As a general rule, the factor comparison method is predicated upon the use of these five factors defined appropriately to make them specifically applicable to the particular company in which the evaluation is being performed. Although it sometimes is necessary to add another factor or two to this basic list in order to encompass all jobs included within the evaluation, the number of factors rarely is permitted to exceed six or seven.

Identifying the Key Jobs. After the committee has selected and defined the factors it will use, it selects a number (generally 15–20) of "key" jobs within the company. These jobs are selected in accord with two primary requirements: (1) They cover virtually the entire range of jobs included in the evaluative plan. The key jobs selected by the committee run the gamut of "overall worth." (2) The committee members agree that the present rates of pay assigned to these jobs are fair in relation to other jobs within the company and the community at large. Thus, the list of key jobs will serve as a frame of reference for the committee in its deliberations about all other jobs included within the evaluation. It should be apparent that the validity of the factor comparison method rests upon the identification of appropriate key jobs. If the rates now paid for these jobs are in error, the entire evaluation for all other jobs may also be invalid.

Ranking the Key Jobs. The factor comparison method requires that the committee members rank the key jobs in two ways. First,

---

[18] E. J. Benge, S. L. H. Burk, and E. N. Hay, *Manual of Job Evaluation* (New York: Harper & Bros., 1941).

each member working independently must rank the jobs with respect to each of the factors. He considers each of these jobs, for example, relative to its mental requirements and orders them from highest to lowest on this factor. This procedure is repeated for each of the other factors with which the committee has agreed to work. Typically these rankings-by-factor are made two or three times with a period of several weeks intervening between rankings. Wide discrepancies between the ranks assigned by individual committee

TABLE 14–2

Average Rankings of Key Jobs on Each of the Critical Factors

			Factors		
Key Job	*Mental Requirements*	*Skill*	*Physical Requirements*	*Responsibilities*	*Working Conditions*
Patternmaker..........	1	1	6	1	7
Electrician.............	3	3	5	2	3
Machinist.............	2	2	7	3	6
Painter...............	4	4	4	4	5
Drill press operator......	7	5	8	6	8
Inspector.............	5	6	10	5	10
Bench assembler........	6	7	9	10	9
Carpenter's helper......	8	8	2	7	4
Janitor...............	9	9	3	8	2
Laborer..............	10	10	1	9	1

members are discussed to correct possible misunderstandings either about the job's requirements or the definitions of the factors. Finally, the average of the ranks assigned by the committee members is computed to yield results similar to those shown in Table 14–2.

The second kind of ranking involves wage apportionment and must be performed without reference to the factor rankings. Each committee member must consider the total hourly rate for each of the key jobs and decide how much of this hourly rate is paid for the possession of each of the factors critical to the job. How much of the patternmaker's hourly rate, for example, is paid for possession of the necessary mental requirements, skill, physical requirements, and so on. The apportionments made individually by the commiteee members are then averaged and these averages are converted to ranks.

The results from the two independent ranking procedures, one based upon wage apportionment (*$ rank*) and the other based upon

TABLE 14–3

Average Money Apportionment, Ranked Money Apportionment, and Overall Rankings Assigned to Key Jobs on Each Factor

Key Job	Average Hourly Rate	Mental Requirements $*	Mental Requirements $ Rank†	Mental Requirements Job Rank‡	Skill $	Skill $ Rank	Skill Job Rank	Physical Requirements $	Physical Requirements $ Rank	Physical Requirements Job Rank	Responsibility $	Responsibility $ Rank	Responsibility Job Rank	Working Conditions $	Working Conditions $ Rank	Working Conditions Job Rank
Patternmaker	$3.05	.95	1	1	.95	1	1	.35	5	6§	.50	1	1	.30	6	7§
Electrician	2.90	.75	3	3	.90	2	3§	.30	6	5§	.45	2	2	.50	3	3
Machinist	2.65	.90	2	2	.85	3	2§	.25	7	7	.40	3	3	.25	7	6§
Painter	2.60	.70	4	4	.80	4	4	.40	4	4	.30	5	4§	.40	5	5
Drill press operator	2.05	.65	5	5	.75	5	5	.20	8	8	.25	6	6	.20	8	8
Inspector	1.90	.60	6	6	.70	6	6	.15	9	10§	.35	4	5§	.10	10	10
Bench assembler	1.50	.55	7	7	.60	7	7	.10	10	9§	.10	9	10§	.15	9	9
Carpenter's helper	1.75	.40	8	8	.15	8	8	.55	2	2	.20	7	7	.45	4	4
Janitor	1.45	.15	9	9	.10	9	9	.50	3	3	.15	8	8	.55	2	2
Laborer	1.40	.10	10	10	.05	10	10	.60	1	1	.05	10	9§	.60	1	1

* Portion of hourly rate paid for this factor.
† Ranking of monetary apportionment.
‡ Job ranking as indicated in Table 14–2.
§ Discrepancy existing between $ rank and job rank must be adjusted.

the jobs' factorial components *(job rank)*, are compared as shown in Table 14–3.

Discrepancies of the order noted in Table 14–3 are to be anticipated. Further discussion by the committee members will frequently lead either to resolution of such discrepancies or to a decision to drop the particular job from the list of key jobs.

Use of the Master Scale. The final list of key jobs and the ranks assigned to them constitutes a master scale for the establishment of wage rates for all other jobs included within the evaluative plan. Let us assume, for example, that the committee wishes to establish a base rate for lathe operators. The factorial composition of this job would be compared with the master scale, perhaps with the following results: The mental requirements for lathe operators fall between those of painters and electricians ($0.72); the skills are roughly comparable to those required of electricians ($0.90); the physical requirements exceed those of drill press operators but not those of machinists ($0.23); the responsibilities involved and the working conditions are about the same as those of machinists ($0.40, $0.25). The total of the base rates apportioned by factors would thus be $2.50.

You will note from examination of Table 14–3 that the factors mental requirements and skill have been weighted more heavily by the committee than have the other three factors. The patternmaker's rate, for example, was broken down to $0.95 for mental requirements and $0.95 for skill, but only $0.50 for responsibility even though this position was ranked highest on all three factors. This tendency by job evaluation committees to weight skill and mental requirements more heavily than most other factors is rather prevalent, and is a matter to which we will return in subsequent discussion.

The Points Method

The points method is used more frequently for job evaluation than any other scheme.[19] The objective of this procedure is to assign to each job a point value representing the committee's opinion about the job's overall worth. The more valuable the job, the higher will be the total number of points assigned to it. The conversion of

---

[19] C. W. Lytle, *Job Evaluation Methods* (New York: The Ronald Press Co., 1946).

points to dollars is not undertaken until point allocations have been made for all jobs included within the evaluation.

The points method and the factor comparison method are similar in that both procedures are based upon the assumption that certain factors are common to all jobs in varying degrees. Thus, the method presently under consideration leads to the assignment of a point total to each job predicated upon the point allocations for each of the specific factors selected for analytic purposes.

Selecting the Factors. The number and type of factors used in various point evaluation plans varies considerably as a function of the specific jobs encompassed by the evaluation. Attempts to formulate a set of general factors applicable to all kinds of jobs, including factory and clerical work, have generally been relatively unsuccessful. A factor like working conditions, for example, may be rather critical in the evaluation of certain kinds of factory work but inconsequential for most clerical work.

Most points plans are based upon the use of about 10 to 15 relatively specific factors like: education, experience, physical effort, mental effort, physical working conditions, hazards, responsibility for equipment, initiative, precision, manual skill, tact, or diplomacy. The foregoing list of factors is by no means exhaustive.

Constructing the Points Table. Since it is anticipated that each of the factors will be present in varying degrees for the different jobs, the committee must decide upon the number of levels to be differentiated for each factor. It is fairly common practice to identify five factor levels, although, on occasion, a particular set of jobs may require as many as seven or eight levels or as few as three levels for each factor.

Once the factors have been agreed upon and the number of levels to be differentiated for each factor is established, the committee is ready to construct a points table. Such a table indicates the number of points to be assigned for possession of a particular factor at a particular level. The points table for the widely used National Electrical Manufacturers' Association (NEMA) plan for shop jobs is shown in Table 14–4.

The NEMA plan is based upon 11 factors, each with five levels. You will note that this plan makes a deliberate attempt to weight the factors unequally: the maximum number of possible points for "experience" exceeds the maximum for any of the other factors.

The decision about whether to weight factors equally or, as in the case of the NEMA plan, to weight them unequally rests squarely with the committee. Its initial decision in this matter may have to be revised if it is found that the plan they establish does not permit for a sufficient point spread between the various jobs included in the evaluation. Furthermore, the practice of establishing differential points allocations for the various factor levels does not guarantee the desired weighting of the factors when points totals are determined.

TABLE 14-4

The Points Allocations and Factor Weights Used in the Plan of the National
Electrical Manufacturers' Association

Factor	First Level	Second Level	Third Level	Fourth Level	Fifth Level	Factor Weight
Skill:						
Education............14	28	42	56	70	14%
Experience.............22	44	66	88	110	22
Initiative and ingenuity.....14	28	42	56	70	14
Effort:						
Physical demands.........10	20	30	40	50	10
Mental/visual demands..... 5	10	15	20	25	5
Responsibility:						
For equipment or process... 5	10	15	20	25	5
For material or product..... 5	10	15	20	25	5
For safety of others......... 5	10	15	20	25	5
For work of others......... 5	10	15	20	25	5
Job conditions:						
Working conditions........10	20	30	40	50	10
Hazards................. 5	10	15	20	25	5

Source: National Electrical Manufacturers Association, New York.

Applying the Points Table. The total number of points allocated to each job is determined by rating the job against the points tables. This rating is performed for each factor, and the points derived from the factor ratings are summed. Differences between the total point allocations by the committee to each of the jobs serve as the basis for establishing wage scales.

The way in which point totals are assigned to the various job in a company is illustrated by referring to a job evaluation for Broward County (Florida) Title Company. This company makes land abstracts and issues title insurance. On the basis of job analyses, 24 different jobs were identified for inclusion in the job evaluation.

TABLE 14-5

The Master Points Table Developed by a Title Company

Factor	Weight	First Level, 10 Points	Second Level, 20 Points	Third Level, 30 Points	Fourth Level, 40 Points	Fifth Level, 50 Points
Employment requirements:						
A. Formal education....10		Grammer school graduation		High school graduation		College graduation
B. Mental requirements....10		Much below average		Average		Much above average
C. Past experience....10		None	6 months or less	6 months to 3 years	3 years to 5 years	More than 5 years
Required knowledge and skill:						
D. Knowledge about the company....10		None required				Knowledge of all departments
E. Specialized knowledge and skills....10		None	Low level typing			
Work performed:						
F. Importance of accuracy....10		Essentially unimportant		Moderately important		Highly critical
G. Decisions and planning....10		None	Slight	Moderate	Great	Free from supervision
H. Supervision exerted....10		None	Slight	Moderate	Great	Extreme
I. Contact with public affecting business....10		None	Slight	Moderate	Great	Extreme
J. How difficult is it to train for this work?....10		Relatively easy				Extremely difficult

TABLE 14-6

Points Totals by Positions

	Factors (Keyed to Letter Designation in Table 14–5)										
	A	B	C	D	E	F	G	H	I	J	Total
Messenger	12	16	14	14	14	22	16	10	30	12	160
Bookkeeper, junior	30	28	30	16	24	48	14	10	12	12	224
Bookkeeper, senior	30	34	38	32	36	48	40	32	28	40	358
Abstract typist	30	30	20	16	20	40	18	10	10	14	208
Abstractor, junior	30	34	34	28	28	46	28	22	16	28	294
Abstractor, senior	30	42	46	34	30	50	42	38	28	42	382
Receptionist	30	30	30	40	20	30	20	10	40	30	280
Receptionist manager	30	30	30	40	20	40	30	20	50	40	330
Closing secretary, junior	30	30	20	20	20	30	10	10	30	20	220
Closing secretary, sr.—main office	30	40	37	50	30	50	40	32	44	43	396
Closing secretary, sr.—branch	30	40	40	50	34	50	46	36	48	46	420
Poster, junior	26	26	10	12	10	43	12	10	14	16	180
Poster, senior	28	32	30	22	10	48	22	20	22	32	266
Posting manager	30	36	42	32	20	48	44	42	34	44	372
Cartographer	30	32	30	16	32	50	30	10	16	30	276
Courthouse searcher	30	32	38	30	24	50	28	12	30	37	311
Tax searcher	30	32	32	26	16	50	24	12	36	34	288
File clerk	20	26	10	14	10	40	12	10	10	12	164
Printer	20	22	22	12	30	16	14	12	12	22	182
Photographer	20	22	22	12	32	16	14	12	12	22	184
Policy writer	20	32	33	32	23	50	26	12	10	28	276
Switchboard operator	26	22	22	30	22	22	14	10	46	30	244
Clerk typist	30	26	10	10	16	32	10	10	10	12	166
Filing manager	30	30	30	40	20	50	30	20	30	20	300

The job evaluation committee developed the points table shown in Table 14–5. Note that this committee decided to weigh each of the 10 factors equally and to classify jobs into five levels for each factor. Thus the range of points possible for any job extended from 100 (ratings at the lowest level for each factor) to 500 (ratings at the highest level for each factor). Note also that this committee provided itself with several "guideposts" in constructing the points table.

After the points table was developed, committee members each independently rated each job within the company on the scales for each of the 10 factors. These ratings were averaged and summarized as shown in Table 14–6.

CONVERTING JOB EVALUATION RESULTS TO WAGES

The job evaluation schemes described thus far, with the exception of the factor comparison method, are designed to order jobs along a continuum of worth without reference to the monetary value that ought to be assigned to each job. The ranking method expresses relative worth in terms of simple ranks; the classification method assigns each job to one of the classifications of the master rating scale; and the points method reflects differential worth in the total number of points allocated to each job. It remains now to convert these numerical indices of worth to hourly, daily, weekly, monthly, or annual rates of pay. The procedures for such conversion will be described for the points method. They are applicable, with minor modifications, to the other evaluative plans.

The Wage Curve for Key Jobs

Certain of the jobs that have been included in the points evaluation are identified as "key" jobs because: (1) they represent a considerable range of total point allocations; (2) they are sufficiently common to exist in many companies other than the one in which the evaluation has been performed; and (3) there is general agreement that the present average pay rate for each of these jobs is a fair one.

The point allocations for these key jobs are plotted against the present average salaries, yielding the kind of wage curve shown in Figure 14–2. The wage curve, shown as a heavy line in this figure, is

FIGURE 14–2

Point Allocations (from Table 14–6) Plotted against Median Biweekly Salary

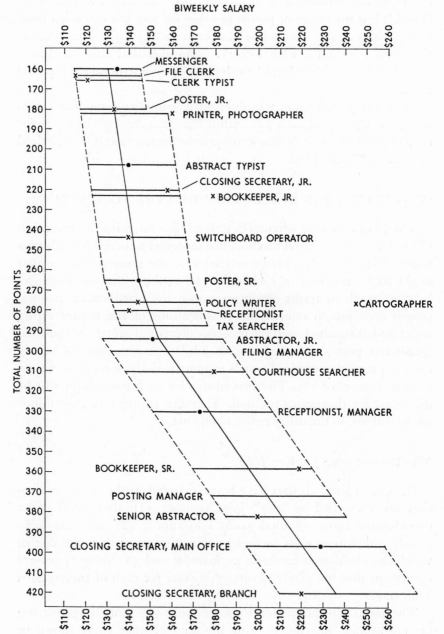

BIWEEKLY SALARY

fitted to the plotted points for the key jobs either statistically or by inspection. The key jobs from which this curve was developed were: messenger, abstract typist, senior poster, junior abstractor, reception-ist-manager, closing secretary (main office). The points allocations for these jobs were taken from Table 14–6; the biweekly salary for these jobs is the median salary paid all persons occupying these positions in the company.

Whereas the points-salary plot for each key job is indicated in Figure 14–2 by a heavy dot, the plot for other positions in the company is indicated by an X. Note especially that current salaries for junior bookkeeper and for cartographer are considerably above the "worth" of these jobs as judged by the job evaluation.

The smoothed wage curve is useful for establishing salaries for newly created jobs. For example, the position posting manager was newly created at the time of this job evaluation. Since the committee assigned it 372 points, an equitable biweekly salary for this position is $205. Likewise, inspection of Figure 14–2 reveals that the bi-weekly salary for another newly created position, filing manager, ought to be $158.

Since it is generally the intent of a job evaluation to determine salary *ranges* rather than a specific wage for the various jobs, the wage curve is usually transformed to a wage band. The band of wages (shown by dotted curves in Figure 14–2) permit for periodic rate increases on the basis of seniority and/or merit without necessi-tating promotion to the next higher level. The structure of wage bands, the desirability of overlapping wages between adjacent posi-tions or labor grades, and the extent of such overlapping if it is permitted are matters that must be decided in the light of past company practices, labor traditions, and union sentiment.

RESEARCH ON JOB EVALUATION

We have described four fundamental plans for job evaluation in the preceding sections. Other plans in current use involve, for the most part, variations in or combinations of these fundamental schemes. Thus, research on job evaluation has involved comparative studies of these schemes in the attempt to identify the "best" plan, and the "ideal" number and type of factors underlying judgments of jobs' overall worth.

No Best Plan

Research comparing the relative efficiency of the several plans for job evaluation has indicated that there is no "best" or "ideal" plan. One such study, for example, compared the results obtained from the plans in use by six different companies: two companies were using factor comparison systems; two were using a point plan based upon 15 factors; one was using a 13-factor point plan; and one was using a combination of the ranking and classification plans. The intercorrelations between the results obtained from these six systems were exceedingly high, ranging between 0.89 to 0.93.[20] It is apparent that as long as the raters are well trained, it makes relatively little difference which system of job evaluation is used. Thus, the actual selection of a particular plan ought to be based on such practical considerations as cost and its adapatibility to company needs rather than upon a desire to use the "best" procedure.

Factors Underlying "Overall Worth"

The issue of the number and type of factors included in the job evaluation scheme has been the subject of considerable study, particularly by Lawshe and his associates. The single factor making the most important contribution to the results of a job evaluation is skill demands. This factor was found to account for between 77.5 percent and 99 percent of the variance in total point ratings for hourly paid jobs,[21] and 95.6 percent of the total variance for salaried jobs.[22] It is apparent from results like these that the number of factors necessary for a satisfactory job evaluation often need not be very large. If skill demands accounts for more than 90 percent of the variance of total point allocations, there is not much additional information that can be obtained from using a large number of other factors.

The number of factors required for a job evaluation increases as a

---

[20] D. J. Chesler, "Reliability and Comparability of Different Job Evaluation Systems," *Journal of Applied Psychology*, Vol. 32 (1948), pp. 465–75.

[21] C. H. Lawshe, Jr., and G. A. Satler, "Studies in Job Evaluation No. 1: Factor Analyses of Point Ratings for Hourly Paid Jobs in Three Industrial Plants," *Journal of Applied Psychology*, Vol. 28 (1944), pp. 189–98.

[22] C. H. Lawshe, Jr., and A. A. Maleski, "Studies in Job Evaluation No. 3: An Analysis of Point Ratings for Salary Paid Jobs in an Industrial Plant," *Journal of Applied Psychology*, Vol. 30 (1946), pp. 117–28.

function of the heterogeneity of the jobs under consideration. However, some abbreviation is possible even here as shown by an investigation wherein a five-factor scale of the factor comparison type was abbreviated to three factors. The results obtained with the abbreviated and the longer scale correlated 0.99.[23] Another study compared the results obtained with an abbreviated points scale and the longer original version of this scale. The scale under investigation was the 11-factor NEMA points scale for hourly paid jobs. The results obtained with the full scale were compared with the results from an abbreviated version of the scale consisting of just three factors: experience, hazards, and initiative. It was found that the abbreviated scale yielded results that would have maintained the same labor grade for 62 percent of the jobs, with virtually all of the remaining jobs being displaced by only one labor grade.[24] Another investigation, this time of the NEMA points scale for salaried employees, found that 3 of the original 11 factors were sufficient to account for 96 percent of the total variance in point allocations. These three factors were experience, complexity of duties, and character of supervision.[25]

The results of such investigations of job evaluation procedures exhibit a high degree of consistency. The frequent practice with the points method, of using 10 or more factors, appears to be relatively inefficient. Such a large number of factors does not contribute either to the overall validity or reliability of the method.[26] Three or four carefully chosen factors would appear to be satisfactory for either a points or a factor comparison evaluation in many circumstances.

SUMMARY

Much of the recent research concerning the relationship between pay and employee attitudes and performance has been conducted in the framework of equity theory. As applied to wages, this theory

---

[23] C. H. Lawshe, Jr., and R. F. Wilson, "Studies in Job Evaluation No. 5: An Analysis of the Factor Comparison System as It Functions in a Paper Mill," *Journal of Applied Psychology*, Vol. 30 (1946), pp. 426–34.

[24] C. H. Lawshe, Jr., "Studies in Job Evaluation No. 2: The Adequacy of Abbreviated Point Ratings for Hourly Paid Jobs in Three Industrial Plants," *Journal of Applied Psychology*, Vol. 29 (1945), pp. 177–84.

[25] Lawshe and Maleski, *op. cit.*

[26] C. H. Lawshe, Jr., and R. F. Wilson, "Studies in Job Evaluation, No. 6: The Reliability of Two Point Rating Systems," *Journal of Applied Psychology*, Vol. 31 (1947), pp. 355–65.

hypothesizes that satisfaction is associated with the perception that the pay received is equitable or fair. Deviations either above or below this equitable point result in dissonant perceptions, and consequent changes in attitude or performance.

The employee's perception of equity rests upon his assessment that the relationship between his job inputs and outcomes is balanced. More research is needed to determine how much inbalance can be tolerated without generating a perception of inequity, and to clarify the nature of specific inequity reduction methods chosen by an individual.

Job evaluation procedures are designed to assist management in establishing equitable rates of pay. The utility of such procedures is limited to rather large companies embodying diverse jobs.

Job evaluation should not be regarded as a panacea for correcting wage inequities. Both management and the union may raise pertinent and valid objections to the procedure and the rationale underlying it. Thus, if a job evaluation is to succeed at all, it must be preceded by a comprehensive program of labor and management preparation. This program must clarify the objectives of the evaluation, and the possible effects of the plan upon individual employees.

Four specific procedures for job evaluation were described in this chapter: the ranking, classification, factor comparison, and points methods. All of these methods order the jobs under consideration along a continuum of overall worth. The position of each job on this continuum is subsequently converted to a monetary value.

Job evaluation is, of necessity, a highly subjective procedure. It is imperative, therefore, that the committee members who actually perform the evaluation be carefully selected and adequately trained.

V.

Organizational Psychology

The preceding chapters have largely concerned the behavior of individuals rather than groups and employees rather than managers. Although some aspects of interpersonal and supervisory behavior were discussed in passing, these matters were not heretofore central to our basic concern for the personal and job-related conditions affecting employee performance and job satisfaction.

The focus changes in Part V from the individual to the organization. The company's structure, goals, and the processes by which it seeks to implement these goals clearly influence the behavior of its members. Each company has a history and a "flavor" which encourages certain kinds of employee action and discourages others. Men grouped as an organization constitute a social system, the nature of which both affects and is affected by the actions of its members.

Certain of the characteristics of industrial organizations as social systems have been singled out for discussion in this part. Chapter 15 concerns the nature of organizational structures, including such things as hierarchical arrangements, size, and communication patterns, and the influence of such structural characteristics upon various aspects of industrial behavior. *Leadership* is discussed as one of the keystones of organizational effectiveness in Chapter 16; this discussion is extended in Chapter 17 to applications of leadership research to the specific problems of selecting and training industrial managers. Two of the outcomes of the continual and dynamic interaction between the organization and its members, morale and industrial relations, are discussed in Chapter 18.

All of the topics considered in Part V involve applications of social psychology to industrial behavior. The importance of this interface between social and industrial psychology was recognized over 40 years ago in consequence of the Hawthorne studies. You will recall from Chapter 10 that these studies called particular attention to the interaction of the social milieu with other features of the work environment as joint determinants of employee performance.

Although evidence about the importance of social factors in industrial behavior has been slowly accumulating since the Hawthorne studies, the decade of the sixties was marked by a dramatic increase in organizational research and by the formal designation of an area of research and theory as "organizational psychology."[1] Organizational psychology has recently been defined as the multidisciplinary and interdisciplinary study of the psychological and social aspects of large-scale organizations;[2] that is, of the milieu in which people work or otherwise function. Activity in this field has so blossomed that for some writers the traditional concerns of industrial psychology are subsumed under this new body of research and theory.[3]

We take a somewhat more moderate position in this book: the organization's structure and goals are regarded as both influencing and influenced by the behavior and needs of its members. Hence, organizational psychology provides insights into industrial behavior complementing the insights from engineering psychology, experimental psychology, the psychology of individual differences, and so on.

---

[1] H. J. Leavitt and B. M. Bass, "Organizational Psychology," *Annual Review of Psychology*, Vol. 15 (1964), pp. 371–98.

[2] R. P. Quinn and R. L. Kahn, "Organizational Psychology," *Annual Review of Psychology*, Vol. 18 (1967), pp. 437–66.

[3] H. J. Leavitt, *Toward Organizational Psychology*, Walter V. Bingham Memorial Lecture, Carnegie Institute of Technology, March 23, 1961.

15. Organizational Theories and Structures

For convenience, our discussion in this and subsequent chapters is restricted to industrial rather than political, social, or other types of organizations. However, the fundamental properties of all organizations are essentially similar irrespective of their goals. Any organization is a social system wherein people are grouped in a structure calculated to facilitate attainment of the organization's goal or goals.

It will aid our consideration of organizational theories and structures to begin by relating the concerns of organizational and personnel psychology.

ORGANIZATIONAL AND PERSONNEL PSYCHOLOGY

It is now generally recognized that few issues in industrial psychology can be comprehensively examined without consideration of the organizational milieu.[1] The interface between personnel and organizational psychology has recently been described with particular reference to issues in personnel selection and placement, training, performance evaluation, and compensation.[2]

---

[1] L. W. Porter, "Personnel Psychology," *Annual Review of Psychology*, Vol. 17 (1966), pp. 395-422.

[2] This section was suggested by B. M. Bass, "Interface between Personnel and Organizational Psychology," *Journal of Applied Psychology*, Vol. 52 (1968), pp. 81-88.

Personal Selection and Placement

There is a substantial technology of selection and placement as discussed in Part II. However, the concerns of personnel psychology are not as immune to organizational influences as the technology might imply.

Consider, for example, the preemployment interview. We stated in Chapter 5 that interviews are widely used for selection in spite of the fact that they often have low, and sometimes negative, validity. Modification of the selection program, entailing either eliminating the preemployment interview or diminishing the weight assigned to it, is an organizational problem. The greatest resistance to this modification often comes from high status organizational members who erroneously pride themselves on their "intuitive insight."

Furthermore, as discussed in Chapters 4, 5, and 6, the technology of personnel selection seems to have reached a plateau as far as validity is concerned. Predictor-criterion correlations above the range of $0.40 - 0.50$ are relatively rare. There is a growing feeling, and some supportive evidence, that further improvements in validity are more likely to follow from an increased focus upon the social and organizational history of the applicant than from yet additional refinements in the traditional technology of personnel selection.

To illustrate, two application blank items when combined yielded a validity of 0.70 against merit ratings for salesmen.[3] These items were unique in that they concerned the relationship between the applicant and the organization by asking whether (*a*) the company could contact the applicant's present boss and (*b*) how soon the applicant could start work. Applicants who subsequently proved to be meritorious employees replied to the first question with an unqualified "yes," and to the second by indicating that they would have to give their present employer at least two weeks' notice. The investigator felt that these items were assessing the sense of responsibility and of security of these applicants—two aspects of the relationship between the man and his organization not usually explored in validating application blanks.

Likewise, this relationship is typically, and perhaps erroneously,

---

[3] *Ibid.*, p. 82.

ignored in preemployment testing. It has been suggested that the generally low validity of personality inventories for predicting job performance is attributable to the fact that they measure characteristics like "neuroticism" instead of characteristics more closely allied to task performance and organizational participation.

Finally, the social milieu itself, including public and organizational policy, may influence the way in which preemployment testing programs are constituted and administered. This is particularly evident, for example, in establishing the selection ratio and setting cutoff scores on tests. It is often possible to eliminate applicants who make "average" test scores by recruiting more applicants and setting the cutoff score higher (exploiting a low selection ratio). However, this procedure may have the secondary effect of eliminating applicants on some such basis as race or sex. When this happens, even though it may be ancillary to the company's concern for making more efficient use of its preemployment tests, it raises important questions about the social impact of company practices.

Training

The point was made in Chapter 8 that no training program can successfully influence job performance if it ignores the organizational setting in which the trainees will finally work. Unless all employees, including top management, are committed to keeping abreast of new developments and procedures, the training program becomes identified as one appropriate for new employees only.

The conflict that may develop under these circumstances is self-evident. Trainees learn new skills and procedures while in the program. However, once on the job, they are instructed by their supervisors to "forget about all that stuff" and learn "how things really are done here." Such discontinuity between training and actual job procedures disrupts morale and performance, and represents a sheer waste of the cost of training.

The introduction of a training program likewise cannot be divorced from the organizational milieu. The continuation of a program, irrespective of its merit, rests in large measure upon trainee acceptance. This has been forcibly demonstrated, for example, in cases where student resistance to undergraduate instruction by television has compelled some universities to abandon TV teaching.

Performance Evaluation

Any evaluation of a particular employee's job performance entails two potential sources of subjectivity.

The first of these may be inherent in the nature of the evaluation procedure itself. When objective criteria are not available, for example, it may be necessary to assess performance by means of ratings.

A second potential source of subjectivity is related to organizational goals and is independent of the evaluation procedure itself. In order to decide whether an employee's performance is satisfactory or unsatisfactory, the company must first define what it means by satisfactory performance. To illustrate, some employees are highly productive but disrupt the activities of others; other employees may produce somewhat less but pose no special social problem within the work unit. In order to judge one as more satisfactory than another, the company must have a clearly expressed preference for high production or smoothly interacting work units. This preference in turn will reflect the relative economic position of the company and its posture toward interpersonal relations.

A further implication of the relationship between organizational goals and performance evaluation is that different kinds of performance may be equally satisfactory, or that the same type of performance, judged satisfactory for one employee, may be judged unsatisfactory for another employee at the same job level. Consider, for example, a company wherein the jobs personnel manager and sales manager are roughly comparable with respect to level. Whereas a criterion of output (total monthly sales) may be an especially important performance criterion for the sales manager, a similar measure (total number of applicants assessed) may be irrelevant for the personnel manager. Different kinds of positions makes different kinds of contributions to the organization; and a meaningful assessment of an individual's performance is possible only when his contribution is interpreted in the light of the intended purpose of his job.

Compensation

No compensation plan is entirely free from organizational decisions. A plan whereby all employees on a given job and at a given level of seniority earn the same income requires a prior decision to ignore differences in merit. Conversely, a plan whereby superior merit is recognized by higher compensation requires a prior decision to reward differentially for performance in spite of seniority. Many of the kinds of decisions entailed in formulating compensation plans were discussed in Chapter 14.

The nature of the decisions made by a particular company is affected by the cultural backgrounds of the decision makers, their attitudes toward different kinds of jobs, and toward men who receive competing job offers. Thus, in an exercise for training managers wherein they each were to award salary increases to 10 engineers differing in merit and other attributes, the following differences were noted: North Europeans believed that an average increase of 4–6 percent was equitable, whereas South Europeans advocated average increases as high as 36 percent; American, British, and Irish managers did not generally believe that competing job offers should be a basis for increasing a man's salary, whereas Flemings, Norwegians, Italians, Indians, and Latin Americans tended to award larger increases to men who had counteroffers. Even among managers from the same company, some preferred to assign different wages to the 10 engineers while others insisted that all ought to receive identical salary increases irrespective of merit or seniority.[4]

BUREAUCRACY: A TRADITIONAL ORGANIZATIONAL CLIMATE

The two characteristics of bureaucracies most frequently noted are (*a*) a hierarchy of authority with (*b*) a clear division of labor among organizational members.[5] These characteristics are expressed through the well-known "organizational chart" wherein every job has its neatly delineated place. Typically, such a chart shows a pyramid-type structure with a single position (for example, "president") at the top and increasing numbers of positions toward the base. The positions are linked together vertically forming a "chain of command" (see Figure 15–1).

---

[4] B. M. Bass, "Combining Management Training and Research," *Training Directors Journal*, Vol. 21 (1967), pp. 2–7.

[5] R. Hall, "The Concept of Bureaucracy: An Empirical Assessment," *American Journal of Sociology*, Vol. 69 (1963), pp. 32–40.

In its pure form, this type of bureaucratic organization permits only certain kinds of activities:

1. Orders are transmitted *down* the chain; reports are transmitted *up* the chain.

2. The greater the importance of the decision, the closer to the apex is the decision-making site.

FIGURE 15–1

The Organizational Pyramid

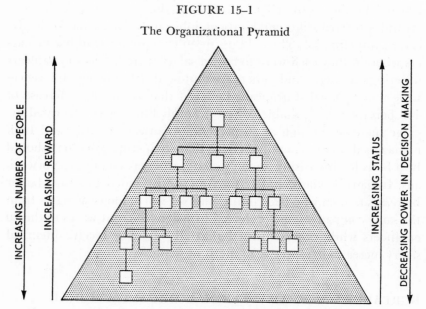

Source: L. R. Sayles and G. Strauss, *Human Behavior in Organizations* (Englewood Cliffs, N.J.: Prentice-Hall, Inc., 1966), p. 349.

3. Each subordinate is directly responsible to only one boss.

4. Each superior supervises only a limited number of subordinates.

5. A person at any level (except the top and bottom) has contact only with his boss above him and his subordinates below him.[6]

The bureaucratic organization is comprised of roles rather than personalities. Its arrangement is logical, impersonal, and entirely dependent upon technical competence. Although no organization adheres rigidly to this kind of structure, some, like the military, come mighty close!

The internal environment of bureaucratic organizations is well

_____

[6] L. R. Sayles and G. Strauss, *Human Behavior in Organizations* (Englewood Cliffs, N.J.: Prentice-Hall, Inc., 1966) .

defined. Each organizational role is accorded certain rights, privileges, and status; likewise, the level of technical competence associated with that role is clearly prescribed. The bureaucratic organization does not recognize or accommodate to the members' needs. On the contrary, whatever accommodation takes place is thoroughly one-sided; the participants tailor themselves to the role they fill.

This organizational structure assumes a stable external environment and holds the simple goal of outselling competitors. Given these conditions, the necessary decisions emanate from the top of the company power structure and tend to reflect a primary concern for maximizing company profits.

NEWER ORGANIZATIONAL THEORIES

As effective as bureaucratic structures were in the past, they seem for the most part now to be outmoded. The world external to the organization increasingly is characterized by change rather than stability, and organizational goals have become much more complex than they once were. Among the factors responsible for the changing nature of society, demanding consequent modifications of organizational structures, are the growth of science and technology, and of research and development activities.[7] It thus has become imperative to develop a harmonious integration between organizational structure and technology.[8]

One meaningful criterion of an efficient organizational structure is its effectiveness for resolving the tension between individual and organizational goals.[9] Proceeding from this view, several writers have proposed organizational theories, each making certain assumptions about the sources of conflict between individual and organizational goals. On the basis of these assumptions, the theories specify the kinds of organizational structures and management behavior that will reduce this tension. For convenience we have grouped these theories into three categories descriptive of the nature of their underlying assumptions: equity, group affiliation, and nature of man.

---

[7] D. Bell, "The Post-Industrial Society," in E. Ginsberg (ed.), *Technology and Social Change* (New York: Columbia University Press, 1964), p. 44.

[8] F. J. Jasinski, "Adapting Organization to New Technology," *Harvard Business Review*, Vol. 37 (1959), pp. 79–86.

[9] W. G. Bennis, "Organizational Developments and the Fate of Bureaucracy," *Industrial Management Review*, Vol. 7 (1966), pp. 41–55.

Equity Theories

These theories assume that the fundamental source of tension between individual and organizational goals is the perceived discrepancy between the value of the outcomes provided by the organization to its members and the inputs required of the employee. Thus, they posit an equilibrium model wherein the organization induces employee participation by providing outcomes with utility value equaling or exceeding his inputs.

The general frame of reference for equity theories was provided in Chapter 14. You will recall from that discussion that the individual strives for balance between his job inputs and the outcomes he derives from work. In a sense he exchanges certain of his activities useful to the organization for attaining *its* goals (his inputs) in return for certain rewards from the organization (the outcomes) which contribute to *his own* goal attainment.

When the employee perceives the outcomes as exceeding the inputs, he is most likely to experience job satisfaction and to behave in the direction of creating equity by complying with organizational demands. Conversely, when he perceives that input exceeds outcomes—in other words, when he feels that he is sacrificing attainment of his own goals in the process of working for organizational goals—equity theory predicts diminished input (a form of psychological withdrawal) or actual physical withdrawal by quitting the organization.

The employee's inputs to organizational goal attainment include his time, effort, skills, knowledge, commitment, educational investment, and so on. What does the organization provide him in exchange for these inputs? Clearly, financial compensation is one aspect of the exchange. In addition, the organization provides such psychological outcomes as an opportunity for personal growth and mastery, a social structure with which to identify, a psychological anchor in times of rapid social change, and so on.[10]

Group Affiliation Theories

These theories emphasize a particular kind of employee need: that for affiliating with other people and participating in a social

---

[10] H. Levinson, "Reciprocation: The Relationship Between Man and Organization" (invited address, Division of Industrial and Business Psychology, American Psychological Association, September 3, 1963).

group. When the organization fails to satisfy this need for group affiliation, usually by emphasizing task accomplishment and minimizing the importance of human interaction, it fosters tension between employee and organizational goal attainment. Following this reasoning, the organization can satisfy the need for group affiliation, hence motivating performance directed toward organizational goals, by developing a spirit of cooperation among the employees.

When originally proposed,[11] this view represented a radical departure from the traditional notion of organizations as economic and technical systems without regard for their social nature. However, its implementation in the original formulation did not require a drastic revision of organizational structure. A sense of group affiliation through employee cooperation was to be accomplished by reorienting managerial activities toward a greater sensitivity to, and concern for, human relations.

More recently a similar awareness of the motivational value of work group affiliation has generated suggestions for changes in organizational structures as well as in management roles.[12] In this view, an attitude of cooperation between organizational members requires that each participant have a sense that he is contributing effectively and importantly to goal attainment by the organization. To encourage each employee to experience this sense of effective participation requires that every level of activity within the organization be articulated both with the next lower and next higher level. Such articulation is described as the "linking pin concept." Each supervisor holds membership in two groups: one consisting of his subordinates and the other consisting of other supervisors at his level plus *their* supervisor.

This dual and overlapping group membership provides the organization with a structure quite different from that of a bureaucracy. In the latter, communication moves in only one direction (down the line), is subject to distortions and misinterpretations by intermediate levels of management and supervision, and requires considerable time to filter down to the bottom rungs of the hierarchy. In contrast, a linking-pin structure facilitates two-way communication and significantly reduces the number of intermediate steps in transmitting communications from top management. Since

---

[11] E. Mayo, *The Social Problems of an Industrial Civilization* (Cambridge, Mass.: Harvard University Press, 1945).

[12] R. Likert, *New Patterns of Management* (New York: McGraw-Hill Book Co., Inc., 1961).

communication is rapid and since every employee, regardless of level, can be heard and exert influence, each employee *is* important to the group.

Nature-of-Man Theories

Whereas group affiliation theories emphasize man's need to identify with and be part of a social group, the theories we have grouped together under the "nature-of-man" heading include the need for

TABLE 15–1

A Traditional versus an Integrated View of Man

	Theory X (Traditional)	*Theory Y (Integrated)*
Attitude toward work.	Man inherently dislikes work and will avoid it when possible.	Expenditure of effort for work is as natural to men as play or rest.
Performance incentives.	Coersion, direction, and threat of punishment are required to induce performance.	Man will exercise self-direction if he is committed to the goal.
Supervision.	Man prefers direction and avoids responsibility; he has little ambition.	Man seeks responsibility and the opportunity for independent and creative action.

Source: D. McGregor, *The Human Side of Enterprise* (New York: McGraw-Hill Book Co., Inc., 1960)

group affiliation as but one of several needs that the organization must satisfy.

Any organizational structure makes certain assumptions about the nature of man. Two contrasting sets of assumptions have been hypothesized in distinguishing between the traditional view of behavior assumed by bureaucratic structures (and designated "Theory X") and a more integrated view of behavior (designated "Theory Y").[13] Some of the essential differences between these two contrasting views of man are summarized in Table 15–1.

Individual differences aside, the importance of this type of comparison is that it calls attention to a potential source of conflict between the organization and its employees and suggests a solution.

---

[13] D. McGregor, *The Human Side of Enterprise* (New York: McGraw-Hill Book Co., Inc., 1960) .

The conflict arises when the organization either neglects employee needs altogether or makes fallacious assumptions about them. The solution is to increase organizational effectiveness by correctly perceiving employee needs and arranging the structure so these needs can be satisfied within the organization itself.

The healthy, mature personality is characterized by such traits as independence, receptivity to challenge which provides opportunities for developing competence, perspective, aspirations for leadership and recognition, and a sense of personal integrity and identity. When, as often occurs in bureaucratic organizations, such employees are asked to behave in ways that are dependent, subordinate, and submissive, friction is inevitable.[14] The behavior valued by bureaucratic organization is in essential conflict with the behavior the individual has learned to value as he matures. The consequent repression and frustration of the individual may result in absenteeism, defensiveness, apathy, and so on.

In the typical bureaucratic organization such unfavorable employee responses are met by establishing additional controls and tightening up the structure. For example, when a high rate of defective output is a problem, the bureaucratic interpretation is likely to be that this behavior confirms that employees are lazy and have been too loosely supervised. The "solution" will entail closer supervision, greater financial and other penalties for rejected work, and, perhaps, further task fragmentation so each man can do his job "better." Hence a repetitive and futile cycle of organizational constraint and employee counteraction is established because management erroneously subscribes to a "Theory X" nature-of-man concept.

Instead, management must learn to encourage and reward independence rather than dependence, expanded competence rather than repetitive pedestrian activity, and individuality rather than unthinking conformity. Proceeding from a "Theory Y" view of the nature of man, solutions to the above-mentioned output reject problem might be sought in job enlargement, improved training, changed patterns of supervision, and in other broad ranging organizational efforts to develop a working climate wherein employees perceive greater congruence between their own goals and those of the organization.

---

[14] C. Argyris, *Integrating the Individual and the Organization* (New York: John Wiley & Sons, Inc., 1964).

THE DYNAMIC NATURE OF ORGANIZATIONS: A CONTEMPORARY VIEW

Two threads are common to the foregoing discussion of organizational theory:

First, much of the difficulty generated within traditionally structured organizations is attributed to their mechanistic nature. Such organizations tend to emphasize skills, authority-obedience relationships, a strict division of labor, centralized decision making, and suppression of individuality. Members are expected to play their roles as if they were cogs in some kind of machine.

Second, there is an increasing emphasis in the recent thinking about organizations on what has been termed "organic" organizational structures, that is, structures which are dynamic and adaptive rather than mechanical.[15] Organic organizations are characterized by less clearly prescribed member roles and greater member participation in control, responsibility, and decision making.

In clarifying contemporary thinking about organizations, it is useful to distinguish between two dimensions of organizational activity: the organization's internal environment and the relationship between the organization and the external environment.[16]

The Internal Environment

Every individual in the organization has his own needs and goals. Some of these may be congruent with those of the organization; some may be dissonant; and some may be relatively inconsequential as far as the organization is concerned.

Clearly, these idiosyncratic needs and goals cannot be permitted full sway if the organization is to realize *its* goals. Imagine the chaos in a military squad, for example, if each soldier were free to fight (or not to fight) his own version of the battle in his own way. The effectiveness of the squad depends upon concerted action; all squad members must cooperate in fulfilling the organizational mission. Likewise, political organizations must finally endorse, through convention, a single presidential nominee in spite of the initially con-

---

[15] H. A. Shepard, "Changing Interpersonal and Intergroup Relationships in Organizations," in J. March (ed.), *Handbook of Organizations* (Chicago: Rand McNally Co., 1965).

[16] Bennis, *op. cit.*

flicting views of the participating delegates. And an industrial organization must ultimately market specified products or services generated by the coordinate efforts of its employees.

Reciprocity. Thus, a characteristic of any organization's internal environment is tension between the goals of the participants and those of the organization. The essential requirement for the organization to function effectively is cooperation by the participants in spite of their diverse needs. Such cooperation depends upon two conditions:

First, the organization members may actually realize certain of their own goals through participation in the organization's goal-directed activities. This occurs, for example, when a player so identifies with his team that he feels a personal stake in its victory. *He* wins when the organization wins. Such congruence between participant and organization goals is characteristic of organizations with high morale.

Second, the participant may perceive his activities on behalf of the organization's goal attainment as providing a vehicle for the secondary attainment of his own personal goals. Thus, the employee may work on behalf of the organization to earn the money with which to satisfy such purely extra-organizational needs as those for a new car and a better home, or for satisfying such personal-social needs as those for status and power.

In either case, the internal environment of the organization exercises a certain degree of constraint upon the participant members. They give up a measure of individual freedom on behalf of the organization. Similarly, the organization gives up a measure of "efficiency" in its goal-directed efforts in order to accommodate to the humanness of its members. This two-sided accommodation is what is meant by *reciprocity.*

Situational Constraints. Granting the importance of the relatively recent emphasis upon individuality and the integration of employee and organizational goals, there are yet circumstances wherein the traditional authoritarian organizational pattern may prove superior to a more participative pattern. The unique combination of employees and tasks defines a special situation for each organization or organizational subunit.[17] Certain tasks, like line assembly, do not lend themselves to task-related decision making. Likewise, employees differ in the strength of their need and capacity

---

[17] H. J. Leavitt, "Unhuman Organization," *Harvard Business Review,* Vol. 40 (1962), pp. 90–98.

for independent action. Therefore, no organizational pattern can be prescribed as "best" under all circumstances.

The External Environment

Organizations function in a dynamic world wherein change is the norm. The company manager must increasingly relate in complex ways to many features of the world outside his company organization including government, distributors, consumers, shareholders, competitors, raw material and power suppliers, sources of employees (for example, colleges) , and trade unions.

Clearly, social institutions are becoming increasingly interdependent; the economic and noneconomic aspects of society have become tightly woven into a single fabric. Technological change cannot be evaluated solely with reference to the company making the change, or on the basis solely of economics. Such change may have social ramifications for the community, curricular ramifications for the schools from which employees ultimately are drawn, and competitive ramifications for other companies in the same industry. Furthermore it may alter demands upon suppliers and distributors, necessitate changed patterns of consumer purchasing, and influence negotiations with the unions. Because activities within the company are no longer restricted in effect pretty much to that organization alone, companies are now increasingly involved in legislation and public regulation.[18]

ORGANIZATIONAL STRUCTURE

The primary criteria of organizational effectiveness are in one form or another measures of job performance and job satisfaction. Such measures are used as dependent variables in assessing the influence of such aspects of organizational structure as size and hierarchical arrangements.

Size

Changes in the size of an organization are accompanied by concomitant changes in patterns of communication and interpersonal

---

[18] F. E. Emory and E. L. Trist, "The Causal Texture of Organizational Environments," (paper read at the International Congress of Psychology, Washington, D.C., September, 1963) .

relationships. Typically, as the organization grows larger, its members become increasingly isolated from one another. Therefore, it seems reasonable to anticipate a negative relationship between organizational size beyond some critical point and effectiveness unless the organization takes steps to counteract the undesirable concomitants of increased size.

Experimental Findings. The expectation stated above has been the subject of considerable research relating size to attitudinal and performance criteria. As groups become larger they tend toward increased bureaucratization. Large groups tend to be less cohesive, more highly organized, and to encourage a greater division of labor.[19] Furthermore, members of larger groups are less likely to ask for information and help, reveal their tensions, give or seek opinions, and express their feelings.[20] Thus, it is not surprising that members of larger groups report less job satisfaction than those of small groups.[21]

In contrast with these generalizations, no consistent pattern of adverse relationships between organizational size and either member or group performance has been discovered. Some studies report greater productivity in smaller groups, others report greater productivity in larger groups, and yet others report a curvilinear relationship; that is, greater productivity in both large and small groups than in groups of intermediate size.[22]

Size Is a Complex Variable. Such inconsistent findings concerning productivity, point to the complexity of size as a variable. In the first place, largeness or smallness of a group is relative rather than absolute. Insertion into a 20-man unit may mean something quite different to an employee who formerly was a member of a 3-man work team and one who was formerly assigned to a 12-man section.

Secondly, there likely are individual differences among group members in the effects of increased size. These differences are obscured in gross comparisons between large and small groups. It has been suggested, for example, that the effects of organizational size

---

[19] E. J. Thomas and C. F. Fink, "Effects of Group Size," *Psychological Bulletin*, Vol. 60 (1963), pp. 371–84.

[20] R. L. Hamblin and L. K. Miller, "Variation Interaction Profiles and Group Size," *Sociological Quarterly*, Vol. 2 (1961), pp. 105–17.

[21] L. W. Porter and E. E. Lawler, III, "Properties of Organization Structure in Relation to Job Attitudes and Job Behavior," *Psychological Bulletin*, Vol. 64 (1965), pp. 23–51.

[22] *Ibid.*

upon the individual may be mediated by his hierarchical position in the company.[23] A reorganization following an increase in company size may enhance or diminish the member's influence with consequent effects upon his reaction to the reorganization. It is likely, also, that the effects of size changes are influenced by the member's former levels of acceptance and interpersonal participation, the strength of his need for social interaction, and so on.

Third, group size is really a cluster of variables rather than a single variable. As was pointed out earlier, changes in size are often accompanied by other organizational changes including modified communication patterns and altered superior-subordinate relationships. It is likely that some findings are erroneously attributed to changes in organizational size when they ought more correctly be attributed to the intermediate effects of these more fundamental consequences of changes in size.[24]

Finally, the research on organizational size has generally failed to recognize that an employee typically is a member of at least three organizational subunits: a primary work group, a department, and a factory or office. It is not presently known whether a size change in any one of these subunits is more important than in the others, or may counteract changes in the others.[25] It is conceivable, for example, that fairly substantial increases in company size might have little effect when work group size is maintained at a constant level, but substantial effects when work group size is also increased.

Optimal Size. The issue of optimal size has been considered both for work groups and for total organizations. Since, as we have seen, size alone cannot be clearly related to performance, generalizations about optimum size are qualified by (*a*) other organizational characteristics, (*b*) task characteristics, (*c*) membership composition of the group, and (*d*) economic considerations.

The latter qualification deserves special mention. Optimal size for a work group must take into consideration the costs to the total organizational system of maintaining the group at that size.[26] Increments in employee satisfaction or output in five- over eight-man work

---

[23] G. A. Forehand and B. v.H. Gilmer, "Environmental Variations in Studies of Organizational Behavior," *Psychological Bulletin*, Vol. 62 (1964), pp. 361–82.

[24] Thomas and Fink, *op. cit.*

[25] Porter and Lawler, *op. cit.*

[26] W. H. Starbuck, "Organizational Growth and Development," in J. G. March (ed.), *Handbook of Organizations* (Chicago: Rand McNally Co., 1965), pp. 451–533.

groups, for example, may not be economically justifiable in the light of savings that might be effected by reducing the total number of work groups and increasing the size of each one.

Thus, what may prove to be an optimal work group size in one company may be far from optimal in another with a different tradition and management style. By analogy, the optimal class size at a small liberal arts college differs from that at a large midwestern university.

Extending the scholastic analogy, optimal class size depends also upon the subject matter to be taught, the objectives of the course, and the student composition of the class. In the same way, the optimum size for a work group depends upon the tasks to be accomplished by the group and the characteristics of the group members. Problem-solving groups seem to function best with five or six members;[27] and the creativity of their solutions is enhanced by grouping persons with dissimilar personality profiles.[28] For more routine kinds of work, it is more efficient to create larger work groups wherein the personalities of the members are more homogeneous.

Although we commonly recognize that organizations can be too large for optimum effectiveness, we must also point out that they can be too small. Any company needs a staff of critical size and diversity before it can efficiently produce or distribute its product or service. Once this critical point is exceeded, further increments in earnings do not require corresponding increments in expenditures for personnel, plant, and materials, *up to a point.*

In this regard, organizational growth has been compared in a very interesting way with biological growth.[29] There is a clear relationship between the size of organisms and their structure and shape. Species survival requires that shape and form accommodate to size and weight. Likewise, as organizations increase in size, their survival depends upon their ability to change organizational forms in the light of new requirements imposed by alterations in size. For example, increased size beyond some point may compel reductions in the size of constituent work units, changed patterns of supervision, and so on.

---

[27] A. Newell, J. C. Shaw, and H. A. Simon, "Elements of a Theory of Human Problem Solving," *Psychological Review,* Vol. 65 (1958), pp. 151–66.

[28] N. R. F. Maier and L. R. Hoffman, "Organization and Creative Problem Solving," *Journal of Applied Psychology,* Vol. 45 (1961), pp. 277–80.

[29] M. Haire, *Psychology in Management* (New York: McGraw-Hill Book Co., Inc., 1964), pp. 224 ff.

Hierarchical Levels

Figure 15–1 describes the type of vertical structure more or less characteristic of all organizations. As shown in this figure, rewards and status are greatest near the top of the influence hierarchy. Therefore, it is not surprising that several studies have consistently shown increased job satisfaction at each higher organizational level.[30]

As organizations become larger the height of the pyramidal structure tends to become more pronounced. This implies that increased job satisfaction may be gained for proportionately few top-level managers in "tall" organizations at the expense of diminished personal involvement and satisfaction of the majority of employees. Furthermore, the narrowing at the top of the influence hierarchy encourages a certain amount of competition for advancement which may well interfere with organizational effectiveness.[31]

Organizational complexity and hierarchical arrangements have been investigated rather extensively at Sears, Roebuck and Company.[32] The results suggest that overcomplexity of organizational structure is a major cause of poor management-employee relations. The workers in such a setting are required to perform highly fragmented and specialized tasks, thereby depriving them of a feeling of goal-directedness. The subunits within a complex organizational structure tend to be poorly integrated, and the supervisors tend, therefore, to exert control by pressures and threats rather than by exhibiting leadership based upon cooperation and team effort.

In summarizing the results of this organizational analysis, the investigator advocates flatter, less complex structures. It is argued that these tend to create a potential for improved attitudes, more effective supervision, and greater individual responsibility and initiative.

Although the foregoing argument is persuasive, subsequent evidence concerning the superiority of flat versus tall structures in terms of member attitudes and performance is not clear-cut.[33] This

[30] Porter and Lawler, *op. cit.*

[31] Leavitt (1962) , *op. cit.*

[32] J. C. Worthy, "Organizational Structure and Employee Morale," *American Sociological Review*, Vol. 15 (1950) , pp. 169–79.

[33] Porter and Lawler, *op. cit.*

further reinforces the point made earlier about the interdependence, and consequent interactive effects, of such organizational variables as hierarchical arrangements, task requirements, employee characteristics, and organizational size. With respect to the latter interaction—that between hierarchical arrangement and size—evidence from a study of managerial job satisfaction[34] can be interpreted as meaning that whereas "taller" structures are accepted as appropriate in organizations with more than 5,000 employees, "flatter" structures were regarded by these managers as more appropriate for smaller companies.

COMMUNICATION

Much of the impact of organizational (and subunit) size and hierarchical arrangements upon member performance and attitudes is mediated by the effectiveness or ineffectiveness of communication within the organization. Ineffective communication can have far-reaching consequences. Erroneous or delayed transmission of facts may serve as the groundwork for rumor. Furthermore, even without rumor, employees who are not well informed about company policies and practices or about their supervisor's evaluation of their performance can hardly develop a sense of identification with the company. Finally, poor communication can lead to an utter breakdown of activities requiring coordinated action.

Directions of Communications Flow

Most writers differentiate between downward, upward, and horizontal communication flows.[35] Downward communication from manager to subordinate is the most prevalent. Such communication typically is effected by issuing management letters to employees, distributing company newsletters, conducting mass meetings, or posting notices on the bulletin board. In upward communication, information is transmitted from subordinates to superiors. Included among the formal mechanisms for upward communication are suggestion systems, grievance procedures, reports from employee

---

[34] L. W. Porter and E. E. Lawler, III, "The Effects of 'Tall' versus 'Flat' Organizational Structures on Managerial Job Satisfactions," *Personnel Psychology*, Vol. 17 (1964), pp. 135–48.

[35] See, for example: B. M. Bass, *Organizational Psychology* (Boston: Allyn & Bacon, Inc., 1965), pp. 285–316.

committees appointed to evaluate various organizational programs, and job satisfaction or morale studies.

Two-Way Communication.   Whereas both downward and upward communication may entail utilization of unidirectional channels (either from manager to subordinate or from subordinate to manager), both the communication accuracy and employee satisfaction are enhanced by two-way communication.

In spite of these advantages, many supervisors inhibit upward communication. In part, this can be attributed to the fact that two-way communication is relatively slow; feedback from the receivers takes time, and some receivers experience difficulty in assimilating and responding to apparently simple messages. Two-way communication may also threaten the supervisor who would prefer to communicate downwards only. Upward feedback may be unflattering to supervisors who make technical errors or are ineffective communicators.

Horizontal Communication.   Although, as was pointed out earlier in this chapter, the typical organizational chart assumes only vertical communication, much of the actual and necessary communication in industry is horizontal. Horizontal communication is required whenever such parallel aspects of an organization as product planning, manufacturing, and sales must be articulated. This is particularly evident when, as in the space program, research and development activities must be coordinated with line or manufacturing services supporting the research and development.[36] Increasingly, all of the newer organizational structures described earlier tend to encourage a greater amount of horizontal communication flow.

Communication Networks

The various forms of communication—downward, upward, and horizontal; one way and two way—have been extensively studied in the laboratory as well as in natural settings. The laboratory studies establish and analyze the effectiveness of communication networks; that is, artificially established pathways for transmitting information among members of the group.[37] Four such networks are shown in

---

[36] B. M. Bass, "Industrial Organization for the Space Age," *Pittsburgh Business Review,* Vol. 34 (1964) pp. 5–13.

[37] A. Bavelas, "Communication Patterns in Task-Oriented Groups," *Journal of Accoustical Society of America,* Vol. 22 (1950), pp. 725–30.

Figure 15–2. To facilitate comparison, each of these illustrative networks includes the same number of participants, and each is shown with a two-way communication flow.

The star group: All information is sent to a central figure (*C*) who in turn relays it to the persons on the periphery of the group (*P*). This is a miniature representation of a simple autocratic communication structure.

The chain: The communication pattern is complicated by placing middlemen (*M*) between the star and the men on the periphery. This is a miniature bureaucratic structure.

FIGURE 15–2

Four Communication Networks

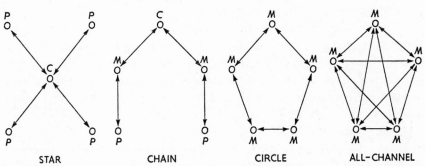

The circle: This pattern permits communication between adjacent group members but lacks centralized organization. It is an artificial pattern useful for research, but not often found in industry.

The all-channel group: In this pattern all members are free to communicate with all other members. This is typical of the communication network among members of a governing board or other group composed of members with equal status and influence.

The relative efficiency of these and other communication networks is typically investigated in a particular kind of laboratory setting. The subjects in each group are seated around a table but are separated from one another by partitions. They can communicate only by passing notes through slots in the partitions and the experimenter establishes the network by opening and closing the slots. The group must solve problems utilizing only the channels of communication open to it.

Dimensions of Networks. The four networks shown in Figure 15-2 differ from each other in three important respects: the number of communication channels provided each member, the amount of information available to each member, and the total number of channels ("links") available for the communication.

With respect to the *number of channels open to each member,* you will note that the circle provides every member two channels of communication; that is, he can communicate directly with only two other members of his group. The all-channel network provides every member with four channels of communication. In the chain, members at the periphery (*P*) have only one channel, whereas each middleman (*M*) has two channels (one to *C* and one to *P*). And in the star, the peripheral members each have one channel while the central figure has four channels.

The *amount of information* available to the participants varies from very partial information possessed by peripheral members of a star or chain, to somewhat more complete information by middlemen in a chain or circle, to complete information by the central figure in either a star or chain and by all members of an all-channel network.

The greater the number of *links* available for transmitting information, the greater is the possibility of overburdening a network with messages. The various five-man networks shown in Figure 15-2 entail 4 links each for the star and chain, 5 links for the circle, and 10 links for the all-channel network.

Relative Effectiveness of Networks. By combining two of the dimensions discussed above—number of channels open to each participant and amount of information available to participants—it is possible to distinguish between networks that are highly centralized and those that are decentralized. Highly centralized networks are those, like the star and chain, wherein one participant (*C*) has more channels of communication and more information than the other participants. Networks low in centralization are those, like the circle and all-channel, wherein all members have an equal number of channels and have access to the same amount of information.

In summarizing the results of several studies of communication networks, the following generalizations emerge:[38]

------

[38] T. W. Costello and S. S. Zalkind, *Psychology in Administration* (Englewood Cliffs, N.J.: Prentice-Hall, Inc., 1963), p. 457.

Highly centralized communication networks facilitate:
1. Efficient performance of routine problem solving of the type involving assembly of information;
2. Development of a strong leadership position for the central figure;
3. Development of a quickly stabilized set of interactions among group members.

Decentralized communication networks facilitate:
1. Development of higher levels of member satisfaction;
2. Handling ambiguous and unpredictable situations;
3. Innovative and creative solutions to problems.

Thus, research does not identify one type of network as uniformly superior to another. Highly centralized and decentralized networks each have unique advantages, depending upon the nature of the task. However, whereas the latter tend to be characterized by high member satisfaction, the former tend to suffer low morale.[39]

The reason for the relative efficiency of highly centralized networks for collating information and using it to solve problems is that the structure of these nets facilitates assemblage of all relevant information with a minimum of communication "overload" (that is, too much and sometimes irrelevant communication) . In contrast, decentralized nets (circle, all-channel) are less efficient in this regard because their arrangement prevents them from developing a hierarchy wherein a central figure collates information,[40] and because they are characterized by more linkages encouraging communication overload.[41]

Evidence for this view comes from a study wherein decentralized groups were deliberately given an opportunity to restructure themselves in order most efficiently to solve assigned problems. They typically elected either a star or chain network.[42] Both of these networks elected by originally decentralized groups are characterized by imposition of a communication hierarchy and a reduction in the number of communication linkages.

---

[39] H. J. Leavitt, "Some Effects of Certain Communication Patterns upon Performance," *Journal of Abnormal and Social Psychology,* Vol. 46 (1951) , pp. 38–50.

[40] H. Guetzkow and H. A. Simon, "The Impact of Certain Communication Nets in Task-Oriented Groups," *Management Science,* Vol. 1 (1955) , pp. 233–50.

[41] R. Dubin, "Stability of Human Organizations," in M. Haire (ed.) , *Modern Organizational Theory* (New York: John Wiley & Sons, Inc., 1959) .

[42] H. Guetzkow and W. R. Dill, "Factors in the Organizational Development of Task-Oriented Groups," *Sociometry,* Vol. 20 (1957) , pp. 175–204.

In summary, generalizations about the superiority of particular kinds of communication networks, judged either by the criterion of task performance or member satisfaction, must be tempered by considering the constituency of the group and the purpose for which it is formed. A highly centralized network is most efficient when the task is routine and collation of individual activities is necessary from the very beginning. However, there are circumstances wherein a freer network permitting more active participation by the group members is highly desirable. It would probably be unwise to impose a rigidly patterned communication network when flexibility is required of the group by virtue of the complexity of the problem confronting it and/or the diversity of knowledges and backgrounds possessed by its members.

Highly centralized and decentralized communication networks can coexist within the same organization. Thus, whereas a decentralized net is highly appropriate to communication between professional and technical personnel in a research, academic, or scientific organization, there is also a need in the same organization for more centralized communication networks for effective support services.

SUMMARY

Traditionally organizational structures have tended to be bureaucratic, emphasizing a hierarchy of authority and a clear division of labor among organizational members. However, the rapid growth of science and technology and of research and development activities have caused far-reaching changes in the society. These changes are reflected in more complex goals for industrial organizations, including the involvement of such organizations in legislation and public regulation, and in new kinds of organizational structures.

Much of the difficulty inherent in traditionally structured organizations is attributed to their mechanistic nature. Such organizations tend to emphasize individual skills, authority-obedience relationships, a strict division of labor, centralized decision making, and suppression of individuality. In contrast, contemporary organizational theory emphasizes the need for structures which are dynamic, adaptive, and responsive to the needs of the participants.

Three aspects of organizational structure are discussed in this chapter: size, hierarchical levels, and communications networks.

Organizational size tends generally to be inversely related to member participation and satisfaction. However, there is no consistent evidence that increased size adversely affects member or organizational performance. The equivocal nature of the relationship between size and performance can be partly attributed to the fact that size is a complex variable. Changes in size are accompanied by concomitant conditions, like changed communication and supervisory patterns, themselves exerting significant influences upon organizational performance. For this reason, generalizations about optimum size must be qualified in terms of other organizational characteristics, task characteristics, membership composition of the group, and economic considerations.

The same sort of qualifications must be applied to generalizations about hierarchical arrangements. As companies become larger, they tend to develop "taller" hierarchies of authority and influence. Unless the organization effects counteractive measures, such tall hierarchies may reduce the participant's initiative and sense of responsibility, and encourage coercive management. However, the contrary conditions of effective leadership and member participation are by no means assured merely because the organization is "flat"; that is, structured with relatively few levels of authority and influence.

Much of the impact of both size and hierarchical arrangement is mediated by the effectiveness or ineffectiveness of communication within the organization. A highly centralized communication network is most efficient when the task is routine and collation of individual activities is necessary from the very beginning. However, such networks do not encourage a high level of participant satisfaction. In contrast, decentralized communication networks are most efficient when flexibility is required of the group by virtue of the complexity of the problem confronting it and/or the diversity of knowledges and backgrounds possessed by its members.

16. Industrial Leadership

The leader is clearly a key figure in any organization. He establishes organizational goals, initiates action toward attainment of these goals, and is largely responsible for maintaining or improving the prevailing level of member satisfactions. As described in the preceding chapter, most industrial leadership is exercised through a chain of command wherein persons at successively lower levels of the hierarchy wield progressively less power and have lesser degrees of status.

TWO LEVELS OF LEADERSHIP ACTIVITY

The present chapter concerns two levels of industrial leadership: line supervision and management. Although leadership is required at both levels, there are important differences between line supervisors and managers in the kinds of things they are expected to accomplish.

Supervisory Roles

The foreman or line supervisor is an intermediate in the relationship between nonsupervisory employees and higher levels of management. He typically has been promoted to his position from the line on the basis of seniority and/or merit, and often receives little or no training for his new leadership role. Although the line supervisor exerts a most direct influence upon the activities of individual employees and is the key figure in implementing decisions originating with management, he often is not accepted as a member either of the management or worker group.

Thus, whereas the supervisor lacks the status and authority associated with management, he must accept responsibilities far exceeding those of line employees. These responsibilities may include inducting the new employee into the work group and providing on-the-job training, encouraging safety, handling grievances, encouraging efficient job behavior, making performance ratings of the men he supervises, and scheduling the work activities in his section. In addition, he must represent the views of management to those he supervises and effectively communicate the needs of his subordinates to higher management.

Managerial Roles

Successively higher levels of industrial leadership (mid- and top management) tend less and less to interact with line employees. Managerial concerns are organizational in the sense that they are oriented more toward the company than toward a component work unit and are directed toward such broad issues as organizational goals, budgets, markets, and so on.

Ten dimensions of management activities identified from questionnaire responses of a sample of executives are:[1]

1. Providing staff service in nonoperational areas—including gathering information, selecting employees, training supervisors.

2. Supervising work of others. (This dimension is characteristic of mid-management and lower positions. It is not a dimension of higher level management positions.)

3. Business control, including cost reduction and budget preparation.

4. Technical concern with products and markets.

5. Concern with human, community, and social affairs in consequence of company activity and policy.

6. Long range planning.

7. Exercise of broad power and authority.

8. Concern with company reputation through public relations and maintenance of product quality.

9. Concern with personal status within the company and community.

10. Preservation of company assets.

All management positions emphasize some of these dimensions more than others. Indeed, certain of these dimensions are relatively incompatible. For example, managers concerned with preserving

[1] J. K. Hemphill, *Dimensions of Executive Positions* (Columbus, Ohio: Ohio State University Press, 1960) .

company assets through manipulating large operating expenses and taxes tend not to be involved in industrial relations or technical operations. Furthermore, these 10 dimensions of management activity are not all-inclusive. Differences in organizational settings, task requirements, and personal predispositions of managers may lead them to engage heavily in such other activities as personnel staffing (including selection, placement, and training), coordination, and communication.

The importance of the interaction between certain organizational characteristics and the primary roles of *mid-management personnel* has been calrified in a study of civilian managers working for the Department of the Army.[2] Nine possible management roles, somewhat overlapping the 10 dimensions listed above, were identified for these employees: (a) long-range planning; (b) staffing; (c) technical consultation; (d) budgeting; (e) responsibility for sharing information versus personal responsibility for taking action; (f) concern for operations versus concern for advising others on technical matters; (g) involvement in technical activity versus administrative activity (coordination, communication, and so on); (h) controlling activities, including cost reduction; and (i) time spent with others.

These nine roles were related to certain organizational characteristics like the organization's mission, level relative to the Department of the Army, location, and size. It was found with respect to mission, for example, that organizations with an administrative mission tended to emphasize the staffing and controlling roles, and to deemphasize long-range planning. In contrast, organizations with a research and development mission tended to deemphasize staffing and controlling roles. With respect to organizational size as an interactive variable, larger organizations tended more than smaller organizations to emphasize the importance of time spent with others, and to deemphasize long-range planning activities by middle managers.

In spite of differences in managerial roles as a function of the organizational setting and of differences in roles between managers and line supervisors, all persons in these positions exercise some

---

[2] R. A. Katzell, R. S. Barrett, D. H. Vann, and J. M. Hogan, "Organizational Correlates of Executive Roles," *Journal of Applied Psychology*, Vol. 52 (1968), pp. 22–28.

form of leadership. Therefore, it is necessary to make some general observations about the leadership process by way of background for the discussion of industrial supervision and management.

NOMINAL VERSUS EFFECTIVE LEADERSHIP

It is considerably easier to describe the ways in which leaders can function than it is to define the personal requirements for effective leadership, or to conceptualize the process of "leading." Investigations in the general area of leadership have pointed to the necessity for differentiating between leadership and status, and abandoning the prevalently held "great man" theory of leadership. Leaders are status figures; they occupy positions of esteem and wield power. However, the converse need not be true. Persons can have considerable status and power without being effective leaders.

Nominal leadership is imposed upon the group. The person occupying a position of nominal leadership has been appointed to this position by his superordinates. His status is generally reinforced by a title and salary sufficient to differentiate between himself and the members of the group he is assigned to head. A "title on the door" and a "carpet on the floor" may denote power as well as status. With enough of each, nominal leaders can command obedience. Whether or not they function as effective leaders, however, is an entirely different matter.

A person cannot be regarded as an *effective* leader unless he has willing followers. Workers who accept their supervisor or manager, and willingly implement his plans, behave and feel quite differently from those who are compelled to do so unwillingly. This is most apparent for elected leaders who are in a position to evoke a high level of subordinate effort and satisfaction by virtue of the fact that they have been chosen by the persons they lead. Elected leaders have behind them a feeling of group solidarity which gives them a powerful edge over a titular head.

Although many companies do take employee preferences into account when making supervisory appointments, the election of leaders is relatively uncommon in industry. Nevertheless, the distinction between nominal and effective leadership is useful because it alerts us to some of the potential difficulties entailed in the imposition of leadership. In order for an appointed leader to function with maximum effectiveness, he must be the sort of person who would have been elected by the group itself if it had been given the opportunity.

The distinction between nominal and effective leadership is perhaps most apparent in the military services. Virtually all enlisted men are obedient when an officer issues commands. Such obedience results from the threat of dire consequences for insubordination. However, the officer who can command on the basis of willing followership and whose men respect his superior knowledge and ability, feeling that they are part of a cohesive group pursuing common goals, is in an enviable position indeed. Unpleasant tasks are performed more willingly by the group members, and the general level of performance and personal feelings of satisfaction are considerably heightened under such circumstances.

From the foregoing discussion, it is evident that nominal leaders must be selected and trained with utmost care if they are to function effectively. Consideration of supervisory and management selection and training procedures is deferred to Chapter 17.

EFFECTIVE INDUSTRIAL LEADERSHIP

Specific techniques aside, what underlying attitudes, objectives, and concerns differentiate effective from ineffective leadership in contemporary society? If it were possible to select only one key phrase in reply to this question, it would have to be "human relations." Effective industrial leadership is concerned with managing the interpersonal relationships at work in ways calculated to encourage both employee satisfaction and organizational goal attainment.

This dual emphasis upon effective human relations and organizational productivity as joint responsibilities of the industrial leader contrasts sharply with the notion of "scientific management" prevalent during the early part of this century. In this earlier view the leader's sole function was to expedite organizational productivity. This was to be accomplished impersonally through refinements in bureaucratic structure and increased efficiency of the methods of work.

The changing nature of society during the past several decades and accompanying changes in perceptions about what constitutes an effective industrial organization were discussed in the previous chapter. The various organizational theories presented there can also be construed as theories of effective supervision and management. Rather than cover this same ground again, and in order to clarify some additional thinking about industrial leadership, our subsequent discussion begins by examining leadership styles and builds toward a situational view of effective leadership.

Leadership Styles

The behavior of leaders is often classified along a continuum ranging from *authoritarian* (or boss-centered) leadership at one pole to *democratic* (or subordinate-centered) leadership at the other (see Figure 16–1). Although the distinction between authori-

FIGURE 16–1

Continuum of Leadership Behavior

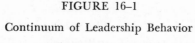

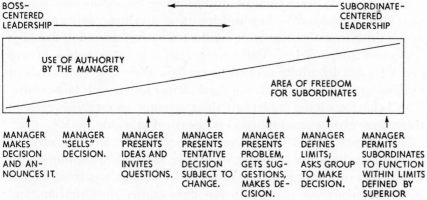

Source: P. Tanenbaum and W. H. Schmidt, "How to Choose a Leadership Pattern," *Harvard Business Review*, Vol. 36 (1958), p. 96.

tarian and democratic leadership is a convenient one, it is apparent that these two styles rarely exist in pure form. It is generally recognized also that classification of leadership solely on this dimension does not do justice to the multidimensional nature of leadership climates.

Authoritarian Leadership. A group operating under authoritarian leadership is wholly dependent on the leader for a determination of policies and goals. The authoritarian leader wields absolute power and is the sole unifying factor within the group. He is the only person within the group who knows the overall plan of activity;

and he alone has the responsibility for assigning tasks to individual members. The morale and productivity of the group deteriorates rapidly when such a leader is temporarily absent because the followers have become wholly dependent upon his direction.

Democratic Leadership. The democratic leader is an agent of the group. He facilitates and encourages the members' involvement and participation in achieving the group's goals and, whenever possible, in actually forming its objectives. Thus, the democratic leader encourages a maximum amount of group solidarity founded upon a network of strong interpersonal relationships between group members. Since each of the members is an active and informed participant in the group's activity, democratically led groups tend to perform quite effectively even during periods when the leader is temporarily absent.

Studies of Leadership Style. The most extensive studies concerning the relative effectiveness of authoritarian and democratic leadership were conducted by Lewin, Lippitt, and White.[3] The groups in which these investigations were conducted each consisted of five boys who were 10 years old. These were extracurricular hobby groups and were led by adults primed to exercise three different kinds of leadership behavior: authoritarian, democratic, and laissez-faire. The behavior of the leaders in their attempt to establish each of these three group "atmospheres" is described in Table 16–1.

The experimental design required that the adult leader be changed periodically in order to expose each hobby group to all three types of leadership. The order of leadership was *rotated:* that is, the sequence for one group was democratic, authoritarian, and laissez-faire leadership; for another it was authoritarian, democratic, and laissez-faire, and so on.

In general, the results indicated that democratic leadership is superior for the purpose of evoking creative behavior and cooperativeness. Productivity and member satisfaction were poorest in the laissez-faire situation. It is important to note, however, that there were exceptions to the generalization that democratic leadership was responsible for the highest level of morale. Some of the youngsters,

---

[3] K. Lewin, R. Lippitt, and R. K. White, "Patterns of Aggressive Behavior in Experimentally Created Social Climates," *Journal of Social Psychology,* Vol. 10 (1939), pp. 271–301; and R. Lippitt, "An Experimental Study of the Effect of Democratic and Authoritarian Group Atmospheres," *University of Iowa Studies,* Vol. 16, No. 3 (1940), pp. 43–198.

TABLE 16-1

Three Types of Leadership

Variable	Leader's Behavior		
	Democratic	Authoritarian	Laissez-faire
1. Control over policy formulation.	All policies a matter of group discussion and decision, encouraged and assisted by the leader.	All determination of policy by the leader.	Complete freedom for group or individual decision with a minimum of leader participation.
2. Control over member's activities.	Activity perspective gained during discussion period. General steps to group goal sketched, and when technical advice was needed, leader suggested two or more alternative procedures from which a choice could be made.	Techniques and activity steps dictated by the authority, one at a time, so that future steps were always uncertain to a large degree.	Various materials supplied by the leader who made it clear that he would supply information when asked to do so. He took no other part in the discussion.
3. Control over working associates.	The members were free to work with whomever they chose, and the division of tasks was left to the group.	The leader usually dictated the particular work task and work companion of each member.	Complete nonparticipation of the leader.
4. Dispensation of praise and criticism.	The leader was "objective" or "fact-minded" in his praise or criticism.	The leader tended to be "personal" in his praise or criticism of each member.	No attempt to appraise or regulate the course of events.
5. Participation by leader.	Leader tried to be a regular group member in spirit without doing too much of the work.	Leader remained aloof from active group participation except when demonstrating.	Infrequent spontaneous comments about members' activities.

Source: R. K. White and R. Lippitt, "Leader Behavior and Member Reaction in Three 'Social Climates,'" in D. Cartwright and A. Zander (eds.), *Group Dynamics* (Evanston, Ill.: Row, Peterson & Co., 1960), p. 528.

particularly those from autocratic homes, were perfectly satisfied to take orders from an authoritarian leader.

Many investigations of industrial leadership styles have been stimulated by this research with children. In general, such studies point to two conclusions:

First, a particular style may be relatively effective for one purpose and relatively ineffective for another. Thus, a style affecting productivity may not influence employee attitudes, and vice versa; and whereas a particular style may increase quantity of output, another may be required to increase quality.[4]

Second, whereas our society tends to give an edge to democratic leadership styles, there are yet circumstances wherein authoritarian leadership may be superior. Persons who are unprepared for democratic group action because of lack of prior exposure to and training for such leadership may feel relatively insecure unless provided with the kind of direction afforded by an authoritarian leader.

Thus, the "best" leadership style is a function of such situational factors as the specific type of problem confronting the group and the group's constituency. With respect to the former, for example, it has been found that problems which depend for their solution upon coordinated action are more efficiently solved when the leadership is centralized and authoritarian than when it is democratic.[5] With respect to group constituency, there is evidence from several studies that individuals vary in their preference for constraining (authoritarian) versus freer (democratic) environments, and that this preference interacts with the leader's style jointly to determine both the employee's level of performance and satisfaction.[6]

Leadership Dimensions

Two dimensions of leader behavior, *consideration* and *initiation of structure,* have been the subject of considerable research. Typically, these dimensions are assessed by means of a questionnaire on

---

[4] L. R. Anderson and F. E. Fiedler, "The Effect of Participatory and Supervisory Leadership on Group Creativity," *Journal of Applied Psychology,* Vol. 48 (1964), pp. 227–36.

[5] T. B. Roby, E. H. Nicol, and F. M. Farrell, "Group Problem Solving under Two Types of Executive Structure," *Journal of Abnormal and Social Psychology,* Vol. 67 (1963), pp. 530–56.

[6] G. A. Forehand and B. v.H. Gilmer, "Environmental Variation in Studies of Organizational Behavior," *Psychological Bulletin,* Vol. 62 (1964), pp. 361–82.

which subordinates describe the way in which their supervisor leads.[7]

Consideration entails awareness by the leader of his subordinates' feelings. It is the dimension of leadership emanating from the "human relations" view and is revealed by affirmative responses to such questionnaire items as:

"He expresses appreciation when one of us does a good job."

"He puts suggestions that are made by foremen under him into operation."

Initiating structure is supervisory behavior facilitating group interaction toward goal attainment. The supervisor may accomplish this by organizing, planning, and scheduling the work or by direct intervention in the group's goal-directed activities.[8] Questionnaire items illustrating this dimension are:

"He offers new approaches to problems."

"He insists that foremen follow standard ways of doing things in every detail."

Dimensions versus Styles. Although there appears superficially to be a parallelism between the dimensions "consideration" and "initiation of structure" and the styles described earlier as "democratic" and "authoritarian," it would be erroneous to equate leadership dimensions and styles. A leader may have *either* a democratic or authoritarian style (to use the extremes of this scale) without his style necessarily implying anything about the dimensions of his leadership behavior. Either style can be exercised in a climate of high or low consideration.

Furthermore, contrary to what one might expect, the dimensions "consideration" and "initiating structure" are independent of each other. Considerate supervisors may or may not avoid initiating structure.

Consideration. The effective supervisor tends to regard his subordinates as individuals, each with his own motives, feelings, and goals. He recognizes that the motives, feelings, and goals of his subordinates are likely to be quite different from those held by himself.[9] Such an attitude of consideration in dealing with subordi-

---

[7] E. A. Fleishman, "The Description of Supervisory Behavior," *Journal of Applied Psychology,* Vol. 38 (1953), pp. 1–6.

[8] E. A. Fleishman, "Leadership Climate, Human Relations Training, and Supervisory Behavior," *Personnel Psychology,* Vol. 6 (1955), pp. 205–22.

[9] H. H. Meyer, "Factors Related to Success in the Human Relations Aspect of Work Group Leadership," *Psychological Monograph,* Vol. 45, No. 3 (1951), 29 pp.

nates has been found to correlate positively both with ratings of supervisory effectiveness[10] and productivity of the work group.[11]

This respect for the individuality of each subordinate probably underlies certain specific behaviors that have been found to differentiate between effective and ineffective supervisors. The former (1) evidence trust in the worker's ability to handle the task by not supervising too closely, (2) communicate effectively, and (3) delegate job tasks and provide the delegated persons with sufficient authority to carry out the tasks with which they are charged.[12]

Initiating Structure. A supervisor who initiates structure actively organizes and defines the group's activities. He assigns tasks, defines roles, plans ahead, and generally establishes ways of getting things done.

Thus, in initiating structure the supervisor behaves in a somewhat authoritarian manner. However, as we have previously said, this need not have any implication for the level of "consideration" displayed by him. It is quite possible for a supervisor to initiate structure and be regarded by his subordinates as high on consideration, low on consideration, or somewhere between these extremes on the consideration dimension.

There is evidence that with respect to at least one criterion of industrial behavior, grievance rate, initiation of structure is an especially important dimension for those supervisors who are "moderately considerate."[13] Those supervisors who were perceived by their subordinates as "highly considerate" generated a low grievance rate irrespective of their score for initiating structure. Also, those supervisors who were perceived as "inconsiderate" generated a high grievance rate irrespective of their score for initiating structure. But of supervisors perceived as being medium in consideration, those low on initiating structure generated a low grievance rate whereas those high on initiating structure generated a high grievance rate. These relationships are shown in Figure 16–2.

---

[10] B. M. Bass, "Leadership Opinions as Forecasts of Supervisory Success: A Replication," *Personnel Psychology,* Vol. 11 (1958) , pp. 515–18.

[11] R. Likert, "Measuring Organizational Performance," *Harvard Business Review,* Vol. 36 (1968) , pp. 41–50.

[12] R. L. Kahn and D. Katz, "Leadership Practices in Relation to Productivity and Morale," in Cartwright and Zander (eds.) , *Group Dynamics* (Evanston, Ill.: Row, Peterson and Co., 1953) , pp. 612–27.

[13] E. A. Fleishman and E. F. Harris, "Patterns of Leadership Behavior Related to Employee Grievance and Turnover," *Personnel Psychology,* Vol. 15 (1962) , pp. 43–56.

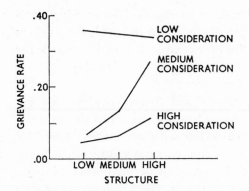

FIGURE 16–2

Interaction of Leadership Dimensions as Joint Determinants of Grievance Rate

Source: E. A. Fleishman and E. F. Harris, "Patterns of Leadership Behavior Related to Employee Grievance and Turnover," *Personnel Psychology,* Vol. 15 (1962), p. 50.

Thus, although initiation of structure *may* contribute to an elevated grievance rate, *it need not.* The determining factor is the interpersonal atmosphere in which the leader provides his direction and structure. If he can develop a climate of consideration, then his efforts to initiate structure can be well received.

Employee Participation

The supervisor's role in initiating structure or, alternatively, in encouraging subordinate participation in setting goals, defining work roles, and so on must be appropriate to situational factors associated with the group's activities and structural properties of the group itself.

This was demonstrated in an investigation of the relationship between the flavor of management policy and the attitudes of supervisors. Two companies, one with democratic management and one with authoritarian management, were compared. The investigator concluded that the success of a democratic approach to leadership rests upon the employees' readiness to accept responsibility and the possession by them of sufficient experience and knowledge to deal with their work problems. If these conditions do not exist, authoritarian leadership proves to be superior to democratic leadership.[14]

One of the important determinants of the effectiveness of employee participation is the legitimacy of such participation as perceived by the workers themselves. Worker attitudes are positively influenced by participating in situations in which they regard it as

---

[14] E. S. Stanton, "Company Policies and Supervisors' Attitudes toward Supervision," *Journal of Applied Psychology,* Vol. 44 (1960) , pp. 22–26.

right and proper for them to engage in the decision-making process.[15] However, there are a variety of situations in which the workers regard such participation as inappropriate and look toward the supervisor for concrete action of a structure-initiating nature.

The tolerance of workers for supervisors who exercise power depends also upon the perceived personal characteristics of the supervisor himself and the psychological needs of each of the subordinates. Workers may express satisfaction with a relatively powerful and directive supervisor who does not encourage much participation, provided such a supervisor is perceived by them as considerate of his men.[16] Furthermore, there are individual differences among workers in their desire for, and hence satisfactions derived from, participation in decision making. Persons who have strong needs for independence react more favorably to participation than do persons with weak independence needs.[17]

Finally, even within a single industrial organization attitudes toward directive and participative supervision may vary because of differences in the structure of various work groups. Large groups characterized by little personal interaction among the workers and between workers and their supervisor were found to favor authoritarian leadership. Conversely, workers within small, highly interactive groups had more positive attitudes toward equalitarian leaders.[18]

It is evident from the foregoing that it is impossible to make blanket generalizations about the most effective supervisory styles. Effective leadership behavior in certain situations may prove relatively ineffective in others because of interactions between variables within the work group. Among others, these include the personal needs of the group members, the tasks in which they are engaged, their perceptions about the legitimacy of participating in decision making, and the structure of the group. These worker and work-group variables are further compounded by the personal characteris-

---

[15] J. R. P. French, J. Israel, and D. Ås, "An Experiment on Participation in a Norwegian Factory: Interpersonal Dimensions of Decision-Making," *Human Relations,* Vol. 13 (1960), pp. 3–19.

[16] F. C. Mann and L. R. Hoffman, *Automation and the Worker: A Study of Social Change in Power Plants* (New York: Henry Holt & Co., 1960).

[17] V. H. Vroom, "Some Personality Determinants of the Effects of Participation," *Journal of Abnormal and Social Psychology,* Vol. 59 (1959), pp. 322–27.

[18] V. H. Vroom and F. C. Mann, "Leader Authoritarianism and Employee Attitudes," *Personnel Psychology,* Vol. 13 (1960), pp. 125–40.

tics, including the needs, attitudes, and perceptions, of the supervisor himself.

A Situational Model

In somewhat oversimplified form, the issues raised thus far in our discussion of effective leadership have contrasted the "human relations" and "scientific management" points of view. We have asked whether it is better for the manager to lead using a democratic or authoritarian style; to evidence a high level of consideration or structure initiation; to encourage or discourage employee participation. To these and similar questions, we have concluded uniformly that the effectiveness of any kind of leader behavior depends upon the configuration of the situation in which leadership is being exercised. The situational factors to be taken into account include characteristics of the task or problem, the participants (both leader and followers), and the organizational environment. Thus, instead of regarding one form of leadership as generally better than another, it is more accurate to speak of types of leadership as being best for particular combinations of circumstances.

Following this conclusion, it remains to identify those combinations of circumstances under which various kinds of leadership are most effective. This is precisely what has been attempted in the "contingency model" described below.[19] This model regards effective leadership as a joint function of three interactive sets of situational variables:

1. *Leader-member relations.* The degree to which group members trust the leader and are willing to follow his guidance.

2. *The task structure.* The extent to which the task can be spelled out step by step and performed according to a standard procedure (as opposed to tasks which must be left nebulous and undefined).

3. *Position power.* The power inherent in the leader's position including his freedom to hire, fire, promote, or demote.

Any group can be classified with respect to these three situational variables in accordance with the model shown in Figure 16–3. Each cell of this model represents the integration of a particular combina-

---

[19] F. E. Fiedler, "A Contingency Model of Leadership Effectiveness," in L. Berkowitz (ed.), *Advances in Experimental Social Psychology* (New York: Academic Press, 1964), pp. 150–90.

tion of these variables. Thus, the shaded cell in the figure identifies a group characterized by distance rather than trusting closeness between the leader and members, working on an unstructured task, and supervised by a powerful leader.

Predictions. Eight different kinds of groups are portrayed in the model shown in Figure 16–3. These groups are ranked in Table

FIGURE 16–3

Situational Determinants of Effective Leadership: A Contingency Model

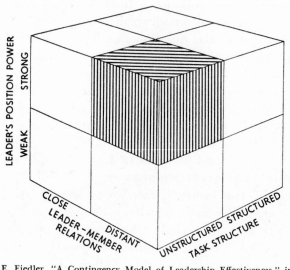

Source: F. E. Fiedler, "A Contingency Model of Leadership Effectiveness," in L. Berkowitz (ed.), *Advances in Experimental Social Psychology* (New York: Academic Press, 1964), pp. 150–90.

16–2 according to whether circumstances in the group are favorable to the leader. (This ranking assumes that "leader-member relations" is the most important and "position power" is the least important of the three situational variables.)

Referring to this table, the easiest group to lead is the one wherein the members like their supervisor, have a highly structured task, and where the supervisor is powerful. The most difficult group to lead is one wherein the members dislike their supervisor, work on an unstructured task, and where the supervisor has little power.

Using this classification of conditions favorable and unfavorable to exercising leadership, the contingency model makes the following two predictions:

1. Autocratic, highly structured leadership will be most effective in situations either very favorable or very unfavorable to exercising supervision. (These are the conditions ranked at the top and bottom of Table 16–2.)

TABLE 16–2

Situational Factors Facilitating and Inhibiting Leadership

| Rank (*Reflecting Ease of Leadership*) | *Situational Variables* | | |
	Leader-Member Relations	*Task Structure*	*Position Power*
1 (Most favorable)	Close	Structured	Strong
2	Close	Structured	Weak
3	Close	Unstructured	Strong
4	Close	Unstructured	Weak
5	Distant	Structured	Strong
6	Distant	Structured	Weak
7	Distant	Unstructured	Strong
8 (Most unfavorable)	Distant	Unstructured	Weak

2. Human-relations oriented, democratic, permissive leadership will be most effective in situations intermediate in favorableness to exercising supervision (that is, the middle ranks in Table 16–2).

Implications. When put to the test, these predictions seem generally to be supported by the data. Although more evidence is needed, the contingency model shows promise of specifying the circumstances wherein the two polar leadership styles, authoritarian and democratic leadership, will each prove most effective.

Using the model, it becomes possible to engineer the situation to fit the manager.[20] The company can most effectively capitalize upon a manager's particular leadership style by arranging an optimal work setting for him; that is, a setting with the proper combination of leader-member relations, task structure, and leader position power. The kinds of modifications that are possible include:

1. *Leader-Member Relations*

To encourage greater closeness—increase homogeneity of the group by including men with attitudes, beliefs, and backgrounds similar to those of the manager.

---

[20] F. E. Fiedler, "Engineer the Job to Fit the Manager," *Harvard Business Review,* Vol. 43 (1965), pp. 115–22.

To encourage greater distance—increase heterogeneity of the group by including men with attitudes, beliefs, and backgrounds dissimilar to those of the manager.

2. *Task Structure*

To increase task structure—give the manager precise operating procedures for the group to follow.

To reduce task structure—assign the manager to groups which perform tasks that cannot be reduced to clearly specified operating procedures.

3. *Position Power*

To increase position power—assign men to the group who are several ranks below the manager; allow communication only through established channels; give the manager greater autonomy.

To decrease position power—assign men to the group who are almost equal to the manager in rank; communicate directly with each group member without going through the manager; require the manager to consult with his subordinates in making work-related decisions.

SUMMARY

The essence of effective leadership is a willing group of followers. This fact is recognized in the distinction sometimes made between "nominal" and "effective" leadership. A nominal leader is invested with power by virtue of his appointment to a status position. However, unless his subordinates willingly follow him, such a person is merely a titular head. He may, to be sure, issue orders and command obedience; but high morale and the maximum expenditure of effort by individuals to achieve the group's goals are beyond the realm of command.

The fact that persons serving as nominal heads may be relatively ineffective as leaders poses a particularly significant problem for industry. The organizational structure of most companies requires that certain individuals be appointed to positions of authority. In order for these nominal heads to function as *effective* leaders, they must be carefully selected and trained. In practice, such selection and training is guided by a situational rather than a trait view of the origins and exercise of leadership.

Effective industrial leadership is concerned with managing the interpersonal relationships at work in ways calculated to encourage both employee satisfaction and organizational goal attainment. Three factors in interpersonal management are discussed in this chapter: leadership style, ranging from authoritarian to democratic; leadership dimensions, including consideration and the initiation of structure; and employee participation. In each instance, conclusions about the effectiveness of particular kinds of leader behavior (for example, democratic *versus* authoritarian) depend upon the configuration of the situation in which leadership is being exercised. The situational factors to be taken into account include characteristics of the task or problem, the participants, and the organizational environment. Thus, instead of regarding one form of leadership as generally better or worse than another, it is more accurate to speak of types of leadership as being most appropriate for particular combinations of circumstances.

17. Management Development

Management development, as considered in this chapter, involves three intimately interrelated applications of basic research on leadership: (a) selection, or the identification of potential managers; (b) assessment, or the evaluation of the performance of currently employed managers and supervisors; and (c) training. Most of the procedures for training managers also provide managerial performance appraisals. And some procedures, like the in-basket test discussed later, can serve all three functions.

The importance of these three aspects of management development is emphasized by an observation made in the previous chapter: industrial managers typically are appointed rather than elected to their positions of leadership. As you will recall from Chapter 16, appointment to nominal leadership may convey power and status but does not insure effectiveness. Hence, the purpose of managerial selection, evaluation, and training programs is to develop the skills and attitudes associated with generating a willing "followership." To introduce the matter of management development, it is instructive to examine the conditions determining which member a group *voluntarily* selects as its leader when given the opportunity.

THEORIES OF LEADERSHIP ELECTION

There are two general views about the conditions responsible for election by a group of one of its members as its leader: trait theories and situational theories.

Trait Theories

As described in the preceding chapter, this approach to leadership maintains that effective leaders possess a unique combination of specific personal characteristics or leadership traits. It is a "great man" concept of leadership; that is, there are some men who are so outstanding, by virtue of their possession of particular traits or trait combinations, that they are "natural" leaders. Other men, according to this theory, are attracted by this generalized leadership quality and willingly follow its possessor regardless of the particular circumstances under which it is displayed. The personal characteristics usually associated with this general leadership quality include such things as aggressiveness, intelligence, and tact.

Trait theories of leadership are now quite generally regarded by psychologists as sterile because they make little contribution to our understanding of the leadership process.[1] The traits explanation of leadership leads to the expectation that persons who are effective leaders in one situation will tend also to be effective leaders in other situations. This kind of generality of effective leadership is, however, open to serious question. It has been estimated that the correlation between leadership ability in *different* situations would not exceed 0.35.[2] The correlations between several measures of leadership ability in a *given* situation, on the other hand, are considerably higher.

Thus, it is apparent that leadership is somehow a function of the particular situation in which it is displayed. Persons who are effective leaders in one group often are ineffective leaders in another group. The finding that leadership is not a generalizable characteristic has led to the more recent emphasis upon situational rather than trait factors in explaining effective leadership.

Situational Theories

This approach to leadership perceives the leader and followers as engaging in a continual and dynamic personal interaction. Hence, a particular person emerges as the leader in response to the particular combination of individuals in the group, and to the particular problem that serves as the focus of group activity.

The predictions that follow from the situational and the trait approaches to leadership are quite different. The expectations stemming from the trait approach are static; that is, it is anticipated that the person who possesses leadership traits will emerge as the leader

---

[1] R. M. Stogdill, "Personal Factors Associated with Leadership: A Survey of the Literature," *Journal of Psychology*, Vol. 25 (1948), pp. 35–71.

[2] J. Matthews, "Research in the Development of Valid Situational Tests, I: Survey of the Literature" (Pittsburgh: American Institute for Research, 1951).

and continue to occupy this position as long as the group exists. The situational approach has a much more dynamic flavor since it anticipates that the leadership of a group will change as the needs of the group members and the problem orientation of the entire group are changed.

The situational explanation of leadership is substantiated by the finding that the group members' attitudes toward the leader are variable rather than constant. Enlisted men, for example, held much less favorable attitudes toward their officers near the end of World War II than at the beginning of the war, even when the matters of longevity and rank were controlled.[3] The particular task orientation of enlisted men during the early phases of the war made military headship quite acceptable to them. As the war neared its conclusion, however, this focusing orientation disappeared, and authoritarian leadership was much less acceptable to the followers.

The work of the Office of Strategic Services also provides evidence for the fact that leadership is a transitory rather than a permanent phenomenon. Groups of men were presented with a complex task and permitted to elect their own leaders. The person originally elected as the leader was retained in this capacity only so long as he was able to meet the demands of the problem. The group replaced him with another leader whenever it became apparent that this would facilitate progress toward the solution of the problem.[4]

The person chosen by the group as its leader has generally given the group some evidence of his superior general or technical competence and knowledge relative to the group's problem or activity.[5] It is interesting to note that the person who emerges as a leader is not necessarily the one who is best liked by the other group members.[6] Rather, he is the person the other members perceive as the best qualified to deal with the particular situation in question.

IDENTIFYING POTENTIAL LEADERS

As we have already said, most industrial supervisors are appointed leaders. Since industrial situations generally preclude the

---

[3] S. A. Stouffer, *et al.*, *The American Soldier* (Princeton, N.J.: Princeton University Press, Vol. I, 1949).

[4] OSS Assessment Staff, *Assessment of Men* (New York: Holt, Rinehart & Winston, Inc., 1948).

[5] W. O. Jenkins, "A Review of Leadership Studies with Particular Reference to Military Problems," *Psychological Bulletin*, Vol. 19 (1947), pp. 54–79.

[6] H. H. Jennings, *Leadership and Isolation* (New York: Longmans, Green & Co., Inc., 1950).

election of a leader by the group itself, it is particularly critical that appointed group heads function so effectively as leaders that they are acceptable to the group. The problem of promoting effective supervision requires that management pursue an active policy of (1) identifying potential leaders within the work force and (2) training these persons in the effective exercise of supervision.

The identification of any ability prior to its emergence or development is, of course, a prediction problem. Thus, the identification of persons who are likely to be effective leaders involves procedures quite similar in nature to those we encountered earlier in our discussion of personnel selection and placement. Nevertheless, certain rather unique problems are encountered in attempts to predict leadership ability. As we have seen, it is virtually impossible, in the first place, to arrive at a uniformly applicable definition of "effective" leadership; hence, predictors of such behavior that are valid in one setting may be quite invalid in some other setting. Secondly, the criteria for "effective" or "ineffective" leader behavior are generally developed from ratings made by subordinates and superordinates. Such subjective criteria are exceedingly unreliable and therefore cannot be predicted very successfully.

The situational explanation of leadership discourages attempts to search for particular traits associated with effective leadership. It suggests, instead, that we must search for persons who demonstrate that they can or do actually emerge as leaders when the circumstances permit for the display of leadership ability. The situational behavior of persons can be studied in its "natural state," that is, as it occurs in real-life situations or in circumstances deliberately contrived for this purpose. This is clearly somewhat easier when the company is searching for potential supervisors or managers from among its present employees than when it is seeking management trainees from among as yet industrially inexperienced college graduates.

Buddy Ratings

The existing work group is a real-life situation. Presumably, the members of such a group have had an ample opportunity to observe each other's behavior under a variety of circumstances. Therefore, they should be in an excellent position to evaluate one another's potential for leadership. Such evaluations are most often made in the form of sociometric ("buddy") ratings, discussed in Chapter 18.

Buddy ratings can, of course, be supplemented by ratings made by the supervisor.

Behavioral Tests

The approach to predicting leadership behavior from contrived situations is an extremely interesting one. Persons may be exposed to actual test situations demanding a display of leadership (that is, *behavioral tests*), or they may be required to respond to a paper-and-pencil inventory posing unique leadership problems. Some indication of the kinds of behavioral predictors that have been explored is provided by the following five measures used in an attempt to differentiate between effective and ineffective civilian supervisors at military depots.[7]

1. A standardized panel interview: The candidate was interviewed informally by three interviewers. Topics and questions related to supervisory performance and attitudes were introduced into the discussion and the candidate's responses were evaluated independently by each interviewer.

2. A standardized individual interview: The candidate was interviewed by just one interviewer.

3. A group discussion problem: Four of the candidates were constituted as a committee with instructions to develop recommendations on a particular aspect of plant management. The quality of the contributions made to this discussion by each candidate was rated by the examiner.

4. A role playing situation: The candidate was required to deal with a "staged" personnel problem. An assistant examiner acted the role of the subordinate and the examiner recorded specific aspects of the candidate's performance.

5. A small job management problem: The candidate was required to demonstrate supervisory ability in a minature work situation. An observer scored the quality of his supervisory behavior and his actual work output.

When these five behavioral test situations were compared, it was found that the group discussion problem was the most efficient predictor of effective leadership while the small job management problem was the least efficient predictor.

------

[7] R. Glaser, P. A. Schwarz, and J. C. Flanagan, "The Contribution of Interview and Situational Performance Procedures to the Selection of Supervisory Personnel," *Journal of Applied Psychology*, Vol. 42 (1958), pp. 69–73.

Paper-and-Pencil Tests

Contrived situations involving supervisory leadership have been presented in paper-and-pencil form in a test of "social attitudes."[8] Each item in this test describes a simple social situation, and the multiple-choice alternatives state various courses of action that might be followed in this situation or feelings about it. The respondent is asked to mark the alternative stating the course of action or attitude he feels is appropriate. The following items about "Harry," a senior accountant, illustrate the content of this test:

29. Harry's supervisor is near the retirement age. Most of the men will be glad when he retires because he is so grouchy. How would you expect Harry to feel toward him?
    a) He probably agrees with the rest of the men.
    b) He probably feels that he might be grouchy, too, if he were as old as the boss.
    c) He probably tries to avoid the boss.
    d) He probably feels that something must be troubling the boss.
36. The group leader who is in charge in the supervisor's absence, is a young, college-trained man with less experience than Harry and some of the others. When the man was appointed group leader, Harry thought to himself,
    a) "I hope he makes out all right."
    b) "The boss is making a mistake in not appointing a senior man."
    c) "That fellow isn't qualified for the job of group leader."
    d) "I like to see a young fellow get ahead."

Encouraging results have been reported for this approach to identifying leadership ability. Scores on the test were found to correlate positively with criterion ratings of leadership ability. One of the very interesting findings of this study was that the test of "social attitudes" was a much more efficient predictor of leadership ability than was a test of knowledge about supervisory skills. Thus, it appears that leadership training might better concentrate on changing the social attitudes of new supervisors than upon teaching specific leadership skills or techniques.

---

[8] H. H. Meyer, "Factors Related to Success in the Human Relations Aspect of Work Group Leadership," *Psychological Monograph,* Vol. 65, No. 3 (1951), 29 pp.

The In-Basket Test

The in-basket test[9] combines elements both of behavioral and paper-and-pencil testing. It has been used for evaluating incumbent managerial performance as well as for assessing the performance of prospective managers and as a training device.

The examinee is confronted with an in-basket filled with realistically assorted items including important memoranda, daily reports, social items, and so on. His task is to go through the items, handling each as if he were on the job. He can refer, delegate, plan meetings, issue memoranda, and write letters. Each of his actions must be taken in writing, thereby providing a record of his test responses. When he finishes with the in-basket materials, he completes a form which allows him to describe his reasons for taking each of his actions.

In-basket responses are "scored" by trained judges who evaluate such things as decisiveness, imagination, courteousness to subordinates, and so on. The test has been found to tap three major areas of behavior: (1) making decisions and taking action *versus* deferring decisions and actions; (2) high work output *versus* low work output; and (3) acting independently *versus* seeking advice and guidance from superiors.[10]

Although these areas of behavior seem clearly related to managerial success, and as intriguing as the technique is, there are two issues needing further attention. First, performance across in-basket tests tends to fluctuate.[11] Thus, extreme care must be taken in selecting items for inclusion in an in-basket test in order to insure that they closely approximate those that would actually be encountered on the job. Because of the tremendous variety of managerial jobs, this poses obvious difficulties for standardizing in-basket tests. Second, the validity of the technique requires further study, with particular reference to test-taking attitudes. Whether a person's real life responses are like those he makes on the in-basket test is still an open question.

---

[9] N. Frederickson, D. R. Saunders, and B. Ward, "The In-Basket Test," *Psychological Monographs,* Vol. 71 (1957) , Whole No. 438.

[10] N. Frederickson, "Factors in In-Basket Performance," *Psychological Monographs,* Vol. 76 (1962) , Whole No. 541.

[11] N. Frederickson, "Consistency of Performance in Simulated Situations," *E.T.S. Res. Bull. 61–22* (Princeton, N.J.: Educational Testing Service) , 1961.

MANAGEMENT AND SUPERVISORY TRAINING

Some of the procedures used for leadership training include: (1) lectures; (2) assigned readings; (3) formal courses in public speaking, human relations, and so on; (4) job rotation providing an overview of company operations; (5) case study; (6) role playing; (7) gaming; (8) sensitivity training; and (9) "managerial grid." The principles of learning discussed in Chapter 8 are applicable to all of these techniques, but most obviously to the first four listed. Therefore in this section, we will consider only the procedures numbered 5–9 in the list above.

A preliminary note about training for line supervisors and foremen is in order. Such employees typically are promoted from the line on the basis of job experience and proficiency. Once in his new position, the supervisor is required to spend much of his time in activities broadly classified as human relations; he must deal with people rather than with machinery or equipment. Although the supervisor needs to have the technical know-how required for the kind of work he supervises, this alone is not enough; he needs also to develop leadership skills.

One of the major problems in leadership training is the distinction made within many companies between supervisory behavior as it is taught in theory or in the classroom and as it is actually practiced in the plant. An excellent training program may be utterly ineffective whenever higher management provides an example of leadership contradicting what the supervisors have been taught in their training classes. It is futile, for example, to attempt to train foremen in techniques of democratic leadership if when they return to the plant they are exposed to autocratic leadership from their superordinates. Thus, it is not surprising to find that some leadership training courses are relatively ineffective; that is, they produce no noticeable changes in foremen's attitudes or behaviors when they return to the plant.[12] One of the implications of a negative evaluation of supervisory training programs is simply that such training cannot be effective if it is conducted solely at the level of the line supervisor. Middle and top management benefit also from participation in leadership training programs.

---

[12] E. A. Fleishman, *Leadership Climate and Supervisory Behavior* (Columbus, Ohio: Personnel Research Board, Ohio State University, 1951).

Case Study

A fundamental objective in training managers and supervisors is to develop an understanding and appreciation of human relations problems and the acquisition of skill in dealing with personnel problems. The case conference method is one way in which these objectives may be realized.

This method involves group discussions of actual business problems or cases. The case is a realistic situation requiring some kind of supervisory action. It lends itself to various solutions, none of which can be judged in absolute terms as being "right" or "wrong." Some solutions are, however, better or more appropriate than others. The following cases designed for line supervisors typify this kind of situation.

Case 1

The other day Miss Black went to the personnel office and asked to be transferred out of your section. Joe, the personnel manager, informed you that she gave as her reason that you are favoring Miss White. According to Miss Black's story, Miss White, who is of the same grade level as she but with six months' seniority, has entrenched herself in your favor by being an informer. As a result, Miss White is allowed to while away the day doing just enough work to make it look good, while she (Miss Black) carries a heavy work load and is closely supervised by you.

This is news to you. You are careful to distribute the work evenly. Miss White has a better aptitude for the work, completes it rapidly, and needs little supervision. On the other hand, Miss Black has difficulties, so you are giving her job training—not close supervision. In relation to the charge of informing, you think this might arise from the fact that Miss White often gives you good suggestions on methods improvement. You think Miss White is supervisory material, while you doubt if Miss Black is.

How are you going to handle this situation? [13]

Case 2

The other day the personnel department informed you that one of your men had quit—Smith, an operator you had hired about a month ago. During the exit interview, he told the personnel interviewer he was quitting because in your section the regular workers were a clique, there

---

[13] William J. McLarney, *Management Training: Cases and Principles* (Homewood, Ill.: Richard D. Irwin, Inc., 1959), p. 334.

were no opportunities for an outsider, and he had been told that he was not wanted.

You began to investigate by talking to Jack White, the old-timer whom you had selected to help Smith get acquainted with the job and with the other men. Jack informed you that he went to lunch with Smith the first day. During the meal Smith kept boasting of how he was going to be top man in the section before long because of his wonderful experience— that you had practically guaranteed him rapid advancement by stating that his past experience would be of great aid to him. Jack claimed that he tried to show Smith that this attitude wouldn't do him any good in getting along with the group. The next day Smith turned down Jack's suggestion that they go to lunch together and went instead with Bill Brown, who had recently been demoted and transferred to your section. Smith and Brown continued going to lunch together.

Then you began to check up on Smith's work. You found that he made less than normal progress during the month he was in your section. You spoke to several of the men who worked with Smith. They told you that none of the men liked him—that he criticized everything and everybody and was constantly saying that in the company where he had worked previously conditions were better and better work was turned out. One of the group said he told Smith that, if he didn't like the way things were done here, he ought to quit.

You review your actions in hiring Smith. You recall from the application blank and the interview that he came to work for a wage that was less than he had received on his previous job, also that he had received no raises on his last two jobs. During the interview he stated that he didn't mind getting less than his previous wage if he had the opportunity to advance—that the reason he quit his last two jobs was the lack of opportunity on them. You told him there were always opportunities in the company for a good man. During the month Smith was on the job, you spoke to him several times, and he told you that he was coming along fine.

1. What might be some of the things wrong with Smith, the man who quit?
2. Which of these might you have uncovered in the interview?
3. What mistakes might you have made in the induction?
4. How should you have inducted Smith?
5. Suppose he is right about the clique—that your group does try to discourage new men who are good workers. How are you going to clean up that situation?
6. What are you looking for in an induction follow-up?
7. How do you get this information? [14]

---

[14] *Ibid.*, p. 358.

The trainees are given a period of time in which to study the case and to think about alternative solutions. They are encouraged, during the conference, to discuss the problem, to suggest solutions, and to evaluate the ramifications of the various solutions.

Role Playing

Role playing is in a way an extension of the case approach. The case conference terminates with a discussion of alternative solutions. Role playing, however, requires that the trainee actually carry out his solution in a supervised practice situation.

A problem for consideration at a role-playing session, for example, might be the case of employee Jones who has an unusually high accident rate. One of the supervisor-trainees would be assigned to the role of the employee and several others would be assigned to the supervisory role. Each of the role players would then act out his solution to the problem with the remainder of the training class as an audience. The class sees several alternative solutions acted out before it and is in a position to compare and evaluate each of them. Furthermore, the role-players have an opportunity to experience the feeling of reacting in a particular way. And the one who is assigned to the role of the employee gains some appreciation of how it feels to be on the receiving end of various kinds of supervisory reaction.

Aside from some embarrassment during the initial role-playing sessions, this technique appears to be quite valuable for helping supervisors gain an understanding of the human element in business and industry. Furthermore, it has been suggested that much of the embarrassment arising from being observed can be sharply reduced by the technique of *multiple role playing*. In this procedure the entire training class is split into small groups, each confronted by the same problem. Since every member of the group is assigned a role to play within his own group, the method tends to reduce feelings of self-consciousness. An additional advantage of multiple role playing is that subsequent discussion across groups often reveals a variety of solutions to the same problem as a function of the particular personalities interacting within each group.[15]

---

[15] N. R. F. Maier and L. F. Zerfoss, "MRP: A Technique for Training Large Groups of Supervisors and Its Potential Use in Social Research," *Human Relations,* Vol. 5 (1952) , pp. 177–86.

Management Gaming

Decision making is one of management's most critical functions. Management games attempt to develop a degree of decision-making facility by constituting groups of trainees as teams, each representing a "company," and requiring them to make decisions governing the company's operations during the next period of play. The outcome of these decisions is evaluated in terms of a "model" of the operation of the industry or economy. This evaluation is fed back to the teams at the end of each period of play and they then make new decisions for the next period. Anywhere from a week to a year of "real time" may be represented in periods of play ranging from a few minutes to several hours.

One such game, developed at the Carnegie Institute of Technology for use by graduate students, is played by three teams constituting the "industry." The complexity of this game is indicated by the fact that each set of decisions, covering a month of "real" time, requires two to three hours. An IBM computer is tied up for about 45 minutes each time the results of a move are computed.[16]

The players in this particular game are provided with many kinds of information, including basic background data on the history of their company's operations and constraints on its policies and operations. They receive quarterly balance sheets and income statements for their competitors. The status of the team's own company is indicated monthly by a variety of reports, including balance sheets, income statements, summaries of financial commitments, cost of raw materials, cost of goods sold, warehouse stocks and shipments, finished product inventories, and work force as well as equipment down time data. Other information including market survey data, availability of financing, results of product preference tests, and so on are available to each team as requested or required.

The teams are required to make a full range of production, marketing, and finance decisions, including such things as price levels, sales, forecasts, amount of production, applications for financing, allocation of products to regions, and others.

---

[16] W. R. Dill, "A New Environment for Training Decision-Makers—The Carnegie Management Game" (originally an unpublished report, Carnegie Institute of Technology, Graduate School of Industrial Administration, 1960). Reprinted in E. A. Fleishman, *Studies in Personnel and Industrial Psychology* (Homewood, Ill.: The Dorsey Press, Inc., 1967), pp. 217–27.

Management gaming has opened tremendous possibilities both for training managerial personnel and for investigating the effectiveness of various industrial policies and practices. The latter application of gaming is, of course, dependent upon the adequacy of the model upon which the game is constructed. To the extent that it realistically simulates industrial conditions, the game itself becomes a research tool whereby answers may be provided to fundamental questions about management theory and practices.

Sensitivity Training

The goals of sensitivity training include the development of (*a*) insight or sensitivity to oneself and others; (*b*) understanding of conditions which inhibit or facilitate effective interpersonal, group, and intergroup functioning; (*c*) and skills in diagnosing individual, group, and organizational behavior. Such training seeks to provide an experience where dependency and control can be reduced in favor of increased interpersonal competence and self esteem and where feelings and emotions are openly recognized and examined rather than suppressed.[17]

Given these objectives, sensitivity training clearly attempts to foster personal development of a type highly relevant to effective managerial behavior. And given the current emphasis in organizational and management theory upon recognition and satisfaction of employee needs through organizational behavior (as discussed in Chapter 15), it is not surprising that such training is much in vogue in many companies. Indeed, there can be little quarrel with the purposes of sensitivity training. Whether or not it achieves these ends is another matter—and one not easily answered.

The T-Group.   Although sensitivity training is essentially a constellation of procedures, sometimes subsumed under a more generic designation of *laboratory training,* an important constituent aspect is the T- (for "training") Group.[18] This is an unstructured group of about 10–15 persons who meet face-to-face. Historically, such groups have been structured heterogeneously; the members represent various occupations and professions, and ordinarily first become ac-

---

[17] C. Argyris, *Integrating the Individual and the Organization* (New York: John Wiley & Sons, Inc., 1964) .

[18] K. D. Benne, L. P. Bradford, and R. Lippitt, "Designing the Laboratory," in L. B. Bradford, J. R. Gibb, and K. D. Benne, *T-Group Theory and Laboratory Method* (New York: John Wiley & Sons, Inc., 1964) , pp. 45–79.

quainted in the T-Group. Although this pattern of T-Group structure is still used, there has been a recent interest in laboratory training for organizational "families" wherein the group members are likely to have had some prior acquaintance.

Typically, the group has no assigned "project" or focus for discussion; the interpersonal processes transpiring within the group are themselves the subject of study by the members. By being a member of the group, each participant can examine the effects he has on other people and the effects they exert upon him. Presumably, he brings with him into the group his characteristic modes of interpersonal behavior in the outside world: assertiveness, hostility, dependency, or whatever. These behavioral modes are examined in the group both as they evoke responses from other participants and are themselves responses to the behavior of the other participants.

Effectiveness. Does sensitivity training accomplish its objectives? The evidence has been slowly accumulating for the past 15 years or so, without definitive conclusions.[19] Clearly, change, when it occurs, is a function of what the person is like when he begins sensitivity training. But such change is difficult to measure. Different participants may learn different things from the experience; and much of what is learned can only be assessed by self-ratings—an admittedly tenuous criterion. The acid test, of course, is whether on-the-job behavior is favorably affected following sensitivity training. In this regard, participants frequently *say* that they were helped to become more effective managers. But hard evidence on this point based upon more objective criteria is difficult to come by. At present, the posture of sensitivity training advocates and detractors with respect to its effects upon job behavior is based more on faith or a lack thereof than on empirical data.[20]

Managerial Grid

The managerial grid[21] is offered to industry as a packaged management development program with a clear-cut financial payoff. In

---

[19] D. Stock, "A Survey of Research on T-Groups," in Bradford, Gibb, and Benne, *ibid.*, pp. 395–441; and G. S. Odiorne, "The Trouble with Sensitivity Training," *Training Directors Journal,* Vol. 17 (1963) , pp. 9–20.

[20] J. P. Campbell and M. D. Dunnette, "Effectiveness of T-Group Experiences in Managerial Training and Development," *Psychological Bulletin,* Vol. 70 (1968) , pp. 73–104.

[21] R. R. Blake, J. S. Mouton, L. B. Barnes, and L. E. Greiner, "Breakthrough in Organization Development," *Harvard Business Review,* Vol. 42 (1964) , pp. 133–55.

view of the limited evidence on its effectiveness, claims for its efficacy seem at this time to be exaggerated.

The rationale for the managerial grid rests on a bipolar conceptualization of leadership dimensions similar to those discussed in Chapter 16. Here, the two key dimensions are designated: (1) concern for people and (2) concern for production. By keying each of these dimensions to a nine-point scale and assuming that the dimensions are uncorrelated, it is possible to classify a manager in terms of his position of the managerial grid. This grid, showing the placement of five hypothetical managers, is illustrated in Figure 17–1. The 1,1 manager behaves in least desirable fashion; the 9,9

FIGURE 17–1

Managerial Grid

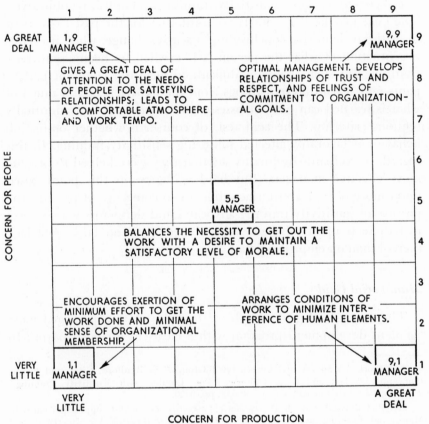

CONCERN FOR PRODUCTION

Source: R. R. Blake, J. S. Mouton, L. B. Barnes, and L. E. Greiner, "Breakthrough in Organization Development," *Harvard Business Review*, Vol. 42 (1964), pp. 133–55.

manager, who is maximally concerned both with production and with the people with whom he interacts, is presumed to behave in optimal fashion.

The managerial grid training program seeks to develop 9,9 managers. This is to be accomplished by a program involving elements of sensitivity training leading both to management development and organizational change.[22]

Whether or not the 9,9 pattern on the managerial grid is, in fact, optimal can be questioned on the basis of evidence presented in Chapter 16. Certainly, this simple view about effective leadership ignores the situational factors that several other writers regard as highly important. Also, the assumption that task and interpersonal orientations are the two most critical dimensions of leadership is merely that—an assumption.

SUMMARY

Many techniques have been developed as aids to identifying potentially effective supervisors and managers. The search for traits, like intelligence or aggressiveness, predisposing their possessor to leadership in virtually all kinds of situations has generally been abandoned as sterile. The trait approach has been replaced by predictive devices permitting an evaluation of leadership ability actually demonstrated in a variety of real-life or especially contrived situations.

Five supervisory and management training procedures are considered in this chapter: case study, role playing, gaming, sensitivity training, and the managerial grid. These procedures are frequently supplemented by more traditional training experiences including lectures, assigned readings, formal courses, and job rotation.

---

[22] R. R. Blake and J. S. Mouton, *The Managerial Grid* (Houston, Texas: Gulf Publishing Co., 1964) .

18. Morale and Industrial Relations

Several factors associated with job satisfaction were considered in Chapter 13. Such satisfaction or dissatisfaction is, as you will recall, a highly individual matter. Its level depends upon the extent to which the job is perceived by the employee as fulfilling his needs and providing the gratifications he desires. Such perceptions are also related to morale. However, the nature of this relationship depends upon the way in which morale is defined.

DEFINITIONS OF MORALE

We can distinguish between two general types of definition: one regarding morale as an *individual* characteristic and the other treating it as a *group* characteristic.

According to the first view, morale is the combination of attitudes held by the employee toward his job, company, and immediate supervisor.[1] In a sense, this is an operational definition, describing the way in which morale is often appraised. An *attitude* predisposes a person to behave in either a favorable or an unfavorable fashion. Thus, a typical approach to assessing morale involves a kind of "averaging" of employee attitudes in several critical areas. Presumably, an employee who is unfavorably disposed toward his job, his company, or his supervisor will lack the sense of company identification that is associated with high morale.

---

[1] R. L. Kahn and D. Katz, "Leadership Practices in Relation to Productivity and Morale," in D. Cartwright and A. Zander (eds.), *Group Dynamics* (Evanston, Ill.: Row, Peterson & Co., 1953), p. 616.

The above definition of morale as a composite of employee attitudes appears to miss two essential components of the concept. First, we generally think of morale as a relatively stable attribute. Employee attitudes toward various aspects of the job, and hence a composite of these attitudes, may be transitory, reflecting conditions of the moment rather than a more basic orientation. Secondly, the view that morale is a combination of job-related attitudes misses the flavor of the interaction between the individual and the group usually associated with morale. High morale implies that ". . . the individual perceives a probability of satisfying his own motives through cooperation with the group."[2] In order for cooperation to occur, the group members must share a common goal which they value and regard as attainable.

Therefore, we take the position in this chapter that morale is a concept more properly applied to groups than to individuals.[3] Characteristically, we associate high morale with team spirit and organized progress toward goal attainment. Groups that are despirited and disorganized are regarded as having low morale.

The distinction between these two kinds of definitions, one referring to an individual's morale and the other to a group's morale, is not merely hairsplitting. It has been shown that research findings relative to morale differ depending upon whether the criterion reflects one or the other definition.[4]

MORALE ASSESSMENT

All approaches to morale assessment study one or more of three components quite uniformly associated with high morale: group cohesiveness, commitment to attainment of organizational goals, and a sense of progress toward goal attainment. The two latter components are, of course, individual matters. Whereas we can speak of a group as being cohesive, we can speak of commitment and participation only in terms of the group's members. Note that this is not the same as endorsing the view that morale is an individual characteristic. To the contrary, one or a few group members (s) may

---

[2] R. Stagner, "Motivational Aspects of Industrial Morale," from "Industrial Morale (A Symposium) ," *Personnel Psychology*, Vol. 11 (1958) , p. 64.

[3] S. A. Stouffer, E. A. Buchanan, *et al.*, *The American Soldier: Adjustment during Army Life* (Princeton, N.J.: Princeton University Press, 1949) , Vol. 1.

[4] T. H. Jerdee, "Work-Group versus Individual Differences in Attitude," *Journal of Applied Psychology*, Vol. 50 (1966) , pp. 431–33.

be highly committed to the organization's goal, and the group may yet be characterized by low morale. Likewise, one (or a few) members may feel the goal is attainable, whereas morale of the *group* may be low. Thus, the enthusiasm of the team captain or section supervisor simply may not accurately mirror the prevailing attitude of the majority of group members.

Because morale has several components, its assessment is best made in multidimensional fashion. The work group must be studied as a unit to determine the extent to which it functions as a cohesive whole; the individuals within the group must be studied to determine the level of their awareness of the existence of a goal and the extent to which they perceive themselves as contributing substantially to the overall group endeavor.

Sociometry

From one viewpoint, high morale depends upon the existence of shared feelings of belonging and participation by the employees. Thus, in a high morale group, we would expect group structure to be relatively cohesive. Conversely, when morale is low, we might anticipate that there will be some employees who are assigned to, but not integrated within, the work unit.

Sociometry is a technique developed by Moreno[5] for studying a variety of group structures. It has been rather extensively used both for assessing morale and suggesting possible modifications in group structure.

When sociometric procedures are utilized in work groups, each individual assigned to the group is asked to name the person who in his judgment would be the best supervisor, makes the greatest contribution to the total group effort, or is the best worker. This fundamental procedure can be modified easily by requiring respondents, for example, to choose two persons rather than one, or by requiring them to "nominate" persons who they feel are inefficient as well as those who are efficient. The application of the latter *nominating technique* is illustrated by the following questions asked during interviews with naval pilots:

---

[5] J. L. Moreno, "Foundations of Sociometry," *Sociometry Monograph*, No. 4 (Boston: Beacon House, 1943) .

Assume that you are to be shifted to a new air group tomorrow and that you may select your own combat mates to go with you to this new air group. Of all the men known to you in Naval Aviation—living or dead—what two men would you like most to fly wing in your new combat assignment? Why would you select these men?

What two men would you least like to have flying wing on you? Why?[6]

The resultant choices and rejections are summarized visually in a map of the group's structure called a *sociogram*. Every person is represented in the sociogram by some kind of symbol, like a circle. Choices and rejections are often represented by connecting pairs of circles with solid lines to represent positive choices and dotted lines to represent negative choices. Some representative sociometric patterns are shown in Figure 18–1.

Application of Sociometric Findings. It is impossible to perform a sociometric analysis of group structure unless the group satisfies certain requirements. The members of the group must be closely associated for a sufficient period of time to have formulated evaluations of each other. The circumstances of their association, furthermore, must be such that they are familiar with one another's capabilities and limitations. Finally, the group must share a common task or objective if sociometric evidence is to be regarded as a valid index of morale.

This latter point is an important one and, perhaps, not self-evident. Workers who are grouped together for administrative purposes but do not share a common objective may have high morale in spite of sociometric evidence for the existence of cliques and self-contained subgroups. These subgroups may have been formed because of common interests and activities. Thus, the very fact of their existence under such circumstances could be indicative of high morale.

The information relative to group structure provided by a sociogram yields valuable clues about ways in which industrial morale may be improved. Any procedure that eliminates cliques or isolates, either by integrating them within the group structure or severing them from the group, may well improve morale by increasing cohesiveness. Furthermore, the sociogram can be extremely potent for the purposes of identifying persons who are potential leaders and

---

[6] J. G. Jenkins, *The Nominating Technique: Its Uses and Limitations* (paper presented to meetings of the Eastern Psychological Association, 1947).

FIGURE 18–1

Some Typical Sociometric Patterns

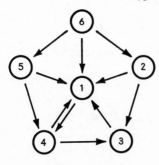

A. A COHESIVE GROUP
WITH A STAR

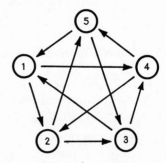

B. A COHESIVE GROUP
WITHOUT A STAR

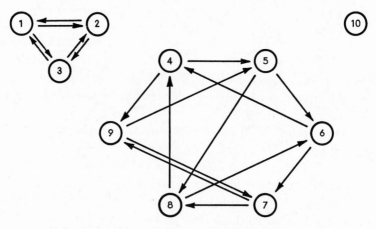

C. A NONCOHESIVE GROUP WITH A CLIQUE (1, 2, AND 3)
AND AN ISOLATE (10)

paving the way for newly assigned supervisors by familiarizing them with the structure of the group they are to lead.

It frequently is desirable to implement sociometric choices by assigning employees to work with the persons whom they have chosen. A good deal of industrial activity is organized about the work team consisting of two or more employees. This is, perhaps, most evident in the case of an aircrew executing a military mission, but is a factor also in many other kinds of settings. When carpenters and bricklayers were permitted to choose their work partners sociometrically, for example, production costs decreased by about 5 percent and the workers reported increased interest in and satisfaction with their work.[7]

Surveys

Morale is, as we have already pointed out, dependent upon certain factors in addition to the one of cohesiveness. Knowledge of the employee's feelings about the job, the company, and the supervisor is important to the assessment of morale. In order for morale to be high, the employees must perceive their job to be of importance to the welfare of the company, the company to be sincerely interested in them as individuals, and the supervisor to be an individual who acts fairly in his role as intermediary between the employee and the company.

Employee attitudes and opinions may be surveyed by a variety of questionnaire, interview, and attitude scaling procedures. Such surveys serve three purposes in addition to the fundamental one of appraising morale. (1) The properly designed morale survey is a diagnostic device which helps to identify some of the sources of friction between management and the worker. (2) Action predicated upon the results of such a survey can do much to improve group solidarity and morale. (3) It provides concrete evidence to the employees that management is really interested in them and in their opinions.

Questionnaires. A questionnaire is the most economical and probably the most frequently used procedure for soliciting employee opinion. The format of the questionnaire can be varied in accord with the kind of information desired from each respondent, the amount of time available for summarizing the responses, and the occupational level of the employees. The principal dimension differentiating between various kinds of formats is the extent to which the questionnaire is structured.

A *highly structured questionnaire* asks very specific questions and limits the nature of the response that can be made by the employee. The percentage of employees marking each alternative of a structured questionnaire can be summarized easily. In addition, such

---

[7] R. H. Van Zelst, "Sociometrically Selected Work Teams Increase Production," *Personnel Psychology,* Vol. 5 (1952) , pp. 175–85.

forms are sometimes "scored" by assigning weights to each of the alternatives and averaging the weights of the alternatives marked by each respondent.

The *Tear Ballot for Industry* is a generalized questionnaire designed for administration in a variety of industrial situations. The test consists of 11 five-alternative items, is simple to administer, and guarantees anonymity to the respondent.[8] Replies to the *Tear Ballot* questions were correlated with job tenure rate for a sample of 98 workers in diverse industries. Job tenure rate was determined by dividing the total time the worker had been in the labor market by the number of different jobs he had held. The resultant correlations for each of the items are shown in Table 18–1.

TABLE 18–1

Correlations between Items in the "Tear Ballot for Industry" and Job Tenure Rate

1. Does the company make you feel that your job is reasonably secure as long as you do good work?...0.45
2. In your opinion, how does this company compare with others in its interest in the welfare of the employees?...0.14
3. How does your immediate supervisor compare with other managers, foremen, or section leaders as to supervisory ability?.......................0.18
4. Consider your work; are your working conditions comfortable and healthful? .0.26
5. Are most of the workers around you the kind who still remember you when you pass them on the street?..0.63
6. Do you think your income is adequate for your living needs?............0.26
7. Do you feel that you have proper opportunity to present a problem, complaint, or suggestion to the management?..............................0.33
8. Do you have confidence in the *good intentions* of management?...........0.33
9. Do you have confidence in the *good sense* of management?..............0.32
10. What effect is your experience with the company having upon your personal happiness?...0.17

Highly structured questionnaires have been criticized on the grounds that the areas of opinion investigated are too narrowly defined by the specific questions asked and the replies are limited by the choices offered by the item. The respondent generally cannot indicate subtle gradations of feeling or qualify his answers. *Unstructured questionnaires* offer the respondent considerably more leeway in making comments related to his attitudes and opinions. An illustrative item from such a questionnaire might read as follows:

---

[8] W. A. Kerr, "On the Validity and Reliability of the Job Satisfaction Tear Ballot," *Journal of Applied Psychology*, Vol. 32 (1948), pp. 275–81.

How do you feel about the flow of information from management? Do you get all of the information you want or need? Does this information reach you rapidly enough or does it come to you to slowly? How could the flow of information in your section be improved?

The response to such a sequence of questions must, of course, be written out. Hence, it is considerably more difficult to summarize and integrate the replies than it is when highly structured questionnaires are administered. This type of open-ended question, however, often elicits considerably more information of greater depth and significance than that obtained from structured morale surveys.

Interviews. The employee interview for the purpose of morale assessment, in a way, involves the verbal administration of a questionnaire. In fact, the two procedures often are combined. The preliminary administration of a questionnaire may suggest areas that merit further discussion during the course of the subsequent interview.

The interview has the unique advantage over the questionnaire of providing direct contact between the employee and the interviewer. Thus, if it is skillfully conducted, the interview will permit considerable probing of feeling and may lead to the discovery of previously unsuspected sources of low morale. The interview, furthermore, provides the employee with opportunities to indicate not only *how* he feels but also *why* he feels the way he does, and to make positive suggestions about the ways in which morale might be improved.

Interviews are, however, subject to a number of sources of difficulty which may interfere with their utility for morale assessment. The validity of the interview is highly dependent upon the establishment of good rapport. Unless this is accomplished, the interviewee may fear reprisals by management and, in consequence, the usefulness of his replies will be diminished.

Successful interviewing requires considerable skill and experience. A number of pitfalls attributable to the extreme subjectivity of this procedure have already been discussed in Chapter 5. Management may decide against using interviews for morale assessment also because of the relative costliness of this procedure in comparison with questionnaire surveys. Questionnaires can be administered simultaneously to groups of employees and on occasion may be given to the employees with instructions to complete the form at home. Interviews, on the other hand, are generally conducted with just one employee at a time and hence entail considerable expense in terms of both released work time and consultant or interviewer time.

Attitude Scales. This approach to morale assessment is founded upon many of the concepts underlying psychological testing procedures. Attitude scaling is a measurement technique as differentiated from procedures, like questionnaires and interviews, that are designed primarily to yield qualitative information about employee opinions. The attitude scale is a psychological yardstick. Employee responses are scored, and the resultant value is indicative of the degree to which the employee holds favorable or unfavorable attitudes. These scores may be averaged for groups of employees, and the attitude scales themselves may be submitted to the same kinds of studies of reliability and validity which are applied to tests. (See Chapter 9 for a further discussion of attitude scaling.)

EFFECTS OF MORALE

As we noted in Chapter 13, it is erroneous to assume that poor productivity, labor turnover, or excessive absenteeism are necessarily associated with job dissatisfaction. It is likewise erroneous to assume that such performance decrements are necessarily associated with low morale. In a comprehensive survey of 26 studies relating morale to productivity, the authors concluded that 14 demonstrated a positive relationship, 9 demonstrated no relationship, and 3 demonstrated a negative relationship.[9] Other investigators have found that certain elements of morale, namely pride in the work group[10] and attitude toward the supervisor,[11] correlate with productivity while other elements appear to be unrelated to output.

Findings like these point to three fundamental conclusions about morale:

First, low morale may itself be a symptom rather than a cause of undesirable industrial behavior. It is significant that often a problem which is presented to the psychologist as evidence of low morale proves upon investigation to stem from deficiencies in other ele-

---

[9] F. Herzberg, B. Mausner, R. O. Peterson, and D. F. Capwell, *Job Attitudes: Review of Research and Opinion* (Pittsburgh: Psychological Service of Pittsburgh, 1957).

[10] D. Katz, N. Maccoby, and N. Morse, *Productivity, Supervision, and Morale in an Office Situation* (Ann Arbor, Mich.: University of Michigan Survey Research Center, 1950).

[11] C. H. Lawshe and B. F. Nagle, "Productivity and Attitude toward Supervisor," *Journal of Applied Psychology,* Vol. 37 (1953), pp. 159–62.

ments of the organizational configuration—a shoddy selection program, improper training procedures, unfavorable working conditions, and so on. Here, instead of the referral problem resulting from poor morale, both it and the low morale level are joint symptoms of a more fundamental problem.

Second, even when morale is a causal factor in industrial performance, its effects may sometimes be opposite to those anticipated from a superficial analysis of the situation. Thus, low morale may actually enhance performance; workers who are too despirited to take assertive action of their own behalf are unlikely to strike! Likewise, high morale can be generated in a work group by virtue of its concerted effort to depose its manager; in spite of high morale so generated, the effects upon productivity can be quite deleterious.

Finally, morale is but one of a multiplex of factors which can influence industrial performance. A poorly led team may lose the game in spite of its high morale. In the final analysis, performance is a function of *effort*.[12] High morale may stimulate the group members to exert more effort, but such effort must be properly directed if it is to be fruitful.

Management is certainly well advised when it is concerned about morale. However, the above conclusions mean that management cannot anticipate that simple prescriptions for morale improvement, like piping music into the plant or repainting the restrooms, will necessarily have noteworthy effects upon performance. Any company seriously interested in improving employee morale must, in effect, be concerned with improving every aspect of its organizational structure and activity.

ORGANIZATIONAL CONDITIONS AND MORALE

As discussed in Chapters 15 and 16, morale has been investigated as a consequence of assorted organizational conditions including size, hierarchical arrangements, communication patterns, and leadership styles. The generalization that emerges from all of this research is that involvement and participation *perceived by the employees as genuine and appropriate* encourages high morale.

Note the italics in the sentence above. The key is *employee perception*. For morale to be high, employees must perceive congru-

---

[12] P. C. Smith and C. J. Cranny, "Psychology of Men at Work," *Annual Review of Psychology*, Vol. 19 (1968), pp. 467–96.

ence between management styles and the requirements of the task. Employee participation or a democratic group structure cannot effectively be superimposed upon circumstances in which it is apparent to the employees that they lack the information required for appropriate decision making and genuine participation.

Employee perception affects morale in yet another way. You will recall that for morale to be high the participants must perceive themselves and each other as contributing to the group effort and as making progress toward the goal. Furthermore, they must perceive the goal as important and worth pursuing. There are, to be sure, individual differences in perceptions of, feelings about, and responses to the same environment. Yet in spite of such individual differences, the organizational setting can encourage or discourage the kinds of perceptions associated with high morale.

This was demonstrated in a comparison of the morale levels of jet engine testers and a control group of welders and grinders.[13] The engine testers worked under adverse conditions: the noise level was extremely high. The noise level for the control group was considerably lower—about average for factory work. The social work settings for the two groups also differed. Whereas engine testers worked as teams and their work was diversified, the welders and grinders worked alone and their work was repetitive. Sociometric and other data indicated that in spite of the more comfortable physical conditions experienced by control group workers, their morale was considerably below that of engine testers. This difference in morale was attributed to the difference between the groups in the way they perceived their job. The engine testers could see that their goal was important—a pilot's life might depend upon the quality of the engine. Furthermore, since engine testers worked as teams, cooperation was required in order to achieve the work goal. In contrast, the welders and grinders worked on parts not clearly identified with total engine function; hence, the goal seemed less important. And since the welders and grinders worked alone, cooperation was not required of them.

In summary, the basic *S-I-R* paradigm is helpful in understanding the relationship between working conditions and morale. As is true of all responses, morale is evoked less by the stimulus condition

---

[13] J. S. Felton and C. Spencer, *Morale of Workers Exposed to High Levels of Occupational Noise* (Norman, Okla.: University of Oklahoma School of Medicine, 1957).

as objectively defined than by employee perceptions about the stimulus condition.

Improving Morale Using Problem Solving

It follows that the steps taken by management to improve morale must be directed toward (*a*) modifying employee perceptions in the direction of increased feelings of cohesiveness and individual identification with the group and (*b*) clarifying the importance of organizational goals and of each member's role in goal attainment. The attainment of these ends requires both effective communication throughout the organizational structure and when possible, employee involvement in solving company problems.

Organizational changes involving alterations in methods of work and established work groups are frequently associated with low morale. Such changes disrupt the cohesiveness of the work unit and engender unfavorable attitudes by virtue of enforced departure from the accustomed way of doing things.

It has been demonstrated that low morale is not an inevitable consequence of organizational change when employees participate in discussions of the necessity for change and alternative solutions. Two problems treated in this fashion by the management of a men's apparel manufacturing company were: (1) supervisors' reluctance to hire female employees and (2) excessive turnover among workers forced to transfer from one job task to another because of changing market conditions. Both problems were successfully resolved by having employees participate in the changes.[14]

When groups of persons work together to arrive at the solution of some common problem, they tend to experience a feeling of solidarity. This, of course, is one of the crucial elements of morale. Moreover, when employees are encouraged to engage in group discussions of work-related problems, they are better able to understand some of the limiting constraints experienced by management, and management in its turn is better able to understand what it is that employees need and want from their job.

Employee discussion groups are not to be confused with gripe sessions. The discussion leader focuses the entire discussion upon the solution of a single problem. He does not lead the discussion to a

---

[14] L. Coch and J. R. P. French, Jr., "Overcoming Resistance to Change," *Human Relations*, Vol. I (1948), pp. 512–32.

preordained conclusion or decision but rather handles it in an entirely democratic fashion. Resource persons with specific areas of competence (consultants, representatives of management or of the union) may be requested by the employees to sit in during the session to clarify matters of policy or to help the discussion group evaluate the feasibility of a number of proposed solutions. If the discussion procedure is to work effectively, however, neither management nor an outside consultant can be permitted to grab the ball and run with it. The employees alone must share the responsibility for developing a final solution to the problem. Once the solution is voted upon and accepted by the group, little if any enforcement by management will be required. It is unnecessary for anyone to see to it that we do something that we ourselves have decided to do.

It cannot be assumed that amount of participation per se determines the level of satisfaction of participants. In fact, a nonindustrial study of this issue led to the suggestion that the *opportunity* to participate rather than the amount of participation may be the critical variable. Small groups of undergraduate students were allotted a specified number of grade points to distribute among the individual group members. These points were added to course examination scores, engendering a conflict of interest. The solution arrived at by three fourths of the groups was to allocate these points according to need. Each member was asked to express his feelings about the decision. The degree of satisfaction reported by individual members was related to the extent to which they felt they had an opportunity to participate in and affect the group's decision. The number of points received and the actual degree of participation were not similarly related to members' feelings.[15]

Participation, or at least the opportunity to participate, is essentially a democratic process. Therefore, there has been some speculation that results favoring participation might be culturally limited to the United States. A review of recent studies in certain other countries, including Norway, Japan, and England, supports a degree of generality for the beneficial effects of participation upon employee attitudes.[16] Whether or not participation would be either

---

[15] L. R. Hoffman and N. R. F. Maier, "The Use of Group Decision to Resolve a Problem of Fairness," *Personnel Psychology*, Vol. 12 (1959), pp. 545–59.

[16] V. H. Vroom and N. R. F. Maier, "Industrial Social Psychology," *Annual Review of Psychology*, Vol. 12 (1961), p. 421.

possible or similarly effective in other more restrictive nations is still an open question.

INDUSTRIAL RELATIONS

Industrial harmony implies cohesiveness across all levels of the organization, providing every participant with a sense of membership in and allegiance to the company group. This superordinate identification with the company, transcending allegiances to management and labor subgroups, is theoretically possible only when all participants pursue common goals.

In spite of the attractiveness of a harmonious relationship between labor and management, this state of affairs is more or less unattainable. The members of a company organization are also members of many other groups both within and outside of the company itself. Even when the internal relations within the company are relatively harmonious, the organization's members tend to identify themselves with management or labor. Each of these subgroups reflect certain member needs and generate vested interests that are unique to that subgroup and affect its members' perceptions. Furthermore, there are superordinate organizations of management (like the American Management Association) and labor (unions) that transcend a particular company and may define conflicting goals for their members.

Sources of Industrial Conflict

We can best approach an understanding of industrial conflict by considering some of the differences in needs and perceptions of the two groups involved in the conflict. This focus upon groups rather than upon individuals does not negate the importance of the individual as a determinant of group action. The leader in particular can exert a powerful influence upon the group members and is in turn responsive to the needs of the individuals constituting the group.

Worker Needs. Labor unions develop and grow because their members perceive them as being the only effective satisfiers of some of their needs. The union can operate as effective need-satisfiers in at least two dimensions: (1) It is a liaison between management and labor, providing the worker with a voice that is heard even by top management. (2) The union is itself a structured group and therefore can provide certain gratifications to its members based upon such internal factors as participation in group activities and personal recognition. We will examine each of these functions of labor unions in more detail.

Employees join labor unions partly because of the external representation made to management by such unions. Such representation satisfies many different needs, two of which are highly important. First, the worker needs to feel that he has a voice in decisions that may affect him. The union provides him with a channel of communication with management, and presents his grievances and desires for him. Thus, instead of being subjected solely to downward communication from various levels of the management hierarchy, the union member is enabled also to communicate upward through the management hierarchy. Secondly, the union is perceived by its members as a power equalizer. The availability of upward communication is of rather dubious value if the communicating voice is a weak one. Thus, although many employees feel that as individuals they are in a disadvantageous power position relative to management, their membership in a union strengthens their voice and puts them in an effective bargaining position.

These needs for representation and power in dealing with management are extremely important. It would be a gross oversimplification, however, to attempt to explain union membership solely on the basis of such needs. The internal dynamics of the union group also satisfy member needs in another direction. The union often provides the worker with a group of his own in which his participation and expression is welcomed; he can speak up without fear of reprisal. In addition, the union provides the member with some status. An employee is a first-rate citizen in his union even though he may feel that he is a second-rate citizen in his company. Unlike the work environment, in which the employee is not consulted on matters of policy, the union *does* consult its members on union-related issues. Union members are provided with avenues for personal recognition, leadership, and authority within the labor organization itself.[17] Finally, the union member feels that he has an organization that is really interested in his feelings and thus provides him with

---

[17] G. Watson, "Labor Unions and Morale," in G. Watson (ed.), *Civilian Morale* (Boston: Houghton Mifflin Co., 1942).

emotional outlets that are impossible for him to attain from either disinterested or overly paternalistic employers.[18]

Management Needs. Unlike the union member who perceives the labor organization as equalizing the balance of power, management may perceive the union as disrupting the balance of power by tipping the scale in favor of the workers. Union demands are often interpreted by management as an encroachment upon its right to run the company. Thus, employers may affiliate with management organizations in order to restore what they perceive to be their rightful prerogatives in the management of the company.

The Power Struggle. If we had to select a dominant thread running through the fabric of industrial conflict, it would be the power struggle between labor and management. This is rooted in emotions and feelings rather than in reason. Unions develop and thrive because they are perceived by their members as removing the power differential between the boss and the worker. Management's antipathy to the union is largely founded upon the belief that its own position of power is weakened by the labor organization.

Although this power struggle between opposing factions has been emphasized, it would be erroneous to regard union affiliation as perforce precluding loyalty to the company. In a survey pertinent to this matter, 73 percent of packing house workers responded favorably *both* to the company and the union.[19] Furthermore, whereas a strike reflects a power struggle at the level of labor and management organizations, this struggle probably is not central to the behavior of the individual participants. Many of the strikers likely do not feel any personal involvement in making a show of strength. They strike simply because they are told to do so by the union and are compelled to do so by the social pressures exerted by co-workers.

Automation. Of the several factors causing displacement or unemployment, the replacement of manpower by machines is seen by unions as a unique threat to job security. Hence, automation has increasingly become an issue in labor-management relations.

The effects of automation are diverse and vary from one industry to another. Sometimes, automation completely eliminates jobs.

---

[18] T. Burling, "Disruptive and Cohesive Forces in Job Situations," in G. W. Hartmann and T. Newcomb (eds.), *Industrial Conflict* (New York: Cordon Co., 1939).

[19] T. V. Purcell, "Dual Allegiance to Company and Union—Packinghouse Workers. A Swift-UPWA Study in a Crisis Situation, 1949–1952," *Personnel Psychology,* Vol. 7 (1954), pp. 48–58.

More often, it reduces job content, thereby creating the technical possibility of combining the fractional remainders into new jobs.[20] Thus, automation often changes personnel requirements and job tasks; however, these changes are not necessarily improvements as far as the employee is concerned. For example, automation in automative assembly has not been found materially to affect the level of employee skills and responsibilities; in fact, it has had the somewhat negative effects, from the employee's viewpoint, of encouraging greater supervision and reducing opportunities for advancement.[21]

In general, automation has led the unions to attempt to advance contractual provisions intended to prevent, or reduce the effects of, unemployment. Such provisions include: (1) aids to worker mobility (transfer to other operations or plants, moving expenses, retraining programs) ; (2) cushions against interrupted employment (supplementary employment benefits, severance pay) ; and (3) reductions in the length of the workweek or work year in order to spread available work among more people.[22]

A number of problems associated with automation require a greater amount of attention than psychologists have heretofore given this matter. To the extent that automation creates changed personnel requirements, it necessitates alterations in selection and training programs; employee resistance to automation may be a component of job dissatisfaction and lowered morale; and since automation tends to transfer control over production rate from the man to the machine, it tends to undermine the rationale of incentive payment and poses special problems for job evaluation schemes.

Patterns of Union-Management Relations

Granting the existence of a certain degree of polarization of participant needs and perceptions, the style of accommodation by labor and management subgroups varies across companies. Such variation in patterns of union-management relationships was evident in an analysis of such things as labor practices, company and union official attitudes, the union contract, company and union

---

[20] C. C. Killingsworth, "Industrial Relations and Automation," *The Annals of Sociology*, Vol. 340 (1962) , pp. 69–80.

[21] W. A. Faunce, "Automation in the Automobile Industry," *American Sociological Review*, Vol. 23 (1958) , pp. 401–7.

[22] Killingsworth, *op. cit.*

organizations, and contract negotiations in 41 Illinois companies.[23]

Information concerning these and related matters was interpreted in terms of three patterns of relationship:

1. *Union influence* in union-management relations.

2. Extent to which settlements were based on the use of *pressure* (such as work stoppages, movement of the plant, and so on).

3. Union-management *attitude* (defined by a composite of the union attitude toward management and management attitude toward the union).

Each participating company was classified with respect to its rank (high or low) on each of these variables, and companies with similar patterns were clustered together. The predominant patterns of union-management relations, each characteristic of 5 or more of the 41 companies studied, were found to be the following:

Pattern A. Aggression and resistance—companies wherein the union is influential and seeks settlement of labor-management disputes through exerting pressure; management is unhappy about the situation.

Pattern B. Quiescence—companies wherein the unions have little influence and where both management and the union prefer their relationship to remain as it is.

Pattern C. Joint participation—companies wherein the union exerts moderate influence in labor-management relations and where both management and the union like the present relationship.

Pattern D. Repressed hostility—companies wherein attitudes are unfavorable on either the management or union side and where union influence is moderate but not exerted through pressure tactics.

Given such variation in the patterns of union-management relations, it is logical to expect differences between companies in the nature and intensity of their labor-management conflicts and in the efficacy of alternative attempts at conflict resolution. It is in this general area—that of investigating the situational determinants of conflict and of procedures for resolving conflicts—that the industrial psychologist can make an especially noteworthy contribution to labor-management relations.

---

[23] M. Derber, W. E. Chalmers, and R. Stagner, *The Local Union-Management Relationship* (Champaign, Ill.: University of Illinois Press, 1960).

Resolving Industrial Conflicts

Strikes or lockouts cannot be explained on purely rational grounds. The "reasons" given by the warring factions do not often stand the test of rational consistency. The assumption, for example, that workers strike primarily to earn more money is an obvious oversimplification. The actual cost to the worker of a lengthy strike may offset his financial gain from the strike for a considerable period of time. Similarly, management may suffer a considerable financial loss far exceeding workers' salary demands during a period of industrial warfare.

If we stand apart from the struggle for power between management and labor and view it in perspective rather than from one side or the other, a rather obvious fact becomes apparent: the fundamental interest of labor and management are highly interdependent. Management has nothing to offer to potential consumers if it does not have an efficiently functioning work force. Likewise, labor's sole means to product and service consumption is provided by management in the form of opportunities to work.

An Overview of Methods.   The most constructive, but as yet unattainable, method of conflict resolution treats an industrial conflict as a problem jointly shared by labor and management. Such a problem-solving approach to industrial conflict rests upon the recognition that the fate of both management and labor is tied to the fate of their company, and hence to the fate of one another. Thus, both conflict prevention and resolution are joint responsibilities.

This kind of constructive solution is rarely implemented. Instead, other methods of conflict resolution varying in destructiveness are used. These have been classified along a continuum, from least to most destructive, as bargaining, limited war, total war, and suppression.[24]

Bargaining is discussed separately below. It is a process of negotiation wherein each party to the dispute gives something in order to gain something. It is regarded as less constructive than "problem solving" because the participants are adversaries negotiating the best agreement obtainable in terms of their own self-interests.

Arbitration is a form of "limited war" with somewhat less poten-

---

[24] H. A. Shepard, "Responses to Situations of Competition and Conflict," in *Conflict Management in Organizations* (Ann Arbor, Mich.: Foundation for Research on Human Behavior, 1961), pp. 33–41.

tial than bargaining for building toward a problem-solving climate. Here there is a clear-cut "winner" and "loser" as determined by a judge or panel of judges. Whereas this approach may settle the dispute in the sense that a decision is made for one of the parties, it can hardly be regarded as a procedure for resolving underlying conflicts.

Collective Bargaining. The purpose of collective bargaining is to permit union and management representatives to work out peaceful solutions to their mutual problems and to formalize their solutions in a contractual agreement. This agreement is a form of treaty. The negotiations preceding contractual agreement permit each side to (*a*) attempt to influence the other's opinions, (*b*) show its strength, and (*c*) discover each other's maximum and minimum expectations.[25]

The bargaining table is inevitably the site of a power struggle. Each side seeks to increase its strength and influence within the company. Also, at a more personal level, the individuals negotiating for labor and for management are driven by a need for continued respect from the groups they each represent. Several impediments to bargaining emanate from and reinforce this conflict of interest: faulty communication between the bargaining participants, incorrect perceptions of the facts and desires presented by the other side, and personality differences between union and management representatives.[26] Although rarely implemented, it has been suggested that clinical psychologists may be in a position to make substantial contributions to the bargaining process itself by facilitating the communication between labor and management. Their special skills might enable them to deal directly with the kinds of misperceptions and seemingly irrational behavior often displayed during bargaining sessions.[27]

Reducing Industrial Conflicts

Although a certain amount of labor-management conflict is inevitable, the intensity and frequency of such conflict can be reduced. In general, this can be accomplished either by modifying the organiza-

[25] E. Peters, *Strategy and Tactics in Labor Negotiations* (New London, Conn.: National Foremen's Institute, 1955).

[26] M. D. Dunnette and W. K. Kirschner, *Psychology Applied to Industry* (New York: Appleton-Century-Crofts Co., Inc., 1965), pp. 188–97.

[27] R. Stagner, "The Psychologist's Function in Union-Management Relations," *Personnel Administration*, Vol. 26 (1963), pp. 24–29.

tional structure or by improving the operation of the present organizational system.[28]

The earlier discussions, particularly in Chapters 15 and 16, are germane to both approaches. Specific techniques (like developing more effective leadership, or decentralizing authority) aside, it is clear that the extent of industrial conflict can be reduced only when labor and management maintain a continuing and relatively informal dialogue. The necessity for such less formal and more frequent contacts than that provided by collective bargaining is evident from a study of the satisfactions sought by union officers.[29] These officers were found to seek satisfactions of two kinds: those stemming from contractual accomplishments and those stemming from daily interactions with management. Although successful collective bargaining may contribute to the former, it alone is not sufficient to reinforce the feeling of day-to-day partnership between labor and management. On the contrary, in view of the characteristics of collective bargaining noted above, issues which have not been resolved informally and without recourse to bargaining emphasize the schism between labor and management.

SUMMARY

High morale is characteristic of groups that are cohesive and wherein the members both are committed to the attainment of organizational goals and have a sense of progress toward goal attainment. Because morale has these three components, it is most appropriately assessed multidimensionally using various kinds of sociometric and survey techniques.

It is erroneous to assume that increased productivity and reduced labor turnover or absenteeism are necessarily associated with high morale. In the final analysis, performance is a function of properly directed effort. High morale may stimulate the group members to exert more effort, but unless this effort is properly channeled it may not be reflected in a performance increment. Furthermore, simple prescriptions for improving morale, like the institution of coffee breaks, have a transitory effect, at best. Any company seriously interested in improving employee morale must, in effect, be con-

[28] D. Katz, "Approaches to Managing Conflict," in *Conflict Management in Organizations*, pp. 13–20.

[29] R. Stagner, M. Derber, and W. E. Chalmers, "The Dimensionality of Union-Management Relations at the Local Level," *Journal of Applied Psychology*, Vol. 43 (1959), pp. 1–7.

cerned with improving every aspect of its organizational structure and activity.

The influence of organizational changes upon morale is mediated by employee perceptions about those changes. For such changes to have the desired effects, employees must perceive them as congruent with the requirements of the task. For example, a democratic group structure cannot effectively be superimposed upon circumstances wherein it is apparent to the employees that they lack the information required for making valid work-related decisions.

Impending organizational changes, particularly of the type involving alterations in work methods and established work groups, may themselves lower morale unless the employees to be affected are permitted to participate in the change process. When employees are encouraged to engage in group discussions of work-related problems, they are better able to understand some of the limiting constraints experienced by management, and management is better able to understand what it is that employees need and want from their job.

In spite of the evident attractiveness of thoroughly harmonious industrial relations, this state of affairs is more or less unattainable. Every company is segmented, to some degree, into labor and management subgroups. These subgroups each have certain needs and vested interests that may, on occasion, be in essential conflict. Unions develop and thrive because they are perceived by their members as removing the power differential between the boss and the worker. Management's antipathy to the union is largely grounded in the belief that its own position of power is weakened by the labor organization. More than anything else, then, industrial conflict represents a power struggle between labor and management.

Such conflicts can be prevented or resolved only when the parties to the conflict become fully aware of the interdependence of their fundamental interests. The fate of both management and labor is tied to the fate of the company and hence they are tied to one another. Ideally, conflicts should be resolved by treating them as problems to be solved jointly by labor and management. Unfortunately, this kind of problem-solving approach to conflict resolution is rarely implemented. Of the remaining procedures for conflict resolution, the least destructive is collective bargaining.

Although a certain amount of industrial conflict is inevitable, the intensity and frequency of such conflict can be reduced by maintaining a continuing and informal dialogue between labor and management.

VI.

Consumer Psychology

We have thus far focused our attention upon two of the three groups of persons involved in any industrial enterprise: employees and management. A smoothly functioning business organization is one in which the efficiency of each of these groups is maximized. Under such circumstances intracompany tensions are reduced, employee and employer satisfactions are heightened, and both the quality and quantity of output may be improved. The economic justification for the existence of a company is, however, ultimately dependent upon the behavior of a third group of persons—the consumers.

You will recall our earlier mention of the fact that psychologists study behavior with a view toward understanding, predicting, and controlling or changing it. The application of these objectives in the realm of consumer behavior is immediately apparent. The purpose of advertising and selling programs is to control or change consumer behavior. The producer, distributor, and advertiser often wish also to predict the way in which poten-

tial consumers will respond to various appeals, products, and packages.

The accuracy of such predictions rests in large measure upon an understanding of consumer motivation. This is particularly evident in the American culture wherein masses of consumers have considerable discretion in economic expenditures. In consequence, consumers desire many things today which were hardly known a few years ago. And because of social changes, including those reflecting altered educational levels, income distribution, increased leisure time, more stable age patterns, governmental intervention on behalf of the consumer, and growth of the mass media, it is likely that these felt needs will continue to proliferate.[1]

Part VI considers the psychologist's contribution to the study of consumer behavior and the understanding of consumer needs; that is, the research methods and behavior principles germane to consumer psychology. The methods particularly stressed in these chapters are (a) surveys of various kinds, (b) "depth procedures" designed to elicit information about underlying consumer motivation, and (c) studies of actual consumer behavior. The range of applications of these procedures is extremely broad and includes studies of the characteristics of consumers and potential consumers, the effectiveness of advertising appeals and alternative distribution channels, product design, and consumer response to available products and services. In addition, consumer psychology has increasingly focused upon the consumer as an organism worthy of study in his own right, with particular attention to improved health and safety and to an increased understanding of the factors involved in consumer decisions and choices.

---

[1] D. W. Twedt, "Consumer Psychology," *Annual Review of Psychology*, Vol. 16 (1965), pp. 268–72.

19. Consumer Research

Two fundamental problems for the producer are: (1) bringing the product to the attention of potential consumers and (2) influencing them to purchase it. Purchase by the consumer involves an element of decision making. The prospective customer must decide on occasion whether or not to buy a product or utilize a service without regard for competing brands. Should he, for example, buy a new car? A new refrigerator? A new coat? He must decide further which of several competing brands or options he ought to select. If he is going to buy a new car, will it be a Chevrolet, Ford, or Pontiac?

Decisions of this kind are not always predicated upon careful consideration of all alternatives. "Impulse buying" results from decisions made precipitously, without much forethought, and in response to factors about which the buyer himself may be quite unaware. Even decisions considered by the consumer to be highly rational may really be based upon irrational factors and unconscious processes.

The complex area of consumer behavior does not fall exclusively within the province of psychology. A comprehensive understanding of consumer behavior must include contributions from such disciplines as sociology, communication, and economics. One of the unique contributions made by the psychologist, however, is the application of rigorous scientific method to consumer research. Psychological methods of inquiry make it possible to replace speculation about consumer behavior with valid and useful information for producers, distributors, and advertisers. Also, because of his knowledge of motivation, perception, decision processes, and learning theory, the psychologist can often interpret the results of a particular study of consumer behavior in a context permitting generalization to other similar consumer problems.

481

SCOPE OF CONSUMER RESEARCH

Consumer studies are often regarded with a high degree of suspicion, particularly when such results are incorporated into an advertising campaign. We have all seen "proof" of product superiority presented as part of a TV commercial or in a full-page magazine spread. This kind of "study" does not fall legitimately within the province of consumer research. It often is loaded, either deliberately or unwittingly, in the direction of supporting a predetermined conclusion indicating superiority of the particular product under consideration. By passing out free samples, it would be a simple matter to arrange for 9 out of 10 women on the campus to own a bottle of EFFLUVIUM perfume. However, an advertising campaign based upon the statement that "90 percent of women in a typical Midwestern college use EFFLUVIUM" would hardly be using the results of a scientifically conducted investigation.

This kind of unethical practice should not be construed as a condemnation either of advertisers or of consumer research. Although many advertising agencies do in fact employ psychologists to study consumer behavior, the objectives of their investigations are to test hypotheses and answer questions. It is perfectly possible to be as objective in making inquiries about consumer behavior as in studying the behavior of any other group of persons. In addition to advertising agencies, sound studies of consumer behavior are sponsored by certain manufacturing companies, publishers, federal departments, and universities. Other organizations not maintaining a consumer-research unit may avail themselves of the services of market research companies or consultants who specialize in this area of investigation.

The legitimate areas of inquiry into consumer behavior are tremendously diverse. The following discussion is intended to be illustrative of activity in this field rather than comprehensive. For convenience, we have grouped consumer studies into three classifications or areas of application: (1) delineating, defining, and describing the market; (2) reaching the market; (3) product design and testing; and (4) consumer motivation.

Delineating the Market

Delineation of the market is of particular interest to manufacturers, distributors, and advertisers as they attempt to forecast the sales potential of a product. Furthermore, the characteristics of the persons within this market will in large measure determine the way in which the product can be most effectively packaged, displayed, advertised, and sold. Thus, research in this area may include studies of consumer needs, preferences, habits, and attitudes, and the influence upon these of such factors as age, education, income level, marital status, and so on.

The Short-Term Market. Information about the relative strength of the market over a relatively brief period of time may be critical to maintaining satisfactory production schedules, arranging distribution facilities, and timing advertising campaigns. This is particularly apparent in the case of certain products, like pleasure boats, having a seasonal appeal.

Other characteristics of the product may lead to relatively high saturation of the market over the short term and consequent resistance to buying. The consumer is not likely to replace durable goods unless the industry succeeds in convincing him that last year's model is out of date, inferior, or unfashionable. This approach to stimulating short-term markets is obviously successful in the case of the automotive, appliance, and apparel industries.

The Long-Term Market. The fact that an excellent market for a product exists at the present time is no assurance that it will persist in the future. Technological advances may completely outmode a product or heighten the demand for it. If there is evidence for the former, the manufacturer must prepare for economic survival by diversification. Otherwise, he will share the fate of the once prosperous buggy-whip manufacturer who refused to adjust to changing modes of transportation.

The possibility of heightened demand over the long-term must similarly be anticipated. A manufacturer who is unable to fill his orders because he underestimated the demand, issues an open invitation to competitors. Persistently increasing consumer demand is dramatically apparent in the case of equipment, gadgets, clothing, and other paraphernalia in the "sports" and "leisure time" classifications. Increased demand for other products like children's clothing and school equipment can be anticipated on the basis of projected population growth.

The Potential Consumer. Although projections about the short- and long-term markets establish the number of potential consumers, they do not clarify the characteristics of these persons. It is important to supplement information about *how many* persons will buy the product with information about *who* will buy the product, if it is to be effectively advertised and promoted.

Virtually all products are limited in appeal to certain groups. The limiting factors may include such variables as age, sex, occupation, geographic location, socioeconomic level, educational background, and marital status, to name just a few. Studies of these limiting factors often assist companies in selecting appropriate advertising media, appeals, and distribution facilities. There is not much point, after all, to attempting to sell lawnmowers to apartment-dwellers or horses to Venetians!

Reaching the Market

Once a manufacturer has ascertained the strength of the market and has learned about its composition, he can take steps appropriate to placing the product before the potential consumers. The two primary areas of investigation relative to this problem include studies of advertising and of distribution channels.

Advertising. The ultimate objectives of advertising are to increase consumer awareness of the product and to impel potential consumers to become actual consumers. The various advertising media are not equally effective for all markets. Thus, comparative studies of the relative effectiveness of advertising media (for example, television versus magazines) and between vehicles within a particular medium (for example, *The New Yorker* versus *Esquire*) may provide valuable clues to the most efficient placement of the advertising dollar.

It is important also to study differences in the relative efficiency of various kinds of advertising copy and appeals. The level of vocabulary utilized and the validity of the appeal for the potential consumer are but two of the vital issues in this regard. One could hardly expect 10-year-old youngsters to be effectively reached by an advertisement for a "prestidigitation kit designed to confound your peers." And an advertisement for an expensive encyclopedia had better not begin, "Boy, oh, boy, Mom, every kid in the neighborhood will want to do his homework at your house when you own this set of books!"

Distribution Channels. The development of appropriate channels for distributing the product must parallel effective advertising. Products with a wide potential market should be made widely available; products with a restricted appeal can best be handled by restricted and carefully selected distribution facilities.

Many of the decisions about channels for distribution can be made without recourse to systematic investigation. However, intuition about appropriate distribution facilities may prove to be misleading either because the product is placed before an inappropriate market or because the market once served by a channel has changed. Not long ago the consumer went to a drugstore to buy pharmaceuticals and to a hardware store to buy small appliances and housewares. Now, however, many drugstores have become extremely efficient channels for distributing not only pharmaceuticals and small electric appliances but a potpourri of other products including such unlikely items as lawn furniture, furnace filters, and potato peelers.

Product Design and Testing

A vigorous company cannot afford to maintain an air of complacency about its sales. A once burgeoning market may become progressively diminished by technological advances and products introduced by competitors. Furthermore, consumer needs and desires and their consequent behavior reflect broad social, economic, and educational changes in society generally. Improved educational levels are associated with altered patterns of taste and increased demand for services; improved economic conditions are associated with increased leisure time and a larger amount of discretionary income for entertainment and leisure activities. Psychologists are uniquely qualified to help in designing products and services that will be attractive to special groups, like the aged.[1]

The manufacturer is understandably concerned about the public's reactions to his product. If the product is a new one, he may find it worthwhile to subject it to a consumer appraisal before it is released for distribution to the public. It may be initially distributed in trial areas only, or submitted to consumer tests either in the laboratory or the field. Product features that are clearly satisfactory or appealing to consumers during these trials may be exploited in the subsequently developed advertising campaign. The discovery of

---

[1] R. Perloff, "Potential Contributions of the Consumer Oriented Psychologist," *Business and Society*, Vol. 4 (1964), pp. 28–34.

unsatisfactory features may indicate a need for modification of the product prior to its release or in extreme cases to its withdrawal from the market.

The utility of product testing is, of course, not limited to new products. Studies of consumer reaction to a well-established product are vital to the maintenance and expansion of the market. A product once regarded by consumers as outstanding may lose ground rapidly in the face of competition. What was good enough 10 years ago, or even last year, may not be good enough for the present market. Consumer's expectations and standards change. It is imperative that the manufacturer be sensitive to these changes.

Consumer Motivation

The matter of sales cannot be reduced simply to considerations of product excellence and appropriateness of advertising media and distribution channels. Human behavior is much more complicated than this. Consumers perceive particular products either as being appropriate or inappropriate to their needs; they purchase need-satisfying products and reject the others.

Studies of the complexities involved in consumer motivation are often subsumed under the heading "motivation research." The intent of such investigation is to discover patterns of underlying consumer needs, both at the conscious and unconscious levels. Such information can provide the manufacturer and advertiser with extremely powerful ammunition for effecting brand changes and reinforcing brand loyalties.

Studies of consumer motivation are not always directed toward the self-interests of particular manufacturers or distributors. There is a growing trend toward research on the consumer as an organism worthy of study in his own right. Such studies focus both on consumer's welfare (for example, improved health and safety)[2] and on developing a better understanding of the factors involved in his economic decisions.[3]

---

[2] R. Perloff, "Consumer Analysis," *Annual Review of Psychology,* Vol. 19 (1968), p. 439.

[3] See, for example, G. Katona, "The Relationship between Psychology and Economics," in S. Koch (ed.), *Psychology: A Study of Science* (New York: McGraw-Hill Book Co., Inc., 1963), Vol. 6, pp. 639–76.

SAMPLING

In consumer research, data are collected from a sample of persons and the findings are generalized to the population from which that sample was drawn. The reason for sampling is efficiency. For example, it usually is infeasible to administer a questionnaire to all consumers or potential consumers (the population). This kind of blanket administration generally proves to be too time-consuming and expensive. Instead, the questionnaire is administered to a sample of consumers. The way in which this sample is drawn is of critical importance because we are not after all interested only in the opinions of the specific group of persons included within the sample. Since the survey findings must be generalized from the sample to the population, the ultimate utility of a survey rests heavily upon the adequacy of its underlying sampling procedures.

Suppose we wished to survey the opinions about fluoridation of the water supply held by eligible voters in a particular midwestern community. The population with which we are concerned (that is, all eligible voters in this community) would be quite large. It would probably be so large, in fact, as to preclude surveying the opinions of everyone in it because of the time and expense involved in such a comprehensive survey.

Rather than solicit expressions of feeling held by all eligible voters, the decision would probably be made to survey the opinions held by a sample of such voters. We would hope to be able to generalize from the opinions held by the population. This intent to generalize from sample results places a very important restriction upon the nature of the sample and hence upon the way in which it is drawn; that is, the persons included within the sample must represent the persons in the population.

The importance of adequate sampling in consumer research is not, of course, restricted to identifying persons to whom to administer questionnaires. It is critical to all of the methods of consumer research discussed subsequently in this chapter.

Furthermore, sampling considerations are not unique to *consumer* research. They are important in any kind of research wherein the investigator wishes to generalize from the data at hand to a more general situation; for example, from a sample of job applicants to

job applicants in general, from a sample of observed job performance to employee job proficiency, or from a sample of achievement
test questions to the respondent's knowledge about the general area
in which he is being tested.

With respect to consumer research, the distinction has been made
between three fundamental techniques for drawing samples: (1)
accidental sampling, (2) random sampling, and (3) stratified sampling.[4] We will discuss each of these procedures in turn and evaluate
the extent to which they provide representative samples.

Accidental Sampling

This is a relatively simple and inexpensive method for obtaining
survey respondents. Once the universe has been defined (for example, eligible voters in a midwestern city) and the questions about
the critical issue (for example, fluoridation) have been phrased, the
interviewers are turned loose with instructions to question 5, 25, or
100 persons from within the universe. Since specific interviewees are
not designated, the interviewer uses his own discretion in selecting
respondents. The structure of the sample of persons surveyed is
beyond the control of the survey director.

It is obvious that accidental sampling provides none of the safe-
guards required to insure representativeness of the sample. Attempts
to generalize from the responses of interviewees to opinions of the
population are thus on very tenuous ground. The sole value of
discussing this procedure is to hold it up to scrutiny as a horrible
example of some of the kinds of errors that may creep into a sample
and destroy its value for consumer research.

Since the interviewer is not told specifically whom he is to interview, he interviews persons who are readily accessible and with
whom he can establish rapport rather easily. This means in effect
that the respondents included within an accidental sample are very
much like the interviewers in such personal characteristics as age,
sex, and socioeconomic level. If the fluoridation survey were conducted by college student interviewers, the results would probably
reflect the opinions of a special group of eligible voters; that is,
persons who are rather young, reasonably well-educated, and above

---

[4] F. Stanton, "Problems of Sampling in Market Research," *Journal of Consulting
Psychology*, Vol. 5 (1941), pp. 154–63.

average in financial means. The sample would probably not include a sufficient representation of persons from socially underprivileged or minority subgroups, of low educational attainment, and earning meager incomes.

Thus, the primary source of bias in the accidentally drawn sample is introduced by the interviewers. They tend to "load" the sample with persons who are like themselves. It might be possible, of course, to compensate for this deficiency of accidental sampling by selecting *interviewers* with extreme care. If the interviewers are themselves representative of the universe, the persons they choose to interview will probably constitute a sample generating more valid findings than if the interviewers are not so selected. There are, however, better and easier methods for obtaining representative samples.

Random Sampling

The selection of respondents by some random procedure overcomes the biases introduced into the sample by the interviewers. The fundamental prerequisite for random sampling is that every member of the population must have an equal opportunity to be included within the sample. Determination of the particular persons selected for inclusion within the sample is made in a totally unbiased fashion.

Random sampling begins with a complete listing of every member of the population. This list must not be arranged or ordered according to such potentially biasing classifications as income level, job status, educational level, or area of residence. The sample is randomly drawn from this complete list by selecting every 10th, 20th, or 50th name, depending upon how many persons are desired.

The rationale behind random sampling is a sound one. If the universe is completely listed without biasing subclassifications, if every person randomly selected for inclusion in the sample is actually surveyed, and if a large enough number of names is drawn, the sample should be representative of the total population listed. These three "ifs" are important ones. Failure to comply with any one of these requirements will introduce bias into the sample. Satisfaction of these requirements is not, however, always a simple matter.

Consider the requirement of availability of a complete and unclassified listing of the persons in the population. Some populations are unlisted. To use a somewhat far-fetched example, how would one go about obtaining a complete list of producers of "home brew" even for survey purposes? Or, to be more realistic, how could a comprehensive list of all persons owning a piano be compiled in advance of conducting a survey?

The second requirement for representativeness of the random sample is that every person selected for inclusion in the sample actually be surveyed. If the survey is conducted by interviewers who canvass during weekdays, they will undoubtedly find that they have much better luck contacting the women than the men assigned for interview. Furthermore, the interviewers will find that it is relatively impossible even to contact some of the women during the day. Some may be away from home because they have jobs, others may be out playing bridge, and a few may be on an extended vacation in the Caribbean. The women who are at home and are willing to answer the interviewer's questions probably represent quite a different social and economic segment of the female population than those who either are away from home or are unwilling to cooperate with the surveyor.

The third prerequisite of adequate sampling (random or otherwise) is sufficient sample size. The size of the sample and its representativeness determine the accuracy with which results obtained from the sample can be generalized to the population. These two factors, size and representativeness, are independent of each other. It is perfectly possible to have a large but unrepresentative sample. It is also possible to draw a representative sample that is, however, too small to permit accurate generalizations to the universe.

There is no simple answer to the question, "How big must the sample be before it is sufficiently large?" Both statistical and economic considerations are involved in the determination of optimal sample size. Although generalizations based upon large representative samples are less subject to statistical error than those based upon small representative samples, the relationship between sample size and statistical error is not an arithmetic one. Improvements in accuracy obtained by increasing the size of the sample reach a point of diminishing returns. Thus, the increased accuracy gained by surveying a larger sample must be weighed against the additional expense entailed by virtue of the increase. Rather accurate nationwide political polls are conducted with 7,500 respondents or less!

Stratified Sampling

We anticipate that a sample drawn by random procedures will be representative because of the lack of systematic bias in identifying the persons to be surveyed. The representativeness of randomly drawn samples is left to "chance." Stratified sampling procedures, however, insure the representativeness of the sample, at least with respect to the characteristics regarded as salient to the investigation. The stratified sample is deliberately structured as a miniature representation of the population with respect to these characteristics.

The population can be stratified, or divided into subgroups, on the basis of such characteristics as geographic distribution, sex, age, educational background, economic level, religion, and so on. Although it is not necessary to stratify the population on all conceivable variables, it is of the utmost importance to stratify on those variables that may be presumed to bear upon the attitudes and opinions under investigation. Population data for many of these variables are available from the U.S. Census Bureau.

Once the significant variables for stratification have been identified, the percentage of the total population within each stratum is determined. These population percentages are used to set sample quotas for each of the strata. The percentages of respondents by sex, age, socioeconomic level, and other salient variables included within the sample duplicates the population percentages.

Stratified sampling must ultimately be combined either with random or accidental procedures. To illustrate, suppose we have stratified a university population on just two variables: sex and fraternity or sorority affiliation. We will assume that 60 percent of the population is male and 40 percent is female; 30 percent belong to a fraternity or sorority and 70 percent is independent. Assuming that each interviewer is assigned to obtain data from 20 students, he must be instructed to select his interviewees so that 12 are men and 8 are women; 6 are fraternity or sorority members and 14 are independents. If, as is often done, the interviewer is permitted to choose his own subjects with the sole restriction that his subsample conform to these stratification requirements, he engages in a kind of accidental sampling. Adherence to the stratification requirements assures representativeness of the sample on the two characteristics under consideration in spite of the fact that the interviewer ultimately determines which persons to survey.

When stratified and accidental sampling procedures are combined in this fashion, there is the danger that bias will be introduced into the sample because of critical variables not anticipated in the original stratification. This danger may be considerably reduced by combining stratified with random sampling techniques. Let us again consider the hypothetical survey of university students stratified on two dimensions. After the population characteristics for each stratum have been determined, the interviewers can be directed to survey specific persons randomly selected from alphabetical lists of male fraternity members, male independents, female sorority members, and female independents. The characteristics of the sample thus constituted would be deliberately controlled on the two variables known to be critical, and free from interviewer bias on other variables that may or may not be critical.

AN OVERVIEW OF METHODS

Consumer research entails special applications of the general methods of psychological investigation described in Chapter 2: naturalistic, experimental, and clinical observation. Likewise, the techniques for obtaining data about consumer behavior involve elaborations of such procedures discussed earlier as interviewing, rating, attitude scaling, and testing.

The remainder of this chapter is devoted to a discussion of three basic approaches to consumer research: opinion and attitude surveys, depth procedures, and behavioral studies. It will be helpful to consider the general characteristics and purposes of each in advance of the more detailed presentation.

Consumer Surveys

A questionnaire or interview survey is conducted for the purpose of ascertaining consumer opinions and attitudes. It often is desirable to find out how consumers feel about the product, the way in which it is advertised, distributed, and serviced, and the company that manufactures it. Survey findings may indicate, for example, that the product is perceived as one of shoddy construction and poor durability; that the service organization is viewed as unequal to the task of repairing the product and obtaining necessary replacement parts speedily and cheerfully; or that there is considerable consumer resistance to purchasing a product made by a company with a widely publicized history of unsatisfactory labor practices. The identification of such unfavorable attitudes can contribute importantly both to understanding and predicting buying behavior.

Depth Procedures

Survey methods sometimes are criticized on the ground that they treat verbalized attitudes and opinions at face value. This argument against the validity of survey findings stems from a distinction between "verbalized" feelings and "real" or underlying feelings. Depth procedures, including projective techniques and probing interviews, are presumed to reveal the more basic and often unconscious values and feelings responsible for consumer behavior.

Behavioral Studies

Opinion surveys and depth studies are alike in that both are concerned with intermediate variables, that is, opinions, attitudes, drives, motives, and so on. The results from such studies contribute to our understanding of consumer behavior and to a certain extent permit us to make some predictions about the behavior. However, since the behavior itself is the ultimate criterion for consumer psychology, studies of what consumers actually *do* and of the choices and decisions they actually make often provide more useful information than do analyses of the intervening variables as provided by survey and depth procedures.

SURVEYING CONSUMER OPINION

One of the assumptions underlying survey procedures is that consumers can verbalize at least some of their attitudes and opinions. Thus, if we wish to discover these feelings, we need only ask respondents to reply to questions contained in some kind of opinionnaire.

The purposes and techniques of consumer surveys are essentially similar to those of political polls. The basic difference between them is that in the former we are generally interested in opinions about products or competing brands, while in the latter we are interested in opinions about political parties or competing candidates.

Assuming that arrangements have been made for obtaining survey responses from a sufficiently large and representative sample, there are yet two factors that may exert a considerable influence upon the survey findings: the structure of the questionnaire (including the way in which questions are phrased and the format) and the method by which it is distributed and administered.

Phrasing the Question

A questionnaire is a sort of self-descriptive inventory. The respondent may be asked to reveal his past behavior ("What brand of bread did you buy most recently?"), his intentions regarding future behavior ("Do you expect to buy a new car this year?"), and his feelings or opinions about something ("Do you prefer to write with a ball-point pen or one that uses ink?"). The phraseology of the questions must meet some of the requirements established for adequate test items: they must be unambiguous, appropriate to the overall purpose of the questionnaire, and free from internal cues that may influence the nature of the reply. The four major bugaboos of effective survey-question writing are (1) ambiguous, (2) non-specific, (3) leading, and (4) restrictive phraseology.

An *ambiguous* question is interpreted differently by various respondents, hence precluding the combination of replies for summary purposes. Ambiguities may be introduced into a question by using words that vary in meaning (like "usually" and "sometimes"), or that have essentially no meaning for the respondent either because they are overly technical or require an unduly high vocabulary level.

Questions that lack sufficient *specificity* are unnecessarily difficult and do not yield useful information. There is no point, for example, to asking a housewife how many hours she spent washing dishes during the past year. It should be possible, instead, to select a representative and more limited time interval current in the respondent's memory. Housewives can probably estimate dishwashing time with a fair degree of accuracy for an interval like "last week" or "yesterday."

The "why" question tends also to be nonspecific and therefore less than maximally productive, even though it often is used. Since a variety of factors, both conscious and unconscious, generally underlie consumer decisions it is doubtful that a respondent could give all

of his reasons for doing something even if he wanted to be cooperative. Furthermore, the reasons cited in response to a "why" question
often lack comparability. One respondent may fixate upon considerations of economy, another upon style, another upon durability, and
so on. In truth, most respondents may have based their decisions
upon all of these factors but may mention only one or two in a
survey in order to get it over with as quickly as possible.

The *leading question* is the most insidious defect in consumer
opinionnaires. Its phraseology distorts the response by cueing the
reply desired by the interviewer, indicating the answer given by the
majority of respondents, or by being emotionally loaded. Few people
indeed could be expected to reply truthfully to leading questions
like the following:

"You are interested in reading good literature, aren't you?"

"We have found that people tend to spend less and less time
watching TV and more time reading. How much time did you
devote to TV viewing yesterday?"

"Do you prefer to buy clothes in the 'shocking' colors and patterns, or do you tend to restrict your clothing purchases to the more
refined colors and patterns?"

Restrictive wording prevents the respondent from considering all
of the possible alternatives. How can the person who intends to buy
a cartridge pen cope with the question, "On your next purchase will
you buy a ball-point pen or a filler pen?" If the questionnaire is
administered by interview, the respondent may protest the inadequacy of a restrictive question. If it is included in a mail survey, the
respondent may be tempted either to omit the question or, in disgust,
to file the entire questionnaire in the trash can.

From the preceding discussion, it should be apparent that there
are elements of both art and skill involved in writing questions for a
consumer survey. One cannot merely write a series of adequate items
"off the top of his head." The preliminary versions of the questions
must undergo a process of continual refinement based upon pretests
and revisions before the questionnaire is structured in its final form.

Format

The organization, arrangement, and mode of presentation of
survey questions have been found to exert some influence upon the
nature of the elicited responses. The order in which questions are

asked may be such that a particular question "sets up" the reply to the next one. You would probably be inclined, for example, to respond more favorably to a question concerning your feelings about the present administrative restrictions upon student behavior if it were preceded by a question suggesting the possibility that such restrictions might be tightened.

A highly structured format providing multiple-choice alternatives for each question may be quite satisfactory for some purposes and misleading for others. If a detergent manufacturer distributes free samples of *Sudsy* to housewives and then asks them to complete an anonymous questionnaire, he might inquire:

How does *Sudsy* compare with the detergent you habitually use?
 a) I haven't tried *Sudsy*.
 b) It is superior to my usual brand.
 c) It is about as good as my usual brand.
 d) It is inferior to my usual brand.

It may appear that all possible opinions are encompassed in the alternatives provided for this question. These alternatives will prove inadequate, however, for a housewife who feels that *Sudsy* is superior for use in her washing machine but not for hand-washable fabrics, or for one who has found that she must use more *Sudsy* to obtain results as good as those obtained with her usual brand.

Some attention has been given to the matter of verbal as opposed to pictorial presentations of questions. A comparison between questionnaires concerning consumer preferences in stove design revealed that the indicated preferences varied with the way in which the questions were presented. The verbal questionnaire consisted of nine items like: "Do you prefer a hinged door or a drawer type storage area?" The pictorial version required the identical discriminations except that the alternatives were presented as drawings rather than verbally. The discrepant results obtained when these two forms of the questionnaire were administered to equated groups of housewives indicated that the two formats under consideration actually yielded statistically different distributions of preference for eight of the nine items. Although the investigation did not demonstrate which of the two versions was more valid for the purpose of actually predicting stove-buying behavior, it provides a convincing demonstration of the potential effects of questionnaire format upon survey responses.[5]

Administering the Questionnaire

Once the questionnaire has been structured in its final form, it may be administered to a sample of consumers in one of three ways: by mail, telephone interview, or personal interview.

Mail Surveys. The primary advantages of mail surveys are simplicity and economy of administration. Using a mailed questionnaire, it is possible economically to survey the opinions of persons in widely separated geographical locations. In addition, the mail survey eliminates one of the potential sources of bias inherent in the other two methods, that is, the interviewer himself.

In spite of these advantages, most mail surveys are inadequate because of the large proportion of persons in the original mailing who fail to return completed questionnaires. Serious errors can be introduced into the study when generalizations are made from the opinions of the persons who *did* reply to the opinions of those who *did not* reply, and thence to the larger population from which the original sample was drawn. There is evidence that respondents to mail questionnaires are higher both in interest in the topic under consideration and in educational level than are nonrespondents.[6]

In addition to these differences between persons who return and fail to return a mail survey, the number of omitted items on those questionnaires that *are* returned is found to increase with the complexity of the questionnaire and to vary with the type of question and the respondent's age, sex, and occupation.[7] Furthermore, there is some evidence for the conclusion that persons who willingly cooperate with a survey tend to have less traditional or conventional value orientations than do noncooperative persons.[8]

Thus, it is unsafe to generalize from mail surveys unless the

---

[5] J. Weitz, "Verbal and Pictorial Questionnaires in Market Research," *Journal of Applied Psychology*, Vol. 34 (1950), pp. 363–66.

[6] R. Franzen and P. L. Lazarsfeld, "Mail Questionnaire as a Research Problem," *Journal of Psychology*, Vol. 20 (1945), pp. 293–310.

[7] R. Ferber, "Item Nonresponse in a Consumer Survey," *Public Opinion Quarterly*, Vol. 30 (1966), pp. 399–415.

[8] L. G. Burchinal, "Personality Characteristics and Sample Bias," *Journal of Applied Psychology*, Vol. 44 (1960), pp. 172–74.

proportion of returns is very high. There are many ways in which to encourage mail questionnaire returns including monetary inducements, simplification of format, preliminary contacts, and skillful follow-ups with persons in the sample.[9] By combining several of these procedures, one investigator reported a rate of completion across 14 surveys (almost 3,000 respondents) of about 74 percent.[10] This is an unusually high rate of return, and still one wonders about the characteristics of the 26 percent who were nonrespondents and the possible sampling biases thus incurred.

Telephone Interviews

Surveys conducted by telephone rarely need be contaminated by nonrespondents. Perseverance in placing telephone calls to persons in the original sample will usually be rewarded by establishing contacts with almost everyone selected for the survey. Other attractive features of telephone surveys in comparison with direct interviewing include the elimination of travel and the reduction of interview costs.[11]

However, there is a rather obvious source of bias in telephone surveys. The sample thus contacted does not include an adequate representation of segments of the population which for economic or other reasons either do not have telephones or who have unlisted telephones. Furthermore, telephone interviewing is unsuitable for lengthy or complex interviews, or for survey problems (like evaluation of advertising copy) requiring subjects to make judgments about materials actually presented to them.[12]

Personal Interviews

Because of the sampling deficiencies already noted as inherent in mail and telephone surveys, the well-conducted personal interview survey tends to produce the most valid findings under most circumstances. However, it must be remembered that the mere fact that personal interviews have been conducted for survey purposes assures

[9] Perloff, *op. cit.* (1968), p. 451.

[10] E. G. Francel, "Mail-Administered Questionnaires: A Success Story," *Journal of Marketing Research*, Vol. 3 (1966), pp. 89–92.

[11] S. Sudman, "New Uses of Telephone Methods in Survey Research," *Journal of Marketing Research*, Vol. 1 (1966), pp. 163–67.

[12] I. C. Kildegaard, "Rejoinder," *Journal of Advertising Research*, Vol. 5 (1965), pp. 40–41.

neither representativeness of the sample interviewed nor freedom of the replies from bias. For such a survey to succeed, the interviewers must be carefully trained in the techniques of interviewing and in the requirements of representative sampling.

DEPTH PROCEDURES

The primary value of survey procedures is the accumulation of "head counting" data and expressions of superficial attitudes and feelings. Survey findings tell us *who* bought a product or intends to buy a product. Such data help clarify the present and anticipated market. Depth procedures, on the other hand, are oriented more toward the *why* of consumer behavior. Hence, the application of depth procedures to consumer studies is sometimes referred to as "motivation research."

Motivation research seeks to probe beneath the surface of consumer attitudes and to reveal the underlying values, images, and unconscious or "hidden" feelings influencing consumer behavior. In essence, the approach of the motivation researcher has much in common with that of the clinical psychologist. His tools frequently are similar to those used for clinical diagnosis; they include depth interviews, projective techniques of various kinds, and personality inventories. The fundamental difference between the application of these tools in clinical and consumer psychology is in the intent or objective of the study. The clinical psychologist is patient oriented; his sole concern is with the patient's welfare. The motivation researcher may be similarly consumer oriented, but the producer or advertising agency paying for the research has just one fundamental objective: that is, selling more goods to more people. The consumer psychologist is also consumer oriented and seeks to provide a communication link between the makers and users of goods.[13] However, the producer or advertising agency may in its effort to sell more goods to more people emphasize the "hidden persuader" components of motivation research.

Some Illustrative Studies

The difference between results obtained from surveys and depth procedures is illustrated by a report of the reasons for reading *Time*

[13] D. W. Twedt, "Consumer Psychology," *Annual Review of Psychology.* Vol. 16 (1965), p. 287.

magazine. Questionnaire responses indicated that *Time* was read for reasons like "It condenses the news for me" or "It is written in brilliant style." When the matter was investigated in greater depth, however, *Time* was found to provide its readers with certain "ego benefits." It conveyed to its readers the feeling that they were busy executives who needed to be well informed. As one reader said in the course of depth study, "When I read *Time* I like myself."[14]

Another illustration of the power of motivation research to reveal hidden and sometimes highly significant factors affecting consumer behavior is apparent in an ingenious study of attitudes toward instant coffee. Instant coffee was available in the stores for a long time before it was accepted by housewives. Women generally indicated on a questionnaire that they did not like its flavor. The investigator decided to use a projective device in order to discover whether some more basic factor might be responsible for unfavorable attitudes toward instant coffee. He devised two shopping lists, identical in all respects except for the fifth item:

List A	*List B*
1½ lb. hamburger	1½ lb. hamburger
2 loaves Wonder bread	2 loaves Wonder bread
Bunch of carrots	Bunch of carrots
1 can Rumford's baking powder	1 can Rumford's baking powder
Nescafe instant coffee	Maxwell House coffee, drip grind
2 cans Del Monte peaches	2 cans Del Monte peaches
5 lb. potatoes	5 lb. potatoes

Samples of housewives were asked to characterize the women who would go to the store with one or the other of these shopping lists. Almost half of the respondents to the list containing *Nescafe* characterized the shopper as lazy and a poor planner, 12 percent indicated that she was a spendthrift, and 16 percent said she was a poor wife. The responses to the *Maxwell House* list were quite different: only 16 percent mentioned laziness or bad planning and none characterized the shopper as a spendthrift or poor wife.[15]

Methods

The two basic methods of motivation research are: depth interviews and projective techniques. These methods have been advo-

---

[14] E. Dichter, "Psychology in Market Research," *Harvard Business Review,* Vol. 25 (1947), pp. 432–43.

[15] M. Haire, "Projective Techniques in Market Research," *Journal of Marketing,* Vol. 14 (1950), p. 649.

cated when (*a*) the information being sought is not available at the conscious or rational level and (*b*) the respondent may consciously or unconsciously block his reply to a survey question.[16]

Depth Interviews. When this form of interview is applied in consumer research, it is designed to elicit the respondent's underlying feelings about products, services, companies, and so on. The interviewer's main role is to establish rapport and provide very general initial guidance; the respondent is encouraged to express himself freely, often with the aid of projective techniques like those described below.

The success of the procedure depends heavily upon the clinical skill of the interviewer and his knowledge of personality dynamics. Although a detailed consideration of these matters is beyond the scope of this book, the comments made earlier (in Chapter 5) about unstructured interviews apply also to depth interviews.

Projective Techniques. The "shopping list" study described earlier illustrates the application of a projective technique. You will recall from Chapter 7 that such procedures are presumed to encourage respondents to project their own thoughts, wishes, desires, fears, and so on upon deliberately vague or ambiguous stimuli like those presented in the Rorschach and Thematic Apperception Tests.

Word association is another such procedure. Here, the respondent typically is asked to reply to a series of stimulus words with the first word or phrase that comes to his mind. The list of stimulus words contains "critical stimuli" (that is, words related to the issue under investigation) embedded in a context of other, noncritical stimulus words. Thus, in a study of advertising copy the researcher may solicit associations to key words taken from possible advertisements (such as *powerful, strong, heavy-duty*) , selecting for the final copy those words which generate the most positive associations.

Yet another form of projective testing involves *sentence completion.* Here the respondent is presented with a series of incomplete sentences related to the problem under consideration and is instructed to complete each sentence. For example: "The thing I like about my present car is _____;" "Wearing a safety belt makes me feel _____;" and so on. As with all projective techniques, the underlying assumption is that a clinical examination of the pat-

---

[16] E. Dichter, "Toward an Understanding of Human Behavior," in R. Ferber and H. G. Wales, *Motivation and Market Behavior* (Homewood, Ill.: Richard D. Irwin, Inc., 1958) .

tern of replies reveals more about the respondent's underlying motives than do his answers to more traditional survey questions.

Evaluation of Motivation Research

There is obvious merit to considering motivation when seeking to
explain behavior. Furthermore, there is ample evidence for the fact
that much human motivation is unconscious. The utilization of
depth procedures for discovering such hidden determinants of consumer behavior, and the subsequent application of these findings to
advertising and selling does, however, raise two important questions.
One of these concerns the validity of the findings uncovered by the
motivation researcher; the other concerns the ethics of motivation
research.

Validity.   Since the procedures employed in motivation research
are somewhat similar to those used for clinical purposes, they are
open to the same criticisms relative to validity. An essential difference between the application of depth procedures in consumer and
clinical studies, however, is that the former usually involves a relatively brief time span (for example, a two-hour "depth" interview
or the administration of a single projective instrument) while clinical diagnoses are based upon long-term studies and administration
of batteries of instruments.

The effect of misusing instruments that are less than maximally
valid to begin with may on occasion lead to distorted or misleading
findings. This point is effectively made in an article intriguingly
subtitled *Is the Prune a Witch?*[17] The author refers in it to a study,
made by Dichter, for the California Prune Advisory Board. This
study reported that prunes are symbols of old age, a scapegoat food,
and that the prune is a witch. In order to sell more prunes, Dichter
advised advertisers to make the pitch that prunes are the black
diamonds of the fruit family. Furthermore, he suggested that women
be reassured that it is perfectly acceptable to serve prunes, and that
they ought not be ashamed because prunes have a cathartic effect.
We must agree that there is much about unconscious motivation
that is as yet unknown. However, it would seem that characterizing
the prune as a witch is carrying things just a bit too far. We cannot

---

[17] A. Graham, "Adman's Nightmare: Is the Prune a Witch?" *Reporter,* Vol. 12
(1953, pp. 27–31. Reported in M. L. Blum, *Industrial Psychology and Its Social
Foundations* (New York: Harper & Bros., 1956), p. 519.

dispute the advertiser's right to combat this witch, if he so chooses; he has paid for it! He should, however, exercise a certain amount of judgment in differentiating between witches or windmills and proper targets for combat.

Ethics. It sometimes is argued that motivation research invades the privacy of our thoughts and leads to insidious marketing and advertising practices against which the consumer has no real defense. On the other side of the coin, the suggestion has been made that motivation research applied to consumer behavior may be merely another manifestation of the "genius of our economy." Industrial survival depends upon giving the people what they want, and motivation research may sometimes be necessary to enable industry to discover these wants.[18]

The ethical controversy over motivation research inevitably involves a certain amount of moral judgment. Investigators in this area point out that their subjects are not coerced into cooperating with them, that consumers are not compelled to make a purchase or succumb to an advertising appeal, and that competitive manufacturers are using the methodology of motivation research anyway. The first of these arguments makes sense, but the second begs the question because it is precisely the matter of susceptibility to advertising appeals to unconscious needs that is in question. Ethical justification for motivation research on the ground that competitors are using it is, of course, specious.

Assuming the validity of the information uncovered by depth studies of consumer motivation, what is the investigator's responsibilities both to the consumer and to the manufacturer or advertiser? Consumer psychologists are ethically bound to use their knowledge of human behavior in a socially responsible manner. This means in effect that the proper application of depth studies should benefit both consumer and manufacturer by helping to assure that (*a*) consumers have available the products and services they need, and (*b*) manufacturers are distributing products that are marketable.

BEHAVIORAL STUDIES

We might anticipate a high degree of relationship between what consumers *say* they will do and what they *actually* do. However,

---

[18] A. W. Rose, "Motivation Research and Subliminal Advertising," *Social Research,* Vol. 25 (1958), pp. 271–84.

there is conflicting evidence regarding this relationship. In one instance, a relatively high level of agreement was found between consumers' reports of the brands of certain products last purchased and sales-slip records of the brands actually purchased.[19] There are many other studies, however, that do not support such a relationship. Behavior and verbal expressions were compared for women who had a choice of two rooms in which to wait before a lecture. One was decorated in functional modern; the other in ornate traditional. Although the room furnished in modern decor filled first, 84 percent of the women chose the traditional room in response to the question, "Which room do you like better?"[20]

This type of discrepancy between verbalized preferences and actual behavior points up the fact that people do not always do what they say they will do, and do not always feel the way they say they feel. Some of this discrepancy is undoubtedly deliberate; much of it is not. In either case, the surest way to gage consumer behavior is to make controlled observations of the behavior itself. Three kinds of criteria have been employed in behavioral studies: records of actual purchases; expressed preferences for, and identification of, competing brands; psychophysiological indicators.

Consumer Purchases

Field studies of consumer purchases would seem to provide an acid test of the acceptability of a product. However, such studies rarely are productive from a research standpoint. Too many uncontrolled factors may influence the behavior of potential purchasers as they go into a store or market. The sales record may reflect the combined influence of such diverse and relatively inseparable factors as amount and type of advertising, pressures exerted by salesmen and clerks, the relative amount of display space allotted to the product, bonuses or premium stamps offered for the purchase of particular products, and the relative size and attractiveness of the package in which the product is presented.

Even if the effects of such factors could be separated, it is doubtful

---

[19] J. G. Jenkins and H. H. Corbin, Jr., "Dependability of Psychological Brand Barometers, II: The Problem of Validity," *Journal of Applied Psychology*, Vol. 22 (1938), pp. 252–60.

[20] V. Packard, *The Hidden Persuaders* (New York: David McKay Co., Inc., 1957), p. 15.

that the kind of sales records maintained by many stores can serve as adequate criteria for consumer research. Difficulty in this regard was experienced in an aborted attempt (later completed) to validate consumers' verbalized brand preferences against actual buying behavior in a particular store. In the authors' words:

> The bookkeeping system of this particular store exhibited a curious lack of objectivity. An entry reading simply "corn flakes," we were told, always meant X-Brand Corn Flakes. This notation was followed, we found, except in the case of certain regular customers, for whom it meant the brand habitually purchased, which might be A-, B-, or Z-Brand. The clerks expressed surprise, indeed, that anyone should question the comprehensibility of such a system.[21]

We will consider one relatively simple study in some detail in order to indicate the kinds of controls that must be exerted when actual buying behavior is under investigation. The purpose of this study was to determine the effect of shelf display width upon the sales of soap in a self-service market.[22]

Two soap products (A and B) were selected, and the shelf arrangements of these products were varied in three ways: three facings of A and one facing of B; two facings of A and two facings of B; one facing of A and three facings of B. The display situations were changed in each store after a total of 10 boxes of both products had been sold.

The following factors had to be controlled in this study:

1. Location of the stores. (Three stores were selected on the basis of the prevailing socioeconomic level of the residents of the area.)
2. Packaging. (Both products A and B were packaged in identically sized boxes, primarily blue in color.)
3. Pricing. (The selling price was identical for both products.)
4. Product classification. (Both products were classified as "all-purpose" detergents.)
5. Promotion. (Neither product was tied in with a sales promotion gimmick at the time of the study.)
6. Location of the displays. (The two products were located side by side toward the middle of the soap section.)

---

[21] Jenkins and Corbin, *op. cit.*, 1938, p. 254.

[22] D. H. Harris, "The Effect of Display Width in Merchandising Soap," *Journal of Applied Psychology*, Vol. 42 (1958), pp. 283–84.

7. Starting time for the study. (Wednesday afternoon for all three stores.)

The results of this study indicated that increases in the relative display width of these products did not increase their sales. This is an interesting finding because it contraindicates the usual practice of increasing shelf display width to "move" slow selling merchandise. The investigator suggests that the value of this procedure for stimulating sales may be limited to infrequently advertised products. In such instances, there is no established feeling of brand loyalty to deter impulse buying.

Brand Identification and Preferences

Studies of consumer behavior are considerably simplified when the criterion is accuracy of brand identification or expressed preferences for particular brands rather than actual purchases. Criterion data of the former type can be accumulated with a greater degree of accuracy than usually is permitted by sales slips and inventory records.

The results of this kind of study most often indicate that consumers experience considerable difficulty in correctly identifying brands and in expressing consistent preferences for one brand over another. A series of studies with cola drinks, for example, demonstrated that (1) respondents could not distinguish between the best-known brands of these beverages solely on the basis of taste; and (2) cola beverages, regardless of brand, were always identified as either Coca-Cola, Pepsi-Cola, or Royal Crown Cola.[23] Similarly negative findings have been reported for perfumes, cigarettes, and other products. In contrast, studies with some products, like beer,[24] have indicated that taste and smell panels can indeed express consistent preferences for particular brands.

When consistent preferences are expressed for certain brands by a consumer jury, one may have reason to wonder about the bases upon which such discriminations are made. A certain amount of accumu-

---

[23] N. H. Pronko and J. W. Bowles, Jr., "Identification of Cola Beverages, I," *Journal of Applied Psychology*, Vol. 32 (1948), pp. 304–12; N. H. Pronko and J. W. Bowles, Jr., "Identification of Cola Beverages, II," *Journal of Applied Psychology*, Vol. 32 (1948), pp. 559–64; and N. H. Pronko and J. H. Bowles, Jr., "Identification of Cola Beverages, III," *Journal of Applied Psychology*, Vol. 33 (1949), pp. 605–8.

[24] E. A. Fleishman, "An Experimental Consumer Panel Technique," *Journal of Applied Psychology*, Vol. 35 (1951), pp. 133–35.

lated evidence seems to indicate that these discriminations are sometimes based upon rather irrelevant considerations. We can assume, for example, that given a choice, consumers would select fresh bread over stale bread. But when loaves of equally fresh bread were wrapped differently for experimental purposes, panels of judges claimed to perceive differences in freshness. Cellophane-wrapped bread felt fresher than bread encased in a wax wrapper.[25]

Psychophysiological Indicators

It has long been known that emotional arousal evokes such largely involuntary effects of the autonomic nervous system and circulatory system as changes in blood pressure, blood volume, heart rate, and galvanic skin response. In fact, the "lie detector" is simply a device for making simultaneous recordings of several of these psychophysiological indices.

Attempts to use these measures as criteria of emotional arousal in consumer research on advertising and packaging have generally been unsuccessful. There are two major reasons for this: First, such indicators are also sensitive to bodily conditions other than emotional arousal. Second, these indicators fail to reveal anything about the quality of the arousal; that is, whether the emotion is pleasant or unpleasant, favorable or unfavorable.

Recently, another psychophysiological measure, pupil dilation, has shown promise as an indicator of the interest value of visual stimuli. Whereas small increases in dilation have been noted for interesting content, pupillary contraction is associated with content that lacks the power to interest or arouse the viewer.[26] The superiority of this measure over verbalized opinions for assessing the emotional appeal of advertisements, packages, and products is self-evident provided it can be reliably made and interpreted, is beyond the deliberate control of the respondents, and predicts relevant consumer behavior. Although studies to date offer tentative support for the reliability of the technique[27] considerably more research is needed on all three of these issues.

[25] R. L. Brown, "Wrapper Influence on the Perception of Freshness in Bread," *Journal of Applied Psychology,* Vol. 42 (1958), pp. 257–60.

[26] E. H. Hess and J. M. Polt, "Pupil Size as Related to Interest Value of Visual Stimuli," *Science,* Vol. 132 (1960), pp. 349–50.

[27] H. E. Krugman, "Some Applications of Pupil Measurement," *Journal of Marketing Research,* Vol. 1 (1964), pp. 15–19.

SUMMARY

All parties to the manufacture, distribution, and sale of products have a vital interest in understanding, predicting, and controlling consumer behavior. One of the unique contributions of the psychologist in this general area in his application of rigorous scientific methods of inquiry. The scope of consumer research utilizing psychological methodology is exceedingly broad. It may include studies of the size and constituency of markets, the effectiveness of advertising campaigns and distribution facilities, consumer reactions to the product and the company that manufactures it, and the needs and motives underlying consumer behavior. Data for such studies are obtained by (1) surveying consumer opinions, (2) applying depth procedures, and (3) observing consumer behavior.

One of the assumptions underlying *survey* procedures is that people can verbalize many of their attitudes and opinions on a questionnaire. In the interest of economy and ease of administration, the survey is generally conducted with a sample of respondents rather than with the entire population or universe. However, since the survey findings must ultimately be generalized to the larger population, the method whereby the sample is drawn is of considerable importance. The sample must be large enough to insure a high level of statistical accuracy and sufficiently representative of the strata or subgroups within the population to permit for such generalizations. The specific sampling procedures discussed in this chapter include accidental, random, and stratified sampling.

Adequate sampling is, however, no guarantee of the validity of survey findings. Survey responses may be affected by the wording of specific questions, the format of the questionnaire, and the way in which it is administered. It is imperative that the entire questionnaire be structured to insure clarity of the questions and freedom from potential sources of internal bias (like cues to "desired" replies, or restriction of the range of possible responses). In addition, the survey must be administered in a way calculated to insure maximal cooperation from all respondents in the sample.

Depth procedures, including probing interviews and projective techniques, are sometimes used to study the underlying values, images, and unconscious feelings affecting consumer behavior. The conduct of such studies and the subsequent application of the findings from "motivation research" raises both technical and ethical issues. The misuse of clinical instruments by some motivation researchers may produce findings of dubious validity. Even when validity of studies of the drives underlying consumer behavior can be assumed, the ethics of the approach are open to question. The psychologist participating in such studies must, of course, heed his paramount responsibility to the welfare of society rather than to particular vested interest groups.

Behavioral studies often involve an analysis of actual sales records. Although buying behavior may be regarded as the ultimate criterion in consumer research, it must be recognized that sales records sometimes are inaccurately kept and reflect the combined influence of a variety of uncontrolled factors. In order to circumvent these difficulties, many behavioral studies forego analysis of sales records in favor of controlled investigations of such criteria as accuracy of brand identification and expressed brand preferences. Recently, attention has been given also to pupil dilation as a potentially useful psychophysiological indicator of the interest value of visual stimuli.

20. Advertising and Selling

In terms of the end result sought, advertising and selling have an identical objective. Both aim to persuade potential consumers to purchase products or avail themselves of services. The fundamental difference between advertising and selling inheres in the personal component of the latter. The salesman does not make a blanket appeal to a mass audience. Instead, he seeks to discover the individual buyer's needs and emphasizes product features appropriate to those needs in order to close the sale.

Thus, advertising is a form of preselling. Advertisements make a one-sided pitch in behalf of a particular product, company, or industry. They are disseminated for the express purpose of persuading persons to behave in accord with the desires of a vested interest group. Viewed this way, the functions and techniques of advertising are in many respects similar to those of propaganda.

In this chapter, it is not our purpose to add further to the controversy over the broad social implications of advertising and selling. Instead, we will be concerned with the psychological principles underlying these activities. As we shall see, these principles are more clearly established for advertising than they are for selling.

ADVERTISING

Most potential consumers have a limited amount of money which they spend for commodities they value highly.[1] According to this model of consumer behavior, it should be possible to predict actual purchases from knowledge of (1) the prices of various commodities and (2) the relative preference values attached to these commodities.

---

[1] P. H. Benson, "A Model for the Analysis of Consumer Preferences and an Exploratory Test," *Journal of Applied Psychology*, Vol. 39 (1955), pp. 375–81.

To the extent that consumers actually do seek to balance available money against commodity preferences, there are two ways in which sales may be increased: either the cost can be reduced or the preference value attached to a product may be heightened. Advertising seeks to accomplish the latter objective; that is, to enhance the preference value attached to a particular brand of product or to a general class of products.

One feature of our economy is the availability of many different *brands* of the same product all priced competitively. There is little difference indeed between the price of various brands of cigarettes, detergents, beer, or gasoline. Hence, the consumer's decision about particular brand purchases probably reflects greater discrepancies in perceived preference values than in actual cost.

Much advertising is specifically devoted to manipulating subjective preferences for one brand over competitive brands. The impression is conveyed that standardized pricing among competitors does not assure standardization of the satisfactions derived from purchasing competing products. In essence, the consumer is encouraged to prefer the advertised brand to all others within the same product classification.

This may be accomplished in a variety of ways. The advertiser may appeal to rational considerations of product superiority like "safety" or "durability." He may, on the other hand, attempt to reinforce preferences by manipulating feeling tone. The advertisement may suggest that purchase and/or use of the particular brand will make the consumer feel good, like himself better, or be better liked by others. Thus, advertising slogans proclaim *Satisfy Yourself, Feel Really Clean,* and *Be Sociable.*

The consumer's choice between competing brands is often preceded by a choice between *products.* He must decide, for example, to buy a car rather than a boat before he is ready to select from among the automobiles offered within a price bracket by various manufacturers.

Here again, advertising seeks to strengthen preference values in relation to cost. The general approach underlying product advertising is that "you will derive the greatest satisfaction from using your money to buy what we have to sell." On occasion, product advertising (and to a certain extent, brand advertising) is directed toward strengthening relatively weak drives and awakening relatively passive ones. This is particularly true when the market is highly saturated. In order to maintain a high volume of automotive sales, the second car must be regarded as a necessity instead of a luxury.

Although it may not be correct to characterize us as a nation of persons primarily concerned with body odor, our flourishing deodorant industry is some kind of tribute to highly effective advertising. As Americans, we seem to be peculiarly preoccupied with product ownership as symbolic of economic, social, and sexual status. This kind of personalization of the products we own is a reflection of the interactive and mutually enhancing effects of our expanding economy, increased leisure time, and vulnerability to advertising appeals. The latter is not simply a fortuitous circumstance. The analysis and improvement of advertising is the subject of voluminous research. In general, such research revolves about four basic questions:[2]

1. What shall be said? (message research)
2. How shall it be said? (copy research)
3. Where and when shall it be said? (media research)
4. How effectively was it said? (evaluative research)

Each of these questions is considered separately in the following sections.

The Message

Every advertisement attempts to tell us something. This *message* may be relatively obvious, as in the case of a simple declaration of product superiority. However, it may be quite subtle, suggesting that our virility, status, or likability will be enhanced by using the product in question.

Regardless of the nature of the message, it must ultimately get us to do something or experience particular feelings. To accomplish this, the advertiser typically either promises to satisfy some already existing need or strengthens weak needs to the point where the promise of their satisfaction assumes real importance to the consumer. This point is made rather succinctly by Dichter as follows:

No item of merchandise is ever sold unless a psychological need exists which it satisfies. In other words, the actual merchandise is secondary.

Advertising's goal has to be the mobilization and manipulation of human needs as they exist in the customer.[3]

For a number of years advertisers sought some kind of magic key to successful appeals by consulting presumably exhaustive compilations of motives, wants, and needs. This tack proved to be relatively fruitless. As discussed in Chapter 13, human motivation is exceedingly complex and therefore defies neat classification and categorization. Even a fundamentally biological drive like hunger, for example, becomes rapidly overlaid with learned preferences and feelings. The food advertiser cannot make a successful appeal to the "need for food." He must appeal, instead, to needs for particular kinds of foods, appetizing in appearance, attractively served, and appropriate to particular circumstances which we have learned to associate with them. Thus, margarine manufacturers learned that they could not compete effectively with butter by emphasizing only the economy and nutritive value of their product. People are reluctant to accept something they can justify solely on the grounds that it is an effective substitute.

We are sometimes led by advertising to invest products and companies with particular "personalities" and to formulate an image of the kind of person for whom the product is appropriate. If we can project ourselves into the advertisement, perceiving ourselves as users of the product, the advertiser has come a long way toward inducing us to make the purchase.

Product Images. The image of the appropriate purchaser of a particular product is conveyed by the dominant verbal and pictorial aspects of its underlying advertising appeal. Pepsi-Cola has never tried to capture the old age retirement market! It has a well-established, youthful, lighthearted, gay, "sociable" image. Similarly, Chrysler Corporation automobiles were perceived for many years as sound, conservative investments in transportation. Prior to the radical change in styling and advertising for the 1957 model, the image of the Plymouth buyer was expressed by such adjectives as "quiet," "careful," "slow," "silent," "moral," "fat," "gentle," and "calm."[4] In 1957, styling changes were accompanied by advertisements peppered

---

[3] E. Dichter, "A Psychological View of Advertising Effectiveness," *Journal of Marketing.* Vol. 14 (1949), pp. 61–66.

[4] W. D. Wells, F. J. Andriuli, F. J. Goi, and S. Seader, "An Adjective Checklist for the Study of 'Product Personality,'" *Journal of Applied Psychology,* Vol. 41 (1957), pp. 317–19.

with references to *The Forward Look, Three Years Ahead, Flight Sweep Styling,* and the *Fabulous Fury* 301 V-8 *Engine.* The effectiveness of this campaign is evident from the findings in a follow-up study that the Plymouth buyer was subsequently characterized by adjectives like "high-class," "important," "rich," "different," and "particular."[5] This more recent image has persisted to the present.

The impact of the message embodied in any advertisement cannot be considered as independent of the total corporate and/or product image effort. People respond to an advertisement for a particular brand of cigarettes, for example, in terms of their assessment of the tobacco industry and their attitudes toward cigarettes as a product class. In this regard, it is worth noting that even an unknown brand may have an image. This image is derived from the image of the general product class, since the unknown brand is assumed to have the same range of uses and satisfactions common to known brands.[6]

Corporate Images. A considerable amount of advertising is devoted to establishing a favorable attitude toward a company and investing the company with a "personality." This advertising approach is particularly useful when the company's products are sold to producers rather than individual consumers (for example, steel, rubber, oil) or when the advertiser sells services like insurance, communications, or travel.

Advertising to develop a corporate image aims to convey to the public that although the company exists for monetary reasons, its concerns extend considerably beyond the balance sheet and the ledger. The company is personalized and humanized. It is transformed by institutional advertising from a huge, impersonal organization controlling the lives of its employees and the tastes of the public to an organization in which employees are partners in an enterprise providing consumers with beneficial goods and services.

Some of the dominant themes of such advertising have been identified as:

1. Elaboration of latent consequences: The company's activities benefit you or some group in which you have a direct and vital interest.

---

[5] W. D. Wells, F. J. Goi, and S. Seader, "A Change in a Product Image," *Journal of Applied Psychology,* Vol. 42 (1958), pp. 120–21.

[6] D. R. Longman, "Foundations of Consumer Buying Behavior," in C. H. Sandage (ed.), *The Promise of Advertising* (Homewood, Ill.: Richard D. Irwin, Inc., 1961), pp. 108–24.

New from Westinghouse

Fresh water
from the sea

Today, in many places throughout the world, the shortage of water is a critical problem.

By 1975, there will be another *billion* people in the world ... and, unless we find "new" water for drinking, irrigation and industry, there won't be enough fresh water for them all.

We are starting to find it in the salt sea. At San Diego, Westinghouse is building the country's largest seawater plant for the U.S. Department of the Interior's Office of Saline Water. This plant will provide 7,000,000 gallons of "new" drinking water a week from the Pacific Ocean.

In the desert of Kuwait, four Westinghouse units are already at work taking in Persian Gulf water and pouring out nearly 17 million gallons of fresh water a week. You can be sure ... if it's Westinghouse.

Westinghouse

FIGURE 20–1—*Continued*

Curator of the mind's riches

No bank holds riches such as this—the great legacy of learning in our libraries. Here every man may maintain an account. Here all may borrow, in any amount, from the endless assets of the mind.

The men and women who create and keep our libraries perform far more than an essential service—they guard a priceless trust. It is to their greater credit that our country's librarians accept their charge as a labor of love as well as a great responsibility. To them a nation is grateful.

Among the books in today's libraries are many published by Rand McNally, or printed and bound by us for other American publishers. Even above our pride in more than a century of fine craftsmanship, we hold this privilege of contributing tangibly to our libraries' inestimable wealth.

RAND McNALLY

PUBLISHERS • PRINTERS • MAP MAKERS • ESTABLISHED 1856 • CHICAGO • NEW YORK • NASHVILLE • SAN FRANCISCO • WASHINGTON

TIME, APRIL 21, 1961   103

Courtesy: Rand McNally

FIGURE 20–1—*Concluded*

JAMES LIND—Conqueror of Scurvy—reproduced here is one of a series of original oil paintings commissioned by Parke-Davis.

Great Moments in Medicine

James Lind, a British Naval Surgeon, in 1747 proved experimentally the value of a treatment for a disease that had incapacitated more seamen than all other diseases, naval engagements, marine mishaps, shipwrecks, and accidents combined. The disease was scurvy . . . a severe vitamin deficiency resulting from sailors' unvaried diet of salt meat and sea biscuits.

Lind's recommendation was the addition of fresh limes, other citrus fruits, and their juices to diets of seamen. Though not adopted generally by the British Navy until after his death, this diet saved countless lives. British seamen, thereafter called "Limeys," were the first men to receive prophylactic vitamin therapy.

Although some vitamin deficiencies in man cannot be prevented or corrected as dramatically and as simply as scurvy, modern medical research is constantly giving physicians better and more effective weapons for use in the fight for better health for people world wide.

Original research, conducted at Parke-Davis laboratories into causes and control of disease, has made significant contributions to world health. These medicines, prescribed by physicians and dispensed by pharmacists, help you to enjoy a healthier, longer life.

PARKE-DAVIS

Pioneers in better medicines

Courtesy: Parke, Davis & Co.

2. Humanization: The company is a warm, friendly, hard-working "individual."
3. Denial and Conversion: Odious charges about big business are either denied or converted to have socially acceptable implications.
4. Sympathy or Ego-Involvement: Since you have a vital stake in the company, it is in your interest to understand and be sympathetic to the company's problems and to appreciate its solutions.[7]

Some of these appeals are illustrated in Figure 20–1.

Public Service. Quite often, institutional advertising takes a less direct approach to developing favorable attitudes. Rather than stressing the company's contribution to your welfare, public service advertising seeks to clarify the company's stake in our society and its role as a "good citizen." The distinction between direct attempts to create a corporate image and the public service approach is a rather fine one. In the latter, the advertisement seeks to establish a rapprochement between the broader interests and welfare of society on the one hand, and the company on the other. It attempts to capitalize upon what has been termed "significant involvement"[8] serving the private interests of the advertiser, the personal interest of the consumer, and the public interest of the nation.

Advertising Copy

The purpose of research on advertising copy is to discover effective means for transmitting messages as a guide to formulating advertisements and evaluating their impact. With respect to the structure of advertising copy, it is important to note that psychologists are not advertising men either by training or, for the most part, by inclination. Developing a good advertisement requires the skills of a number of specialists, including copywriters, artists, layout specialists, and others. The unique contributions of psychologists stem from their fundamental concern with human behavior and familiarity with techniques for investigating changes in behavior.

Copy Format. Advertisements are structured in a manner calculated to attract and maintain attention, spotlight the salient aspects of the message, and encourage retention of the message as well as

---

[7] L. I. Pearlin and M. Rosenberg, "Propaganda Techniques in Institutional Advertising," *Public Opinion Quarterly,* Vol. 16 (1952), pp. 5–26.

[8] W. D. Patterson, "The Power of Significant Involvement," *Saturday Review,* April 22, 1961, pp. 41–46.

subsequent action in accord with it. We will briefly review some evidence concerning the effects of several format variables upon the realization of these objectives.

1. Color. The legibility of colored lettering is less dependent upon the specific colors used than upon the brightness differential between the colored letter and the background. In general, the most satisfactory background for colored lettering is grey, and dark colors on a light background are most legible in daylight.[9]

The value of color in advertising for attracting and maintaining interest is somewhat obscured by such other considerations as the skill with which the color is used, its appropriateness to the product being advertised, and the fundamental purpose of the advertisement. In the latter regard, it has been suggested that color is maximally valuable for advertising an established brand and not much superior to black-and-white advertising for promoting a new brand.[10] Furthermore, contrary to belief, it does not necessarily follow that advertisers whose advertisements are in color are perceived as more prestigious than advertisers whose advertisements are in black and white.[11]

2. Movement. The fact that a moving object attracts more attention than a stationary one is well known. Youngsters playing hide-and-seek remain as motionless as possible in their hiding place in order to avoid detection. The student who wants desperately to be recognized by his instructor does not merely raise his arm; he often waves his hand rather frantically.

The primary applications of the principle of movement in advertising occur in television and in the outdoor spectacular signs showing bread being sliced, bottles pouring liquid, and water cascading over a dam. In most TV advertising, the movement is "real." The viewer watches a skin diver plunging under water to shave, or observes the needle pointer swing revealing the deodorizing power of a mouthwash. The outdoor spectacular signs make use of "apparent" movement created by lights successively illuminated in sequence with a brief time interval between them. It makes no dif-

---

[9] E. H. Jones and F. C. Sumner, "Relation of Brightness Differences of Colors to Their Apparent Distances," *Journal of Applied Psychology,* Vol. 26 (1948), pp. 25–29.

[10] L. Warner and R. Franzen, "Value of Color in Advertising," *Journal of Applied Psychology,* Vol. 31 (1947), pp. 260–70.

[11] L. Guest, "Status Enhancement as a Function of Color in Advertising," *Journal of Advertising Research,* Vol. 6 (1966), pp. 40–44.

ference to the observer whether the movement is real or apparent. Movement attracts attention.

3. Repetition.   Much advertising is repetitive in nature. The slogan, jingle, or catchy tune repeated over and over again capitalizes upon certain well established psychological principles. Frequency of presentation both attracts attention and leads to overlearning. Thus, if you let your thoughts wander during a TV commercial, an insistent chant like "Double the flavor, double the fun, with Doublemint, Doublemint, Doublemint gum" is bound to part your intellectual curtain and bring you back to the realities of the world of commercialism. Repetition can, of course, be overdone. Its value is likely to be greatest when the audience's initial level of interest in the subject material is low.[12]

4. Novelty.   Things that appear to be new and different contrast markedly with the old and familiar and hence stand out in bold relief. The extent to which product novelty is stressed in magazine advertising is evident from the frequent use of words and phrases like "New!" "No more (messy hands, and so on) " "Revolutionary," "Now! At Last!" "Never before!"[13]

In addition to showing that they have a product that is "new" or "different," many advertisers attempt to advertise in novel ways. There is after all something rather compelling about seeing a miniature butler dispensing paper napkins or omnipotent Mr. Clean springing to life.

Copy Research.   The effectiveness of alternative forms of advertising copy often is evaluated before the advertisement is widely disseminated. This can be accomplished either by pretesting the alternative forms with samples of subjects or by actually running limited editions of the alternative advertisements prior to selecting the final form for widespread dissemination.

The assessment of copy may be conducted by interview and/or questionnaire and by behavioral test. It is directed toward determining the relative effectiveness of the copy for (*a*) attracting and maintaining attention and (*b*) evoking the desired feelings and initiating the intended action.

Recall and recognition tests of various kinds are particularly ap-

---

[12] A. Greenberg and N. Garfinkle, "Delayed Recall of Magazine Articles," *Journal of Advertising Research*, Vol. 3 (1962) , pp. 28–31.

[13] W. H. Whyte, Jr., "The Language of Advertising," *Fortune,* September, 1952, p. 99.

propriate for assessing attentiveness to advertisements in the printed media. Subscribers to a particular magazine may be asked to recall as many advertisements as they can from a recent issue or to select from a scrapbook (that is, recognize) those advertisements that have actually appeared in the magazine. An interesting finding with reference to the scrapbook technique is that a correction must be made for persons claiming to "recognize" advertisements that have not yet appeared in print! The proportion of such false identifications was found in one study to be as high as 15–20 percent.[14]

Even if we were somehow to "correct" for such false identifications, thereby obtaining a reasonably accurate recall or recognition measure, this measure may have little bearing upon the ultimate criterion of copy effectiveness, that is, subsequent purchasing behavior.[15] It clearly is possible to be aware of an advertisement without being motivated to buy the advertised product.

Behavioral criteria sometimes used to test copy effectiveness include coupon returns and contest entries. Two or more versions of the same basic advertisement are run in alternate copies of a particular publication (*split-run*). Although the contents of these versions are different, all forms of the advertisement contain a coupon to be sent to the company or taken to the dealer, or a suggestion that the reader telephone or write regarding the product. The relative effectiveness of the several versions of the advertisement is determined by comparing the rate of consumer replies evoked by each one.

Audience reaction to TV and radio programs and commercials is automatically recorded by a mechanical device called the *Program Analyzer* developed by Stanton and Lazarsfeld.[16] This device is used exclusively by the Columbia Broadcasting System and the McCann-Erickson advertising agency.[17] During a test session, members of the audience react to various portions of the program by pressing "like" or "dislike" buttons. Their responses are recorded and supplemented by replies to questionnaires and interviews.

Another approach to both program and commercial testing is that

---

[14] E. B. Lucas and M. J. Murphy, "Faults of Identification of Advertisements in Recognition Tests," *Journal of Applied Psychology*, Vol. 23 (1939), pp. 264–69.

[15] J. B. Haskins, "Factual Recall as a Measure of Advertising Effectiveness," *Journal of Advertising Research*, Vol. 4 (1964), pp. 2–8.

[16] P. F. Lazarsfeld and F. N. Stanton, *Radio Research* (New York: Duell, Sloan & Pearce, Inc., 1944).

[17] G. F. Seehafer and J. W. Laemmar, *Successful Television and Radio Advertising* (New York: McGraw-Hill Book Co., Inc, 1959).

employed by the Schwerin Research Corporation. The Schwerin system exposes a preselected test audience to the program under study and each member of the audience records his reaction on a three-point scale *(interesting, mildly interesting, not interesting)* at selected points in the program. Tabulations and summaries of these reactions are used to construct a "profile" of audience reaction during the program. Recall data and changes in preference for particular products are used also to evaluate the effectiveness of the commercials.

The Medium

Where advertising is placed (the medium or vehicle) influences the size of the audience and its composition. In the interest of economy, advertisers seek to place their messages before the "right" prospects, in terms of age, sex, educational level, and so on, and in the "right" context.

There is a growing body of evidence that the context is particularly important in the case of television advertising. For example, changes in mood during a TV showing of the film "The Nuremburg Trial" were found to be associated with changes in attitude toward products.[18] In another study, it was demonstrated that women may be more susceptible than men to the influence of program context upon attitudes toward commercials.[19] With further research in this direction, we can anticipate the possibility of selecting programs and places within programs which are most suitable for advertising particular products.

Audience Research. Another kind of media research is directed toward estimating the size and characteristics of the audience exposed to the advertiser's message. This problem can be attacked somewhat more easily for the printed media than for the broadcast media because the number of issues of a particular magazine or newspaper sold can be determined with a fair degree of accuracy.

However, even in the case of printed media, there are certain difficulties in estimating the size of the audience reached by an advertisement. The fact that a particular magazine is purchased

---

[18] J. N. Axelrod, "Induced Moods and Attitudes Toward Products," *Journal of Advertising Research,* Vol. 3 (1963), pp. 19–24.

[19] L. E. Crane, "How Product Appeal and Program Affect Attitudes Toward Commercials," *Journal of Advertising Research,* Vol. 4 (1964), pp. 15–18.

does not mean that it is read; conversely, a substantial number of persons read magazines they do not actually purchase. Estimates of audience exposure to printed media are further complicated by the fact that there is a certain amount of duplication between the readership of various magazines carrying the same advertisement. It is likely that simple consideration of the circulation of a particular publication without regard for overlapping publications carrying the same advertisement leads to an overestimate of the size of the advertiser's audience.

The audience reached by the broadcast media (radio and TV) is even more difficult to estimate. The program rating services gather their information in a variety of ways, each with unique shortcomings. The A. C. Nielson Company, for example, compiles its basic data for program ratings from mechanical recorders attached to radio and TV receivers. This device maintains a continuous record of set usage throughout the day for a sample of homes. However, the fact that a receiver is tuned to a particular program is itself no assurance that anyone in the home is actually viewing or listening to the program and its accompanying commercials.

Hooper ratings for radio and Trendex ratings for TV are based upon the "coincidental telephone" survey. Telephone interviews are conducted with a sample of persons while the program under consideration is in progress. In addition to sample bias introduced by limiting the rating to results obtained from telephone-owning homes, this procedure cannot be used for early morning or late evening programs. One just doesn't place telephone calls at 6:00 A.M. or midnight to randomly selected persons inquiring whether they have their TV receiver on and, if so, which program they are watching.

Other rating services conduct coincidental personal (rather than telephone) interviews and use the diary method. In the latter procedure, a sample of respondents is requested to keep a log of all viewing or listening activities. The effect of keeping such a diary upon program selection, and the accuracy of the logs themselves, are both open questions.

Subliminal Advertising.   Subliminal perception is a well-established psychological phenomenon. We sometimes respond to stimuli that are below the threshold of awareness. In the tradition of experimental psychology, the *limen,* or threshold of awareness, is defined as a stimulus intensity perceived exactly half the time.

Quite a furor developed about 10 years ago when an apparently successful attempt to capitalize upon subliminal perception for advertising purposes was reported by Vicary.[20] The procedure consisted of flashing the phrases "Eat Popcorn" and "Drink Coca-Cola" at 0.003 second on a movie screen during the showing of a film. According to the report, Coca-Cola sales increased 18 percent and popcorn sales increased 57 percent although the audience did not suspect they were participating in a deliberate attempt to influence their behavior. Thus, the application of subliminal perception in advertising has been aptly termed "the little ad that isn't there."[21]

Vicary's procedure and findings were never reported in any professional publication. Hence, it is impossible to evaluate the validity of his results. The implications of this technique for presenting advertisements would if it worked be at once startling and frightening. It is repugnant enough to some people to be bombarded by advertisements they can see and hear. But to be victimized by advertising below the threshold of awareness raises such serious moral concerns that it has been banned from both TV and radio.

Both public and professional concern for subliminal advertising have diminished in recent years, largely because of evidence that (a) individual differences and variability in the limen make applications of subliminal advertising technically infeasible and (b) such advertising is of dubious value for generating needs or changing established behavior patterns.

Evaluating Advertising Effectiveness

It is clear from the foregoing discussion that considerable research using a variation of "attentiveness" as a criterion is often entailed in developing the message, structuring the copy, and selecting an appropriate medium. However, considering all aspects of the advertisement together, the ultimate test of its impact is its effect upon sales.

Certain difficulties inherent in developing a sales criterion for consumer studies generally were described in Chapter 19. That discussion emphasized potential sources of contamination of sales

---

[20] Results obtained by James M. Vicary and reported in a memorandum from Subliminal Projection Co., Inc., to the Federal Communications Commission, January 13, 1958. Cited by R. Wilhelm, "Are Subliminal Commercials Bad?" *Michigan Business Review*, January, 1958, p. 26.

[21] J. Brooks, *Consumer Reports*, Vol. 23, No. 1 (1958), pp. 7–10.

data such as seasonal and economic variations and inadequate record-keeping.

Another difficulty, specifically related to the use of sales records for evaluating advertising effectiveness, is that the effects of advertising upon sales are delayed. Most sustained advertising does not show significant effects until some time after the campaign has started, and the effects may persist for some time after it has stopped.[22]

This phenomenon has a dual implication. For the researcher, it means that the sales impact of an advertisement or campaign cannot properly be gaged without attention to long-term sales trends suitably corrected for possible sources of contamination. For the advertiser, it suggests that substantial repetition of an advertisement, involving 15 or more presentations in the case of newspaper advertising, may be required to achieve efficient purchase results.[23]

SELLING

We have attempted throughout this book to develop a feeling for psychology as a science. Psychologists' conclusions about human behavior are based upon careful investigation under controlled circumstances. Casual observation, armchair speculation, and hunches "off the top of the head" may occasionally serve as a starting point for subsequent investigation. They do not, however, constitute a reasonable basis for scientific conclusions without empirical verification. A "psychology" of anything lacking an experimental literature reflecting a history of careful investigation is not psychology at all; it is common sense. And the wisdom of common sense often is open to question.

A designation like "the psychology of selling" exemplifies a tendency to confuse commonsense analyses of human behavior with a rigorous scientific approach to inquiry. For the present, salesmanship must be regarded pretty much as an art to which psychologists have devoted relatively little attention. The effectiveness of various sales approaches has been demonstrated in the past by experience rather than controlled investigation. This is an area in which there is a serious need for scientific study.

---

[22] F. Meissner, "Sales and Advertising of Lettuce," *Journal of Advertising Research,* Vol. 1 (1961), pp. 1–10.

[23] J. B. Stewart, *Repetitive Advertising in Newspapers* (Boston: Harvard Business School, 1964).

Two Views of Salesmanship

One of the effects of even the sparse amount of attention thus far given by psychologists to the selling process has been to alter the view of the nature of the salesman-prospect interaction. The older, psychologically naive view emphasizes the buyer's passivity and the consequent value of "selling formulas" calculated to manipulate his behavior in the desired direction. The more recent and sophisticated view emphasizes the salesman's role in correctly identifying and satisfying the prospect's needs, desires, and preferences.

The Older View. Here, the salesman and prospect are regarded as antagonists in a struggle. The salesman is seen as attempting, by virtually any means, to persuade a reluctant prospect to make a purchase. High-pressure tactics, deviousness, and deceitfulness are justified when necessary to force a sale. This view likens the prospect to an almost inanimate and unresponsive recipient of the sales "pitch" who remains relatively passive while something is *done to* him. Proceeding from the assumption of buyer passivity during the sales interaction, several writers have proposed "selling formulas" designed to lead any prospect through a sequence of steps terminating in his purchase of the product.

One such prescription for salesmanship, proposed before the turn of the century, is the A-I-D-A formula: Attention-Interest-Desire-Action. This formula assumes that all prospects think alike and that the nature of this stream of thought proceeds in orderly fashion through the four stages embodied in the formula. It disregards such important considerations as: the buyer's perceived need for the product (we desire many things we do not buy because we do not need them) ; his ability to make a purchase (including his authority to buy and the availability of sufficient funds) ; counterpressures upon him *not* to buy the product in spite of his desire and need for it (including his reactions to the salesperson) ; conflicting desires for several purchases all of which cannot be simultaneously gratified; and so on. It is naive to assume that the thinking process can be reduced to the uniformly applicable sequential stream hypothesized by the A-I-D-A formula.

Need Satisfaction. Salesmanship viewed as a process of need-satisfaction focuses more upon the buying process than the selling process. This approach to salesmanship rejects selling formulas as stilted, oversimplified, and unduly concerned with the actions of the seller.

A need-satisfaction point of view is accepted by virtually all sound recent writers on salesmanship. As one author states, salesmanship is ". . . the process whereby the seller ascertains and activates the needs or wants of the buyer and satisfies these needs or wants to the mutual, continuous advantage of both the buyer and the seller."[24] Thus, the buyer's needs are regarded as central to the selling process; the salesman's behavior assumes importance only as a vehicle for promising and providing need satisfaction.

There are a number of practical implications of the need-satisfaction approach to salesmanship. Since every prospective buyer is a unique individual with unique needs and perceptions, every sales presentation must be somewhat different. A particular prospect may need assurance that he is getting maximum value for his money; another may need to derive feelings of heightened status by virtue of his dealings with the salesman; yet another may be particularly concerned about the reliability of the company with respect to customer service or its reputation for prompt delivery. The salesman's initial endeavor must be in the direction of discovering the prospect's needs and/or stimulating needs appropriate to whatever he is selling.

Both need discovery and need stimulation require a high degree of sensitivity. The salesman must be a careful listener and an astute observer of the prospect's behavior.

Once the particular buyer's needs are evident, the salesman is in a position to demonstrate and discuss his product or service as a need satisfier. He must be exceedingly flexible, realizing that whatever he is selling can be presented from numerous aspects, each satisfying to particular needs. The salesman attempts to stress those particular satisfactions appropriate to the buyer's needs.

Assuming that the product or service is properly presented, the prospect will want it. He has not been hoodwinked, high-pressured, or embarrassed into making the purchase; he has been convinced that he will benefit from it. It is not surprising, then, that the most effective salesmen tend themselves to be convinced of the value of whatever it is they are selling. A study of variables contributing to

---

[24] C. A. Pederson and M. D. Wright, *Salesmanship: Principles and Methods* (3d ed.; Homewood, Ill.: Richard D. Irwin, Inc., 1961) , pp. 45–46.

success of life insurance salesmen, for example, determined that the amount of life insurance owned by the agent (indicating belief in the value of his product) correlated more significantly with a composite criterion of selling effectiveness than several other factors, including product knowledge and length of service.[25]

Finally, the salesman's responsibility extends beyond closing the sale to assuring customer satisfaction with his purchase. This is particularly important when repeat sales are desired. Satisfied customers tend to make additional purchases of the product perceived as satisfying. Further, since such customers are favorably disposed to the salesman and the organization he represents, they are an excellent form of word-of-mouth advertising.

The importance of buyer satisfaction was illustrated in an analysis of recordings of the actual selling behavior of expert department store sales personnel. Personal selling of the department store variety is very often a rather routine affair. The customer sees what she likes on the rack, the clerk proffers it for her inspection, shows variations in color, style, and so on, upon request, and ultimately either wraps it and accepts the cash, or replaces it on the rack. Analysis of the recordings of expert salespersons, however, indicated that the most effective personal selling goes an important step beyond facilitating the customer's purchase. The ingredient added by these salespersons is that they help the customer obtain maximum personal satisfaction for the money she spends.[26]

The Selling-Buying Process

We have already indicated that a need-satisfactions approach to salesmanship leads necessarily to a flexible view of selling. Each sales appeal must be individually tailored to the needs of the individual prospect. In this regard it is useful to make a few observations about the reasons for making a purchase and the nature of the sales presentation.

Why People Buy.   Here again there is considerable conflict between a common sense analysis and a psychological analysis of human behavior. It seems just plain good common sense that people

---

[25] D. E. Baier and R. D. Dugan, "Factors in Sales Success," *Journal of Applied Psychology*, Vol. 41 (1957), pp. 37–40.

[26] W. M. Thompson, "How Expert Salespeople Sell," *Journal of Retailing*, 1955, p. 150.

buy food to prepare for hunger, new appliances to replace ones that are worn out or defective, and bigger houses to accommodate larger families. Further, assuming the decision has been made, for example, to buy a refrigerator, it is common sense to buy the make and model offering maximum value for the money. Such factors as initial cost, reputation of the manufacturer and retail outlet, and availability of servicing ought to be critical to such a purchase.

Common sense assumes a highly rational basis for buying behavior. However, the point was made in Chapter 19 that buyers often behave rather irrationally by external standards. The reasons given for making a purchase may not be the really operative reasons at all. Thus, although unverbalized as needs, the purchaser may seek to identify with persons whom he respects by buying products endorsed by them. He may seek social approval by purchasing in conformance with certain stereotypes of the "well-groomed" or "masculine" man; heightened status by buying expensive or "exclusive" items; or simply a "bargain." Derived (learned) needs for social approval and status rarely are verbalized. Instead, the purchaser prefers to think he is a highly rational buyer basing his decisions upon a careful consideration of the available alternatives. Thus, the salesman must often provide the customer with such *rationalizations* (acceptable "reasons") as "economy," "low upkeep," and "once-in-a-lifetime value" if he is to close the sale successfully.

The Sales Presentation. Much more research has been devoted to selecting and training salesmen than to the sales presentation itself. The relative lack of research activity in the latter area is attributable to a number of factors. Laboratory studies of the sales interview suffer rather seriously from a sense of artificiality. Field studies, on the other hand, are difficult to conduct because of the enormous range of variation in prospect needs and personalities necessitating a high degree of flexibility in sales presentations. Such flexibility probably increases the number of sales closed but precludes the kinds of control necessary to conduct satisfactory investigations.

Occasionally the sales presentation is atomized for the purpose of study. One investigator, for example, found that department store sales were increased when clerks kept their voices up on the last syllable of the "Good Morning" greeting.[27] Another found that superior and inferior salesclerks could be differentiated on the basis

---

[27] J. N. Bauman, "How the Professional Salesman Makes His Approach," *Sales Management,* June 15, 1955, p. 58.

of ratings of voice transcriptions. The recordings of voices of superior clerks were rated higher by a group of college students on "enthusiasm," "convincingness," and "sales ability."[28]

Studies like these barely scratch the surface of the sales presentation. At the present time, effective salesmanship must be regarded as an art refined by experience rather than by experimentation, and heavily dependent upon general skills in human relations.

Selecting Salesmen

Three general approaches to selecting personnel, including salesmen, were described in earlier chapters: weighted application blanks, standardized interviews, and psychological tests of various kinds. Rather than review these selection procedures, we will direct our attention to some of the special problems indigenous to selecting salesmen.

Kinds of Salesmen.   Salesmanship is not a homogeneous activity. The available classifications of sales occupations generally reflect either the nature of the goods and services sold or the type of employer the salesman represents. Although we need not be concerned with particular classificatory schemes, certain distinctions have important implications for selection.

Manufacturer's salesmen represent the manufacturer to wholesalers, retailers, and others who sell to the ultimate consumer. The manufacturer may be represented in a variety of ways: sales engineers generally assist with improving factory operations; merchandising salesmen engage in sales promotion encouraging greater efforts in selling the company's goods; and so on. *Retail salesmen* sell to customers who come into a store generally committed to the purchase of a product. The retail salesman's primary function is to help the customer make the purchase. The skills and requirements for retail salesmen vary considerably from one store to another. In some, he is essentially a purchase-wrapper and change-maker. In others, particularly where a significant amount of brand competition exists, he must engage in a high level of salesmanship.

These differences in function between salesman servicing industry and those serving retail customers are reinforced by the self-percep-

---

[28] E. J. Fay and W. C. Middleton, "Relationship between Sales Ability and Rating of Transcribed Voices of Salesmen," *Journal of Applied Psychology*, Vol. 26 (1942), pp. 499–509.

tions of salesmen in these two classifications. Industrial salesmen see their job as placing a heavy emphasis upon ingenuity and inventiveness. Retail salesmen see, as prime requirements for success in their job: planning, hard work, and persuading people to their point of view or way of doing things.[29]

Interesting differences between specialty salesmen, route salesmen, and sales engineers emerged from a comparison of Strong Vocational Interest Blank scores earned by representatives of these three groups. The route salesmen tended to display greater interest than either of the other groups in "business details"; the sales engineers tended to be less interested than either of the other groups in "salesmanship" as measured by two subscales of this inventory.[30] The latter finding is understandable when we recall that sales engineers are technically trained manufacturer's representatives rather than salesmen in the traditional sense.

Results like these support a trend away from the concept of salesmen as a general occupational category and toward the concept of special, more homogeneous, sales occupational groups. In view of the functional differences between various kinds of salesmen, it is unreasonable to expect a single predictor or combination of predictors to be universally applicable for selecting salesmen. Selection procedures must be tailored to the specific requirements and activities of particular sales positions.

Criteria of Sales Success. As of 1945 it was concluded by one reviewer that all claims to the contrary, no one selection technique had emerged as clearly superior to all others.[31] The emphasis in predicting sales personnel success has shifted somewhat during the past 20 years, with considerable attention devoted recently to biographical inventories and personal history blanks. Newer tests, like those measuring sales comprehension and sales motivation, have also been proposed.[32] However, to the author's knowledge, the conclusion of 1945 is still applicable today.

---

[29] M. D. Dunnette and W. K. Kirchner, "Psychological Test Differences between Industrial Salesmen and Retail Salesmen," *Journal of Applied Psychology,* Vol. 44 (1960), pp. 121–25.

[30] A. A. Witkin, "Differential Interest Patterns in Salesmen," *Journal of Applied Psychology,* Vol. 40 (1956), pp. 338–40.

[31] E. A. Cleveland, "Sales Personnel Research, 1935–1945: A Review," *Personnel Psychology,* Vol. I (1948), pp. 211–55.

[32] M. M. Bruce, "A Sales Comprehension Test," *Journal of Applied Psychology,* Vol. 38 (1954), pp. 302–4; and M. M. Bruce, *Examiner's Manual, Sales Motivation Inventory* (New Rochelle, N.Y.: Author, 1953).

Why is it that no one outstanding type of predictor of sales success has been discovered? Part of the answer has already been given in the previous discussion of the heterogeneous nature of positions designated "salesman." A related factor is the problem of identifying a satisfactory criterion of job performance for salesmen.

You will recall from Chapter 4 that behavioral predictions are impossible in the absence of suitable criteria against which to validate the predictors. The criterion problem for selecting salesmen may not seem especially formidable at first glance. It would seem that we could use a measure of productivity, like gross sales per unit of time, for evaluating the effectiveness of a particular salesman in comparison with others in a similar position. However, the development of a suitable sales criterion entails certain complexities. Although sales data usually are readily available, they must be corrected for a number of factors in order to make them meaningful as criteria. One such factor is job experience. Salesmen with some experience tend to make more sales per unit of time than inexperienced salesmen, other things being equal. Secondly, it would be necessary to adjust for the potential of the sales territory or outlet. Certain geographical areas, cities, and neighborhoods are more likely to be productive for the salesman than others both because of population density and receptivity to the particular commodity being sold. Third, a correction must be applied for orders that are later rescinded or upon which payment is defaulted. It would probably be wise also to adjust gross sales per unit of time for such factors as repeat orders subsequently placed, and the productivity of a particular territory prior to the time the salesman in question acquired it.

Assuming that a reasonably adequate correction could be devised and applied to a record of gross sales, there is yet the issue of appropriateness of such a criterion. Adjusted sales is ony a partial index of success because when considered alone, it neglects the important factor of termination/survival. The effective salesman, defined by adjusted gross sales, who remains with the company for a long period of time is a greater asset to that company than the equally effective salesman who terminates his employment after relatively brief tenure. Predictors of adjusted gross sales may be relatively ineffective for a termination/survival criterion and vice versa.

It is obvious that as the time interval between initial selection and measurement of a performance criterion increases, the criterion itself becomes increasingly contaminated by the factor of voluntary job termination. It has been hypothesized that for studies involving a relatively brief time interval between selection and criterion measurement (that is, when voluntary termination is not a significant factor) successful prediction will depend much more upon measures of *ability* than interest. Conversely, predictions made against a delayed criterion will depend more upon *interest* than ability since the former reflects a desire to stay with a particular company or in a particular position.[33] Regardless of the merits of this suggestion for improving the accuracy of selecting salesmen, it calls attention to the issue of criterion contamination and the consequence of such contamination for reducing predictive efficiency.

SUMMARY

Advertising and selling are closely related in that both aim to persuade potential buyers to purchase products or avail themselves of services. However, while advertising appeals to the mass market, selling appeals to the individual consumer. Thus, advertising is a form of preselling whereby the buying public is informed about the existence and special features of a product or service. The salesman attempts to personalize the attractive features of the product or service so it is perceived as highly desirable by individual consumers.

Although psychologists are not advertising specialists, they have a fundamental interest in virtually any attempt to influence human behavior. Successful advertisements capitalize upon certain psychological principles related to attentiveness. These relate to such format characteristics as color, movement, repetition, and novelty. Beyond this, the successful advertisement makes an appeal to human needs and motives. If we can project ourselves into the advertisement and perceive ourselves as users of the product, the advertiser has come a long way toward inducing us to make the purchase.

In addition to investigating the effectiveness of advertising copy, the consumer psychologist may study the medium for dissemination of the advertisement, responsiveness to advertising as a function of certain audience characteristics (like age, educational level, and so on), and the impact of advertising upon consumer behavior.

---

[33] L. W. Ferguson, "Ability, Interest and Aptitude," *Journal of Applied Psychology*, Vol. 44 (1960), pp. 126–31.

To the present, psychologists have devoted much less research to selling than to advertising. Whatever research has been done on selling has been directed almost exclusively to the matters of selecting and training salesmen. Current thinking about the conduct of sales interviews and the effectiveness of various kinds of sales presentations is based more upon experience than upon the results of carefully controlled investigation.

Early approaches to salesmanship capitalized upon the use of selling formulas. These formulas assumed that buyers are relatively passive and that their thinking proceeded in a uniform and predictable stream through several rather distinct stages.

More recently this rather naive approach to salesmanship has been replaced by one capitalizing upon need satisfaction. The buyer's needs are regarded as central to the selling process. The salesman's behavior assumes importance only as a vehicle for promising and providing need-satisfaction. The fundamental implication of this approach to salesmanship is that since every prospect is a unique individual with unique needs, every sales presentation must be custom-tailored to him.

Two problems of particular significance to selecting effective salesmen are (1) the diversity of duties of and requirements for different kinds of salesmen and (2) the inadequacies of various criteria of selling "success." Thus, it is unreasonable to expect a single predictor or combination of predictors to be universally applicable for selecting salesmen. Selection procedures must be tailored to the specific requirements of particular sales positions.

Appendixes

A. Statistical Computation

This discussion of computational procedures is not comprehensive. It is limited in scope to certain statistics most frequently encountered by undergraduate students in industrial psychology courses. Furthermore only selected computational formulas are presented, and these without consideration for their derivation. The student who is interested in a more comprehensive discussion of statistical procedures is referred to any one of a number of excellent statistics texts.[1]

RAW DATA

The discussion in this Appendix revolves about the analysis of a single set of raw data. These data were obtained from a personnel testing program wherein a measure of clerical aptitude was administered as a preemployment test to all job applicants. The first 50 applicants were hired regardless of test score. Three months after she was hired, each employee was rated on work proficiency by her supervisor. The supervisor making the proficiency rating had no knowledge about the employee's preemployment test scores. The range of possible test scores extended from a low of 0 to a maximum

---

[1] See, for example, A. L. Edwards, *Statistical Methods for the Behavioral Sciences* (New York: Rinehart & Co., 1954); J. P. Guilford, *Fundamental Statistics in Psychology and Education* (New York: McGraw-Hill Book Co., Inc., 1965); W. L. Hays, *Statistics for Psychologists* (New York: Holt, Rinehart & Winston, 1963); J. G. Peatman, *Descriptive and Sampling Statistics* (New York: Harper & Row, 1947); and R. P. Runyan, and A. Haber, *Fundamentals of Behavioral Statistics* (Reading, Mass.: Addison-Wesley Publishing Co., 1967).

TABLE A–1

Preemployment Test Scores and Supervisory Ratings for 50 Employees

Employee	Preemployment Test	Supervisory Rating	Employee	Preemployment Test	Supervisory Rating
A..........40	3.0	Z..........63	9.0
B..........35	6.0	AA.........41	8.0
C..........49	5.0	BB.........50	7.0
D..........48	4.0	CC.........42	3.0
E..........52	6.0	DD.........49	5.0
F..........46	3.0	EE.........48	5.0
G..........58	3.0	FF.........35	2.0
H..........57	7.0	GG.........53	2.0
I..........53	6.0	HH.........45	4.0
J..........40	4.0	II..........62	9.0
K..........56	7.0	JJ..........68	9.0
L..........60	8.0	KK.........44	4.0
M..........37	5.0	LL.........64	8.0
N..........65	7.0	MM.......42	2.0
O..........55	9.0	NN.........54	2.0
P..........44	4.0	OO.........51	6.0
Q..........47	5.0	PP.........46	5.0
R..........63	8.0	QQ.........49	3.0
S..........50	6.0	RR.........56	7.0
T..........49	5.0	SS.........38	3.0
U..........39	2.0	TT.........51	6.0
V..........31	1.0	UU.........49	5.0
W.........50	5.0	VV.........32	1.0
X..........47	5.0	WW.......47	4.0
Y..........47	5.0	XX.........43	5.0

of 70; the range of possible ratings extended from a low of 1.0 to a maximum of 9.0. The resultant data are summarized in Table A–1.

This table indicates that employee A earned a preemployment test score of 40 and a supervisory rating three months later of 3.0; employee B earned a preemployment test score of 35 and a supervisory rating of 6.0; and so on.

FREQUENCY DISTRIBUTION

We can ask a number of descriptive questions about the data displayed in Table A–1. For example, what were the lowest and highest preemployment test scores earned by persons in this sample? How many persons earned a test score of, say, 49, or a supervisory rating of, say, 5.0? What was the most commonly earned test score? Although these questions can be answered by examining the raw data, they can be answered more easily by examining a *frequency distribution* prepared from these data. Such a distribution is merely a tabulation of the number of persons (*frequency*) earning each raw score.

Frequency Distributions from Raw Scores

To prepare a frequency distribution, the raw scores are arranged in order, usually from highest to lowest score, with the appropriate frequency indicated for each score. This procedure has been followed in preparing the two frequency distributions (one for preemployment test scores and one for supervisory ratings) shown in Table A–2. Note that a raw score is designated in statistical terminology by a capital letter (X or Y); frequency is designated f.

Now it is apparent at a glance that preemployment test scores ranged between 31 and 68 and that a score of 49 was earned by more people ($f = 5$) than any other single score. Similarly, the supervisory ratings ranged between 1.0 and 9.0 with 5.0 being the single most frequently assigned rating.

Grouped Data

The frequency distributions in Table A–2 required frequency tallies for each raw score. Although this produced a compact distribution for the supervisory ratings, the distribution for the preemployment test was quite lengthy, involving tabulations for each of 38 separate raw scores.

A distribution with about 15 raw score steps is regarded as optimal for computational convenience. In order to collapse a distribution like the one shown for preemployment scores in Table A–2 into about 15 raw score steps, each step must contain more than one raw score unit. Since every step in a frequency distribution must contain the same number of raw score units as every other step, there are two possibilities for this particular set of data: each step can consist of three raw score units (that is, have an interval of 3); or each step can consist of four raw score units (that is, have an interval of 4). An interval (i) of 3 would generate 16 steps in order to encompass all raw scores from the lowest (31) to the highest (68). An i of 4 would generate 12 steps.

The frequency distribution for preemployment test scores

TABLE A–2

Frequency Distributions for Preemployment Test Scores (X)
and Supervisory Ratings (Y)

Preemployment Test			Supervisory Rating		
X	Tally	f_x	Y	Tally	f_y
68	/	1	9.0	////	4
67		0	8.0	////	4
66		0	7.0	////	5
65	/	1	6.0	//// /	6
64	/	1	5.0	//// //// //	12
63	//	2	4.0	//// /	6
62	/	1	3.0	//// /	6
61		0	2.0	////	5
60	/	1	1 0	//	2
59		0			$N = 50$
58	/	1			
57	/	1			
56	//	2			
55	/	1			
54	/	1			
53	//	2			
52	/	1			
51	//	2			
50	///	3			
49	////	5			
48	//	2			
47	////	4			
46	//	2			
45	/	1			
44	//	2			
43	/	1			
42	//	2			
41	/	1			
40	//	2			
39	/	1			
38	/	1			
37	/	1			
36		0			
35	//	2			
34		0			
33		0			
32	/	1			
31	/	1			
		$N = 50$			

wherein data are grouped with an interval of 3 is shown in Table A–3.

Note that the raw data from which the distributions in Tables A–3 and A–2 were generated are identical. The only difference between these distributions is that in the latter raw scores were used whereas in the former the raw scores were grouped into intervals of three points each.

TABLE A–3

Frequency Distribution for Pre-employment Test Scores When $i = 3$

c.i.	Tally	f
66–68 .... /		1
63–65 .... ////		4
60–62 .... //		2
57–59 .... //		2
54–56 .... ////		4
51–53 .... ///		5
48–50 .... /// ///	10
45–47 .... /// //	7
42–44 .... ///	5
39–41 .... ////		4
36–38 .... //		2
33–35 .... //		2
30–32 .... //		2

Certain features of these data are more apparent when they are grouped (Table A–3) than when they are ungrouped (Table A–2). In particular, it is easier to identify by inspection the most "typical" or most "nearly average" scores. The peak frequency is obtained for scores in the *class interval* (c.i.) 48–50.

CENTRAL TENDENCY

The discussion of statistics in Chapter 2 defined three primary measures of central tendency: mean, median, and mode. The ensuing discussion concerns the computation of these measures.

Mean

The mean (X) is defined as the arithmetic average. Thus it is computed by adding (Σ) the raw scores (X) and dividing by the total number of observations (N). The computational formula is written:

$$\bar{X} = \frac{\Sigma X}{N_x} \quad \text{or} \quad \bar{Y} = \frac{\Sigma Y}{N_y} \,.$$

This formula is the "raw score formula" for calculating the mean. The calculation can be made easily from the raw data presented in Table A–1.

For the preemployment test, the sum of the raw scores is 2,440 and the number of observations is 50. Substituting in the formula above,

$$\bar{X} = \frac{2{,}440}{50} = 48.8 \,.$$

Substituting in similar fashion to calculate the mean supervisory rating, we have

$$\bar{Y} = \frac{253}{50} = 5.0 \,.$$

Using the Frequency Distribution. The work involved in making these calculations can be somewhat simplified by using the appropriate frequency distribution instead of the unorganized listing of raw scores.

Consider the distribution of supervisory ratings in Table A–2. Since each raw score occurs more than once, one need only sum the products of each raw score and its frequency to obtain the same value as ΣY. In other words, since a rating of 9.0 was given to four persons, it contributes 36.0 to the total ΣY. This value can be obtained either by adding 9.0 four times or by multiplying 9.0 by its frequency (4).

Thus the computational formula using data organized in the form of a frequency distribution like the one in Table A–2 for supervisory ratings is

$$\bar{Y} = \frac{\Sigma f Y}{N_y} \quad \text{or} \quad \bar{X} = \frac{\Sigma f X}{N} \,.$$

This computation is illustrated for supervisory ratings in Table A–4.

Grouped Data. The procedure just illustrated is quite convenient for ungrouped data. However, how can we compute the mean when data are grouped into class intervals?

TABLE A–4

Calculating the Mean Using a Frequency
Distribution
(Y = supervisory ratings)

Y	f	fY	
9.0	4	36.0	
8.0	4	32.0	
7.0	5	35.0	$\bar{Y} = \dfrac{\Sigma fY}{N_y}$
6.0	6	36.0	
5.0	12	60.0	
4.0	6	24.0	$\bar{Y} = \dfrac{253}{50}$
3.0	6	18.0	
2.0	5	10.0	$\bar{Y} = 5.0$
1.0	2	2.0	
	$N_y = 50$	$\Sigma fY = 253.0$	

One approach is to assume that all scores within a class interval
are equally distributed about the midpoint of that interval. Thus
the midpoint can be treated as the "score" to be assigned to all
frequencies in that interval.

To illustrate: Referring to Table A–3, one person earned a score
somewhere between 66 and 68. The best assumption we can make
about that person's score is that it was 67 (the midpoint of the class
interval). If our assumption is incorrect (that is, if he actually
earned a score of 66 or 68), our maximum error cannot exceed one
point. Either of the other possible assumptions (that he earned a
score of 66 or of 68) would open the way for a possible error of two
points.

Now consider the next lower class interval in Table A–3: 63–65.
The best assumption we can make about the four persons in this
interval is that their scores are distributed in balanced fashion with
two above the midpoint of the interval (64) and two below this midpoint. That being the case, all four cases converge upon the midpoint for computational purposes.

Thus when data are grouped into class intervals, the computational formula for the mean is stated as follows:

$$\bar{X} = \frac{\Sigma f \text{ mid.}}{N_x}.$$

TABLE A–5

Calculating the Mean from Grouped Data with $i = 3$
(X = preemployment test scores)

ci.	mid.	f	f mid.	
66–68...........	67	1	67	
63–65...........	64	4	256	$\bar{X} = \dfrac{\Sigma f \text{ mid.}}{N}$
60–62...........	61	2	122	
57–59...........	58	2	116	
54–56...........	55	4	220	$\bar{X} = \dfrac{2{,}432}{50}$
51–53...........	52	5	260	
48–50...........	49	10	490	
45–47...........	46	7	322	
42–44...........	43	5	215	$\bar{X} = 48.64$
39–41...........	40	4	160	
36–38...........	37	2	74	
33–35...........	34	2	68	
30–32...........	31	2	62	
		$N_x = \overline{50}$	Σf mid. $= \overline{2{,}432}$	

The procedure for computing the mean preemployment test score using the frequency distribution from Table A–3 is shown in Table A–5.

Note that the arithmetic simplification by this procedure entails some sacrifice of accuracy. The mean calculated directly from the raw data is 48.8; from the grouped data it is 48.6. However a loss of accuracy of this magnitude is usually regarded as unimportant in view of the convenience of the simplified procedure for hand computation.

Median

The median (*med*) is defined as the middle score in the distribution. It is that score which separates the highest 50 percent of the scores from the lowest 50 percent of the scores. Thus, when considering a set of raw scores arranged in order from highest to lowest (or from lowest to highest), the median score is the one earned by the $N/2$ person. With a set of 50 scores, as in our illustration, arranged in ascending or descending order, the median score is the one earned by the 25th person.

If you list the raw preemployment test scores from Table A–1 in order, you will note that the 25th person earned a score of 49. In the same way, you can determine that the median supervisory rating is 5.0.

Grouped Data. Clearly, the arrangement of raw scores required to carry out the procedure described above becomes increasingly laborious as the N increases. Therefore, it is usually simpler to calculate the median from data grouped into class intervals than from raw data.

Consider the distribution in Table A–3. By inspection, the median falls somewhere within the interval 48–50. That interval con-

TABLE A–6

Calculating the Median from Grouped Data
(X = Preemployment Test Scores)

Class Interval	f	cf	
66–68................	1	50	
63–65................	4	49	Median case $= \dfrac{N}{2} = 25$
60–62................	2	45	
57–59................	2	43	$l = 47.5$
54–56................	4	41	$n_m = 3$
51–53................	5	37	$f_m = 10$
48–50................	10	32	
45–47................	7	22	$\text{Med} = l + \dfrac{n_m}{f_m}\,(i)$
42–44................	5	15	
39–41................	4	10	$= 47.5 + \dfrac{3}{10}\,(3)$
36–38................	2	6	
33–35................	2	4	$= 47.5 + 0.3\,(3)$
30–32................	2	2	$= 47.5 + 0.9$
			$= 48.4$

tains the 25th case. But *where* within that interval does the 25th case fall?

Examine the *cumulative frequency (cf)* column of Table A–6. This column simply shows the total frequencies at and below a particular class interval. The *cf* entry for the class interval 45–47 indicates that 22 persons earned test scores of 47 or less. Likewise 32 persons earned test scores of 50 (the upper limit of the class interval 48–50) or less.

Since there are 50 cases in the sample and the median is given by the 25th case, inspection of the cumulative frequency column of Table A–6 confirms that the median is closer to the lower limit of the class interval 48–50 than to the upper limit of that interval. The lower limit lacks three cases of being the median; the upper limit exceeds the median by seven cases.

In order to locate the median within this class interval, we must invoke the assumption about the distribution of cases in a class interval discussed earlier. You will recall that all cases in a class interval are assumed to be distributed equidistantly throughout that interval. Thus, since there are 10 cases in the interval 48–50, that interval is assumed to be divided into tenths as shown below.

Note that the class interval 48–50 is treated as designating a continuum of scores extending from 0.5 score unit below its lower limit of 48 to 0.5 score unit above its upper limit of 50. The next higher class interval, 51–53, is regarded as extending from 50.5 to 53.5. If this were not done, the score continuum would have gaps between the top of one class interval (for example, 50) and the bottom of the next interval (for example, 51).

The computation of the median as shown in Table A–6 involves the following steps:

1. Identify the median case. This case is given by $N/2 = 50/2 = 25$. Thus the median is that score earned by the 25th person.

2. The lower limit (l) of the class interval containing the median case is 47.5. (The median case falls in the class interval 47.5–50.5.)

3. The number of cases needed from the class interval containing the median (n_m) is 3. Since there are 22 cases below this class interval and the median is given by the 25th case, $25 - 22 = 3$.

4. The number of cases in the class interval containing the median (f_m) is 10.

5. The median $= 48.4$. Since the median case is three tenths of the distance between 47.5 and 50.5 and the total distance of this class interval is three points, the median is located within the class interval at a distance of 3/10 (3), or 0.9, above the lower limit of the interval.

Related Calculations. The two designations, median and 50th percentile, are synonymous. The median score separates the upper and lower 50 percent of the cases in a distribution; the 50th percentile corresponds to that score and all lower ones earned by 50 percent of the persons in a sample.

Thus the procedure outlined above can be readily used for determining scores corresponding to any percentile. For example, what score corresponds to each 10th percentile (that is, the 10th, 20th, 30th, and so on, percentiles) of the distribution shown in Table A–6?

For the *10th* percentile we will be looking for the case that separates the bottom 10 percent of the cases from the highest 90 percent of the cases. In other words, we will be looking for the fifth case from the bottom of the cumulative frequency distribution (10 percent of $N = N/10 = 50/10 = 5$). For the *20th* percentile, we will be looking for the 10th case from the bottom of the cumulative frequency distribution (20 percent of $N = N/5 = 50/5 = 10$).

These calculations are worked below for each 10th percentile of the distribution shown in Table A–6. The computational formula is identical to that used to calculate the median:

$$\text{Percentile score} = l + \frac{n}{f}(i),$$

where l is the lower limit of the interval containing the desired percentile score; n is the number of cases needed from that interval; f is the frequency in that interval; and i is the size of the interval.

Tenth percentile (5th case) $= 35.5 + \frac{1}{2}(3) = 37.0$
Twentieth percentile (10th case) $= 38.5 + \frac{4}{4}(3) = 41.5$
Thirtieth percentile (15th case) $= 41.5 + \frac{5}{5}(3) = 44.5$
Fortieth percentile (20th case) $= 44.5 + \frac{5}{7}(3) = 46.6$
Fiftieth percentile (median) $= 47.5 + \frac{3}{10}(3) = 48.4$
Sixtieth percentile (30th case) $= 47.5 + \frac{8}{10}(3) = 49.9$
Seventieth percentile (35th case) $= 50.5 + \frac{3}{5}(3) = 52.3$
Eightieth percentile (40th case) $= 53.5 + \frac{3}{4}(3) = 55.8$
Ninetieth percentile (45th case) $= 59.5 + \frac{2}{2}(3) = 62.5$

In similar fashion you can calculate from Table A–6 that the 25th percentile is given by a test score of 43.0 and the 75th percentile by a score of 53.9.

Mode

Since the modal score is the one occurring most frequently, it can be easily identified by inspection. From Table A–2 it is evident that the mode for supervisory ratings is 5.0. In the same table the modal preemployment test score is seen to be 49. However this is somewhat misleading because the distribution does not really have a clear-cut mode; a score of 47 was earned almost as frequently as was 49.

If we were to identify the mode for the preemployment test data grouped as in Table A–6, we would regard the mode as the midpoint of the class interval with the highest frequency, that is, 49.

VARIABILITY

We have already discussed the need for describing a set of data both in terms of its central tendency and its variability (or spread away from the mean). As shown in Chapter 2, distributions may have identical means but differ markedly in their variabilities.

Although there are several statistics of variability, the only one that will concern us here is *standard deviation* (s.d.). The scores defining the range between ± 1 s.d. (one standard deviation either side of the mean) include the middle 68 percent of the cases in a normal distribution.

Computing Standard Deviation from Raw Scores

The raw score formula for standard deviation is

$$\text{s.d.} = \sqrt{\frac{\Sigma D^2}{N}},$$

where D is the difference between each raw score and the mean of the distribution. The following steps are required for this calculation:

1. Calculate the mean $(\overline{X})$ of the scores.
2. Calculate the D for each score $(X - \overline{X})$.
3. Square each D value.
4. Sum the squared D values.
5. Divide this sum by N.
6. Extract the square root.

These steps are illustrated in Table A–7 for the set of raw preemployment test scores listed in Table A–1. This distribution is shown to have a mean of 49 (actually, 48.8) and a standard deviation of 8.6.

TABLE A-7

Standard Deviation Calculated from Raw Scores
$(X = \text{preemployment test})$

Employee	X	$D = X - \bar{X}$	D^2
A............	40	−9	81
B............	35	−14	196
C............	49	0	0
D............	48	−1	1
E............	52	3	9
F............	46	−3	9
G............	58	9	81
H............	57	8	64
I............	53	4	16
J............	40	−9	81
K............	56	7	49
L............	60	11	121
M............	37	−12	144
N............	65	16	256
O............	55	6	36
P............	44	−5	25
Q............	47	−2	4
R............	63	14	196
S............	50	1	1
T............	49	0	0
U............	39	−10	100
V............	31	−18	324
W............	50	1	1
X............	47	−2	4
Y............	47	−2	4
Z............	63	14	196
AA............	41	−8	64
BB............	50	1	1
CC............	42	−7	49
DD............	49	0	0
EE............	48	−1	1
FF............	35	−14	196
GG............	53	4	16
HH............	45	−4	16
II............	62	13	169
JJ............	68	19	361
KK............	44	−5	25
LL............	64	15	225
MM............	42	−7	49
NN............	54	5	25
OO............	51	2	4
PP............	46	−3	9
QQ............	49	0	0
RR............	56	7	49
SS............	38	−11	121
TT............	51	2	4
UU............	49	0	0
VV............	32	−17	289
WW............	47	−2	4
XX............	43	−6	36
	$\Sigma X = 2,440$		$\Sigma D^2 = 3,712$

$$\bar{X} = \frac{\Sigma X}{N} = \frac{2,440}{50} = 48.8 = 49$$

$$\text{s.d.} = \sqrt{\frac{\Sigma D^2}{N}}$$

$$= \sqrt{\frac{3,712}{50}} = \sqrt{74.24}$$

$$= 8.6$$

Computing Standard Deviation from Grouped Data

The laborious calculation for standard deviation described above is considerably simplified when the data are grouped as in Table A–3. The arithmetic operations for such grouped data are shown in Table A–8.

TABLE A–8

Standard Deviation Calculated from Grouped Data
(X = preemployment test score)

ci	f	x	x^2	fx	fx^2
66–68........... 1		12	144	12	144
63–65........... 4		11	121	44	484
60–62........... 2		10	100	20	200
57–59........... 2		9	81	18	162
54–56........... 4		8	64	32	256
51–53........... 5		7	49	35	245
48–50...........10		6	36	60	360
45–47........... 7		5	25	35	175
42–44........... 5		4	16	20	80
39–41........... 4		3	9	12	36
36–38........... 2		2	4	4	8
33–35........... 2		1	1	2	2
30–32........... 2		0	0	0	0
$N = 50$				$\Sigma fx = 294$	$\Sigma fx^2 = 2,152$

$$s.d. = ci\sqrt{\frac{\Sigma fx^2}{N} - \left(\frac{\Sigma fx}{N}\right)^2}$$

$$= 3\sqrt{\frac{2,152}{50} - \left(\frac{294}{50}\right)^2}$$

$$= 3\sqrt{43.04 - (5.88)^2} = 3\sqrt{43.04 - 34.57} = 3\sqrt{8.47} = 3(2.91)$$

$$= 8.7$$

What have we done to modify the raw score standard deviation formula to the formula shown in Table A–8 for grouped data?

You will recall that the raw score formula is

$$s.d. = \sqrt{\frac{\Sigma D^2}{N}}$$

where $D = (X - \overline{X})$. Thus by substituting $(X - \overline{X})$ for D, this formula can be rewritten

$$\text{s.d.} = \sqrt{\frac{\Sigma(X - \bar{X})^2}{N}} = \sqrt{\frac{\Sigma_A^2}{N} - \left(\frac{\Sigma X}{N}\right)^2}$$

As discussed earlier, when calculations are made from raw score frequency distributions, it is easier to sum the fX values than to sum each of the X values. Thus the formula for standard deviation given above may be rewritten as

$$\text{s.d.} = \sqrt{\frac{\Sigma fX^2}{N} - \left(\frac{\Sigma fX}{N}\right)^2}$$

The calculation shown in Table A–8 involves a further simplification of the arithmetic processes. Note particularly that the work sheet in this table codes the class intervals (the x column) in numerical order starting with 0 for the interval 30–32, 1 for the interval 33–35, and so on. We have used the symbol x to represent a coded score, in contrast with X which represents an actual raw score.

When computations are based upon these coded scores rather than raw scores, the formula for standard deviation when the class interval is 1 must be rewritten:

$$\text{s.d.} = \sqrt{\frac{\Sigma fx^2}{N} - \left(\frac{\Sigma fx}{N}\right)^2}$$

One final modification is necessitated by the fact that the scores in Table A–8 are organized into intervals of 3. The above formula would in this case give an estimate of $\frac{1}{3}$ s.d. To make this formula generally applicable regardless of the size of the class interval, requires restatement as follows:

$$\text{s.d.} = ci \sqrt{\frac{\Sigma fx^2}{N} - \left(\frac{\Sigma fx}{N}\right)^2}$$

TRANSFORMATIONS OF RAW SCORES

The discussion of test norming in Chapter 6 clarified the need for transforming raw scores to some sort of common base for comparative purposes. Referring to Table A–1, did person A score "better" on the preemployment test or on the supervisory rating? His raw score on the former was 40; on the latter 3.0. We have already

TABLE A–9

Transformation of Raw Scores to Numerical Ranks

Employee	Preemployment Test		Supervisory Rating	
	X	$Rank_x$	Y	$Rank_y$
A	40	42.5	3.0	40.5
B	35	47.5	6.0	16.5
C	49	24.0	5.0	25.5
D	48	27.5	4.0	34.5
E	52	16.0	6.0	16.5
F	46	33.5	3.0	40.5
G	58	8.0	3.0	40.5
H	57	9.0	7.0	11.0
I	53	14.5	6.0	16.5
J	40	42.5	4.0	34.5
K	56	10.5	7.0	11.0
L	60	7.0	8.0	6.5
M	37	46.0	5.0	25.5
N	65	2.0	7.0	11.0
O	55	12.0	9.0	2.5
P	44	36.5	4.0	34.5
Q	47	30.5	5.0	25.5
R	63	4.5	8.0	6.5
S	50	20.0	6.0	16.5
T	49	24.0	5.0	25.5
U	39	44.0	2.0	46.0
V	31	50.0	1.0	49.5
W	50	20.0	5.0	25.5
X	47	30.5	5.0	25.5
Y	47	37.5	5.0	25.5
Z	63	4.5	9.0	2.5
AA	41	41.0	8.0	6.5
BB	50	20.0	7.0	11.0
CC	42	39.5	3.0	40.5
DD	49	24.0	5.0	25.5
EE	48	27.5	5.0	25.5
FF	35	47.5	2.0	46.0
GG	53	14.5	2.0	46.0
HH	45	35.0	4.0	34.5
II	62	6.0	9.0	2.5
JJ	68	1.0	9.0	2.5
KK	44	36.5	4.0	34.5
LL	64	3.0	8.0	6.5
MM	42	39.5	2.0	46.0
NN	54	13.0	2.0	46.0
OO	51	17.5	6.0	16.5
PP	46	33.5	5.0	25.5
QQ	49	24.0	3.0	40.5
RR	56	10.5	7.0	11.0
SS	38	45.0	3.0	40.5
TT	51	17.5	6.0	16.5
UU	49	24.0	5.0	25.5
VV	32	49.0	1.0	49.5
WW	47	30.5	4.0	34.5
XX	43	38.0	5.0	25.5

calculated the mean as 48.8 for the preemployment test and 5.0 for the supervisory rating. Hence, person A scored below the mean on both measures. But how far below each mean were his scores? The difference between his raw test score and its mean (8.8 points) cannot be compared with the difference between his raw rating and *its* mean (2.0 units) without transforming both sets of scores to a common yardstick.

The particular kinds of transformations with which we will here be concerned are numerical rank, percentile rank, and standard score.

Numerical Rank

Raw scores are numerically ranked by arranging them in order from highest to lowest and assigning a rank of *1* to the highest raw score, *2* to the second highest score, and so on. This has been done in Table A–9 for the raw scores listed in Table A–1.

Note the procedure for assigning ranks when two or more persons have the same raw score. Two persons (*R* and *Z*) for example, earned preemployment test scores of 63. Since three persons had scores higher than 63, we had previously assigned the ranks 1, 2, and 3. Therefore a rank of 4.5 (midway between ranks 4 and 5) is assigned to persons *R* and *Z,* and the next lower raw score (62, earned by II) is assigned a rank of 6.

Percentile Rank

A percentile rank states the percent of persons scoring at or below the raw score to which it corresponds. Thus if we are told that a given raw score corresponds to the 72nd percentile, we know that 72 percent of the persons taking this test earned scores at or below that raw score. By transforming raw scores from two or more tests to a percentile rank yardstick, it becomes possible to make direct comparisons between a person's performance across these tests.

The easiest method for computing percentile ranks is to begin with a frequency distribution using raw scores rather than class intervals. Cumulative frequencies (*cf*) are next computed for each raw score. The cumulative frequency is the number of persons earning that particular score or lower. These cumulative frequencies are then easily converted to percentile ranks by

$$\%\text{ile rank} = \frac{cf}{N}$$

The procedure is illustrated in Table A–10, taking the frequency distribution from Table A–2. The arrangement of the display in Table A–10 clarifies the usefulness of percentile ranks as raw score transformations. Note, for example, that a raw preemployment test score of 57 carries the same percentile rank as a raw supervisory rating of 7.0. And, returning to our initial question about person A's performance, we note that whereas his preemployment test score ranks at the 18th percentile, his supervisory rating ranks at the 26th percentile.

Standard Score

It is often useful to transform scores in such a way that they can both be directly compared and combined into a single composite score. Whereas percentile ranks permit direct comparisons of raw scores, such ranks cannot be averaged or summed to yield a single composite score. To achieve this end, it is necessary to effect a standard score transformation.

One kind of standard score is the Z score, defined by the formula

$$Z_x = \frac{X - \bar{X}}{sd_x} \quad \text{or} \quad Z_y = \frac{Y - \bar{Y}}{sd_y}$$

Appropriate Z score transformations of the raw preemployment test and supervisory rating scores are shown in Table A–11. Once again, to clarify the utility of such transformations, the raw scores on both measures are aligned in terms of their Z score equivalents.

CORRELATION

A correlation coefficient indicates both the magnitude and direction of the relationship between two or more sets of scores (see Chapter 2). The discussion in this section is restricted to correlations involving two variables only.

The Scattergram

The meaning of correlation is clarified by plotting a scattergram (or cross-tally) of each person's score on the two variables under

TABLE A–10

Transforming Raw Scores to Percentile Ranks

Preemployment Test				Supervisory Rating			
X	f	cf	%ile Rank	Y	f	cf	%ile Rank
68	1	50		9.0	4	50	
67	0	49	98				
66	0	49	98				
65	1	49	98				
64	1	48	96				
63	2	47	94				
62	1	45	90	8.0	4	46	92
61	0	44	88				
60	1	44	88				
59	0	43	86				
58	1	43	86				
57	1	42	84	7.0	5	42	84
56	2	41	82				
55	1	39	78				
54	1	38	76				
53	2	37	74	6.0	6	37	74
52	1	35	70				
51	2	34	68				
50	3	32	64	5.0	12	31	62
49	5	29	58				
48	2	24	48				
47	4	22	44	4.0	6	19	38
46	2	18	36				
45	1	16	32				
44	2	15	30				
43	1	13	26	3.0	6	13	26
42	2	12	24				
41	1	10	20				
40	2	9	18				
39	1	7	14	2.0	5	7	14
38	1	6	12				
37	1	5	10				
36	0	4	8				
35	2	4	8				
34	0	2	4				
33	0	2	4				
32	1	2	4	1.0	2	2	4
31	1	1	2				

TABLE A–11

Z Score Transformations of Raw Scores

Preemployment Test $(\bar{X} = 49; sd_x = 8.7)$			Supervisory Ratings $(\bar{Y} = 5.0; sd_y = 2.2)$		
X	$X - \bar{X}$	z_x	Y	$Y - \bar{Y}$	z_y
68	19	2.19			
67	18	2.07			
66	17	1.96			
65	16	1.84	9.0	4	1.82
64	15	1.73			
63	14	1.61			
62	13	1.50			
61	12	1.38	8.0	3	1.37
60	11	1.27			
59	10	1.15			
58	9	1.04			
57	8	0.92	7.0	2	0.91
56	7	0.81			
55	6	0.69			
54	5	0.58			
53	4	0.46	6.0	1	0.46
52	3	0.35			
51	2	0.23			
50	1	0.12			
49	0	0.00	5.0	0	0.00
48	−1	−0.12			
47	−2	−0.23			
46	−3	−0.35			
45	−4	−0.46	4.0	−1	−0.46
44	−5	−0.58			
43	−6	−0.69			
42	−7	−0.81			
41	−8	−0.92	3.0	−2	−0.91
40	−9	−1.04			
39	−10	−1.15			
38	−11	−1.27			
37	−12	−1.38	2.0	−3	−1.37
36	−13	−1.50			
35	−14	−1.61			
34	−15	−1.73			
33	−16	−1.84	1.0	−4	−1.82
32	−17	−1.96			
31	−18	−2.07			

FIGURE A-1

Scattergram Showing the Relationship between Preemployment Test
Scores (X) and Supervisory Ratings (Y)

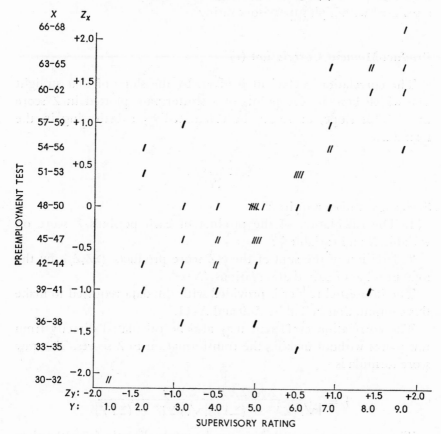

consideration. This has been done in Figure A-1 for the raw score
data taken from Table A-9. Person A's scores $(X = 40; Y = 3.0)$ are
represented by a tally mark at the intersection of the two appropriate base line intervals (39–41 for X; 3.0 for Y); person B's scores
$(X = 35; Y = 2.0)$ are indicated by a tally at the intersection of the
33–35 interval for X and the 2.0 interval for Y; and so on.

We have already shown, in the previous discussion of standard
scores, that preemployment test raw score units are not equivalent to
supervisory rating raw score units. Therefore the raw scores along
the axes of Figure A-1 are spaced proportionally to their Z score
transformations (as given in Table A-11).

From the discussion in Chapter 2 you will undoubtedly recognize that this particular scattergram provides evidence for a moderately high and positive correlation. High preemployment test scores are associated with high supervisory ratings.

Product-Moment Correlation (r)

The correlation coefficient is given by the slope of that straight line which best fits the points of a scattergram plotted in Z score units. This slope, or r, can be calculated by substituting in the formula

$$r = \frac{\Sigma Z_x Z_y}{N} .$$

Such substitution requires:

1. The calculation of the product of each person's Z score on variable X and variable $Y;$
2. Division of the sum of these Z score products $(\Sigma Z_x Z_y)$ by the total number of paired observations (N) .

The interested reader is provided with the data required to make this computation in Tables A–9 and A–11.

The correlation coefficient may also be calculated directly from raw scores without making the transformation to Z scores. The raw score formula is

$$r = \frac{N\Sigma XY - \Sigma X\Sigma Y}{[\sqrt{N\Sigma X^2 - (\Sigma X)^2}][\sqrt{N\Sigma Y^2 - (\Sigma Y)^2}]}$$

The necessary computations can be made directly from the data in Table A–1 by—

1. Adding all X scores $(\Sigma X = 2{,}440)$.
2. Adding all Y scores $(\Sigma Y = 253)$.
3. Adding the products of each pair of X and Y scores $(\Sigma XY = 13{,}001)$.
4. Adding the squares of each X score $(\Sigma X^2 = 122{,}782)$.
5. Adding the squares of each Y score $(\Sigma Y^2 = 1{,}513)$.
6. Squaring the ΣX to obtain $(\Sigma X)^2 = 5{,}953{,}600$.
7. Squaring the ΣY to obtain $(\Sigma Y)^2 = 64{,}009$.
8. Substituting the values above in the raw score formula for r. The resultant value of r is 0.73.

Rank-Difference Correlation

The simplest method for estimating correlation coefficients when the number of paired observations is not too large is the rank-difference method. The formula for this estimate of correlation (ρ:rho) is

$$\rho = 1 - \frac{6\Sigma D^2}{N(N^2 - 1)},$$

where D is the difference in numerical ranks of the two scores comprising each pair. An illustrative computation using the rank data from Table A-9 is given in Table A-12.

THE MEAN DIFFERENCE

The correlation between preemployment test scores and supervisory ratings as in the preceding illustration is a validity coefficient. The value *0.68* tells us that the two measures, one obtained prior to employment (the predictor) and the other three months after employment (the criterion), are related.

Another evidence of this relationship may be obtained by examining the predictor scores of persons judged after three months to perform satisfactorily and unsatisfactorily. Specifically, this procedure involves (*a*) separating groups of persons eventually earning "high" and "low" criterion ratings and (*b*) comparing the mean predictor scores for these groups. If the preemployment test were valid, then persons receiving "favorable" supervisory ratings should as a group have earned higher test scores than persons receiving "unfavorable" ratings.

Of the several techniques for interpreting an obtained difference between means, the simplest provides an estimate of the percentage overlap between the two distributions from which the means were calculated. (Another statistic, the *t* ratio, although commonly used, is beyond the scope of the present discussion.)

In order to apply the percentage overlap procedure to our data, we must first separate the persons in the total sample into "high" and "low" subgroups based upon criterion ratings. Since the supervisory ratings were essentially normally distributed about a mean rating of 5.0 ("average performance"), we can regard ratings be-

TABLE A–12

Calculating the Rank-Difference Correlation between Preemployment
Test Score (X) and Supervisory Rating (Y)

Employee	$Rank_x$	$Rank_y$	D	D^2	Employee	$Rank_x$	$Rank_y$	D	D^2
A.........42.5		40.5	2.0	4.00	Z.........	4.5	2.5	2.0	4.00
B.........47.5		16.5	31.0	961.00	AA........	41.0	6.5	34.5	1,190.25
C.........24.0		25.5	1.5	1.25	BB........	20.0	11.0	9.0	81.00
D.........27.5		34.5	7.0	49.00	CC........	39.5	40.5	1.0	1.00
E.........16.0		16.5	0.5	0.25	DD........	24.0	25.5	1.5	2.25
F.........33.5		40.5	6.5	42.25	EE........	27.5	25.5	2.0	4.00
G......... 8.0		40.5	32.5	1,056.25	FF........	47.5	46.0	1.5	2.25
H......... 9.0		11.0	2.0	4.00	GG........	14.5	46.0	31.5	992.25
I.........14.5		16.5	2.0	4.00	HH........	35.0	34.5	0.5	0.25
J.........42.5		34.5	8.0	64.00	II.........	6.0	2.5	3.5	12.25
K.........10.5		11.0	0.5	0.25	JJ.........	1.0	2.5	1.5	2.25
L......... 7.0		6.5	0.5	0.25	KK........	36.5	34.5	2.0	4.00
M.........46.0		25.5	21.5	462.25	LL........	3.0	6.5	3.5	12.25
N......... 2.0		11.0	9.0	81.00	MM........	39.5	46.0	6.5	42.25
O.........12.0		2.5	9.5	90.25	NN........	13.0	46.0	33.0	1,089.00
P.........36.5		34.5	2.0	4.00	OO........	17.5	16.5	1.0	1.00
Q.........30.5		25.5	5.0	25.00	PP........	33.5	25.5	8.0	64.00
R......... 4.5		6.5	2.0	4.00	QQ........	24.0	40.5	15.5	240.25
S.........20.0		16.5	3.5	12.25	RR........	10.5	11.0	0.5	0.25
T.........24.0		25.5	1.5	2.25	SS........	45.0	40.5	4.5	20.25
U.........44.0		46.0	2.0	4.00	TT........	17.5	16.5	1.0	1.00
V.........50.0		49.5	0.5	0.25	UU........	24.0	25.5	1.5	2.25
W.........20.0		25.5	5.5	30.25	VV........	49.0	49.5	0.5	0.25
X.........30.5		25.5	5.0	25.00	WW........	30.5	34.5	4.0	16.00
Y.........30.5		25.5	5.0	25.00	XX........	38.0	34.5	3.5	12.25

$$\Sigma D^2 = 6{,}748.75$$

$$= 1 - \frac{6\Sigma D^2}{N(N^2 - 1)}$$

$$= 1 - \frac{6(6{,}748.75)}{50(2{,}500 - 1)}$$

$$= 1 - \frac{40{,}492.5}{124{,}950.0}$$

$$= 1 - 0.32$$

$$= 0.68$$

tween 6.0–9.0 as "favorable" and those between 1.0–4.0 as "unfavorable."

Having thus defined the high ("favorable" ratings) and low ("unfavorable" ratings) criterion subgroups, the next step is to determine the percentage overlap *(0)* in the distributions of preemployment test scores for these subgroups. This requires a reorganization of the raw data originally presented in Table A–1 in the form shown in Table A–13.

TABLE A–13

Calculating the Percentage Overlap

High Criterion Group (Supervisory Ratings: 6.0–9.0)		Low Criterion Group (Supervisory Ratings: 1.0–4.0)		
Employee	*Preemployment Test Score*	*Employee*	*Preemployment Test Score*	
B.............35		A.............40		
E.............52		D.............48		
H.............57		F.............46		
I.............53		G.............58		
K.............56	$N = 19$	J.............40	$N = 19$	
L.............60	$\bar{X}_h = 55.4$	P.............40	$\bar{X}_l = 43.3$	
N.............65	$sd_h = 7.9$	U.............39	$sd_l = 7.1$	
O.............55		V.............31		
R.............63		CC.............42		
S.............50		FF.............35		
Z.............63		GG.............53		
AA.............41		HH.............45		
BB.............50		KK.............44		
II.............62		MM.............42		
JJ.............68		NN.............54		
LL.............64		QQ.............49		
OO.............51		SS.............38		
RR.............56		VV.............32		
TT.............51		WW.............47		

$$\bar{X}_h - \bar{X}_l = 55.4 - 43.3 = 12.1$$

$$sd_{av} = \frac{sd_h + sd_l}{2} = \frac{7.9 + 7.1}{2} = 7.5$$

$$\frac{\bar{X}_h - \bar{X}_l}{sd_{av}} = \frac{12.1}{7.5} = 1.61$$

The mean and standard deviation is calculated separately for the high and low criterion subgroups. (Verification of these values as shown in Table A–13 constitutes an easy review exercise.) To estimate the percentage overlap between the two preemployment test distributions, the difference between the two means is divided by the

TABLE A–14

Estimation of Percentage Overlap, 0, between Two Distributions from Means and Standard Deviations

$\dfrac{\bar{X}_h - \bar{X}_l}{sd_{av.}}$*	Percentage Overlap, 0	$\dfrac{\bar{X}_h - \bar{X}_l}{sd_{av.}}$*	Percentage Overlap, 0	$\dfrac{X_h - X_l}{sd_{av.}}$*	Percentage Overlap, 0
0.000	100	0.880	66	1.948	33
0.025	99	0.908	65	1.989	32
0.050	98	0.935	64	2.030	31
0.075	97	0.963	63	2.073	30
0.100	96	0.992	62	2.116	29
0.125	95	1.020	61	2.161	28
0.151	94	1.049	60	2.206	27
0.176	93	1.078	59	2.253	26
0.201	92	1.107	58	2.301	25
0.226	91	1.136	57	2.350	24
0.251	90	1.166	56	2.401	23
0.277	89	1.197	55	2.453	22
0.302	88	1.226	54	2.507	21
0.327	87	1.256	53	2.563	20
0.353	86	1.287	52	2.621	19
0.378	85	1.318	51	2.682	18
0.403	84	1.349	50	2.744	17
0.429	83	1.381	49	2.810	16
0.455	82	1.413	48	2.879	15
0.481	81	1.445	47	2.952	14
0.507	80	1.478	46	3.028	13
0.533	79	1.511	45	3.110	12
0.559	78	1.544	44	3.196	11
0.585	77	1.578	43	3.290	10
0.611	76	1.613	42	3.391	9
0.637	75	1.648	41	3.501	8
0.664	74	1.683	40	3.624	7
0.690	73	1.719	39	3.762	6
0.717	72	1.756	38	3.920	5
0.744	71	1.793	37	4.107	4
0.771	70	1.831	36	4.340	3
0.798	69	1.869	35	4.653	2
0.825	68	1.908	34	5.152	1
0.852	67				

* sd_{av} = average of the standard deviations = $\dfrac{sd_2 + sd_1}{2}$

Source: J. W. Tilton, "The Measurement of Overlapping," *Journal of Educational Psychology*, Vol. 28, (1937) 656–62.

average of the two standard deviations and the resultant quotient is entered into Table A–14.[2]

Table A–14 estimates that distributions yielding a quotient of 1.61 overlap 42 percent. In other words, it is estimated that for 42 percent of the cases, the predictor scores will *not* distinguish between satisfactory and unsatisfactory criterion ratings. Conversely, it is estimated that the preemployment test can effectively separate potentially satisfactory from potentially unsatisfactory employees 58 percent of the time.

If a predictor were totally invalid, the estimate of 0 would, of course, be 100 percent. In this case, there would be complete overlapping between the distributions of predictor scores for the two criterion groups. The greater the validity, the lower the 0 until with perfect validity the two distributions of predictor scores are totally independent $(0 = 0.00)$.

---

[2] J. W. Tilton, "The Measurement of Overlapping," *Journal of Educational Psychology*, Vol. 28 (1937), pp. 656–62.

B. Taylor-Russell Tables[1] for Group Prediction[2]

---

[1] H. C. Taylor and J. T. Russell, "The Relationship of Validity Coefficients to the Practical Effectiveness of Tests in Selection: Discussion and Tables," *Journal of Applied Psychology*, Vol. 23 (1939) , pp. 565–78.

[2] Entries are the proportions of employees who will be satisfactory among those selected under specified conditions.

Proportion of Employees Considered Satisfactory = 0.05

	Selection Ratio										
r	*0.05*	*0.10*	*0.20*	*0.30*	*0.40*	*0.50*	*0.60*	*0.70*	*0.80*	*0.90*	*0.95*
0.00	0.05	0.05	0.05	0.05	0.05	0.05	0.05	0.05	0.05	0.05	0.05
0.05	0.06	0.06	0.06	0.06	0.06	0.05	0.05	0.05	0.05	0.05	0.05
0.10	0.07	0.07	0.07	0.06	0.06	0.06	0.06	0.05	0.05	0.05	0.05
0.15	0.09	0.08	0.07	0.07	0.07	0.06	0.06	0.06	0.05	0.05	0.05
0.20	0.11	0.09	0.08	0.08	0.07	0.07	0.06	0.06	0.06	0.05	0.05
0.25	0.12	0.11	0.09	0.08	0.08	0.07	0.07	0.06	0.06	0.05	0.05
0.30	0.14	0.12	0.10	0.09	0.08	0.07	0.07	0.06	0.06	0.05	0.05
0.35	0.17	0.14	0.11	0.10	0.09	0.08	0.07	0.06	0.06	0.05	0.05
0.40	0.19	0.16	0.12	0.10	0.09	0.08	0.07	0.07	0.06	0.05	0.05
0.45	0.22	0.17	0.13	0.11	0.10	0.08	0.08	0.07	0.06	0.06	0.05
0.50	0.24	0.19	0.15	0.12	0.10	0.09	0.08	0.07	0.06	0.06	0.05
0.55	0.28	0.22	0.16	0.13	0.11	0.09	0.08	0.07	0.06	0.06	0.05
0.60	0.31	0.24	0.17	0.13	0.11	0.09	0.08	0.07	0.06	0.06	0.05
0.65	0.35	0.26	0.18	0.14	0.11	0.10	0.08	0.07	0.06	0.06	0.05
0.70	0.39	0.29	0.20	0.15	0.12	0.10	0.08	0.07	0.06	0.06	0.05
0.75	0.44	0.32	0.21	0.15	0.12	0.10	0.08	0.07	0.06	0.06	0.05
0.80	0.50	0.35	0.22	0.16	0.12	0.10	0.08	0.07	0.06	0.06	0.05
0.85	0.56	0.39	0.23	0.16	0.12	0.10	0.08	0.07	0.06	0.06	0.05
0.90	0.64	0.43	0.24	0.17	0.13	0.10	0.08	0.07	0.06	0.06	0.05
0.95	0.73	0.47	0.25	0.17	0.13	0.10	0.08	0.07	0.06	0.06	0.05
1.00	1.00	0.50	0.25	0.17	0.13	0.10	0.08	0.07	0.06	0.06	0.05

Proportion of Employees Considered Satisfactory = 0.10

	Selection Ratio										
r	0.05	0.10	0.20	0.30	0.40	0.50	0.60	0.70	0.80	0.90	0.95
0.00	0.10	0.10	0.10	0.10	0.10	0.10	0.10	0.10	0.10	0.10	0.10
0.05	0.12	0.12	0.11	0.11	0.11	0.11	0.11	0.10	0.10	0.10	0.10
0.10	0.14	0.13	0.13	0.12	0.12	0.11	0.11	0.11	0.11	0.10	0.10
0.15	0.16	0.15	0.14	0.13	0.13	0.12	0.12	0.11	0.11	0.10	0.10
0.20	0.19	0.17	0.15	0.14	0.14	0.13	0.12	0.12	0.11	0.11	0.10
0.25	0.22	0.19	0.17	0.16	0.14	0.13	0.13	0.12	0.11	0.11	0.10
0.30	0.25	0.22	0.19	0.17	0.15	0.14	0.13	0.12	0.12	0.11	0.10
0.35	0.28	0.24	0.20	0.18	0.16	0.15	0.14	0.13	0.12	0.11	0.10
0.40	0.31	0.27	0.22	0.19	0.17	0.16	0.14	0.13	0.12	0.11	0.10
0.45	0.35	0.29	0.24	0.20	0.18	0.16	0.15	0.13	0.12	0.11	0.10
0.50	0.39	0.32	0.26	0.22	0.19	0.17	0.15	0.13	0.12	0.11	0.11
0.55	0.43	0.36	0.28	0.23	0.20	0.17	0.15	0.14	0.12	0.11	0.11
0.60	0.48	0.39	0.30	0.25	0.21	0.18	0.16	0.14	0.12	0.11	0.11
0.65	0.53	0.43	0.32	0.26	0.22	0.18	0.16	0.14	0.12	0.11	0.11
0.70	0.58	0.47	0.35	0.27	0.22	0.19	0.16	0.14	0.12	0.11	0.11
0.75	0.64	0.51	0.37	0.29	0.23	0.19	0.16	0.14	0.12	0.11	0.11
0.80	0.71	0.56	0.40	0.30	0.24	0.20	0.17	0.14	0.12	0.11	0.11
0.85	0.78	0.62	0.43	0.31	0.25	0.20	0.17	0.14	0.12	0.11	0.11
0.90	0.86	0.69	0.46	0.33	0.25	0.20	0.17	0.14	0.12	0.11	0.11
0.95	0.95	0.78	0.49	0.33	0.25	0.20	0.17	0.14	0.12	0.11	0.11
1.00	1.00	1.00	0.50	0.33	0.25	0.20	0.17	0.14	0.13	0.11	0.11

Proportion of Employees Considered Satisfactory = 0.20

						Selection Ratio					
r	0.05	0.10	0.20	0.30	0.40	0.50	0.60	0.70	0.80	0.90	0.95
0.00	0.20	0.20	0.20	0.20	0.20	0.20	0.20	0.20	0.20	0.20	0.20
0.05	0.23	0.23	0.22	0.22	0.21	0.21	0.21	0.21	0.20	0.20	0.20
0.10	0.26	0.25	0.24	0.23	0.23	0.22	0.22	0.21	0.21	0.21	0.20
0.15	0.30	0.28	0.26	0.25	0.24	0.23	0.23	0.22	0.21	0.21	0.20
0.20	0.33	0.31	0.28	0.27	0.26	0.25	0.24	0.23	0.22	0.21	0.21
0.25	0.37	0.34	0.31	0.29	0.27	0.26	0.24	0.23	0.22	0.21	0.21
0.30	0.41	0.37	0.33	0.30	0.28	0.27	0.25	0.24	0.23	0.21	0.21
0.35	0.45	0.41	0.36	0.32	0.30	0.28	0.26	0.24	0.23	0.22	0.21
0.40	0.49	0.44	0.38	0.34	0.31	0.29	0.27	0.25	0.23	0.22	0.21
0.45	0.54	0.48	0.41	0.36	0.33	0.30	0.28	0.26	0.24	0.22	0.21
0.50	0.59	0.52	0.44	0.38	0.35	0.31	0.29	0.26	0.24	0.22	0.21
0.55	0.63	0.56	0.47	0.41	0.36	0.32	0.29	0.27	0.24	0.22	0.21
0.60	0.68	0.60	0.50	0.43	0.38	0.34	0.30	0.27	0.24	0.22	0.21
0.65	0.73	0.64	0.53	0.45	0.39	0.35	0.31	0.27	0.25	0.22	0.21
0.70	0.79	0.69	0.56	0.48	0.41	0.36	0.31	0.28	0.25	0.22	0.21
0.75	0.84	0.74	0.60	0.50	0.43	0.37	0.32	0.28	0.25	0.22	0.21
0.80	0.89	0.79	0.64	0.53	0.45	0.38	0.33	0.28	0.25	0.22	0.21
0.85	0.94	0.85	0.69	0.56	0.47	0.39	0.33	0.28	0.25	0.22	0.21
0.90	0.98	0.91	0.75	0.60	0.48	0.40	0.33	0.29	0.25	0.22	0.21
0.95	1.00	0.97	0.82	0.64	0.50	0.40	0.33	0.29	0.25	0.22	0.21
1.00	1.00	1.00	1.00	0.67	0.50	0.40	0.33	0.29	0.25	0.22	0.21

Proportion of Employees Considered Satisfactory = 0.30

					Selection Ratio						
r	0.05	0.10	0.20	0.30	0.40	0.50	0.60	0.70	0.80	0.90	0.95
0.00	0.30	0.30	0.30	0.30	0.30	0.30	0.30	0.30	0.30	0.30	0.30
0.05	0.34	0.33	0.33	0.32	0.32	0.31	0.31	0.31	0.31	0.30	0.30
0.10	0.38	0.36	0.35	0.34	0.33	0.33	0.32	0.32	0.31	0.31	0.30
0.15	0.42	0.40	0.38	0.36	0.35	0.34	0.33	0.33	0.32	0.31	0.31
0.20	0.46	0.43	0.40	0.38	0.37	0.36	0.34	0.33	0.32	0.31	0.31
0.25	0.50	0.47	0.43	0.41	0.39	0.37	0.36	0.34	0.33	0.32	0.31
0.30	0.54	0.50	0.46	0.43	0.40	0.38	0.37	0.35	0.33	0.32	0.31
0.35	0.58	0.54	0.49	0.45	0.42	0.40	0.38	0.36	0.34	0.32	0.31
0.40	0.63	0.58	0.51	0.47	0.44	0.41	0.39	0.37	0.34	0.32	0.31
0.45	0.67	0.61	0.55	0.50	0.46	0.43	0.40	0.37	0.35	0.32	0.31
0.50	0.72	0.65	0.58	0.52	0.48	0.44	0.41	0.38	0.35	0.33	0.31
0.55	0.76	0.69	0.61	0.55	0.50	0.46	0.42	0.39	0.36	0.33	0.31
0.60	0.81	0.74	0.64	0.58	0.52	0.47	0.43	0.40	0.36	0.33	0.31
0.65	0.85	0.78	0.68	0.60	0.54	0.49	0.44	0.40	0.37	0.33	0.32
0.70	0.89	0.82	0.72	0.63	0.57	0.51	0.46	0.41	0.37	0.33	0.32
0.75	0.93	0.86	0.76	0.67	0.59	0.52	0.47	0.42	0.37	0.33	0.32
0.80	0.96	0.90	0.80	0.70	0.62	0.54	0.48	0.42	0.37	0.33	0.32
0.85	0.99	0.94	0.85	0.74	0.65	0.56	0.49	0.43	0.37	0.33	0.32
0.90	1.00	0.98	0.90	0.79	0.68	0.58	0.49	0.43	0.37	0.33	0.32
0.95	1.00	1.00	0.96	0.85	0.72	0.60	0.50	0.43	0.37	0.33	0.32
1.00	1.00	1.00	1.00	1.00	0.75	0.60	0.50	0.43	0.38	0.33	0.32

Proportion of Employees Considered Satisfactory = 0.40

	Selection Ratio										
r	0.05	0.10	0.20	0.30	0.40	0.50	0.60	0.70	0.80	0.90	0.95
0.00	0.40	0.40	0.40	0.40	0.40	0.40	0.40	0.40	0.40	0.40	0.40
0.05	0.44	0.43	0.43	0.42	0.42	0.42	0.41	0.41	0.41	0.40	0.40
0.10	0.48	0.47	0.46	0.45	0.44	0.43	0.42	0.42	0.41	0.41	0.40
0.15	0.52	0.50	0.48	0.47	0.46	0.45	0.44	0.43	0.42	0.41	0.41
0.20	0.57	0.54	0.51	0.49	0.48	0.46	0.45	0.44	0.43	0.41	0.41
0.25	0.61	0.58	0.54	0.51	0.49	0.48	0.46	0.45	0.43	0.42	0.41
0.30	0.65	0.61	0.57	0.54	0.51	0.49	0.47	0.46	0.44	0.42	0.41
0.35	0.69	0.65	0.60	0.56	0.53	0.51	0.49	0.47	0.45	0.42	0.41
0.40	0.73	0.69	0.63	0.59	0.56	0.53	0.50	0.48	0.45	0.43	0.41
0.45	0.77	0.72	0.66	0.61	0.58	0.54	0.51	0.49	0.46	0.43	0.42
0.50	0.81	0.76	0.69	0.64	0.60	0.56	0.53	0.49	0.46	0.43	0.42
0.55	0.85	0.79	0.72	0.67	0.62	0.58	0.54	0.50	0.47	0.44	0.42
0.60	0.89	0.83	0.75	0.69	0.64	0.60	0.55	0.51	0.48	0.44	0.42
0.65	0.92	0.87	0.79	0.72	0.67	0.62	0.57	0.52	0.48	0.44	0.42
0.70	0.95	0.90	0.82	0.76	0.69	0.64	0.58	0.53	0.49	0.44	0.42
0.75	0.97	0.93	0.86	0.79	0.72	0.66	0.60	0.54	0.49	0.44	0.42
0.80	0.99	0.96	0.89	0.82	0.75	0.68	0.61	0.55	0.49	0.44	0.42
0.85	1.00	0.98	0.93	0.86	0.79	0.71	0.63	0.56	0.50	0.44	0.42
0.90	1.00	1.00	0.97	0.91	0.82	0.74	0.65	0.57	0.50	0.44	0.42
0.95	1.00	1.00	0.99	0.96	0.87	0.77	0.66	0.57	0.50	0.44	0.42
1.00	1.00	1.00	1.00	1.00	1.00	0.80	0.67	0.57	0.50	0.44	0.42

| | Proportion of Employees Considered Satisfactory = 0.50 | | | | | | | | | | |
| | | | | | Selection Ratio | | | | | | |
r	0.05	0.10	0.20	0.30	0.40	0.50	0.60	0.70	0.80	0.90	0.95
0.00	0.50	0.50	0.50	0.50	0.50	0.50	0.50	0.50	0.50	0.50	0.50
0.05	0.54	0.54	0.53	0.52	0.52	0.52	0.51	0.51	0.51	0.50	0.50
0.10	0.58	0.57	0.56	0.55	0.54	0.53	0.53	0.52	0.51	0.51	0.50
0.15	0.63	0.61	0.58	0.57	0.56	0.55	0.54	0.53	0.52	0.51	0.51
0.20	0.67	0.64	0.61	0.59	0.58	0.56	0.55	0.54	0.53	0.52	0.51
0.25	0.70	0.67	0.64	0.62	0.60	0.58	0.56	0.55	0.54	0.52	0.51
0.30	0.74	0.71	0.67	0.64	0.62	0.60	0.58	0.56	0.54	0.52	0.51
0.35	0.78	0.74	0.70	0.66	0.64	0.61	0.59	0.57	0.55	0.53	0.51
0.40	0.82	0.78	0.73	0.69	0.66	0.63	0.61	0.58	0.56	0.53	0.52
0.45	0.85	0.81	0.75	0.71	0.68	0.65	0.62	0.59	0.56	0.53	0.52
0.50	0.88	0.84	0.78	0.74	0.70	0.67	0.63	0.60	0.57	0.54	0.52
0.55	0.91	0.87	0.81	0.76	0.72	0.69	0.65	0.61	0.58	0.54	0.52
0.60	0.94	0.90	0.84	0.79	0.75	0.70	0.66	0.62	0.59	0.54	0.52
0.65	0.96	0.92	0.87	0.82	0.77	0.73	0.68	0.64	0.59	0.55	0.52
0.70	0.98	0.95	0.90	0.85	0.80	0.75	0.70	0.65	0.60	0.55	0.53
0.75	0.99	0.97	0.92	0.87	0.82	0.77	0.72	0.66	0.61	0.55	0.53
0.80	1.00	0.99	0.95	0.90	0.85	0.80	0.73	0.67	0.61	0.55	0.53
0.85	1.00	0.99	0.97	0.94	0.88	0.82	0.76	0.69	0.62	0.55	0.53
0.90	1.00	1.00	0.99	0.97	0.92	0.86	0.78	0.70	0.62	0.56	0.53
0.95	1.00	1.00	1.00	0.99	0.96	0.90	0.81	0.71	0.63	0.56	0.53
1.00	1.00	1.00	1.00	1.00	1.00	1.00	0.83	0.71	0.63	0.56	0.53

Proportion of Employees Considered Satisfactory = 0.60

	Selection Ratio										
r	0.05	0.10	0.20	0.30	0.40	0.50	0.60	0.70	0.80	0.90	0.95
0.00	0.60	0.60	0.60	0.60	0.60	0.60	0.60	0.60	0.60	0.60	0.60
0.05	0.64	0.63	0.63	0.62	0.62	0.62	0.61	0.61	0.61	0.60	0.60
0.10	0.68	0.67	0.65	0.64	0.64	0.63	0.63	0.62	0.61	0.61	0.60
0.15	0.71	0.70	0.68	0.67	0.66	0.65	0.64	0.63	0.62	0.61	0.61
0.20	0.75	0.73	0.71	0.69	0.67	0.66	0.65	0.64	0.63	0.62	0.61
0.25	0.78	0.76	0.73	0.71	0.69	0.68	0.66	0.65	0.63	0.62	0.61
0.30	0.82	0.79	0.76	0.73	0.71	0.69	0.68	0.66	0.64	0.62	0.61
0.35	0.85	0.82	0.78	0.75	0.73	0.71	0.69	0.67	0.65	0.63	0.62
0.40	0.88	0.85	0.81	0.78	0.75	0.73	0.70	0.68	0.66	0.63	0.62
0.45	0.90	0.87	0.83	0.80	0.77	0.74	0.72	0.69	0.66	0.64	0.62
0.50	0.93	0.90	0.86	0.82	0.79	0.76	0.73	0.70	0.67	0.64	0.62
0.55	0.95	0.92	0.88	0.84	0.81	0.78	0.75	0.71	0.68	0.64	0.62
0.60	0.96	0.94	0.90	0.87	0.83	0.80	0.76	0.73	0.69	0.65	0.63
0.65	0.98	0.96	0.92	0.89	0.85	0.82	0.78	0.74	0.70	0.65	0.63
0.70	0.99	0.97	0.94	0.91	0.87	0.84	0.80	0.75	0.71	0.66	0.63
0.75	0.99	0.99	0.96	0.93	0.90	0.86	0.81	0.77	0.71	0.66	0.63
0.80	1.00	0.99	0.98	0.95	0.92	0.88	0.83	0.78	0.72	0.66	0.63
0.85	1.00	1.00	0.99	0.97	0.95	0.91	0.86	0.80	0.73	0.66	0.63
0.90	1.00	1.00	1.00	0.99	0.97	0.94	0.88	0.82	0.74	0.67	0.63
0.95	1.00	1.00	1.00	1.00	0.99	0.97	0.92	0.84	0.75	0.67	0.63
1.00	1.00	1.00	1.00	1.00	1.00	1.00	1.00	0.86	0.75	0.67	0.63

Proportion of Employees Considered Satisfactory = 0.70

r	Selection Ratio										
	0.05	0.10	0.20	0.30	0.40	0.50	0.60	0.70	0.80	0.90	0.95
0.00	0.70	0.70	0.70	0.70	0.70	0.70	0.70	0.70	0.70	0.70	0.70
0.05	0.73	0.73	0.72	0.72	0.72	0.71	0.71	0.71	0.71	0.70	0.70
0.10	0.77	0.76	0.75	0.74	0.73	0.73	0.72	0.72	0.71	0.71	0.70
0.15	0.80	0.79	0.77	0.76	0.75	0.74	0.73	0.73	0.72	0.71	0.71
0.20	0.83	0.81	0.79	0.78	0.77	0.76	0.75	0.74	0.73	0.71	0.71
0.25	0.86	0.84	0.81	0.80	0.78	0.77	0.76	0.75	0.73	0.72	0.71
0.30	0.88	0.86	0.84	0.82	0.80	0.78	0.77	0.75	0.74	0.72	0.71
0.35	0.91	0.89	0.86	0.83	0.82	0.80	0.78	0.76	0.75	0.73	0.71
0.40	0.93	0.91	0.88	0.85	0.83	0.81	0.79	0.77	0.75	0.73	0.72
0.45	0.94	0.93	0.90	0.87	0.85	0.83	0.81	0.78	0.76	0.73	0.72
0.50	0.96	0.94	0.91	0.89	0.87	0.84	0.82	0.80	0.77	0.74	0.72
0.55	0.97	0.96	0.93	0.91	0.88	0.86	0.83	0.81	0.78	0.74	0.72
0.60	0.98	0.97	0.95	0.92	0.90	0.87	0.85	0.82	0.79	0.75	0.73
0.65	0.99	0.98	0.96	0.94	0.92	0.89	0.86	0.83	0.80	0.75	0.73
0.70	1.00	0.99	0.97	0.96	0.93	0.91	0.88	0.84	0.80	0.76	0.73
0.75	1.00	1.00	0.98	0.97	0.95	0.92	0.89	0.86	0.81	0.76	0.73
0.80	1.00	1.00	0.99	0.98	0.97	0.94	0.91	0.87	0.82	0.77	0.73
0.85	1.00	1.00	1.00	0.99	0.98	0.96	0.93	0.89	0.84	0.77	0.74
0.90	1.00	1.00	1.00	1.00	0.99	0.98	0.95	0.91	0.85	0.78	0.74
0.95	1.00	1.00	1.00	1.00	1.00	0.99	0.98	0.94	0.86	0.78	0.74
1.00	1.00	1.00	1.00	1.00	1.00	1.00	1.00	1.00	0.88	0.78	0.74

Proportion of Employees Considered Satisfactory = 0.80

r	Selection Ratio										
	0.05	0.10	0.20	0.30	0.40	0.50	0.60	0.70	0.80	0.90	0.95
0.00	0.80	0.80	0.80	0.80	0.80	0.80	0.80	0.80	0.80	0.80	0.80
0.05	0.83	0.82	0.82	0.82	0.81	0.81	0.81	0.81	0.81	0.80	0.80
0.10	0.85	0.85	0.84	0.83	0.83	0.82	0.82	0.81	0.81	0.81	0.80
0.15	0.88	0.87	0.86	0.85	0.84	0.83	0.83	0.82	0.82	0.81	0.81
0.20	0.90	0.89	0.87	0.86	0.85	0.84	0.84	0.83	0.82	0.81	0.81
0.25	0.92	0.91	0.89	0.88	0.87	0.86	0.85	0.84	0.83	0.82	0.81
0.30	0.94	0.92	0.90	0.89	0.88	0.87	0.86	0.84	0.83	0.82	0.81
0.35	0.95	0.94	0.92	0.90	0.89	0.89	0.87	0.85	0.84	0.82	0.81
0.40	0.96	0.95	0.93	0.92	0.90	0.89	0.88	0.86	0.85	0.83	0.82
0.45	0.97	0.96	0.95	0.93	0.92	0.90	0.89	0.87	0.85	0.83	0.82
0.50	0.98	0.97	0.96	0.94	0.93	0.91	0.90	0.88	0.86	0.84	0.82
0.55	0.99	0.98	0.97	0.95	0.94	0.92	0.91	0.89	0.87	0.84	0.82
0.60	0.99	0.99	0.98	0.96	0.95	0.94	0.92	0.90	0.87	0.84	0.83
0.65	1.00	0.99	0.98	0.97	0.96	0.95	0.93	0.91	0.88	0.85	0.83
0.70	1.00	1.00	0.99	0.98	0.97	0.96	0.94	0.92	0.89	0.85	0.83
0.75	1.00	1.00	1.00	0.99	0.98	0.97	0.95	0.93	0.90	0.86	0.83
0.80	1.00	1.00	1.00	1.00	0.99	0.98	0.96	0.94	0.91	0.87	0.84
0.85	1.00	1.00	1.00	1.00	1.00	0.99	0.98	0.96	0.92	0.87	0.84
0.90	1.00	1.00	1.00	1.00	1.00	1.00	0.99	0.97	0.94	0.88	0.84
0.95	1.00	1.00	1.00	1.00	1.00	1.00	1.00	0.99	0.96	0.89	0.84
1.00	1.00	1.00	1.00	1.00	1.00	1.00	1.00	1.00	1.00	0.89	0.84

Proportion of Employees Considered Satisfactory = 0.90

r	Selection Ratio										
	0.05	0.10	0.20	0.30	0.40	0.50	0.60	0.70	0.80	0.90	0.95
0.00	0.90	0.90	0.90	0.90	0.90	0.90	0.90	0.90	0.90	0.90	0.90
0.05	0.92	0.91	0.91	0.91	0.91	0.91	0.91	0.90	0.90	0.90	0.90
0.10	0.93	0.93	0.92	0.92	0.92	0.91	0.91	0.91	0.91	0.90	0.90
0.15	0.95	0.94	0.93	0.93	0.92	0.92	0.92	0.91	0.91	0.91	0.90
0.20	0.96	0.95	0.94	0.94	0.93	0.93	0.92	0.92	0.91	0.91	0.90
0.25	0.97	0.96	0.95	0.95	0.94	0.93	0.93	0.92	0.92	0.91	0.91
0.30	0.98	0.97	0.96	0.95	0.95	0.94	0.94	0.93	0.92	0.91	0.91
0.35	0.98	0.98	0.97	0.96	0.95	0.95	0.94	0.93	0.93	0.92	0.91
0.40	0.99	0.98	0.98	0.97	0.96	0.95	0.95	0.94	0.93	0.92	0.91
0.45	0.99	0.99	0.98	0.98	0.97	0.96	0.95	0.94	0.93	0.92	0.91
0.50	1.00	0.99	0.99	0.98	0.97	0.97	0.96	0.95	0.94	0.92	0.92
0.55	1.00	1.00	0.99	0.99	0.98	0.97	0.97	0.96	0.94	0.93	0.92
0.60	1.00	1.00	0.99	0.99	0.99	0.98	0.97	0.96	0.95	0.93	0.92
0.65	1.00	1.00	1.00	0.99	0.99	0.98	0.98	0.97	0.96	0.94	0.92
0.70	1.00	1.00	1.00	1.00	0.99	0.99	0.98	0.97	0.96	0.94	0.93
0.75	1.00	1.00	1.00	1.00	1.00	0.99	0.99	0.98	0.97	0.95	0.93
0.80	1.00	1.00	1.00	1.00	1.00	1.00	0.99	0.99	0.97	0.95	0.93
0.85	1.00	1.00	1.00	1.00	1.00	1.00	1.00	0.99	0.98	0.96	0.94
0.90	1.00	1.00	1.00	1.00	1.00	1.00	1.00	1.00	0.99	0.97	0.94
0.95	1.00	1.00	1.00	1.00	1.00	1.00	1.00	1.00	1.00	0.98	0.94
1.00	1.00	1.00	1.00	1.00	1.00	1.00	1.00	1.00	1.00	1.00	0.95

C. Expectancy Tables[1] for Individual Prediction[2]

Percent of Employees Considered Satisfactory = 30%

	Predictor Category				
	Upper $\frac{1}{5}$	Next $\frac{1}{5}$	Middle $\frac{1}{5}$	Next $\frac{1}{5}$	Bottom $\frac{1}{5}$
r					
0.15	38	32	30	28	22
0.20	40	34	29	26	21
0.25	43	35	29	24	19
0.30	46	35	29	24	16
0.35	49	36	29	22	14
0.40	51	37	28	21	12
0.45	55	38	28	20	10
0.50	58	38	27	18	09
0.55	61	39	27	17	07
0.60	64	40	26	15	05
0.65	68	41	25	13	04
0.70	72	42	23	11	03
0.75	76	43	22	09	02
0.80	80	44	20	06	01
0.85	85	45	17	04	00
0.90	90	46	12	02	00
0.95	96	48	07	00	00

[1] C. H. Lawshe, R. A. Bolda, R. L. Brune, and G. Auclair, "Expectancy Charts III, Their Theoretical Development," *Personnel Psychology*, Vol. 11 (1958), pp. 545–99.

[2] Entries are the probabilities of success of individual employees under specified conditions.

575

Percent of Employees Considered Satisfactory = 40%

	Predictor Category				
r	Upper ⅕	Next ⅕	Middle ⅕	Next ⅕	Bottom ⅕
0.15	48	44	40	36	32
0.20	51	45	40	35	30
0.25	54	44	40	34	28
0.30	57	46	40	33	24
0.35	60	47	39	32	22
0.40	63	48	39	31	19
0.45	66	49	39	29	17
0.50	69	50	39	28	14
0.55	72	53	38	26	12
0.60	75	53	38	24	10
0.65	79	55	37	22	08
0.70	82	58	36	19	06
0.75	86	59	35	17	04
0.80	89	61	34	14	02
0.85	93	64	32	10	01
0.90	97	69	29	06	00
0.95	100	76	23	02	00

Percent of Employees Considered Satisfactory = 50%

	Predictor Category				
r	Upper ⅕	Next ⅕	Middle ⅕	Next ⅕	Bottom ⅕
0.15	58	54	50	46	42
0.20	61	55	50	45	39
0.25	64	56	50	44	36
0.30	67	57	50	43	33
0.35	70	58	50	42	30
0.40	73	59	50	41	28
0.45	75	60	50	40	25
0.50	78	62	50	38	22
0.55	81	64	50	36	19
0.60	84	65	50	35	16
0.65	87	67	50	33	13
0.70	90	70	50	30	10
0.75	92	72	50	28	08
0.80	95	75	50	25	05
0.85	97	80	50	20	03
0.90	99	85	50	15	01
0.95	100	93	50	08	00

Percent of Employees Considered Satisfactory = 60%

r	Predictor Category				
	Upper $\frac{1}{5}$	Next $\frac{1}{5}$	Middle $\frac{1}{5}$	Next $\frac{1}{5}$	Bottom $\frac{1}{5}$
0.15	68	64	60	57	52
0.20	71	63	60	56	48
0.25	73	65	60	55	48
0.30	76	66	61	54	44
0.35	78	68	61	53	40
0.40	81	69	61	52	37
0.45	83	71	61	51	34
0.50	86	72	62	50	31
0.55	88	74	62	48	28
0.60	90	76	62	47	25
0.65	92	78	63	45	21
0.70	94	80	64	43	18
0.75	96	83	65	42	14
0.80	98	86	66	39	11
0.85	99	90	68	36	07
0.90	100	94	71	31	03
0.95	100	98	77	24	00

Percent of Employees Considered Satisfactory = 70%

r	Predictor Category				
	Upper $\frac{1}{5}$	Next $\frac{1}{5}$	Middle $\frac{1}{5}$	Next $\frac{1}{5}$	Bottom $\frac{1}{5}$
0.15	77	73	69	69	62
0.20	79	75	70	67	59
0.25	81	75	71	65	58
0.30	84	76	71	65	54
0.35	86	78	71	64	52
0.40	88	79	72	63	49
0.45	90	80	72	63	46
0.50	91	82	73	62	42
0.55	93	83	73	61	39
0.60	95	85	74	60	36
0.65	96	87	75	59	32
0.70	97	89	77	58	29
0.75	98	91	78	57	25
0.80	99	94	80	56	20
0.85	100	96	83	55	16
0.90	100	98	88	54	10
0.95	100	100	93	52	04

Indexes

Name Index

Subject Index

*This book has been set in 11 and 10 point
Baskerville, leaded 2 points. Part and
chapter numbers are in 66 point Weiss
Series I. Part and chapter titles are in 24
point Goudy Handtooled. The size of the
type page is 27 by 45 picas.*